ALGEBRA AND TRIGONOMETRY

SENIOR CONTRIBUTING AUTHOR

JAY ABRAMSON, ARIZONA STATE UNIVERSITY

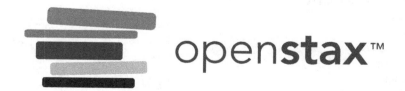

About Our Team

Lead Author, Senior Content Expert

Jay Abramson has been teaching Algebra and Trigonometry for 33 years, the last 14 at Arizona State University, where he is a principal lecturer in the School of Mathematics and Statistics. His accomplishments at ASU include co-developing the university's first hybrid and online math courses as well as an extensive library of video lectures and tutorials. In addition, he has served as a contributing author for two of Pearson Education's math programs, NovaNet Precalculus and Trigonometry. Prior to coming to ASU, Jay taught at Texas State Technical College and Amarillo College. He received Teacher of the Year awards at both institutions.

The following faculty contributed to the development of OpenStax *Algebra and Trigonometry*, the text from which this product was updated and derived.

Honorable Mention:

Nina Alketa, Cecil College
Kiran Bhutani, Catholic University of America
Brandie Biddy, Cecil College
Lisa Blank, Lyme Central School
Bryan Blount, Kentucky Wesleyan College
Jessica Bolz, The Bryn Mawr School
Sheri Boyd, Rollins College
Sarah Brewer, Alabama School of Math and Science
Charles Buckley, St. Gregory's University
Michael Cohen, Hofstra University
Kenneth Crane, Texarkana College
Rachel Cywinski, Alamo Colleges
Nathan Czuba
Srabasti Dutta, Ashford University
Kristy Erickson, Cecil College
Nicole Fernandez, Georgetown University / Kent State University
David French, Tidewater Community College
Douglas Furman, SUNY Ulster
Lance Hemlow, Raritan Valley Community College
Erinn Izzo, Nicaragua Christian Academy
John Jaffe
Jerry Jared, Blue Ridge School
Stan Kopec, Mount Wachusett Community College
Kathy Kovacs
Cynthia Landrigan, Erie Community College
Sara Lenhart, Christopher Newport University
Wendy Lightheart, Lane Community College
Joanne Manville, Bunker Hill Community College
Karla McCavit, Albion College
Cynthia McGinnis, Northwest Florida State College
Lana Neal, University of Texas at Austin
Rhonda Porter, Albany State University
Steven Purtee, Valencia College
William Radulovich, Florida State College Jacksonville
Alice Ramos, Bethel College
Nick Reynolds, Montgomery Community College
Amanda Ross, A. A. Ross Consulting and Research, LLC
Erica Rutter, Arizona State University
Sutandra Sarkar, Georgia State University
Willy Schild, Wentworth Institute of Technology
Todd Stephen, Cleveland State University
Scott Sykes, University of West Georgia
Linda Tansil, Southeast Missouri State University
John Thomas, College of Lake County
Diane Valade, Piedmont Virginia Community College
Allen Wolmer, Atlanta Jewish Academy

Contributing Authors:

Valeree Falduto, Palm Beach State College
Rachael Gross, Towson University
David Lippman, Pierce College
Melonie Rasmussen, Pierce College
Rick Norwood, East Tennessee State University
Nicholas Belloit, Florida State College Jacksonville
Jean-Marie Magnier, Springfield Technical Community College
Harold Whipple
Christina Fernandez

Faculty Reviewers and Consultants:

Phil Clark, Scottsdale Community College
Michael Cohen, Hofstra University
Charles Conrad, Volunteer State Community College
David French, Tidewater Community College
Matthew Goodell, SUNY Ulster
Lance Hemlow, Raritan Valley Community College
Dongrin Kim, Arizona State University
Cynthia Landrigan, Eerie Community College
Wendy Lightheart, Lane Community College
Chinenye Ofodile, Albany State University
Carl Penziul, Tompkins-Cortland Community College
Sandra Nite, Texas A&M University
Eugenia Peterson, Richard J. Daley College
Rhonda Porter, Albany State University
Michael Price, University of Oregon
Steven Purtee, Valencia College
William Radulovich, Florida State College Jacksonville
Camelia Salajean, City Colleges of Chicago
Katy Shields, Oakland Community College
Nathan Schrenk, ECPI University
Pablo Suarez, Delaware State University
Allen Wolmer, Atlanta Jewish Academy

ALGEBRA AND TRIGONOMETRY

Volume 2

Chapters 8–13

530 Great Road
Acton, MA 01720
800-562-2147
www.xanedu.com

OpenStax College

OpenStax College is a non-profit organization committed to improving student access to quality learning materials. Our free textbooks are developed and peer-reviewed by educators to ensure they are readable, accurate, and meet the scope and sequence requirements of modern college courses. Through our partnerships with companies and foundations committed to reducing costs for students, OpenStax College is working to improve access to higher education for all.

OpenStax CNX

The technology platform supporting OpenStax College is OpenStax CNX (http://cnx.org), one of the world's first and largest open education projects. OpenStax CNX provides students with free online and low-cost print editions of the OpenStax College library and provides instructors with tools to customize the content so that they can have the perfect book for their course.

Rice University

OpenStax College and OpenStax CNX are initiatives of Rice University. As a leading research university with a distinctive commitment to undergraduate education, Rice University aspires to path-breaking research, unsurpassed teaching, and contributions to the betterment of our world. It seeks to fulfill this mission by cultivating a diverse community of learning and discovery that produces leaders across the spectrum of human endeavor.

Foundation Support

OpenStax College is grateful for the tremendous support of our sponsors. Without their strong engagement, the goal of free access to high-quality textbooks would remain just a dream.

Laura and John Arnold Foundation (LJAF) actively seeks opportunities to invest in organizations and thought leaders that have a sincere interest in implementing fundamental changes that not only yield immediate gains, but also repair broken systems for future generations. LJAF currently focuses its strategic investments on education, criminal justice, research integrity, and public accountability.

The William and Flora Hewlett Foundation has been making grants since 1967 to help solve social and environmental problems at home and around the world. The Foundation concentrates its resources on activities in education, the environment, global development and population, performing arts, and philanthropy, and makes grants to support disadvantaged communities in the San Francisco Bay Area.

Guided by the belief that every life has equal value, the Bill & Melinda Gates Foundation works to help all people lead healthy, productive lives. In developing countries, it focuses on improving people's health with vaccines and other life-saving tools and giving them the chance to lift themselves out of hunger and extreme poverty. In the United States, it seeks to significantly improve education so that all young people have the opportunity to reach their full potential. Based in Seattle, Washington, the foundation is led by CEO Jeff Raikes and Co-chair William H. Gates Sr., under the direction of Bill and Melinda Gates and Warren Buffett.

The Maxfield Foundation supports projects with potential for high impact in science, education, sustainability, and other areas of social importance.

Our mission at the Twenty Million Minds Foundation is to grow access and success by eliminating unnecessary hurdles to affordability. We support the creation, sharing, and proliferation of more effective, more affordable educational content by leveraging disruptive technologies, open educational resources, and new models for collaboration between for-profit, nonprofit, and public entities.

OpenStax College

Rice University
6100 Main Street MS-375
Houston, Texas 77005

To learn more about OpenStax College, visit **http://openstaxcollege.org**.
Individual print copies and bulk orders can be purchased through our
website.

ISBN-10   1-938168-37-2
ISBN-13   978-1-938168-37-6
Revision   AT-2015-002(03/17)-BW

Brief Contents

1 Prerequisites   1

2 Equations and Inequalities   73

3 Functions   159

4 Linear Functions   279

5 Polynomial and Rational Functions   343

6 Exponential and Logarithmic Functions   463

7 The Unit Circle: Sine and Cosine Functions   575

8 Periodic Functions   641

9 Trigonometric Identities and Equations   695

10 Further Applications of Trigonometry   761

11 Systems of Equations and Inequalities   875

12 Analytic Geometry   981

13 Sequences, Probability and Counting Theory   1055

Contents

Preface   vii

1   Prerequisites   1

1.1   Real Numbers: Algebra Essentials   2
1.2   Exponents and Scientific Notation   17
1.3   Radicals and Rational Expressions   31
1.4   Polynomials   41
1.5   Factoring Polynomials   49
1.6   Rational Expressions   58
Chapter 1 Review   66
Chapter 1 Review Exercises   70
Chapter 1 Practice Test   72

2   Equations and Inequalities   73

2.1   The Rectangular Coordinate Systems and Graphs   74
2.2   Linear Equations in One Variable   87
2.3   Models and Applications   102
2.4   Complex Numbers   111
2.5   Quadratic Equations   119
2.6   Other Types of Equations   131
2.7   Linear Inequalities and Absolute Value Inequalities   142
Chapter 2 Review   151
Chapter 2 Review Exercises   155
Chapter 2 Practice Test   158

3   Functions   159

3.1   Functions and Function Notation   160
3.2   Domain and Range   180
3.3   Rates of Change and Behavior of Graphs   196
3.4   Composition of Functions   209
3.5   Transformation of Functions   222
3.6   Absolute Value Functions   247
3.7   Inverse Functions   254
Chapter 3 Review   267
Chapter 3 Review Exercises   272
Chapter 3 Practice Test   277

4   Linear Functions   279

4.1   Linear Functions   280
4.2   Modeling with Linear Functions   309
4.3   Fitting Linear Models to Data   322
Chapter 4 Review   334
Chapter 4 Review Exercises   336
Chapter 4 Practice Test   340

5   Polynomial and Rational Functions   343

5.1   Quadratic Functions   344
5.2   Power Functions and Polynomial Functions   360
5.3   Graphs of Polynomial Functions   375
5.4   Dividing Polynomials   393
5.5   Zeros of Polynomial Functions   402
5.6   Rational Functions   414
5.7   Inverses and Radical Functions   435
5.8   Modeling Using Variation   446
Chapter 5 Review   453
Chapter 5 Review Exercises   458
Chapter 5 Practice Test   461

6   Exponential and Logarithmic Functions   463

6.1   Exponential Functions   464
6.2   Graphs of Exponential Functions   479
6.3   Logarithmic Functions   491
6.4   Graphs of Logarithmic Functions   499
6.5   Logarithmic Properties   516
6.6   Exponential and Logarithmic Equations   526
6.7   Exponential and Logarithmic Models   537
6.8   Fitting Exponential Models to Data   552
Chapter 6 Review   565
Chapter 6 Review Exercises   570
Chapter 6 Practice Test   573

7 The Unit Circle: Sine and Cosine Functions   575

7.1 Angles   576
7.2 Right Triangle Trigonometry   593
7.3 Unit Circle   604
7.4 The Other Trigonometric Functions   620
Chapter 7 Review   633
Chapter 7 Review Exercises   637
Chapter 7 Practice Test   639

8 Periodic Functions   641

8.1 Graphs of the Sine and Cosine Functions   642
8.2 Graphs of the Other Trigonometric Functions   659
8.3 Inverse Trigonometric Functions   677
Chapter 8 Review   688
Chapter 8 Review Exercises   690
Chapter 8 Practice Test   692

9 Trigonometric Identities and Equations   695

9.1 Solving Trigonometric Equations with Identities   696
9.2 Sum and Difference Identities   706
9.3 Double-Angle, Half-Angle, and Reduction Formulas   720
9.4 Sum-to-Product and Product-to-Sum Formulas   732
9.5 Solving Trigonometric Equations   739
Chapter 9 Review   753
Chapter 9 Review Exercises   757
Chapter 9 Practice Test   759

10 Further Applications of Trigonometry   761

10.1 Non-right Triangles: Law of Sines   762
10.2 Non-right Triangles: Law of Cosines   776
10.3 Polar Coordinates   788
10.4 Polar Coordinates: Graphs   799
10.5 Polar Form of Complex Numbers   815
10.6 Parametric Equations   826
10.7 Parametric Equations: Graphs   837
10.8 Vectors   847
Chapter 10 Review   865
Chapter 10 Review Exercises   870
Chapter 10 Practice Test   873

11 Systems of Equations and Inequalities   875

11.1 Systems of Linear Equations: Two Variables   876
11.2 Systems of Linear Equations: Three Variables   892
11.3 Systems of Nonlinear Equations and Inequalities: Two Variables   903
11.4 Partial Fractions   913
11.5 Matrices and Matrix Operations   923
11.6 Solving Systems with Gaussian Elimination   934
11.7 Solving Systems with Inverses   947
11.8 Solving Systems with Cramer's Rule   961
Chapter 11 Review   972
Chapter 11 Review Exercises   976
Chapter 11 Practice Test   979

12 Analytic Geometry   981

12.1 The Ellipse   982
12.2 The Hyperbola   997
12.3 The Parabola   1014
12.4 Rotation of Axis   1027
12.5 Conic Sections in Polar Coordinates   1040
Chapter 12 Review   1049
Chapter 12 Review Exercises   1052
Chapter 12 Practice Test   1054

13 Sequences, Probability and Counting Theory   1055

13.1 Sequences and Their Notations   1056
13.2 Arithmetic Sequences   1069
13.3 Geometric Sequences   1079
13.4 Series and Their Notations   1087
13.5 Counting Principles   1100
13.6 Binomial Theorem   1110
13.7 Probability   1117
Chapter 13 Review   1126
Chapter 13 Review Exercises   1130
Chapter 13 Practice Test   1133

Appendix   A-1

Try It Answers   B-1

Odd Answers   C-1

Index   D-1

8

Periodic Functions

Figure 1 (credit: "Maxxer_", Flickr)

CHAPTER OUTLINE

8.1 Graphs of the Sine and Cosine Functions

8.2 Graphs of the Other Trigonometric Functions

8.3 Inverse Trigonometric Functions

Introduction

Each day, the sun rises in an easterly direction, approaches some maximum height relative to the celestial equator, and sets in a westerly direction. The celestial equator is an imaginary line that divides the visible universe into two halves in much the same way Earth's equator is an imaginary line that divides the planet into two halves. The exact path the sun appears to follow depends on the exact location on Earth, but each location observes a predictable pattern over time.

The pattern of the sun's motion throughout the course of a year is a periodic function. Creating a visual representation of a periodic function in the form of a graph can help us analyze the properties of the function. In this chapter, we will investigate graphs of sine, cosine, and other trigonometric functions.

LEARNING OBJECTIVES

In this section, you will:

- Graph variations of $y = \sin(x)$ and $y = \cos(x)$.
- Use phase shifts of sine and cosine curves.

8.1   GRAPHS OF THE SINE AND COSINE FUNCTIONS

Figure 1 Light can be separated into colors because of its wavelike properties. (credit: "wonderferret"/ Flickr)

White light, such as the light from the sun, is not actually white at all. Instead, it is a composition of all the colors of the rainbow in the form of waves. The individual colors can be seen only when white light passes through an optical prism that separates the waves according to their wavelengths to form a rainbow.

Light waves can be represented graphically by the sine function. In the chapter on **Trigonometric Functions**, we examined trigonometric functions such as the sine function. In this section, we will interpret and create graphs of sine and cosine functions.

Graphing Sine and Cosine Functions

Recall that the sine and cosine functions relate real number values to the x- and y-coordinates of a point on the unit circle. So what do they look like on a graph on a coordinate plane? Let's start with the sine function. We can create a table of values and use them to sketch a graph. **Table 1** lists some of the values for the sine function on a unit circle.

x	0	$\dfrac{\pi}{6}$	$\dfrac{\pi}{4}$	$\dfrac{\pi}{3}$	$\dfrac{\pi}{2}$	$\dfrac{2\pi}{3}$	$\dfrac{3\pi}{4}$	$\dfrac{5\pi}{6}$	π
$\sin(x)$	0	$\dfrac{1}{2}$	$\dfrac{\sqrt{2}}{2}$	$\dfrac{\sqrt{3}}{2}$	1	$\dfrac{\sqrt{3}}{2}$	$\dfrac{\sqrt{2}}{2}$	$\dfrac{1}{2}$	0

Table 1

Plotting the points from the table and continuing along the x-axis gives the shape of the sine function. See **Figure 2**.

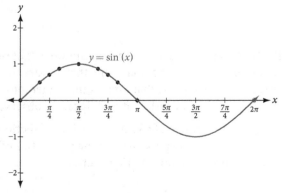

Figure 2 The sine function

Notice how the sine values are positive between 0 and π, which correspond to the values of the sine function in quadrants I and II on the unit circle, and the sine values are negative between π and 2π, which correspond to the values of the sine function in quadrants III and IV on the unit circle. See **Figure 3**.

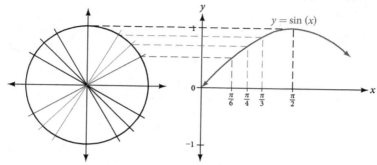

Figure 3 Plotting values of the sine function

Now let's take a similar look at the cosine function. Again, we can create a table of values and use them to sketch a graph. **Table 2** lists some of the values for the cosine function on a unit circle.

x	0	$\dfrac{\pi}{6}$	$\dfrac{\pi}{4}$	$\dfrac{\pi}{3}$	$\dfrac{\pi}{2}$	$\dfrac{2\pi}{3}$	$\dfrac{3\pi}{4}$	$\dfrac{5\pi}{6}$	π
$\cos(x)$	1	$\dfrac{\sqrt{3}}{2}$	$\dfrac{\sqrt{2}}{2}$	$\dfrac{1}{2}$	0	$-\dfrac{1}{2}$	$-\dfrac{\sqrt{2}}{2}$	$-\dfrac{\sqrt{3}}{2}$	-1

Table 2

As with the sine function, we can plots points to create a graph of the cosine function as in *Figure 4*.

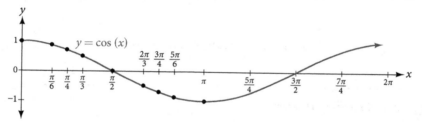

Figure 4 The cosine function

Because we can evaluate the sine and cosine of any real number, both of these functions are defined for all real numbers. By thinking of the sine and cosine values as coordinates of points on a unit circle, it becomes clear that the range of both functions must be the interval $[-1, 1]$.

In both graphs, the shape of the graph repeats after 2π, which means the functions are periodic with a period of 2π. A **periodic function** is a function for which a specific horizontal shift, P, results in a function equal to the original function: $f(x + P) = f(x)$ for all values of x in the domain of f. When this occurs, we call the smallest such horizontal shift with $P > 0$ the period of the function. **Figure 5** shows several periods of the sine and cosine functions.

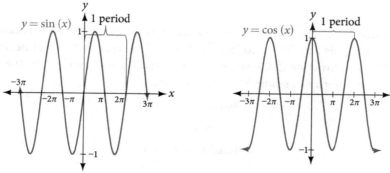

Figure 5

Looking again at the sine and cosine functions on a domain centered at the y-axis helps reveal symmetries. As we can see in **Figure 6**, the sine function is symmetric about the origin. Recall from **The Other Trigonometric Functions** that we determined from the unit circle that the sine function is an odd function because $\sin(-x) = -\sin x$. Now we can clearly see this property from the graph.

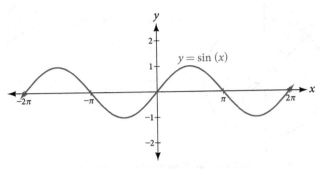

Figure 6 Odd symmetry of the sine function

Figure 7 shows that the cosine function is symmetric about the y-axis. Again, we determined that the cosine function is an even function. Now we can see from the graph that $\cos(-x) = \cos x$.

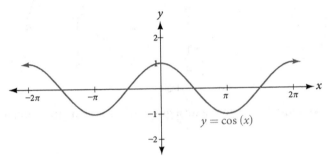

Figure 7 Even symmetry of the cosine function

> *characteristics of sine and cosine functions*
> The sine and cosine functions have several distinct characteristics:
> - They are periodic functions with a period of 2π.
> - The domain of each function is $(-\infty, \infty)$ and the range is $[-1, 1]$.
> - The graph of $y = \sin x$ is symmetric about the origin, because it is an odd function.
> - The graph of $y = \cos x$ is symmetric about the y- axis, because it is an even function.

Investigating Sinusoidal Functions

As we can see, sine and cosine functions have a regular period and range. If we watch ocean waves or ripples on a pond, we will see that they resemble the sine or cosine functions. However, they are not necessarily identical. Some are taller or longer than others. A function that has the same general shape as a sine or cosine function is known as a **sinusoidal function**. The general forms of sinusoidal functions are

$$y = A\sin(Bx - C) + D$$

and

$$y = A\cos(Bx - C) + D$$

Determining the Period of Sinusoidal Functions

Looking at the forms of sinusoidal functions, we can see that they are transformations of the sine and cosine functions. We can use what we know about transformations to determine the period.

In the general formula, B is related to the period by $P = \dfrac{2\pi}{|B|}$. If $|B| > 1$, then the period is less than 2π and the function undergoes a horizontal compression, whereas if $|B| < 1$, then the period is greater than 2π and the function undergoes a horizontal stretch. For example, $f(x) = \sin(x)$, $B = 1$, so the period is 2π, which we knew. If $f(x) = \sin(2x)$, then $B = 2$, so the period is π and the graph is compressed. If $f(x) = \sin\left(\dfrac{x}{2}\right)$, then $B = \dfrac{1}{2}$, so the period is 4π and the graph is stretched. Notice in **Figure 8** how the period is indirectly related to $|B|$.

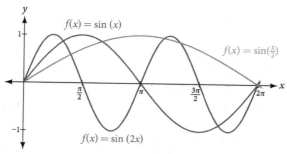

Figure 8

---

period of sinusoidal functions

If we let $C = 0$ and $D = 0$ in the general form equations of the sine and cosine functions, we obtain the forms

$$y = A\sin(Bx) \qquad y = A\cos(Bx)$$

The period is $\dfrac{2\pi}{|B|}$.

Example 1   Identifying the Period of a Sine or Cosine Function

Determine the period of the function $f(x) = \sin\left(\dfrac{\pi}{6}x\right)$.

Solution   Let's begin by comparing the equation to the general form $y = A\sin(Bx)$.

In the given equation, $B = \dfrac{\pi}{6}$, so the period will be

$$
\begin{aligned}
P &= \frac{2\pi}{|B|} \\
&= \frac{2\pi}{\frac{\pi}{6}} \\
&= 2\pi \cdot \frac{6}{\pi} \\
&= 12
\end{aligned}
$$

Try It #1

Determine the period of the function $g(x) = \left(\cos\dfrac{x}{3}\right)$.

Determining Amplitude

Returning to the general formula for a sinusoidal function, we have analyzed how the variable B relates to the period. Now let's turn to the variable A so we can analyze how it is related to the **amplitude**, or greatest distance from rest. A represents the vertical stretch factor, and its absolute value $|A|$ is the amplitude. The local maxima will be a distance $|A|$ above the vertical **midline** of the graph, which is the line $x = D$; because $D = 0$ in this case, the midline is the x-axis. The local minima will be the same distance below the midline. If $|A| > 1$, the function is stretched. For example, the amplitude of $f(x) = 4\sin x$ is twice the amplitude of $f(x) = 2\sin x$. If $|A| < 1$, the function is compressed. **Figure 9** compares several sine functions with different amplitudes.

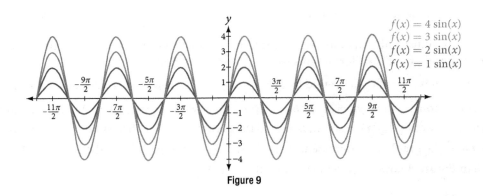

Figure 9

---

amplitude of sinusoidal functions

If we let $C = 0$ and $D = 0$ in the general form equations of the sine and cosine functions, we obtain the forms

$$y = A\sin(Bx) \text{ and } y = A\cos(Bx)$$

The **amplitude** is A, and the vertical height from the **midline** is $|A|$. In addition, notice in the example that

$$|A| = \text{amplitude} = \frac{1}{2}|\text{maximum} - \text{minimum}|$$

Example 2   **Identifying the Amplitude of a Sine or Cosine Function**

What is the amplitude of the sinusoidal function $f(x) = -4\sin(x)$? Is the function stretched or compressed vertically?

Solution   Let's begin by comparing the function to the simplified form $y = A\sin(Bx)$.

In the given function, $A = -4$, so the amplitude is $|A| = |-4| = 4$. The function is stretched.

Analysis   *The negative value of A results in a reflection across the x-axis of the sine function, as shown in* **Figure 10**.

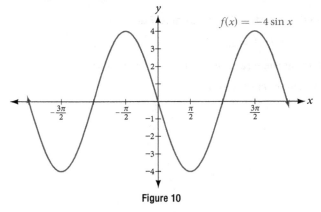

Figure 10

Try It #2

What is the amplitude of the sinusoidal function $f(x) = \frac{1}{2}\sin(x)$? Is the function stretched or compressed vertically?

Analyzing Graphs of Variations of $y = \sin x$ and $y = \cos x$

Now that we understand how A and B relate to the general form equation for the sine and cosine functions, we will explore the variables C and D. Recall the general form:

$$y = A\sin(Bx - C) + D \text{ and } y = A\cos(Bx - C) + D$$

or

$$y = A\sin\left(B\left(x - \frac{C}{B}\right)\right) + D \text{ and } y = A\cos\left(B\left(x - \frac{C}{B}\right)\right) + D$$

The value $\frac{C}{B}$ for a sinusoidal function is called the **phase shift**, or the horizontal displacement of the basic sine or cosine function. If $C > 0$, the graph shifts to the right. If $C < 0$, the graph shifts to the left. The greater the value of $|C|$, the more the graph is shifted. *Figure 11* shows that the graph of $f(x) = \sin(x - \pi)$ shifts to the right by π units, which is more than we see in the graph of $f(x) = \sin\left(x - \frac{\pi}{4}\right)$, which shifts to the right by $\frac{\pi}{4}$ units.

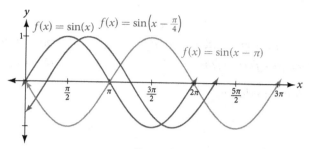

Figure 11

While C relates to the horizontal shift, D indicates the vertical shift from the midline in the general formula for a sinusoidal function. See **Figure 12**. The function $y = \cos(x) + D$ has its midline at $y = D$.

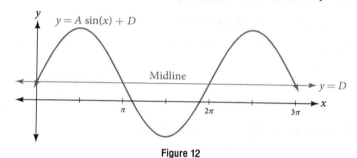

Figure 12

Any value of D other than zero shifts the graph up or down. *Figure 13* compares $f(x) = \sin x$ with $f(x) = \sin x + 2$, which is shifted 2 units up on a graph.

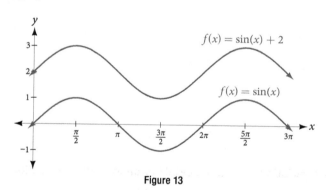

Figure 13

---

variations of sine and cosine functions

Given an equation in the form $f(x) = A\sin(Bx - C) + D$ or $f(x) = A\cos(Bx - C) + D$, $\frac{C}{B}$ is the **phase shift** and D is the vertical shift.

Example 3   **Identifying the Phase Shift of a Function**

Determine the direction and magnitude of the phase shift for $f(x) = \sin\left(x + \frac{\pi}{6}\right) - 2$.

Solution   Let's begin by comparing the equation to the general form $y = A\sin(Bx - C) + D$.

In the given equation, notice that $B = 1$ and $C = -\frac{\pi}{6}$. So the phase shift is

$$\frac{C}{B} = -\frac{\frac{\pi}{6}}{1}$$

$$= -\frac{\pi}{6}$$

or $\frac{\pi}{6}$ units to the left.

Analysis We must pay attention to the sign in the equation for the general form of a sinusoidal function. The equation shows a minus sign before C. Therefore $f(x) = \sin\left(x + \frac{\pi}{6}\right) - 2$ can be rewritten as $f(x) = \sin\left(x - \left(-\frac{\pi}{6}\right)\right) - 2$.

If the value of C is negative, the shift is to the left.

Try It #3

Determine the direction and magnitude of the phase shift for $f(x) = 3\cos\left(x - \frac{\pi}{2}\right)$.

Example 4   **Identifying the Vertical Shift of a Function**

Determine the direction and magnitude of the vertical shift for $f(x) = \cos(x) - 3$.

Solution   Let's begin by comparing the equation to the general form $y = A\cos(Bx - C) + D$.

In the given equation, $D = -3$ so the shift is 3 units downward.

Try It #4

Determine the direction and magnitude of the vertical shift for $f(x) = 3\sin(x) + 2$.

How To...

Given a sinusoidal function in the form $f(x) = A\sin(Bx - C) + D$, identify the midline, amplitude, period, and phase shift.

1. Determine the amplitude as $|A|$.

2. Determine the period as $P = \frac{2\pi}{|B|}$.

3. Determine the phase shift as $\frac{C}{B}$.

4. Determine the midline as $y = D$.

Example 5   **Identifying the Variations of a Sinusoidal Function from an Equation**

Determine the midline, amplitude, period, and phase shift of the function $y = 3\sin(2x) + 1$.

Solution   Let's begin by comparing the equation to the general form $y = A\sin(Bx - C) + D$.

$A = 3$, so the amplitude is $|A| = 3$.

Next, $B = 2$, so the period is $P = \frac{2\pi}{|B|} = \frac{2\pi}{2} = \pi$.

There is no added constant inside the parentheses, so $C = 0$ and the phase shift is $\frac{C}{B} = \frac{0}{2} = 0$.

Finally, $D = 1$, so the midline is $y = 1$.

Analysis Inspecting the graph, we can determine that the period is π, the midline is $y = 1$, and the amplitude is 3. See **Figure 14.**

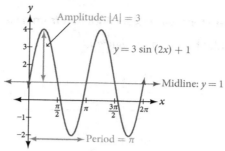

Figure 14

Try It #5

Determine the midline, amplitude, period, and phase shift of the function $y = \frac{1}{2}\cos\left(\frac{x}{3} - \frac{\pi}{3}\right)$.

Example 6   **Identifying the Equation for a Sinusoidal Function from a Graph**

Determine the formula for the cosine function in *Figure 15*.

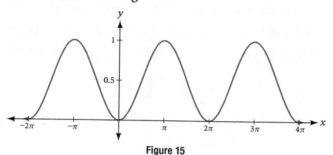

Figure 15

Solution   To determine the equation, we need to identify each value in the general form of a sinusoidal function.

$$y = A\sin(Bx - C) + D \qquad\qquad y = A\cos(Bx - C) + D$$

The graph could represent either a sine or a cosine function that is shifted and/or reflected. When $x = 0$, the graph has an extreme point, (0, 0). Since the cosine function has an extreme point for $x = 0$, let us write our equation in terms of a cosine function.

Let's start with the midline. We can see that the graph rises and falls an equal distance above and below $y = 0.5$. This value, which is the midline, is D in the equation, so $D = 0.5$.

The greatest distance above and below the midline is the amplitude. The maxima are 0.5 units above the midline and the minima are 0.5 units below the midline. So $|A| = 0.5$. Another way we could have determined the amplitude is by recognizing that the difference between the height of local maxima and minima is 1, so $|A| = \frac{1}{2} = 0.5$. Also, the graph is reflected about the x-axis so that $A = -0.5$.

The graph is not horizontally stretched or compressed, so $B = 1$; and the graph is not shifted horizontally, so $C = 0$. Putting this all together,

$$g(x) = -0.5\cos(x) + 0.5$$

Try It #6

Determine the formula for the sine function in *Figure 16*.

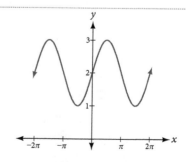

Figure 16

Example 7   **Identifying the Equation for a Sinusoidal Function from a Graph**

Determine the equation for the sinusoidal function in *Figure 17*.

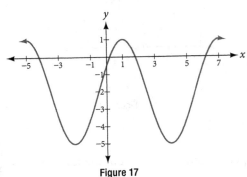

Figure 17

Solution   With the highest value at 1 and the lowest value at -5, the midline will be halfway between at -2. So $D = -2$.

The distance from the midline to the highest or lowest value gives an amplitude of $|A| = 3$.

The period of the graph is 6, which can be measured from the peak at $x = 1$ to the next peak at $x = 7$, or from the distance between the lowest points. Therefore, $P = \frac{2\pi}{|B|} = 6$. Using the positive value for B, we find that

$$B = \frac{2\pi}{P} = \frac{2\pi}{6} = \frac{\pi}{3}$$

So far, our equation is either $y = 3\sin\left(\frac{\pi}{3}x - C\right) - 2$ or $y = 3\cos\left(\frac{\pi}{3}x - C\right) - 2$. For the shape and shift, we have more than one option. We could write this as any one of the following:

- a cosine shifted to the right
- a negative cosine shifted to the left
- a sine shifted to the left
- a negative sine shifted to the right

While any of these would be correct, the cosine shifts are easier to work with than the sine shifts in this case because they involve integer values. So our function becomes

$$y = 3\cos\left(\frac{\pi}{3}x - \frac{\pi}{3}\right) - 2 \text{ or } y = -3\cos\left(\frac{\pi}{3}x + \frac{2\pi}{3}\right) - 2$$

Again, these functions are equivalent, so both yield the same graph.

Try It #7

Write a formula for the function graphed in *Figure 18*.

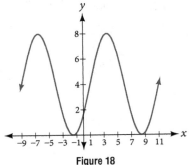

Figure 18

Graphing Variations of $y = \sin x$ and $y = \cos x$

Throughout this section, we have learned about types of variations of sine and cosine functions and used that information to write equations from graphs. Now we can use the same information to create graphs from equations.

Instead of focusing on the general form equations

$$y = A\sin(Bx - C) + D \text{ and } y = A\cos(Bx - C) + D,$$

we will let $C = 0$ and $D = 0$ and work with a simplified form of the equations in the following examples.

How To…

Given the function $y = A\sin(Bx)$, sketch its graph.

1. Identify the amplitude, $|A|$.

2. Identify the period, $P = \dfrac{2\pi}{|B|}$.

3. Start at the origin, with the function increasing to the right if A is positive or decreasing if A is negative.

4. At $x = \dfrac{\pi}{2|B|}$ there is a local maximum for $A > 0$ or a minimum for $A < 0$, with $y = A$.

5. The curve returns to the x-axis at $x = \dfrac{\pi}{|B|}$.

6. There is a local minimum for $A > 0$ (maximum for $A < 0$) at $x = \dfrac{3\pi}{2|B|}$ with $y = -A$.

7. The curve returns again to the x-axis at $x = \dfrac{\pi}{2|B|}$.

Example 8   **Graphing a Function and Identifying the Amplitude and Period**

Sketch a graph of $f(x) = -2\sin\left(\dfrac{\pi x}{2}\right)$.

Solution   Let's begin by comparing the equation to the form $y = A\sin(Bx)$.

Step 1. We can see from the equation that $A = -2$, so the amplitude is 2.

$$|A| = 2$$

Step 2. The equation shows that $B = \dfrac{\pi}{2}$, so the period is

$$P = \frac{2\pi}{\frac{\pi}{2}}$$
$$= 2\pi \cdot \frac{2}{\pi}$$
$$= 4$$

Step 3. Because A is negative, the graph descends as we move to the right of the origin.

Step 4–7. The x-intercepts are at the beginning of one period, $x = 0$, the horizontal midpoints are at $x = 2$ and at the end of one period at $x = 4$.

The quarter points include the minimum at $x = 1$ and the maximum at $x = 3$. A local minimum will occur 2 units below the midline, at $x = 1$, and a local maximum will occur at 2 units above the midline, at $x = 3$. **Figure 19** shows the graph of the function.

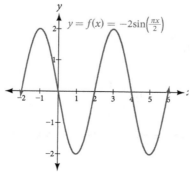

Figure 19

Try It #8

Sketch a graph of $g(x) = -0.8\cos(2x)$. Determine the midline, amplitude, period, and phase shift.

How To...

Given a sinusoidal function with a phase shift and a vertical shift, sketch its graph.

1. Express the function in the general form $y = A\sin(Bx - C) + D$ or $y = A\cos(Bx - C) + D$.

2. Identify the amplitude, $|A|$.

3. Identify the period, $P = \dfrac{2\pi}{|B|}$.

4. Identify the phase shift, $\dfrac{C}{B}$.

5. Draw the graph of $f(x) = A\sin(Bx)$ shifted to the right or left by $\dfrac{C}{B}$ and up or down by D.

Example 9　**Graphing a Transformed Sinusoid**

Sketch a graph of $f(x) = 3\sin\left(\dfrac{\pi}{4}x - \dfrac{\pi}{4}\right)$.

Solution

Step 1. The function is already written in general form: $f(x) = 3\sin\left(\dfrac{\pi}{4}x - \dfrac{\pi}{4}\right)$. This graph will have the shape of a sine function, starting at the midline and increasing to the right.

Step 2. $|A| = |3| = 3$. The amplitude is 3.

Step 3. Since $|B| = \left|\dfrac{\pi}{4}\right| = \dfrac{\pi}{4}$, we determine the period as follows.

$$P = \frac{2\pi}{|B|} = \frac{2\pi}{\frac{\pi}{4}} = 2\pi \cdot \frac{4}{\pi} = 8$$

The period is 8.

Step 4. Since $C = \dfrac{\pi}{4}$, the phase shift is

$$\frac{C}{B} = \frac{\frac{\pi}{4}}{\frac{\pi}{4}} = 1.$$

The phase shift is 1 unit.

Step 5. **Figure 20** shows the graph of the function.

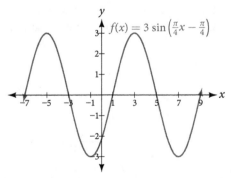

Figure 20 A horizontally compressed, vertically stretched, and horizontally shifted sinusoid

Try It #9

Draw a graph of $g(x) = -2\cos\left(\frac{\pi}{3}x + \frac{\pi}{6}\right)$. Determine the midline, amplitude, period, and phase shift.

Example 10 Identifying the Properties of a Sinusoidal Function

Given $y = -2\cos\left(\frac{\pi}{2}x + \pi\right) + 3$, determine the amplitude, period, phase shift, and horizontal shift. Then graph the function.

Solution Begin by comparing the equation to the general form and use the steps outlined in **Example 9**.

$$y = A\cos(Bx - C) + D$$

Step 1. The function is already written in general form.

Step 2. Since $A = -2$, the amplitude is $|A| = 2$.

Step 3. $|B| = \frac{\pi}{2}$, so the period is $P = \frac{2\pi}{|B|} = \frac{2\pi}{\frac{\pi}{2}} = 2\pi \cdot \frac{2}{\pi} = 4$. The period is 4.

Step 4. $C = -\pi$, so we calculate the phase shift as $\frac{C}{B} = \frac{-\pi}{\frac{\pi}{2}} = -\pi \cdot \frac{2}{\pi} = -2$. The phase shift is -2.

Step 5. $D = 3$, so the midline is $y = 3$, and the vertical shift is up 3.

Since A is negative, the graph of the cosine function has been reflected about the x-axis. **Figure 21** shows one cycle of the graph of the function.

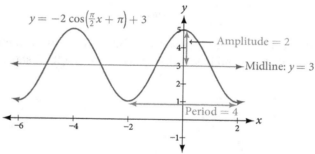

$$y = -2\cos\left(\frac{\pi}{2}x + \pi\right) + 3$$

Amplitude = 2

Midline: $y = 3$

Period = 4

Figure 21

Using Transformations of Sine and Cosine Functions

We can use the transformations of sine and cosine functions in numerous applications. As mentioned at the beginning of the chapter, circular motion can be modeled using either the sine or cosine function.

Example 11 Finding the Vertical Component of Circular Motion

A point rotates around a circle of radius 3 centered at the origin. Sketch a graph of the y-coordinate of the point as a function of the angle of rotation.

Solution Recall that, for a point on a circle of radius r, the y-coordinate of the point is $y = r\sin(x)$, so in this case, we get the equation $y(x) = 3\sin(x)$. The constant 3 causes a vertical stretch of the y-values of the function by a factor of 3, which we can see in the graph in **Figure 22**.

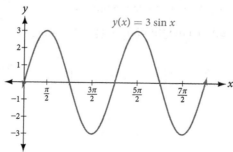

$y(x) = 3\sin x$

Figure 22

Analysis　Notice that the period of the function is still 2π; as we travel around the circle, we return to the point $(3, 0)$ for $x = 2\pi, 4\pi, 6\pi, \dots$ Because the outputs of the graph will now oscillate between -3 and 3, the amplitude of the sine wave is 3.

Try It #10

What is the amplitude of the function $f(x) = 7\cos(x)$? Sketch a graph of this function.

Example 12　**Finding the Vertical Component of Circular Motion**

A circle with radius 3 ft is mounted with its center 4 ft off the ground. The point closest to the ground is labeled *P*, as shown in **Figure 23**. Sketch a graph of the height above the ground of the point *P* as the circle is rotated; then find a function that gives the height in terms of the angle of rotation.

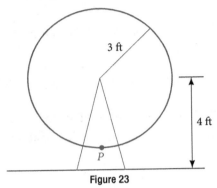

Figure 23

Solution　Sketching the height, we note that it will start 1 ft above the ground, then increase up to 7 ft above the ground, and continue to oscillate 3 ft above and below the center value of 4 ft, as shown in **Figure 24**.

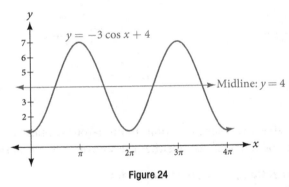

Figure 24

Although we could use a transformation of either the sine or cosine function, we start by looking for characteristics that would make one function easier to use than the other. Let's use a cosine function because it starts at the highest or lowest value, while a sine function starts at the middle value. A standard cosine starts at the highest value, and this graph starts at the lowest value, so we need to incorporate a vertical reflection.

Second, we see that the graph oscillates 3 above and below the center, while a basic cosine has an amplitude of 1, so this graph has been vertically stretched by 3, as in the last example.

Finally, to move the center of the circle up to a height of 4, the graph has been vertically shifted up by 4. Putting these transformations together, we find that

$$y = -3\cos(x) + 4$$

Try It #11

A weight is attached to a spring that is then hung from a board, as shown in **Figure 25**. As the spring oscillates up and down, the position y of the weight relative to the board ranges from -1 in. (at time $x = 0$) to -7 in. (at time $x = \pi$) below the board. Assume the position of y is given as a sinusoidal function of x. Sketch a graph of the function, and then find a cosine function that gives the position y in terms of x.

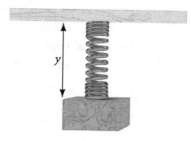

Figure 25

Example 13   **Determining a Rider's Height on a Ferris Wheel**

The London Eye is a huge Ferris wheel with a diameter of 135 meters (443 feet). It completes one rotation every 30 minutes. Riders board from a platform 2 meters above the ground. Express a rider's height above ground as a function of time in minutes.

Solution   With a diameter of 135 m, the wheel has a radius of 67.5 m. The height will oscillate with amplitude 67.5 m above and below the center.

Passengers board 2 m above ground level, so the center of the wheel must be located $67.5 + 2 = 69.5$ m above ground level. The midline of the oscillation will be at 69.5 m.

The wheel takes 30 minutes to complete 1 revolution, so the height will oscillate with a period of 30 minutes.

Lastly, because the rider boards at the lowest point, the height will start at the smallest value and increase, following the shape of a vertically reflected cosine curve.

- Amplitude: 67.5, so $A = 67.5$
- Midline: 69.5, so $D = 69.5$
- Period: 30, so $B = \dfrac{2\pi}{30} = \dfrac{\pi}{15}$
- Shape: $-\cos(t)$

An equation for the rider's height would be

$$y = -67.5\cos\left(\frac{\pi}{15}t\right) + 69.5$$

where t is in minutes and y is measured in meters.

Access these online resources for additional instruction and practice with graphs of sine and cosine functions.

- Amplitude and Period of Sine and Cosine (http://openstaxcollege.org/l/ampperiod)
- Translations of Sine and Cosine (http://openstaxcollege.org/l/translasincos)
- Graphing Sine and Cosine Transformations (http://openstaxcollege.org/l/transformsincos)
- Graphing the Sine Function (http://openstaxcollege.org/l/graphsinefunc)

8.1   SECTION EXERCISES

VERBAL

1. Why are the sine and cosine functions called periodic functions?

2. How does the graph of $y = \sin x$ compare with the graph of $y = \cos x$? Explain how you could horizontally translate the graph of $y = \sin x$ to obtain $y = \cos x$.

3. For the equation $A\cos(Bx + C) + D$, what constants affect the range of the function and how do they affect the range?

4. How does the range of a translated sine function relate to the equation $y = A\sin(Bx + C) + D$?

5. How can the unit circle be used to construct the graph of $f(t) = \sin t$?

GRAPHICAL

For the following exercises, graph two full periods of each function and state the amplitude, period, and midline. State the maximum and minimum y-values and their corresponding x-values on one period for $x > 0$. Round answers to two decimal places if necessary.

6. $f(x) = 2\sin x$

7. $f(x) = \dfrac{2}{3}\cos x$

8. $f(x) = -3\sin x$

9. $f(x) = 4\sin x$

10. $f(x) = 2\cos x$

11. $f(x) = \cos(2x)$

12. $f(x) = 2\sin\left(\dfrac{1}{2}x\right)$

13. $f(x) = 4\cos(\pi x)$

14. $f(x) = 3\cos\left(\dfrac{6}{5}x\right)$

15. $y = 3\sin(8(x + 4)) + 5$

16. $y = 2\sin(3x - 21) + 4$

17. $y = 5\sin(5x + 20) - 2$

For the following exercises, graph one full period of each function, starting at $x = 0$. For each function, state the amplitude, period, and midline. State the maximum and minimum y-values and their corresponding x-values on one period for $x > 0$. State the phase shift and vertical translation, if applicable. Round answers to two decimal places if necessary.

18. $f(t) = 2\sin\left(t - \dfrac{5\pi}{6}\right)$

19. $f(t) = -\cos\left(t + \dfrac{\pi}{3}\right) + 1$

20. $f(t) = 4\cos\left(2\left(t + \dfrac{\pi}{4}\right)\right) - 3$

21. $f(t) = -\sin\left(\dfrac{1}{2}t + \dfrac{5\pi}{3}\right)$

22. $f(x) = 4\sin\left(\dfrac{\pi}{2}(x - 3)\right) + 7$

23. Determine the amplitude, midline, period, and an equation involving the sine function for the graph shown in **Figure 26**.

24. Determine the amplitude, period, midline, and an equation involving cosine for the graph shown in **Figure 27**.

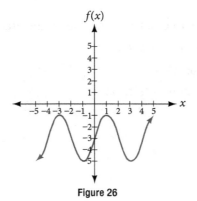

Figure 26

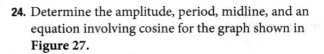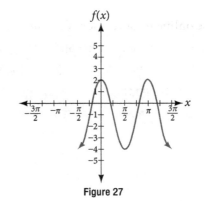

Figure 27

25. Determine the amplitude, period, midline, and an equation involving cosine for the graph shown in **Figure 28.**

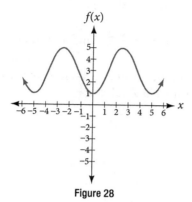

Figure 28

26. Determine the amplitude, period, midline, and an equation involving sine for the graph shown in **Figure 29.**

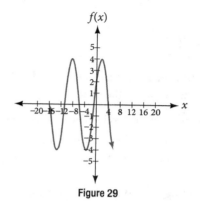

Figure 29

27. Determine the amplitude, period, midline, and an equation involving cosine for the graph shown in **Figure 30.**

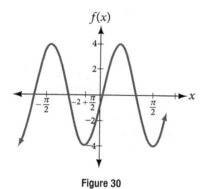

Figure 30

28. Determine the amplitude, period, midline, and an equation involving sine for the graph shown in **Figure 31.**

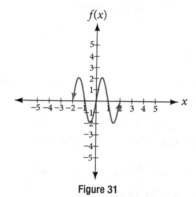

Figure 31

29. Determine the amplitude, period, midline, and an equation involving cosine for the graph shown in **Figure 32.**

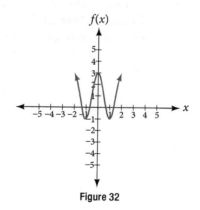

Figure 32

30. Determine the amplitude, period, midline, and an equation involving sine for the graph shown in **Figure 33.**

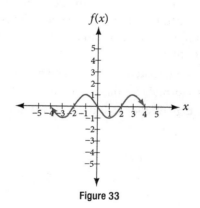

Figure 33

ALGEBRAIC

For the following exercises, let $f(x) = \sin x$.

31. On $[0, 2\pi)$, solve $f(x) = 0$.

32. On $[0, 2\pi)$, solve $f(x) = \frac{1}{2}$.

33. Evaluate $f\left(\frac{\pi}{2}\right)$.

34. On $[0, 2\pi)$, $f(x) = \frac{\sqrt{2}}{2}$. Find all values of x.

35. On $[0, 2\pi)$, the maximum value(s) of the function occur(s) at what x-value(s)?

36. On $[0, 2\pi)$, the minimum value(s) of the function occur(s) at what x-value(s)?

37. Show that $f(-x) = -f(x)$. This means that $f(x) = \sin x$ is an odd function and possesses symmetry with respect to _____.

For the following exercises, let $f(x) = \cos x$.

38. On $[0, 2\pi)$, solve the equation $f(x) = \cos x = 0$.

39. On $[0, 2\pi)$, solve $f(x) = \frac{1}{2}$.

40. On $[0, 2\pi)$, find the x-intercepts of $f(x) = \cos x$.

41. On $[0, 2\pi)$, find the x-values at which the function has a maximum or minimum value.

42. On $[0, 2\pi)$, solve the equation $f(x) = \frac{\sqrt{3}}{2}$.

TECHNOLOGY

43. Graph $h(x) = x + \sin x$ on $[0, 2\pi]$. Explain why the graph appears as it does.

44. Graph $h(x) = x + \sin x$ on $[-100, 100]$. Did the graph appear as predicted in the previous exercise?

45. Graph $f(x) = x \sin x$ on $[0, 2\pi]$ and verbalize how the graph varies from the graph of $f(x) = \sin x$.

46. Graph $f(x) = x \sin x$ on the window $[-10, 10]$ and explain what the graph shows.

47. Graph $f(x) = \frac{\sin x}{x}$ on the window $[-5\pi, 5\pi]$ and explain what the graph shows.

REAL-WORLD APPLICATIONS

48. A Ferris wheel is 25 meters in diameter and boarded from a platform that is 1 meter above the ground. The six o'clock position on the Ferris wheel is level with the loading platform. The wheel completes 1 full revolution in 10 minutes. The function $h(t)$ gives a person's height in meters above the ground t minutes after the wheel begins to turn.

   a. Find the amplitude, midline, and period of $h(t)$.

   b. Find a formula for the height function $h(t)$.

   c. How high off the ground is a person after 5 minutes?

LEARNING OBJECTIVES

In this section, you will:

- Analyze the graph of $y = \tan x$.
- Graph variations of $y = \tan x$.
- Analyze the graphs of $y = \sec x$ and $y = \csc x$.
- Graph variations of $y = \sec x$ and $y = \csc x$.
- Analyze the graph of $y = \cot x$.
- Graph variations of $y = \cot x$.

8.2 GRAPHS OF THE OTHER TRIGONOMETRIC FUNCTIONS

We know the tangent function can be used to find distances, such as the height of a building, mountain, or flagpole. But what if we want to measure repeated occurrences of distance? Imagine, for example, a police car parked next to a warehouse. The rotating light from the police car would travel across the wall of the warehouse in regular intervals. If the input is time, the output would be the distance the beam of light travels. The beam of light would repeat the distance at regular intervals. The tangent function can be used to approximate this distance. Asymptotes would be needed to illustrate the repeated cycles when the beam runs parallel to the wall because, seemingly, the beam of light could appear to extend forever. The graph of the tangent function would clearly illustrate the repeated intervals. In this section, we will explore the graphs of the tangent and other trigonometric functions.

Analyzing the Graph of $y = \tan x$

We will begin with the graph of the tangent function, plotting points as we did for the sine and cosine functions. Recall that

$$\tan x = \frac{\sin x}{\cos x}$$

The period of the tangent function is π because the graph repeats itself on intervals of $k\pi$ where k is a constant. If we graph the tangent function on $-\frac{\pi}{2}$ to $\frac{\pi}{2}$, we can see the behavior of the graph on one complete cycle. If we look at any larger interval, we will see that the characteristics of the graph repeat.

We can determine whether tangent is an odd or even function by using the definition of tangent.

$$\tan(-x) = \frac{\sin(-x)}{\cos(-x)} \qquad \text{Definition of tangent.}$$

$$= \frac{-\sin x}{\cos x} \qquad \text{Sine is an odd function, cosine is even.}$$

$$= -\frac{\sin x}{\cos x} \qquad \begin{array}{l}\text{The quotient of an odd and an even}\\\text{function is odd.}\end{array}$$

$$= -\tan x \qquad \text{Definition of tangent.}$$

Therefore, tangent is an odd function. We can further analyze the graphical behavior of the tangent function by looking at values for some of the special angles, as listed in **Table 1.**

x	$-\frac{\pi}{2}$	$-\frac{\pi}{3}$	$-\frac{\pi}{4}$	$-\frac{\pi}{6}$	0	$\frac{\pi}{6}$	$\frac{\pi}{4}$	$\frac{\pi}{3}$	$\frac{\pi}{2}$
$\tan(x)$	undefined	$-\sqrt{3}$	-1	$-\frac{\sqrt{3}}{3}$	0	$\frac{\sqrt{3}}{3}$	1	$\sqrt{3}$	undefined

Table 1

These points will help us draw our graph, but we need to determine how the graph behaves where it is undefined. If we look more closely at values when $\frac{\pi}{3} < x < \frac{\pi}{2}$, we can use a table to look for a trend. Because $\frac{\pi}{3} \approx 1.05$ and $\frac{\pi}{2} \approx 1.57$, we will evaluate x at radian measures $1.05 < x < 1.57$ as shown in **Table 2.**

x	1.3	1.5	1.55	1.56
tan x	3.6	14.1	48.1	92.6

Table 2

As x approaches $\frac{\pi}{2}$, the outputs of the function get larger and larger. Because $y = \tan x$ is an odd function, we see the corresponding table of negative values in **Table 3**.

x	−1.3	−1.5	−1.55	−1.56
tan x	−3.6	−14.1	−48.1	−92.6

Table 3

We can see that, as x approaches $-\frac{\pi}{2}$, the outputs get smaller and smaller. Remember that there are some values of x for which $\cos x = 0$. For example, $\cos\left(\frac{\pi}{2}\right) = 0$ and $\cos\left(\frac{3\pi}{2}\right) = 0$. At these values, the tangent function is undefined, so the graph of $y = \tan x$ has discontinuities at $x = \frac{\pi}{2}$ and $\frac{3\pi}{2}$. At these values, the graph of the tangent has vertical asymptotes. **Figure 1** represents the graph of $y = \tan(x)$. The tangent is positive from 0 to $\frac{\pi}{2}$ and from π to $\frac{3\pi}{2}$, corresponding to quadrants I and III of the unit circle.

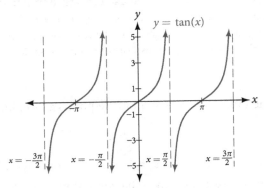

Figure 1 Graph of the tangent function

Graphing Variations of $y = \tan x$

As with the sine and cosine functions, the tangent function can be described by a general equation.

$$y = A\tan(Bx)$$

We can identify horizontal and vertical stretches and compressions using values of A and B. The horizontal stretch can typically be determined from the period of the graph. With tangent graphs, it is often necessary to determine a vertical stretch using a point on the graph.

Because there are no maximum or minimum values of a tangent function, the term *amplitude* cannot be interpreted as it is for the sine and cosine functions. Instead, we will use the phrase *stretching/compressing factor* when referring to the constant A.

---

features of the graph of $y = A\tan(Bx)$

- The stretching factor is $|A|$.
- The period is $P = \dfrac{\pi}{|B|}$.
- The domain is all real numbers x, where $x \neq \dfrac{\pi}{2|B|} + \dfrac{\pi}{|B|}k$ such that k is an integer.
- The range is $(-\infty, \infty)$.
- The asymptotes occur at $x = \dfrac{\pi}{2|B|} + \dfrac{\pi}{|B|}k$, where k is an integer.
- $y = A\tan(Bx)$ is an odd function.

Graphing One Period of a Stretched or Compressed Tangent Function

We can use what we know about the properties of the tangent function to quickly sketch a graph of any stretched and/ or compressed tangent function of the form $f(x) = A\tan(Bx)$. We focus on a single period of the function including the origin, because the periodic property enables us to extend the graph to the rest of the function's domain if we wish. Our limited domain is then the interval $\left(-\dfrac{P}{2}, \dfrac{P}{2}\right)$ and the graph has vertical asymptotes at $\pm\dfrac{P}{2}$ where $P = \dfrac{\pi}{B}$. On $\left(-\dfrac{\pi}{2}, \dfrac{\pi}{2}\right)$, the graph will come up from the left asymptote at $x = -\dfrac{\pi}{2}$, cross through the origin, and continue to increase as it approaches the right asymptote at $x = \dfrac{\pi}{2}$. To make the function approach the asymptotes at the correct rate, we also need to set the vertical scale by actually evaluating the function for at least one point that the graph will pass through. For example, we can use

$$f\left(\frac{P}{4}\right) = A\tan\left(B\frac{P}{4}\right) = A\tan\left(B\frac{\pi}{4B}\right) = A$$

because $\tan\left(\dfrac{\pi}{4}\right) = 1$.

How To...

Given the function $f(x) = A\tan(Bx)$, graph one period.

1. Identify the stretching factor, $|A|$.

2. Identify B and determine the period, $P = \dfrac{\pi}{|B|}$.

3. Draw vertical asymptotes at $x = -\dfrac{P}{2}$ and $x = \dfrac{P}{2}$.

4. For $A > 0$, the graph approaches the left asymptote at negative output values and the right asymptote at positive output values (reverse for $A < 0$).

5. Plot reference points at $\left(\dfrac{P}{4}, A\right)$, $(0, 0)$, and $\left(-\dfrac{P}{4}, -A\right)$, and draw the graph through these points.

Example 1   **Sketching a Compressed Tangent**

Sketch a graph of one period of the function $y = 0.5\tan\left(\dfrac{\pi}{2}x\right)$.

Solution   First, we identify A and B.

$$y = 0.5\,\tan\left(\frac{\pi}{2}x\right)$$
$$\uparrow \qquad \nearrow$$
$$y = A\tan(Bx)$$

Because $A = 0.5$ and $B = \dfrac{\pi}{2}$, we can find the stretching/compressing factor and period. The period is $\dfrac{\pi}{\frac{\pi}{2}} = 2$, so the asymptotes are at $x = \pm 1$. At a quarter period from the origin, we have

$$f(0.5) = 0.5\tan\left(\frac{0.5\pi}{2}\right)$$

$$= 0.5\tan\left(\frac{\pi}{4}\right)$$

$$= 0.5$$

This means the curve must pass through the points $(0.5, 0.5)$, $(0, 0)$, and $(-0.5, -0.5)$. The only inflection point is at the origin. **Figure 2** shows the graph of one period of the function.

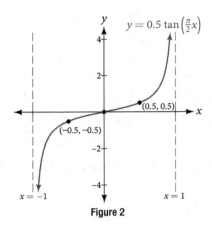

Figure 2

Try It #1

Sketch a graph of $f(x) = 3\tan\left(\dfrac{\pi}{6}x\right)$.

Graphing One Period of a Shifted Tangent Function

Now that we can graph a tangent function that is stretched or compressed, we will add a vertical and/or horizontal (or phase) shift. In this case, we add C and D to the general form of the tangent function.

$$f(x) = A\tan(Bx - C) + D$$

The graph of a transformed tangent function is different from the basic tangent function $\tan x$ in several ways:

---

features of the graph of $y = A\tan(Bx - C) + D$

- The stretching factor is $|A|$.
- The period is $\dfrac{\pi}{|B|}$.
- The domain is $x \neq \dfrac{C}{B} + \dfrac{\pi}{2|B|}k$, where k is an odd integer.
- The range is $(-\infty, \infty)$.
- The vertical asymptotes occur at $x = \dfrac{C}{B} + \dfrac{\pi}{2|B|}k$, where k is an odd integer.
- There is no amplitude.
- $y = A\tan(Bx)$ is an odd function because it is the quotient of odd and even functions (sine and cosine respectively).

How To...

Given the function $y = A\tan(Bx - C) + D$, sketch the graph of one period.

1. Express the function given in the form $y = A\tan(Bx - C) + D$.

2. Identify the stretching/compressing factor, $|A|$.

3. Identify B and determine the period, $P = \dfrac{\pi}{|B|}$.

4. Identify C and determine the phase shift, $\dfrac{C}{B}$.

5. Draw the graph of $y = A\tan(Bx)$ shifted to the right by $\dfrac{C}{B}$ and up by D.

6. Sketch the vertical asymptotes, which occur at $x = \dfrac{C}{B} + \dfrac{\pi}{2|B|}k$, where k is an odd integer.

7. Plot any three reference points and draw the graph through these points.

Example 2 Graphing One Period of a Shifted Tangent Function

Graph one period of the function $y = -2\tan(\pi x + \pi) - 1$.

Solution

Step 1. The function is already written in the form $y = A\tan(Bx - C) + D$.

Step 2. $A = -2$, so the stretching factor is $|A| = 2$.

Step 3. $B = \pi$, so the period is $P = \dfrac{\pi}{|B|} = \dfrac{\pi}{\pi} = 1$.

Step 4. $C = -\pi$, so the phase shift is $\dfrac{C}{B} = \dfrac{-\pi}{\pi} = -1$.

Step 5-7. The asymptotes are at $x = -\dfrac{3}{2}$ and $x = -\dfrac{1}{2}$ and the three recommended reference points are $(-1.25, 1)$, $(-1, -1)$, and $(-0.75, -3)$. The graph is shown in **Figure 3**.

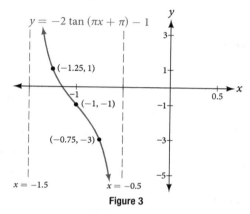

Figure 3

Analysis Note that this is a decreasing function because $A < 0$.

Try It #2

How would the graph in **Example 2** look different if we made $A = 2$ instead of -2?

How To...

Given the graph of a tangent function, identify horizontal and vertical stretches.

1. Find the period P from the spacing between successive vertical asymptotes or x-intercepts.

2. Write $f(x) = A\tan\left(\dfrac{\pi}{P}x\right)$.

3. Determine a convenient point $(x, f(x))$ on the given graph and use it to determine A.

Example 3 Identifying the Graph of a Stretched Tangent

Find a formula for the function graphed in **Figure 4**.

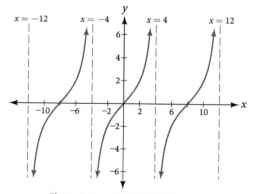

Figure 4 A stretched tangent function

Solution   The graph has the shape of a tangent function.

Step 1. One cycle extends from −4 to 4, so the period is $P = 8$. Since $P = \dfrac{\pi}{|B|}$, we have $B = \dfrac{\pi}{P} = \dfrac{\pi}{8}$.

Step 2. The equation must have the form $f(x) = A\tan\left(\dfrac{\pi}{8}x\right)$.

Step 3. To find the vertical stretch A, we can use the point $(2, 2)$.

$$2 = A\tan\left(\dfrac{\pi}{8} \cdot 2\right) = A\tan\left(\dfrac{\pi}{4}\right)$$

Because $\tan\left(\dfrac{\pi}{4}\right) = 1$, $A = 2$.

This function would have a formula $f(x) = 2\tan\left(\dfrac{\pi}{8}x\right)$.

Try It #3

Find a formula for the function in **Figure 5**.

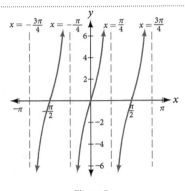

Figure 5

Analyzing the Graphs of $y = \sec x$ and $y = \csc x$

The secant was defined by the reciprocal identity $\sec x = \dfrac{1}{\cos x}$. Notice that the function is undefined when the cosine is 0, leading to vertical asymptotes at $\dfrac{\pi}{2}$, $\dfrac{3\pi}{2}$, etc. Because the cosine is never more than 1 in absolute value, the secant, being the reciprocal, will never be less than 1 in absolute value.

We can graph $y = \sec x$ by observing the graph of the cosine function because these two functions are reciprocals of one another. See **Figure 6**. The graph of the cosine is shown as a blue wave so we can see the relationship. Where the graph of the cosine function decreases, the graph of the secant function increases. Where the graph of the cosine function increases, the graph of the secant function decreases. When the cosine function is zero, the secant is undefined.

The secant graph has vertical asymptotes at each value of x where the cosine graph crosses the x-axis; we show these in the graph below with dashed vertical lines, but will not show all the asymptotes explicitly on all later graphs involving the secant and cosecant.

Note that, because cosine is an even function, secant is also an even function. That is, $\sec(-x) = \sec x$.

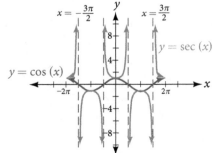

Figure 6 Graph of the secant function, $f(x) = \sec x = \dfrac{1}{\cos x}$

As we did for the tangent function, we will again refer to the constant $|A|$ as the stretching factor, not the amplitude.

features of the graph of $y = A\sec(Bx)$

- The stretching factor is $|A|$.
- The period is $\dfrac{2\pi}{|B|}$.
- The domain is $x \neq \dfrac{\pi}{2|B|}k$, where k is an odd integer.
- The range is $(-\infty, -|A|] \cup [|A|, \infty)$.
- The vertical asymptotes occur at $x = \dfrac{\pi}{2|B|}k$, where k is an odd integer.
- There is no amplitude.
- $y = A\sec(Bx)$ is an even function because cosine is an even function.

Similar to the secant, the cosecant is defined by the reciprocal identity $\csc x = \dfrac{1}{\sin x}$. Notice that the function is undefined when the sine is 0, leading to a vertical asymptote in the graph at $0, \pi$, etc. Since the sine is never more than 1 in absolute value, the cosecant, being the reciprocal, will never be less than 1 in absolute value.

We can graph $y = \csc x$ by observing the graph of the sine function because these two functions are reciprocals of one another. See **Figure 7**. The graph of sine is shown as a blue wave so we can see the relationship. Where the graph of the sine function decreases, the graph of the cosecant function increases. Where the graph of the sine function increases, the graph of the cosecant function decreases.

The cosecant graph has vertical asymptotes at each value of x where the sine graph crosses the x-axis; we show these in the graph below with dashed vertical lines.

Note that, since sine is an odd function, the cosecant function is also an odd function. That is, $\csc(-x) = -\csc x$.

The graph of cosecant, which is shown in **Figure 7**, is similar to the graph of secant.

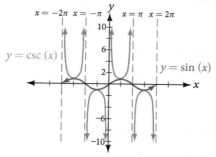

Figure 7 The graph of the cosecant function, $f(x) = \csc x = \dfrac{1}{\sin x}$

features of the graph of $y = A\csc(Bx)$

- The stretching factor is $|A|$.
- The period is $\dfrac{2\pi}{|B|}$.
- The domain is $x \neq \dfrac{\pi}{|B|}k$, where k is an integer.
- The range is $(-\infty, -|A|] \cup [|A|, \infty)$.
- The asymptotes occur at $x = \dfrac{\pi}{|B|}k$, where k is an integer.
- $y = A\csc(Bx)$ is an odd function because sine is an odd function.

Graphing Variations of $y = \sec x$ and $y = \csc x$

For shifted, compressed, and/or stretched versions of the secant and cosecant functions, we can follow similar methods to those we used for tangent and cotangent. That is, we locate the vertical asymptotes and also evaluate the functions for a few points (specifically the local extrema). If we want to graph only a single period, we can choose the interval for the period in more than one way. The procedure for secant is very similar, because the cofunction identity means that the secant graph is the same as the cosecant graph shifted half a period to the left. Vertical and phase shifts may be applied to the cosecant function in the same way as for the secant and other functions. The equations become the following.

$$y = A\sec(Bx - C) + D \qquad y = A\csc(Bx - C) + D$$

---

features of the graph of $y = A\sec(Bx - C) + D$

- The stretching factor is $|A|$.
- The period is $\dfrac{2\pi}{|B|}$.
- The domain is $x \neq \dfrac{C}{B} + \dfrac{\pi}{2|B|}k$, where k is an odd integer.
- The range is $(-\infty, -|A| + D] \cup [|A| + D, \infty)$.
- The vertical asymptotes occur at $x = \dfrac{C}{B} + \dfrac{\pi}{2|B|}k$, where k is an odd integer.
- There is no amplitude.
- $y = A\sec(Bx)$ is an even function because cosine is an even function.

---

features of the graph of $y = A\csc(Bx - C) + D$

- The stretching factor is $|A|$.
- The period is $\dfrac{2\pi}{|B|}$.
- The domain is $x \neq \dfrac{C}{B} + \dfrac{\pi}{|B|}k$, where k is an integer.
- The range is $(-\infty, -|A| + D] \cup [|A| + D, \infty)$.
- The vertical asymptotes occur at $x = \dfrac{C}{B} + \dfrac{\pi}{|B|}k$, where k is an integer.
- There is no amplitude.
- $y = A\csc(Bx)$ is an odd function because sine is an odd function.

How To...

Given a function of the form $y = A\sec(Bx)$, graph one period.

1. Express the function given in the form $y = A\sec(Bx)$.
2. Identify the stretching/compressing factor, $|A|$.
3. Identify B and determine the period, $P = \dfrac{2\pi}{|B|}$.
4. Sketch the graph of $y = A\cos(Bx)$.
5. Use the reciprocal relationship between $y = \cos x$ and $y = \sec x$ to draw the graph of $y = A\sec(Bx)$.
6. Sketch the asymptotes.
7. Plot any two reference points and draw the graph through these points.

Example 4   **Graphing a Variation of the Secant Function**

Graph one period of $f(x) = 2.5\sec(0.4x)$.

Solution

Step 1. The given function is already written in the general form, $y = A\sec(Bx)$.

Step 2. $A = 2.5$ so the stretching factor is 2.5.

Step 3. $B = 0.4$ so $P = \dfrac{2\pi}{0.4} = 5\pi$. The period is 5π units.

Step 4. Sketch the graph of the function $g(x) = 2.5\cos(0.4x)$.

Step 5. Use the reciprocal relationship of the cosine pend secant functions to draw the cosecant function.

Steps 6–7. Sketch two asymptotes at $x = 1.25\pi$ and $x = 3.75\pi$. We can use two reference points, the local minimum at $(0, 2.5)$ and the local maximum at $(2.5\pi, -2.5)$. **Figure 8** shows the graph.

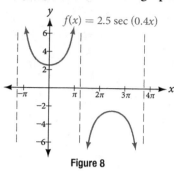

Figure 8

Try It #4

Graph one period of $f(x) = -2.5\sec(0.4x)$.

Q & A...

Do the vertical shift and stretch/compression affect the secant's range?

Yes. The range of $f(x) = A\sec(Bx - C) + D$ is $(-\infty, -|A| + D] \cup [|A| + D, \infty)$.

How To...

Given a function of the form $f(x) = A\sec(Bx - C) + D$, graph one period.

1. Express the function given in the form $y = A\sec(Bx - C) + D$.

2. Identify the stretching/compressing factor, $|A|$.

3. Identify B and determine the period, $\dfrac{2\pi}{|B|}$.

4. Identify C and determine the phase shift, $\dfrac{C}{B}$.

5. Draw the graph of $y = A\sec(Bx)$ but shift it to the right by $\dfrac{C}{B}$ and up by D.

6. Sketch the vertical asymptotes, which occur at $x = \dfrac{C}{B} + \dfrac{\pi}{2|B|}k$, where k is an odd integer.

Example 5   **Graphing a Variation of the Secant Function**

Graph one period of $y = 4\sec\left(\dfrac{\pi}{3}x - \dfrac{\pi}{2}\right) + 1$.

Solution

Step 1. Express the function given in the form $y = 4\sec\left(\dfrac{\pi}{3}x - \dfrac{\pi}{2}\right) + 1$.

Step 2. The stretching/compressing factor is $|A| = 4$.

Step 3. The period is

$$\frac{2\pi}{|B|} = \frac{2\pi}{\dfrac{\pi}{3}}$$

$$= \frac{2\pi}{1} \cdot \frac{3}{\pi}$$

$$= 6$$

Step 4. The phase shift is

$$\frac{C}{B} = \frac{\dfrac{\pi}{2}}{\dfrac{\pi}{3}}$$

$$= \frac{\pi}{2} \cdot \frac{3}{\pi}$$

$$= 1.5$$

Step 5. Draw the graph of $y = A\sec(Bx)$, but shift it to the right by $\dfrac{C}{B} = 1.5$ and up by $D = 6$.

Step 6. Sketch the vertical asymptotes, which occur at $x = 0, x = 3$, and $x = 6$. There is a local minimum at $(1.5, 5)$ and a local maximum at $(4.5, -3)$. **Figure 9** shows the graph.

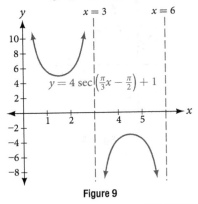

Figure 9

Try It #5

Graph one period of $f(x) = -6\sec(4x + 2) - 8$.

Q & A...

The domain of csc x was given to be all x such that $x \neq k\pi$ for any integer k. Would the domain of $y = A\csc(Bx - C) + D$ be $x \neq \dfrac{C + k\pi}{B}$?

Yes. The excluded points of the domain follow the vertical asymptotes. Their locations show the horizontal shift and compression or expansion implied by the transformation to the original function's input.

How To...

Given a function of the form $y = A\csc(Bx)$, graph one period.

1. Express the function given in the form $y = A\csc(Bx)$.
2. Identify the stretching/compressing factor, $|A|$.
3. Identify B and determine the period, $P = \dfrac{2\pi}{|B|}$.
4. Draw the graph of $y = A\sin(Bx)$.
5. Use the reciprocal relationship between $y = \sin x$ and $y = \csc x$ to draw the graph of $y = A\csc(Bx)$.
6. Sketch the asymptotes.
7. Plot any two reference points and draw the graph through these points.

Example 6   **Graphing a Variation of the Cosecant Function**

Graph one period of $f(x) = -3\csc(4x)$.

Solution

Step 1. The given function is already written in the general form, $y = A\csc(Bx)$.

Step 2. $|A| = |-3| = 3$, so the stretching factor is 3.

Step 3. $B = 4$, so $P = \dfrac{2\pi}{4} = \dfrac{\pi}{2}$. The period is $\dfrac{\pi}{2}$ units.

Step 4. Sketch the graph of the function $g(x) = -3\sin(4x)$.

Step 5. Use the reciprocal relationship of the sine and cosecant functions to draw the cosecant function.

Steps 6–7. Sketch three asymptotes at $x = 0$, $x = \dfrac{\pi}{4}$, and $x = \dfrac{\pi}{2}$. We can use two reference points, the local maximum at $\left(\dfrac{\pi}{8}, -3\right)$ and the local minimum at $\left(\dfrac{3\pi}{8}, 3\right)$. **Figure 10** shows the graph.

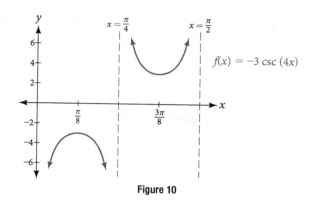

Figure 10

Try It #6

Graph one period of $f(x) = 0.5\csc(2x)$.

How To...

Given a function of the form $f(x) = A\csc(Bx - C) + D$, graph one period.

1. Express the function given in the form $y = A\csc(Bx - C) + D$.
2. Identify the stretching/compressing factor, $|A|$.
3. Identify B and determine the period, $\dfrac{2\pi}{|B|}$.
4. Identify C and determine the phase shift, $\dfrac{C}{B}$.
5. Draw the graph of $y = A\csc(Bx)$ but shift it to the right by $\dfrac{C}{B}$ and up by D.
6. Sketch the vertical asymptotes, which occur at $x = \dfrac{C}{B} + \dfrac{\pi}{|B|}k$, where k is an integer.

Example 7 **Graphing a Vertically Stretched, Horizontally Compressed, and Vertically Shifted Cosecant**

Sketch a graph of $y = 2\csc\left(\dfrac{\pi}{2}x\right) + 1$. What are the domain and range of this function?

Solution

Step 1. Express the function given in the form $y = 2\csc\left(\dfrac{\pi}{2}x\right) + 1$.

Step 2. Identify the stretching/compressing factor, $|A| = 2$.

Step 3. The period is $\dfrac{2\pi}{|B|} = \dfrac{2\pi}{\dfrac{\pi}{2}} = \dfrac{2\pi}{1} \cdot \dfrac{2}{\pi} = 4$.

Step 4. The phase shift is $\dfrac{0}{\dfrac{\pi}{2}} = 0$.

Step 5. Draw the graph of $y = A\csc(Bx)$ but shift it up $D = 1$.

Step 6. Sketch the vertical asymptotes, which occur at $x = 0$, $x = 2$, $x = 4$.

The graph for this function is shown in **Figure 11**.

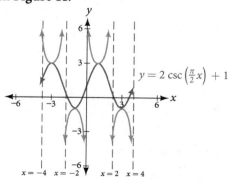

Figure 11 A transformed cosecant function

Analysis The vertical asymptotes shown on the graph mark off one period of the function, and the local extrema in this interval are shown by dots. Notice how the graph of the transformed cosecant relates to the graph of $f(x) = 2\sin\left(\dfrac{\pi}{2}x\right) + 1$, shown as the blue wave.

Try It #7

Given the graph of $f(x) = 2\cos\left(\dfrac{\pi}{2}x\right) + 1$ shown in **Figure 12**, sketch the graph of $g(x) = 2\sec\left(\dfrac{\pi}{2}x\right) + 1$ on the same axes.

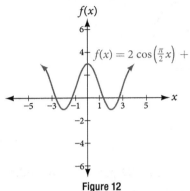

Figure 12

Analyzing the Graph of $y = \cot x$

The last trigonometric function we need to explore is cotangent. The cotangent is defined by the reciprocal identity $\cot x = \dfrac{1}{\tan x}$. Notice that the function is undefined when the tangent function is 0, leading to a vertical asymptote in the graph at 0, π, etc. Since the output of the tangent function is all real numbers, the output of the cotangent function is also all real numbers.

We can graph $y = \cot x$ by observing the graph of the tangent function because these two functions are reciprocals of one another. See **Figure 13**. Where the graph of the tangent function decreases, the graph of the cotangent function increases. Where the graph of the tangent function increases, the graph of the cotangent function decreases.

The cotangent graph has vertical asymptotes at each value of x where $\tan x = 0$; we show these in the graph below with dashed lines. Since the cotangent is the reciprocal of the tangent, $\cot x$ has vertical asymptotes at all values of x where $\tan x = 0$, and $\cot x = 0$ at all values of x where $\tan x$ has its vertical asymptotes.

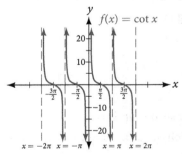

Figure 13 The cotangent function

---

features of the graph of $y = A\cot(Bx)$

- The stretching factor is $|A|$.
- The period is $P = \dfrac{\pi}{|B|}$.
- The domain is $x \neq \dfrac{\pi}{|B|}k$, where k is an integer.
- The range is $(-\infty, \infty)$.
- The asymptotes occur at $x = \dfrac{\pi}{|B|}k$, where k is an integer.
- $y = A\cot(Bx)$ is an odd function.

Graphing Variations of $y = \cot x$

We can transform the graph of the cotangent in much the same way as we did for the tangent. The equation becomes the following.

$$y = A\cot(Bx - C) + D$$

---

features of the graph of $y = A\cot(Bx - C) + D$

- The stretching factor is $|A|$.
- The period is $\dfrac{\pi}{|B|}$.
- The domain is $x \neq \dfrac{C}{B} + \dfrac{\pi}{|B|}k$, where k is an integer.
- The range is $(-\infty, \infty)$.
- The vertical asymptotes occur at $x = \dfrac{C}{B} + \dfrac{\pi}{|B|}k$, where k is an integer.
- There is no amplitude.
- $y = A\cot(Bx)$ is an odd function because it is the quotient of even and odd functions (cosine and sine, respectively)

How To...

Given a modified cotangent function of the form $f(x) = A\cot(Bx)$, graph one period.

1. Express the function in the form $f(x) = A\cot(Bx)$.
2. Identify the stretching factor, $|A|$.
3. Identify the period, $P = \dfrac{\pi}{|B|}$.
4. Draw the graph of $y = A\tan(Bx)$.
5. Plot any two reference points.
6. Use the reciprocal relationship between tangent and cotangent to draw the graph of $y = A\cot(Bx)$.
7. Sketch the asymptotes.

Example 8   **Graphing Variations of the Cotangent Function**

Determine the stretching factor, period, and phase shift of $y = 3\cot(4x)$, and then sketch a graph.

Solution

Step 1. Expressing the function in the form $f(x) = A\cot(Bx)$ gives $f(x) = 3\cot(4x)$.

Step 2. The stretching factor is $|A| = 3$.

Step 3. The period is $P = \dfrac{\pi}{4}$.

Step 4. Sketch the graph of $y = 3\tan(4x)$.

Step 5. Plot two reference points. Two such points are $\left(\dfrac{\pi}{16}, 3\right)$ and $\left(\dfrac{3\pi}{16}, -3\right)$.

Step 6. Use the reciprocal relationship to draw $y = 3\cot(4x)$.

Step 7. Sketch the asymptotes, $x = 0$, $x = \dfrac{\pi}{4}$.

The blue graph in **Figure 14** shows $y = 3\tan(4x)$ and the red graph shows $y = 3\cot(4x)$.

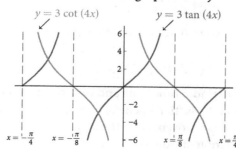

Figure 14

How To...

Given a modified cotangent function of the form $f(x) = A\cot(Bx - C) + D$, graph one period.

1. Express the function in the form $f(x) = A\cot(Bx - C) + D$.
2. Identify the stretching factor, $|A|$.
3. Identify the period, $P = \dfrac{\pi}{|B|}$.
4. Identify the phase shift, $\dfrac{C}{B}$.
5. Draw the graph of $y = A\tan(Bx)$ shifted to the right by $\dfrac{C}{B}$ and up by D.
6. Sketch the asymptotes $x = \dfrac{C}{B} + \dfrac{\pi}{|B|}k$, where k is an integer.
7. Plot any three reference points and draw the graph through these points.

Example 9   Graphing a Modified Cotangent

Sketch a graph of one period of the function $f(x) = 4\cot\left(\dfrac{\pi}{8}x - \dfrac{\pi}{2}\right) - 2$.

Solution

Step 1. The function is already written in the general form $f(x) = A\cot(Bx - C) + D$.

Step 2. $A = 4$, so the stretching factor is 4.

Step 3. $B = \dfrac{\pi}{8}$, so the period is $P = \dfrac{\pi}{|B|} = \dfrac{\pi}{\frac{\pi}{8}} = 8$.

Step 4. $C = \dfrac{\pi}{2}$, so the phase shift is $\dfrac{C}{B} = \dfrac{\frac{\pi}{2}}{\frac{\pi}{8}} = 4$.

Step 5. We draw $f(x) = 4\tan\left(\dfrac{\pi}{8}x - \dfrac{\pi}{2}\right) - 2$.

Step 6-7. Three points we can use to guide the graph are $(6, 2)$, $(8, -2)$, and $(10, -6)$. We use the reciprocal relationship of tangent and cotangent to draw $f(x) = 4\cot\left(\dfrac{\pi}{8}x - \dfrac{\pi}{2}\right) - 2$.

Step 8. The vertical asymptotes are $x = 4$ and $x = 12$.

The graph is shown in **Figure 15**.

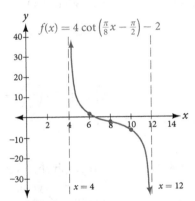

Figure 15 One period of a modified cotangent function

Using the Graphs of Trigonometric Functions to Solve Real-World Problems

Many real-world scenarios represent periodic functions and may be modeled by trigonometric functions. As an example, let's return to the scenario from the section opener. Have you ever observed the beam formed by the rotating light on a police car and wondered about the movement of the light beam itself across the wall? The periodic behavior of the distance the light shines as a function of time is obvious, but how do we determine the distance? We can use the tangent function.

Example 10 Using Trigonometric Functions to Solve Real-World Scenarios

Suppose the function $y = 5\tan\left(\frac{\pi}{4}t\right)$ marks the distance in the movement of a light beam from the top of a police car across a wall where t is the time in seconds and y is the distance in feet from a point on the wall directly across from the police car.

 a. Find and interpret the stretching factor and period.

 b. Graph on the interval $[0, 5]$.

 c. Evaluate $f(1)$ and discuss the function's value at that input.

Solution

 a. We know from the general form of $y = A\tan(Bt)$ that $|A|$ is the stretching factor and $\frac{\pi}{B}$ is the period.

$$y = 5\tan\left(\frac{\pi}{4}t\right)$$
$$\uparrow \qquad \uparrow$$
$$A \qquad B$$

Figure 16

We see that the stretching factor is 5. This means that the beam of light will have moved 5 ft after half the period.

The period is $\dfrac{\pi}{\frac{\pi}{4}} = \dfrac{\pi}{1} \cdot \dfrac{4}{\pi} = 4$. This means that every 4 seconds, the beam of light sweeps the wall. The distance from the spot across from the police car grows larger as the police car approaches.

 b. To graph the function, we draw an asymptote at $t = 2$ and use the stretching factor and period. See **Figure 17**.

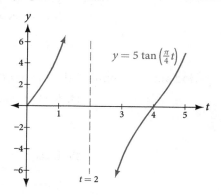

Figure 17

 c. period: $f(1) = 5\tan\left(\frac{\pi}{4}(1)\right) = 5(1) = 5$; after 1 second, the beam of has moved 5 ft from the spot across from the police car.

Access these online resources for additional instruction and practice with graphs of other trigonometric functions.

 • Graphing the Tangent (http://openstaxcollege.org/l/graphtangent)

 • Graphing Cosecant and Secant (http://openstaxcollege.org/l/graphcscsec)

 • Graphing the Cotangent (http://openstaxcollege.org/l/graphcot)

8.2   SECTION EXERCISES

VERBAL

1. Explain how the graph of the sine function can be used to graph $y = \csc x$.

2. How can the graph of $y = \cos x$ be used to construct the graph of $y = \sec x$?

3. Explain why the period of $\tan x$ is equal to π.

4. Why are there no intercepts on the graph of $y = \csc x$?

5. How does the period of $y = \csc x$ compare with the period of $y = \sin x$?

ALGEBRAIC

For the following exercises, match each trigonometric function with one of the graphs in **Figure 18**.

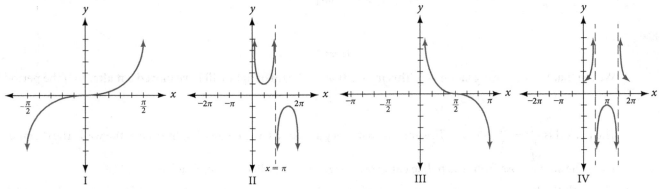

Figure 18

6. $f(x) = \tan x$

7. $f(x) = \sec x$

8. $f(x) = \csc x$

9. $f(x) = \cot x$

For the following exercises, find the period and horizontal shift of each of the functions.

10. $f(x) = 2\tan(4x - 32)$

11. $h(x) = 2\sec\left(\dfrac{\pi}{4}(x + 1)\right)$

12. $m(x) = 6\csc\left(\dfrac{\pi}{3}x + \pi\right)$

13. If $\tan x = -1.5$, find $\tan(-x)$.

14. If $\sec x = 2$, find $\sec(-x)$.

15. If $\csc x = -5$, find $\csc(-x)$.

16. If $x\sin x = 2$, find $(-x)\sin(-x)$.

For the following exercises, rewrite each expression such that the argument x is positive.

17. $\cot(-x)\cos(-x) + \sin(-x)$

18. $\cos(-x) + \tan(-x)\sin(-x)$

GRAPHICAL

For the following exercises, sketch two periods of the graph for each of the following functions. Identify the stretching factor, period, and asymptotes.

19. $f(x) = 2\tan(4x - 32)$

20. $h(x) = 2\sec\left(\dfrac{\pi}{4}(x + 1)\right)$

21. $m(x) = 6\csc\left(\dfrac{\pi}{3}x + \pi\right)$

22. $j(x) = \tan\left(\dfrac{\pi}{2}x\right)$

23. $p(x) = \tan\left(x - \dfrac{\pi}{2}\right)$

24. $f(x) = 4\tan(x)$

25. $f(x) = \tan\left(x + \dfrac{\pi}{4}\right)$

26. $f(x) = \pi\tan(\pi x - \pi) - \pi$

27. $f(x) = 2\csc(x)$

28. $f(x) = -\dfrac{1}{4}\csc(x)$

29. $f(x) = 4\sec(3x)$

30. $f(x) = -3\cot(2x)$

31. $f(x) = 7\sec(5x)$

32. $f(x) = \dfrac{9}{10}\csc(\pi x)$

33. $f(x) = 2\csc\left(x + \dfrac{\pi}{4}\right) - 1$

34. $f(x) = -\sec\left(x - \dfrac{\pi}{3}\right) - 2$

35. $f(x) = \dfrac{7}{5}\csc\left(x - \dfrac{\pi}{4}\right)$

36. $f(x) = 5\left(\cot\left(x + \dfrac{\pi}{2}\right) - 3\right)$

For the following exercises, find and graph two periods of the periodic function with the given stretching factor, $|A|$, period, and phase shift.

37. A tangent curve, $A = 1$, period of $\frac{\pi}{3}$; and phase shift $(h, k) = \left(\frac{\pi}{4}, 2\right)$

38. A tangent curve, $A = -2$, period of $\frac{\pi}{4}$, and phase shift $(h, k) = \left(-\frac{\pi}{4}, -2\right)$

For the following exercises, find an equation for the graph of each function.

39.

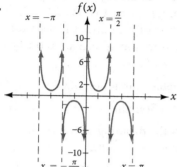

40.

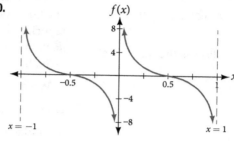

41.

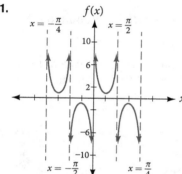

42.

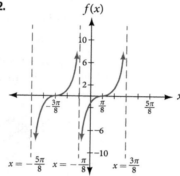

43.

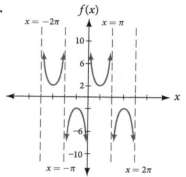

44.

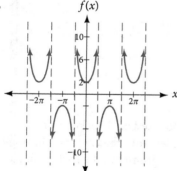

45.

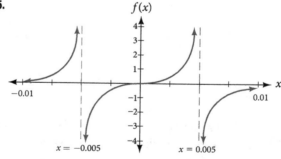

TECHNOLOGY

For the following exercises, use a graphing calculator to graph two periods of the given function. Note: most graphing calculators do not have a cosecant button; therefore, you will need to input $\csc x$ as $\frac{1}{\sin x}$.

46. $f(x) = |\csc(x)|$

47. $f(x) = |\cot(x)|$

48. $f(x) = 2^{\csc(x)}$

49. $f(x) = \dfrac{\csc(x)}{\sec(x)}$

50. Graph $f(x) = 1 + \sec^2(x) - \tan^2(x)$. What is the function shown in the graph?

51. $f(x) = \sec(0.001x)$

52. $f(x) = \cot(100\pi x)$

53. $f(x) = \sin^2 x + \cos^2 x$

REAL-WORLD APPLICATIONS

54. The function $f(x) = 20\tan\left(\dfrac{\pi}{10}x\right)$ marks the distance in the movement of a light beam from a police car across a wall for time x, in seconds, and distance $f(x)$, in feet.

   a. Graph on the interval $[0, 5]$.

   b. Find and interpret the stretching factor, period, and asymptote.

   c. Evaluate $f(1)$ and $f(2.5)$ and discuss the function's values at those inputs.

55. Standing on the shore of a lake, a fisherman sights a boat far in the distance to his left. Let x, measured in radians, be the angle formed by the line of sight to the ship and a line due north from his position. Assume due north is 0 and x is measured negative to the left and positive to the right. (See **Figure 19**.) The boat travels from due west to due east and, ignoring the curvature of the Earth, the distance $d(x)$, in kilometers, from the fisherman to the boat is given by the function $d(x) = 1.5\sec(x)$.

   a. What is a reasonable domain for $d(x)$?

   b. Graph $d(x)$ on this domain.

   c. Find and discuss the meaning of any vertical asymptotes on the graph of $d(x)$.

   d. Calculate and interpret $d\left(-\dfrac{\pi}{3}\right)$. Round to the second decimal place.

   e. Calculate and interpret $d\left(\dfrac{\pi}{6}\right)$. Round to the second decimal place.

   f. What is the minimum distance between the fisherman and the boat? When does this occur?

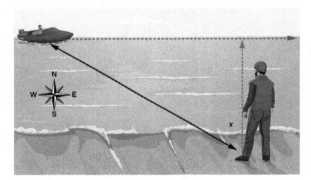

Figure 19

56. A laser rangefinder is locked on a comet approaching Earth. The distance $g(x)$, in kilometers, of the comet after x days, for x in the interval 0 to 30 days, is given by $g(x) = 250{,}000\csc\left(\dfrac{\pi}{30}x\right)$.

   a. Graph $g(x)$ on the interval $[0, 35]$.

   b. Evaluate $g(5)$ and interpret the information.

   c. What is the minimum distance between the comet and Earth? When does this occur? To which constant in the equation does this correspond?

   d. Find and discuss the meaning of any vertical asymptotes.

57. A video camera is focused on a rocket on a launching pad 2 miles from the camera. The angle of elevation from the ground to the rocket after x seconds is $\dfrac{\pi}{120}x$.

   a. Write a function expressing the altitude $h(x)$, in miles, of the rocket above the ground after x seconds. Ignore the curvature of the Earth.

   b. Graph $h(x)$ on the interval $(0, 60)$.

   c. Evaluate and interpret the values $h(0)$ and $h(30)$.

   d. What happens to the values of $h(x)$ as x approaches 60 seconds? Interpret the meaning of this in terms of the problem.

LEARNING OBJECTIVES

In this section, you will:

- Understand and use the inverse sine, cosine, and tangent functions.
- Find the exact value of expressions involving the inverse sine, cosine, and tangent functions.
- Use a calculator to evaluate inverse trigonometric functions.
- Find exact values of composite functions with inverse trigonometric functions.

8.3 INVERSE TRIGONOMETRIC FUNCTIONS

For any right triangle, given one other angle and the length of one side, we can figure out what the other angles and sides are. But what if we are given only two sides of a right triangle? We need a procedure that leads us from a ratio of sides to an angle. This is where the notion of an inverse to a trigonometric function comes into play. In this section, we will explore the inverse trigonometric functions.

Understanding and Using the Inverse Sine, Cosine, and Tangent Functions

In order to use inverse trigonometric functions, we need to understand that an inverse trigonometric function "undoes" what the original trigonometric function "does," as is the case with any other function and its inverse. In other words, the domain of the inverse function is the range of the original function, and vice versa, as summarized in **Figure 1**.

Trig Functions
Domain: Measure of an angle
Range: Ratio

Inverse Trig Functions
Domain: Ratio
Range: Measure of an angle

Figure 1

For example, if $f(x) = \sin x$, then we would write $f^{-1}(x) = \sin^{-1}x$. Be aware that $\sin^{-1} x$ does not mean $\dfrac{1}{\sin x}$. The following examples illustrate the inverse trigonometric functions:

- Since $\sin\left(\dfrac{\pi}{6}\right) = \dfrac{1}{2}$, then $\dfrac{\pi}{6} = \sin^{-1}\left(\dfrac{1}{2}\right)$.
- Since $\cos(\pi) = -1$, then $\pi = \cos^{-1}(-1)$.
- Since $\tan\left(\dfrac{\pi}{4}\right) = 1$, then $\dfrac{\pi}{4} = \tan^{-1}(1)$.

In previous sections, we evaluated the trigonometric functions at various angles, but at times we need to know what angle would yield a specific sine, cosine, or tangent value. For this, we need inverse functions. Recall that, for a one-to-one function, if $f(a) = b$, then an inverse function would satisfy $f^{-1}(b) = a$.

Bear in mind that the sine, cosine, and tangent functions are not one-to-one functions. The graph of each function would fail the horizontal line test. In fact, no periodic function can be one-to-one because each output in its range corresponds to at least one input in every period, and there are an infinite number of periods. As with other functions that are not one-to-one, we will need to restrict the domain of each function to yield a new function that is one-to-one. We choose a domain for each function that includes the number 0. **Figure 2** shows the graph of the sine function limited to $\left[-\dfrac{\pi}{2}, \dfrac{\pi}{2}\right]$ and the graph of the cosine function limited to $[0, \pi]$.

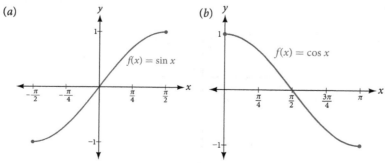

Figure 2 (a) Sine function on a restricted domain of $\left[-\dfrac{\pi}{2}, \dfrac{\pi}{2}\right]$; (b) Cosine function on a restricted domain of $[0, \pi]$

Figure 3 shows the graph of the tangent function limited to $\left(-\dfrac{\pi}{2}, \dfrac{\pi}{2}\right)$.

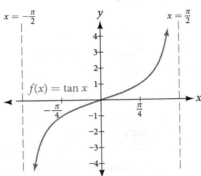

Figure 3 Tangent function on a restricted domain of $\left(-\dfrac{\pi}{2}, \dfrac{\pi}{2}\right)$

These conventional choices for the restricted domain are somewhat arbitrary, but they have important, helpful characteristics. Each domain includes the origin and some positive values, and most importantly, each results in a one-to-one function that is invertible. The conventional choice for the restricted domain of the tangent function also has the useful property that it extends from one vertical asymptote to the next instead of being divided into two parts by an asymptote.

On these restricted domains, we can define the inverse trigonometric functions.

- The **inverse sine function** $y = \sin^{-1} x$ means $x = \sin y$. The inverse sine function is sometimes called the **arcsine function**, and notated arcsin$x$.

$$y = \sin^{-1} x \text{ has domain } [-1, 1] \text{ and range } \left[-\frac{\pi}{2}, \frac{\pi}{2}\right]$$

- The **inverse cosine function** $y = \cos^{-1} x$ means $x = \cos y$. The inverse cosine function is sometimes called the **arccosine** function, and notated arccos x.

$$y = \cos^{-1} x \text{ has domain } [-1, 1] \text{ and range } [0, \pi]$$

- The **inverse tangent function** $y = \tan^{-1} x$ means $x = \tan y$. The inverse tangent function is sometimes called the **arctangent** function, and notated arctan x.

$$y = \tan^{-1} x \text{ has domain } (-\infty, \infty) \text{ and range } \left(-\frac{\pi}{2}, \frac{\pi}{2}\right)$$

The graphs of the inverse functions are shown in **Figure 4, Figure 5,** and **Figure 6**. Notice that the output of each of these inverse functions is a number, an angle in radian measure. We see that $\sin^{-1} x$ has domain $[-1, 1]$ and range $\left[-\dfrac{\pi}{2}, \dfrac{\pi}{2}\right]$, $\cos^{-1} x$ has domain $[-1, 1]$ and range $[0, \pi]$, and $\tan^{-1} x$ has domain of all real numbers and range $\left(-\dfrac{\pi}{2}, \dfrac{\pi}{2}\right)$. To find the domain and range of inverse trigonometric functions, switch the domain and range of the original functions. Each graph of the inverse trigonometric function is a reflection of the graph of the original function about the line $y = x$.

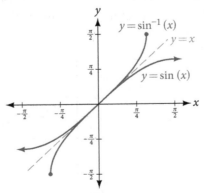

Figure 4 The sine function and inverse sine (or arcsine) function

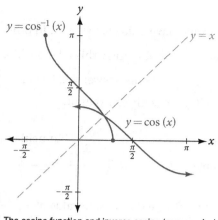

Figure 5 The cosine function and inverse cosine (or arccosine) function

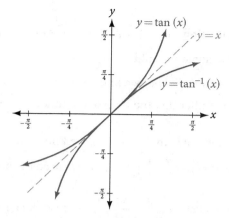

Figure 6 The tangent function and inverse tangent (or arctangent) function

---

relations for inverse sine, cosine, and tangent functions

For angles in the interval $\left[-\frac{\pi}{2}, \frac{\pi}{2}\right]$, if $\sin y = x$, then $\sin^{-1} x = y$.

For angles in the interval $[0, \pi]$, if $\cos y = x$, then $\cos^{-1} x = y$.

For angles in the interval $\left(-\frac{\pi}{2}, \frac{\pi}{2}\right)$, if $\tan y = x$, then $\tan^{-1} x = y$.

Example 1 Writing a Relation for an Inverse Function

Given $\sin\left(\frac{5\pi}{12}\right) \approx 0.96593$, write a relation involving the inverse sine.

Solution Use the relation for the inverse sine. If $\sin y = x$, then $\sin^{-1} x = y$.
In this problem, $x = 0.96593$, and $y = \frac{5\pi}{12}$.

$$\sin^{-1}(0.96593) \approx \frac{5\pi}{12}$$

Try It #1

Given $\cos(0.5) \approx 0.8776$, write a relation involving the inverse cosine.

Finding the Exact Value of Expressions Involving the Inverse Sine, Cosine, and Tangent Functions

Now that we can identify inverse functions, we will learn to evaluate them. For most values in their domains, we must evaluate the inverse trigonometric functions by using a calculator, interpolating from a table, or using some other numerical technique. Just as we did with the original trigonometric functions, we can give exact values for the inverse functions when we are using the special angles, specifically $\frac{\pi}{6}$ (30°), $\frac{\pi}{4}$ (45°), and $\frac{\pi}{3}$ (60°), and their reflections into other quadrants.

How To...

Given a "special" input value, evaluate an inverse trigonometric function.

1. Find angle x for which the original trigonometric function has an output equal to the given input for the inverse trigonometric function.
2. If x is not in the defined range of the inverse, find another angle y that is in the defined range and has the same sine, cosine, or tangent as x, depending on which corresponds to the given inverse function.

Example 2 Evaluating Inverse Trigonometric Functions for Special Input Values

Evaluate each of the following.

a. $\sin^{-1}\left(\frac{1}{2}\right)$ b. $\sin^{-1}\left(-\frac{\sqrt{2}}{2}\right)$ c. $\cos^{-1}\left(-\frac{\sqrt{3}}{2}\right)$ d. $\tan^{-1}(1)$

Solution

a. Evaluating $\sin^{-1}\left(\frac{1}{2}\right)$ is the same as determining the angle that would have a sine value of $\frac{1}{2}$. In other words, what angle x would satisfy $\sin(x) = \frac{1}{2}$? There are multiple values that would satisfy this relationship, such as $\frac{\pi}{6}$ and $\frac{5\pi}{6}$, but we know we need the angle in the interval $\left[-\frac{\pi}{2}, \frac{\pi}{2}\right]$, so the answer will be $\sin^{-1}\left(\frac{1}{2}\right) = \frac{\pi}{6}$. Remember that the inverse is a function, so for each input, we will get exactly one output.

b. To evaluate $\sin^{-1}\left(-\frac{\sqrt{2}}{2}\right)$, we know that $\frac{5\pi}{4}$ and $\frac{7\pi}{4}$ both have a sine value of $-\frac{\sqrt{2}}{2}$, but neither is in the interval $\left[-\frac{\pi}{2}, \frac{\pi}{2}\right]$. For that, we need the negative angle coterminal with $\frac{7\pi}{4}$: $\sin^{-1}\left(-\frac{\sqrt{2}}{2}\right) = -\frac{\pi}{4}$.

c. To evaluate $\cos^{-1}\left(-\frac{\sqrt{3}}{2}\right)$, we are looking for an angle in the interval $[0, \pi]$ with a cosine value of $-\frac{\sqrt{3}}{2}$. The angle that satisfies this is $\cos^{-1}\left(-\frac{\sqrt{3}}{2}\right) = \frac{5\pi}{6}$.

d. Evaluating $\tan^{-1}(1)$, we are looking for an angle in the interval $\left(-\frac{\pi}{2}, \frac{\pi}{2}\right)$ with a tangent value of 1. The correct angle is $\tan^{-1}(1) = \frac{\pi}{4}$.

Try It #2

Evaluate each of the following.

a. $\sin^{-1}(-1)$ **b.** $\tan^{-1}(-1)$ **c.** $\cos^{-1}(-1)$ **d.** $\cos^{-1}\left(\frac{1}{2}\right)$

Using a Calculator to Evaluate Inverse Trigonometric Functions

To evaluate inverse trigonometric functions that do not involve the special angles discussed previously, we will need to use a calculator or other type of technology. Most scientific calculators and calculator-emulating applications have specific keys or buttons for the inverse sine, cosine, and tangent functions. These may be labeled, for example, **SIN-1**, **ARCSIN**, or **ASIN**.

In the previous chapter, we worked with trigonometry on a right triangle to solve for the sides of a triangle given one side and an additional angle. Using the inverse trigonometric functions, we can solve for the angles of a right triangle given two sides, and we can use a calculator to find the values to several decimal places.

In these examples and exercises, the answers will be interpreted as angles and we will use θ as the independent variable. The value displayed on the calculator may be in degrees or radians, so be sure to set the mode appropriate to the application.

Example 3   Evaluating the Inverse Sine on a Calculator

Evaluate $\sin^{-1}(0.97)$ using a calculator.

Solution   Because the output of the inverse function is an angle, the calculator will give us a degree value if in degree mode and a radian value if in radian mode. Calculators also use the same domain restrictions on the angles as we are using.

In radian mode, $\sin^{-1}(0.97) \approx 1.3252$. In degree mode, $\sin^{-1}(0.97) \approx 75.93°$. Note that in calculus and beyond we will use radians in almost all cases.

Try It #3

Evaluate $\cos^{-1}(-0.4)$ using a calculator.

How To...

Given two sides of a right triangle like the one shown in **Figure 7**, find an angle.

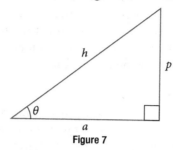

Figure 7

1. If one given side is the hypotenuse of length h and the side of length a adjacent to the desired angle is given, use the equation $\theta = \cos^{-1}\left(\dfrac{a}{h}\right)$.

2. If one given side is the hypotenuse of length h and the side of length p opposite to the desired angle is given, use the equation $\theta = \sin^{-1}\left(\dfrac{p}{h}\right)$

3. If the two legs (the sides adjacent to the right angle) are given, then use the equation $\theta = \tan^{-1}\left(\dfrac{p}{a}\right)$.

Example 4   **Applying the Inverse Cosine to a Right Triangle**

Solve the triangle in **Figure 8** for the angle θ.

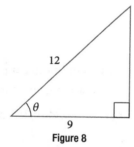

Figure 8

Solution   Because we know the hypotenuse and the side adjacent to the angle, it makes sense for us to use the cosine function.

$$\cos \theta = \frac{9}{12}$$

$$\theta = \cos^{-1}\left(\frac{9}{12}\right) \qquad \text{Apply definition of the inverse.}$$

$$\theta \approx 0.7227 \text{ or about } 41.4096° \qquad \text{Evaluate.}$$

Try It #4

Solve the triangle in **Figure 9** for the angle θ.

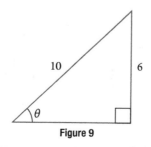

Figure 9

Finding Exact Values of Composite Functions with Inverse Trigonometric Functions

There are times when we need to compose a trigonometric function with an inverse trigonometric function. In these cases, we can usually find exact values for the resulting expressions without resorting to a calculator. Even when the input to the composite function is a variable or an expression, we can often find an expression for the output. To help sort out different cases, let $f(x)$ and $g(x)$ be two different trigonometric functions belonging to the set $\{\sin(x), \cos(x), \tan(x)\}$ and let $f^{-1}(y)$ and $g^{-1}(y)$ be their inverses.

Evaluating Compositions of the Form $f(f^{-1}(y))$ and $f^{-1}(f(x))$

For any trigonometric function, $f(f^{-1}(y)) = y$ for all y in the proper domain for the given function. This follows from the definition of the inverse and from the fact that the range of f was defined to be identical to the domain of f^{-1}. However, we have to be a little more careful with expressions of the form $f^{-1}(f(x))$.

---

compositions of a trigonometric function and its inverse

$$\sin(\sin^{-1} x) = x \text{ for } -1 \leq x \leq 1$$
$$\cos(\cos^{-1} x) = x \text{ for } -1 \leq x \leq 1$$
$$\tan(\tan^{-1} x) = x \text{ for } -\infty < x < \infty$$

$$\sin^{-1}(\sin x) = x \text{ only for } -\frac{\pi}{2} \leq x \leq \frac{\pi}{2}$$
$$\cos^{-1}(\cos x) = x \text{ only for } 0 \leq x \leq \pi$$
$$\tan^{-1}(\tan x) = x \text{ only for } -\frac{\pi}{2} < x < \frac{\pi}{2}$$

Q & A...
Is it correct that $\sin^{-1}(\sin x) = x$?

No. This equation is correct if x belongs to the restricted domain $\left[-\frac{\pi}{2}, \frac{\pi}{2} \right]$, but sine is defined for all real input values, and for x outside the restricted interval, the equation is not correct because its inverse always returns a value in $\left[-\frac{\pi}{2}, \frac{\pi}{2} \right]$. The situation is similar for cosine and tangent and their inverses. For example, $\sin^{-1}\left(\sin\left(\frac{3\pi}{4} \right) \right) = \frac{\pi}{4}$.

How To...
Given an expression of the form $f^{-1}(f(\theta))$ where $f(\theta) = \sin \theta$, $\cos \theta$, or $\tan \theta$, evaluate.

1. If θ is in the restricted domain of f, then $f^{-1}(f(\theta)) = \theta$.
2. If not, then find an angle ϕ within the restricted domain of f such that $f(\phi) = f(\theta)$. Then $f^{-1}(f(\theta)) = \phi$.

Example 5   Using Inverse Trigonometric Functions

Evaluate the following:

    a. $\sin^{-1}\left(\sin\left(\frac{\pi}{3} \right) \right)$
    b. $\sin^{-1}\left(\sin\left(\frac{2\pi}{3} \right) \right)$
    c. $\cos^{-1}\left(\cos\left(\frac{2\pi}{3} \right) \right)$
    d. $\cos^{-1}\left(\cos\left(-\frac{\pi}{3} \right) \right)$

Solution

    a. $\frac{\pi}{3}$ is in $\left[-\frac{\pi}{2}, \frac{\pi}{2} \right]$, so $\sin^{-1}\left(\sin\left(\frac{\pi}{3} \right) \right) = \frac{\pi}{3}$.

    b. $\frac{2\pi}{3}$ is not in $\left[-\frac{\pi}{2}, \frac{\pi}{2} \right]$, but $\sin\left(\frac{2\pi}{3} \right) = \sin\left(\frac{\pi}{3} \right)$, so $\sin^{-1}\left(\sin\left(\frac{2\pi}{3} \right) \right) = \frac{\pi}{3}$.

    c. $\frac{2\pi}{3}$ is in $[0, \pi]$, so $\cos^{-1}\left(\cos\left(\frac{2\pi}{3} \right) \right) = \frac{2\pi}{3}$.

    d. $-\frac{\pi}{3}$ is not in $[0, \pi]$, but $\cos\left(-\frac{\pi}{3} \right) = \cos\left(\frac{\pi}{3} \right)$ because cosine is an even function. $\frac{\pi}{3}$ is in $[0, \pi]$, so $\cos^{-1}\left(\cos\left(-\frac{\pi}{3} \right) \right) = \frac{\pi}{3}$.

Try It #5

Evaluate $\tan^{-1}\left(\tan\left(\frac{\pi}{8}\right)\right)$ and $\tan^{-1}\left(\tan\left(\frac{11\pi}{9}\right)\right)$.

Evaluating Compositions of the Form $f^{-1}(g(x))$

Now that we can compose a trigonometric function with its inverse, we can explore how to evaluate a composition of a trigonometric function and the inverse of another trigonometric function. We will begin with compositions of the form $f^{-1}(g(x))$. For special values of x, we can exactly evaluate the inner function and then the outer, inverse function. However, we can find a more general approach by considering the relation between the two acute angles of a right triangle where one is θ, making the other $\frac{\pi}{2} - \theta$. Consider the sine and cosine of each angle of the right triangle in **Figure 10**.

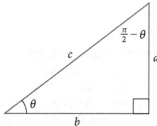

Figure 10 Right triangle illustrating the cofunction relationships

Because $\cos\theta = \frac{b}{c} = \sin\left(\frac{\pi}{2} - \theta\right)$, we have $\sin^{-1}(\cos\theta) = \frac{\pi}{2} - \theta$ if $0 \leq \theta \leq \pi$. If θ is not in this domain, then we need to find another angle that has the same cosine as θ and does belong to the restricted domain; we then subtract this angle from $\frac{\pi}{2}$. Similarly, $\sin\theta = \frac{a}{c} = \cos\left(\frac{\pi}{2} - \theta\right)$, so $\cos^{-1}(\sin\theta) = \frac{\pi}{2} - \theta$ if $-\frac{\pi}{2} \leq \theta \leq \frac{\pi}{2}$. These are just the function-cofunction relationships presented in another way.

How To...

Given functions of the form $\sin^{-1}(\cos x)$ and $\cos^{-1}(\sin x)$, evaluate them.

1. If x is in $[0, \pi]$, then $\sin^{-1}(\cos x) = \frac{\pi}{2} - x$.
2. If x is not in $[0, \pi]$, then find another angle y in $[0, \pi]$ such that $\cos y = \cos x$.
$$\sin^{-1}(\cos x) = \frac{\pi}{2} - y$$
3. If x is in $\left[-\frac{\pi}{2}, \frac{\pi}{2}\right]$, then $\cos^{-1}(\sin x) = \frac{\pi}{2} - x$.
4. If x is not in $\left[-\frac{\pi}{2}, \frac{\pi}{2}\right]$, then find another angle y in $\left[-\frac{\pi}{2}, \frac{\pi}{2}\right]$ such that $\sin y = \sin x$.
$$\cos^{-1}(\sin x) = \frac{\pi}{2} - y$$

Example 6   Evaluating the Composition of an Inverse Sine with a Cosine

Evaluate $\sin^{-1}\left(\cos\left(\frac{13\pi}{6}\right)\right)$

    a. by direct evaluation.   **b.** by the method described previously.

Solution

    a. Here, we can directly evaluate the inside of the composition.

$$\cos\left(\frac{13\pi}{6}\right) = \cos\left(\frac{\pi}{6} + 2\pi\right)$$
$$= \cos\left(\frac{\pi}{6}\right)$$
$$= \frac{\sqrt{3}}{2}$$

Now, we can evaluate the inverse function as we did earlier.

$$\sin^{-1}\left(\frac{\sqrt{3}}{2}\right) = \frac{\pi}{3}$$

b. We have $x = \frac{13\pi}{6}, y = \frac{\pi}{6}$, and

$$\sin^{-1}\left(\cos\left(\frac{13\pi}{6}\right)\right) = \frac{\pi}{2} - \frac{\pi}{6}$$

$$= \frac{\pi}{3}$$

Try It #6

Evaluate $\cos^{-1}\left(\sin\left(-\frac{11\pi}{4}\right)\right)$.

Evaluating Compositions of the Form $f(g^{-1}(x))$

To evaluate compositions of the form $f(g^{-1}(x))$, where f and g are any two of the functions sine, cosine, or tangent and x is any input in the domain of g^{-1}, we have exact formulas, such as $\sin(\cos^{-1} x) = \sqrt{1 - x^2}$. When we need to use them, we can derive these formulas by using the trigonometric relations between the angles and sides of a right triangle, together with the use of Pythagoras's relation between the lengths of the sides. We can use the Pythagorean identity, $\sin^2 x + \cos^2 x = 1$, to solve for one when given the other. We can also use the inverse trigonometric functions to find compositions involving algebraic expressions.

Example 7   Evaluating the Composition of a Sine with an Inverse Cosine

Find an exact value for $\sin\left(\cos^{-1}\left(\frac{4}{5}\right)\right)$.

Solution   Beginning with the inside, we can say there is some angle such that $\theta = \cos^{-1}\left(\frac{4}{5}\right)$, which means $\cos\theta = \frac{4}{5}$, and we are looking for $\sin\theta$. We can use the Pythagorean identity to do this.

$$\sin^2\theta + \cos^2\theta = 1 \qquad \text{Use our known value for cosine.}$$

$$\sin^2\theta + \left(\frac{4}{5}\right)^2 = 1 \qquad \text{Solve for sine.}$$

$$\sin^2\theta = 1 - \frac{16}{25}$$

$$\sin\theta = \pm\sqrt{\frac{9}{25}} = \pm\frac{3}{5}$$

Since $\theta = \cos^{-1}\left(\frac{4}{5}\right)$ is in quadrant I, $\sin\theta$ must be positive, so the solution is $\frac{3}{5}$. See **Figure 11**.

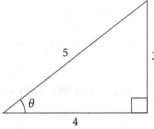

Figure 11 Right triangle illustrating that if $\cos\theta = \frac{4}{5}$, then $\sin\theta = \frac{3}{5}$

We know that the inverse cosine always gives an angle on the interval $[0, \pi]$, so we know that the sine of that angle must be positive; therefore $\sin\left(\cos^{-1}\left(\frac{4}{5}\right)\right) = \sin\theta = \frac{3}{5}$.

Try It #7

Evaluate $\cos\left(\tan^{-1}\left(\frac{5}{12}\right)\right)$.

Example 8   **Evaluating the Composition of a Sine with an Inverse Tangent**

Find an exact value for $\sin\left(\tan^{-1}\left(\frac{7}{4}\right)\right)$.

Solution   While we could use a similar technique as in **Example 6**, we will demonstrate a different technique here.

From the inside, we know there is an angle such that $\tan\theta = \frac{7}{4}$. We can envision this as the opposite and adjacent sides on a right triangle, as shown in **Figure 12.**

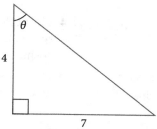

Figure 12 A right triangle with two sides known

Using the Pythagorean Theorem, we can find the hypotenuse of this triangle.

$$4^2 + 7^2 = \text{hypotenuse}^2$$
$$\text{hypotenuse} = \sqrt{65}$$

Now, we can evaluate the sine of the angle as the opposite side divided by the hypotenuse.

$$\sin\theta = \frac{7}{\sqrt{65}}$$

This gives us our desired composition.

$$\sin\left(\tan^{-1}\left(\frac{7}{4}\right)\right) = \sin\theta$$
$$= \frac{7}{\sqrt{65}}$$
$$= \frac{7\sqrt{65}}{65}$$

Try It #8

Evaluate $\cos\left(\sin^{-1}\left(\frac{7}{9}\right)\right)$.

Example 9   **Finding the Cosine of the Inverse Sine of an Algebraic Expression**

Find a simplified expression for $\cos\left(\sin^{-1}\left(\frac{x}{3}\right)\right)$ for $-3 \leq x \leq 3$.

Solution   We know there is an angle θ such that $\sin\theta = \frac{x}{3}$.

$$\sin^2\theta + \cos^2\theta = 1 \qquad \text{Use the Pythagorean Theorem.}$$
$$\left(\frac{x}{3}\right)^2 + \cos^2\theta = 1 \qquad \text{Solve for cosine.}$$
$$\cos^2\theta = 1 - \frac{x^2}{9}$$
$$\cos\theta = \pm\sqrt{\frac{9-x^2}{9}} = \pm\frac{\sqrt{9-x^2}}{3}$$

Because we know that the inverse sine must give an angle on the interval $\left[-\frac{\pi}{2}, \frac{\pi}{2}\right]$, we can deduce that the cosine of that angle must be positive.

$$\cos\left(\sin^{-1}\left(\frac{x}{3}\right)\right) = \frac{\sqrt{9-x^2}}{3}$$

Try It #9

Find a simplified expression for $\sin(\tan^{-1}(4x))$ for $-\frac{1}{4} \leq x \leq \frac{1}{4}$.

Access this online resource for additional instruction and practice with inverse trigonometric functions.

- Evaluate Expressions Involving Inverse Trigonometric Functions (http://openstaxcollege.org/l/evalinverstrig)

8.3   SECTION EXERCISES

VERBAL

1. Why do the functions $f(x) = \sin^{-1} x$ and $g(x) = \cos^{-1} x$ have different ranges?

2. Since the functions $y = \cos x$ and $y = \cos^{-1} x$ are inverse functions, why is $\cos^{-1}\left(\cos\left(-\dfrac{\pi}{6}\right)\right)$ not equal to $-\dfrac{\pi}{6}$?

3. Explain the meaning of $\dfrac{\pi}{6} = \arcsin(0.5)$.

4. Most calculators do not have a key to evaluate $\sec^{-1}(2)$. Explain how this can be done using the cosine function or the inverse cosine function.

5. Why must the domain of the sine function, $\sin x$, be restricted to $\left[-\dfrac{\pi}{2}, \dfrac{\pi}{2}\right]$ for the inverse sine function to exist?

6. Discuss why this statement is incorrect: $\arccos(\cos x) = x$ for all x.

7. Determine whether the following statement is true or false and explain your answer: $\arccos(-x) = \pi - \arccos x$.

ALGEBRAIC

For the following exercises, evaluate the expressions.

8. $\sin^{-1}\left(\dfrac{\sqrt{2}}{2}\right)$

9. $\sin^{-1}\left(-\dfrac{1}{2}\right)$

10. $\cos^{-1}\left(\dfrac{1}{2}\right)$

11. $\cos^{-1}\left(-\dfrac{\sqrt{2}}{2}\right)$

12. $\tan^{-1}(1)$

13. $\tan^{-1}(-\sqrt{3})$

14. $\tan^{-1}(-1)$

15. $\tan^{-1}(\sqrt{3})$

16. $\tan^{-1}\left(\dfrac{-1}{\sqrt{3}}\right)$

For the following exercises, use a calculator to evaluate each expression. Express answers to the nearest hundredth.

17. $\cos^{-1}(-0.4)$

18. $\arcsin(0.23)$

19. $\arccos\left(\dfrac{3}{5}\right)$

20. $\cos^{-1}(0.8)$

21. $\tan^{-1}(6)$

For the following exercises, find the angle θ in the given right triangle. Round answers to the nearest hundredth.

22.

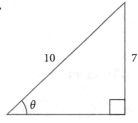

10   7

θ

23.

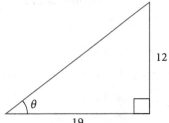

12

θ

19

For the following exercises, find the exact value, if possible, without a calculator. If it is not possible, explain why.

24. $\sin^{-1}(\cos(\pi))$

25. $\tan^{-1}(\sin(\pi))$

26. $\cos^{-1}\left(\sin\left(\dfrac{\pi}{3}\right)\right)$

27. $\tan^{-1}\left(\sin\left(\dfrac{\pi}{3}\right)\right)$

28. $\sin^{-1}\left(\cos\left(\dfrac{-\pi}{2}\right)\right)$

29. $\tan^{-1}\left(\sin\left(\dfrac{4\pi}{3}\right)\right)$

30. $\sin^{-1}\left(\sin\left(\dfrac{5\pi}{6}\right)\right)$

31. $\tan^{-1}\left(\sin\left(\dfrac{-5\pi}{2}\right)\right)$

32. $\cos\left(\sin^{-1}\left(\dfrac{4}{5}\right)\right)$

33. $\sin\left(\cos^{-1}\left(\dfrac{3}{5}\right)\right)$

34. $\sin\left(\tan^{-1}\left(\dfrac{4}{3}\right)\right)$

35. $\cos\left(\tan^{-1}\left(\dfrac{12}{5}\right)\right)$

36. $\cos\left(\sin^{-1}\left(\dfrac{1}{2}\right)\right)$

For the following exercises, find the exact value of the expression in terms of x with the help of a reference triangle.

37. $\tan(\sin^{-1}(x-1))$

38. $\sin(\cos^{-1}(1-x))$

39. $\cos\left(\sin^{-1}\left(\frac{1}{x}\right)\right)$

40. $\cos(\tan^{-1}(3x-1))$

41. $\tan\left(\sin^{-1}\left(x+\frac{1}{2}\right)\right)$

EXTENSIONS

For the following exercise, evaluate the expression without using a calculator. Give the exact value.

42. $\dfrac{\sin^{-1}\left(\frac{1}{2}\right) - \cos^{-1}\left(\frac{\sqrt{2}}{2}\right) + \sin^{-1}\left(\frac{\sqrt{3}}{2}\right) - \cos^{-1}(1)}{\cos^{-1}\left(\frac{\sqrt{3}}{2}\right) - \sin^{-1}\left(\frac{\sqrt{2}}{2}\right) + \cos^{-1}\left(\frac{1}{2}\right) - \sin^{-1}(0)}$

For the following exercises, find the function if $\sin t = \dfrac{x}{x+1}$.

43. $\cos t$

44. $\sec t$

45. $\cot t$

46. $\cos\left(\sin^{-1}\left(\frac{x}{x+1}\right)\right)$

47. $\tan^{-1}\left(\frac{x}{\sqrt{2x+1}}\right)$

GRAPHICAL

48. Graph $y = \sin^{-1} x$ and state the domain and range of the function.

49. Graph $y = \arccos x$ and state the domain and range of the function.

50. Graph one cycle of $y = \tan^{-1} x$ and state the domain and range of the function.

51. For what value of x does $\sin x = \sin^{-1} x$? Use a graphing calculator to approximate the answer.

52. For what value of x does $\cos x = \cos^{-1} x$? Use a graphing calculator to approximate the answer.

REAL-WORLD APPLICATIONS

53. Suppose a 13-foot ladder is leaning against a building, reaching to the bottom of a second-floor window 12 feet above the ground. What angle, in radians, does the ladder make with the building?

54. Suppose you drive 0.6 miles on a road so that the vertical distance changes from 0 to 150 feet. What is the angle of elevation of the road?

55. An isosceles triangle has two congruent sides of length 9 inches. The remaining side has a length of 8 inches. Find the angle that a side of 9 inches makes with the 8-inch side.

56. Without using a calculator, approximate the value of arctan(10,000). Explain why your answer is reasonable.

57. A truss for the roof of a house is constructed from two identical right triangles. Each has a base of 12 feet and height of 4 feet. Find the measure of the acute angle adjacent to the 4-foot side.

58. The line $y = \frac{3}{5}x$ passes through the origin in the x,y-plane. What is the measure of the angle that the line makes with the positive x-axis?

59. The line $y = -\frac{3}{7}x$ passes through the origin in the x,y-plane. What is the measure of the angle that the line makes with the negative x-axis?

60. What percentage grade should a road have if the angle of elevation of the road is 4 degrees? (The percentage grade is defined as the change in the altitude of the road over a 100-foot horizontal distance. For example a 5% grade means that the road rises 5 feet for every 100 feet of horizontal distance.)

61. A 20-foot ladder leans up against the side of a building so that the foot of the ladder is 10 feet from the base of the building. If specifications call for the ladder's angle of elevation to be between 35 and 45 degrees, does the placement of this ladder satisfy safety specifications?

62. Suppose a 15-foot ladder leans against the side of a house so that the angle of elevation of the ladder is 42 degrees. How far is the foot of the ladder from the side of the house?

CHAPTER 8 REVIEW

Key Terms

amplitude the vertical height of a function; the constant A appearing in the definition of a sinusoidal function

arccosine another name for the inverse cosine; $\arccos x = \cos^{-1} x$

arcsine another name for the inverse sine; $\arcsin x = \sin^{-1} x$

arctangent another name for the inverse tangent; $\arctan x = \tan^{-1} x$

inverse cosine function the function $\cos^{-1} x$, which is the inverse of the cosine function and the angle that has a cosine equal to a given number

inverse sine function the function $\sin^{-1} x$, which is the inverse of the sine function and the angle that has a sine equal to a given number

inverse tangent function the function $\tan^{-1} x$, which is the inverse of the tangent function and the angle that has a tangent equal to a given number

midline the horizontal line $y = D$, where D appears in the general form of a sinusoidal function

periodic function a function $f(x)$ that satisfies $f(x + P) = f(x)$ for a specific constant P and any value of x

phase shift the horizontal displacement of the basic sine or cosine function; the constant $\frac{C}{B}$

sinusoidal function any function that can be expressed in the form $f(x) = A\sin(Bx - C) + D$ or $f(x) = A\cos(Bx - C) + D$

Key Equations

Sinusoidal functions	$f(x) = A\sin(Bx - C) + D$
	$f(x) = A\cos(Bx - C) + D$
Shifted, compressed, and/or stretched tangent function	$y = A\tan(Bx - C) + D$
Shifted, compressed, and/or stretched secant function	$y = A\sec(Bx - C) + D$
Shifted, compressed, and/or stretched cosecant function	$y = A\csc(Bx - C) + D$
Shifted, compressed, and/or stretched cotangent function	$y = A\cot(Bx - C) + D$

Key Concepts

8.1 Graphs of the Sine and Cosine Functions

- Periodic functions repeat after a given value. The smallest such value is the period. The basic sine and cosine functions have a period of 2π.
- The function $\sin x$ is odd, so its graph is symmetric about the origin. The function $\cos x$ is even, so its graph is symmetric about the y-axis.
- The graph of a sinusoidal function has the same general shape as a sine or cosine function.
- In the general formula for a sinusoidal function, the period is $P = \frac{2\pi}{|B|}$. See **Example 1**.
- In the general formula for a sinusoidal function, $|A|$ represents amplitude. If $|A| > 1$, the function is stretched, whereas if $|A| < 1$, the function is compressed. See **Example 2**.
- The value $\frac{C}{B}$ in the general formula for a sinusoidal function indicates the phase shift. See **Example 3**.
- The value D in the general formula for a sinusoidal function indicates the vertical shift from the midline. See **Example 4**.
- Combinations of variations of sinusoidal functions can be detected from an equation. See **Example 5**.
- The equation for a sinusoidal function can be determined from a graph. See **Example 6** and **Example 7**.
- A function can be graphed by identifying its amplitude and period. See **Example 8** and **Example 9**.
- A function can also be graphed by identifying its amplitude, period, phase shift, and horizontal shift. See **Example 10**.
- Sinusoidal functions can be used to solve real-world problems. See **Example 11**, **Example 12**, and **Example 13**.

8.2 Graphs of the Other Trigonometric Functions

- The tangent function has period π.

- $f(x) = A\tan(Bx - C) + D$ is a tangent with vertical and/or horizontal stretch/compression and shift. See **Example 1**, **Example 2**, and **Example 3**.

- The secant and cosecant are both periodic functions with a period of 2π. $f(x) = A\sec(Bx - C) + D$ gives a shifted, compressed, and/or stretched secant function graph. See **Example 4** and **Example 5**.

- $f(x) = A\csc(Bx - C) + D$ gives a shifted, compressed, and/or stretched cosecant function graph. See **Example 6** and **Example 7**.

- The cotangent function has period π and vertical asymptotes at $0, \pm\pi, \pm 2\pi, \ldots$

- The range of cotangent is $(-\infty, \infty)$, and the function is decreasing at each point in its range.

- The cotangent is zero at $\pm\dfrac{\pi}{2}, \pm\dfrac{3\pi}{2}, \ldots$

- $f(x) = A\cot(Bx - C) + D$ is a cotangent with vertical and/or horizontal stretch/compression and shift. See **Example 8** and **Example 9**.

- Real-world scenarios can be solved using graphs of trigonometric functions. See **Example 10**.

8.3 Inverse Trigonometric Functions

- An inverse function is one that "undoes" another function. The domain of an inverse function is the range of the original function and the range of an inverse function is the domain of the original function.

- Because the trigonometric functions are not one-to-one on their natural domains, inverse trigonometric functions are defined for restricted domains.

- For any trigonometric function $f(x)$, if $x = f^{-1}(y)$, then $f(x) = y$. However, $f(x) = y$ only implies $x = f^{-1}(y)$ if x is in the restricted domain of f. See **Example 1**.

- Special angles are the outputs of inverse trigonometric functions for special input values; for example, $\dfrac{\pi}{4} = \tan^{-1}(1)$ and $\dfrac{\pi}{6} = \sin^{-1}\left(\dfrac{1}{2}\right)$. See **Example 2**.

- A calculator will return an angle within the restricted domain of the original trigonometric function. See **Example 3**.

- Inverse functions allow us to find an angle when given two sides of a right triangle. See **Example 4**.

- In function composition, if the inside function is an inverse trigonometric function, then there are exact expressions; for example, $\sin(\cos^{-1}(x)) = \sqrt{1 - x^2}$. See **Example 5**.

- If the inside function is a trigonometric function, then the only possible combinations are $\sin^{-1}(\cos x) = \dfrac{\pi}{2} - x$ if $0 \le x \le \pi$ and $\cos^{-1}(\sin x) = \dfrac{\pi}{2} - x$ if $-\dfrac{\pi}{2} \le x \le \dfrac{\pi}{2}$. See **Example 6** and **Example 7**.

- When evaluating the composition of a trigonometric function with an inverse trigonometric function, draw a reference triangle to assist in determining the ratio of sides that represents the output of the trigonometric function. See **Example 8**.

- When evaluating the composition of a trigonometric function with an inverse trigonometric function, you may use trig identities to assist in determining the ratio of sides. See **Example 9**.

CHAPTER 8 REVIEW EXERCISES

GRAPHS OF THE SINE AND COSINE FUNCTIONS

For the following exercises, graph the functions for two periods and determine the amplitude or stretching factor, period, midline equation, and asymptotes.

1. $f(x) = -3\cos x + 3$

2. $f(x) = \frac{1}{4}\sin x$

3. $f(x) = 3\cos\left(x + \frac{\pi}{6}\right)$

4. $f(x) = -2\sin\left(x - \frac{2\pi}{3}\right)$

5. $f(x) = 3\sin\left(x - \frac{\pi}{4}\right) - 4$

6. $f(x) = 2\left(\cos\left(x - \frac{4\pi}{3}\right) + 1\right)$

7. $f(x) = 6\sin\left(3x - \frac{\pi}{6}\right) - 1$

8. $f(x) = -100\sin(50x - 20)$

GRAPHS OF THE OTHER TRIGONOMETRIC FUNCTIONS

For the following exercises, graph the functions for two periods and determine the amplitude or stretching factor, period, midline equation, and asymptotes.

9. $f(x) = \tan x - 4$

10. $f(x) = 2\tan\left(x - \frac{\pi}{6}\right)$

11. $f(x) = -3\tan(4x) - 2$

12. $f(x) = 0.2\cos(0.1x) + 0.3$

For the following exercises, graph two full periods. Identify the period, the phase shift, the amplitude, and asymptotes.

13. $f(x) = \frac{1}{3}\sec x$

14. $f(x) = 3\cot x$

15. $f(x) = 4\csc(5x)$

16. $f(x) = 8\sec\left(\frac{1}{4}x\right)$

17. $f(x) = \frac{2}{3}\csc\left(\frac{1}{2}x\right)$

18. $f(x) = -\csc(2x + \pi)$

For the following exercises, use this scenario: The population of a city has risen and fallen over a 20-year interval. Its population may be modeled by the following function: $y = 12{,}000 + 8{,}000\sin(0.628x)$, where the domain is the years since 1980 and the range is the population of the city.

19. What is the largest and smallest population the city may have?

20. Graph the function on the domain of $[0, 40]$.

21. What are the amplitude, period, and phase shift for the function?

22. Over this domain, when does the population reach 18,000? 13,000?

23. What is the predicted population in 2007? 2010?

For the following exercises, suppose a weight is attached to a spring and bobs up and down, exhibiting symmetry.

24. Suppose the graph of the displacement function is shown in **Figure 1**, where the values on the x-axis represent the time in seconds and the y-axis represents the displacement in inches. Give the equation that models the vertical displacement of the weight on the spring.

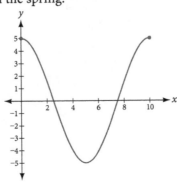

Figure 1

25. At time = 0, what is the displacement of the weight?

26. At what time does the displacement from the equilibrium point equal zero?

27. What is the time required for the weight to return to its initial height of 5 inches? In other words, what is the period for the displacement function?

INVERSE TRIGONOMETRIC FUNCTIONS

For the following exercises, find the exact value without the aid of a calculator.

28. $\sin^{-1}(1)$

29. $\cos^{-1}\left(\dfrac{\sqrt{3}}{2}\right)$

30. $\tan^{-1}(-1)$

31. $\cos^{-1}\left(\dfrac{1}{\sqrt{2}}\right)$

32. $\sin^{-1}\left(\dfrac{-\sqrt{3}}{2}\right)$

33. $\sin^{-1}\left(\cos\left(\dfrac{\pi}{6}\right)\right)$

34. $\cos^{-1}\left(\tan\left(\dfrac{3\pi}{4}\right)\right)$

35. $\sin\left(\sec^{-1}\left(\dfrac{3}{5}\right)\right)$

36. $\cot\left(\sin^{-1}\left(\dfrac{3}{5}\right)\right)$

37. $\tan\left(\cos^{-1}\left(\dfrac{5}{13}\right)\right)$

38. $\sin\left(\cos^{-1}\left(\dfrac{x}{x+1}\right)\right)$

39. Graph $f(x) = \cos x$ and $f(x) = \sec x$ on the interval $[0, 2\pi)$ and explain any observations.

40. Graph $f(x) = \sin x$ and $f(x) = \csc x$ and explain any observations.

41. Graph the function $f(x) = \dfrac{x}{1} - \dfrac{x^3}{3!} + \dfrac{x^5}{5!} - \dfrac{x^7}{7!}$ on the interval $[-1, 1]$ and compare the graph to the graph of $f(x) = \sin x$ on the same interval. Describe any observations.

CHAPTER 8 PRACTICE TEST

For the following exercises, sketch the graph of each function for two full periods. Determine the amplitude, the period, and the equation for the midline.

1. $f(x) = 0.5\sin x$

2. $f(x) = 5\cos x$

3. $f(x) = 5\sin x$

4. $f(x) = \sin(3x)$

5. $f(x) = -\cos\left(x + \dfrac{\pi}{3}\right) + 1$

6. $f(x) = 5\sin\left(3\left(x - \dfrac{\pi}{6}\right)\right) + 4$

7. $f(x) = 3\cos\left(\dfrac{1}{3}x - \dfrac{5\pi}{6}\right)$

8. $f(x) = \tan(4x)$

9. $f(x) = -2\tan\left(x - \dfrac{7\pi}{6}\right) + 2$

10. $f(x) = \pi\cos(3x + \pi)$

11. $f(x) = 5\csc(3x)$

12. $f(x) = \pi\sec\left(\dfrac{\pi}{2}x\right)$

13. $f(x) = 2\csc\left(x + \dfrac{\pi}{4}\right) - 3$

For the following exercises, determine the amplitude, period, and midline of the graph, and then find a formula for the function.

14. Give in terms of a sine function.

15. Give in terms of a sine function.

16. Give in terms of a tangent function.

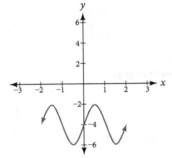 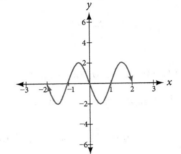 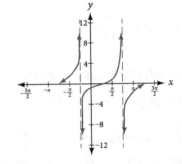

For the following exercises, find the amplitude, period, phase shift, and midline.

17. $y = \sin\left(\dfrac{\pi}{6}x + \pi\right) - 3$

18. $y = 8\sin\left(\dfrac{7\pi}{6}x + \dfrac{7\pi}{2}\right) + 6$

19. The outside temperature over the course of a day can be modeled as a sinusoidal function. Suppose you know the temperature is 68°F at midnight and the high and low temperatures during the day are 80°F and 56°F, respectively. Assuming t is the number of hours since midnight, find a function for the temperature, D, in terms of t.

20. Water is pumped into a storage bin and empties according to a periodic rate. The depth of the water is 3 feet at its lowest at 2:00 a.m. and 71 feet at its highest, which occurs every 5 hours. Write a cosine function that models the depth of the water as a function of time, and then graph the function for one period.

For the following exercises, find the period and horizontal shift of each function.

21. $g(x) = 3\tan(6x + 42)$

22. $n(x) = 4\csc\left(\dfrac{5\pi}{3}x - \dfrac{20\pi}{3}\right)$

23. Write the equation for the graph in **Figure 1** in terms of the secant function and give the period and phase shift.

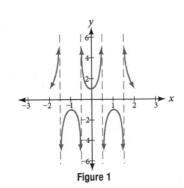

Figure 1

24. If $\tan x = 3$, find $\tan(-x)$.

25. If $\sec x = 4$, find $\sec(-x)$.

For the following exercises, graph the functions on the specified window and answer the questions.

26. Graph $m(x) = \sin(2x) + \cos(3x)$ on the viewing window $[-10, 10]$ by $[-3, 3]$. Approximate the graph's period.

27. Graph $n(x) = 0.02\sin(50\pi x)$ on the following domains in x: $[0, 1]$ and $[0, 3]$. Suppose this function models sound waves. Why would these views look so different?

28. Graph $f(x) = \dfrac{\sin x}{x}$ on $[-0.5, 0.5]$ and explain any observations.

For the following exercises, let $f(x) = \dfrac{3}{5}\cos(6x)$.

29. What is the largest possible value for $f(x)$?

30. What is the smallest possible value for $f(x)$?

31. Where is the function increasing on the interval $[0, 2\pi]$?

For the following exercises, find and graph one period of the periodic function with the given amplitude, period, and phase shift.

32. Sine curve with amplitude 3, period $\dfrac{\pi}{3}$, and phase shift $(h, k) = \left(\dfrac{\pi}{4}, 2\right)$

33. Cosine curve with amplitude 2, period $\dfrac{\pi}{6}$, and phase shift $(h, k) = \left(-\dfrac{\pi}{4}, 3\right)$

For the following exercises, graph the function. Describe the graph and, wherever applicable, any periodic behavior, amplitude, asymptotes, or undefined points.

34. $f(x) = 5\cos(3x) + 4\sin(2x)$

35. $f(x) = e^{\sin t}$

For the following exercises, find the exact value.

36. $\sin^{-1}\left(\dfrac{\sqrt{3}}{2}\right)$

37. $\tan^{-1}\left(\sqrt{3}\right)$

38. $\cos^{-1}\left(-\dfrac{\sqrt{3}}{2}\right)$

39. $\cos^{-1}(\sin(\pi))$

40. $\cos^{-1}\left(\tan\left(\dfrac{7\pi}{4}\right)\right)$

41. $\cos(\sin^{-1}(1 - 2x))$

42. $\cos^{-1}(-0.4)$

43. $\cos(\tan^{-1}(x^2))$

For the following exercises, suppose $\sin t = \dfrac{x}{x + 1}$.

44. $\tan t$

45. $\csc t$

46. Given **Figure 2**, find the measure of angle θ to three decimal places. Answer in radians.

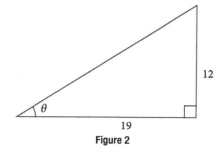

Figure 2

For the following exercises, determine whether the equation is true or false.

47. $\arcsin\left(\sin\left(\dfrac{5\pi}{6}\right)\right) = \dfrac{5\pi}{6}$

48. $\arccos\left(\cos\left(\dfrac{5\pi}{6}\right)\right) = \dfrac{5\pi}{6}$

49. The grade of a road is 7%. This means that for every horizontal distance of 100 feet on the road, the vertical rise is 7 feet. Find the angle the road makes with the horizontal in radians.

Trigonometric Identities and Equations

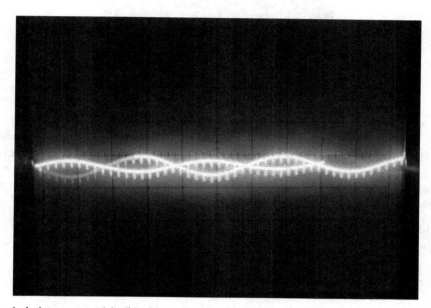

Figure 1 A sine wave models disturbance. (credit: modification of work by Mikael Altemark, Flickr).

CHAPTER OUTLINE

9.1 Solving Trigonometric Equations with Identities

9.2 Sum and Difference Identities

9.3 Double-Angle, Half-Angle, and Reduction Formulas

9.4 Sum-to-Product and Product-to-Sum Formulas

9.5 Solving Trigonometric Equations

Introduction

Math is everywhere, even in places we might not immediately recognize. For example, mathematical relationships describe the transmission of images, light, and sound. The sinusoidal graph in **Figure 1** models music playing on a phone, radio, or computer. Such graphs are described using trigonometric equations and functions. In this chapter, we discuss how to manipulate trigonometric equations algebraically by applying various formulas and trigonometric identities. We will also investigate some of the ways that trigonometric equations are used to model real-life phenomena.

LEARNING OBJECTIVES

In this section, you will:

- Verify the fundamental trigonometric identities.
- Simplify trigonometric expressions using algebra and the identities.

9.1   SOLVING TRIGONOMETRIC EQUATIONS WITH IDENTITIES

Figure 1 International passports and travel documents

In espionage movies, we see international spies with multiple passports, each claiming a different identity. However, we know that each of those passports represents the same person. The trigonometric identities act in a similar manner to multiple passports—there are many ways to represent the same trigonometric expression. Just as a spy will choose an Italian passport when traveling to Italy, we choose the identity that applies to the given scenario when solving a trigonometric equation.

In this section, we will begin an examination of the fundamental trigonometric identities, including how we can verify them and how we can use them to simplify trigonometric expressions.

Verifying the Fundamental Trigonometric Identities

Identities enable us to simplify complicated expressions. They are the basic tools of trigonometry used in solving trigonometric equations, just as factoring, finding common denominators, and using special formulas are the basic tools of solving algebraic equations. In fact, we use algebraic techniques constantly to simplify trigonometric expressions. Basic properties and formulas of algebra, such as the difference of squares formula and the perfect squares formula, will simplify the work involved with trigonometric expressions and equations. We already know that all of the trigonometric functions are related because they all are defined in terms of the unit circle. Consequently, any trigonometric identity can be written in many ways.

To verify the trigonometric identities, we usually start with the more complicated side of the equation and essentially rewrite the expression until it has been transformed into the same expression as the other side of the equation. Sometimes we have to factor expressions, expand expressions, find common denominators, or use other algebraic strategies to obtain the desired result. In this first section, we will work with the fundamental identities: the Pythagorean identities, the even-odd identities, the reciprocal identities, and the quotient identities.

We will begin with the **Pythagorean identities** (see **Table 1**), which are equations involving trigonometric functions based on the properties of a right triangle. We have already seen and used the first of these identifies, but now we will also use additional identities.

Pythagorean Identities		
$\sin^2 \theta + \cos^2 \theta = 1$	$1 + \cot^2 \theta = \csc^2 \theta$	$1 + \tan^2 \theta = \sec^2 \theta$

Table 1

The second and third identities can be obtained by manipulating the first. The identity $1 + \cot^2 \theta = \csc^2 \theta$ is found by rewriting the left side of the equation in terms of sine and cosine.

Prove: $1 + \cot^2 \theta = \csc^2 \theta$

$$1 + \cot^2 \theta = \left(1 + \frac{\cos^2 \theta}{\sin^2 \theta}\right) \qquad \text{Rewrite the left side.}$$

$$= \left(\frac{\sin^2 \theta}{\sin^2 \theta}\right) + \left(\frac{\cos^2 \theta}{\sin^2 \theta}\right) \qquad \text{Write both terms with the common denominator.}$$

$$= \frac{\sin^2 \theta + \cos^2 \theta}{\sin^2 \theta}$$

$$= \frac{1}{\sin^2 \theta}$$

$$= \csc^2 \theta$$

Similarly, $1 + \tan^2 \theta = \sec^2 \theta$ can be obtained by rewriting the left side of this identity in terms of sine and cosine. This gives

$$1 + \tan^2 \theta = 1 + \left(\frac{\sin \theta}{\cos \theta}\right)^2 \qquad \text{Rewrite left side.}$$

$$= \left(\frac{\cos \theta}{\cos \theta}\right)^2 + \left(\frac{\sin \theta}{\cos \theta}\right)^2 \qquad \text{Write both terms with the common denominator.}$$

$$= \frac{\cos^2 \theta + \sin^2 \theta}{\cos^2 \theta}$$

$$= \frac{1}{\cos^2 \theta}$$

$$= \sec^2 \theta$$

Recall that we determined which trigonometric functions are odd and which are even. The next set of fundamental identities is the set of **even-odd identities**. The even-odd identities relate the value of a trigonometric function at a given angle to the value of the function at the opposite angle. (See **Table 2**).

Even-Odd Identities		
$\tan(-\theta) = -\tan \theta$	$\sin(-\theta) = -\sin \theta$	$\cos(-\theta) = \cos \theta$
$\cot(-\theta) = -\cot \theta$	$\csc(-\theta) = -\csc \theta$	$\sec(-\theta) = \sec \theta$

Table 2

Recall that an odd function is one in which $f(-x) = -f(x)$ for all x in the domain of f. The sine function is an odd function because $\sin(-\theta) = -\sin \theta$. The graph of an odd function is symmetric about the origin. For example, consider corresponding inputs of $\frac{\pi}{2}$ and $-\frac{\pi}{2}$. The output of $\sin\left(\frac{\pi}{2}\right)$ is opposite the output of $\sin\left(-\frac{\pi}{2}\right)$. Thus,

$$\sin\left(\frac{\pi}{2}\right) = 1$$

and

$$\sin\left(-\frac{\pi}{2}\right) = -\sin\left(\frac{\pi}{2}\right)$$

$$= -1$$

This is shown in **Figure 2**.

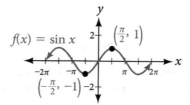

Figure 2 Graph of $y = \sin \theta$

Recall that an even function is one in which

$$f(-x) = f(x) \text{ for all } x \text{ in the domain of } f$$

The graph of an even function is symmetric about the y-axis. The cosine function is an even function because $\cos(-\theta) = \cos \theta$. For example, consider corresponding inputs $\frac{\pi}{4}$ and $-\frac{\pi}{4}$. The output of $\cos\left(\frac{\pi}{4}\right)$ is the same as the output of $\cos\left(-\frac{\pi}{4}\right)$. Thus,

$$\cos\left(-\frac{\pi}{4}\right) = \cos\left(\frac{\pi}{4}\right)$$
$$\approx 0.707$$

See **Figure 3**.

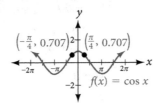

Figure 3 Graph of $y = \cos \theta$

For all θ in the domain of the sine and cosine functions, respectively, we can state the following:

- Since $\sin(-\theta) = -\sin \theta$, sine is an odd function.
- Since, $\cos(-\theta) = \cos \theta$, cosine is an even function.

The other even-odd identities follow from the even and odd nature of the sine and cosine functions. For example, consider the tangent identity, $\tan(-\theta) = -\tan \theta$. We can interpret the tangent of a negative angle as $\tan(-\theta) = \frac{\sin(-\theta)}{\cos(-\theta)} = \frac{-\sin \theta}{\cos \theta} = -\tan \theta$. Tangent is therefore an odd function, which means that $\tan(-\theta) = -\tan(\theta)$ for all θ in the domain of the tangent function.

The cotangent identity, $\cot(-\theta) = -\cot \theta$, also follows from the sine and cosine identities. We can interpret the cotangent of a negative angle as $\cot(-\theta) = \frac{\cos(-\theta)}{\sin(-\theta)} = \frac{\cos \theta}{-\sin \theta} = -\cot \theta$. Cotangent is therefore an odd function, which means that $\cot(-\theta) = -\cot(\theta)$ for all θ in the domain of the cotangent function.

The cosecant function is the reciprocal of the sine function, which means that the cosecant of a negative angle will be interpreted as $\csc(-\theta) = \frac{1}{\sin(-\theta)} = \frac{1}{-\sin \theta} = -\csc \theta$. The cosecant function is therefore odd.

Finally, the secant function is the reciprocal of the cosine function, and the secant of a negative angle is interpreted as $\sec(-\theta) = \frac{1}{\cos(-\theta)} = \frac{1}{\cos \theta} = \sec \theta$. The secant function is therefore even.

To sum up, only two of the trigonometric functions, cosine and secant, are even. The other four functions are odd, verifying the even-odd identities.

The next set of fundamental identities is the set of **reciprocal identities**, which, as their name implies, relate trigonometric functions that are reciprocals of each other. See **Table 3**. Recall that we first encountered these identities when defining trigonometric functions from right angles in **Right Angle Trigonometry**.

Reciprocal Identities	
$\sin \theta = \dfrac{1}{\csc \theta}$	$\csc \theta = \dfrac{1}{\sin \theta}$
$\cos \theta = \dfrac{1}{\sec \theta}$	$\sec \theta = \dfrac{1}{\cos \theta}$
$\tan \theta = \dfrac{1}{\cot \theta}$	$\cot \theta = \dfrac{1}{\tan \theta}$

Table 3

The final set of identities is the set of quotient identities, which define relationships among certain trigonometric functions and can be very helpful in verifying other identities. See **Table 4**.

Quotient Identities	
$\tan \theta = \dfrac{\sin \theta}{\cos \theta}$	$\cot \theta = \dfrac{\cos \theta}{\sin \theta}$

Table 4

The reciprocal and quotient identities are derived from the definitions of the basic trigonometric functions.

---

summarizing trigonometric identities

The **Pythagorean identities** are based on the properties of a right triangle.

$$\cos^2\theta + \sin^2\theta = 1$$

$$1 + \cot^2\theta = \csc^2\theta$$

$$1 + \tan^2\theta = \sec^2\theta$$

The **even-odd identities** relate the value of a trigonometric function at a given angle to the value of the function at the opposite angle.

$$\tan(-\theta) = -\tan\theta$$

$$\cot(-\theta) = -\cot\theta$$

$$\sin(-\theta) = -\sin\theta$$

$$\csc(-\theta) = -\csc\theta$$

$$\cos(-\theta) = \cos\theta$$

$$\sec(-\theta) = \sec\theta$$

The **reciprocal identities** define reciprocals of the trigonometric functions.

$$\sin\theta = \frac{1}{\csc\theta}$$

$$\cos\theta = \frac{1}{\sec\theta}$$

$$\tan\theta = \frac{1}{\cot\theta}$$

$$\csc\theta = \frac{1}{\sin\theta}$$

$$\sec\theta = \frac{1}{\cos\theta}$$

$$\cot\theta = \frac{1}{\tan\theta}$$

The **quotient identities** define the relationship among the trigonometric functions.

$$\tan\theta = \frac{\sin\theta}{\cos\theta}$$

$$\cot\theta = \frac{\cos\theta}{\sin\theta}$$

Example 1 **Graphing the Equations of an Identity**

Graph both sides of the identity $\cot\theta = \dfrac{1}{\tan\theta}$. In other words, on the graphing calculator, graph $y = \cot\theta$ and $y = \dfrac{1}{\tan\theta}$.

Solution See **Figure 4**.

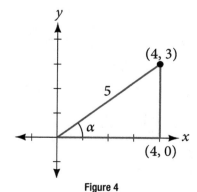

Figure 4

Analysis We see only one graph because both expressions generate the same image. One is on top of the other. This is a good way to prove any identity. If both expressions give the same graph, then they must be identities.

How To...
Given a trigonometric identity, verify that it is true.

1. Work on one side of the equation. It is usually better to start with the more complex side, as it is easier to simplify than to build.
2. Look for opportunities to factor expressions, square a binomial, or add fractions.
3. Noting which functions are in the final expression, look for opportunities to use the identities and make the proper substitutions.
4. If these steps do not yield the desired result, try converting all terms to sines and cosines.

Example 2   Verifying a Trigonometric Identity

Verify $\tan \theta \cos \theta = \sin \theta$.

Solution We will start on the left side, as it is the more complicated side:

$$\tan \theta \cos \theta = \left(\frac{\sin \theta}{\cos \theta} \right) \cos \theta$$
$$= \left(\frac{\sin \theta}{\cancel{\cos \theta}} \right) \cancel{\cos \theta}$$
$$= \sin \theta$$

Analysis This identity was fairly simple to verify, as it only required writing $\tan \theta$ in terms of $\sin \theta$ and $\cos \theta$.

Try It #1
Verify the identity $\csc \theta \cos \theta \tan \theta = 1$.

Example 3   Verifying the Equivalency Using the Even-Odd Identities

Verify the following equivalency using the even-odd identities:

$$(1 + \sin x)[1 + \sin(-x)] = \cos^2 x$$

Solution Working on the left side of the equation, we have

$$(1 + \sin x)[1 + \sin(-x)] = (1 + \sin x)(1 - \sin x) \qquad \text{Since } \sin(-x) = -\sin x$$
$$= 1 - \sin^2 x \qquad\qquad\qquad \text{Difference of squares}$$
$$= \cos^2 x \qquad\qquad\qquad \cos^2 x = 1 - \sin^2 x$$

Example 4   Verifying a Trigonometric Identity Involving sec² θ

Verify the identity $\dfrac{\sec^2 \theta - 1}{\sec^2 \theta} = \sin^2 \theta$

Solution As the left side is more complicated, let's begin there.

$$\frac{\sec^2 \theta - 1}{\sec^2 \theta} = \frac{(\tan^2 \theta + 1) - 1}{\sec^2 \theta} \qquad \sec^2 \theta = \tan^2 \theta + 1$$
$$= \frac{\tan^2 \theta}{\sec^2 \theta}$$
$$= \tan^2 \theta \left(\frac{1}{\sec^2 \theta} \right)$$
$$= \tan^2 \theta (\cos^2 \theta) \qquad\qquad \cos^2 \theta = \frac{1}{\sec^2 \theta}$$
$$= \left(\frac{\sin^2 \theta}{\cos^2 \theta} \right)(\cos^2 \theta) \qquad\qquad \tan^2 \theta = \frac{\sin^2 \theta}{\cos^2 \theta}$$
$$= \left(\frac{\sin^2 \theta}{\cancel{\cos^2 \theta}} \right)(\cancel{\cos^2 \theta})$$
$$= \sin^2 \theta$$

There is more than one way to verify an identity. Here is another possibility. Again, we can start with the left side.

$$\frac{\sec^2 \theta - 1}{\sec^2 \theta} = \frac{\sec^2 \theta}{\sec^2 \theta} - \frac{1}{\sec^2 \theta}$$
$$= 1 - \cos^2 \theta$$
$$= \sin^2 \theta$$

Analysis In the first method, we used the identity $\sec^2 \theta = \tan^2 \theta + 1$ and continued to simplify. In the second method, we split the fraction, putting both terms in the numerator over the common denominator. This problem illustrates that there are multiple ways we can verify an identity. Employing some creativity can sometimes simplify a procedure. As long as the substitutions are correct, the answer will be the same.

Try It #2

Show that $\dfrac{\cot \theta}{\csc \theta} = \cos \theta$.

Example 5   **Creating and Verifying an Identity**

Create an identity for the expression $2\tan \theta \sec \theta$ by rewriting strictly in terms of sine.

Solution   There are a number of ways to begin, but here we will use the quotient and reciprocal identities to rewrite the expression:

$$2 \tan \theta \sec \theta = 2\left(\frac{\sin \theta}{\cos \theta}\right)\left(\frac{1}{\cos \theta}\right)$$
$$= \frac{2 \sin \theta}{\cos^2 \theta}$$
$$= \frac{2 \sin \theta}{1 - \sin^2 \theta} \qquad \text{Substitute } 1 - \sin^2 \theta \text{ for } \cos^2 \theta$$

Thus,

$$2\tan \theta \sec \theta = \frac{2 \sin \theta}{1 - \sin^2 \theta}$$

Example 6   **Verifying an Identity Using Algebra and Even/Odd Identities**

Verify the identity:

$$\frac{\sin^2(-\theta) - \cos^2(-\theta)}{\sin(-\theta) - \cos(-\theta)} = \cos \theta - \sin \theta$$

Solution   Let's start with the left side and simplify:

$$\frac{\sin^2(-\theta) - \cos^2(-\theta)}{\sin(-\theta) - \cos(-\theta)} = \frac{[\sin(-\theta)]^2 - [\cos(-\theta)]^2}{\sin(-\theta) - \cos(-\theta)}$$
$$= \frac{(-\sin \theta)^2 - (\cos \theta)^2}{-\sin \theta - \cos \theta} \qquad \sin(-x) = -\sin x \text{ and } \cos(-x) = \cos x$$
$$= \frac{(\sin \theta)^2 - (\cos \theta)^2}{-\sin \theta - \cos \theta} \qquad \text{Difference of squares}$$
$$= \frac{(\sin \theta - \cos \theta)(\sin \theta + \cos \theta)}{-(\sin \theta + \cos \theta)}$$
$$= \frac{(\sin \theta - \cos \theta)(\sin \theta + \cos \theta)}{-(\sin \theta + \cos \theta)}$$
$$= \cos \theta - \sin \theta$$

Try It #3

Verify the identity $\dfrac{\sin^2 \theta - 1}{\tan \theta \sin \theta - \tan \theta} = \dfrac{\sin \theta + 1}{\tan \theta}$.

Example 7   Verifying an Identity Involving Cosines and Cotangents

Verify the identity: $(1 - \cos^2 x)(1 + \cot^2 x) = 1$.

Solution   We will work on the left side of the equation

$$(1 - \cos^2 x)(1 + \cot^2 x) = (1 - \cos^2 x)\left(1 + \frac{\cos^2 x}{\sin^2 x}\right)$$

$$= (1 - \cos^2 x)\left(\frac{\sin^2 x}{\sin^2 x} + \frac{\cos^2 x}{\sin^2 x}\right) \quad \text{Find the common denominator.}$$

$$= (1 - \cos^2 x)\left(\frac{\sin^2 x + \cos^2 x}{\sin^2 x}\right)$$

$$= (\sin^2 x)\left(\frac{1}{\sin^2 x}\right)$$

$$= 1$$

Using Algebra to Simplify Trigonometric Expressions

We have seen that algebra is very important in verifying trigonometric identities, but it is just as critical in simplifying trigonometric expressions before solving. Being familiar with the basic properties and formulas of algebra, such as the difference of squares formula, the perfect square formula, or substitution, will simplify the work involved with trigonometric expressions and equations.

For example, the equation $(\sin x + 1)(\sin x - 1) = 0$ resembles the equation $(x + 1)(x - 1) = 0$, which uses the factored form of the difference of squares. Using algebra makes finding a solution straightforward and familiar. We can set each factor equal to zero and solve. This is one example of recognizing algebraic patterns in trigonometric expressions or equations.

Another example is the difference of squares formula, $a^2 - b^2 = (a - b)(a + b)$, which is widely used in many areas other than mathematics, such as engineering, architecture, and physics. We can also create our own identities by continually expanding an expression and making the appropriate substitutions. Using algebraic properties and formulas makes many trigonometric equations easier to understand and solve.

Example 8   Writing the Trigonometric Expression as an Algebraic Expression

Write the following trigonometric expression as an algebraic expression: $2\cos^2 \theta + \cos \theta - 1$.

Solution   Notice that the pattern displayed has the same form as a standard quadratic expression, $ax^2 + bx + c$. Letting $\cos \theta = x$, we can rewrite the expression as follows:

$$2x^2 + x - 1$$

This expression can be factored as $(2x + 1)(x - 1)$. If it were set equal to zero and we wanted to solve the equation, we would use the zero factor property and solve each factor for x. At this point, we would replace x with $\cos \theta$ and solve for θ.

Example 9   Rewriting a Trigonometric Expression Using the Difference of Squares

Rewrite the trigonometric expression: $4 \cos^2 \theta - 1$.

Solution   Notice that both the coefficient and the trigonometric expression in the first term are squared, and the square of the number 1 is 1. This is the difference of squares.

$$4 \cos^2 \theta - 1 = (2 \cos \theta)^2 - 1$$

$$= (2 \cos \theta - 1)(2 \cos \theta + 1)$$

Analysis   *If this expression were written in the form of an equation set equal to zero, we could solve each factor using the zero factor property. We could also use substitution like we did in the previous problem and let $\cos \theta = x$, rewrite the expression as $4x^2 - 1$, and factor $(2x - 1)(2x + 1)$. Then replace x with $\cos \theta$ and solve for the angle.*

Try It #4

Rewrite the trigonometric expression using the difference of squares: $25 - 9 \sin^2 \theta$.

Example 10   **Simplify by Rewriting and Using Substitution**

Simplify the expression by rewriting and using identities:

$$\csc^2 \theta - \cot^2 \theta$$

Solution   We can start with the Pythagorean Identity.

$$1 + \cot^2 \theta = \csc^2 \theta$$

Now we can simplify by substituting $1 + \cot^2 \theta$ for $\csc^2 \theta$. We have

$$\csc^2 \theta - \cot^2 \theta = 1 + \cot^2 \theta - \cot^2 \theta$$

$$= 1$$

Try It #5

Use algebraic techniques to verify the identity: $\dfrac{\cos \theta}{1 + \sin \theta} = \dfrac{1 - \sin \theta}{\cos \theta}$.

(Hint: Multiply the numerator and denominator on the left side by $1 - \sin \theta$.)

Access these online resources for additional instruction and practice with the fundamental trigonometric identities.

- Fundamental Trigonometric Identities (http://openstaxcollege.org/l/funtrigiden)
- Verifying Trigonometric Identities (http://openstaxcollege.org/l/verifytrigiden)

9.1   SECTION EXERCISES

VERBAL

1. We know $g(x) = \cos x$ is an even function, and $f(x) = \sin x$ and $h(x) = \tan x$ are odd functions. What about $G(x) = \cos^2 x$, $F(x) = \sin^2 x$, and $H(x) = \tan^2 x$? Are they even, odd, or neither? Why?

2. Examine the graph of $f(x) = \sec x$ on the interval $[-\pi, \pi]$. How can we tell whether the function is even or odd by only observing the graph of $f(x) = \sec x$?

3. After examining the reciprocal identity for $\sec t$, explain why the function is undefined at certain points.

4. All of the Pythagorean identities are related. Describe how to manipulate the equations to get from $\sin^2 t + \cos^2 t = 1$ to the other forms.

ALGEBRAIC

For the following exercises, use the fundamental identities to fully simplify the expression.

5. $\sin x \cos x \sec x$

6. $\sin(-x)\cos(-x)\csc(-x)$

7. $\tan x \sin x + \sec x \cos^2 x$

8. $\csc x + \cos x \cot(-x)$

9. $\dfrac{\cot t + \tan t}{\sec(-t)}$

10. $3 \sin^3 t \csc t + \cos^2 t + 2 \cos(-t)\cos t$

11. $-\tan(-x)\cot(-x)$

12. $\dfrac{-\sin(-x)\cos x \sec x \csc x \tan x}{\cot x}$

13. $\dfrac{1 + \tan^2 \theta}{\csc^2 \theta} + \sin^2 \theta + \dfrac{1}{\sec^2 \theta}$

14. $\left(\dfrac{\tan x}{\csc^2 x} + \dfrac{\tan x}{\sec^2 x} \right)\left(\dfrac{1 + \tan x}{1 + \cot x} \right) - \dfrac{1}{\cos^2 x}$

15. $\dfrac{1 - \cos^2 x}{\tan^2 x} + 2 \sin^2 x$

For the following exercises, simplify the first trigonometric expression by writing the simplified form in terms of the second expression.

16. $\dfrac{\tan x + \cot x}{\csc x}$; $\cos x$

17. $\dfrac{\sec x + \csc x}{1 + \tan x}$; $\sin x$

18. $\dfrac{\cos x}{1 + \sin x} + \tan x$; $\cos x$

19. $\dfrac{1}{\sin x \cos x} - \cot x$; $\cot x$

20. $\dfrac{1}{1 - \cos x} - \dfrac{\cos x}{1 + \cos x}$; $\csc x$

21. $(\sec x + \csc x)(\sin x + \cos x) - 2 - \cot x$; $\tan x$

22. $\dfrac{1}{\csc x - \sin x}$; $\sec x$ and $\tan x$

23. $\dfrac{1 - \sin x}{1 + \sin x} - \dfrac{1 + \sin x}{1 - \sin x}$; $\sec x$ and $\tan x$

24. $\tan x$; $\sec x$

25. $\sec x$; $\cot x$

26. $\sec x$; $\sin x$

27. $\cot x$; $\sin x$

28. $\cot x$; $\csc x$

For the following exercises, verify the identity.

29. $\cos x - \cos^3 x = \cos x \sin^2 x$

30. $\cos x(\tan x - \sec(-x)) = \sin x - 1$

31. $\dfrac{1 + \sin^2 x}{\cos^2 x} = \dfrac{1}{\cos^2 x} + \dfrac{\sin^2 x}{\cos^2 x} = 1 + 2 \tan^2 x$

32. $(\sin x + \cos x)^2 = 1 + 2 \sin x \cos x$

33. $\cos^2 x - \tan^2 x = 2 - \sin^2 x - \sec^2 x$

EXTENSIONS

For the following exercises, prove or disprove the identity.

34. $\dfrac{1}{1 + \cos x} - \dfrac{1}{1 - \cos(-x)} = -2 \cot x \csc x$ **35.** $\csc^2 x(1 + \sin^2 x) = \cot^2 x$

36. $\left(\dfrac{\sec^2(-x) - \tan^2 x}{\tan x} \right)\left(\dfrac{2 + 2 \tan x}{2 + 2 \cot x} \right) - 2 \sin^2 x = \cos 2x$

37. $\dfrac{\tan x}{\sec x} \sin(-x) = \cos^2 x$ **38.** $\dfrac{\sec(-x)}{\tan x + \cot x} = -\sin(-x)$

39. $\dfrac{1 + \sin x}{\cos x} = \dfrac{\cos x}{1 + \sin(-x)}$

For the following exercises, determine whether the identity is true or false. If false, find an appropriate equivalent expression.

40. $\dfrac{\cos^2 \theta - \sin^2 \theta}{1 - \tan^2 \theta} = \sin^2 \theta$ **41.** $3 \sin^2 \theta + 4 \cos^2 \theta = 3 + \cos^2 \theta$

42. $\dfrac{\sec \theta + \tan \theta}{\cot \theta + \cos \theta} = \sec^2 \theta$

LEARNING OBJECTIVES

In this section, you will:
- Use sum and difference formulas for cosine.
- Use sum and difference formulas for sine.
- Use sum and difference formulas for tangent.
- Use sum and difference formulas for cofunctions.
- Use sum and difference formulas to verify identities.

9.2   SUM AND DIFFERENCE IDENTITIES

Figure 1 Mount McKinley, in Denali National Park, Alaska, rises 20,237 feet (6,168 m) above sea level. It is the highest peak in North America. (credit: Daniel A. Leifheit, Flickr)

How can the height of a mountain be measured? What about the distance from Earth to the sun? Like many seemingly impossible problems, we rely on mathematical formulas to find the answers. The trigonometric identities, commonly used in mathematical proofs, have had real-world applications for centuries, including their use in calculating long distances.

The trigonometric identities we will examine in this section can be traced to a Persian astronomer who lived around 950 AD, but the ancient Greeks discovered these same formulas much earlier and stated them in terms of chords. These are special equations or postulates, true for all values input to the equations, and with innumerable applications.

In this section, we will learn techniques that will enable us to solve problems such as the ones presented above. The formulas that follow will simplify many trigonometric expressions and equations. Keep in mind that, throughout this section, the term *formula* is used synonymously with the word *identity*.

Using the Sum and Difference Formulas for Cosine

Finding the exact value of the sine, cosine, or tangent of an angle is often easier if we can rewrite the given angle in terms of two angles that have known trigonometric values. We can use the special angles, which we can review in the unit circle shown in **Figure 2**.

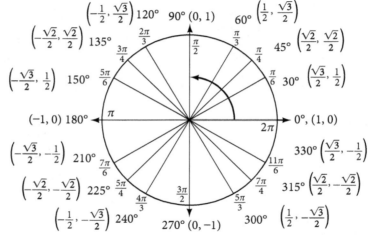

Figure 2 The Unit Circle

We will begin with the sum and difference formulas for cosine, so that we can find the cosine of a given angle if we can break it up into the sum or difference of two of the special angles. See **Table 1**.

Sum formula for cosine	$\cos(\alpha + \beta) = \cos\alpha\cos\beta - \sin\alpha\sin\beta$
Difference formula for cosine	$\cos(\alpha - \beta) = \cos\alpha\cos\beta + \sin\alpha\sin\beta$

Table 1

First, we will prove the difference formula for cosines. Let's consider two points on the unit circle. See **Figure 3**. Point P is at an angle α from the positive x-axis with coordinates $(\cos\alpha, \sin\alpha)$ and point Q is at an angle of β from the positive x-axis with coordinates $(\cos\beta, \sin\beta)$. Note the measure of angle POQ is $\alpha - \beta$.

Label two more points: A at an angle of $(\alpha - \beta)$ from the positive x-axis with coordinates $(\cos(\alpha - \beta), \sin(\alpha - \beta))$; and point B with coordinates $(1, 0)$. Triangle POQ is a rotation of triangle AOB and thus the distance from P to Q is the same as the distance from A to B.

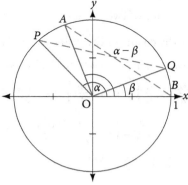

Figure 3

We can find the distance from P to Q using the distance formula.

$$d_{PQ} = \sqrt{(\cos\alpha - \cos\beta)^2 + (\sin\alpha - \sin\beta)^2}$$
$$= \sqrt{\cos^2\alpha - 2\cos\alpha\cos\beta + \cos^2\beta + \sin^2\alpha - 2\sin\alpha\sin\beta + \sin^2\beta}$$

Then we apply the Pythagorean Identity and simplify.

$$= \sqrt{(\cos^2\alpha + \sin^2\alpha) + (\cos^2\beta + \sin^2\beta) - 2\cos\alpha\cos\beta - 2\sin\alpha\sin\beta}$$
$$= \sqrt{1 + 1 - 2\cos\alpha\cos\beta - 2\sin\alpha\sin\beta}$$
$$= \sqrt{2 - 2\cos\alpha\cos\beta - 2\sin\alpha\sin\beta}$$

Similarly, using the distance formula we can find the distance from A to B.

$$d_{AB} = \sqrt{(\cos(\alpha - \beta) - 1)^2 + (\sin(\alpha - \beta) - 0)^2}$$
$$= \sqrt{\cos^2(\alpha - \beta) - 2\cos(\alpha - \beta) + 1 + \sin^2(\alpha - \beta)}$$

Applying the Pythagorean Identity and simplifying we get:

$$= \sqrt{(\cos^2(\alpha - \beta) + \sin^2(\alpha - \beta)) - 2\cos(\alpha - \beta) + 1}$$
$$= \sqrt{1 - 2\cos(\alpha - \beta) + 1}$$
$$= \sqrt{2 - 2\cos(\alpha - \beta)}$$

Because the two distances are the same, we set them equal to each other and simplify.

$$\sqrt{2 - 2\cos\alpha\cos\beta - 2\sin\alpha\sin\beta} = \sqrt{2 - 2\cos(\alpha - \beta)}$$
$$2 - 2\cos\alpha\cos\beta - 2\sin\alpha\sin\beta = 2 - 2\cos(\alpha - \beta)$$

Finally we subtract 2 from both sides and divide both sides by -2.

$$\cos\alpha\cos\beta + \sin\alpha\sin\beta = \cos(\alpha - \beta)$$

Thus, we have the difference formula for cosine. We can use similar methods to derive the cosine of the sum of two angles.

---

sum and difference formulas for cosine

These formulas can be used to calculate the cosine of sums and differences of angles.

$$\cos(\alpha + \beta) = \cos\alpha\cos\beta - \sin\alpha\sin\beta \qquad \cos(\alpha - \beta) = \cos\alpha\cos\beta + \sin\alpha\sin\beta$$

How To...

Given two angles, find the cosine of the difference between the angles.

1. Write the difference formula for cosine.

2. Substitute the values of the given angles into the formula.

3. Simplify.

Example 1   **Finding the Exact Value Using the Formula for the Cosine of the Difference of Two Angles**

Using the formula for the cosine of the difference of two angles, find the exact value of $\cos\left(\dfrac{5\pi}{4} - \dfrac{\pi}{6}\right)$.

Solution   Begin by writing the formula for the cosine of the difference of two angles. Then substitute the given values.

$$\cos(\alpha - \beta) = \cos\alpha\cos\beta + \sin\alpha\sin\beta$$

$$\cos\left(\frac{5\pi}{4} - \frac{\pi}{6}\right) = \cos\left(\frac{5\pi}{4}\right)\cos\left(\frac{\pi}{6}\right) + \sin\left(\frac{5\pi}{4}\right)\sin\left(\frac{\pi}{6}\right)$$

$$= \left(-\frac{\sqrt{2}}{2}\right)\left(\frac{\sqrt{3}}{2}\right) - \left(\frac{\sqrt{2}}{2}\right)\left(\frac{1}{2}\right)$$

$$= -\frac{\sqrt{6}}{4} - \frac{\sqrt{2}}{4}$$

$$= \frac{-\sqrt{6} - \sqrt{2}}{4}$$

Keep in mind that we can always check the answer using a graphing calculator in radian mode.

Try It #1

Find the exact value of $\cos\left(\dfrac{\pi}{3} - \dfrac{\pi}{4}\right)$.

Example 2   **Finding the Exact Value Using the Formula for the Sum of Two Angles for Cosine**

Find the exact value of $\cos(75°)$.

Solution   As $75° = 45° + 30°$, we can evaluate $\cos(75°)$ as $\cos(45° + 30°)$.

$$\cos(\alpha + \beta) = \cos\alpha\cos\beta - \sin\alpha\sin\beta$$

$$\cos(45° + 30°) = \cos(45°)\cos(30°) - \sin(45°)\sin(30°)$$

$$= \frac{\sqrt{2}}{2}\left(\frac{\sqrt{3}}{2}\right) - \frac{\sqrt{2}}{2}\left(\frac{1}{2}\right)$$

$$= \frac{\sqrt{6}}{4} - \frac{\sqrt{2}}{4}$$

$$= \frac{\sqrt{6} - \sqrt{2}}{4}$$

Keep in mind that we can always check the answer using a graphing calculator in degree mode.

Analysis   Note that we could have also solved this problem using the fact that $75° = 135° - 60°$.

$$\cos(\alpha - \beta) = \cos\alpha\cos\beta + \sin\alpha\sin\beta$$

$$\cos(135° - 60°) = \cos(135°)\cos(60°) - \sin(135°)\sin(60°)$$

$$= \left(-\frac{\sqrt{2}}{2}\right)\left(\frac{1}{2}\right) + \left(\frac{\sqrt{2}}{2}\right)\left(\frac{\sqrt{3}}{2}\right)$$

$$= \left(-\frac{\sqrt{2}}{4}\right) + \left(\frac{\sqrt{6}}{4}\right)$$

$$= \frac{\sqrt{6} - \sqrt{2}}{4}$$

Try It #2

Find the exact value of cos(105°).

Using the Sum and Difference Formulas for Sine

The sum and difference formulas for sine can be derived in the same manner as those for cosine, and they resemble the cosine formulas.

> **sum and difference formulas for sine**
>
> These formulas can be used to calculate the sines of sums and differences of angles.
>
> $$\sin(\alpha + \beta) = \sin \alpha \cos \beta + \cos \alpha \sin \beta \qquad \sin(\alpha - \beta) = \sin \alpha \cos \beta - \cos \alpha \sin \beta$$

How To...

Given two angles, find the sine of the difference between the angles.

1. Write the difference formula for sine.
2. Substitute the given angles into the formula.
3. Simplify.

Example 3   **Using Sum and Difference Identities to Evaluate the Difference of Angles**

Use the sum and difference identities to evaluate the difference of the angles and show that part *a* equals part *b*.

    a. $\sin(45° - 30°)$ **b.** $\sin(135° - 120°)$

Solution

a. Let's begin by writing the formula and substitute the given angles.

$$\sin(\alpha - \beta) = \sin \alpha \cos \beta - \cos \alpha \sin \beta$$
$$\sin(45° - 30°) = \sin(45°)\cos(30°) - \cos(45°)\sin(30°)$$

Next, we need to find the values of the trigonometric expressions.

$$\sin(45°) = \frac{\sqrt{2}}{2}, \cos(30°) = \frac{\sqrt{3}}{2}, \cos(45°) = \frac{\sqrt{2}}{2}, \sin(30°) = \frac{1}{2}$$

Now we can substitute these values into the equation and simplify.

$$\sin(45° - 30°) = \frac{\sqrt{2}}{2}\left(\frac{\sqrt{3}}{2}\right) - \frac{\sqrt{2}}{2}\left(\frac{1}{2}\right)$$
$$= \frac{\sqrt{6} - \sqrt{2}}{4}$$

b. Again, we write the formula and substitute the given angles.

$$\sin(\alpha - \beta) = \sin \alpha \cos \beta - \cos \alpha \sin \beta$$
$$\sin(135° - 120°) = \sin(135°)\cos(120°) - \cos(135°)\sin(120°)$$

Next, we find the values of the trigonometric expressions.

$$\sin(135°) = \frac{\sqrt{2}}{2}, \cos(120°) = -\frac{1}{2}, \cos(135°) = -\frac{\sqrt{2}}{2}, \sin(120°) = \frac{\sqrt{3}}{2}$$

Now we can substitute these values into the equation and simplify.

$$\sin(135° - 120°) = \frac{\sqrt{2}}{2}\left(-\frac{1}{2}\right) - \left(-\frac{\sqrt{2}}{2}\right)\left(\frac{\sqrt{3}}{2}\right)$$
$$= \frac{-\sqrt{2} + \sqrt{6}}{4}$$
$$= \frac{\sqrt{6} - \sqrt{2}}{4}$$

$$\sin(135° - 120°) = \frac{\sqrt{2}}{2}\left(-\frac{1}{2}\right) - \left(-\frac{\sqrt{2}}{2}\right)\left(\frac{\sqrt{3}}{2}\right)$$

$$= \frac{-\sqrt{2} + \sqrt{6}}{4}$$

$$= \frac{\sqrt{6} - \sqrt{2}}{4}$$

Example 4   **Finding the Exact Value of an Expression Involving an Inverse Trigonometric Function**

Find the exact value of $\sin\left(\cos^{-1}\frac{1}{2} + \sin^{-1}\frac{3}{5}\right)$. Then check the answer with a graphing calculator.

Solution   The pattern displayed in this problem is $\sin(\alpha + \beta)$. Let $\alpha = \cos^{-1}\frac{1}{2}$ and $\beta = \sin^{-1}\frac{3}{5}$. Then we can write

$$\cos\alpha = \frac{1}{2}, 0 \le \alpha \le \pi$$

$$\sin\beta = \frac{3}{5}, -\frac{\pi}{2} \le \beta \le \frac{\pi}{2}$$

We will use the Pythagorean identities to find $\sin\alpha$ and $\cos\beta$.

$$\sin\alpha = \sqrt{1 - \cos^2\alpha} \qquad\qquad \cos\beta = \sqrt{1 - \sin^2\beta}$$

$$= \sqrt{1 - \frac{1}{4}} \qquad\qquad\qquad = \sqrt{1 - \frac{9}{25}}$$

$$= \sqrt{\frac{3}{4}} \qquad\qquad\qquad\qquad = \sqrt{\frac{16}{25}}$$

$$= \frac{\sqrt{3}}{2} \qquad\qquad\qquad\qquad = \frac{4}{5}$$

Using the sum formula for sine,

$$\sin\left(\cos^{-1}\frac{1}{2} + \sin^{-1}\frac{3}{5}\right) = \sin(\alpha + \beta)$$

$$= \sin\alpha\cos\beta + \cos\alpha\sin\beta$$

$$= \frac{\sqrt{3}}{2}\cdot\frac{4}{5} + \frac{1}{2}\cdot\frac{3}{5}$$

$$= \frac{4\sqrt{3} + 3}{10}$$

Using the Sum and Difference Formulas for Tangent

Finding exact values for the tangent of the sum or difference of two angles is a little more complicated, but again, it is a matter of recognizing the pattern.

Finding the sum of two angles formula for tangent involves taking quotient of the sum formulas for sine and cosine and simplifying. Recall, $\tan x = \frac{\sin x}{\cos x}$, $\cos x \ne 0$.

Let's derive the sum formula for tangent.

$$\tan(\alpha + \beta) = \frac{\sin(\alpha + \beta)}{\cos(\alpha + \beta)}$$

$$= \frac{\sin\alpha\cos\beta + \cos\alpha\sin\beta}{\cos\alpha\cos\beta - \sin\alpha\sin\beta}$$

$$= \frac{\dfrac{\sin\alpha\cos\beta + \cos\alpha\sin\beta}{\cos\alpha\cos\beta}}{\dfrac{\cos\alpha\cos\beta - \sin\alpha\sin\beta}{\cos\alpha\cos\beta}} \qquad \text{Divide the numerator and denominator by } \cos\alpha\cos\beta$$

$$= \frac{\dfrac{\sin\alpha\cancel{\cos\beta}}{\cos\alpha\cancel{\cos\beta}} + \dfrac{\cancel{\cos\alpha}\sin\beta}{\cancel{\cos\alpha}\cos\beta}}{\dfrac{\cancel{\cos\alpha}\cancel{\cos\beta}}{\cancel{\cos\alpha}\cancel{\cos\beta}} - \dfrac{\sin\alpha\sin\beta}{\cos\alpha\cos\beta}}$$

$$= \frac{\dfrac{\sin \alpha}{\cos \alpha} + \dfrac{\sin \beta}{\cos \beta}}{1 - \dfrac{\sin \alpha \sin \beta}{\cos \alpha \cos \beta}}$$

$$= \frac{\tan \alpha + \tan \beta}{1 - \tan \alpha \tan \beta}$$

We can derive the difference formula for tangent in a similar way.

---

sum and difference formulas for tangent

The sum and difference formulas for tangent are:

$$\tan(\alpha + \beta) = \frac{\tan \alpha + \tan \beta}{1 - \tan \alpha \tan \beta} \qquad \tan(\alpha - \beta) = \frac{\tan \alpha - \tan \beta}{1 + \tan \alpha \tan \beta}$$

How To…

Given two angles, find the tangent of the sum of the angles.

1. Write the sum formula for tangent.
2. Substitute the given angles into the formula.
3. Simplify.

Example 5   **Finding the Exact Value of an Expression Involving Tangent**

Find the exact value of $\tan\left(\dfrac{\pi}{6} + \dfrac{\pi}{4}\right)$.

Solution   Let's first write the sum formula for tangent and substitute the given angles into the formula.

$$\tan(\alpha + \beta) = \frac{\tan \alpha + \tan \beta}{1 - \tan \alpha \tan \beta}$$

$$\tan\left(\frac{\pi}{6} + \frac{\pi}{4}\right) = \frac{\tan\left(\dfrac{\pi}{6}\right) + \tan\left(\dfrac{\pi}{4}\right)}{1 - \left(\tan\left(\dfrac{\pi}{6}\right)\tan\left(\dfrac{\pi}{4}\right)\right)}$$

Next, we determine the individual tangents within the formulas:

$$\tan\left(\frac{\pi}{6}\right) = \frac{1}{\sqrt{3}} \qquad \tan\left(\frac{\pi}{4}\right) = 1$$

So we have

$$\tan\left(\frac{\pi}{6} + \frac{\pi}{4}\right) = \frac{\dfrac{1}{\sqrt{3}} + 1}{1 - \left(\dfrac{1}{\sqrt{3}}\right)(1)}$$

$$= \frac{\dfrac{1 + \sqrt{3}}{\sqrt{3}}}{\dfrac{\sqrt{3} - 1}{\sqrt{3}}}$$

$$= \frac{1 + \sqrt{3}}{\sqrt{3}}\left(\frac{\sqrt{3}}{\sqrt{3} - 1}\right)$$

$$= \frac{\sqrt{3} + 1}{\sqrt{3} - 1}$$

Try It #3

Find the exact value of $\tan\left(\dfrac{2\pi}{3} + \dfrac{\pi}{4}\right)$.

Example 6   Finding Multiple Sums and Differences of Angles

Given $\sin\alpha = \dfrac{3}{5}, 0 < \alpha < \dfrac{\pi}{2}, \cos\beta = -\dfrac{5}{13}, \pi < \beta < \dfrac{3\pi}{2}$, find

    a. $\sin(\alpha+\beta)$ **b.** $\cos(\alpha+\beta)$ **c.** $\tan(\alpha+\beta)$ **d.** $\tan(\alpha-\beta)$

Solution   We can use the sum and difference formulas to identify the sum or difference of angles when the ratio of sine, cosine, or tangent is provided for each of the individual angles. To do so, we construct what is called a reference triangle to help find each component of the sum and difference formulas.

    a. To find $\sin(\alpha+\beta)$, we begin with $\sin\alpha = \dfrac{3}{5}$ and $0 < \alpha < \dfrac{\pi}{2}$. The side opposite α has length 3, the hypotenuse has length 5, and α is in the first quadrant. See **Figure 4**. Using the Pythagorean Theorem, we can find the length of side a:

$$a^2 + 3^2 = 5^2$$
$$a^2 = 16$$
$$a = 4$$

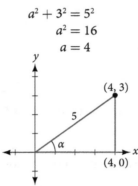

Figure 4

Since $\cos\beta = -\dfrac{5}{13}$ and $\pi < \beta < \dfrac{3\pi}{2}$, the side adjacent to β is -5, the hypotenuse is 13, and β is in the third quadrant. See **Figure 5**. Again, using the Pythagorean Theorem, we have

$$(-5)^2 + a^2 = 13^2$$
$$25 + a^2 = 169$$
$$a^2 = 144$$
$$a = \pm 12$$

Since β is in the third quadrant, $a = -12$.

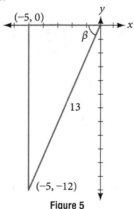

Figure 5

The next step is finding the cosine of α and the sine of β. The cosine of α is the adjacent side over the hypotenuse. We can find it from the triangle in **Figure 5**: $\cos\alpha = \dfrac{4}{5}$. We can also find the sine of β from the triangle in **Figure 5**, as opposite side over the hypotenuse: $\sin\beta = -\dfrac{12}{13}$. Now we are ready to evaluate $\sin(\alpha+\beta)$.

$$\sin(\alpha + \beta) = \sin \alpha \cos \beta + \cos \alpha \sin \beta$$

$$= \left(\frac{3}{5}\right)\left(-\frac{5}{13}\right) + \left(\frac{4}{5}\right)\left(-\frac{12}{13}\right)$$

$$= -\frac{15}{65} - \frac{48}{65}$$

$$= -\frac{63}{65}$$

b. We can find $\cos(\alpha + \beta)$ in a similar manner. We substitute the values according to the formula.

$$\cos(\alpha + \beta) = \cos \alpha \cos \beta - \sin \alpha \sin \beta$$

$$= \left(\frac{4}{5}\right)\left(-\frac{5}{13}\right) - \left(\frac{3}{5}\right)\left(-\frac{12}{13}\right)$$

$$= -\frac{20}{65} + \frac{36}{65}$$

$$= \frac{16}{65}$$

c. For $\tan(\alpha + \beta)$, if $\sin \alpha = \frac{3}{5}$ and $\cos \alpha = \frac{4}{5}$, then

$$\tan \alpha = \frac{\frac{3}{5}}{\frac{4}{5}} = \frac{3}{4}$$

If $\sin \beta = -\frac{12}{13}$ and $\cos \beta = -\frac{5}{13}$, then

$$\tan \beta = \frac{\frac{-12}{13}}{\frac{-5}{13}} = \frac{12}{5}$$

Then,

$$\tan(\alpha + \beta) = \frac{\tan \alpha + \tan \beta}{1 - \tan \alpha \tan \beta}$$

$$= \frac{\frac{3}{4} + \frac{12}{5}}{1 - \frac{3}{4}\left(\frac{12}{5}\right)}$$

$$= \frac{\frac{63}{20}}{-\frac{16}{20}}$$

$$= -\frac{63}{16}$$

d. To find $\tan(\alpha - \beta)$, we have the values we need. We can substitute them in and evaluate.

$$\tan(\alpha - \beta) = \frac{\tan \alpha - \tan \beta}{1 + \tan \alpha \tan \beta}$$

$$= \frac{\frac{3}{4} - \frac{12}{5}}{1 + \frac{3}{4}\left(\frac{12}{5}\right)}$$

$$= \frac{-\frac{33}{20}}{\frac{56}{20}}$$

$$= -\frac{33}{56}$$

Analysis　A common mistake when addressing problems such as this one is that we may be tempted to think that α and β are angles in the same triangle, which of course, they are not. Also note that

$$\tan(\alpha + \beta) = \frac{\sin(\alpha + \beta)}{\cos(\alpha + \beta)}$$

Using Sum and Difference Formulas for Cofunctions

Now that we can find the sine, cosine, and tangent functions for the sums and differences of angles, we can use them to do the same for their cofunctions. You may recall from **Right Triangle Trigonometry** that, if the sum of two positive angles is $\frac{\pi}{2}$, those two angles are complements, and the sum of the two acute angles in a right triangle is $\frac{\pi}{2}$, so they are also complements. In **Figure 6**, notice that if one of the acute angles is labeled as θ, then the other acute angle must be labeled $\left(\frac{\pi}{2} - \theta\right)$.

Notice also that $\sin \theta = \cos\left(\frac{\pi}{2} - \theta\right)$: opposite over hypotenuse. Thus, when two angles are complimentary, we can say that the sine of θ equals the cofunction of the complement of θ. Similarly, tangent and cotangent are cofunctions, and secant and cosecant are cofunctions.

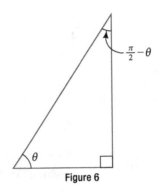

Figure 6

From these relationships, the cofunction identities are formed. Recall that you first encountered these identities in **The Unit Circle: Sine and Cosine Functions**.

---

cofunction identities
The cofunction identities are summarized in **Table 2**.

$\sin \theta = \cos\left(\frac{\pi}{2} - \theta\right)$	$\cos \theta = \sin\left(\frac{\pi}{2} - \theta\right)$	$\tan \theta = \cot\left(\frac{\pi}{2} - \theta\right)$
$\sec \theta = \csc\left(\frac{\pi}{2} - \theta\right)$	$\csc \theta = \sec\left(\frac{\pi}{2} - \theta\right)$	$\cot \theta = \tan\left(\frac{\pi}{2} - \theta\right)$

Table 2

Notice that the formulas in the table may also be justified algebraically using the sum and difference formulas. For example, using

$$\cos(\alpha - \beta) = \cos \alpha \cos \beta + \sin \alpha \sin \beta,$$

we can write

$$\cos\left(\frac{\pi}{2} - \theta\right) = \cos\frac{\pi}{2} \cos \theta + \sin\frac{\pi}{2} \sin \theta$$

$$= (0)\cos \theta + (1)\sin \theta$$

$$= \sin \theta$$

Example 7   **Finding a Cofunction with the Same Value as the Given Expression**

Write $\tan \frac{\pi}{9}$ in terms of its cofunction.

Solution   The cofunction of $\tan \theta = \cot\left(\frac{\pi}{2} - \theta\right)$. Thus,

$$\tan\left(\frac{\pi}{9}\right) = \cot\left(\frac{\pi}{2} - \frac{\pi}{9}\right)$$

$$= \cot\left(\frac{9\pi}{18} - \frac{2\pi}{18}\right)$$

$$= \cot\left(\frac{7\pi}{18}\right)$$

Try It #4

Write $\sin \frac{\pi}{7}$ in terms of its cofunction.

Using the Sum and Difference Formulas to Verify Identities

Verifying an identity means demonstrating that the equation holds for all values of the variable. It helps to be very familiar with the identities or to have a list of them accessible while working the problems. Reviewing the general rules presented earlier may help simplify the process of verifying an identity.

How To...

Given an identity, verify using sum and difference formulas.

1. Begin with the expression on the side of the equal sign that appears most complex. Rewrite that expression until it matches the other side of the equal sign. Occasionally, we might have to alter both sides, but working on only one side is the most efficient.
2. Look for opportunities to use the sum and difference formulas.
3. Rewrite sums or differences of quotients as single quotients.
4. If the process becomes cumbersome, rewrite the expression in terms of sines and cosines.

Example 8   **Verifying an Identity Involving Sine**

Verify the identity $\sin(\alpha + \beta) + \sin(\alpha - \beta) = 2 \sin \alpha \cos \beta$.

Solution   We see that the left side of the equation includes the sines of the sum and the difference of angles.

$$\sin(\alpha + \beta) = \sin \alpha \cos \beta + \cos \alpha \sin \beta$$
$$\sin(\alpha - \beta) = \sin \alpha \cos \beta - \cos \alpha \sin \beta$$

We can rewrite each using the sum and difference formulas.

$$\sin(\alpha + \beta) + \sin(\alpha - \beta) = \sin \alpha \cos \beta + \cos \alpha \sin \beta + \sin \alpha \cos \beta - \cos \alpha \sin \beta$$

$$= 2 \sin \alpha \cos \beta$$

We see that the identity is verified.

Example 9   **Verifying an Identity Involving Tangent**

Verify the following identity.

$$\frac{\sin(\alpha - \beta)}{\cos \alpha \cos \beta} = \tan \alpha - \tan \beta$$

Solution   We can begin by rewriting the numerator on the left side of the equation.

$$\frac{\sin(\alpha - \beta)}{\cos \alpha \cos \beta} = \frac{\sin \alpha \cos \beta - \cos \alpha \sin \beta}{\cos \alpha \cos \beta}$$

$$= \frac{\sin \alpha \cos \beta}{\cos \alpha \cos \beta} - \frac{\cos \alpha \sin \beta}{\cos \alpha \cos \beta} \qquad \text{Rewrite using a common denominator.}$$

$$= \frac{\sin \alpha}{\cos \alpha} - \frac{\sin \beta}{\cos \beta} \qquad \text{Cancel.}$$

$$= \tan \alpha - \tan \beta \qquad \text{Rewrite in terms of tangent.}$$

We see that the identity is verified. In many cases, verifying tangent identities can successfully be accomplished by writing the tangent in terms of sine and cosine.

Try It #5

Verify the identity: $\tan(\pi - \theta) = -\tan \theta$.

Example 10   **Using Sum and Difference Formulas to Solve an Application Problem**

Let L_1 and L_2 denote two non-vertical intersecting lines, and let θ denote the acute angle between L_1 and L_2. See **Figure 7**. Show that

$$\tan \theta = \frac{m_2 - m_1}{1 + m_1 m_2}$$

where m_1 and m_2 are the slopes of L_1 and L_2 respectively. (**Hint:** Use the fact that $\tan \theta_1 = m_1$ and $\tan \theta_2 = m_2$.)

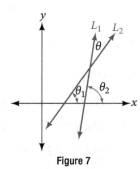

Figure 7

Solution   Using the difference formula for tangent, this problem does not seem as daunting as it might.

$$\tan \theta = \tan(\theta_2 - \theta_1)$$

$$= \frac{\tan \theta_2 - \tan \theta_1}{1 + \tan \theta_1 \tan \theta_2}$$

$$= \frac{m_2 - m_1}{1 + m_1 m_2}$$

Example 11   Investigating a Guy-wire Problem

For a climbing wall, a guy-wire R is attached 47 feet high on a vertical pole. Added support is provided by another guy-wire S attached 40 feet above ground on the same pole. If the wires are attached to the ground 50 feet from the pole, find the angle α between the wires. See **Figure 8**.

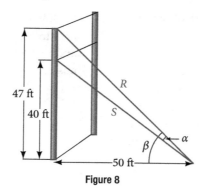

Figure 8

Solution   Let's first summarize the information we can gather from the diagram. As only the sides adjacent to the right angle are known, we can use the tangent function. Notice that $\tan \beta = \dfrac{47}{50}$, and $\tan(\beta - \alpha) = \dfrac{40}{50} = \dfrac{4}{5}$. We can then use difference formula for tangent.

$$\tan(\beta - \alpha) = \frac{\tan \beta - \tan \alpha}{1 + \tan \beta \tan \alpha}$$

Now, substituting the values we know into the formula, we have

$$\frac{4}{5} = \frac{\dfrac{47}{50} - \tan \alpha}{1 + \dfrac{47}{50}\tan \alpha}$$

$$4\left(1 + \frac{47}{50}\tan \alpha\right) = 5\left(\frac{47}{50} - \tan \alpha\right)$$

Use the distributive property, and then simplify the functions.

$$4(1) + 4\left(\frac{47}{50}\right)\tan \alpha = 5\left(\frac{47}{50}\right) - 5\tan \alpha$$

$$4 + 3.76\tan \alpha = 4.7 - 5\tan \alpha$$

$$5\tan \alpha + 3.76\tan \alpha = 0.7$$

$$8.76\tan \alpha = 0.7$$

$$\tan \alpha \approx 0.07991$$

$$\tan^{-1}(0.07991) \approx .079741$$

Now we can calculate the angle in degrees.

$$\alpha \approx 0.079741\left(\frac{180}{\pi}\right) \approx 4.57°$$

Analysis   *Occasionally, when an application appears that includes a right triangle, we may think that solving is a matter of applying the Pythagorean Theorem. That may be partially true, but it depends on what the problem is asking and what information is given.*

Access these online resources for additional instruction and practice with sum and difference identities.

- Sum and Difference Identities for Cosine (http://openstaxcollege.org/l/sumdifcos)
- Sum and Difference Identities for Sine (http://openstaxcollege.org/l/sumdifsin)
- Sum and Difference Identities for Tangent (http://openstaxcollege.org/l/sumdiftan)

9.2 SECTION EXERCISES

VERBAL

1. Explain the basis for the cofunction identities and when they apply.

2. Is there only one way to evaluate $\cos\left(\dfrac{5\pi}{4}\right)$? Explain how to set up the solution in two different ways, and then compute to make sure they give the same answer.

3. Explain to someone who has forgotten the even-odd properties of sinusoidal functions how the addition and subtraction formulas can determine this characteristic for $f(x) = \sin(x)$ and $g(x) = \cos(x)$. (Hint: $0 - x = -x$)

ALGEBRAIC

For the following exercises, find the exact value.

4. $\cos\left(\dfrac{7\pi}{12}\right)$
5. $\cos\left(\dfrac{\pi}{12}\right)$
6. $\sin\left(\dfrac{5\pi}{12}\right)$
7. $\sin\left(\dfrac{11\pi}{12}\right)$

8. $\tan\left(-\dfrac{\pi}{12}\right)$
9. $\tan\left(\dfrac{19\pi}{12}\right)$

For the following exercises, rewrite in terms of $\sin x$ and $\cos x$.

10. $\sin\left(x + \dfrac{11\pi}{6}\right)$
11. $\sin\left(x - \dfrac{3\pi}{4}\right)$
12. $\cos\left(x - \dfrac{5\pi}{6}\right)$
13. $\cos\left(x + \dfrac{2\pi}{3}\right)$

For the following exercises, simplify the given expression.

14. $\csc\left(\dfrac{\pi}{2} - t\right)$
15. $\sec\left(\dfrac{\pi}{2} - \theta\right)$
16. $\cot\left(\dfrac{\pi}{2} - x\right)$
17. $\tan\left(\dfrac{\pi}{2} - x\right)$

18. $\sin(2x)\cos(5x) - \sin(5x)\cos(2x)$

19. $\dfrac{\tan\left(\dfrac{3}{2}x\right) - \tan\left(\dfrac{7}{5}x\right)}{1 + \tan\left(\dfrac{3}{2}x\right)\tan\left(\dfrac{7}{5}x\right)}$

For the following exercises, find the requested information.

20. Given that $\sin a = \dfrac{2}{3}$ and $\cos b = -\dfrac{1}{4}$, with a and b both in the interval $\left[\dfrac{\pi}{2}, \pi\right)$, find $\sin(a + b)$ and $\cos(a - b)$.

21. Given that $\sin a = \dfrac{4}{5}$, and $\cos b = \dfrac{1}{3}$, with a and b both in the interval $\left[0, \dfrac{\pi}{2}\right)$, find $\sin(a - b)$ and $\cos(a + b)$.

For the following exercises, find the exact value of each expression.

22. $\sin\left(\cos^{-1}(0) - \cos^{-1}\left(\dfrac{1}{2}\right)\right)$

23. $\cos\left(\cos^{-1}\left(\dfrac{\sqrt{2}}{2}\right) + \sin^{-1}\left(\dfrac{\sqrt{3}}{2}\right)\right)$

24. $\tan\left(\sin^{-1}\left(\dfrac{1}{2}\right) - \cos^{-1}\left(\dfrac{1}{2}\right)\right)$

GRAPHICAL

For the following exercises, simplify the expression, and then graph both expressions as functions to verify the graphs are identical. Confirm your answer using a graphing calculator.

25. $\cos\left(\dfrac{\pi}{2} - x\right)$ **26.** $\sin(\pi - x)$ **27.** $\tan\left(\dfrac{\pi}{3} + x\right)$ **28.** $\sin\left(\dfrac{\pi}{3} + x\right)$

29. $\tan\left(\dfrac{\pi}{4} - x\right)$ **30.** $\cos\left(\dfrac{7\pi}{6} + x\right)$ **31.** $\sin\left(\dfrac{\pi}{4} + x\right)$ **32.** $\cos\left(\dfrac{5\pi}{4} + x\right)$

For the following exercises, use a graph to determine whether the functions are the same or different. If they are the same, show why. If they are different, replace the second function with one that is identical to the first. (Hint: think $2x = x + x$.)

33. $f(x) = \sin(4x) - \sin(3x)\cos x,\ g(x) = \sin x \cos(3x)$ **34.** $f(x) = \cos(4x) + \sin x \sin(3x),\ g(x) = -\cos x \cos(3x)$

35. $f(x) = \sin(3x)\cos(6x),\ g(x) = -\sin(3x)\cos(6x)$ **36.** $f(x) = \sin(4x),\ g(x) = \sin(5x)\cos x - \cos(5x)\sin x$

37. $f(x) = \sin(2x),\ g(x) = 2 \sin x \cos x$ **38.** $f(\theta) = \cos(2\theta),\ g(\theta) = \cos^2 \theta - \sin^2 \theta$

39. $f(\theta) = \tan(2\theta),\ g(\theta) = \dfrac{\tan \theta}{1 + \tan^2\theta}$ **40.** $f(x) = \sin(3x)\sin x,$
$g(x) = \sin^2(2x)\cos^2 x - \cos^2(2x)\sin^2 x$

41. $f(x) = \tan(-x),\ g(x) = \dfrac{\tan x - \tan(2x)}{1 - \tan x \tan(2x)}$

TECHNOLOGY

For the following exercises, find the exact value algebraically, and then confirm the answer with a calculator to the fourth decimal point.

42. $\sin(75°)$ **43.** $\sin(195°)$ **44.** $\cos(165°)$ **45.** $\cos(345°)$

46. $\tan(-15°)$

EXTENSIONS

For the following exercises, prove the identities provided.

47. $\tan\left(x + \dfrac{\pi}{4}\right) = \dfrac{\tan x + 1}{1 - \tan x}$ **48.** $\dfrac{\tan(a + b)}{\tan(a - b)} = \dfrac{\sin a \cos a + \sin b \cos b}{\sin a \cos a - \sin b \cos b}$

49. $\dfrac{\cos(a + b)}{\cos a \cos b} = 1 - \tan a \tan b$ **50.** $\cos(x + y)\cos(x - y) = \cos^2 x - \sin^2 y$

51. $\dfrac{\cos(x + h) - \cos x}{h} = \cos x \dfrac{\cos h - 1}{h} - \sin x \dfrac{\sin h}{h}$

For the following exercises, prove or disprove the statements.

52. $\tan(u + v) = \dfrac{\tan u + \tan v}{1 - \tan u \tan v}$ **53.** $\tan(u - v) = \dfrac{\tan u - \tan v}{1 + \tan u \tan v}$

54. $\dfrac{\tan(x + y)}{1 + \tan x \tan x} = \dfrac{\tan x + \tan y}{1 - \tan^2 x \tan^2 y}$ **55.** If α, β, and γ are angles in the same triangle, then prove or disprove $\sin(\alpha + \beta) = \sin \gamma$.

56. If α, β, and γ are angles in the same triangle, then prove or disprove:
$\tan \alpha + \tan \beta + \tan \gamma = \tan \alpha \tan \beta \tan \gamma$.

LEARNING OBJECTIVES

In this section, you will:
- Use double-angle formulas to find exact values.
- Use double-angle formulas to verify identities.
- Use reduction formulas to simplify an expression.
- Use half-angle formulas to find exact values.

9.3   DOUBLE-ANGLE, HALF-ANGLE, AND REDUCTION FORMULAS

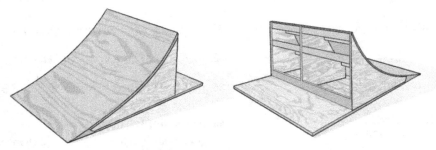

Figure 1 Bicycle ramps for advanced riders have a steeper incline than those designed for novices.

Bicycle ramps made for competition (see **Figure 1**) must vary in height depending on the skill level of the competitors. For advanced competitors, the angle formed by the ramp and the ground should be θ such that $\tan \theta = \dfrac{5}{3}$. The angle is divided in half for novices. What is the steepness of the ramp for novices? In this section, we will investigate three additional categories of identities that we can use to answer questions such as this one.

Using Double-Angle Formulas to Find Exact Values

In the previous section, we used addition and subtraction formulas for trigonometric functions. Now, we take another look at those same formulas. The double-angle formulas are a special case of the sum formulas, where $\alpha = \beta$. Deriving the double-angle formula for sine begins with the sum formula,

$$\sin(\alpha + \beta) = \sin \alpha \cos \beta + \cos \alpha \sin \beta$$

If we let $\alpha = \beta = \theta$, then we have

$$\sin(\theta + \theta) = \sin \theta \cos \theta + \cos \theta \sin \theta$$

$$\sin(2\theta) = 2\sin \theta \cos \theta$$

Deriving the double-angle for cosine gives us three options. First, starting from the sum formula, $\cos(\alpha + \beta) = \cos \alpha \cos \beta - \sin \alpha \sin \beta$, and letting $\alpha = \beta = \theta$, we have

$$\cos(\theta + \theta) = \cos \theta \cos \theta - \sin \theta \sin \theta$$

$$\cos(2\theta) = \cos^2 \theta - \sin^2 \theta$$

Using the Pythagorean properties, we can expand this double-angle formula for cosine and get two more interpretations. The first one is:

$$\cos(2\theta) = \cos^2 \theta - \sin^2 \theta$$
$$= (1 - \sin^2 \theta) - \sin^2 \theta$$
$$= 1 - 2\sin^2 \theta$$

The second variation is:

$$\cos(2\theta) = \cos^2 \theta - \sin^2 \theta$$
$$= \cos^2 \theta - (1 - \cos^2 \theta)$$
$$= 2\cos^2 \theta - 1$$

Similarly, to derive the double-angle formula for tangent, replacing $\alpha = \beta = \theta$ in the sum formula gives

$$\tan(\alpha + \beta) = \frac{\tan \alpha + \tan \beta}{1 - \tan \alpha \tan \beta}$$

$$\tan(\theta + \theta) = \frac{\tan \theta + \tan \theta}{1 - \tan \theta \tan \theta}$$

$$\tan(2\theta) = \frac{2\tan \theta}{1 - \tan^2 \theta}$$

> ### *double-angle formulas*
> The **double-angle formulas** are summarized as follows:
>
> $$\sin(2\theta) = 2 \sin \theta \cos \theta$$
>
> $$\cos(2\theta) = \cos^2 \theta - \sin^2 \theta$$
>
> $$= 1 - 2 \sin^2 \theta$$
>
> $$= 2 \cos^2 \theta - 1$$
>
> $$\tan(2\theta) = \frac{2 \tan \theta}{1 - \tan^2 \theta}$$

How To...

Given the tangent of an angle and the quadrant in which it is located, use the double-angle formulas to find the exact value.

1. Draw a triangle to reflect the given information.
2. Determine the correct double-angle formula.
3. Substitute values into the formula based on the triangle.
4. Simplify.

Example 1   **Using a Double-Angle Formula to Find the Exact Value Involving Tangent**

Given that $\tan \theta = -\frac{3}{4}$ and θ is in quadrant II, find the following:

    a. $\sin(2\theta)$ **b.** $\cos(2\theta)$ **c.** $\tan(2\theta)$

Solution   If we draw a triangle to reflect the information given, we can find the values needed to solve the problems on the image. We are given $\tan \theta = -\frac{3}{4}$, such that θ is in quadrant II. The tangent of an angle is equal to the opposite side over the adjacent side, and because θ is in the second quadrant, the adjacent side is on the x-axis and is negative. Use the Pythagorean Theorem to find the length of the hypotenuse:

$$(-4)^2 + (3)^2 = c^2$$

$$16 + 9 = c^2$$

$$25 = c^2$$

$$c = 5$$

Now we can draw a triangle similar to the one shown in **Figure 2**.

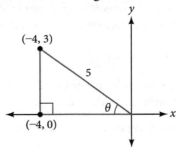

Figure 2

a. Let's begin by writing the double-angle formula for sine.

$$\sin(2\theta) = 2\sin\theta\cos\theta$$

We see that we to need to find $\sin\theta$ and $\cos\theta$. Based on **Figure 2**, we see that the hypotenuse equals 5, so $\sin\theta = \dfrac{3}{5}$, and $\cos\theta = -\dfrac{4}{5}$. Substitute these values into the equation, and simplify.

Thus,

$$\sin(2\theta) = 2\left(\frac{3}{5}\right)\left(-\frac{4}{5}\right)$$
$$= -\frac{24}{25}$$

b. Write the double-angle formula for cosine.

$$\cos(2\theta) = \cos^2\theta - \sin^2\theta$$

Again, substitute the values of the sine and cosine into the equation, and simplify.

$$\cos(2\theta) = \left(-\frac{4}{5}\right)^2 - \left(\frac{3}{5}\right)^2$$
$$= \frac{16}{25} - \frac{9}{25}$$
$$= \frac{7}{25}$$

c. Write the double-angle formula for tangent.

$$\tan(2\theta) = \frac{2\tan\theta}{1 - \tan^2\theta}$$

In this formula, we need the tangent, which we were given as $\tan\theta = -\dfrac{3}{4}$. Substitute this value into the equation, and simplify.

$$\tan(2\theta) = \frac{2\left(-\dfrac{3}{4}\right)}{1 - \left(-\dfrac{3}{4}\right)^2}$$
$$= \frac{-\dfrac{3}{2}}{1 - \dfrac{9}{16}}$$
$$= -\frac{3}{2}\left(\frac{16}{7}\right)$$
$$= -\frac{24}{7}$$

Try It #1

Given $\sin\alpha = \dfrac{5}{8}$, with θ in quadrant I, find $\cos(2\alpha)$.

Example 2   Using the Double-Angle Formula for Cosine without Exact Values

Use the double-angle formula for cosine to write $\cos(6x)$ in terms of $\cos(3x)$.

Solution

$$\cos(6x) = \cos(2(3x))$$
$$= \cos^2 3x - \sin^2 3x$$
$$= 2\cos^2 3x - 1$$

Analysis   *This example illustrates that we can use the double-angle formula without having exact values. It emphasizes that the pattern is what we need to remember and that identities are true for all values in the domain of the trigonometric function.*

Using Double-Angle Formulas to Verify Identities

Establishing identities using the double-angle formulas is performed using the same steps we used to derive the sum and difference formulas. Choose the more complicated side of the equation and rewrite it until it matches the other side.

Example 3   Using the Double-Angle Formulas to Verify an Identity

Verify the following identity using double-angle formulas: $1 + \sin(2\theta) = (\sin\theta + \cos\theta)^2$

Solution   We will work on the right side of the equal sign and rewrite the expression until it matches the left side.

$$(\sin\theta + \cos\theta)^2 = \sin^2\theta + 2\sin\theta\cos\theta + \cos^2\theta$$
$$= (\sin^2\theta + \cos^2\theta) + 2\sin\theta\cos\theta$$
$$= 1 + 2\sin\theta\cos\theta$$
$$= 1 + \sin(2\theta)$$

Analysis   *This process is not complicated, as long as we recall the perfect square formula from algebra:*

$$(a \pm b)^2 = a^2 \pm 2ab + b^2$$

where $a = \sin\theta$ and $b = \cos\theta$. Part of being successful in mathematics is the ability to recognize patterns. While the terms or symbols may change, the algebra remains consistent.

Try It #2

Verify the identity: $\cos^4\theta - \sin^4\theta = \cos(2\theta)$.

Example 4   Verifying a Double-Angle Identity for Tangent

Verify the identity:

$$\tan(2\theta) = \frac{2}{\cot\theta - \tan\theta}$$

Solution   In this case, we will work with the left side of the equation and simplify or rewrite until it equals the right side of the equation.

$$\tan(2\theta) = \frac{2\tan\theta}{1 - \tan^2\theta} \qquad \text{Double-angle formula}$$

$$= \frac{2\tan\theta\left(\dfrac{1}{\tan\theta}\right)}{(1 - \tan^2\theta)\left(\dfrac{1}{\tan\theta}\right)} \qquad \text{Multiply by a term that results in desired numerator.}$$

$$= \frac{2}{\dfrac{1}{\tan\theta} - \dfrac{\tan^2\theta}{\tan\theta}}$$

$$= \frac{2}{\cot\theta - \tan\theta} \qquad \text{Use reciprocal identity for } \dfrac{1}{\tan\theta}.$$

Analysis   *Here is a case where the more complicated side of the initial equation appeared on the right, but we chose to work the left side. However, if we had chosen the left side to rewrite, we would have been working backwards to arrive at the equivalency. For example, suppose that we wanted to show*

$$\frac{2\tan\theta}{1 - \tan^2\theta} = \frac{2}{\cot\theta - \tan\theta}$$

Let's work on the right side.

$$\frac{2}{\cot\theta - \tan\theta} = \frac{2}{\dfrac{1}{\tan\theta} - \tan\theta}\left(\frac{\tan\theta}{\tan\theta}\right)$$

$$= \frac{2\tan\theta}{\dfrac{1}{\tan\theta}(\tan\theta) - \tan\theta(\tan\theta)}$$

$$= \frac{2\tan\theta}{1 - \tan^2\theta}$$

When using the identities to simplify a trigonometric expression or solve a trigonometric equation, there are usually several paths to a desired result. There is no set rule as to what side should be manipulated. However, we should begin with the guidelines set forth earlier.

Try It #3

Verify the identity: $\cos(2\theta)\cos\theta = \cos^3\theta - \cos\theta\sin^2\theta$.

Use Reduction Formulas to Simplify an Expression

The double-angle formulas can be used to derive the reduction formulas, which are formulas we can use to reduce the power of a given expression involving even powers of sine or cosine. They allow us to rewrite the even powers of sine or cosine in terms of the first power of cosine. These formulas are especially important in higher-level math courses, calculus in particular. Also called the power-reducing formulas, three identities are included and are easily derived from the double-angle formulas.

We can use two of the three double-angle formulas for cosine to derive the reduction formulas for sine and cosine. Let's begin with $\cos(2\theta) = 1 - 2\sin^2\theta$. Solve for $\sin^2\theta$:

$$\cos(2\theta) = 1 - 2\sin^2\theta$$
$$2\sin^2\theta = 1 - \cos(2\theta)$$
$$\sin^2\theta = \frac{1 - \cos(2\theta)}{2}$$

Next, we use the formula $\cos(2\theta) = 2\cos^2\theta - 1$. Solve for $\cos^2\theta$:

$$\cos(2\theta) = 2\cos^2\theta - 1$$
$$1 + \cos(2\theta) = 2\cos^2\theta$$
$$\frac{1 + \cos(2\theta)}{2} = \cos^2\theta$$

The last reduction formula is derived by writing tangent in terms of sine and cosine:

$$\tan^2\theta = \frac{\sin^2\theta}{\cos^2\theta}$$

$$= \frac{\dfrac{1 - \cos(2\theta)}{2}}{\dfrac{1 + \cos(2\theta)}{2}} \qquad \text{Substitute the reduction formulas.}$$

$$= \left(\frac{1 - \cos(2\theta)}{2}\right)\left(\frac{2}{1 + \cos(2\theta)}\right)$$

$$= \frac{1 - \cos(2\theta)}{1 + \cos(2\theta)}$$

---

reduction formulas

The **reduction formulas** are summarized as follows:

$$\sin^2\theta = \frac{1 - \cos(2\theta)}{2} \qquad \cos^2\theta = \frac{1 + \cos(2\theta)}{2} \qquad \tan^2\theta = \frac{1 - \cos(2\theta)}{1 + \cos(2\theta)}$$

Example 5   **Writing an Equivalent Expression Not Containing Powers Greater Than 1**

Write an equivalent expression for $\cos^4 x$ that does not involve any powers of sine or cosine greater than 1.

Solution   We will apply the reduction formula for cosine twice.

$$\cos^4 x = (\cos^2 x)^2$$

$$= \left(\frac{1 + \cos(2x)}{2}\right)^2 \qquad \text{Substitute reduction formula for } \cos^2 x.$$

$$= \frac{1}{4}(1 + 2\cos(2x) + \cos^2(2x))$$

$$= \frac{1}{4} + \frac{1}{2}\cos(2x) + \frac{1}{4}\left(\frac{1 + \cos2(2x)}{2}\right) \qquad \text{Substitute reduction formula for } \cos^2 x.$$

$$= \frac{1}{4} + \frac{1}{2}\cos(2x) + \frac{1}{8} + \frac{1}{8}\cos(4x)$$

$$= \frac{3}{8} + \frac{1}{2}\cos(2x) + \frac{1}{8}\cos(4x)$$

Analysis   *The solution is found by using the reduction formula twice, as noted, and the perfect square formula from algebra.*

Example 6   Using the Power-Reducing Formulas to Prove an Identity

Use the power-reducing formulas to prove
$$\sin^3(2x) = \left[\frac{1}{2}\sin(2x)\right][1 - \cos(4x)]$$

Solution   We will work on simplifying the left side of the equation:

$$\sin^3(2x) = [\sin(2x)][\sin^2(2x)]$$

$$= \sin(2x)\left[\frac{1 - \cos(4x)}{2}\right] \qquad \text{Substitute the power-reduction formula.}$$

$$= \sin(2x)\left(\frac{1}{2}\right)[1 - \cos(4x)]$$

$$= \frac{1}{2}[\sin(2x)][1 - \cos(4x)]$$

Analysis   *Note that in this example, we substituted*

$$\frac{1 - \cos(4x)}{2}$$

for $\sin^2(2x)$. *The formula states*

$$\sin^2\theta = \frac{1 - \cos(2\theta)}{2}$$

We let $\theta = 2x$, *so* $2\theta = 4x$.

Try It #4

Use the power-reducing formulas to prove that $10\cos^4 x = \frac{15}{4} + 5\cos(2x) + \frac{5}{4}\cos(4x)$.

Using Half-Angle Formulas to Find Exact Values

The next set of identities is the set of **half-angle formulas**, which can be derived from the reduction formulas and we can use when we have an angle that is half the size of a special angle. If we replace θ with $\frac{\alpha}{2}$, the half-angle formula for sine is found by simplifying the equation and solving for $\sin\left(\frac{\alpha}{2}\right)$. Note that the half-angle formulas are preceded by a $\pm$ sign.

This does not mean that both the positive and negative expressions are valid. Rather, it depends on the quadrant in which $\frac{\alpha}{2}$ terminates.

The half-angle formula for sine is derived as follows:

$$\sin^2\theta = \frac{1 - \cos(2\theta)}{2}$$

$$\sin^2\left(\frac{\alpha}{2}\right) = \frac{1 - \cos\left(2 \cdot \frac{\alpha}{2}\right)}{2}$$

$$= \frac{1 - \cos\alpha}{2}$$

$$\sin\left(\frac{\alpha}{2}\right) = \pm\sqrt{\frac{1 - \cos\alpha}{2}}$$

To derive the half-angle formula for cosine, we have

$$\cos^2\theta = \frac{1 + \cos(2\theta)}{2}$$

$$\cos^2\left(\frac{\alpha}{2}\right) = \frac{1 + \cos\left(2 \cdot \frac{\alpha}{2}\right)}{2}$$

$$= \frac{1 + \cos\alpha}{2}$$

$$\cos\left(\frac{\alpha}{2}\right) = \pm\sqrt{\frac{1 + \cos\alpha}{2}}$$

For the tangent identity, we have

$$\tan^2 \theta = \frac{1 - \cos(2\theta)}{1 + \cos(2\theta)}$$

$$\tan^2\left(\frac{\alpha}{2}\right) = \frac{1 - \cos\left(2 \cdot \frac{\alpha}{2}\right)}{1 + \cos\left(2 \cdot \frac{\alpha}{2}\right)}$$

$$= \frac{1 - \cos \alpha}{1 + \cos \alpha}$$

$$\tan\left(\frac{\alpha}{2}\right) = \pm\sqrt{\frac{1 - \cos \alpha}{1 + \cos \alpha}}$$

---

half-angle formulas

The **half-angle formulas** are as follows:

$$\sin\left(\frac{\alpha}{2}\right) = \pm\sqrt{\frac{1 - \cos \alpha}{2}}$$

$$\cos\left(\frac{\alpha}{2}\right) = \pm\sqrt{\frac{1 + \cos \alpha}{2}}$$

$$\tan\left(\frac{\alpha}{2}\right) = \pm\sqrt{\frac{1 - \cos \alpha}{1 + \cos \alpha}}$$

$$= \frac{\sin \alpha}{1 + \cos \alpha}$$

$$= \frac{1 - \cos \alpha}{\sin \alpha}$$

Example 7   Using a Half-Angle Formula to Find the Exact Value of a Sine Function

Find $\sin(15°)$ using a half-angle formula.

Solution   Since $15° = \dfrac{30°}{2}$, we use the half-angle formula for sine:

$$\sin\frac{30°}{2} = \sqrt{\frac{1 - \cos 30°}{2}}$$

$$= \sqrt{\frac{1 - \dfrac{\sqrt{3}}{2}}{2}}$$

$$= \sqrt{\frac{\dfrac{2 - \sqrt{3}}{2}}{2}}$$

$$= \sqrt{\frac{2 - \sqrt{3}}{4}}$$

$$= \frac{\sqrt{2 - \sqrt{3}}}{2}$$

Remember that we can check the answer with a graphing calculator.

Analysis   Notice that we used only the positive root because $\sin(15°)$ is positive.

How To...

Given the tangent of an angle and the quadrant in which the angle lies, find the exact values of trigonometric functions of half of the angle.

1. Draw a triangle to represent the given information.
2. Determine the correct half-angle formula.
3. Substitute values into the formula based on the triangle.
4. Simplify.

Example 8 **Finding Exact Values Using Half-Angle Identities**

Given that $\tan \alpha = \dfrac{8}{15}$ and α lies in quadrant III, find the exact value of the following:

a. $\sin\left(\dfrac{\alpha}{2}\right)$ **b.** $\cos\left(\dfrac{\alpha}{2}\right)$ **c.** $\tan\left(\dfrac{\alpha}{2}\right)$

Solution Using the given information, we can draw the triangle shown in **Figure 3**. Using the Pythagorean Theorem, we find the hypotenuse to be 17. Therefore, we can calculate $\sin \alpha = -\dfrac{8}{17}$ and $\cos \alpha = -\dfrac{15}{17}$.

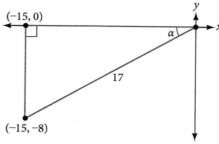

Figure 3

a. Before we start, we must remember that, if α is in quadrant III, then $180° < \alpha < 270°$, so $\dfrac{180°}{2} < \dfrac{\alpha}{2} < \dfrac{270°}{2}$. This means that the terminal side of $\dfrac{\alpha}{2}$ is in quadrant II, since $90° < \dfrac{\alpha}{2} < 135°$. To find $\sin \dfrac{\alpha}{2}$, we begin by writing the half-angle formula for sine. Then we substitute the value of the cosine we found from the triangle in **Figure 3** and simplify.

$$\sin \frac{\alpha}{2} = \pm \sqrt{\frac{1 - \cos \alpha}{2}}$$

$$= \pm \sqrt{\frac{1 - \left(-\dfrac{15}{17}\right)}{2}}$$

$$= \pm \sqrt{\frac{\dfrac{32}{17}}{2}}$$

$$= \pm \sqrt{\frac{32}{17} \cdot \frac{1}{2}}$$

$$= \pm \sqrt{\frac{16}{17}}$$

$$= \pm \frac{4}{\sqrt{17}}$$

$$= \frac{4\sqrt{17}}{17}$$

We choose the positive value of $\sin \dfrac{\alpha}{2}$ because the angle terminates in quadrant II and sine is positive in quadrant II.

b. To find $\cos \dfrac{\alpha}{2}$, we will write the half-angle formula for cosine, substitute the value of the cosine we found from the triangle in **Figure 3**, and simplify.

$$\cos\left(\frac{\alpha}{2}\right) = \pm\sqrt{\frac{1+\cos\alpha}{2}}$$

$$= \pm\sqrt{\frac{1+\left(-\frac{15}{17}\right)}{2}}$$

$$= \pm\sqrt{\frac{\frac{2}{17}}{2}}$$

$$= \pm\sqrt{\frac{2}{17}\cdot\frac{1}{2}}$$

$$= \pm\sqrt{\frac{1}{17}}$$

$$= -\frac{\sqrt{17}}{17}$$

We choose the negative value of $\cos\frac{\alpha}{2}$ because the angle is in quadrant II because cosine is negative in quadrant II.

c. To find $\tan\frac{\alpha}{2}$, we write the half-angle formula for tangent. Again, we substitute the value of the cosine we found from the triangle in **Figure 3** and simplify.

$$\tan\frac{\alpha}{2} = \pm\sqrt{\frac{1-\cos\alpha}{1+\cos\alpha}}$$

$$= \pm\sqrt{\frac{1-\left(-\frac{15}{17}\right)}{1+\left(-\frac{15}{17}\right)}}$$

$$= \pm\sqrt{\frac{\frac{32}{17}}{\frac{2}{17}}}$$

$$= \pm\sqrt{\frac{32}{2}}$$

$$= -\sqrt{16}$$

$$= -4$$

We choose the negative value of $\tan\frac{\alpha}{2}$ because $\frac{\alpha}{2}$ lies in quadrant II, and tangent is negative in quadrant II.

Try It #5

Given that $\sin\alpha = -\frac{4}{5}$ and α lies in quadrant IV, find the exact value of $\cos\left(\frac{\alpha}{2}\right)$.

Example 9   **Finding the Measurement of a Half Angle**

Now, we will return to the problem posed at the beginning of the section. A bicycle ramp is constructed for high-level competition with an angle of θ formed by the ramp and the ground. Another ramp is to be constructed half as steep for novice competition. If $\tan\theta = \frac{5}{3}$ for higher-level competition, what is the measurement of the angle for novice competition?

Solution   Since the angle for novice competition measures half the steepness of the angle for the high-level competition, and $\tan\theta = \dfrac{5}{3}$ for high-level competition, we can find $\cos\theta$ from the right triangle and the Pythagorean theorem so that we can use the half-angle identities. See **Figure 4**.

$$3^2 + 5^2 = 34$$

$$c = \sqrt{34}$$

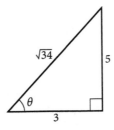

Figure 4

We see that $\cos\theta = \dfrac{3}{\sqrt{34}} = \dfrac{3\sqrt{34}}{34}$. We can use the half-angle formula for tangent: $\tan\dfrac{\theta}{2} = \sqrt{\dfrac{1 - \cos\theta}{1 + \cos\theta}}$. Since $\tan\theta$ is in the first quadrant, so is $\tan\dfrac{\theta}{2}$. Thus,

$$\tan\frac{\theta}{2} = \sqrt{\dfrac{1 - \dfrac{3\sqrt{34}}{34}}{1 + \dfrac{3\sqrt{34}}{34}}}$$

$$= \sqrt{\dfrac{\dfrac{34 - 3\sqrt{34}}{34}}{\dfrac{34 + 3\sqrt{34}}{34}}}$$

$$= \sqrt{\dfrac{34 - 3\sqrt{34}}{34 + 3\sqrt{34}}}$$

$$\approx 0.57$$

We can take the inverse tangent to find the angle: $\tan^{-1}(0.57) \approx 29.7°$. So the angle of the ramp for novice competition is $\approx 29.7°$.

Access these online resources for additional instruction and practice with double-angle, half-angle, and reduction formulas.

- Double-Angle Identities (http://openstaxcollege.org/l/doubleangiden)
- Half-Angle Identities (http://openstaxcollege.org/l/halfangleident)

9.3 SECTION EXERCISES

VERBAL

1. Explain how to determine the reduction identities from the double-angle identity $\cos(2x) = \cos^2 x - \sin^2 x$.

2. Explain how to determine the double-angle formula for $\tan(2x)$ using the double-angle formulas for $\cos(2x)$ and $\sin(2x)$.

3. We can determine the half-angle formula for tan $\left(\dfrac{x}{2}\right) = \pm \dfrac{\sqrt{1 - \cos x}}{\sqrt{1 + \cos x}}$ by dividing the formula for $\sin\left(\dfrac{x}{2}\right)$ by $\cos\left(\dfrac{x}{2}\right)$. Explain how to determine two formulas for $\tan\left(\dfrac{x}{2}\right)$ that do not involve any square roots.

4. For the half-angle formula given in the previous exercise for $\tan\left(\dfrac{x}{2}\right)$, explain why dividing by 0 is not a concern. (Hint: examine the values of $\cos x$ necessary for the denominator to be 0.)

ALGEBRAIC

For the following exercises, find the exact values of a) $\sin(2x)$, b) $\cos(2x)$, and c) $\tan(2x)$ without solving for x.

5. If $\sin x = \dfrac{1}{8}$, and x is in quadrant I.

6. If $\cos x = \dfrac{2}{3}$, and x is in quadrant I.

7. If $\cos x = -\dfrac{1}{2}$, and x is in quadrant III.

8. If $\tan x = -8$, and x is in quadrant IV.

For the following exercises, find the values of the six trigonometric functions if the conditions provided hold.

9. $\cos(2\theta) = \dfrac{3}{5}$ and $90° \leq \theta \leq 180°$

10. $\cos(2\theta) = \dfrac{1}{\sqrt{2}}$ and $180° \leq \theta \leq 270°$

For the following exercises, simplify to one trigonometric expression.

11. $2\sin\left(\dfrac{\pi}{4}\right) 2\cos\left(\dfrac{\pi}{4}\right)$

12. $4\sin\left(\dfrac{\pi}{8}\right)\cos\left(\dfrac{\pi}{8}\right)$

For the following exercises, find the exact value using half-angle formulas.

13. $\sin\left(\dfrac{\pi}{8}\right)$

14. $\cos\left(-\dfrac{11\pi}{12}\right)$

15. $\sin\left(\dfrac{11\pi}{12}\right)$

16. $\cos\left(\dfrac{7\pi}{8}\right)$

17. $\tan\left(\dfrac{5\pi}{12}\right)$

18. $\tan\left(-\dfrac{3\pi}{12}\right)$

19. $\tan\left(-\dfrac{3\pi}{8}\right)$

For the following exercises, find the exact values of a) $\sin\left(\dfrac{x}{2}\right)$, b) $\cos\left(\dfrac{x}{2}\right)$, and c) $\tan\left(\dfrac{x}{2}\right)$ without solving for x, when $0 \leq x \leq 360°$.

20. If $\tan x = -\dfrac{4}{3}$, and x is in quadrant IV.

21. If $\sin x = -\dfrac{12}{13}$, and x is in quadrant III.

22. If $\csc x = 7$, and x is in quadrant II.

23. If $\sec x = -4$, and x is in quadrant II.

For the following exercises, use **Figure 5** to find the requested half and double angles.

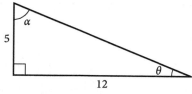

Figure 5

24. Find $\sin(2\theta)$, $\cos(2\theta)$, and $\tan(2\theta)$.

25. Find $\sin(2\alpha)$, $\cos(2\alpha)$, and $\tan(2\alpha)$.

26. Find $\sin\left(\dfrac{\theta}{2}\right)$, $\cos\left(\dfrac{\theta}{2}\right)$, and $\tan\left(\dfrac{\theta}{2}\right)$.

27. Find $\sin\left(\dfrac{\alpha}{2}\right)$, $\cos\left(\dfrac{\alpha}{2}\right)$, and $\tan\left(\dfrac{\alpha}{2}\right)$.

For the following exercises, simplify each expression. Do not evaluate.

28. $\cos^2(28°) - \sin^2(28°)$

29. $2\cos^2(37°) - 1$

30. $1 - 2\sin^2(17°)$

31. $\cos^2(9x) - \sin^2(9x)$

32. $4\sin(8x)\cos(8x)$

33. $6\sin(5x)\cos(5x)$

For the following exercises, prove the identity given.

34. $(\sin t - \cos t)^2 = 1 - \sin(2t)$

35. $\sin(2x) = -2\sin(-x)\cos(-x)$

36. $\cot x - \tan x = 2\cot(2x)$

37. $\dfrac{\sin(2\theta)}{1 + \cos(2\theta)}\tan^2\theta = \tan^3\theta$

For the following exercises, rewrite the expression with an exponent no higher than 1.

38. $\cos^2(5x)$

39. $\cos^2(6x)$

40. $\sin^4(8x)$

41. $\sin^4(3x)$

42. $\cos^2 x \sin^4 x$

43. $\cos^4 x \sin^2 x$

44. $\tan^2 x \sin^2 x$

TECHNOLOGY

For the following exercises, reduce the equations to powers of one, and then check the answer graphically.

45. $\tan^4 x$

46. $\sin^2(2x)$

47. $\sin^2 x \cos^2 x$

48. $\tan^2 x \sin x$

49. $\tan^4 x \cos^2 x$

50. $\cos^2 x \sin(2x)$

51. $\cos^2(2x)\sin x$

52. $\tan^2\left(\dfrac{x}{2}\right)\sin x$

For the following exercises, algebraically find an equivalent function, only in terms of $\sin x$ and/or $\cos x$, and then check the answer by graphing both equations.

53. $\sin(4x)$

54. $\cos(4x)$

EXTENSIONS

For the following exercises, prove the identities.

55. $\sin(2x) = \dfrac{2\tan x}{1 + \tan^2 x}$

56. $\cos(2\alpha) = \dfrac{1 - \tan^2\alpha}{1 + \tan^2\alpha}$

57. $\tan(2x) = \dfrac{2\sin x \cos x}{2\cos^2 x - 1}$

58. $(\sin^2 x - 1)^2 = \cos(2x) + \sin^4 x$

59. $\sin(3x) = 3\sin x\cos^2 x - \sin^3 x$

60. $\cos(3x) = \cos^3 x - 3\sin^2 x\cos x$

61. $\dfrac{1 + \cos(2t)}{\sin(2t) - \cos t} = \dfrac{2\cos t}{2\sin t - 1}$

62. $\sin(16x) = 16\sin x\cos x\cos(2x)\cos(4x)\cos(8x)$

63. $\cos(16x) = (\cos^2(4x) - \sin^2(4x) - \sin(8x))(\cos^2(4x) - \sin^2(4x) + \sin(8x))$

LEARNING OBJECTIVES

In this section, you will:

- Express products as sums.
- Express sums as products.

9.4   SUM-TO-PRODUCT AND PRODUCT-TO-SUM FORMULAS

Figure 1 The UCLA marching band (credit: Eric Chan, Flickr).

A band marches down the field creating an amazing sound that bolsters the crowd. That sound travels as a wave that can be interpreted using trigonometric functions. For example, **Figure 2** represents a sound wave for the musical note A. In this section, we will investigate trigonometric identities that are the foundation of everyday phenomena such as sound waves.

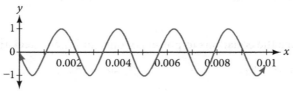

Figure 2

Expressing Products as Sums

We have already learned a number of formulas useful for expanding or simplifying trigonometric expressions, but sometimes we may need to express the product of cosine and sine as a sum. We can use the product-to-sum formulas, which express products of trigonometric functions as sums. Let's investigate the cosine identity first and then the sine identity.

Expressing Products as Sums for Cosine

We can derive the product-to-sum formula from the sum and difference identities for cosine. If we add the two equations, we get:

$$
\begin{aligned}
\cos \alpha \cos \beta + \sin \alpha \sin \beta &= \cos(\alpha - \beta) \\
+ \cos \alpha \cos \beta - \sin \alpha \sin \beta &= \cos(\alpha + \beta) \\
\hline
2 \cos \alpha \cos \beta &= \cos(\alpha - \beta) + \cos(\alpha + \beta)
\end{aligned}
$$

Then, we divide by 2 to isolate the product of cosines:

$$
\cos \alpha \cos \beta = \frac{1}{2}\left[\cos(\alpha - \beta) + \cos(\alpha + \beta)\right]
$$

How To...

Given a product of cosines, express as a sum.

1. Write the formula for the product of cosines.
2. Substitute the given angles into the formula.
3. Simplify.

Example 1 **Writing the Product as a Sum Using the Product-to-Sum Formula for Cosine**

Write the following product of cosines as a sum: $2 \cos\left(\dfrac{7x}{2}\right) \cos \dfrac{3x}{2}$.

Solution We begin by writing the formula for the product of cosines:

$$\cos \alpha \cos \beta = \frac{1}{2}[\cos(\alpha - \beta) + \cos(\alpha + \beta)]$$

We can then substitute the given angles into the formula and simplify.

$$2 \cos\left(\frac{7x}{2}\right) \cos\left(\frac{3x}{2}\right) = (2)\left(\frac{1}{2}\right)\left[\cos\left(\frac{7x}{2} - \frac{3x}{2}\right) + \cos\left(\frac{7x}{2} + \frac{3x}{2}\right)\right]$$

$$= \left[\cos\left(\frac{4x}{2}\right) + \cos\left(\frac{10x}{2}\right)\right]$$

$$= \cos 2x + \cos 5x$$

Try It #1

Use the product-to-sum formula to write the product as a sum or difference: $\cos(2\theta)\cos(4\theta)$.

Expressing the Product of Sine and Cosine as a Sum

Next, we will derive the product-to-sum formula for sine and cosine from the sum and difference formulas for sine. If we add the sum and difference identities, we get:

$$\sin(\alpha + \beta) = \sin \alpha \cos \beta + \cos \alpha \sin \beta$$
$$+ \qquad \sin(\alpha - \beta) = \sin \alpha \cos \beta - \cos \alpha \sin \beta$$
$$\overline{\sin(\alpha + \beta) + \sin(\alpha - \beta) = 2 \sin \alpha \cos \beta}$$

Then, we divide by 2 to isolate the product of cosine and sine:

$$\sin \alpha \cos \beta = \frac{1}{2}[\sin(\alpha + \beta) + \sin(\alpha - \beta)]$$

Example 2 **Writing the Product as a Sum Containing only Sine or Cosine**

Express the following product as a sum containing only sine or cosine and no products: $\sin(4\theta)\cos(2\theta)$.

Solution Write the formula for the product of sine and cosine. Then substitute the given values into the formula and simplify.

$$\sin \alpha \cos \beta = \frac{1}{2}[\sin(\alpha + \beta) + \sin(\alpha - \beta)]$$

$$\sin(4\theta)\cos(2\theta) = \frac{1}{2}[\sin(4\theta + 2\theta) + \sin(4\theta - 2\theta)]$$

$$= \frac{1}{2}[\sin(6\theta) + \sin(2\theta)]$$

Try It #2

Use the product-to-sum formula to write the product as a sum: $\sin(x + y)\cos(x - y)$.

Expressing Products of Sines in Terms of Cosine

Expressing the product of sines in terms of cosine is also derived from the sum and difference identities for cosine. In this case, we will first subtract the two cosine formulas:

$$\cos(\alpha - \beta) = \cos \alpha \cos \beta + \sin \alpha \sin \beta$$
$$- \qquad \cos(\alpha + \beta) = -(\cos \alpha \cos \beta - \sin \alpha \sin \beta)$$
$$\overline{\cos(\alpha - \beta) - \cos(\alpha + \beta) = 2 \sin \alpha \sin \beta}$$

Then, we divide by 2 to isolate the product of sines:

$$\sin \alpha \sin \beta = \frac{1}{2}[\cos(\alpha - \beta) - \cos(\alpha + \beta)]$$

Similarly we could express the product of cosines in terms of sine or derive other product-to-sum formulas.

---

the product-to-sum formulas

The **product-to-sum formulas** are as follows:

$$\cos \alpha \cos \beta = \frac{1}{2}[\cos(\alpha - \beta) + \cos(\alpha + \beta)] \qquad \sin \alpha \cos \beta = \frac{1}{2}[\sin(\alpha + \beta) + \sin(\alpha - \beta)]$$

$$\sin \alpha \sin \beta = \frac{1}{2}[\cos(\alpha - \beta) - \cos(\alpha + \beta)] \qquad \cos \alpha \sin \beta = \frac{1}{2}[\sin(\alpha + \beta) - \sin(\alpha - \beta)]$$

Example 3   Express the Product as a Sum or Difference

Write $\cos(3\theta) \cos(5\theta)$ as a sum or difference.

Solution   We have the product of cosines, so we begin by writing the related formula. Then we substitute the given angles and simplify.

$$\cos \alpha \cos \beta = \frac{1}{2}[\cos(\alpha - \beta) + \cos(\alpha + \beta)]$$

$$\cos(3\theta)\cos(5\theta) = \frac{1}{2}[\cos(3\theta - 5\theta) + \cos(3\theta + 5\theta)]$$

$$= \frac{1}{2}[\cos(2\theta) + \cos(8\theta)] \qquad \text{Use even-odd identity.}$$

Try It #3

Use the product-to-sum formula to evaluate $\cos \dfrac{11\pi}{12} \cos \dfrac{\pi}{12}$.

Expressing Sums as Products

Some problems require the reverse of the process we just used. The sum-to-product formulas allow us to express sums of sine or cosine as products. These formulas can be derived from the product-to-sum identities. For example, with a few substitutions, we can derive the sum-to-product identity for sine. Let $\dfrac{u + v}{2} = \alpha$ and $\dfrac{u - v}{2} = \beta$.

Then,

$$\alpha + \beta = \frac{u + v}{2} + \frac{u - v}{2}$$

$$= \frac{2u}{2}$$

$$= u$$

$$\alpha - \beta = \frac{u + v}{2} - \frac{u - v}{2}$$

$$= \frac{2v}{2}$$

$$= v$$

Thus, replacing α and β in the product-to-sum formula with the substitute expressions, we have

$$\sin \alpha \cos \beta = \frac{1}{2}[\sin(\alpha + \beta) + \sin(\alpha - \beta)]$$

$$\sin\left(\frac{u+v}{2}\right)\cos\left(\frac{u-v}{2}\right) = \frac{1}{2}[\sin u + \sin v] \qquad \text{Substitute for } (\alpha + \beta) \text{ and } (\alpha - \beta)$$

$$2\sin\left(\frac{u+v}{2}\right)\cos\left(\frac{u-v}{2}\right) = \sin u + \sin v$$

The other sum-to-product identities are derived similarly.

---

sum-to-product formulas

The **sum-to-product formulas** are as follows:

$$\sin \alpha + \sin \beta = 2\sin\left(\frac{\alpha+\beta}{2}\right)\cos\left(\frac{\alpha-\beta}{2}\right) \qquad \sin \alpha - \sin \beta = 2\sin\left(\frac{\alpha-\beta}{2}\right)\cos\left(\frac{\alpha+\beta}{2}\right)$$

$$\cos \alpha - \cos \beta = -2\sin\left(\frac{\alpha+\beta}{2}\right)\sin\left(\frac{\alpha-\beta}{2}\right) \qquad \cos \alpha + \cos \beta = 2\cos\left(\frac{\alpha+\beta}{2}\right)\cos\left(\frac{\alpha-\beta}{2}\right)$$

Example 4   **Writing the Difference of Sines as a Product**

Write the following difference of sines expression as a product: $\sin(4\theta) - \sin(2\theta)$.

Solution   We begin by writing the formula for the difference of sines.

$$\sin \alpha - \sin \beta = 2\sin\left(\frac{\alpha-\beta}{2}\right)\cos\left(\frac{\alpha+\beta}{2}\right)$$

Substitute the values into the formula, and simplify.

$$\sin(4\theta) - \sin(2\theta) = 2\sin\left(\frac{4\theta - 2\theta}{2}\right)\cos\left(\frac{4\theta + 2\theta}{2}\right)$$

$$= 2\sin\left(\frac{2\theta}{2}\right)\cos\left(\frac{6\theta}{2}\right)$$

$$= 2\sin\theta\cos(3\theta)$$

Try It #4

Use the sum-to-product formula to write the sum as a product: $\sin(3\theta) + \sin(\theta)$.

Example 5   **Evaluating Using the Sum-to-Product Formula**

Evaluate $\cos(15°) - \cos(75°)$. Check the answer with a graphing calculator.

Solution   We begin by writing the formula for the difference of cosines.

$$\cos \alpha - \cos \beta = -2\sin\left(\frac{\alpha+\beta}{2}\right)\sin\left(\frac{\alpha-\beta}{2}\right)$$

Then we substitute the given angles and simplify.

$$\cos(15°) - \cos(75°) = -2\sin\left(\frac{15° + 75°}{2}\right)\sin\left(\frac{15° - 75°}{2}\right)$$

$$= -2\sin(45°)\sin(-30°)$$

$$= -2\left(\frac{\sqrt{2}}{2}\right)\left(-\frac{1}{2}\right)$$

$$= \frac{\sqrt{2}}{2}$$

Example 6   Proving an Identity

Prove the identity:

$$\frac{\cos(4t) - \cos(2t)}{\sin(4t) + \sin(2t)} = -\tan t$$

Solution   We will start with the left side, the more complicated side of the equation, and rewrite the expression until it matches the right side.

$$\frac{\cos(4t) - \cos(2t)}{\sin(4t) + \sin(2t)} = \frac{-2\sin\left(\dfrac{4t + 2t}{2}\right)\sin\left(\dfrac{4t - 2t}{2}\right)}{2\sin\left(\dfrac{4t + 2t}{2}\right)\cos\left(\dfrac{4t - 2t}{2}\right)}$$

$$= \frac{-2\sin(3t)\sin t}{2\sin(3t)\cos t}$$

$$= \frac{-\cancel{2}\,\cancel{\sin(3t)}\sin t}{\cancel{2}\,\cancel{\sin(3t)}\cos t}$$

$$= -\frac{\sin t}{\cos t}$$

$$= -\tan t$$

Analysis   Recall that verifying trigonometric identities has its own set of rules. The procedures for solving an equation are not the same as the procedures for verifying an identity. When we prove an identity, we pick one side to work on and make substitutions until that side is transformed into the other side.

Example 7   Verifying the Identity Using Double-Angle Formulas and Reciprocal Identities

Verify the identity $\csc^2\theta - 2 = \dfrac{\cos(2\theta)}{\sin^2\theta}$.

Solution   For verifying this equation, we are bringing together several of the identities. We will use the double-angle formula and the reciprocal identities. We will work with the right side of the equation and rewrite it until it matches the left side.

$$\frac{\cos(2\theta)}{\sin^2\theta} = \frac{1 - 2\sin^2\theta}{\sin^2\theta}$$

$$= \frac{1}{\sin^2\theta} - \frac{2\sin^2\theta}{\sin^2\theta}$$

$$= \csc^2\theta - 2$$

Try It #5

Verify the identity $\tan\theta\cot\theta - \cos^2\theta = \sin^2\theta$.

Access these online resources for additional instruction and practice with the product-to-sum and sum-to-product identities.

- Sum to Product Identities (http://openstaxcollege.org/l/sumtoprod)
- Sum to Product and Product to Sum Identities (http://openstaxcollege.org/l/sumtpptsum)

9.4 SECTION EXERCISES

VERBAL

1. Starting with the product to sum formula $\sin \alpha \cos \beta = \frac{1}{2}[\sin(\alpha + \beta) + \sin(\alpha - \beta)]$, explain how to determine the formula for $\cos \alpha \sin \beta$.

2. Provide two different methods of calculating $\cos(195°)\cos(105°)$, one of which uses the product to sum. Which method is easier?

3. Describe a situation where we would convert an equation from a sum to a product and give an example.

4. Describe a situation where we would convert an equation from a product to a sum, and give an example.

ALGEBRAIC

For the following exercises, rewrite the product as a sum or difference.

5. $16\sin(16x)\sin(11x)$

6. $20\cos(36t)\cos(6t)$

7. $2\sin(5x)\cos(3x)$

8. $10\cos(5x)\sin(10x)$

9. $\sin(-x)\sin(5x)$

10. $\sin(3x)\cos(5x)$

For the following exercises, rewrite the sum or difference as a product.

11. $\cos(6t) + \cos(4t)$

12. $\sin(3x) + \sin(7x)$

13. $\cos(7x) + \cos(-7x)$

14. $\sin(3x) - \sin(-3x)$

15. $\cos(3x) + \cos(9x)$

16. $\sin h - \sin(3h)$

For the following exercises, evaluate the product using a sum or difference of two functions. Evaluate exactly.

17. $\cos(45°)\cos(15°)$

18. $\cos(45°)\sin(15°)$

19. $\sin(-345°)\sin(-15°)$

20. $\sin(195°)\cos(15°)$

21. $\sin(-45°)\sin(-15°)$

For the following exercises, evaluate the product using a sum or difference of two functions. Leave in terms of sine and cosine.

22. $\cos(23°)\sin(17°)$

23. $2\sin(100°)\sin(20°)$

24. $2\sin(-100°)\sin(-20°)$

25. $\sin(213°)\cos(8°)$

26. $2\cos(56°)\cos(47°)$

For the following exercises, rewrite the sum as a product of two functions. Leave in terms of sine and cosine.

27. $\sin(76°) + \sin(14°)$

28. $\cos(58°) - \cos(12°)$

29. $\sin(101°) - \sin(32°)$

30. $\cos(100°) + \cos(200°)$

31. $\sin(-1°) + \sin(-2°)$

For the following exercises, prove the identity.

32. $\dfrac{\cos(a + b)}{\cos(a - b)} = \dfrac{1 - \tan a \tan b}{1 + \tan a \tan b}$

33. $4\sin(3x)\cos(4x) = 2\sin(7x) - 2\sin x$

34. $\dfrac{6\cos(8x)\sin(2x)}{\sin(-6x)} = -3\sin(10x)\csc(6x) + 3$

35. $\sin x + \sin(3x) = 4\sin x \cos^2 x$

36. $2(\cos^3 x - \cos x \sin^2 x) = \cos(3x) + \cos x$

37. $2\tan x \cos(3x) = \sec x(\sin(4x) - \sin(2x))$

38. $\cos(a + b) + \cos(a - b) = 2\cos a \cos b$

NUMERIC

For the following exercises, rewrite the sum as a product of two functions or the product as a sum of two functions. Give your answer in terms of sines and cosines. Then evaluate the final answer numerically, rounded to four decimal places.

39. $\cos(58°) + \cos(12°)$

40. $\sin(2°) - \sin(3°)$

41. $\cos(44°) - \cos(22°)$

42. $\cos(176°)\sin(9°)$

43. $\sin(-14°)\sin(85°)$

TECHNOLOGY

For the following exercises, algebraically determine whether each of the given expressions is a true identity. If it is not an identity, replace the right-hand side with an expression equivalent to the left side. Verify the results by graphing both expressions on a calculator.

44. $2\sin(2x)\sin(3x) = \cos x - \cos(5x)$

45. $\dfrac{\cos(10\theta) + \cos(6\theta)}{\cos(6\theta) - \cos(10\theta)} = \cot(2\theta)\cot(8\theta)$

46. $\dfrac{\sin(3x) - \sin(5x)}{\cos(3x) + \cos(5x)} = \tan x$

47. $2\cos(2x)\cos x + \sin(2x)\sin x = 2 \sin x$

48. $\dfrac{\sin(2x) + \sin(4x)}{\sin(2x) - \sin(4x)} = -\tan(3x)\cot x$

For the following exercises, simplify the expression to one term, then graph the original function and your simplified version to verify they are identical.

49. $\dfrac{\sin(9t) - \sin(3t)}{\cos(9t) + \cos(3t)}$

50. $2\sin(8x)\cos(6x) - \sin(2x)$

51. $\dfrac{\sin(3x) - \sin x}{\sin x}$

52. $\dfrac{\cos(5x) + \cos(3x)}{\sin(5x) + \sin(3x)}$

53. $\sin x\cos(15x) - \cos x \sin(15x)$

EXTENSIONS

For the following exercises, prove the following sum-to-product formulas.

54. $\sin x - \sin y = 2 \sin\left(\dfrac{x - y}{2}\right)\cos\left(\dfrac{x + y}{2}\right)$

55. $\cos x + \cos y = 2\cos\left(\dfrac{x + y}{2}\right)\cos\left(\dfrac{x - y}{2}\right)$

For the following exercises, prove the identity.

56. $\dfrac{\sin(6x) + \sin(4x)}{\sin(6x) - \sin(4x)} = \tan (5x)\cot x$

57. $\dfrac{\cos(3x) + \cos x}{\cos(3x) - \cos x} = -\cot (2x)\cot x$

58. $\dfrac{\cos(6y) + \cos(8y)}{\sin(6y) - \sin(4y)} = \cot y \cos(7y) \sec(5y)$

59. $\dfrac{\cos(2y) - \cos(4y)}{\sin(2y) + \sin(4y)} = \tan y$

60. $\dfrac{\sin(10x) - \sin(2x)}{\cos(10x) + \cos(2x)} = \tan(4x)$

61. $\cos x - \cos(3x) = 4 \sin^2 x \cos x$

62. $(\cos(2x) - \cos(4x))^2 + (\sin(4x) + \sin(2x))^2 = 4 \sin^2(3x)$

63. $\tan\left(\dfrac{\pi}{4} - t\right) = \dfrac{1 - \tan t}{1 + \tan t}$

LEARNING OBJECTIVES

In this section, you will:

- Solve linear trigonometric equations in sine and cosine.
- Solve equations involving a single trigonometric function.
- Solve trigonometric equations using a calculator.
- Solve trigonometric equations that are quadratic in form.
- Solve trigonometric equations using fundamental identities.
- Solve trigonometric equations with multiple angles.
- Solve right triangle problems.

9.5 SOLVING TRIGONOMETRIC EQUATIONS

Figure 1 Egyptian pyramids standing near a modern city. (credit: Oisin Mulvihill)

Thales of Miletus (circa 625–547 BC) is known as the founder of geometry. The legend is that he calculated the height of the Great Pyramid of Giza in Egypt using the theory of *similar triangles*, which he developed by measuring the shadow of his staff. Based on proportions, this theory has applications in a number of areas, including fractal geometry, engineering, and architecture. Often, the angle of elevation and the angle of depression are found using similar triangles.

In earlier sections of this chapter, we looked at trigonometric identities. Identities are true for all values in the domain of the variable. In this section, we begin our study of trigonometric equations to study real-world scenarios such as the finding the dimensions of the pyramids.

Solving Linear Trigonometric Equations in Sine and Cosine

Trigonometric equations are, as the name implies, equations that involve trigonometric functions. Similar in many ways to solving polynomial equations or rational equations, only specific values of the variable will be solutions, if there are solutions at all. Often we will solve a trigonometric equation over a specified interval. However, just as often, we will be asked to find all possible solutions, and as trigonometric functions are periodic, solutions are repeated within each period. In other words, trigonometric equations may have an infinite number of solutions. Additionally, like rational equations, the domain of the function must be considered before we assume that any solution is valid. The period of both the sine function and the cosine function is 2π. In other words, every 2π units, the y-values repeat. If we need to find all possible solutions, then we must add $2\pi k$, where k is an integer, to the initial solution. Recall the rule that gives the format for stating all possible solutions for a function where the period is 2π:

$$\sin\theta = \sin(\theta \pm 2k\pi)$$

There are similar rules for indicating all possible solutions for the other trigonometric functions. Solving trigonometric equations requires the same techniques as solving algebraic equations. We read the equation from left to right, horizontally, like a sentence. We look for known patterns, factor, find common denominators, and substitute certain expressions with a variable to make solving a more straightforward process. However, with trigonometric equations, we also have the advantage of using the identities we developed in the previous sections.

Example 1   **Solving a Linear Trigonometric Equation Involving the Cosine Function**

Find all possible exact solutions for the equation $\cos\theta = \frac{1}{2}$.

Solution   From the unit circle, we know that

$$\cos\theta = \frac{1}{2}$$

$$\theta = \frac{\pi}{3}, \frac{5\pi}{3}$$

These are the solutions in the interval $[0, 2\pi]$. All possible solutions are given by

$$\theta = \frac{\pi}{3} \pm 2k\pi \text{ and } \theta = \frac{5\pi}{3} \pm 2k\pi$$

where k is an integer.

Example 2   **Solving a Linear Equation Involving the Sine Function**

Find all possible exact solutions for the equation $\sin t = \frac{1}{2}$.

Solution   Solving for all possible values of t means that solutions include angles beyond the period of 2π. From **Section 9.2 Figure 2**, we can see that the solutions are $t = \frac{\pi}{6}$ and $t = \frac{5\pi}{6}$. But the problem is asking for all possible values that solve the equation. Therefore, the answer is

$$t = \frac{\pi}{6} \pm 2\pi k \quad \text{and} \quad t = \frac{5\pi}{6} \pm 2\pi k$$

where k is an integer.

How To...

Given a trigonometric equation, solve using algebra.

1. Look for a pattern that suggests an algebraic property, such as the difference of squares or a factoring opportunity.
2. Substitute the trigonometric expression with a single variable, such as x or u.
3. Solve the equation the same way an algebraic equation would be solved.
4. Substitute the trigonometric expression back in for the variable in the resulting expressions.
5. Solve for the angle.

Example 3   **Solve the Trigonometric Equation in Linear Form**

Solve the equation exactly: $2\cos\theta - 3 = -5, 0 \le \theta < 2\pi$.

Solution   Use algebraic techniques to solve the equation.

$$2\cos\theta - 3 = -5$$

$$2\cos\theta = -2$$

$$\cos\theta = -1$$

$$\theta = \pi$$

Try It #1

Solve exactly the following linear equation on the interval $[0, 2\pi)$: $2\sin x + 1 = 0$.

Solving Equations Involving a Single Trigonometric Function

When we are given equations that involve only one of the six trigonometric functions, their solutions involve using algebraic techniques and the unit circle (see **Section 9.2 Figure 2**). We need to make several considerations when the equation involves trigonometric functions other than sine and cosine. Problems involving the reciprocals of the primary trigonometric functions need to be viewed from an algebraic perspective. In other words, we will write the reciprocal function, and solve for the angles using the function. Also, an equation involving the tangent function is slightly different from one containing a sine or cosine function. First, as we know, the period of tangent is π, not 2π. Further, the domain of tangent is all real numbers with the exception of odd integer multiples of $\frac{\pi}{2}$, unless, of course, a problem places its own restrictions on the domain.

Example 4 Solving a Problem Involving a Single Trigonometric Function

Solve the problem exactly: $2\sin^2\theta - 1 = 0, 0 \leq \theta < 2\pi$.

Solution As this problem is not easily factored, we will solve using the square root property. First, we use algebra to isolate $\sin\theta$. Then we will find the angles.

$$2\sin^2\theta - 1 = 0$$
$$2\sin^2\theta = 1$$
$$\sin^2\theta = \frac{1}{2}$$
$$\sqrt{\sin^2\theta} = \pm\sqrt{\frac{1}{2}}$$
$$\sin\theta = \pm\frac{1}{\sqrt{2}} = \pm\frac{\sqrt{2}}{2}$$
$$\theta = \frac{\pi}{4}, \frac{3\pi}{4}, \frac{5\pi}{4}, \frac{7\pi}{4}$$

Example 5 Solving a Trigonometric Equation Involving Cosecant

Solve the following equation exactly: $\csc\theta = -2, 0 \leq \theta < 4\pi$.

Solution We want all values of θ for which $\csc\theta = -2$ over the interval $0 \leq \theta < 4\pi$.

$$\csc\theta = -2$$
$$\frac{1}{\sin\theta} = -2$$
$$\sin\theta = -\frac{1}{2}$$
$$\theta = \frac{7\pi}{6}, \frac{11\pi}{6}, \frac{19\pi}{6}, \frac{23\pi}{6}$$

Analysis As $\sin\theta = -\frac{1}{2}$, *notice that all four solutions are in the third and fourth quadrants.*

Example 6 Solving an Equation Involving Tangent

Solve the equation exactly: $\tan\left(\theta - \frac{\pi}{2}\right) = 1, 0 \leq \theta < 2\pi$.

Solution Recall that the tangent function has a period of π. On the interval $[0, \pi)$, and at the angle of $\frac{\pi}{4}$, the tangent has a value of 1. However, the angle we want is $\left(\theta - \frac{\pi}{2}\right)$. Thus, if $\tan\left(\frac{\pi}{4}\right) = 1$, then

$$\theta - \frac{\pi}{2} = \frac{\pi}{4}$$
$$\theta = \frac{3\pi}{4} \pm k\pi$$

Over the interval $[0, 2\pi)$, we have two solutions:

$$\theta = \frac{3\pi}{4} \text{ and } \theta = \frac{3\pi}{4} + \pi = \frac{7\pi}{4}$$

Try It #2

Find all solutions for $\tan x = \sqrt{3}$.

Example 7 Identify all Solutions to the Equation Involving Tangent

Identify all exact solutions to the equation $2(\tan x + 3) = 5 + \tan x, 0 \leq x < 2\pi$.

Solution   We can solve this equation using only algebra. Isolate the expression $\tan x$ on the left side of the equals sign.

$$2(\tan x) + 2(3) = 5 + \tan x$$

$$2\tan x + 6 = 5 + \tan x$$

$$2\tan x - \tan x = 5 - 6$$

$$\tan x = -1$$

There are two angles on the unit circle that have a tangent value of -1: $\theta = \dfrac{3\pi}{4}$ and $\theta = \dfrac{7\pi}{4}$.

Solve Trigonometric Equations Using a Calculator

Not all functions can be solved exactly using only the unit circle. When we must solve an equation involving an angle other than one of the special angles, we will need to use a calculator. Make sure it is set to the proper mode, either degrees or radians, depending on the criteria of the given problem.

Example 8   Using a Calculator to Solve a Trigonometric Equation Involving Sine

Use a calculator to solve the equation $\sin \theta = 0.8$, where θ is in radians.

Solution   Make sure mode is set to radians. To find θ, use the inverse sine function. On most calculators, you will need to push the **2ND** button and then the **SIN** button to bring up the $\sin^{-1}$ function. What is shown on the screen is $\sin^{-1}($. The calculator is ready for the input within the parentheses. For this problem, we enter $\sin^{-1}$ **(0.8)**, and press **ENTER**. Thus, to four decimals places,

$$\sin^{-1}(0.8) \approx 0.9273$$

The solution is

$$\theta \approx 0.9273 \pm 2\pi k$$

The angle measurement in degrees is

$$\theta \approx 53.1°$$

$$\theta \approx 180° - 53.1°$$

$$\approx 126.9°$$

Analysis   Note that a calculator will only return an angle in quadrants I or IV for the sine function, since that is the range of the inverse sine. The other angle is obtained by using $\pi - \theta$.

Example 9   Using a Calculator to Solve a Trigonometric Equation Involving Secant

Use a calculator to solve the equation $\sec \theta = -4$, giving your answer in radians.

Solution   We can begin with some algebra.

$$\sec \theta = -4$$

$$\frac{1}{\cos \theta} = -4$$

$$\cos \theta = -\frac{1}{4}$$

Check that the MODE is in radians. Now use the inverse cosine function.

$$\cos^{-1}\left(-\frac{1}{4}\right) \approx 1.8235$$

$$\theta \approx 1.8235 + 2\pi k$$

Since $\dfrac{\pi}{2} \approx 1.57$ and $\pi \approx 3.14$, 1.8235 is between these two numbers, thus $\theta \approx 1.8235$ is in quadrant II.

Cosine is also negative in quadrant III. Note that a calculator will only return an angle in quadrants I or II for the cosine function, since that is the range of the inverse cosine. See **Figure 2**.

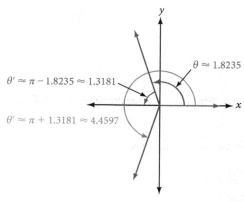

Figure 2

So, we also need to find the measure of the angle in quadrant III. In quadrant III, the reference angle is $\theta' \approx \pi - 1.8235 \approx 1.3181$. The other solution in quadrant III is $\theta' \approx \pi + 1.3181 \approx 4.4597$.

The solutions are $\theta \approx 1.8235 \pm 2\pi k$ and $\theta \approx 4.4597 \pm 2\pi k$.

Try It #3

Solve $\cos \theta = -0.2$.

Solving Trigonometric Equations in Quadratic Form

Solving a quadratic equation may be more complicated, but once again, we can use algebra as we would for any quadratic equation. Look at the pattern of the equation. Is there more than one trigonometric function in the equation, or is there only one? Which trigonometric function is squared? If there is only one function represented and one of the terms is squared, think about the standard form of a quadratic. Replace the trigonometric function with a variable such as x or u. If substitution makes the equation look like a quadratic equation, then we can use the same methods for solving quadratics to solve the trigonometric equations.

Example 10   **Solving a Trigonometric Equation in Quadratic Form**

Solve the equation exactly: $\cos^2 \theta + 3 \cos \theta - 1 = 0, 0 \leq \theta < 2\pi$.

Solution   We begin by using substitution and replacing $\cos \theta$ with x. It is not necessary to use substitution, but it may make the problem easier to solve visually. Let $\cos \theta = x$. We have

$$x^2 + 3x - 1 = 0$$

The equation cannot be factored, so we will use the quadratic formula $x = \dfrac{-b \pm \sqrt{b^2 - 4ac}}{2a}$.

$$x = \frac{-3 \pm \sqrt{(-3)^2 - 4(1)(-1)}}{2}$$

$$= \frac{-3 \pm \sqrt{13}}{2}$$

Replace x with $\cos \theta$, and solve. Thus,

$$\cos \theta = \frac{-3 \pm \sqrt{13}}{2}$$

$$\theta = \cos^{-1}\left(\frac{-3 + \sqrt{13}}{2}\right)$$

Note that only the $+$ sign is used. This is because we get an error when we solve $\theta = \cos^{-1}\left(\dfrac{-3 - \sqrt{13}}{2}\right)$ on a calculator, since the domain of the inverse cosine function is $[-1, 1]$. However, there is a second solution:

$$\theta = \cos^{-1}\left(\frac{-3 + \sqrt{13}}{2}\right)$$

$$\approx 1.26$$

This terminal side of the angle lies in quadrant I. Since cosine is also positive in quadrant IV, the second solution is

$$\theta = 2\pi - \cos^{-1}\left(\frac{-3 + \sqrt{13}}{2}\right)$$
$$\approx 5.02$$

Example 11   Solving a Trigonometric Equation in Quadratic Form by Factoring

Solve the equation exactly: $2\sin^2\theta - 5\sin\theta + 3 = 0, 0 \leq \theta \leq 2\pi$.

Solution   Using grouping, this quadratic can be factored. Either make the real substitution, $\sin\theta = u$, or imagine it, as we factor:

$$2\sin^2\theta - 5\sin\theta + 3 = 0$$
$$(2\sin\theta - 3)(\sin\theta - 1) = 0$$

Now set each factor equal to zero.

$$2\sin\theta - 3 = 0$$
$$2\sin\theta = 3$$
$$\sin\theta = \frac{3}{2}$$

$$\sin\theta - 1 = 0$$
$$\sin\theta = 1$$

Next solve for θ: $\sin\theta \neq \frac{3}{2}$, as the range of the sine function is $[-1, 1]$. However, $\sin\theta = 1$, giving the solution $\theta = \frac{\pi}{2}$.

Analysis   *Make sure to check all solutions on the given domain as some factors have no solution.*

Try It #4

Solve $\sin^2\theta = 2\cos\theta + 2, 0 \leq \theta \leq 2\pi$. [Hint: Make a substitution to express the equation only in terms of cosine.]

Example 12   Solving a Trigonometric Equation Using Algebra

Solve exactly:

$$2\sin^2\theta + \sin\theta = 0; 0 \leq \theta < 2\pi$$

Solution   This problem should appear familiar as it is similar to a quadratic. Let $\sin\theta = x$. The equation becomes $2x^2 + x = 0$. We begin by factoring:

$$2x^2 + x = 0$$
$$x(2x + 1) = 0$$

Set each factor equal to zero.

$$x = 0$$
$$(2x + 1) = 0$$
$$x = -\frac{1}{2}$$

Then, substitute back into the equation the original expression $\sin\theta$ for x. Thus,

$$\sin\theta = 0$$
$$\theta = 0, \pi$$

$$\sin\theta = -\frac{1}{2}$$
$$\theta = \frac{7\pi}{6}, \frac{11\pi}{6}$$

The solutions within the domain $0 \leq \theta < 2\pi$ are $\theta = 0, \pi, \frac{7\pi}{6}, \frac{11\pi}{6}$.

If we prefer not to substitute, we can solve the equation by following the same pattern of factoring and setting each factor equal to zero.

$$2\sin^2\theta + \sin\theta = 0$$
$$\sin\theta(2\sin\theta + 1) = 0$$

$$\sin \theta = 0$$

$$\theta = 0, \pi$$

$$2\sin \theta + 1 = 0$$

$$2\sin \theta = -1$$

$$\sin \theta = -\frac{1}{2}$$

$$\theta = \frac{7\pi}{6}, \frac{11\pi}{6}$$

Analysis   We can see the solutions on the graph in **Figure 3**. On the interval $0 \le \theta < 2\pi$, the graph crosses the x-axis four times, at the solutions noted. Notice that trigonometric equations that are in quadratic form can yield up to four solutions instead of the expected two that are found with quadratic equations. In this example, each solution (angle) corresponding to a positive sine value will yield two angles that would result in that value.

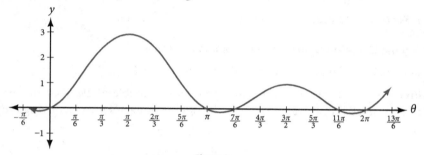

Figure 3

We can verify the solutions on the unit circle in **Section 9.2 Figure 2** as well.

Example 13   Solving a Trigonometric Equation Quadratic in Form

Solve the equation quadratic in form exactly: $2\sin^2 \theta - 3\sin \theta + 1 = 0, 0 \le \theta < 2\pi$.

Solution   We can factor using grouping. Solution values of θ can be found on the unit circle:

$$(2\sin \theta - 1)(\sin \theta - 1) = 0$$

$$2\sin \theta - 1 = 0$$

$$\sin \theta = \frac{1}{2}$$

$$\theta = \frac{\pi}{6}, \frac{5\pi}{6}$$

$$\sin \theta = 1$$

$$\theta = \frac{\pi}{2}$$

Try It #5

Solve the quadratic equation $2\cos^2 \theta + \cos \theta = 0$.

Solving Trigonometric Equations Using Fundamental Identities

While algebra can be used to solve a number of trigonometric equations, we can also use the fundamental identities because they make solving equations simpler. Remember that the techniques we use for solving are not the same as those for verifying identities. The basic rules of algebra apply here, as opposed to rewriting one side of the identity to match the other side. In the next example, we use two identities to simplify the equation.

Example 14   Use Identities to Solve an Equation

Use identities to solve exactly the trigonometric equation over the interval $0 \le x < 2\pi$.

$$\cos x \cos(2x) + \sin x \sin(2x) = \frac{\sqrt{3}}{2}$$

Solution   Notice that the left side of the equation is the difference formula for cosine.

$$\cos x \cos(2x) + \sin x \sin(2x) = \frac{\sqrt{3}}{2}$$

$$\cos(x - 2x) = \frac{\sqrt{3}}{2} \qquad \text{Difference formula for cosine}$$

$$\cos(-x) = \frac{\sqrt{3}}{2} \qquad \text{Use the negative angle identity.}$$

$$\cos x = \frac{\sqrt{3}}{2}$$

From the unit circle in **Section 9.2 Figure 2**, we see that $\cos x = \frac{\sqrt{3}}{2}$ when $x = \frac{\pi}{6}, \frac{11\pi}{6}$.

Example 15   Solving the Equation Using a Double-Angle Formula

Solve the equation exactly using a double-angle formula: $\cos(2\theta) = \cos \theta$.

Solution   We have three choices of expressions to substitute for the double-angle of cosine. As it is simpler to solve for one trigonometric function at a time, we will choose the double-angle identity involving only cosine:

$$\cos(2\theta) = \cos \theta$$

$$2\cos^2 \theta - 1 = \cos \theta$$

$$2\cos^2 \theta - \cos \theta - 1 = 0$$

$$(2\cos \theta + 1)(\cos \theta - 1) = 0$$

$$2\cos \theta + 1 = 0$$

$$\cos \theta = -\frac{1}{2}$$

$$\cos \theta - 1 = 0$$

$$\cos \theta = 1$$

So, if $\cos \theta = -\frac{1}{2}$, then $\theta = \frac{2\pi}{3} \pm 2\pi k$ and $\theta = \frac{4\pi}{3} \pm 2\pi k$; if $\cos \theta = 1$, then $\theta = 0 \pm 2\pi k$.

Example 16   Solving an Equation Using an Identity

Solve the equation exactly using an identity: $3\cos \theta + 3 = 2\sin^2 \theta, \ 0 \le \theta < 2\pi$.

Solution   If we rewrite the right side, we can write the equation in terms of cosine:

$$3\cos \theta + 3 = 2\sin^2 \theta$$

$$3\cos \theta + 3 = 2(1 - \cos^2 \theta)$$

$$3\cos \theta + 3 = 2 - 2\cos^2 \theta$$

$$2\cos^2 \theta + 3\cos \theta + 1 = 0$$

$$(2\cos \theta + 1)(\cos \theta + 1) = 0$$

$$2\cos \theta + 1 = 0$$

$$\cos \theta = -\frac{1}{2}$$

$$\theta = \frac{2\pi}{3}, \frac{4\pi}{3}$$

$$\cos \theta + 1 = 0$$

$$\cos \theta = -1$$

$$\theta = \pi$$

Our solutions are $\theta = \frac{2\pi}{3}, \frac{4\pi}{3}, \pi$

Solving Trigonometric Equations with Multiple Angles

Sometimes it is not possible to solve a trigonometric equation with identities that have a multiple angle, such as $\sin(2x)$ or $\cos(3x)$. When confronted with these equations, recall that $y = \sin(2x)$ is a horizontal compression by a factor of 2 of the function $y = \sin x$. On an interval of 2π, we can graph two periods of $y = \sin(2x)$, as opposed to one cycle of $y = \sin x$. This compression of the graph leads us to believe there may be twice as many x-intercepts or solutions to $\sin(2x) = 0$ compared to $\sin x = 0$. This information will help us solve the equation.

Example 17   **Solving a Multiple Angle Trigonometric Equation**

Solve exactly: $\cos(2x) = \dfrac{1}{2}$ on $[0, 2\pi)$.

Solution   We can see that this equation is the standard equation with a multiple of an angle. If $\cos(\alpha) = \dfrac{1}{2}$, we know α is in quadrants I and IV. While $\theta = \cos^{-1}\dfrac{1}{2}$ will only yield solutions in quadrants I and II, we recognize that the solutions to the equation $\cos\theta = \dfrac{1}{2}$ will be in quadrants I and IV.

Therefore, the possible angles are $\theta = \dfrac{\pi}{3}$ and $\theta = \dfrac{5\pi}{3}$. So, $2x = \dfrac{\pi}{3}$ or $2x = \dfrac{5\pi}{3}$, which means that $x = \dfrac{\pi}{6}$ or $x = \dfrac{5\pi}{6}$. Does this make sense? Yes, because $\cos\left(2\left(\dfrac{\pi}{6}\right)\right) = \cos\left(\dfrac{\pi}{3}\right) = \dfrac{1}{2}$.

Are there any other possible answers? Let us return to our first step.

In quadrant I, $2x = \dfrac{\pi}{3}$, so $x = \dfrac{\pi}{6}$ as noted. Let us revolve around the circle again:

$$2x = \frac{\pi}{3} + 2\pi$$

$$= \frac{\pi}{3} + \frac{6\pi}{3}$$

$$= \frac{7\pi}{3}$$

so $x = \dfrac{7\pi}{6}$.

One more rotation yields

$$2x = \frac{\pi}{3} + 4\pi$$

$$= \frac{\pi}{3} + \frac{12\pi}{3}$$

$$= \frac{13\pi}{3}$$

$x = \dfrac{13\pi}{6} > 2\pi$, so this value for x is larger than 2π, so it is not a solution on $[0, 2\pi)$.

In quadrant IV, $2x = \dfrac{5\pi}{3}$, so $x = \dfrac{5\pi}{6}$ as noted. Let us revolve around the circle again:

$$2x = \frac{5\pi}{3} + 2\pi$$

$$= \frac{5\pi}{3} + \frac{6\pi}{3}$$

$$= \frac{11\pi}{3}$$

so $x = \dfrac{11\pi}{6}$.

One more rotation yields

$$2x = \frac{5\pi}{3} + 4\pi$$

$$= \frac{5\pi}{3} + \frac{12\pi}{3}$$

$$= \frac{17\pi}{3}$$

$x = \frac{17\pi}{6} > 2\pi$, so this value for x is larger than 2π, so it is not a solution on $[0, 2\pi)$.

Our solutions are $x = \frac{\pi}{6}, \frac{5\pi}{6}, \frac{7\pi}{6}$, and $\frac{11\pi}{6}$. Note that whenever we solve a problem in the form of $\sin(nx) = c$, we must go around the unit circle n times.

Solving Right Triangle Problems

We can now use all of the methods we have learned to solve problems that involve applying the properties of right triangles and the Pythagorean Theorem. We begin with the familiar Pythagorean Theorem, $a^2 + b^2 = c^2$, and model an equation to fit a situation.

Example 18   **Using the Pythagorean Theorem to Model an Equation**

Use the Pythagorean Theorem, and the properties of right triangles to model an equation that fits the problem. One of the cables that anchors the center of the London Eye Ferris wheel to the ground must be replaced. The center of the Ferris wheel is 69.5 meters above the ground, and the second anchor on the ground is 23 meters from the base of the Ferris wheel. Approximately how long is the cable, and what is the angle of elevation (from ground up to the center of the Ferris wheel)? See **Figure 4.**

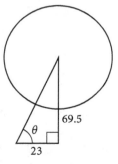

Figure 4

Solution   Using the information given, we can draw a right triangle. We can find the length of the cable with the Pythagorean Theorem.

$$a^2 + b^2 = c^2$$

$$(23)^2 + (69.5)^2 \approx 5359$$

$$\sqrt{5359} \approx 73.2 \text{ m}$$

The angle of elevation is θ, formed by the second anchor on the ground and the cable reaching to the center of the wheel. We can use the tangent function to find its measure. Round to two decimal places.

$$\tan \theta = \frac{69.5}{23}$$

$$\tan^{-1}\left(\frac{69.5}{23}\right) \approx 1.2522$$

$$\approx 71.69°$$

The angle of elevation is approximately 71.7°, and the length of the cable is 73.2 meters.

Example 19 **Using the Pythagorean Theorem to Model an Abstract Problem**

OSHA safety regulations require that the base of a ladder be placed 1 foot from the wall for every 4 feet of ladder length. Find the angle that a ladder of any length forms with the ground and the height at which the ladder touches the wall.

Solution For any length of ladder, the base needs to be a distance from the wall equal to one fourth of the ladder's length. Equivalently, if the base of the ladder is "a" feet from the wall, the length of the ladder will be $4a$ feet. See **Figure 5**.

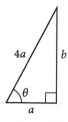

Figure 5

The side adjacent to θ is a and the hypotenuse is $4a$. Thus,

$$\cos \theta = \frac{a}{4a} = \frac{1}{4}$$

$$\cos^{-1}\left(\frac{1}{4}\right) \approx 75.5°$$

The elevation of the ladder forms an angle of 75.5° with the ground. The height at which the ladder touches the wall can be found using the Pythagorean Theorem:

$$a^2 + b^2 = (4a)^2$$

$$b^2 = (4a)^2 - a^2$$

$$b^2 = 16a^2 - a^2$$

$$b^2 = 15a^2$$

$$b = a\sqrt{15}$$

Thus, the ladder touches the wall at $a\sqrt{15}$ feet from the ground.

Access these online resources for additional instruction and practice with solving trigonometric equations.

- Solving Trigonometric Equations I (http://openstaxcollege.org/l/solvetrigeqI)
- Solving Trigonometric Equations II (http://openstaxcollege.org/l/solvetrigeqII)
- Solving Trigonometric Equations III (http://openstaxcollege.org/l/solvetrigeqIII)
- Solving Trigonometric Equations IV (http://openstaxcollege.org/l/solvetrigeqIV)
- Solving Trigonometric Equations V (http://openstaxcollege.org/l/solvetrigeqV)
- Solving Trigonometric Equations VI (http://openstaxcollege.org/l/solvetrigeqVI)

9.5   SECTION EXERCISES

VERBAL

1. Will there always be solutions to trigonometric function equations? If not, describe an equation that would not have a solution. Explain why or why not.

2. When solving a trigonometric equation involving more than one trig function, do we always want to try to rewrite the equation so it is expressed in terms of one trigonometric function? Why or why not?

3. When solving linear trig equations in terms of only sine or cosine, how do we know whether there will be solutions?

ALGEBRAIC

For the following exercises, find all solutions exactly on the interval $0 \leq \theta < 2\pi$.

4. $2\sin \theta = -\sqrt{2}$

5. $2\sin \theta = \sqrt{3}$

6. $2\cos \theta = 1$

7. $2\cos \theta = -\sqrt{2}$

8. $\tan \theta = -1$

9. $\tan x = 1$

10. $\cot x + 1 = 0$

11. $4\sin^2 x - 2 = 0$

12. $\csc^2 x - 4 = 0$

For the following exercises, solve exactly on $[0, 2\pi)$.

13. $2\cos \theta = \sqrt{2}$

14. $2\cos \theta = -1$

15. $2\sin \theta = -1$

16. $2\sin \theta = -\sqrt{3}$

17. $2\sin(3\theta) = 1$

18. $2\sin(2\theta) = \sqrt{3}$

19. $2\cos(3\theta) = -\sqrt{2}$

20. $\cos(2\theta) = -\dfrac{\sqrt{3}}{2}$

21. $2\sin(\pi\theta) = 1$

22. $2\cos\left(\dfrac{\pi}{5}\theta\right) = \sqrt{3}$

For the following exercises, find all exact solutions on $[0, 2\pi)$.

23. $\sec(x)\sin(x) - 2\sin(x) = 0$

24. $\tan(x) - 2\sin(x)\tan(x) = 0$

25. $2\cos^2 t + \cos(t) = 1$

26. $2\tan^2(t) = 3\sec(t)$

27. $2\sin(x)\cos(x) - \sin(x) + 2\cos(x) - 1 = 0$

28. $\cos^2 \theta = \dfrac{1}{2}$

29. $\sec^2 x = 1$

30. $\tan^2(x) = -1 + 2\tan(-x)$

31. $8\sin^2(x) + 6\sin(x) + 1 = 0$

32. $\tan^5(x) = \tan(x)$

For the following exercises, solve with the methods shown in this section exactly on the interval $[0, 2\pi)$.

33. $\sin(3x)\cos(6x) - \cos(3x)\sin(6x) = -0.9$

34. $\sin(6x)\cos(11x) - \cos(6x)\sin(11x) = -0.1$

35. $\cos(2x)\cos x + \sin(2x)\sin x = 1$

36. $6\sin(2t) + 9\sin t = 0$

37. $9\cos(2\theta) = 9\cos^2 \theta - 4$

38. $\sin(2t) = \cos t$

39. $\cos(2t) = \sin t$

40. $\cos(6x) - \cos(3x) = 0$

For the following exercises, solve exactly on the interval $[0, 2\pi)$. Use the quadratic formula if the equations do not factor.

41. $\tan^2 x - \sqrt{3}\tan x = 0$

42. $\sin^2 x + \sin x - 2 = 0$

43. $\sin^2 x - 2\sin x - 4 = 0$

44. $5\cos^2 x + 3\cos x - 1 = 0$

45. $3\cos^2 x - 2\cos x - 2 = 0$

46. $5\sin^2 x + 2\sin x - 1 = 0$

47. $\tan^2 x + 5\tan x - 1 = 0$

48. $\cot^2 x = -\cot x$

49. $-\tan^2 x - \tan x - 2 = 0$

For the following exercises, find exact solutions on the interval $[0, 2\pi)$. Look for opportunities to use trigonometric identities.

50. $\sin^2 x - \cos^2 x - \sin x = 0$

51. $\sin^2 x + \cos^2 x = 0$

52. $\sin(2x) - \sin x = 0$

53. $\cos(2x) - \cos x = 0$

54. $\dfrac{2 \tan x}{2 - \sec^2 x} - \sin^2 x = \cos^2 x$

55. $1 - \cos(2x) = 1 + \cos(2x)$

56. $\sec^2 x = 7$

57. $10\sin x \cos x = 6\cos x$

58. $-3\sin t = 15\cos t \sin t$

59. $4\cos^2 x - 4 = 15\cos x$

60. $8\sin^2 x + 6\sin x + 1 = 0$

61. $8\cos^2 \theta = 3 - 2\cos \theta$

62. $6\cos^2 x + 7\sin x - 8 = 0$

63. $12\sin^2 t + \cos t - 6 = 0$

64. $\tan x = 3\sin x$

65. $\cos^3 t = \cos t$

GRAPHICAL

For the following exercises, algebraically determine all solutions of the trigonometric equation exactly, then verify the results by graphing the equation and finding the zeros.

66. $6\sin^2 x - 5\sin x + 1 = 0$

67. $8\cos^2 x - 2\cos x - 1 = 0$

68. $100\tan^2 x + 20\tan x - 3 = 0$

69. $2\cos^2 x - \cos x + 15 = 0$

70. $20\sin^2 x - 27\sin x + 7 = 0$

71. $2\tan^2 x + 7\tan x + 6 = 0$

72. $130\tan^2 x + 69\tan x - 130 = 0$

TECHNOLOGY

For the following exercises, use a calculator to find all solutions to four decimal places.

73. $\sin x = 0.27$

74. $\sin x = -0.55$

75. $\tan x = -0.34$

76. $\cos x = 0.71$

For the following exercises, solve the equations algebraically, and then use a calculator to find the values on the interval $[0, 2\pi)$. Round to four decimal places.

77. $\tan^2 x + 3\tan x - 3 = 0$

78. $6\tan^2 x + 13\tan x = -6$

79. $\tan^2 x - \sec x = 1$

80. $\sin^2 x - 2\cos^2 x = 0$

81. $2\tan^2 x + 9\tan x - 6 = 0$

82. $4\sin^2 x + \sin(2x)\sec x - 3 = 0$

EXTENSIONS

For the following exercises, find all solutions exactly to the equations on the interval $[0, 2\pi)$.

83. $\csc^2 x - 3\csc x - 4 = 0$

84. $\sin^2 x - \cos^2 x - 1 = 0$

85. $\sin^2 x(1 - \sin^2 x) + \cos^2 x(1 - \sin^2 x) = 0$

86. $3\sec^2 x + 2 + \sin^2 x - \tan^2 x + \cos^2 x = 0$

87. $\sin^2 x - 1 + 2\cos(2x) - \cos^2 x = 1$

88. $\tan^2 x - 1 - \sec^3 x \cos x = 0$

89. $\dfrac{\sin(2x)}{\sec^2 x} = 0$

90. $\dfrac{\sin(2x)}{2 \csc^2 x} = 0$

91. $2\cos^2 x - \sin^2 x - \cos x - 5 = 0$

92. $\dfrac{1}{\sec^2 x} + 2 + \sin^2 x + 4\cos^2 x = 4$

REAL-WORLD APPLICATIONS

93. An airplane has only enough gas to fly to a city 200 miles northeast of its current location. If the pilot knows that the city is 25 miles north, how many degrees north of east should the airplane fly?

94. If a loading ramp is placed next to a truck, at a height of 4 feet, and the ramp is 15 feet long, what angle does the ramp make with the ground?

95. If a loading ramp is placed next to a truck, at a height of 2 feet, and the ramp is 20 feet long, what angle does the ramp make with the ground?

96. A woman is watching a launched rocket currently 11 miles in altitude. If she is standing 4 miles from the launch pad, at what angle is she looking up from horizontal?

97. An astronaut is in a launched rocket currently 15 miles in altitude. If a man is standing 2 miles from the launch pad, at what angle is she looking down at him from horizontal? (Hint: this is called the angle of depression.)

98. A woman is standing 8 meters away from a 10-meter tall building. At what angle is she looking to the top of the building?

99. A man is standing 10 meters away from a 6-meter tall building. Someone at the top of the building is looking down at him. At what angle is the person looking at him?

100. A 20-foot tall building has a shadow that is 55 feet long. What is the angle of elevation of the sun?

101. A 90-foot tall building has a shadow that is 2 feet long. What is the angle of elevation of the sun?

102. A spotlight on the ground 3 meters from a 2-meter tall man casts a 6 meter shadow on a wall 6 meters from the man. At what angle is the light?

103. A spotlight on the ground 3 feet from a 5-foot tall woman casts a 15-foot tall shadow on a wall 6 feet from the woman. At what angle is the light?

For the following exercises, find a solution to the word problem algebraically. Then use a calculator to verify the result. Round the answer to the nearest tenth of a degree.

104. A person does a handstand with his feet touching a wall and his hands 1.5 feet away from the wall. If the person is 6 feet tall, what angle do his feet make with the wall?

105. A person does a handstand with her feet touching a wall and her hands 3 feet away from the wall. If the person is 5 feet tall, what angle do her feet make with the wall?

106. A 23-foot ladder is positioned next to a house. If the ladder slips at 7 feet from the house when there is not enough traction, what angle should the ladder make with the ground to avoid slipping?

CHAPTER 9 REVIEW

Key Terms

double-angle formulas identities derived from the sum formulas for sine, cosine, and tangent in which the angles are equal

even-odd identities set of equations involving trigonometric functions such that if $f(-x) = -f(x)$, the identity is odd, and if $f(-x) = f(x)$, the identity is even

half-angle formulas identities derived from the reduction formulas and used to determine half-angle values of trigonometric functions

product-to-sum formula a trigonometric identity that allows the writing of a product of trigonometric functions as a sum or difference of trigonometric functions

Pythagorean identities set of equations involving trigonometric functions based on the right triangle properties

quotient identities pair of identities based on the fact that tangent is the ratio of sine and cosine, and cotangent is the ratio of cosine and sine

reciprocal identities set of equations involving the reciprocals of basic trigonometric definitions

reduction formulas identities derived from the double-angle formulas and used to reduce the power of a trigonometric function

sum-to-product formula a trigonometric identity that allows, by using substitution, the writing of a sum of trigonometric functions as a product of trigonometric functions

Key Equations

Pythagorean identities	$\sin^2 \theta + \cos^2 \theta = 1$
	$1 + \cot^2 \theta = \csc^2 \theta$
	$1 + \tan^2 \theta = \sec^2 \theta$
Even-odd identities	$\tan(-\theta) = -\tan \theta$
	$\cot(-\theta) = -\cot \theta$
	$\sin(-\theta) = -\sin \theta$
	$\csc(-\theta) = -\csc \theta$
	$\cos(-\theta) = \cos \theta$
	$\sec(-\theta) = \sec \theta$
Reciprocal identities	$\sin \theta = \dfrac{1}{\csc \theta}$
	$\cos \theta = \dfrac{1}{\sec \theta}$
	$\tan \theta = \dfrac{1}{\cot \theta}$
	$\csc \theta = \dfrac{1}{\sin \theta}$
	$\sec \theta = \dfrac{1}{\cos \theta}$
	$\cot \theta = \dfrac{1}{\tan \theta}$
Quotient identities	$\tan \theta = \dfrac{\sin \theta}{\cos \theta}$
	$\cot \theta = \dfrac{\cos \theta}{\sin \theta}$

Sum Formula for Cosine

$$\cos(\alpha + \beta) = \cos\alpha\cos\beta - \sin\alpha\sin\beta$$

Difference Formula for Cosine

$$\cos(\alpha - \beta) = \cos\alpha\cos\beta + \sin\alpha\sin\beta$$

Sum Formula for Sine

$$\sin(\alpha + \beta) = \sin\alpha\cos\beta + \cos\alpha\sin\beta$$

Difference Formula for Sine

$$\sin(\alpha - \beta) = \sin\alpha\cos\beta - \cos\alpha\sin\beta$$

Sum Formula for Tangent

$$\tan(\alpha + \beta) = \frac{\tan\alpha + \tan\beta}{1 - \tan\alpha\tan\beta}$$

Difference Formula for Tangent

$$\tan(\alpha - \beta) = \frac{\tan\alpha - \tan\beta}{1 + \tan\alpha\tan\beta}$$

Cofunction identities

$$\sin\theta = \cos\left(\frac{\pi}{2} - \theta\right)$$

$$\cos\theta = \sin\left(\frac{\pi}{2} - \theta\right)$$

$$\tan\theta = \cot\left(\frac{\pi}{2} - \theta\right)$$

$$\cot\theta = \tan\left(\frac{\pi}{2} - \theta\right)$$

$$\sec\theta = \csc\left(\frac{\pi}{2} - \theta\right)$$

$$\csc\theta = \sec\left(\frac{\pi}{2} - \theta\right)$$

Double-angle formulas

$$\sin(2\theta) = 2\sin\theta\cos\theta$$
$$\cos(2\theta) = \cos^2\theta - \sin^2\theta$$
$$= 1 - 2\sin^2\theta$$
$$= 2\cos^2\theta - 1$$
$$\tan(2\theta) = \frac{2\tan\theta}{1 - \tan^2\theta}$$

Reduction formulas

$$\sin^2\theta = \frac{1 - \cos(2\theta)}{2}$$

$$\cos^2\theta = \frac{1 + \cos(2\theta)}{2}$$

$$\tan^2\theta = \frac{1 - \cos(2\theta)}{1 + \cos(2\theta)}$$

Half-angle formulas

$$\sin\frac{\alpha}{2} = \pm\sqrt{\frac{1 - \cos\alpha}{2}}$$

$$\cos\frac{\alpha}{2} = \pm\sqrt{\frac{1 + \cos\alpha}{2}}$$

$$\tan\frac{\alpha}{2} = \pm\sqrt{\frac{1 - \cos\alpha}{1 + \cos\alpha}}$$

$$= \frac{\sin\alpha}{1 + \cos\alpha}$$

$$= \frac{1 - \cos\alpha}{\sin\alpha}$$

Product-to-sum Formulas

$$\cos \alpha \cos \beta = \frac{1}{2}[\cos(\alpha - \beta) + \cos(\alpha + \beta)]$$

$$\sin \alpha \cos \beta = \frac{1}{2}[\sin(\alpha + \beta) + \sin(\alpha - \beta)]$$

$$\sin \alpha \sin \beta = \frac{1}{2}[\cos(\alpha - \beta) - \cos(\alpha + \beta)]$$

$$\cos \alpha \sin \beta = \frac{1}{2}[\sin(\alpha + \beta) - \sin(\alpha - \beta)]$$

Sum-to-product Formulas

$$\sin \alpha + \sin \beta = 2 \sin\left(\frac{\alpha + \beta}{2}\right)\cos\left(\frac{\alpha - \beta}{2}\right)$$

$$\sin \alpha - \sin \beta = 2 \sin\left(\frac{\alpha - \beta}{2}\right)\cos\left(\frac{\alpha + \beta}{2}\right)$$

$$\cos \alpha - \cos \beta = -2 \sin\left(\frac{\alpha + \beta}{2}\right)\sin\left(\frac{\alpha - \beta}{2}\right)$$

$$\cos \alpha + \cos \beta = 2\cos\left(\frac{\alpha + \beta}{2}\right)\cos\left(\frac{\alpha - \beta}{2}\right)$$

Key Concepts

9.1 Solving Trigonometric Equations with Identities

- There are multiple ways to represent a trigonometric expression. Verifying the identities illustrates how expressions can be rewritten to simplify a problem.
- Graphing both sides of an identity will verify it. See **Example 1**.
- Simplifying one side of the equation to equal the other side is another method for verifying an identity. See **Example 2** and **Example 3**.
- The approach to verifying an identity depends on the nature of the identity. It is often useful to begin on the more complex side of the equation. See **Example 4**.
- We can create an identity by simplifying an expression and then verifying it. See **Example 5**.
- Verifying an identity may involve algebra with the fundamental identities. See **Example 6** and **Example 7**.
- Algebraic techniques can be used to simplify trigonometric expressions. We use algebraic techniques throughout this text, as they consist of the fundamental rules of mathematics. See **Example 8**, **Example 9**, and **Example 10**.

9.2 Sum and Difference Identities

- The sum formula for cosines states that the cosine of the sum of two angles equals the product of the cosines of the angles minus the product of the sines of the angles. The difference formula for cosines states that the cosine of the difference of two angles equals the product of the cosines of the angles plus the product of the sines of the angles.
- The sum and difference formulas can be used to find the exact values of the sine, cosine, or tangent of an angle. See **Example 1** and **Example 2**.
- The sum formula for sines states that the sine of the sum of two angles equals the product of the sine of the first angle and cosine of the second angle plus the product of the cosine of the first angle and the sine of the second angle. The difference formula for sines states that the sine of the difference of two angles equals the product of the sine of the first angle and cosine of the second angle minus the product of the cosine of the first angle and the sine of the second angle. See **Example 3**.
- The sum and difference formulas for sine and cosine can also be used for inverse trigonometric functions. See **Example 4**.

- The sum formula for tangent states that the tangent of the sum of two angles equals the sum of the tangents of the angles divided by 1 minus the product of the tangents of the angles. The difference formula for tangent states that the tangent of the difference of two angles equals the difference of the tangents of the angles divided by 1 plus the product of the tangents of the angles. See **Example 5**.

- The Pythagorean Theorem along with the sum and difference formulas can be used to find multiple sums and differences of angles. See **Example 6**.

- The cofunction identities apply to complementary angles and pairs of reciprocal functions. See **Example 7**.

- Sum and difference formulas are useful in verifying identities. See **Example 8** and **Example 9**.

- Application problems are often easier to solve by using sum and difference formulas. See **Example 10** and **Example 11**.

9.3 Double-Angle, Half-Angle, and Reduction Formulas

- Double-angle identities are derived from the sum formulas of the fundamental trigonometric functions: sine, cosine, and tangent. See **Example 1**, **Example 2**, **Example 3**, and **Example 4**.

- Reduction formulas are especially useful in calculus, as they allow us to reduce the power of the trigonometric term. See **Example 5** and **Example 6**.

- Half-angle formulas allow us to find the value of trigonometric functions involving half-angles, whether the original angle is known or not. See **Example 7**, **Example 8**, and **Example 9**.

9.4 Sum-to-Product and Product-to-Sum Formulas

- From the sum and difference identities, we can derive the product-to-sum formulas and the sum-to-product formulas for sine and cosine.

- We can use the product-to-sum formulas to rewrite products of sines, products of cosines, and products of sine and cosine as sums or differences of sines and cosines. See **Example 1**, **Example 2**, and **Example 3**.

- We can also derive the sum-to-product identities from the product-to-sum identities using substitution.

- We can use the sum-to-product formulas to rewrite sum or difference of sines, cosines, or products sine and cosine as products of sines and cosines. See **Example 4**.

- Trigonometric expressions are often simpler to evaluate using the formulas. See **Example 5**.

- The identities can be verified using other formulas or by converting the expressions to sines and cosines. To verify an identity, we choose the more complicated side of the equals sign and rewrite it until it is transformed into the other side. See **Example 6** and **Example 7**.

9.5 Solving Trigonometric Equations

- When solving linear trigonometric equations, we can use algebraic techniques just as we do solving algebraic equations. Look for patterns, like the difference of squares, quadratic form, or an expression that lends itself well to substitution. See **Example 1**, **Example 2**, and **Example 3**.

- Equations involving a single trigonometric function can be solved or verified using the unit circle. See **Example 4**, **Example 5**, and **Example 6**, and **Example 7**.

- We can also solve trigonometric equations using a graphing calculator. See **Example 8** and **Example 9**.

- Many equations appear quadratic in form. We can use substitution to make the equation appear simpler, and then use the same techniques we use solving an algebraic quadratic: factoring, the quadratic formula, etc. See **Example 10**, **Example 11**, **Example 12**, and **Example 13**.

- We can also use the identities to solve trigonometric equation. See **Example 14**, **Example 15**, and **Example 16**.

- We can use substitution to solve a multiple-angle trigonometric equation, which is a compression of a standard trigonometric function. We will need to take the compression into account and verify that we have found all solutions on the given interval. See **Example 17**.

- Real-world scenarios can be modeled and solved using the Pythagorean Theorem and trigonometric functions. See **Example 18**.

CHAPTER 9 REVIEW EXERCISES

SOLVING TRIGONOMETRIC EQUATIONS WITH IDENTITIES

For the following exercises, find all solutions exactly that exist on the interval $[0, 2\pi)$.

1. $\csc^2 t = 3$

2. $\cos^2 x = \dfrac{1}{4}$

3. $2\sin\theta = -1$

4. $\tan x \sin x + \sin(-x) = 0$

5. $9\sin\omega - 2 = 4\sin^2\omega$

6. $1 - 2\tan(\omega) = \tan^2(\omega)$

For the following exercises, use basic identities to simplify the expression.

7. $\sec x \cos x + \cos x - \dfrac{1}{\sec x}$

8. $\sin^3 x + \cos^2 x \sin x$

For the following exercises, determine if the given identities are equivalent.

9. $\sin^2 x + \sec^2 x - 1 = \dfrac{(1 - \cos^2 x)(1 + \cos^2 x)}{\cos^2 x}$

10. $\tan^3 x \csc^2 x \cot^2 x \cos x \sin x = 1$

SUM AND DIFFERENCE IDENTITIES

For the following exercises, find the exact value.

11. $\tan\left(\dfrac{7\pi}{12}\right)$

12. $\cos\left(\dfrac{25\pi}{12}\right)$

13. $\sin(70°)\cos(25°) - \cos(70°)\sin(25°)$

14. $\cos(83°)\cos(23°) + \sin(83°)\sin(23°)$

For the following exercises, prove the identity.

15. $\cos(4x) - \cos(3x)\cos x = \sin^2 x - 4\cos^2 x \sin^2 x$

16. $\cos(3x) - \cos^3 x = -\cos x \sin^2 x - \sin x \sin(2x)$

For the following exercise, simplify the expression.

17. $\dfrac{\tan\left(\dfrac{1}{2}x\right) + \tan\left(\dfrac{1}{8}x\right)}{1 - \tan\left(\dfrac{1}{8}x\right)\tan\left(\dfrac{1}{2}x\right)}$

For the following exercises, find the exact value.

18. $\cos\left(\sin^{-1}(0) - \cos^{-1}\left(\dfrac{1}{2}\right)\right)$

19. $\tan\left(\sin^{-1}(0) + \sin^{-1}\left(\dfrac{1}{2}\right)\right)$

DOUBLE-ANGLE, HALF-ANGLE, AND REDUCTION FORMULAS

For the following exercises, find the exact value.

20. Find $\sin(2\theta)$, $\cos(2\theta)$, and $\tan(2\theta)$ given $\cos\theta = -\dfrac{1}{3}$ and θ is in the interval $\left[\dfrac{\pi}{2}, \pi\right]$

21. Find $\sin(2\theta)$, $\cos(2\theta)$, and $\tan(2\theta)$ given $\sec\theta = -\dfrac{5}{3}$ and θ is in the interval $\left[\dfrac{\pi}{2}, \pi\right]$

22. $\sin\left(\dfrac{7\pi}{8}\right)$

23. $\sec\left(\dfrac{3\pi}{8}\right)$

For the following exercises, use **Figure 1** to find the desired quantities.

24. $\sin(2\beta)$, $\cos(2\beta)$, $\tan(2\beta)$, $\sin(2\alpha)$, $\cos(2\alpha)$, and $\tan(2\alpha)$

25. $\sin\left(\dfrac{\beta}{2}\right)$, $\cos\left(\dfrac{\beta}{2}\right)$, $\tan\left(\dfrac{\beta}{2}\right)$, $\sin\left(\dfrac{\alpha}{2}\right)$, $\cos\left(\dfrac{\alpha}{2}\right)$, and $\tan\left(\dfrac{\alpha}{2}\right)$

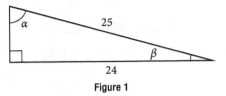

Figure 1

For the following exercises, prove the identity.

26. $\dfrac{2\cos(2x)}{\sin(2x)} = \cot x - \tan x$

27. $\cot x \cos(2x) = -\sin(2x) + \cot x$

For the following exercises, rewrite the expression with no powers.

28. $\cos^2 x \sin^4(2x)$

29. $\tan^2 x \sin^3 x$

SUM-TO-PRODUCT AND PRODUCT-TO-SUM FORMULAS

For the following exercises, evaluate the product for the given expression using a sum or difference of two functions. Write the exact answer.

30. $\cos\left(\dfrac{\pi}{3}\right)\sin\left(\dfrac{\pi}{4}\right)$

31. $2\sin\left(\dfrac{2\pi}{3}\right)\sin\left(\dfrac{5\pi}{6}\right)$

32. $2\cos\left(\dfrac{\pi}{5}\right)\cos\left(\dfrac{\pi}{3}\right)$

For the following exercises, evaluate the sum by using a product formula. Write the exact answer.

33. $\sin\left(\dfrac{\pi}{12}\right) - \sin\left(\dfrac{7\pi}{12}\right)$

34. $\cos\left(\dfrac{5\pi}{12}\right) + \cos\left(\dfrac{7\pi}{12}\right)$

For the following exercises, change the functions from a product to a sum or a sum to a product.

35. $\sin(9x)\cos(3x)$

36. $\cos(7x)\cos(12x)$

37. $\sin(11x) + \sin(2x)$

38. $\cos(6x) + \cos(5x)$

SOLVING TRIGONOMETRIC EQUATIONS

For the following exercises, find all exact solutions on the interval $[0, 2\pi)$.

39. $\tan x + 1 = 0$

40. $2\sin(2x) + \sqrt{2} = 0$

For the following exercises, find all exact solutions on the interval $[0, 2\pi)$.

41. $2\sin^2 x - \sin x = 0$

42. $\cos^2 x - \cos x - 1 = 0$

43. $2\sin^2 x + 5\sin x + 3 = 0$

44. $\cos x - 5\sin(2x) = 0$

45. $\dfrac{1}{\sec^2 x} + 2 + \sin^2 x + 4\cos^2 x = 0$

For the following exercises, simplify the equation algebraically as much as possible. Then use a calculator to find the solutions on the interval $[0, 2\pi)$. Round to four decimal places.

46. $\sqrt{3}\cot^2 x + \cot x = 1$

47. $\csc^2 x - 3\csc x - 4 = 0$

For the following exercises, graph each side of the equation to find the zeroes on the interval $[0, 2\pi)$.

48. $20\cos^2 x + 21\cos x + 1 = 0$

49. $\sec^2 x - 2\sec x = 15$

CHAPTER 9 PRACTICE TEST

For the following exercises, simplify the given expression.

1. $\cos(-x)\sin x \cot x + \sin^2 x$

2. $\sin(-x)\cos(-2x) - \sin(-x)\cos(-2x)$

3. $\csc(\theta)\cot(\theta)(\sec^2 \theta - 1)$

4. $\cos^2(\theta)\sin^2(\theta)(1 + \cot^2(\theta))(1 + \tan^2(\theta))$

For the following exercises, find the exact value.

5. $\cos\left(\dfrac{7\pi}{12}\right)$

6. $\tan\left(\dfrac{3\pi}{8}\right)$

7. $\tan\left(\sin^{-1}\left(\dfrac{\sqrt{2}}{2}\right) + \tan^{-1}\sqrt{3}\right)$

8. $2\sin\left(\dfrac{\pi}{4}\right)\sin\left(\dfrac{\pi}{6}\right)$

9. $\cos\left(\dfrac{4\pi}{3} + \theta\right)$

10. $\tan\left(-\dfrac{\pi}{4} + \theta\right)$

For the following exercises, simplify each expression. Do not evaluate.

11. $\cos^2(32°)\tan^2(32°)$

12. $\cot\left(\dfrac{\theta}{2}\right)$

For the following exercises, find all exact solutions to the equation on $[0, 2\pi)$.

13. $\cos^2 x - \sin^2 x - 1 = 0$

14. $\cos^2 x = \cos x \ 4\sin^2 x + 2\sin x - 3 = 0$

15. $\cos(2x) + \sin^2 x = 0$

16. $2\sin^2 x - \sin x = 0$

17. Rewrite the sum as a product: $\cos(2x) + \cos(-8x)$.

18. Rewrite the product as a sum or difference: $8\cos(15x)\sin(3x)$

19. Rewrite the difference as a product: $2\sin(8\theta) - \sin(4\theta)$

20. Find all solutions of $\tan(x) - \sqrt{3} = 0$.

21. Find the solutions of $\sec^2 x - 2\sec x = 15$ on the interval $[0, 2\pi)$ algebraically; then graph both sides of the equation to determine the answer.

For the following exercises, find all exact solutions to the equation on $[0, 2\pi)$.

22. $2\cos\left(\dfrac{\theta}{2}\right) = 1$

23. $\sqrt{3}\cot(y) = 1$

24. Find $\sin(2\theta)$, $\cos(2\theta)$, and $\tan(2\theta)$ given $\cot \theta = -\dfrac{3}{4}$ and θ is on the interval $\left[\dfrac{\pi}{2}, \pi\right]$.

25. Find $\sin\left(\dfrac{\theta}{2}\right)$, $\cos\left(\dfrac{\theta}{2}\right)$, and $\tan\left(\dfrac{\theta}{2}\right)$ given $\cos \theta = \dfrac{7}{25}$ and θ is in quadrant IV.

26. Rewrite the expression $\sin^4 x$ with no powers greater than 1.

For the following exercises, prove the identity.

27. $\tan^3 x - \tan x \sec^2 x = \tan(-x)$

28. $\sin(3x) - \cos x \sin(2x) = \cos^2 x \sin x - \sin^3 x$

29. $\dfrac{\sin(2x)}{\sin x} - \dfrac{\cos(2x)}{\cos x} = \sec x$

30. Plot the points and find a function of the form $y = A\cos(Bx + C) + D$ that fits the given data.

x	0	1	2	3	4	5
y	-2	2	-2	2	-2	2

31. The displacement $h(t)$ in centimeters of a mass suspended by a spring is modeled by the function $h(t) = \frac{1}{4}\sin(120\pi t)$, where t is measured in seconds. Find the amplitude, period, and frequency of this displacement.

32. A woman is standing 300 feet away from a 2,000-foot building. If she looks to the top of the building, at what angle above horizontal is she looking? A bored worker looks down at her from the 15th floor (1,500 feet above her). At what angle is he looking down at her? Round to the nearest tenth of a degree.

33. Two frequencies of sound are played on an instrument governed by the equation $n(t) = 8\cos(20\pi t)\cos(1{,}000\pi t)$. What are the period and frequency of the "fast" and "slow" oscillations? What is the amplitude?

34. The average monthly snowfall in a small village in the Himalayas is 6 inches, with the low of 1 inch occurring in July. Construct a function that models this behavior. During what period is there more than 10 inches of snowfall?

35. A spring attached to a ceiling is pulled down 20 cm. After 3 seconds, wherein it completes 6 full periods, the amplitude is only 15 cm. Find the function modeling the position of the spring t seconds after being released. At what time will the spring come to rest? In this case, use 1 cm amplitude as rest.

36. Water levels near a glacier currently average 9 feet, varying seasonally by 2 inches above and below the average and reaching their highest point in January. Due to global warming, the glacier has begun melting faster than normal. Every year, the water levels rise by a steady 3 inches. Find a function modeling the depth of the water t months from now. If the docks are 2 feet above current water levels, at what point will the water first rise above the docks?

10

Further Applications of Trigonometry

Figure 1 General Sherman, the world's largest living tree. (credit: Mike Baird, Flickr)

CHAPTER OUTLINE

10.1 Non-right Triangles: Law of Sines
10.2 Non-right Triangles: Law of Cosines
10.3 Polar Coordinates
10.4 Polar Coordinates: Graphs
10.5 Polar Form of Complex Numbers
10.6 Parametric Equations
10.7 Parametric Equations: Graphs
10.8 Vectors

Introduction

The world's largest tree by volume, named General Sherman, stands 274.9 feet tall and resides in Northern California.[27] Just how do scientists know its true height? A common way to measure the height involves determining the angle of elevation, which is formed by the tree and the ground at a point some distance away from the base of the tree. This method is much more practical than climbing the tree and dropping a very long tape measure.

In this chapter, we will explore applications of trigonometry that will enable us to solve many different kinds of problems, including finding the height of a tree. We extend topics we introduced in **Trigonometric Functions** and investigate applications more deeply and meaningfully.

27 Source: National Park Service. "The General Sherman Tree." http://www.nps.gov/seki/naturescience/sherman.htm. Accessed April 25, 2014.

LEARNING OBJECTIVES

In this section, you will:

- Use the Law of Sines to solve oblique triangles.
- Find the area of an oblique triangle using the sine function.
- Solve applied problems using the Law of Sines.

10.1   NON-RIGHT TRIANGLES: LAW OF SINES

Suppose two radar stations located 20 miles apart each detect an aircraft between them. The angle of elevation measured by the first station is 35 degrees, whereas the angle of elevation measured by the second station is 15 degrees. How can we determine the altitude of the aircraft? We see in **Figure 1** that the triangle formed by the aircraft and the two stations is not a right triangle, so we cannot use what we know about right triangles. In this section, we will find out how to solve problems involving non-right triangles.

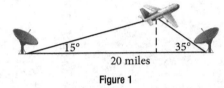

Figure 1

Using the Law of Sines to Solve Oblique Triangles

In any triangle, we can draw an **altitude**, a perpendicular line from one vertex to the opposite side, forming two right triangles. It would be preferable, however, to have methods that we can apply directly to non-right triangles without first having to create right triangles.

Any triangle that is not a right triangle is an **oblique triangle**. Solving an oblique triangle means finding the measurements of all three angles and all three sides. To do so, we need to start with at least three of these values, including at least one of the sides. We will investigate three possible oblique triangle problem situations:

1. **ASA (angle-side-angle)** We know the measurements of two angles and the included side. See **Figure 2**.

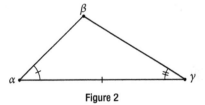

Figure 2

2. **AAS (angle-angle-side)** We know the measurements of two angles and a side that is not between the known angles. See **Figure 3**.

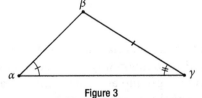

Figure 3

3. **SSA (side-side-angle)** We know the measurements of two sides and an angle that is not between the known sides. See **Figure 4**.

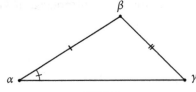

Figure 4

Knowing how to approach each of these situations enables us to solve oblique triangles without having to drop a perpendicular to form two right triangles. Instead, we can use the fact that the ratio of the measurement of one of the angles to the length of its opposite side will be equal to the other two ratios of angle measure to opposite side. Let's see how this statement is derived by considering the triangle shown in **Figure 5**.

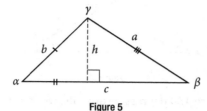

Figure 5

Using the right triangle relationships, we know that $\sin \alpha = \dfrac{h}{b}$ and $\sin \beta = \dfrac{h}{a}$. Solving both equations for h gives two different expressions for h.

$$h = b\sin \alpha \text{ and } h = a\sin \beta$$

We then set the expressions equal to each other.

$$b\sin \alpha = a\sin \beta$$

$$\left(\dfrac{1}{ab}\right)(b\sin \alpha) = (a\sin \beta)\left(\dfrac{1}{ab}\right) \qquad \text{Multiply both sides by } \dfrac{1}{ab}.$$

$$\dfrac{\sin \alpha}{a} = \dfrac{\sin \beta}{b}$$

Similarly, we can compare the other ratios.

$$\dfrac{\sin \alpha}{a} = \dfrac{\sin \gamma}{c} \text{ and } \dfrac{\sin \beta}{b} = \dfrac{\sin \gamma}{c}$$

Collectively, these relationships are called the **Law of Sines.**

$$\dfrac{\sin \alpha}{a} = \dfrac{\sin \beta}{b} = \dfrac{\sin \gamma}{c}$$

Note the standard way of labeling triangles: angle α (alpha) is opposite side a; angle β (beta) is opposite side b; and angle γ (gamma) is opposite side c. See **Figure 6**.

While calculating angles and sides, be sure to carry the exact values through to the final answer. Generally, final answers are rounded to the nearest tenth, unless otherwise specified.

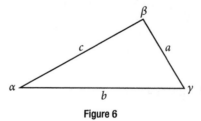

Figure 6

Law of Sines

Given a triangle with angles and opposite sides labeled as in **Figure 6**, the ratio of the measurement of an angle to the length of its opposite side will be equal to the other two ratios of angle measure to opposite side. All proportions will be equal. The **Law of Sines** is based on proportions and is presented symbolically two ways.

$$\dfrac{\sin \alpha}{a} = \dfrac{\sin \beta}{b} = \dfrac{\sin \gamma}{c}$$

$$\dfrac{a}{\sin \alpha} = \dfrac{b}{\sin \beta} = \dfrac{c}{\sin \gamma}$$

To solve an oblique triangle, use any pair of applicable ratios.

Example 1   **Solving for Two Unknown Sides and Angle of an AAS Triangle**

Solve the triangle shown in **Figure 7** to the nearest tenth.

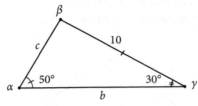

Figure 7

Solution   The three angles must add up to 180 degrees. From this, we can determine that

$$\beta = 180° - 50° - 30°$$
$$= 100°$$

To find an unknown side, we need to know the corresponding angle and a known ratio. We know that angle $\alpha = 50°$ and its corresponding side $a = 10$. We can use the following proportion from the Law of Sines to find the length of c.

$$\frac{\sin(50°)}{10} = \frac{\sin(30°)}{c}$$

$$c\frac{\sin(50°)}{10} = \sin(30°) \qquad \text{Multiply both sides by } c.$$

$$c = \sin(30°)\frac{10}{\sin(50°)} \qquad \text{Multiply by the reciprocal to isolate } c.$$

$$c \approx 6.5$$

Similarly, to solve for b, we set up another proportion.

$$\frac{\sin(50°)}{10} = \frac{\sin(100°)}{b}$$

$$b\sin(50°) = 10\sin(100°) \qquad \text{Multiply both sides by } b.$$

$$b = \frac{10\sin(100°)}{\sin(50°)} \qquad \text{Multiply by the reciprocal to isolate } b.$$

$$b \approx 12.9$$

Therefore, the complete set of angles and sides is

$$\alpha = 50° \qquad a = 10$$
$$\beta = 100° \qquad b \approx 12.9$$
$$\gamma = 30° \qquad c \approx 6.5$$

Try It #1

Solve the triangle shown in **Figure 8** to the nearest tenth.

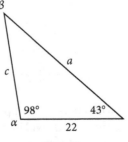

Figure 8

Using The Law of Sines to Solve SSA Triangles

We can use the Law of Sines to solve any oblique triangle, but some solutions may not be straightforward. In some cases, more than one triangle may satisfy the given criteria, which we describe as an **ambiguous case**. Triangles classified as SSA, those in which we know the lengths of two sides and the measurement of the angle opposite one of the given sides, may result in one or two solutions, or even no solution.

possible outcomes for SSA triangles

Oblique triangles in the category SSA may have four different outcomes. **Figure 9** illustrates the solutions with the known sides *a* and *b* and known angle *α*.

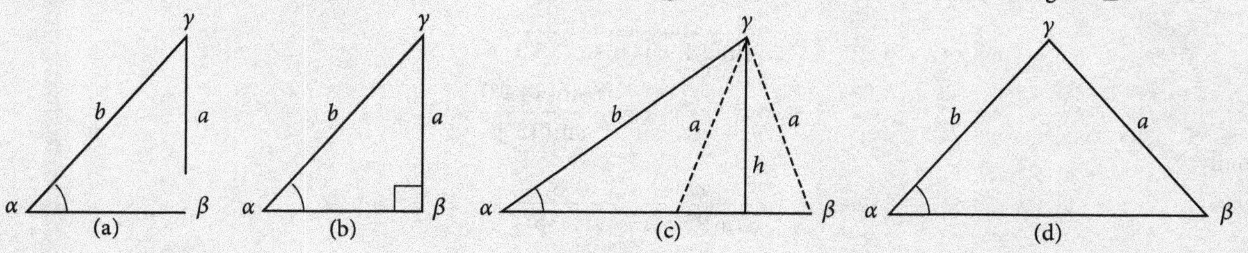

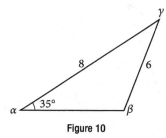

No triangle, *a* < *h*   Right triangle, *a* = *h*   Two triangles, *a* > *h*, *a* < *b*   One triangle, *a* ≥ *b*

Figure 9

Example 2   **Solving an Oblique SSA Triangle**

Solve the triangle in **Figure 10** for the missing side and find the missing angle measures to the nearest tenth.

Figure 10

Solution   Use the Law of Sines to find angle *β* and angle *γ*, and then side *c*. Solving for *β*, we have the proportion

$$\frac{\sin \alpha}{a} = \frac{\sin \beta}{b}$$

$$\frac{\sin(35°)}{6} = \frac{\sin \beta}{8}$$

$$\frac{8\sin(35°)}{6} = \sin \beta$$

$$0.7648 \approx \sin \beta$$

$$\sin^{-1}(0.7648) \approx 49.9°$$

$$\beta \approx 49.9°$$

However, in the diagram, angle *β* appears to be an obtuse angle and may be greater than 90°. How did we get an acute angle, and how do we find the measurement of *β*? Let's investigate further. Dropping a perpendicular from *γ* and viewing the triangle from a right angle perspective, we have **Figure 11**. It appears that there may be a second triangle that will fit the given criteria.

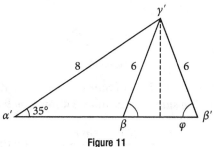

Figure 11

The angle supplementary to *β* is approximately equal to 49.9°, which means that *β* = 180° − 49.9° = 130.1°. (Remember that the sine function is positive in both the first and second quadrants.) Solving for *γ*, we have

$$\gamma = 180° − 35° − 130.1° \approx 14.9°$$

We can then use these measurements to solve the other triangle. Since γ' is supplementary to α' and β', we have

$$\gamma' = 180° - 35° - 49.9° \approx 95.1°$$

Now we need to find c and c'.

We have

$$\frac{c}{\sin(14.9°)} = \frac{6}{\sin(35°)}$$

$$c = \frac{6\sin(14.9°)}{\sin(35°)} \approx 2.7$$

Finally,

$$\frac{c'}{\sin(95.1°)} = \frac{6}{\sin(35°)}$$

$$c' = \frac{6\sin(95.1°)}{\sin(35°)} \approx 10.4$$

To summarize, there are two triangles with an angle of 35°, an adjacent side of 8, and an opposite side of 6, as shown in **Figure 12**.

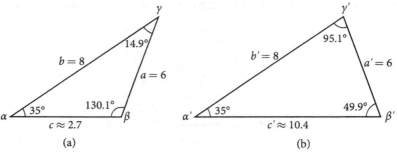

Figure 12

However, we were looking for the values for the triangle with an obtuse angle β. We can see them in the first triangle (*a*) in **Figure 12**.

Try It #2

Given $\alpha = 80°$, $a = 120$, and $b = 121$, find the missing side and angles. If there is more than one possible solution, show both.

Example 3   **Solving for the Unknown Sides and Angles of a SSA Triangle**

In the triangle shown in **Figure 13**, solve for the unknown side and angles. Round your answers to the nearest tenth.

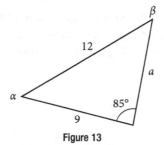

Figure 13

Solution   In choosing the pair of ratios from the Law of Sines to use, look at the information given. In this case, we know the angle $\gamma = 85°$, and its corresponding side $c = 12$, and we know side $b = 9$. We will use this proportion to solve for β.

$$\frac{\sin(85°)}{12} = \frac{\sin \beta}{9} \qquad \text{Isolate the unknown.}$$

$$\frac{9\sin(85°)}{12} = \sin \beta$$

To find β, apply the inverse sine function. The inverse sine will produce a single result, but keep in mind that there may be two values for β. It is important to verify the result, as there may be two viable solutions, only one solution (the usual case), or no solutions.

$$\beta = \sin^{-1}\left(\frac{9\sin(85°)}{12}\right)$$
$$\beta \approx \sin^{-1}(0.7471)$$
$$\beta \approx 48.3°$$

In this case, if we subtract β from 180°, we find that there may be a second possible solution. Thus, $\beta = 180° - 48.3° \approx 131.7°$. To check the solution, subtract both angles, 131.7° and 85°, from 180°. This gives

$$\alpha = 180° - 85° - 131.7° \approx -36.7°,$$

which is impossible, and so $\beta \approx 48.3°$.

To find the remaining missing values, we calculate $\alpha = 180° - 85° - 48.3° \approx 46.7°$. Now, only side a is needed. Use the Law of Sines to solve for a by one of the proportions.

$$\frac{\sin(85°)}{12} = \frac{\sin(46.7°)}{a}$$
$$a\frac{\sin(85°)}{12} = \sin(46.7°)$$
$$a = \frac{12\sin(46.7°)}{\sin(85°)} \approx 8.8$$

The complete set of solutions for the given triangle is

$$\alpha \approx 46.7° \qquad a \approx 8.8$$
$$\beta \approx 48.3° \qquad b = 9$$
$$\gamma = 85° \qquad c = 12$$

Try It #3

Given $\alpha = 80°$, $a = 100$, $b = 10$, find the missing side and angles. If there is more than one possible solution, show both. Round your answers to the nearest tenth.

Example 4   **Finding the Triangles That Meet the Given Criteria**

Find all possible triangles if one side has length 4 opposite an angle of 50°, and a second side has length 10.

Solution   Using the given information, we can solve for the angle opposite the side of length 10. See **Figure 14**.

$$\frac{\sin \alpha}{10} = \frac{\sin(50°)}{4}$$
$$\sin \alpha = \frac{10\sin(50°)}{4}$$
$$\sin \alpha \approx 1.915$$

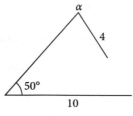

Figure 14

We can stop here without finding the value of α. Because the range of the sine function is $[-1, 1]$, it is impossible for the sine value to be 1.915. In fact, inputting $\sin^{-1}(1.915)$ in a graphing calculator generates an **ERROR DOMAIN**. Therefore, no triangles can be drawn with the provided dimensions.

Try It #4

Determine the number of triangles possible given $a = 31$, $b = 26$, $\beta = 48°$.

Finding the Area of an Oblique Triangle Using the Sine Function

Now that we can solve a triangle for missing values, we can use some of those values and the sine function to find the area of an oblique triangle. Recall that the area formula for a triangle is given as Area $= \frac{1}{2}bh$, where b is base and h is height. For oblique triangles, we must find h before we can use the area formula. Observing the two triangles in **Figure 15**, one acute and one obtuse, we can drop a perpendicular to represent the height and then apply the trigonometric property $\sin \alpha = \dfrac{\text{opposite}}{\text{hypotenuse}}$ to write an equation for area in oblique triangles. In the acute triangle, we have $\sin \alpha = \dfrac{h}{c}$ or $c\sin \alpha = h$. However, in the obtuse triangle, we drop the perpendicular outside the triangle and extend the base b to form a right triangle. The angle used in calculation is α', or $180 - \alpha$.

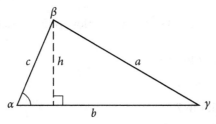
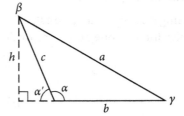

Figure 15

Thus,
$$\text{Area} = \frac{1}{2}(\text{base})(\text{height}) = \frac{1}{2}b(c\sin \alpha)$$

Similarly,
$$\text{Area} = \frac{1}{2}a(b\sin \gamma) = \frac{1}{2}a(c\sin \beta)$$

---

area of an oblique triangle

The formula for the area of an oblique triangle is given by

$$\text{Area} = \frac{1}{2}bc\sin \alpha$$

$$= \frac{1}{2}ac\sin \beta$$

$$= \frac{1}{2}ab\sin \gamma$$

This is equivalent to one-half of the product of two sides and the sine of their included angle.

Example 5 Finding the Area of an Oblique Triangle

Find the area of a triangle with sides $a = 90$, $b = 52$, and angle $\gamma = 102°$. Round the area to the nearest integer.

Solution   Using the formula, we have

$$\text{Area} = \frac{1}{2}ab\sin \gamma$$

$$\text{Area} = \frac{1}{2}(90)(52)\sin(102°)$$

$$\text{Area} \approx 2289 \text{ square units}$$

Try It #5

Find the area of the triangle given $\beta = 42°$, $a = 7.2$ ft, $c = 3.4$ ft. Round the area to the nearest tenth.

Solving Applied Problems Using the Law of Sines

The more we study trigonometric applications, the more we discover that the applications are countless. Some are flat, diagram-type situations, but many applications in calculus, engineering, and physics involve three dimensions and motion.

Example 6   Finding an Altitude

Find the altitude of the aircraft in the problem introduced at the beginning of this section, shown in **Figure 16**. Round the altitude to the nearest tenth of a mile.

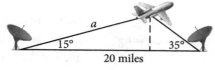

a

$15°$ $35°$

20 miles

Figure 16

Solution   To find the elevation of the aircraft, we first find the distance from one station to the aircraft, such as the side a, and then use right triangle relationships to find the height of the aircraft, h.

Because the angles in the triangle add up to 180 degrees, the unknown angle must be $180° - 15° - 35° = 130°$. This angle is opposite the side of length 20, allowing us to set up a Law of Sines relationship.

$$\frac{\sin(130°)}{20} = \frac{\sin(35°)}{a}$$

$$a\sin(130°) = 20\sin(35°)$$

$$a = \frac{20\sin(35°)}{\sin(130°)}$$

$$a \approx 14.98$$

The distance from one station to the aircraft is about 14.98 miles.

Now that we know a, we can use right triangle relationships to solve for h.

$$\sin(15°) = \frac{\text{opposite}}{\text{hypotenuse}}$$

$$\sin(15°) = \frac{h}{a}$$

$$\sin(15°) = \frac{h}{14.98}$$

$$h = 14.98\sin(15°)$$

$$h \approx 3.88$$

The aircraft is at an altitude of approximately 3.9 miles.

Try It #6

The diagram shown in **Figure 17** represents the height of a blimp flying over a football stadium. Find the height of the blimp if the angle of elevation at the southern end zone, point A, is 70°, the angle of elevation from the northern end zone, point B, is 62°, and the distance between the viewing points of the two end zones is 145 yards.

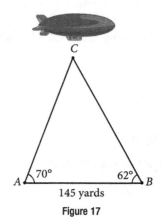

C

A $70°$ $62°$ B

145 yards

Figure 17

Access the following online resources for additional instruction and practice with trigonometric applications.

- Law of Sines: The Basics (http://openstaxcollege.org/l/sinesbasic)
- Law of Sines: The Ambiguous Case (http://openstaxcollege.org/l/sinesambiguous)

10.1   SECTION EXERCISES

VERBAL

1. Describe the altitude of a triangle.

2. Compare right triangles and oblique triangles.

3. When can you use the Law of Sines to find a missing angle?

4. In the Law of Sines, what is the relationship between the angle in the numerator and the side in the denominator?

5. What type of triangle results in an ambiguous case?

ALGEBRAIC

For the following exercises, assume α is opposite side a, β is opposite side b, and γ is opposite side c. Solve each triangle, if possible. Round each answer to the nearest tenth.

6. $\alpha = 43°, \gamma = 69°, a = 20$

7. $\alpha = 35°, \gamma = 73°, c = 20$

8. $\alpha = 60°, \beta = 60°, \gamma = 60°$

9. $a = 4, \alpha = 60°, \beta = 100°$

10. $b = 10, \beta = 95°, \gamma = 30°$

For the following exercises, use the Law of Sines to solve for the missing side for each oblique triangle. Round each answer to the nearest hundredth. Assume that angle A is opposite side a, angle B is opposite side b, and angle C is opposite side c.

11. Find side b when $A = 37°, B = 49°, c = 5$.

12. Find side a when $A = 132°, C = 23°, b = 10$.

13. Find side c when $B = 37°, C = 21, b = 23$.

For the following exercises, assume α is opposite side a, β is opposite side b, and γ is opposite side c. Determine whether there is no triangle, one triangle, or two triangles. Then solve each triangle, if possible. Round each answer to the nearest tenth.

14. $\alpha = 119°, a = 14, b = 26$

15. $\gamma = 113°, b = 10, c = 32$

16. $b = 3.5, c = 5.3, \gamma = 80°$

17. $a = 12, c = 17, \alpha = 35°$

18. $a = 20.5, b = 35.0, \beta = 25°$

19. $a = 7, c = 9, \alpha = 43°$

20. $a = 7, b = 3, \beta = 24°$

21. $b = 13, c = 5, \gamma = 10°$

22. $a = 2.3, c = 1.8, \gamma = 28°$

23. $\beta = 119°, b = 8.2, a = 11.3$

For the following exercises, use the Law of Sines to solve, if possible, the missing side or angle for each triangle or triangles in the ambiguous case. Round each answer to the nearest tenth.

24. Find angle A when $a = 24, b = 5, B = 22°$.

25. Find angle A when $a = 13, b = 6, B = 20°$.

26. Find angle B when $A = 12°, a = 2, b = 9$.

For the following exercises, find the area of the triangle with the given measurements. Round each answer to the nearest tenth.

27. $a = 5, c = 6, \beta = 35°$

28. $b = 11, c = 8, \alpha = 28°$

29. $a = 32, b = 24, \gamma = 75°$

30. $a = 7.2, b = 4.5, \gamma = 43°$

GRAPHICAL

For the following exercises, find the length of side x. Round to the nearest tenth.

31.

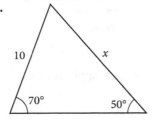

32.

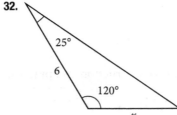

33.

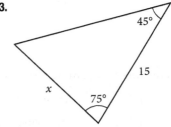

34.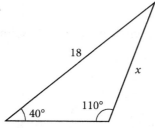

35.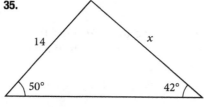

36.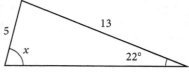

For the following exercises, find the measure of angle x, if possible. Round to the nearest tenth.

37.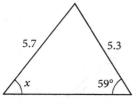

38.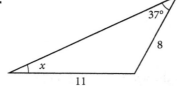

39.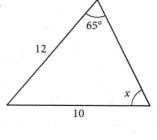

40.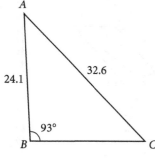

41. Notice that x is an obtuse angle.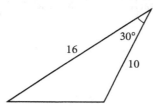

42.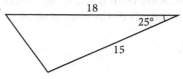

For the following exercises, find the area of each triangle. Round each answer to the nearest tenth.

43.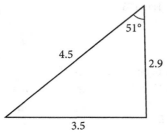

44.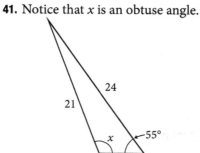

45.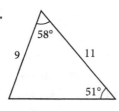

46.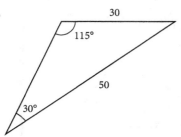

47.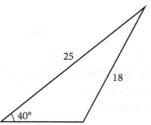

48.

49.

EXTENSIONS

50. Find the radius of the circle in **Figure 18**. Round to the nearest tenth.

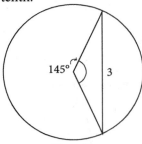

Figure 18

51. Find the diameter of the circle in **Figure 19**. Round to the nearest tenth.

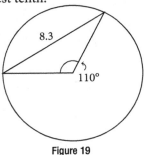

Figure 19

52. Find $m\angle ADC$ in **Figure 20**. Round to the nearest tenth.

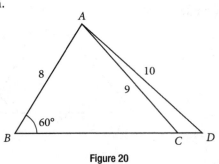

Figure 20

53. Find AD in **Figure 21**. Round to the nearest tenth.

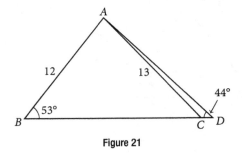

Figure 21

54. Solve both triangles in **Figure 22**. Round each answer to the nearest tenth.

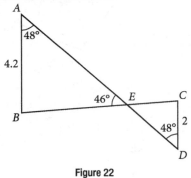

Figure 22

55. Find AB in the parallelogram shown in **Figure 23**.

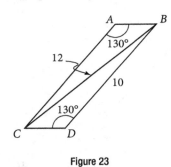

Figure 23

56. Solve the triangle in **Figure 24**. (Hint: Draw a perpendicular from H to JK). Round each answer to the nearest tenth.

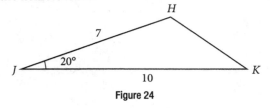

Figure 24

57. Solve the triangle in **Figure 25**. (Hint: Draw a perpendicular from N to LM). Round each answer to the nearest tenth.

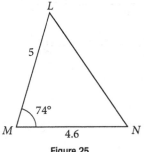

Figure 25

58. In **Figure 26**, *ABCD* is not a parallelogram. ∠*m* is obtuse. Solve both triangles. Round each answer to the nearest tenth.

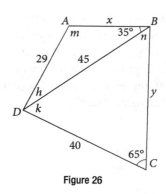

Figure 26

REAL-WORLD APPLICATIONS

59. A pole leans away from the sun at an angle of 7° to the vertical, as shown in **Figure 27**. When the elevation of the sun is 55°, the pole casts a shadow 42 feet long on the level ground. How long is the pole? Round the answer to the nearest tenth.

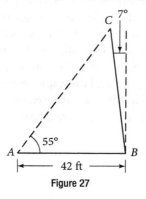

Figure 27

60. To determine how far a boat is from shore, two radar stations 500 feet apart find the angles out to the boat, as shown in **Figure 28**. Determine the distance of the boat from station *A* and the distance of the boat from shore. Round your answers to the nearest whole foot.

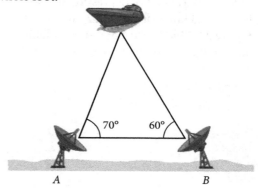

Figure 28

61. **Figure 29** shows *a* satellite orbiting Earth. The satellite passes directly over two tracking stations *A* and *B*, which are 69 miles apart. When the satellite is on one side of the two stations, the angles of elevation at *A* and *B* are measured to be 86.2° and 83.9°, respectively. How far is the satellite from station *A* and how high is the satellite above the ground? Round answers to the nearest whole mile.

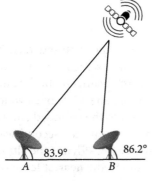

Figure 29

62. A communications tower is located at the top of a steep hill, as shown in **Figure 30**. The angle of inclination of the hill is 67°. A guy wire is to be attached to the top of the tower and to the ground, 165 meters downhill from the base of the tower. The angle formed by the guy wire and the hill is 16°. Find the length of the cable required for the guy wire to the nearest whole meter.

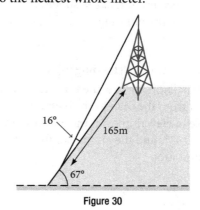

Figure 30

63. The roof of a house is at a 20° angle. An 8-foot solar panel is to be mounted on the roof and should be angled 38° relative to the horizontal for optimal results. (See **Figure 31**). How long does the vertical support holding up the back of the panel need to be? Round to the nearest tenth.

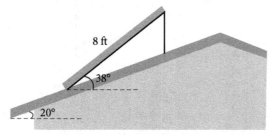

Figure 31

64. Similar to an angle of elevation, an *angle of depression* is the acute angle formed by a horizontal line and an observer's line of sight to an object below the horizontal. A pilot is flying over a straight highway. He determines the angles of depression to two mileposts, 6.6 km apart, to be 37° and 44°, as shown in **Figure 32**. Find the distance of the plane from point *A* to the nearest tenth of a kilometer.

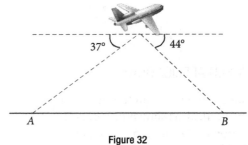

Figure 32

65. A pilot is flying over a straight highway. He determines the angles of depression to two mileposts, 4.3 km apart, to be 32° and 56°, as shown in **Figure 33**. Find the distance of the plane from point *A* to the nearest tenth of a kilometer.

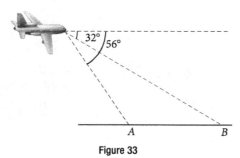

Figure 33

66. In order to estimate the height of a building, two students stand at a certain distance from the building at street level. From this point, they find the angle of elevation from the street to the top of the building to be 39°. They then move 300 feet closer to the building and find the angle of elevation to be 50°. Assuming that the street is level, estimate the height of the building to the nearest foot.

67. In order to estimate the height of a building, two students stand at a certain distance from the building at street level. From this point, they find the angle of elevation from the street to the top of the building to be 35°. They then move 250 feet closer to the building and find the angle of elevation to be 53°. Assuming that the street is level, estimate the height of the building to the nearest foot.

68. Points *A* and *B* are on opposite sides of a lake. Point *C* is 97 meters from *A*. The measure of angle *BAC* is determined to be 101°, and the measure of angle *ACB* is determined to be 53°. What is the distance from *A* to *B*, rounded to the nearest whole meter?

69. A man and a woman standing $3\frac{1}{2}$ miles apart spot a hot air balloon at the same time. If the angle of elevation from the man to the balloon is 27°, and the angle of elevation from the woman to the balloon is 41°, find the altitude of the balloon to the nearest foot.

70. Two search teams spot a stranded climber on a mountain. The first search team is 0.5 miles from the second search team, and both teams are at an altitude of 1 mile. The angle of elevation from the first search team to the stranded climber is 15°. The angle of elevation from the second search team to the climber is 22°. What is the altitude of the climber? Round to the nearest tenth of a mile.

71. A street light is mounted on a pole. A 6-foot-tall man is standing on the street a short distance from the pole, casting a shadow. The angle of elevation from the tip of the man's shadow to the top of his head of 28°. A 6-foot-tall woman is standing on the same street on the opposite side of the pole from the man. The angle of elevation from the tip of her shadow to the top of her head is 28°. If the man and woman are 20 feet apart, how far is the street light from the tip of the shadow of each person? Round the distance to the nearest tenth of a foot.

72. Three cities, A, B, and C, are located so that city A is due east of city B. If city C is located 35° west of north from city B and is 100 miles from city A and 70 miles from city B, how far is city A from city B? Round the distance to the nearest tenth of a mile.

73. Two streets meet at an 80° angle. At the corner, a park is being built in the shape of a triangle. Find the area of the park if, along one road, the park measures 180 feet, and along the other road, the park measures 215 feet.

74. Brian's house is on a corner lot. Find the area of the front yard if the edges measure 40 and 56 feet, as shown in **Figure 34**.

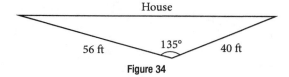

Figure 34

75. The Bermuda triangle is a region of the Atlantic Ocean that connects Bermuda, Florida, and Puerto Rico. Find the area of the Bermuda triangle if the distance from Florida to Bermuda is 1030 miles, the distance from Puerto Rico to Bermuda is 980 miles, and the angle created by the two distances is 62°.

76. A yield sign measures 30 inches on all three sides. What is the area of the sign?

77. Naomi bought a modern dining table whose top is in the shape of a triangle. Find the area of the table top if two of the sides measure 4 feet and 4.5 feet, and the smaller angles measure 32° and 42°, as shown in **Figure 35**.

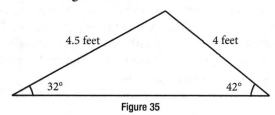

Figure 35

LEARNING OBJECTIVES

In this section, you will:

- Use the Law of Cosines to solve oblique triangles.
- Solve applied problems using the Law of Cosines.
- Use Heron's formula to find the area of a triangle.

10.2   NON-RIGHT TRIANGLES: LAW OF COSINES

Suppose a boat leaves port, travels 10 miles, turns 20 degrees, and travels another 8 miles as shown in **Figure 1**. How far from port is the boat?

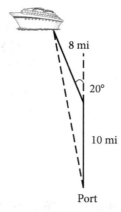

8 mi

20°

10 mi

Port

Figure 1

Unfortunately, while the Law of Sines enables us to address many non-right triangle cases, it does not help us with triangles where the known angle is between two known sides, a SAS (side-angle-side) triangle, or when all three sides are known, but no angles are known, a SSS (side-side-side) triangle. In this section, we will investigate another tool for solving oblique triangles described by these last two cases.

Using the Law of Cosines to Solve Oblique Triangles

The tool we need to solve the problem of the boat's distance from the port is the **Law of Cosines**, which defines the relationship among angle measurements and side lengths in oblique triangles. Three formulas make up the Law of Cosines. At first glance, the formulas may appear complicated because they include many variables. However, once the pattern is understood, the Law of Cosines is easier to work with than most formulas at this mathematical level.

Understanding how the Law of Cosines is derived will be helpful in using the formulas. The derivation begins with the **Generalized Pythagorean Theorem**, which is an extension of the Pythagorean Theorem to non-right triangles. Here is how it works: An arbitrary non-right triangle *ABC* is placed in the coordinate plane with vertex *A* at the origin, side *c* drawn along the *x*-axis, and vertex *C* located at some point (x, y) in the plane, as illustrated in **Figure 2**. Generally, triangles exist anywhere in the plane, but for this explanation we will place the triangle as noted.

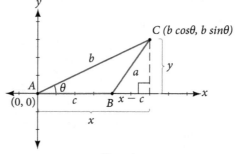

Figure 2

We can drop a perpendicular from C to the x-axis (this is the altitude or height). Recalling the basic trigonometric identities, we know that

$$\cos \theta = \frac{x(\text{adjacent})}{b(\text{hypotenuse})} \text{ and } \sin \theta = \frac{y(\text{opposite})}{b(\text{hypotenuse})}$$

In terms of θ, $x = b\cos \theta$ and $y = b\sin \theta$. The (x, y) point located at C has coordinates $(b\cos \theta, b\sin \theta)$. Using the side $(x - c)$ as one leg of a right triangle and y as the second leg, we can find the length of hypotenuse a using the Pythagorean Theorem. Thus,

$$a^2 = (x - c)^2 + y^2$$

$\quad = (b\cos \theta - c)^2 + (b\sin \theta)^2$ Substitute $(b\cos \theta)$ for x and $(b\sin \theta)$ for y.

$\quad = (b^2 \cos^2 \theta - 2bc\cos \theta + c^2) + b^2 \sin^2 \theta$ Expand the perfect square.

$\quad = b^2 \cos^2 \theta + b^2 \sin^2 \theta + c^2 - 2bc\cos \theta$ Group terms noting that $\cos^2 \theta + \sin^2 \theta = 1$.

$\quad = b^2(\cos^2 \theta + \sin^2 \theta) + c^2 - 2bc\cos \theta$ Factor out b^2.

$$a^2 = b^2 + c^2 - 2bc\cos \theta$$

The formula derived is one of the three equations of the Law of Cosines. The other equations are found in a similar fashion.

Keep in mind that it is always helpful to sketch the triangle when solving for angles or sides. In a real-world scenario, try to draw a diagram of the situation. As more information emerges, the diagram may have to be altered. Make those alterations to the diagram and, in the end, the problem will be easier to solve.

Law of Cosines

The **Law of Cosines** states that the square of any side of a triangle is equal to the sum of the squares of the other two sides minus twice the product of the other two sides and the cosine of the included angle. For triangles labeled as in **Figure 3**, with angles α, β, and γ, and opposite corresponding sides a, b, and c, respectively, the Law of Cosines is given as three equations.

$a^2 = b^2 + c^2 - 2bc \cos \alpha$

$b^2 = a^2 + c^2 - 2ac \cos \beta$

$c^2 = a^2 + b^2 - 2ab \cos \gamma$

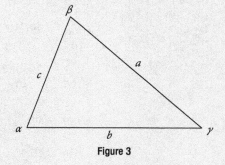

Figure 3

To solve for a missing side measurement, the corresponding opposite angle measure is needed.

When solving for an angle, the corresponding opposite side measure is needed. We can use another version of the Law of Cosines to solve for an angle.

$$\cos \alpha = \frac{b^2 + c^2 - a^2}{2bc} \qquad \cos \beta = \frac{a^2 + c^2 - b^2}{2ac} \qquad \cos \gamma = \frac{a^2 + b^2 - c^2}{2ab}$$

How To...

Given two sides and the angle between them (SAS), find the measures of the remaining side and angles of a triangle.

1. Sketch the triangle. Identify the measures of the known sides and angles. Use variables to represent the measures of the unknown sides and angles.

2. Apply the Law of Cosines to find the length of the unknown side or angle.

3. Apply the Law of Sines or Cosines to find the measure of a second angle.

4. Compute the measure of the remaining angle.

Example 1　**Finding the Unknown Side and Angles of a SAS Triangle**

Find the unknown side and angles of the triangle in **Figure 4**.

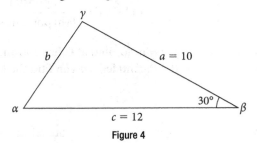

Figure 4

Solution　First, make note of what is given: two sides and the angle between them. This arrangement is classified as SAS and supplies the data needed to apply the Law of Cosines.

Each one of the three laws of cosines begins with the square of an unknown side opposite a known angle. For this example, the first side to solve for is side b, as we know the measurement of the opposite angle β.

$$b^2 = a^2 + c^2 - 2ac\cos\beta$$

$$b^2 = 10^2 + 12^2 - 2(10)(12)\cos(30°) \qquad \text{Substitute the measurements for the known quantities.}$$

$$b^2 = 100 + 144 - 240\left(\frac{\sqrt{3}}{2}\right) \qquad \text{Evaluate the cosine and begin to simplify.}$$

$$b^2 = 244 - 120\sqrt{3}$$

$$b = \sqrt{244 - 120\sqrt{3}} \qquad \text{Use the square root property.}$$

$$b \approx 6.013$$

Because we are solving for a length, we use only the positive square root. Now that we know the length b, we can use the Law of Sines to fill in the remaining angles of the triangle. Solving for angle α, we have

$$\frac{\sin\alpha}{a} = \frac{\sin\beta}{b}$$

$$\frac{\sin\alpha}{10} = \frac{\sin(30°)}{6.013}$$

$$\sin\alpha = \frac{10\sin(30°)}{6.013} \qquad \text{Multiply both sides of the equation by 10.}$$

$$\alpha = \sin^{-1}\left(\frac{10\sin(30°)}{6.013)}\right) \qquad \text{Find the inverse sine of } \frac{10\sin(30°)}{6.013}.$$

$$\alpha \approx 56.3°$$

The other possibility for α would be $\alpha = 180° - 56.3° \approx 123.7°$. In the original diagram, α is adjacent to the longest side, so α is an acute angle and, therefore, 123.7° does not make sense. Notice that if we choose to apply the Law of Cosines, we arrive at a unique answer. We do not have to consider the other possibilities, as cosine is unique for angles between 0° and 180°. Proceeding with $\alpha \approx 56.3°$, we can then find the third angle of the triangle.

$$\gamma = 180° - 30° - 56.3° \approx 93.7°$$

The complete set of angles and sides is

$$\alpha \approx 56.3° \qquad\qquad a = 10$$
$$\beta = 30° \qquad\qquad b \approx 6.013$$
$$\gamma \approx 93.7° \qquad\qquad c = 12$$

Try It #1

Find the missing side and angles of the given triangle: $\alpha = 30°$, $b = 12$, $c = 24$.

Example 2　**Solving for an Angle of a SSS Triangle**

Find the angle α for the given triangle if side $a = 20$, side $b = 25$, and side $c = 18$.

Solution　For this example, we have no angles. We can solve for any angle using the Law of Cosines. To solve for angle α, we have

$$a^2 = b^2 + c^2 - 2bc\cos\alpha$$

$$20^2 = 25^2 + 18^2 - 2(25)(18)\cos\alpha \qquad \text{Substitute the appropriate measurements.}$$

$$400 = 625 + 324 - 900\cos\alpha \qquad \text{Simplify in each step.}$$

$$400 = 949 - 900\cos\alpha$$

$$-549 = -900\cos\alpha \qquad\qquad \text{Isolate } \cos\alpha.$$

$$\frac{-549}{-900} = \cos\alpha$$

$$0.61 \approx \cos\alpha$$

$$\cos^{-1}(0.61) \approx \alpha \qquad\qquad \text{Find the inverse cosine.}$$

$$\alpha \approx 52.4°$$

See **Figure 5**.

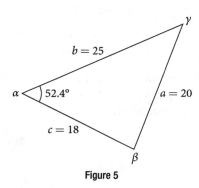

Figure 5

Analysis　*Because the inverse cosine can return any angle between 0 and 180 degrees, there will not be any ambiguous cases using this method.*

Try It #2

Given $a = 5$, $b = 7$, and $c = 10$, find the missing angles.

Solving Applied Problems Using the Law of Cosines

Just as the Law of Sines provided the appropriate equations to solve a number of applications, the Law of Cosines is applicable to situations in which the given data fits the cosine models. We may see these in the fields of navigation, surveying, astronomy, and geometry, just to name a few.

Example 3　**Using the Law of Cosines to Solve a Communication Problem**

On many cell phones with GPS, an approximate location can be given before the GPS signal is received. This is accomplished through a process called triangulation, which works by using the distances from two known points. Suppose there are two cell phone towers within range of a cell phone. The two towers are located 6,000 feet apart along a straight highway, running east to west, and the cell phone is north of the highway. Based on the signal delay, it can be determined that the signal is 5,050 feet from the first tower and 2,420 feet from the second tower. Determine the position of the cell phone north and east of the first tower, and determine how far it is from the highway.

Solution   For simplicity, we start by drawing a diagram similar to **Figure 6** and labeling our given information.

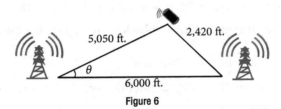

Figure 6

Using the Law of Cosines, we can solve for the angle θ. Remember that the Law of Cosines uses the square of one side to find the cosine of the opposite angle. For this example, let $a = 2420$, $b = 5050$, and $c = 6000$. Thus, θ corresponds to the opposite side $a = 2420$.

$$a^2 = b^2 + c^2 - 2bc\cos\theta$$

$$(2420)^2 = (5050)^2 + (6000)^2 - 2(5050)(6000)\cos\theta$$

$$(2420)^2 - (5050)^2 - (6000)^2 = -2(5050)(6000)\cos\theta$$

$$\frac{(2420)^2 - (5050)^2 - (6000)^2}{-2(5050)(6000)} = \cos\theta$$

$$\cos\theta \approx 0.9183$$

$$\theta \approx \cos^{-1}(0.9183)$$

$$\theta \approx 23.3°$$

To answer the questions about the phone's position north and east of the tower, and the distance to the highway, drop a perpendicular from the position of the cell phone, as in **Figure 7**. This forms two right triangles, although we only need the right triangle that includes the first tower for this problem.

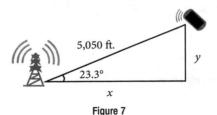

Figure 7

Using the angle $\theta = 23.3°$ and the basic trigonometric identities, we can find the solutions. Thus

$$\cos(23.3°) = \frac{x}{5050}$$

$$x = 5050\cos(23.3°)$$

$$x \approx 4638.15 \text{ feet}$$

$$\sin(23.3°) = \frac{y}{5050}$$

$$y = 5050\sin(23.3°)$$

$$y \approx 1997.5 \text{ feet}$$

The cell phone is approximately 4,638 feet east and 1,998 feet north of the first tower, and 1,998 feet from the highway.

Example 4   **Calculating Distance Traveled Using a SAS Triangle**

Returning to our problem at the beginning of this section, suppose a boat leaves port, travels 10 miles, turns 20 degrees, and travels another 8 miles. How far from port is the boat? The diagram is repeated here in **Figure 8**.

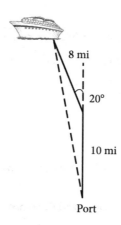

Figure 8

Solution   The boat turned 20 degrees, so the obtuse angle of the non-right triangle is the supplemental angle, $180° - 20° = 160°$. With this, we can utilize the Law of Cosines to find the missing side of the obtuse triangle—the distance of the boat to the port.

$$x^2 = 8^2 + 10^2 - 2(8)(10)\cos(160°)$$
$$x^2 = 314.35$$
$$x = \sqrt{314.35}$$
$$x \approx 17.7 \text{ miles}$$

The boat is about 17.7 miles from port.

Using Heron's Formula to Find the Area of a Triangle

We already learned how to find the area of an oblique triangle when we know two sides and an angle. We also know the formula to find the area of a triangle using the base and the height. When we know the three sides, however, we can use Heron's formula instead of finding the height. Heron of Alexandria was a geometer who lived during the first century A.D. He discovered a formula for finding the area of oblique triangles when three sides are known.

Heron's formula

Heron's formula finds the area of oblique triangles in which sides a, b, and c are known.

$$\text{Area} = \sqrt{s(s-a)(s-b)(s-c)}$$

where $s = \dfrac{(a+b+c)}{2}$ is one half of the perimeter of the triangle, sometimes called the semi-perimeter.

Example 5   **Using Heron's Formula to Find the Area of a Given Triangle**

Find the area of the triangle in **Figure 9** using Heron's formula.

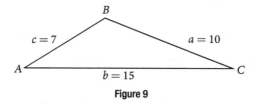

Figure 9

Solution   First, we calculate s.

$$s = \frac{(a+b+c)}{2}$$
$$s = \frac{(10+15+7)}{2} = 16$$

Then we apply the formula.

$$\text{Area} = \sqrt{s(s-a)(s-b)(s-c)}$$
$$\text{Area} = \sqrt{16(16-10)(16-15)(16-7)}$$
$$\text{Area} \approx 29.4$$

The area is approximately 29.4 square units.

Try It #3

Use Heron's formula to find the area of a triangle with sides of lengths $a = 29.7$ ft, $b = 42.3$ ft, and $c = 38.4$ ft.

Example 6   **Applying Heron's Formula to a Real-World Problem**

A Chicago city developer wants to construct a building consisting of artist's lofts on a triangular lot bordered by Rush Street, Wabash Avenue, and Pearson Street. The frontage along Rush Street is approximately 62.4 meters, along Wabash Avenue it is approximately 43.5 meters, and along Pearson Street it is approximately 34.1 meters. How many square meters are available to the developer? See **Figure 10** for a view of the city property.

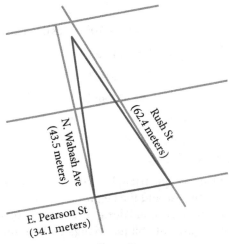

Figure 10

Solution   Find the measurement for s, which is one-half of the perimeter.

$$s = \frac{62.4 + 43.5 + 34.1}{2}$$
$$s = 70 \text{ m}$$

Apply Heron's formula.

$$\text{Area} = \sqrt{70(70-62.4)(70-43.5)(70-34.1)}$$
$$\text{Area} = \sqrt{506,118.2}$$
$$\text{Area} \approx 711.4$$

The developer has about 711.4 square meters.

Try It #4

Find the area of a triangle given $a = 4.38$ ft , $b = 3.79$ ft, and $c = 5.22$ ft.

Access these online resources for additional instruction and practice with the Law of Cosines.

- Law of Cosines (http://openstaxcollege.org/l/lawcosines)
- Law of Cosines: Applications (http://openstaxcollege.org/l/cosineapp)
- Law of Cosines: Applications 2 (http://openstaxcollege.org/l/cosineapp2)

10.2 SECTION EXERCISES

VERBAL

1. If you are looking for a missing side of a triangle, what do you need to know when using the Law of Cosines?

2. If you are looking for a missing angle of a triangle, what do you need to know when using the Law of Cosines?

3. Explain what s represents in Heron's formula.

4. Explain the relationship between the Pythagorean Theorem and the Law of Cosines.

5. When must you use the Law of Cosines instead of the Pythagorean Theorem?

ALGEBRAIC

For the following exercises, assume α is opposite side a, β is opposite side b, and γ is opposite side c. If possible, solve each triangle for the unknown side. Round to the nearest tenth.

6. $\gamma = 41.2°$, $a = 2.49$, $b = 3.13$

7. $\alpha = 120°$, $b = 6$, $c = 7$

8. $\beta = 58.7°$, $a = 10.6$, $c = 15.7$

9. $\gamma = 115°$, $a = 18$, $b = 23$

10. $\alpha = 119°$, $a = 26$, $b = 14$

11. $\gamma = 113°$, $b = 10$, $c = 32$

12. $\beta = 67°$, $a = 49$, $b = 38$

13. $\alpha = 43.1°$, $a = 184.2$, $b = 242.8$

14. $\alpha = 36.6°$, $a = 186.2$, $b = 242.2$

15. $\beta = 50°$, $a = 105$, $b = 45$

For the following exercises, use the Law of Cosines to solve for the missing angle of the oblique triangle. Round to the nearest tenth.

16. $a = 42$, $b = 19$, $c = 30$; find angle A.

17. $a = 14$, $b = 13$, $c = 20$; find angle C.

18. $a = 16$, $b = 31$, $c = 20$; find angle B.

19. $a = 13$, $b = 22$, $c = 28$; find angle A.

20. $a = 108$, $b = 132$, $c = 160$; find angle C.

For the following exercises, solve the triangle. Round to the nearest tenth.

21. $A = 35°$, $b = 8$, $c = 11$

22. $B = 88°$, $a = 4.4$, $c = 5.2$

23. $C = 121°$, $a = 21$, $b = 37$

24. $a = 13$, $b = 11$, $c = 15$

25. $a = 3.1$, $b = 3.5$, $c = 5$

26. $a = 51$, $b = 25$, $c = 29$

For the following exercises, use Heron's formula to find the area of the triangle. Round to the nearest hundredth.

27. Find the area of a triangle with sides of length 18 in, 21 in, and 32 in. Round to the nearest tenth.

28. Find the area of a triangle with sides of length 20 cm, 26 cm, and 37 cm. Round to the nearest tenth.

29. $a = \dfrac{1}{2}\, m$, $b = \dfrac{1}{3}\, m$, $c = \dfrac{1}{4}\, m$

30. $a = 12.4$ ft, $b = 13.7$ ft, $c = 20.2$ ft

31. $a = 1.6$ yd, $b = 2.6$ yd, $c = 4.1$ yd

GRAPHICAL

For the following exercises, find the length of side x. Round to the nearest tenth.

32.

33.

34.

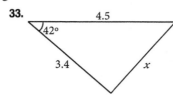

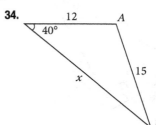

35.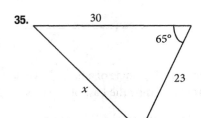

36.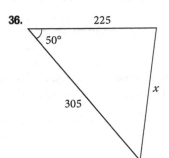

37.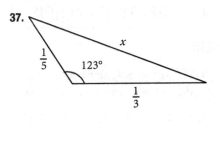

For the following exercises, find the measurement of angle *A*.

38.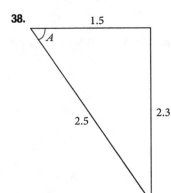

39.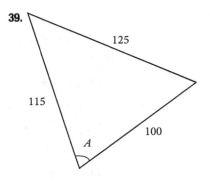

40.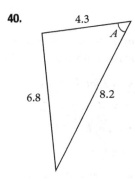

41.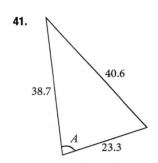

42. Find the measure of each angle in the triangle shown in **Figure 11**. Round to the nearest tenth.

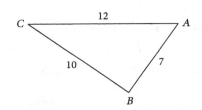

Figure 11

For the following exercises, solve for the unknown side. Round to the nearest tenth.

43.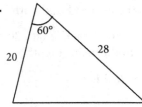

44.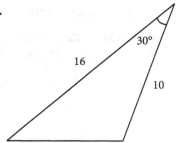

45.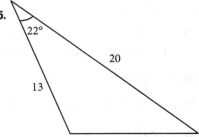

46.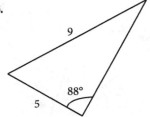

For the following exercises, find the area of the triangle. Round to the nearest hundredth.

47.

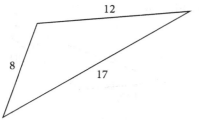

48.

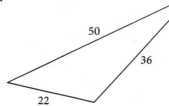

49.

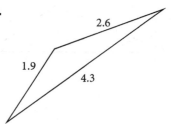

50.

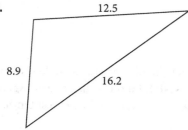

51.

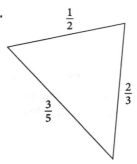

EXTENSIONS

52. A parallelogram has sides of length 16 units and 10 units. The shorter diagonal is 12 units. Find the measure of the longer diagonal.

53. The sides of a parallelogram are 11 feet and 17 feet. The longer diagonal is 22 feet. Find the length of the shorter diagonal.

54. The sides of a parallelogram are 28 centimeters and 40 centimeters. The measure of the larger angle is 100°. Find the length of the shorter diagonal.

55. A regular octagon is inscribed in a circle with a radius of 8 inches. (See **Figure 12**.) Find the perimeter of the octagon.

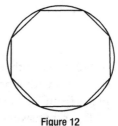

Figure 12

56. A regular pentagon is inscribed in a circle of radius 12 cm. (See **Figure 13**.) Find the perimeter of the pentagon. Round to the nearest tenth of a centimeter.

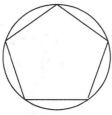

Figure 13

For the following exercises, suppose that $x^2 = 25 + 36 - 60 \cos(52)$ represents the relationship of three sides of a triangle and the cosine of an angle.

57. Draw the triangle.

58. Find the length of the third side.

For the following exercises, find the area of the triangle.

59.

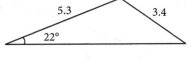

60.

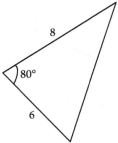

61.

REAL-WORLD APPLICATIONS

62. A surveyor has taken the measurements shown in **Figure 14**. Find the distance across the lake. Round answers to the nearest tenth.

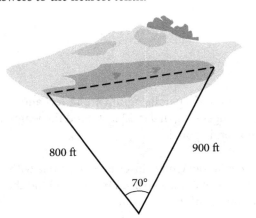

Figure 14

63. A satellite calculates the distances and angle shown in **Figure 15** (not to scale). Find the distance between the two cities. Round answers to the nearest tenth.

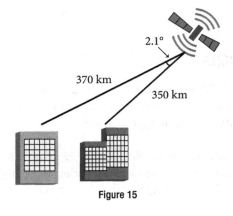

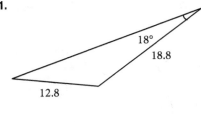

Figure 15

64. An airplane flies 220 miles with a heading of 40°, and then flies 180 miles with a heading of 170°. How far is the plane from its starting point, and at what heading? Round answers to the nearest tenth.

65. A 113-foot tower is located on a hill that is inclined 34° to the horizontal, as shown in **Figure 16**. A guy-wire is to be attached to the top of the tower and anchored at a point 98 feet uphill from the base of the tower. Find the length of wire needed.

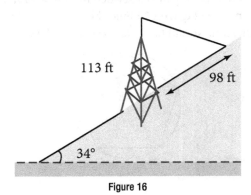

Figure 16

66. Two ships left a port at the same time. One ship traveled at a speed of 18 miles per hour at a heading of 320°. The other ship traveled at a speed of 22 miles per hour at a heading of 194°. Find the distance between the two ships after 10 hours of travel.

67. The graph in **Figure 17** represents two boats departing at the same time from the same dock. The first boat is traveling at 18 miles per hour at a heading of 327° and the second boat is traveling at 4 miles per hour at a heading of 60°. Find the distance between the two boats after 2 hours.

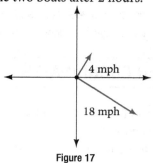

Figure 17

68. A triangular swimming pool measures 40 feet on one side and 65 feet on another side. These sides form an angle that measures 50°. How long is the third side (to the nearest tenth)?

69. A pilot flies in a straight path for 1 hour 30 min. She then makes a course correction, heading 10° to the right of her original course, and flies 2 hours in the new direction. If she maintains a constant speed of 680 miles per hour, how far is she from her starting position?

70. Los Angeles is 1,744 miles from Chicago, Chicago is 714 miles from New York, and New York is 2,451 miles from Los Angeles. Draw a triangle connecting these three cities, and find the angles in the triangle.

71. Philadelphia is 140 miles from Washington, D.C., Washington, D.C. is 442 miles from Boston, and Boston is 315 miles from Philadelphia. Draw a triangle connecting these three cities and find the angles in the triangle.

72. Two planes leave the same airport at the same time. One flies at 20° east of north at 500 miles per hour. The second flies at 30° east of south at 600 miles per hour. How far apart are the planes after 2 hours?

73. Two airplanes take off in different directions. One travels 300 mph due west and the other travels 25° north of west at 420 mph. After 90 minutes, how far apart are they, assuming they are flying at the same altitude?

74. A parallelogram has sides of length 15.4 units and 9.8 units. Its area is 72.9 square units. Find the measure of the longer diagonal.

75. The four sequential sides of a quadrilateral have lengths 4.5 cm, 7.9 cm, 9.4 cm, and 12.9 cm. The angle between the two smallest sides is 117°. What is the area of this quadrilateral?

76. The four sequential sides of a quadrilateral have lengths 5.7 cm, 7.2 cm, 9.4 cm, and 12.8 cm. The angle between the two smallest sides is 106°. What is the area of this quadrilateral?

77. Find the area of a triangular piece of land that measures 30 feet on one side and 42 feet on another; the included angle measures 132°. Round to the nearest whole square foot.

78. Find the area of a triangular piece of land that measures 110 feet on one side and 250 feet on another; the included angle measures 85°. Round to the nearest whole square foot.

LEARNING OBJECTIVES

In this section, you will:

- Plot points using polar coordinates.
- Convert from polar coordinates to rectangular coordinates.
- Convert from rectangular coordinates to polar coordinates.
- Transform equations between polar and rectangular forms.
- Identify and graph polar equations by converting to rectangular equations.

10.3   POLAR COORDINATES

Over 12 kilometers from port, a sailboat encounters rough weather and is blown off course by a 16-knot wind (see **Figure 1**). How can the sailor indicate his location to the Coast Guard? In this section, we will investigate a method of representing location that is different from a standard coordinate grid.

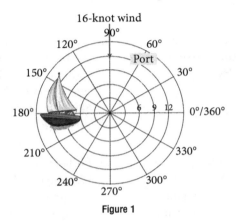

Figure 1

Plotting Points Using Polar Coordinates

When we think about plotting points in the plane, we usually think of rectangular coordinates (x, y) in the Cartesian coordinate plane. However, there are other ways of writing a coordinate pair and other types of grid systems. In this section, we introduce to **polar coordinates**, which are points labeled (r, θ) and plotted on a polar grid. The polar grid is represented as a series of concentric circles radiating out from the **pole**, or the origin of the coordinate plane.

The polar grid is scaled as the unit circle with the positive x-axis now viewed as the **polar axis** and the origin as the pole. The first coordinate r is the radius or length of the directed line segment from the pole. The angle θ, measured in radians, indicates the direction of r. We move counterclockwise from the polar axis by an angle of θ, and measure a directed line segment the length of r in the direction of θ. Even though we measure θ first and then r, the polar point is written with the r-coordinate first. For example, to plot the point $\left(2, \dfrac{\pi}{4}\right)$, we would move $\dfrac{\pi}{4}$ units in the counterclockwise direction and then a length of 2 from the pole. This point is plotted on the grid in **Figure 2**.

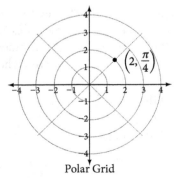

Polar Grid

Figure 2

Example 1   **Plotting a Point on the Polar Grid**

Plot the point $\left(3, \frac{\pi}{2}\right)$ on the polar grid.

Solution   The angle $\frac{\pi}{2}$ is found by sweeping in a counterclockwise direction 90° from the polar axis. The point is located at a length of 3 units from the pole in the $\frac{\pi}{2}$ direction, as shown in **Figure 3**.

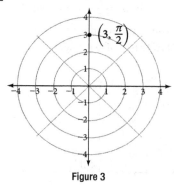

Figure 3

Try It #1

Plot the point $\left(2, \frac{\pi}{3}\right)$ in the polar grid.

Example 2   **Plotting a Point in the Polar Coordinate System with a Negative Component**

Plot the point $\left(-2, \frac{\pi}{6}\right)$ on the polar grid.

Solution   We know that $\frac{\pi}{6}$ is located in the first quadrant. However, $r = -2$. We can approach plotting a point with a negative r in two ways:

1.   Plot the point $\left(2, \frac{\pi}{6}\right)$ by moving $\frac{\pi}{6}$ in the counterclockwise direction and extending a directed line segment 2 units into the first quadrant. Then retrace the directed line segment back through the pole, and continue 2 units into the third quadrant;

2.   Move $\frac{\pi}{6}$ in the counterclockwise direction, and draw the directed line segment from the pole 2 units in the negative direction, into the third quadrant.

See **Figure 4(a)**. Compare this to the graph of the polar coordinate $\left(2, \frac{\pi}{6}\right)$ shown in **Figure 4(b)**.

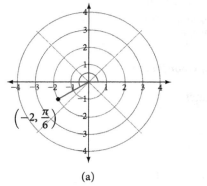

(a)   (b)

Figure 4

Try It #2

Plot the points $\left(3, -\frac{\pi}{6}\right)$ and $\left(2, \frac{9\pi}{4}\right)$ on the same polar grid.

Converting from Polar Coordinates to Rectangular Coordinates

When given a set of polar coordinates, we may need to convert them to rectangular coordinates. To do so, we can recall the relationships that exist among the variables x, y, r, and θ.

$$\cos \theta = \frac{x}{r} \rightarrow x = r\cos \theta$$
$$\sin \theta = \frac{y}{r} \rightarrow y = r\sin \theta$$

Dropping a perpendicular from the point in the plane to the x-axis forms a right triangle, as illustrated in **Figure 5**. An easy way to remember the equations above is to think of $\cos \theta$ as the adjacent side over the hypotenuse and $\sin \theta$ as the opposite side over the hypotenuse.

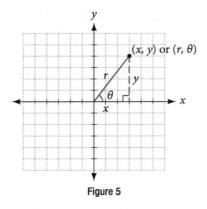

Figure 5

---

converting from polar coordinates to rectangular coordinates

To convert polar coordinates (r, θ) to rectangular coordinates (x, y), let

$$\cos \theta = \frac{x}{r} \rightarrow x = r\cos \theta$$

$$\sin \theta = \frac{y}{r} \rightarrow y = r\sin \theta$$

How To…

Given polar coordinates, convert to rectangular coordinates.

1. Given the polar coordinate (r, θ), write $x = r\cos \theta$ and $y = r\sin \theta$.
2. Evaluate $\cos \theta$ and $\sin \theta$.
3. Multiply $\cos \theta$ by r to find the x-coordinate of the rectangular form.
4. Multiply $\sin \theta$ by r to find the y-coordinate of the rectangular form.

Example 3   **Writing Polar Coordinates as Rectangular Coordinates**

Write the polar coordinates $\left(3, \frac{\pi}{2}\right)$ as rectangular coordinates.

Solution   Use the equivalent relationships.

$$x = r\cos \theta$$

$$x = 3\cos \frac{\pi}{2} = 0$$

$$y = r\sin \theta$$

$$y = 3\sin \frac{\pi}{2} = 3$$

The rectangular coordinates are (0, 3). See **Figure 6**.

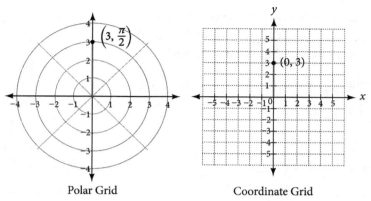

Polar Grid   Coordinate Grid

Figure 6

Example 4   **Writing Polar Coordinates as Rectangular Coordinates**

Write the polar coordinates $(-2, 0)$ as rectangular coordinates.

Solution   See **Figure 7**. Writing the polar coordinates as rectangular, we have

$$x = r\cos\theta$$
$$x = -2\cos(0) = -2$$
$$y = r\sin\theta$$
$$y = -2\sin(0) = 0$$

The rectangular coordinates are also $(-2, 0)$.

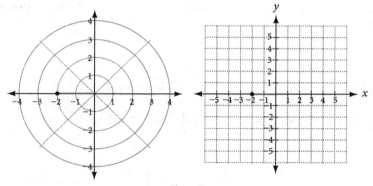

Figure 7

Try It #3

Write the polar coordinates $\left(-1, \dfrac{2\pi}{3}\right)$ as rectangular coordinates.

Converting from Rectangular Coordinates to Polar Coordinates

To convert rectangular coordinates to polar coordinates, we will use two other familiar relationships. With this conversion, however, we need to be aware that a set of rectangular coordinates will yield more than one polar point.

---

converting from rectangular coordinates to polar coordinates

Converting from rectangular coordinates to polar coordinates requires the use of one or more of the relationships illustrated in **Figure 8**.

$$\cos \theta = \frac{x}{r} \text{ or } x = r\cos \theta$$

$$\sin \theta = \frac{y}{r} \text{ or } y = r\sin \theta$$

$$r^2 = x^2 + y^2$$

$$\tan \theta = \frac{y}{x}$$

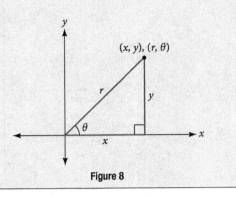

Figure 8

Example 5   **Writing Rectangular Coordinates as Polar Coordinates**

Convert the rectangular coordinates (3, 3) to polar coordinates.

Solution   We see that the original point (3, 3) is in the first quadrant. To find θ, use the formula $\tan \theta = \frac{y}{x}$. This gives

$$\tan \theta = \frac{3}{3}$$

$$\tan \theta = 1$$

$$\theta = \tan^{-1}(1)$$

$$\theta = \frac{\pi}{4}$$

To find r, we substitute the values for x and y into the formula $r = \sqrt{x^2 + y^2}$. We know that r must be positive, as $\frac{\pi}{4}$ is in the first quadrant. Thus

$$r = \sqrt{3^2 + 3^2}$$

$$r = \sqrt{9 + 9}$$

$$r = \sqrt{18} = 3\sqrt{2}$$

So, $r = 3\sqrt{2}$ and $\theta = \frac{\pi}{4}$, giving us the polar point $\left(3\sqrt{2}, \frac{\pi}{4}\right)$. See **Figure 9**.

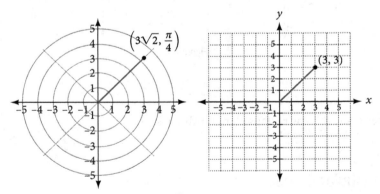

Figure 9

Analysis *There are other sets of polar coordinates that will be the same as our first solution. For example, the points* $\left(-3\sqrt{2}, \frac{5\pi}{4}\right)$ *and* $\left(3\sqrt{2}, -\frac{7\pi}{4}\right)$ *and will coincide with the original solution of* $\left(3\sqrt{2}, \frac{\pi}{4}\right)$. *The point* $\left(-3\sqrt{2}, \frac{5\pi}{4}\right)$ *indicates a move further counterclockwise by* π, *which is directly opposite* $\frac{\pi}{4}$. *The radius is expressed as* $-3\sqrt{2}$. *However, the angle* $\frac{5\pi}{4}$ *is located in the third quadrant and, as r is negative, we extend the directed line segment in the opposite direction, into the first quadrant. This is the same point as* $\left(3\sqrt{2}, \frac{\pi}{4}\right)$. *The point* $\left(3\sqrt{2}, -\frac{7\pi}{4}\right)$ *is a move further clockwise by* $-\frac{7\pi}{4}$, *from* $\frac{\pi}{4}$. *The radius,* $3\sqrt{2}$, *is the same.*

Transforming Equations between Polar and Rectangular Forms

We can now convert coordinates between polar and rectangular form. Converting equations can be more difficult, but it can be beneficial to be able to convert between the two forms. Since there are a number of polar equations that cannot be expressed clearly in Cartesian form, and vice versa, we can use the same procedures we used to convert points between the coordinate systems. We can then use a graphing calculator to graph either the rectangular form or the polar form of the equation.

How To...

Given an equation in polar form, graph it using a graphing calculator.

1. Change the **MODE** to **POL**, representing polar form.
2. Press the **Y=** button to bring up a screen allowing the input of six equations: $r_1, r_2, \ldots, r_6$.
3. Enter the polar equation, set equal to r.
4. Press **GRAPH**.

Example 6 Writing a Cartesian Equation in Polar Form

Write the Cartesian equation $x^2 + y^2 = 9$ in polar form.

Solution The goal is to eliminate x and y from the equation and introduce r and θ. Ideally, we would write the equation r as a function of θ. To obtain the polar form, we will use the relationships between (x, y) and (r, θ). Since $x = r\cos \theta$ and $y = r\sin \theta$, we can substitute and solve for r.

$$(r\cos \theta)^2 + (r\sin \theta)^2 = 9$$
$$r^2\cos^2 \theta + r^2 \sin^2 \theta = 9$$
$$r^2(\cos^2 \theta + \sin^2 \theta) = 9$$
$$r^2(1) = 9 \qquad \text{Substitute } \cos^2 \theta + \sin^2 \theta = 1.$$
$$r = \pm 3 \qquad \text{Use the square root property.}$$

Thus, $x^2 + y^2 = 9$, $r = 3$, and $r = -3$ should generate the same graph. See **Figure 10**.

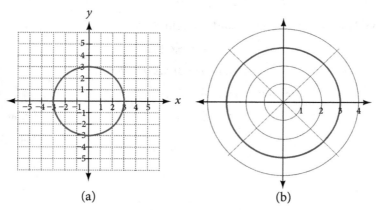

(a)   (b)

Figure 10 (a) Cartesian form $x^2 + y^2 = 9$ (b) Polar form $r = 3$

To graph a circle in rectangular form, we must first solve for y.

$$x^2 + y^2 = 9$$
$$y^2 = 9 - x^2$$
$$y = \pm \sqrt{9 - x^2}$$

Note that this is two separate functions, since a circle fails the vertical line test. Therefore, we need to enter the positive and negative square roots into the calculator separately, as two equations in the form $Y_1 = \sqrt{9 - x^2}$ and $Y_2 = -\sqrt{9 - x^2}$. Press **GRAPH**.

Example 7   **Rewriting a Cartesian Equation as a Polar Equation**

Rewrite the Cartesian equation $x^2 + y^2 = 6y$ as a polar equation.

Solution   This equation appears similar to the previous example, but it requires different steps to convert the equation. We can still follow the same procedures we have already learned and make the following substitutions:

$$r^2 = 6y \qquad \text{Use } x^2 + y^2 = r^2.$$
$$r^2 = 6r\sin\theta \qquad \text{Substitute } y = r\sin\theta.$$
$$r^2 - 6r\sin\theta = 0 \qquad \text{Set equal to 0.}$$
$$r(r - 6\sin\theta) = 0 \qquad \text{Factor and solve.}$$
$$r = 0 \qquad \text{We reject } r = 0, \text{ as it only represents one point, } (0, 0).$$
$$\text{or } r = 6\sin\theta$$

Therefore, the equations $x^2 + y^2 = 6y$ and $r = 6\sin\theta$ should give us the same graph. See **Figure 11**.

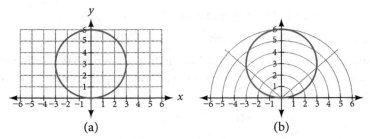

(a)   (b)

Figure 11   (a) Cartesian form $x^2 + y^2 = 6y$ (b) polar form $r = 6\sin\theta$

The Cartesian or rectangular equation is plotted on the rectangular grid, and the polar equation is plotted on the polar grid. Clearly, the graphs are identical.

Example 8   **Rewriting a Cartesian Equation in Polar Form**

Rewrite the Cartesian equation $y = 3x + 2$ as a polar equation.

Solution   We will use the relationships $x = r\cos\theta$ and $y = r\sin\theta$.

$$y = 3x + 2$$
$$r\sin\theta = 3r\cos\theta + 2$$
$$r\sin\theta - 3r\cos\theta = 2$$
$$r(\sin\theta - 3\cos\theta) = 2 \qquad\qquad \text{Isolate } r.$$
$$r = \frac{2}{\sin\theta - 3\cos\theta} \qquad\qquad \text{Solve for } r.$$

Try It #4

Rewrite the Cartesian equation $y^2 = 3 - x^2$ in polar form.

Identify and Graph Polar Equations by Converting to Rectangular Equations

We have learned how to convert rectangular coordinates to polar coordinates, and we have seen that the points are indeed the same. We have also transformed polar equations to rectangular equations and vice versa. Now we will demonstrate that their graphs, while drawn on different grids, are identical.

Example 9 **Graphing a Polar Equation by Converting to a Rectangular Equation**

Covert the polar equation $r = 2\sec\theta$ to a rectangular equation, and draw its corresponding graph.

Solution The conversion is

$$r = 2\sec\theta$$

$$r = \frac{2}{\cos\theta}$$

$$r\cos\theta = 2$$

$$x = 2$$

Notice that the equation $r = 2\sec\theta$ drawn on the polar grid is clearly the same as the vertical line $x = 2$ drawn on the rectangular grid (see **Figure 12**). Just as $x = c$ is the standard form for a vertical line in rectangular form, $r = c\sec\theta$ is the standard form for a vertical line in polar form.

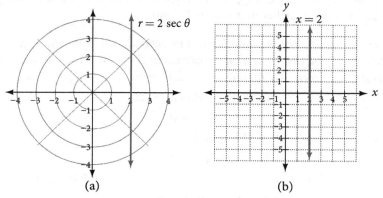

(a)   (b)

Figure 12 (a) Polar grid (b) Rectangular coordinate system

A similar discussion would demonstrate that the graph of the function $r = 2\csc\theta$ will be the horizontal line $y = 2$. In fact, $r = c\csc\theta$ is the standard form for a horizontal line in polar form, corresponding to the rectangular form $y = c$.

Example 10 **Rewriting a Polar Equation in Cartesian Form**

Rewrite the polar equation $r = \dfrac{3}{1 - 2\cos\theta}$ as a Cartesian equation.

Solution The goal is to eliminate θ and r, and introduce x and y. We clear the fraction, and then use substitution. In order to replace r with x and y, we must use the expression $x^2 + y^2 = r^2$.

$$r = \frac{3}{1 - 2\cos\theta}$$

$$r(1 - 2\cos\theta) = 3$$

$$r\left(1 - 2\left(\frac{x}{r}\right)\right) = 3 \qquad \text{Use } \cos\theta = \frac{x}{r} \text{ to eliminate } \theta.$$

$$r - 2x = 3$$

$$r = 3 + 2x \qquad \text{Isolate } r.$$

$$r^2 = (3 + 2x)^2 \qquad \text{Square both sides.}$$

$$x^2 + y^2 = (3 + 2x)^2 \qquad \text{Use } x^2 + y^2 = r^2.$$

The Cartesian equation is $x^2 + y^2 = (3 + 2x)^2$. However, to graph it, especially using a graphing calculator or computer program, we want to isolate y.

$$x^2 + y^2 = (3 + 2x)^2$$

$$y^2 = (3 + 2x)^2 - x^2$$

$$y = \pm\sqrt{(3 + 2x)^2 - x^2}$$

When our entire equation has been changed from r and θ to x and y, we can stop, unless asked to solve for y or simplify. See **Figure 13**.

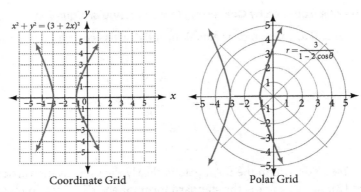

Figure 13

The "hour-glass" shape of the graph is called a *hyperbola*. Hyperbolas have many interesting geometric features and applications, which we will investigate further in **Analytic Geometry**.

Analysis   In this example, the right side of the equation can be expanded and the equation simplified further, as shown above. However, the equation cannot be written as a single function in Cartesian form. We may wish to write the rectangular equation in the hyperbola's standard form. To do this, we can start with the initial equation.

$$x^2 + y^2 = (3 + 2x)^2$$

$$x^2 + y^2 - (3 + 2x)^2 = 0$$

$$x^2 + y^2 - (9 + 12x + 4x^2) = 0$$

$$x^2 + y^2 - 9 - 12x - 4x^2 = 0$$

$$-3x^2 - 12x + y^2 = 9 \qquad \text{Multiply through by } -1.$$

$$3x^2 + 12x - y^2 = -9$$

$$3(x^2 + 4x +) - y^2 = -9 \qquad \text{Organize terms to complete the square for } x.$$

$$3(x^2 + 4x + 4) - y^2 = -9 + 12$$

$$3(x + 2)^2 - y^2 = 3$$

$$(x + 2)^2 - \frac{y^2}{3} = 1$$

Try It #5

Rewrite the polar equation $r = 2\sin\theta$ in Cartesian form.

Example 11   **Rewriting a Polar Equation in Cartesian Form**

Rewrite the polar equation $r = \sin(2\theta)$ in Cartesian form.

Solution

$$r = \sin(2\theta) \qquad \text{Use the double angle identity for sine.}$$

$$r = 2\sin\theta\cos\theta \qquad \text{Use } \cos\theta = \frac{x}{r} \text{ and } \sin\theta = \frac{y}{r}.$$

$$r = 2\left(\frac{x}{r}\right)\left(\frac{y}{r}\right) \qquad \text{Simplify.}$$

$$r = \frac{2xy}{r^2} \qquad \text{Multiply both sides by } r^2.$$

$$r^3 = 2xy$$

$$\left(\sqrt{x^2 + y^2}\right)^3 = 2xy \qquad \text{As } x^2 + y^2 = r^2, r = \sqrt{x^2 + y^2}.$$

This equation can also be written as

$$(x^2 + y^2)^{\frac{3}{2}} = 2xy \text{ or } x^2 + y^2 = (2xy)^{\frac{2}{3}}.$$

Access these online resources for additional instruction and practice with polar coordinates.

- Introduction to Polar Coordinates (http://openstaxcollege.org/l/intropolar)
- Comparing Polar and Rectangular Coordinates (http://openstaxcollege.org/l/polarrect)

10.3 SECTION EXERCISES

VERBAL

1. How are polar coordinates different from rectangular coordinates?

2. How are the polar axes different from the x- and y-axes of the Cartesian plane?

3. Explain how polar coordinates are graphed.

4. How are the points $\left(3, \frac{\pi}{2}\right)$ and $\left(-3, \frac{\pi}{2}\right)$ related?

5. Explain why the points $\left(-3, \frac{\pi}{2}\right)$ and $\left(3, -\frac{\pi}{2}\right)$ are the same.

ALGEBRAIC

For the following exercises, convert the given polar coordinates to Cartesian coordinates with $r > 0$ and $0 \leq \theta \leq 2\pi$. Remember to consider the quadrant in which the given point is located when determining θ for the point.

6. $\left(7, \frac{7\pi}{6}\right)$ **7.** $(5, \pi)$ **8.** $\left(6, -\frac{\pi}{4}\right)$ **9.** $\left(-3, \frac{\pi}{6}\right)$ **10.** $\left(4, \frac{7\pi}{4}\right)$

For the following exercises, convert the given Cartesian coordinates to polar coordinates with $r > 0$, $0 \leq \theta < 2\pi$. Remember to consider the quadrant in which the given point is located.

11. $(4, 2)$ **12.** $(-4, 6)$ **13.** $(3, -5)$ **14.** $(-10, -13)$ **15.** $(8, 8)$

For the following exercises, convert the given Cartesian equation to a polar equation.

16. $x = 3$ **17.** $y = 4$ **18.** $y = 4x^2$ **19.** $y = 2x^4$

20. $x^2 + y^2 = 4y$ **21.** $x^2 + y^2 = 3x$ **22.** $x^2 - y^2 = x$ **23.** $x^2 - y^2 = 3y$

24. $x^2 + y^2 = 9$ **25.** $x^2 = 9y$ **26.** $y^2 = 9x$ **27.** $9xy = 1$

For the following exercises, convert the given polar equation to a Cartesian equation. Write in the standard form of a conic if possible, and identify the conic section represented.

28. $r = 3\sin\theta$ **29.** $r = 4\cos\theta$ **30.** $r = \dfrac{4}{\sin\theta + 7\cos\theta}$ **31.** $r = \dfrac{6}{\cos\theta + 3\sin\theta}$

32. $r = 2\sec\theta$ **33.** $r = 3\csc\theta$ **34.** $r = \sqrt{r\cos\theta + 2}$ **35.** $r^2 = 4\sec\theta\csc\theta$

36. $r = 4$ **37.** $r^2 = 4$ **38.** $r = \dfrac{1}{4\cos\theta - 3\sin\theta}$ **39.** $r = \dfrac{3}{\cos\theta - 5\sin\theta}$

GRAPHICAL

For the following exercises, find the polar coordinates of the point.

40.

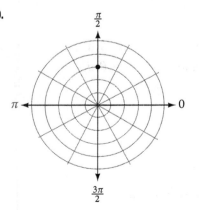

41.

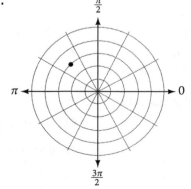

42.

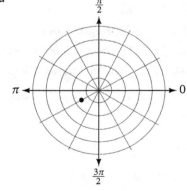

43.

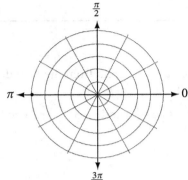

44.

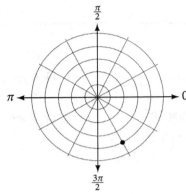

For the following exercises, plot the points.

45. $\left(-2, \dfrac{\pi}{3}\right)$ **46.** $\left(-1, -\dfrac{\pi}{2}\right)$ **47.** $\left(3.5, \dfrac{7\pi}{4}\right)$ **48.** $\left(-4, \dfrac{\pi}{3}\right)$ **49.** $\left(5, \dfrac{\pi}{2}\right)$

50. $\left(4, \dfrac{-5\pi}{4}\right)$ **51.** $\left(3, \dfrac{5\pi}{6}\right)$ **52.** $\left(-1.5, \dfrac{7\pi}{6}\right)$ **53.** $\left(-2, \dfrac{\pi}{4}\right)$ **54.** $\left(1, \dfrac{3\pi}{2}\right)$

For the following exercises, convert the equation from rectangular to polar form and graph on the polar axis.

55. $5x - y = 6$ **56.** $2x + 7y = -3$ **57.** $x^2 + (y - 1)^2 = 1$ **58.** $(x + 2)^2 + (y + 3)^2 = 13$

59. $x = 2$ **60.** $x^2 + y^2 = 5y$ **61.** $x^2 + y^2 = 3x$

For the following exercises, convert the equation from polar to rectangular form and graph on the rectangular plane.

62. $r = 6$ **63.** $r = -4$ **64.** $\theta = -\dfrac{2\pi}{3}$ **65.** $\theta = \dfrac{\pi}{4}$

66. $r = \sec \theta$ **67.** $r = -10\sin \theta$ **68.** $r = 3\cos \theta$

TECHNOLOGY

69. Use a graphing calculator to find the rectangular coordinates of $\left(2, -\dfrac{\pi}{5}\right)$. Round to the nearest thousandth.

70. Use a graphing calculator to find the rectangular coordinates of $\left(-3, \dfrac{3\pi}{7}\right)$. Round to the nearest thousandth.

71. Use a graphing calculator to find the polar coordinates of $(-7, 8)$ in degrees. Round to the nearest thousandth.

72. Use a graphing calculator to find the polar coordinates of $(3, -4)$ in degrees. Round to the nearest hundredth.

73. Use a graphing calculator to find the polar coordinates of $(-2, 0)$ in radians. Round to the nearest hundredth.

EXTENSIONS

74. Describe the graph of $r = a\sec \theta;\ a > 0$.

75. Describe the graph of $r = a\sec \theta;\ a < 0$.

76. Describe the graph of $r = a\csc \theta;\ a > 0$.

77. Describe the graph of $r = a\csc \theta;\ a < 0$.

78. What polar equations will give an oblique line?

For the following exercises, graph the polar inequality.

79. $r < 4$

80. $0 \le \theta \le \dfrac{\pi}{4}$

81. $\theta = \dfrac{\pi}{4}, r \ge 2$

82. $\theta = \dfrac{\pi}{4}, r \ge -3$

83. $0 \le \theta \le \dfrac{\pi}{3}, r < 2$

84. $-\dfrac{\pi}{6} < \theta \le \dfrac{\pi}{3}, -3 < r < 2$

LEARNING OBJECTIVES

In this section, you will:

- Test polar equations for symmetry.
- Graph polar equations by plotting points.

10.4   POLAR COORDINATES: GRAPHS

The planets move through space in elliptical, periodic orbits about the sun, as shown in **Figure 1**. They are in constant motion, so fixing an exact position of any planet is valid only for a moment. In other words, we can fix only a planet's *instantaneous* position. This is one application of polar coordinates, represented as (r, θ). We interpret r as the distance from the sun and θ as the planet's angular bearing, or its direction from a fixed point on the sun. In this section, we will focus on the polar system and the graphs that are generated directly from polar coordinates.

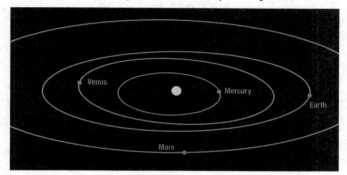

Figure 1 Planets follow elliptical paths as they orbit around the Sun. (credit: modification of work by NASA/JPL-Caltech)

Testing Polar Equations for Symmetry

Just as a rectangular equation such as $y = x^2$ describes the relationship between x and y on a Cartesian grid, a **polar equation** describes a relationship between r and θ on a polar grid. Recall that the coordinate pair (r, θ) indicates that we move counterclockwise from the polar axis (positive x-axis) by an angle of θ, and extend a ray from the pole (origin) r units in the direction of θ. All points that satisfy the polar equation are on the graph.

Symmetry is a property that helps us recognize and plot the graph of any equation. If an equation has a graph that is symmetric with respect to an axis, it means that if we folded the graph in half over that axis, the portion of the graph on one side would coincide with the portion on the other side. By performing three tests, we will see how to apply the properties of symmetry to polar equations. Further, we will use symmetry (in addition to plotting key points, zeros, and maximums of r) to determine the graph of a polar equation.

In the first test, we consider symmetry with respect to the line $\theta = \dfrac{\pi}{2}$ (y-axis). We replace (r, θ) with $(-r, -\theta)$ to determine if the new equation is equivalent to the original equation. For example, suppose we are given the equation $r = 2\sin \theta$;

$$r = 2\sin \theta$$
$$-r = 2\sin(-\theta) \qquad \text{Replace } (r, \theta) \text{ with } (-r, -\theta).$$
$$-r = -2\sin \theta \qquad \text{Identity: } \sin(-\theta) = -\sin \theta.$$
$$r = 2\sin \theta \qquad \text{Multiply both sides by} -1.$$

This equation exhibits symmetry with respect to the line $\theta = \dfrac{\pi}{2}$.

In the second test, we consider symmetry with respect to the polar axis (x-axis). We replace (r, θ) with $(r, -\theta)$ or $(-r, \pi - \theta)$ to determine equivalency between the tested equation and the original. For example, suppose we are given the equation $r = 1 - 2\cos \theta$.

$$r = 1 - 2\cos \theta$$
$$r = 1 - 2\cos(-\theta) \qquad \text{Replace } (r, \theta) \text{ with } (r, -\theta).$$
$$r = 1 - 2\cos \theta \qquad \text{Even/Odd identity}$$

The graph of this equation exhibits symmetry with respect to the polar axis. In the third test, we consider symmetry with respect to the pole (origin). We replace (r, θ) with $(-r, \theta)$ to determine if the tested equation is equivalent to the original equation. For example, suppose we are given the equation $r = 2\sin(3\theta)$.

$$r = 2\sin(3\theta)$$
$$-r = 2\sin(3\theta)$$

The equation has failed the symmetry test, but that does not mean that it is not symmetric with respect to the pole. Passing one or more of the symmetry tests verifies that symmetry will be exhibited in a graph. However, failing the symmetry tests does not necessarily indicate that a graph will not be symmetric about the line $\theta = \frac{\pi}{2}$, the polar axis, or the pole. In these instances, we can confirm that symmetry exists by plotting reflecting points across the apparent axis of symmetry or the pole. Testing for symmetry is a technique that simplifies the graphing of polar equations, but its application is not perfect.

---

symmetry tests

A **polar equation** describes a curve on the polar grid. The graph of a polar equation can be evaluated for three types of symmetry, as shown in **Figure 2**.

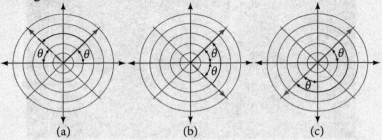

(a)   (b)   (c)

Figure 2 (a) A graph is symmetric with respect to the line $\theta = \frac{\pi}{2}$ (y-axis) if replacing (r, θ) with $(-r, -\theta)$ yields an equivalent equation.
(b) A graph is symmetric with respect to the polar axis (x-axis) if replacing (r, θ) with $(r, -\theta)$ or $(-r, \pi-\theta)$ yields an equivalent equation.
(c) A graph is symmetric with respect to the pole (origin) if replacing (r, θ) with $(-r, \theta)$ yields an equivalent equation.

How To...

Given a polar equation, test for symmetry.

1. Substitute the appropriate combination of components for (r, θ): $(-r, -\theta)$ for $\theta = \frac{\pi}{2}$ symmetry; $(r, -\theta)$ for polar axis symmetry; and $(-r, \theta)$ for symmetry with respect to the pole.
2. If the resulting equations are equivalent in one or more of the tests, the graph produces the expected symmetry.

Example 1   **Testing a Polar Equation for Symmetry**

Test the equation $r = 2\sin\theta$ for symmetry.

Solution   Test for each of the three types of symmetry.

1) Replacing (r, θ) with $(-r, -\theta)$ yields the same result. Thus, the graph is symmetric with respect to the line $\theta = \frac{\pi}{2}$.	$-r = 2\sin(-\theta)$ $-r = -2\sin\theta$ Even-odd identity $r = 2\sin\theta$ Multiply by -1 Passed
2) Replacing θ with $-\theta$ does not yield the same equation. Therefore, the graph fails the test and may or may not be symmetric with respect to the polar axis.	$r = 2\sin(-\theta)$ $r = -2\sin\theta$ Even-odd identity $r = -2\sin\theta \neq 2\sin\theta$ Failed
3) Replacing r with $-r$ changes the equation and fails the test. The graph may or may not be symmetric with respect to the pole.	$-r = 2\sin\theta$ $r = -2\sin\theta \neq 2\sin\theta$ Failed

Table 1

Analysis   Using a graphing calculator, we can see that the equation $r = 2\sin \theta$ is a circle centered at $(0, 1)$ with radius $r = 1$ and is indeed symmetric to the line $\theta = \dfrac{\pi}{2}$. We can also see that the graph is not symmetric with the polar axis or the pole. See **Figure 3**.

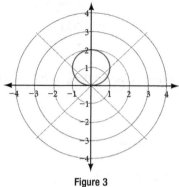

Figure 3

Try It #1

Test the equation for symmetry: $r = -2\cos \theta$.

Graphing Polar Equations by Plotting Points

To graph in the rectangular coordinate system we construct a table of x and y values. To graph in the polar coordinate system we construct a table of θ and r values. We enter values of θ into a polar equation and calculate r. However, using the properties of symmetry and finding key values of θ and r means fewer calculations will be needed.

Finding Zeros and Maxima

To find the zeros of a polar equation, we solve for the values of θ that result in $r = 0$. Recall that, to find the zeros of polynomial functions, we set the equation equal to zero and then solve for x. We use the same process for polar equations. Set $r = 0$, and solve for θ.

For many of the forms we will encounter, the maximum value of a polar equation is found by substituting those values of θ into the equation that result in the maximum value of the trigonometric functions. Consider $r = 5\cos \theta$; the maximum distance between the curve and the pole is 5 units. The maximum value of the cosine function is 1 when $\theta = 0$, so our polar equation is $5\cos \theta$, and the value $\theta = 0$ will yield the maximum $|r|$.

Similarly, the maximum value of the sine function is 1 when $\theta = \dfrac{\pi}{2}$, and if our polar equation is $r = 5\sin \theta$, the value $\theta = \dfrac{\pi}{2}$ will yield the maximum $|r|$. We may find additional information by calculating values of r when $\theta = 0$. These points would be polar axis intercepts, which may be helpful in drawing the graph and identifying the curve of a polar equation.

Example 2   **Finding Zeros and Maximum Values for a Polar Equation**

Using the equation in **Example 1**, find the zeros and maximum $|r|$ and, if necessary, the polar axis intercepts of $r = 2\sin \theta$.

Solution   To find the zeros, set r equal to zero and solve for θ.

$$2\sin \theta = 0$$
$$\sin \theta = 0$$
$$\theta = \sin^{-1} 0$$
$$\theta = n\pi \qquad\qquad \text{where } n \text{ is an integer}$$

Substitute any one of the θ values into the equation. We will use 0.

$$r = 2\sin(0)$$
$$r = 0$$

The points $(0, 0)$ and $(0, \pm n\pi)$ are the zeros of the equation. They all coincide, so only one point is visible on the graph. This point is also the only polar axis intercept.

To find the maximum value of the equation, look at the maximum value of the trigonometric function $\sin\theta$, which occurs when $\theta = \frac{\pi}{2} \pm 2k\pi$ resulting in $\sin\left(\frac{\pi}{2}\right) = 1$. Substitute $\frac{\pi}{2}$ for θ.

$$r = 2\sin\left(\frac{\pi}{2}\right)$$
$$r = 2(1)$$
$$r = 2$$

Analysis   *The point* $\left(2, \frac{\pi}{2}\right)$ *will be the maximum value on the graph. Let's plot a few more points to verify the graph of a circle. See* **Table 2** *and* **Figure 4**.

θ	$r = 2\sin\theta$	r
0	$r = 2\sin(0) = 0$	0
$\dfrac{\pi}{6}$	$r = 2\sin\left(\dfrac{\pi}{6}\right) = 1$	1
$\dfrac{\pi}{3}$	$r = 2\sin\left(\dfrac{\pi}{3}\right) \approx 1.73$	1.73
$\dfrac{\pi}{2}$	$r = 2\sin\left(\dfrac{\pi}{2}\right) = 2$	2
$\dfrac{2\pi}{3}$	$r = 2\sin\left(\dfrac{2\pi}{3}\right) \approx 1.73$	1.73
$\dfrac{5\pi}{6}$	$r = 2\sin\left(\dfrac{5\pi}{6}\right) = 1$	1
π	$r = 2\sin(\pi) = 0$	0

Table 2

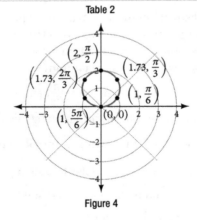

Figure 4

Try It #2

Without converting to Cartesian coordinates, test the given equation for symmetry and find the zeros and maximum values of $|r|$: $r = 3\cos\theta$.

Investigating Circles

Now we have seen the equation of a circle in the polar coordinate system. In the last two examples, the same equation was used to illustrate the properties of symmetry and demonstrate how to find the zeros, maximum values, and plotted points that produced the graphs. However, the circle is only one of many shapes in the set of polar curves.

There are five classic polar curves: **cardioids, limaçons, lemniscates, rose curves,** and **Archimedes' spirals.** We will briefly touch on the polar formulas for the circle before moving on to the classic curves and their variations.

> ### formulas for the equation of a circle
> Some of the formulas that produce the graph of a circle in polar coordinates are given by $r = a\cos\theta$ and $r = a\sin\theta$, where a is the diameter of the circle or the distance from the pole to the farthest point on the circumference. The radius is $\frac{|a|}{2}$, or one-half the diameter. For $r = a\cos\theta$, the center is $\left(\frac{a}{2}, 0\right)$. For $r = a\sin\theta$, the center is $\left(\frac{a}{2}, \pi\right)$.
> **Figure 5** shows the graphs of these four circles.
>
>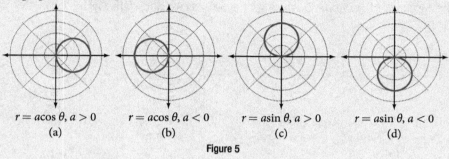
>
> $r = a\cos\theta, a > 0$ $r = a\cos\theta, a < 0$ $r = a\sin\theta, a > 0$ $r = a\sin\theta, a < 0$
> (a)   (b)   (c)   (d)
>
> Figure 5

Example 3   **Sketching the Graph of a Polar Equation for a Circle**

Sketch the graph of $r = 4\cos\theta$.

Solution   First, testing the equation for symmetry, we find that the graph is symmetric about the polar axis. Next, we find the zeros and maximum $|r|$ for $r = 4\cos\theta$. First, set $r = 0$, and solve for θ. Thus, a zero occurs at $\theta = \frac{\pi}{2} \pm k\pi$. A key point to plot is $\left(0, \frac{\pi}{2}\right)$

To find the maximum value of r, note that the maximum value of the cosine function is 1 when $\theta = 0 \pm 2k\pi$. Substitute $\theta = 0$ into the equation:

$$r = 4\cos\theta$$
$$r = 4\cos(0)$$
$$r = 4(1) = 4$$

The maximum value of the equation is 4. A key point to plot is $(4, 0)$.

As $r = 4\cos\theta$ is symmetric with respect to the polar axis, we only need to calculate r-values for θ over the interval $[0, \pi]$. Points in the upper quadrant can then be reflected to the lower quadrant. Make a table of values similar to **Table 3**. The graph is shown in **Figure 6**.

θ	0	$\frac{\pi}{6}$	$\frac{\pi}{4}$	$\frac{\pi}{3}$	$\frac{\pi}{2}$	$\frac{2\pi}{3}$	$\frac{3\pi}{4}$	$\frac{5\pi}{6}$	π
r	4	3.46	2.83	2	0	−2	−2.83	−3.46	4

Table 3

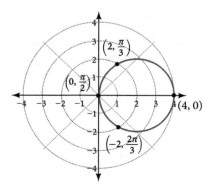

Figure 6

Investigating Cardioids

While translating from polar coordinates to Cartesian coordinates may seem simpler in some instances, graphing the classic curves is actually less complicated in the polar system. The next curve is called a cardioid, as it resembles a heart. This shape is often included with the family of curves called limaçons, but here we will discuss the cardioid on its own.

---

formulas for a cardioid

The formulas that produce the graphs of a **cardioid** are given by $r = a \pm b\cos\theta$ and $r = a \pm b\sin\theta$ where $a > 0$, $b > 0$, and $\frac{a}{b} = 1$. The cardioid graph passes through the pole, as we can see in **Figure 7**.

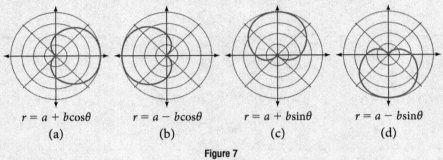

| $r = a + b\cos\theta$ | $r = a - b\cos\theta$ | $r = a + b\sin\theta$ | $r = a - b\sin\theta$ |
| (a) | (b) | (c) | (d) |

Figure 7

How To...

Given the polar equation of a cardioid, sketch its graph.

1. Check equation for the three types of symmetry.
2. Find the zeros. Set $r = 0$.
3. Find the maximum value of the equation according to the maximum value of the trigonometric expression.
4. Make a table of values for r and θ.
5. Plot the points and sketch the graph.

Example 4   **Sketching the Graph of a Cardioid**

Sketch the graph of $r = 2 + 2\cos\theta$.

Solution   First, testing the equation for symmetry, we find that the graph of this equation will be symmetric about the polar axis. Next, we find the zeros and maximums. Setting $r = 0$, we have $\theta = \pi + 2k\pi$. The zero of the equation is located at $(0, \pi)$. The graph passes through this point.

The maximum value of $r = 2 + 2\cos\theta$ occurs when $\cos\theta$ is a maximum, which is when $\cos\theta = 1$ or when $\theta = 0$. Substitute $\theta = 0$ into the equation, and solve for r.

$$r = 2 + 2\cos(0)$$
$$r = 2 + 2(1) = 4$$

The point $(4, 0)$ is the maximum value on the graph.

We found that the polar equation is symmetric with respect to the polar axis, but as it extends to all four quadrants, we need to plot values over the interval $[0, \pi]$. The upper portion of the graph is then reflected over the polar axis. Next, we make a table of values, as in **Table 4**, and then we plot the points and draw the graph. See **Figure 8**.

θ	0	$\frac{\pi}{4}$	$\frac{\pi}{2}$	$\frac{2\pi}{3}$	π
r	4	3.41	2	1	0

Table 4

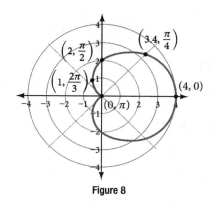

Figure 8

Investigating Limaçons

The word limaçon is Old French for "snail," a name that describes the shape of the graph. As mentioned earlier, the cardioid is a member of the limaçon family, and we can see the similarities in the graphs. The other images in this category include the one-loop limaçon and the two-loop (or inner-loop) limaçon. **One-loop limaçons** are sometimes referred to as **dimpled limaçons** when $1 < \dfrac{a}{b} < 2$ and **convex limaçons** when $\dfrac{a}{b} \geq 2$.

---

formulas for one-loop limaçons

The formulas that produce the graph of a dimpled **one-loop limaçon** are given by $r = a \pm b\cos\theta$ and $r = a \pm b\sin\theta$ where $a > 0$, $b > 0$, and $1 < \dfrac{a}{b} < 2$. All four graphs are shown in **Figure 9**.

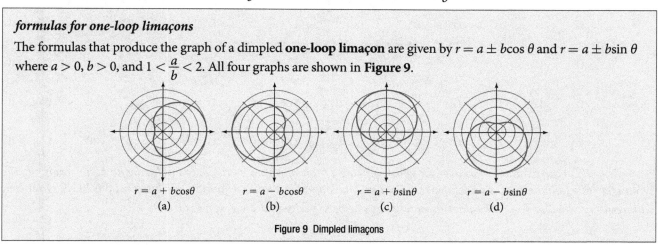

$r = a + b\cos\theta$ $r = a - b\cos\theta$ $r = a + b\sin\theta$ $r = a - b\sin\theta$
(a)   (b)   (c)   (d)

Figure 9 Dimpled limaçons

How To...

Given a polar equation for a one-loop limaçon, sketch the graph.

1. Test the equation for symmetry. Remember that failing a symmetry test does not mean that the shape will not exhibit symmetry. Often the symmetry may reveal itself when the points are plotted.
2. Find the zeros.
3. Find the maximum values according to the trigonometric expression.
4. Make a table.
5. Plot the points and sketch the graph.

Example 5   **Sketching the Graph of a One-Loop Limaçon**

Graph the equation $r = 4 - 3\sin\theta$.

Solution   First, testing the equation for symmetry, we find that it fails all three symmetry tests, meaning that the graph may or may not exhibit symmetry, so we cannot use the symmetry to help us graph it. However, this equation has a graph that clearly displays symmetry with respect to the line $\theta = \dfrac{\pi}{2}$, yet it fails all the three symmetry tests. A graphing calculator will immediately illustrate the graph's reflective quality.

Next, we find the zeros and maximum, and plot the reflecting points to verify any symmetry. Setting $r = 0$ results in θ being undefined. What does this mean? How could θ be undefined? The angle θ is undefined for any value of $\sin\theta > 1$. Therefore, θ is undefined because there is no value of θ for which $\sin\theta > 1$. Consequently, the graph does not pass through the pole. Perhaps the graph does cross the polar axis, but not at the pole. We can investigate other intercepts by calculating r when $\theta = 0$.

$$r(0) = 4 - 3\sin(0)$$
$$r = 4 - 3 \cdot 0 = 4$$

So, there is at least one polar axis intercept at $(4, 0)$.

Next, as the maximum value of the sine function is 1 when $\theta = \frac{\pi}{2}$, we will substitute $\theta = \frac{\pi}{2}$ into the equation and solve for r. Thus, $r = 1$.

Make a table of the coordinates similar to **Table 5**.

θ	0	$\frac{\pi}{6}$	$\frac{\pi}{3}$	$\frac{\pi}{2}$	$\frac{2\pi}{3}$	$\frac{5\pi}{6}$	π	$\frac{7\pi}{6}$	$\frac{4\pi}{3}$	$\frac{3\pi}{2}$	$\frac{5\pi}{3}$	$\frac{11\pi}{6}$	2π
r	4	2.5	1.4	1	1.4	2.5	4	5.5	6.6	7	6.6	5.5	4

Table 5

The graph is shown in **Figure 10**.

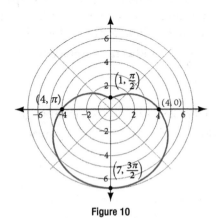

Figure 10

Analysis   *This is an example of a curve for which making a table of values is critical to producing an accurate graph. The symmetry tests fail; the zero is undefined. While it may be apparent that an equation involving sin θ is likely symmetric with respect to the line $\theta = \frac{\pi}{2}$, evaluating more points helps to verify that the graph is correct.*

Try It #3

Sketch the graph of $r = 3 - 2\cos \theta$.

Another type of limaçon, the **inner-loop limaçon**, is named for the loop formed inside the general limaçon shape. It was discovered by the German artist Albrecht Dürer(1471-1528), who revealed a method for drawing the inner-loop limaçon in his 1525 book *Underweysung der Messing*. A century later, the father of mathematician Blaise Pascal, Étienne Pascal(1588-1651), rediscovered it.

formulas for inner-loop limaçons

The formulas that generate the **inner-loop limaçons** are given by $r = a \pm b\cos \theta$ and $r = a \pm b\sin \theta$ where $a > 0$, $b > 0$, and $a < b$. The graph of the inner-loop limaçon passes through the pole twice: once for the outer loop, and once for the inner loop. See **Figure 11** for the graphs.

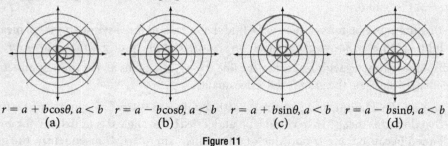

$r = a + b\cos\theta, a < b$	$r = a - b\cos\theta, a < b$	$r = a + b\sin\theta, a < b$	$r = a - b\sin\theta, a < b$
(a)	(b)	(c)	(d)

Figure 11

Example 6   Sketching the Graph of an Inner-Loop Limaçon

Sketch the graph of $r = 2 + 5\cos\theta$.

Solution   Testing for symmetry, we find that the graph of the equation is symmetric about the polar axis. Next, finding the zeros reveals that when $r = 0$, $\theta = 1.98$. The maximum $|r|$ is found when $\cos\theta = 1$ or when $\theta = 0$. Thus, the maximum is found at the point $(7, 0)$.

Even though we have found symmetry, the zero, and the maximum, plotting more points will help to define the shape, and then a pattern will emerge.

See **Table 6**.

θ	0	$\dfrac{\pi}{6}$	$\dfrac{\pi}{3}$	$\dfrac{\pi}{2}$	$\dfrac{2\pi}{3}$	$\dfrac{5\pi}{6}$	π	$\dfrac{7\pi}{6}$	$\dfrac{4\pi}{3}$	$\dfrac{3\pi}{2}$	$\dfrac{5\pi}{3}$	$\dfrac{11\pi}{6}$	2π
r	7	6.3	4.5	2	−0.5	−2.3	−3	−2.3	−0.5	2	4.5	6.3	7

Table 6

As expected, the values begin to repeat after $\theta = \pi$. The graph is shown in **Figure 12**.

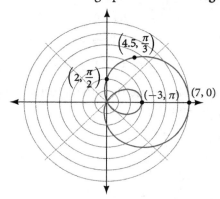

Figure 12 Inner-loop limaçon

Investigating Lemniscates

The lemniscate is a polar curve resembling the infinity symbol ∞ or a figure 8. Centered at the pole, a lemniscate is symmetrical by definition.

---

formulas for lemniscates

The formulas that generate the graph of a **lemniscate** are given by $r^2 = a^2\cos 2\theta$ and $r^2 = a^2\sin 2\theta$ where $a \neq 0$. The formula $r^2 = a^2\sin 2\theta$ is symmetric with respect to the pole. The formula $r^2 = a^2\cos 2\theta$ is symmetric with respect to the pole, the line $\theta = \dfrac{\pi}{2}$, and the polar axis. See **Figure 13** for the graphs.

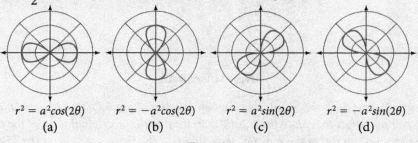

$r^2 = a^2\cos(2\theta)$ $r^2 = -a^2\cos(2\theta)$ $r^2 = a^2\sin(2\theta)$ $r^2 = -a^2\sin(2\theta)$
(a)   (b)   (c)   (d)

Figure 13

Example 7   Sketching the Graph of a Lemniscate

Sketch the graph of $r^2 = 4\cos 2\theta$.

Solution   The equation exhibits symmetry with respect to the line $\theta = \dfrac{\pi}{2}$, the polar axis, and the pole.

Let's find the zeros. It should be routine by now, but we will approach this equation a little differently by making the substitution $u = 2\theta$.

$$0 = 4\cos 2\theta$$

$$0 = 4\cos u$$

$$0 = \cos u$$

$$\cos^{-1} 0 = \frac{\pi}{2}$$

$$u = \frac{\pi}{2} \qquad \text{Substitute } 2\theta \text{ back in for } u.$$

$$2\theta = \frac{\pi}{2}$$

$$\theta = \frac{\pi}{4}$$

So, the point $\left(0, \dfrac{\pi}{4}\right)$ is a zero of the equation.

Now let's find the maximum value. Since the maximum of $\cos u = 1$ when $u = 0$, the maximum $\cos 2\theta = 1$ when $2\theta = 0$. Thus,

$$r^2 = 4\cos(0)$$

$$r^2 = 4(1) = 4$$

$$r = \pm\sqrt{4} = 2$$

We have a maximum at $(2, 0)$. Since this graph is symmetric with respect to the pole, the line $\theta = \dfrac{\pi}{2}$, and the polar axis, we only need to plot points in the first quadrant.

Make a table similar to **Table 7**.

θ	0	$\dfrac{\pi}{6}$	$\dfrac{\pi}{4}$	$\dfrac{\pi}{3}$	$\dfrac{\pi}{2}$
r	2	$\sqrt{2}$	0	$\sqrt{2}$	0

Table 7

Plot the points on the graph, such as the one shown in **Figure 14**.

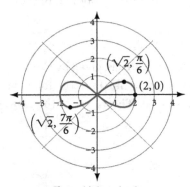

Figure 14 Lemniscate

Analysis   *Making a substitution such as $u = 2\theta$ is a common practice in mathematics because it can make calculations simpler. However, we must not forget to replace the substitution term with the original term at the end, and then solve for the unknown. Some of the points on this graph may not show up using the Trace function on the TI-84 graphing calculator, and the calculator table may show an error for these same points of r. This is because there are no real square roots for these values of θ. In other words, the corresponding r-values of $\sqrt{4\cos(2\theta)}$ are complex numbers because there is a negative number under the radical.*

Investigating Rose Curves

The next type of polar equation produces a petal-like shape called a rose curve. Although the graphs look complex, a simple polar equation generates the pattern.

rose curves

The formulas that generate the graph of a **rose curve** are given by $r = a\cos n\theta$ and $r = a\sin n\theta$ where $a \neq 0$. If n is even, the curve has $2n$ petals. If n is odd, the curve has n petals. See **Figure 15**.

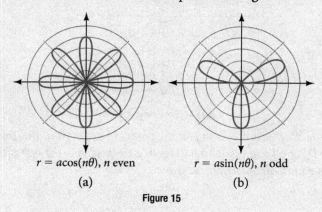

$r = a\cos(n\theta)$, n even $r = a\sin(n\theta)$, n odd

(a) (b)

Figure 15

Example 8   **Sketching the Graph of a Rose Curve (*n* Even)**

Sketch the graph of $r = 2\cos 4\theta$.

Solution   Testing for symmetry, we find again that the symmetry tests do not tell the whole story. The graph is not only symmetric with respect to the polar axis, but also with respect to the line $\theta = \frac{\pi}{2}$ and the pole.

Now we will find the zeros. First make the substitution $u = 4\theta$.

$$0 = 2\cos 4\theta$$

$$0 = \cos 4\theta$$

$$0 = \cos u$$

$$\cos^{-1} 0 = u$$

$$u = \frac{\pi}{2}$$

$$4\theta = \frac{\pi}{2}$$

$$\theta = \frac{\pi}{8}$$

The zero is $\theta = \frac{\pi}{8}$. The point $\left(0, \frac{\pi}{8}\right)$ is on the curve.

Next, we find the maximum $|r|$. We know that the maximum value of $\cos u = 1$ when $\theta = 0$. Thus,

$$r = 2\cos(4 \cdot 0)$$

$$r = 2\cos(0)$$

$$r = 2(1) = 2$$

The point $(2, 0)$ is on the curve.

The graph of the rose curve has unique properties, which are revealed in **Table 8**.

θ	0	$\frac{\pi}{8}$	$\frac{\pi}{4}$	$\frac{3\pi}{8}$	$\frac{\pi}{2}$	$\frac{5\pi}{8}$	$\frac{3\pi}{4}$
r	2	0	-2	0	2	0	-2

Table 8

As $r = 0$ when $\theta = \frac{\pi}{8}$, it makes sense to divide values in the table by $\frac{\pi}{8}$ units. A definite pattern emerges. Look at the range of r-values: 2, 0, -2, 0, 2, 0, -2, and so on. This represents the development of the curve one petal at a time. Starting at $r = 0$, each petal extends out a distance of $r = 2$, and then turns back to zero $2n$ times for a total of eight petals. See the graph in **Figure 16**.

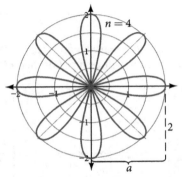

Figure 16 Rose curve, *n* even

Analysis   When these curves are drawn, it is best to plot the points in order, as in the **Table 8**. This allows us to see how the graph hits a maximum (the tip of a petal), loops back crossing the pole, hits the opposite maximum, and loops back to the pole. The action is continuous until all the petals are drawn.

Try It #4

Sketch the graph of $r = 4\sin(2\theta)$.

Example 9   **Sketching the Graph of a Rose Curve (*n* Odd)**

Sketch the graph of $r = 2\sin(5\theta)$.

Solution   The graph of the equation shows symmetry with respect to the line $\theta = \frac{\pi}{2}$. Next, find the zeros and maximum. We will want to make the substitution $u = 5\theta$.

$$0 = 2\sin(5\theta)$$
$$0 = \sin u$$
$$\sin^{-1} 0 = 0$$
$$u = 0$$
$$5\theta = 0$$
$$\theta = 0$$

The maximum value is calculated at the angle where $\sin \theta$ is a maximum. Therefore,

$$r = 2\sin\left(5 \cdot \frac{\pi}{2}\right)$$
$$r = 2(1) = 2$$

Thus, the maximum value of the polar equation is 2. This is the length of each petal. As the curve for *n* odd yields the same number of petals as *n*, there will be five petals on the graph. See **Figure 17**.

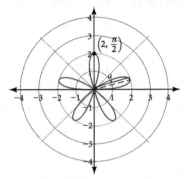

Figure 17 Rose curve, n odd

Create a table of values similar to **Table 9**.

θ	0	$\frac{\pi}{6}$	$\frac{\pi}{3}$	$\frac{\pi}{2}$	$\frac{2\pi}{3}$	$\frac{5\pi}{6}$	π
r	0	1	−1.73	2	−1.73	1	0

Table 9

Try It #5

Sketch the graph of $r = 3\cos(3\theta)$.

Investigating the Archimedes' Spiral

The final polar equation we will discuss is the Archimedes' spiral, named for its discoverer, the Greek mathematician Archimedes (c. 287 BCE–c. 212 BCE), who is credited with numerous discoveries in the fields of geometry and mechanics.

> *Archimedes' spiral*
> The formula that generates the graph of the **Archimedes' spiral** is given by $r = \theta$ for $\theta \geq 0$. As θ increases, r increases at a constant rate in an ever-widening, never-ending, spiraling path. See **Figure 18**.
>
>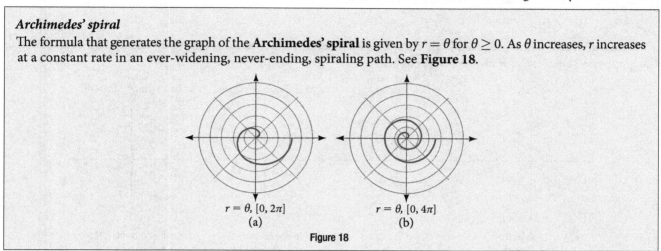
>
> $r = \theta$, $[0, 2\pi]$ $r = \theta$, $[0, 4\pi]$
> (a)   (b)
>
> **Figure 18**

How To...

Given an Archimedes' spiral over $[0, 2\pi]$, sketch the graph.

1. Make a table of values for r and θ over the given domain.
2. Plot the points and sketch the graph.

Example 10   Sketching the Graph of an Archimedes' Spiral

Sketch the graph of $r = \theta$ over $[0, 2\pi]$.

Solution   As r is equal to θ, the plot of the Archimedes' spiral begins at the pole at the point $(0, 0)$. While the graph hints of symmetry, there is no formal symmetry with regard to passing the symmetry tests. Further, there is no maximum value, unless the domain is restricted.

Create a table such as **Table 10**.

θ	$\dfrac{\pi}{4}$	$\dfrac{\pi}{2}$	π	$\dfrac{3\pi}{2}$	$\dfrac{7\pi}{4}$	2π
r	0.785	1.57	3.14	4.71	5.50	6.28

Table 10

Notice that the r-values are just the decimal form of the angle measured in radians. We can see them on a graph in **Figure 19**.

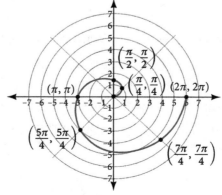

Figure 19 Archimedes' spiral

Analysis   *The domain of this polar curve is $[0, 2\pi]$. In general, however, the domain of this function is $(-\infty, \infty)$. Graphing the equation of the Archimedes' spiral is rather simple, although the image makes it seem like it would be complex.*

Try It #6

Sketch the graph of $r = -\theta$ over the interval $[0, 4\pi]$.

Summary of Curves

We have explored a number of seemingly complex polar curves in this section. **Figure 20** and **Figure 21** summarize the graphs and equations for each of these curves.

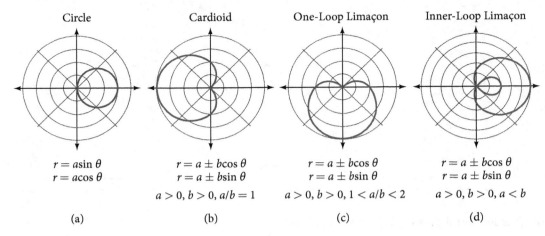

Circle

$r = a\sin\theta$
$r = a\cos\theta$

(a)

Cardioid

$r = a \pm b\cos\theta$
$r = a \pm b\sin\theta$

$a > 0, b > 0, a/b = 1$

(b)

One-Loop Limaçon

$r = a \pm b\cos\theta$
$r = a \pm b\sin\theta$

$a > 0, b > 0, 1 < a/b < 2$

(c)

Inner-Loop Limaçon

$r = a \pm b\cos\theta$
$r = a \pm b\sin\theta$

$a > 0, b > 0, a < b$

(d)

Figure 20

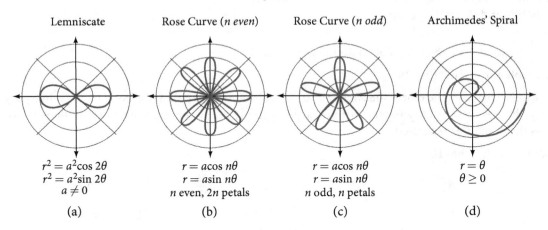

Lemniscate

$r^2 = a^2\cos 2\theta$
$r^2 = a^2\sin 2\theta$
$a \neq 0$

(a)

Rose Curve (*n even*)

$r = a\cos n\theta$
$r = a\sin n\theta$
n even, 2*n* petals

(b)

Rose Curve (*n odd*)

$r = a\cos n\theta$
$r = a\sin n\theta$
n odd, *n* petals

(c)

Archimedes' Spiral

$r = \theta$
$\theta \geq 0$

(d)

Figure 21

Access these online resources for additional instruction and practice with graphs of polar coordinates.

- Graphing Polar Equations Part 1 (http://openstaxcollege.org/l/polargraph1)
- Graphing Polar Equations Part 2 (http://openstaxcollege.org/l/polargraph2)
- Animation: The Graphs of Polar Equations (http://openstaxcollege.org/l/polaranim)
- Graphing Polar Equations on the TI-84 (http://openstaxcollege.org/l/polarTI84)

10.4 SECTION EXERCISES

VERBAL

1. Describe the three types of symmetry in polar graphs, and compare them to the symmetry of the Cartesian plane.

2. Which of the three types of symmetries for polar graphs correspond to the symmetries with respect to the x-axis, y-axis, and origin?

3. What are the steps to follow when graphing polar equations?

4. Describe the shapes of the graphs of cardioids, limaçons, and lemniscates.

5. What part of the equation determines the shape of the graph of a polar equation?

GRAPHICAL

For the following exercises, test the equation for symmetry.

6. $r = 5\cos 3\theta$

7. $r = 3 - 3\cos \theta$

8. $r = 3 + 2\sin \theta$

9. $r = 3\sin 2\theta$

10. $r = 4$

11. $r = 2\theta$

12. $r = 4\cos \dfrac{\theta}{2}$

13. $r = \dfrac{2}{\theta}$

14. $r = 3\sqrt{1-\cos^2\theta}$

15. $r = \sqrt{5\sin 2\theta}$

For the following exercises, graph the polar equation. Identify the name of the shape.

16. $r = 3\cos \theta$

17. $r = 4\sin \theta$

18. $r = 2 + 2\cos \theta$

19. $r = 2 - 2\cos \theta$

20. $r = 5 - 5\sin \theta$

21. $r = 3 + 3\sin \theta$

22. $r = 3 + 2\sin \theta$

23. $r = 7 + 4\sin \theta$

24. $r = 4 + 3\cos \theta$

25. $r = 5 + 4\cos \theta$

26. $r = 10 + 9\cos \theta$

27. $r = 1 + 3\sin \theta$

28. $r = 2 + 5\sin \theta$

29. $r = 5 + 7\sin \theta$

30. $r = 2 + 4\cos \theta$

31. $r = 5 + 6\cos \theta$

32. $r^2 = 36\cos(2\theta)$

33. $r^2 = 10\cos(2\theta)$

34. $r^2 = 4\sin(2\theta)$

35. $r^2 = 10\sin(2\theta)$

36. $r = 3\sin(2\theta)$

37. $r = 3\cos(2\theta)$

38. $r = 5\sin(3\theta)$

39. $r = 4\sin(4\theta)$

40. $r = 4\sin(5\theta)$

41. $r = -\theta$

42. $r = 2\theta$

43. $r = -3\theta$

TECHNOLOGY

For the following exercises, use a graphing calculator to sketch the graph of the polar equation.

44. $r = \dfrac{1}{\theta}$

45. $r = \dfrac{1}{\sqrt{\theta}}$

46. $r = 2\sin \theta \tan \theta$, a cissoid

47. $r = 2\sqrt{1 - \sin^2 \theta}$, a hippopede

48. $r = 5 + \cos(4\theta)$

49. $r = 2 - \sin(2\theta)$

50. $r = \theta^2$

51. $r = \theta + 1$

52. $r = \theta\sin \theta$

53. $r = \theta\cos \theta$

For the following exercises, use a graphing utility to graph each pair of polar equations on a domain of $[0, 4\pi]$ and then explain the differences shown in the graphs.

54. $r = \theta,\ r = -\theta$

55. $r = \theta,\ r = \theta + \sin \theta$

56. $r = \sin \theta + \theta,\ r = \sin \theta - \theta$

57. $r = 2\sin\left(\dfrac{\theta}{2}\right),\ r = \theta\sin\left(\dfrac{\theta}{2}\right)$

58. $r = \sin(\cos(3\theta))\ r = \sin(3\theta)$

59. On a graphing utility, graph $r = \sin\left(\frac{16}{5}\theta\right)$ on $[0, 4\pi]$, $[0, 8\pi]$, $[0, 12\pi]$, and $[0, 16\pi]$. Describe the effect of increasing the width of the domain.

60. On a graphing utility, graph and sketch $r = \sin\theta + \left(\sin\left(\frac{5}{2}\theta\right)\right)^3$ on $[0, 4\pi]$.

61. On a graphing utility, graph each polar equation. Explain the similarities and differences you observe in the graphs.

$$r_1 = 3\sin(3\theta)$$
$$r_2 = 2\sin(3\theta)$$
$$r_3 = \sin(3\theta)$$

62. On a graphing utility, graph each polar equation. Explain the similarities and differences you observe in the graphs.

$$r_1 = 3 + 3\cos\theta$$
$$r_2 = 2 + 2\cos\theta$$
$$r_3 = 1 + \cos\theta$$

63. On a graphing utility, graph each polar equation. Explain the similarities and differences you observe in the graphs.

$$r_1 = 3\theta$$
$$r_2 = 2\theta$$
$$r_3 = \theta$$

EXTENSIONS

For the following exercises, draw each polar equation on the same set of polar axes, and find the points of intersection.

64. $r_1 = 3 + 2\sin\theta$, $r_2 = 2$

65. $r_1 = 6 - 4\cos\theta$, $r_2 = 4$

66. $r_1 = 1 + \sin\theta$, $r_2 = 3\sin\theta$

67. $r_1 = 1 + \cos\theta$, $r_2 = 3\cos\theta$

68. $r_1 = \cos(2\theta)$, $r_2 = \sin(2\theta)$

69. $r_1 = \sin^2(2\theta)$, $r_2 = 1 - \cos(4\theta)$

70. $r_1 = \sqrt{3}$, $r_2 = 2\sin(\theta)$

71. $r_1^2 = \sin\theta$, $r_2^2 = \cos\theta$

72. $r_1 = 1 + \cos\theta$, $r_2 = 1 - \sin\theta$

LEARNING OBJECTIVES

In this section, you will:

- Plot complex numbers in the complex plane.
- Find the absolute value of a complex number.
- Write complex numbers in polar form.
- Convert a complex number from polar to rectangular form.
- Find products of complex numbers in polar form.
- Find quotients of complex numbers in polar form.
- Find powers of complex numbers in polar form.
- Find roots of complex numbers in polar form.

10.5 POLAR FORM OF COMPLEX NUMBERS

"God made the integers; all else is the work of man." This rather famous quote by nineteenth-century German mathematician Leopold Kronecker sets the stage for this section on the polar form of a complex number. Complex numbers were invented by people and represent over a thousand years of continuous investigation and struggle by mathematicians such as Pythagoras, Descartes, De Moivre, Euler, Gauss, and others. Complex numbers answered questions that for centuries had puzzled the greatest minds in science.

We first encountered complex numbers in **Complex Numbers**. In this section, we will focus on the mechanics of working with complex numbers: translation of complex numbers from polar form to rectangular form and vice versa, interpretation of complex numbers in the scheme of applications, and application of De Moivre's Theorem.

Plotting Complex Numbers in the Complex Plane

Plotting a complex number $a + bi$ is similar to plotting a real number, except that the horizontal axis represents the real part of the number, a, and the vertical axis represents the imaginary part of the number, bi.

How To...

Given a complex number $a + bi$, plot it in the complex plane.

1. Label the horizontal axis as the *real* axis and the vertical axis as the *imaginary axis*.
2. Plot the point in the complex plane by moving a units in the horizontal direction and b units in the vertical direction.

Example 1   **Plotting a Complex Number in the Complex Plane**

Plot the complex number $2 - 3i$ in the complex plane.

Solution   From the origin, move two units in the positive horizontal direction and three units in the negative vertical direction. See **Figure 1**.

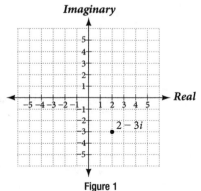

Figure 1

Try It #1

Plot the point $1 + 5i$ in the complex plane.

Finding the Absolute Value of a Complex Number

The first step toward working with a complex number in polar form is to find the absolute value. The absolute value of a complex number is the same as its magnitude, or $|z|$. It measures the distance from the origin to a point in the plane. For example, the graph of $z = 2 + 4i$, in **Figure 2**, shows $|z|$.

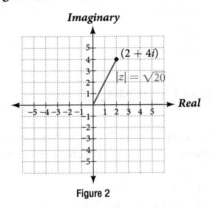

Figure 2

---

absolute value of a complex number

Given $z = x + yi$, a complex number, the absolute value of z is defined as

$$|z| = \sqrt{x^2 + y^2}$$

It is the distance from the origin to the point (x, y).

Notice that the absolute value of a real number gives the distance of the number from 0, while the absolute value of a complex number gives the distance of the number from the origin, $(0, 0)$.

Example 2   **Finding the Absolute Value of a Complex Number with a Radical**

Find the absolute value of $z = \sqrt{5} - i$.

Solution   Using the formula, we have

$$|z| = \sqrt{x^2 + y^2}$$
$$|z| = \sqrt{\sqrt{5}^2 + (-1)^2}$$
$$|z| = \sqrt{5 + 1}$$
$$|z| = \sqrt{6}$$

See **Figure 3**.

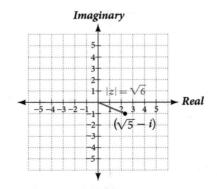

Figure 3

Try It #2

Find the absolute value of the complex number $z = 12 - 5i$.

Example 3   **Finding the Absolute Value of a Complex Number**

Given $z = 3 - 4i$, find $|z|$.

Solution   Using the formula, we have

$$|z| = \sqrt{x^2 + y^2}$$
$$|z| = \sqrt{(3)^2 + (-4)^2}$$
$$|z| = \sqrt{9 + 16}$$
$$|z| = \sqrt{25}$$
$$|z| = 5$$

The absolute value of z is 5. See **Figure 4**.

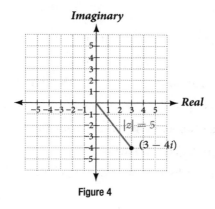

Figure 4

Try It #3

Given $z = 1 - 7i$, find $|z|$.

Writing Complex Numbers in Polar Form

The **polar form of a complex number** expresses a number in terms of an angle θ and its distance from the origin r. Given a complex number in rectangular form expressed as $z = x + yi$, we use the same conversion formulas as we do to write the number in trigonometric form:

$$x = r\cos\theta$$
$$y = r\sin\theta$$
$$r = \sqrt{x^2 + y^2}$$

We review these relationships in **Figure 5**.

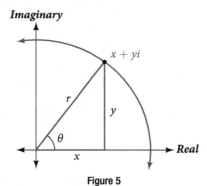

Figure 5

We use the term **modulus** to represent the absolute value of a complex number, or the distance from the origin to the point (x, y). The modulus, then, is the same as r, the radius in polar form. We use θ to indicate the angle of direction (just as with polar coordinates). Substituting, we have

$$z = x + yi$$
$$z = r\cos\theta + (r\sin\theta)i$$
$$z = r(\cos\theta + i\sin\theta)$$

---

polar form of a complex number

Writing a complex number in polar form involves the following conversion formulas:

$$x = r\cos\theta$$
$$y = r\sin\theta$$
$$r = \sqrt{x^2 + y^2}$$

Making a direct substitution, we have

$$z = x + yi$$
$$z = (r\cos\theta) + i(r\sin\theta)$$
$$z = r(\cos\theta + i\sin\theta)$$

where r is the **modulus** and θ is the **argument**. We often use the abbreviation $r\text{cis}\,\theta$ to represent $r(\cos\theta + i\sin\theta)$.

Example 4   Expressing a Complex Number Using Polar Coordinates

Express the complex number $4i$ using polar coordinates.

Solution   On the complex plane, the number $z = 4i$ is the same as $z = 0 + 4i$. Writing it in polar form, we have to calculate r first.

$$r = \sqrt{x^2 + y^2}$$
$$r = \sqrt{0^2 + 4^2}$$
$$r = \sqrt{16}$$
$$r = 4$$

Next, we look at x. If $x = r\cos\theta$, and $x = 0$, then $\theta = \dfrac{\pi}{2}$. In polar coordinates, the complex number $z = 0 + 4i$ can be written as $z = 4\left(\cos\left(\dfrac{\pi}{2}\right) + i\sin\left(\dfrac{\pi}{2}\right)\right)$ or $4\text{cis}\left(\dfrac{\pi}{2}\right)$. See **Figure 6**.

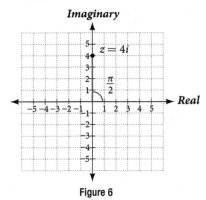

Figure 6

....

Try It #4

Express $z = 3i$ as $r\text{cis}\,\theta$ in polar form.

....

Example 5   **Finding the Polar Form of a Complex Number**

Find the polar form of $-4 + 4i$.

Solution   First, find the value of r.

$$r = \sqrt{x^2 + y^2}$$
$$r = \sqrt{(-4)^2 + (4^2)}$$
$$r = \sqrt{32}$$
$$r = 4\sqrt{2}$$

Find the angle θ using the formula:

$$\cos\theta = \frac{x}{r}$$

$$\cos\theta = \frac{-4}{4\sqrt{2}}$$

$$\cos\theta = -\frac{1}{\sqrt{2}}$$

$$\theta = \cos^{-1}\left(-\frac{1}{\sqrt{2}}\right) = \frac{3\pi}{4}$$

Thus, the solution is $4\sqrt{2}\,\text{cis}\left(\dfrac{3\pi}{4}\right)$.

Try It #5

Write $z = \sqrt{3} + i$ in polar form.

Converting a Complex Number from Polar to Rectangular Form

Converting a complex number from polar form to rectangular form is a matter of evaluating what is given and using the distributive property. In other words, given $z = r(\cos\theta + i\sin\theta)$, first evaluate the trigonometric functions $\cos\theta$ and $\sin\theta$. Then, multiply through by r.

Example 6   **Converting from Polar to Rectangular Form**

Convert the polar form of the given complex number to rectangular form:

$$z = 12\left(\cos\left(\frac{\pi}{6}\right) + i\sin\left(\frac{\pi}{6}\right)\right)$$

Solution   We begin by evaluating the trigonometric expressions.

$$\cos\left(\frac{\pi}{6}\right) = \frac{\sqrt{3}}{2} \text{ and } \sin\left(\frac{\pi}{6}\right) = \frac{1}{2}$$

After substitution, the complex number is

$$z = 12\left(\frac{\sqrt{3}}{2} + \frac{1}{2}i\right)$$

We apply the distributive property:

$$z = 12\left(\frac{\sqrt{3}}{2} + \frac{1}{2}i\right)$$
$$= (12)\frac{\sqrt{3}}{2} + (12)\frac{1}{2}i$$
$$= 6\sqrt{3} + 6i$$

The rectangular form of the given point in complex form is $6\sqrt{3} + 6i$.

Example 7   **Finding the Rectangular Form of a Complex Number**

Find the rectangular form of the complex number given $r = 13$ and $\tan \theta = \dfrac{5}{12}$.

Solution   If $\tan \theta = \dfrac{5}{12}$, and $\tan \theta = \dfrac{y}{x}$, we first determine $r = \sqrt{x^2 + y^2} = \sqrt{12^2 + 5^2} = 13$. We then find $\cos \theta = \dfrac{x}{r}$ and $\sin \theta = \dfrac{y}{r}$.

$$z = 13(\cos \theta + i\sin \theta)$$

$$= 13\left(\frac{12}{13} + \frac{5}{13}i \right)$$

$$= 12 + 5i$$

The rectangular form of the given number in complex form is $12 + 5i$.

Try It #6

Convert the complex number to rectangular form:

$$z = 4\left(\cos \frac{11\pi}{6} + i\sin \frac{11\pi}{6} \right)$$

Finding Products of Complex Numbers in Polar Form

Now that we can convert complex numbers to polar form we will learn how to perform operations on complex numbers in polar form. For the rest of this section, we will work with formulas developed by French mathematician Abraham De Moivre (1667–1754). These formulas have made working with products, quotients, powers, and roots of complex numbers much simpler than they appear. The rules are based on multiplying the moduli and adding the arguments.

> **products of complex numbers in polar form**
>
> If $z_1 = r_1(\cos \theta_1 + i\sin \theta_1)$ and $z_2 = r_2(\cos \theta_2 + i\sin \theta_2)$, then the product of these numbers is given as:
>
> $$z_1 z_2 = r_1 r_2[\cos(\theta_1 + \theta_2) + i\sin(\theta_1 + \theta_2)]$$
>
> $$z_1 z_2 = r_1 r_2 \text{cis}(\theta_1 + \theta_2)$$
>
> Notice that the product calls for multiplying the moduli and adding the angles.

Example 8   **Finding the Product of Two Complex Numbers in Polar Form**

Find the product of $z_1 z_2$, given $z_1 = 4(\cos(80°) + i\sin(80°))$ and $z_2 = 2(\cos(145°) + i\sin(145°))$.

Solution   Follow the formula

$$z_1 z_2 = 4 \cdot 2[\cos(80° + 145°) + i\sin(80° + 145°)]$$

$$z_1 z_2 = 8[\cos(225°) + i\sin(225°)]$$

$$z_1 z_2 = 8\left[\cos\left(\frac{5\pi}{4} \right) + i\sin\left(\frac{5\pi}{4} \right) \right]$$

$$z_1 z_2 = 8\left[-\frac{\sqrt{2}}{2} + i\left(-\frac{\sqrt{2}}{2} \right) \right]$$

$$z_1 z_2 = -4\sqrt{2} - 4i\sqrt{2}$$

Finding Quotients of Complex Numbers in Polar Form

The quotient of two complex numbers in polar form is the quotient of the two moduli and the difference of the two arguments.

> *quotients of complex numbers in polar form*
>
> If $z_1 = r_1(\cos\theta_1 + i\sin\theta_1)$ and $z_2 = r_2(\cos\theta_2 + i\sin\theta_2)$, then the quotient of these numbers is
>
> $$\frac{z_1}{z_2} = \frac{r_1}{r_2}[\cos(\theta_1 - \theta_2) + i\sin(\theta_1 - \theta_2)], z_2 \neq 0$$
>
> $$\frac{z_1}{z_2} = \frac{r_1}{r_2}\operatorname{cis}(\theta_1 - \theta_2), z_2 \neq 0$$
>
> Notice that the moduli are divided, and the angles are subtracted.

How To...

Given two complex numbers in polar form, find the quotient.

1. Divide $\dfrac{r_1}{r_2}$.

2. Find $\theta_1 - \theta_2$.

3. Substitute the results into the formula: $z = r(\cos\theta + i\sin\theta)$. Replace r with $\dfrac{r_1}{r_2}$, and replace θ with $\theta_1 - \theta_2$.

4. Calculate the new trigonometric expressions and multiply through by r.

Example 9   **Finding the Quotient of Two Complex Numbers**

Find the quotient of $z_1 = 2(\cos(213°) + i\sin(213°))$ and $z_2 = 4(\cos(33°) + i\sin(33°))$.

Solution   Using the formula, we have

$$\frac{z_1}{z_2} = \frac{2}{4}[\cos(213° - 33°) + i\sin(213° - 33°)]$$

$$\frac{z_1}{z_2} = \frac{1}{2}[\cos(180°) + i\sin(180°)]$$

$$\frac{z_1}{z_2} = \frac{1}{2}[-1 + 0i]$$

$$\frac{z_1}{z_2} = -\frac{1}{2} + 0i$$

$$\frac{z_1}{z_2} = -\frac{1}{2}$$

Try It #7

Find the product and the quotient of $z_1 = 2\sqrt{3}(\cos(150°) + i\sin(150°))$ and $z_2 = 2(\cos(30°) + i\sin(30°))$.

Finding Powers of Complex Numbers in Polar Form

Finding powers of complex numbers is greatly simplified using **De Moivre's Theorem**. It states that, for a positive integer n, z^n is found by raising the modulus to the nth power and multiplying the argument by n. It is the standard method used in modern mathematics.

> *De Moivre's Theorem*
>
> If $z = r(\cos\theta + i\sin\theta)$ is a complex number, then
>
> $$z^n = r^n[\cos(n\theta) + i\sin(n\theta)]$$
>
> $$z^n = r^n\operatorname{cis}(n\theta)$$
>
> where n is a positive integer.

Example 10   **Evaluating an Expression Using De Moivre's Theorem**

Evaluate the expression $(1 + i)^5$ using De Moivre's Theorem.

Solution   Since De Moivre's Theorem applies to complex numbers written in polar form, we must first write $(1 + i)$ in polar form. Let us find r.

$$r = \sqrt{x^2 + y^2}$$

$$r = \sqrt{(1)^2 + (1)^2}$$

$$r = \sqrt{2}$$

Then we find θ. Using the formula $\tan \theta = \dfrac{y}{x}$ gives

$$\tan \theta = \frac{1}{1}$$

$$\tan \theta = 1$$

$$\theta = \frac{\pi}{4}$$

Use De Moivre's Theorem to evaluate the expression.

$$(a + bi)^n = r^n[\cos(n\theta) + i\sin(n\theta)]$$

$$(1 + i)^5 = (\sqrt{2})^5\left[\cos\left(5 \cdot \frac{\pi}{4}\right) + i\sin\left(5 \cdot \frac{\pi}{4}\right)\right]$$

$$(1 + i)^5 = 4\sqrt{2}\left[\cos\left(\frac{5\pi}{4}\right) + i\sin\left(\frac{5\pi}{4}\right)\right]$$

$$(1 + i)^5 = 4\sqrt{2}\left[-\frac{\sqrt{2}}{2} + i\left(-\frac{\sqrt{2}}{2}\right)\right]$$

$$(1 + i)^5 = -4 - 4i$$

Finding Roots of Complex Numbers in Polar Form

To find the nth root of a complex number in polar form, we use the nth Root Theorem or De Moivre's Theorem and raise the complex number to a power with a rational exponent. There are several ways to represent a formula for finding nth roots of complex numbers in polar form.

---

the nth root theorem

To find the nth root of a complex number in polar form, use the formula given as

$$z^{\frac{1}{n}} = r^{\frac{1}{n}}\left[\cos\left(\frac{\theta}{n} + \frac{2k\pi}{n}\right) + i\sin\left(\frac{\theta}{n} + \frac{2k\pi}{n}\right)\right]$$

where $k = 0, 1, 2, 3, \ldots, n - 1$. We add $\dfrac{2k\pi}{n}$ to $\dfrac{\theta}{n}$ in order to obtain the periodic roots.

Example 11   **Finding the *n*th Root of a Complex Number**

Evaluate the cube roots of $z = 8\left(\cos\left(\dfrac{2\pi}{3}\right) + i\sin\left(\dfrac{2\pi}{3}\right)\right)$.

Solution   We have

$$z^{\frac{1}{3}} = 8^{\frac{1}{3}}\left[\cos\left(\dfrac{\dfrac{2\pi}{3}}{3} + \dfrac{2k\pi}{3}\right) + i\sin\left(\dfrac{\dfrac{2\pi}{3}}{3} + \dfrac{2k\pi}{3}\right)\right]$$

$$z^{\frac{1}{3}} = 2\left[\cos\left(\dfrac{2\pi}{9} + \dfrac{2k\pi}{3}\right) + i\sin\left(\dfrac{2\pi}{9} + \dfrac{2k\pi}{3}\right)\right]$$

There will be three roots: $k = 0, 1, 2$. When $k = 0$, we have

$$z^{\frac{1}{3}} = 2\left(\cos\left(\dfrac{2\pi}{9}\right) + i\sin\left(\dfrac{2\pi}{9}\right)\right)$$

When $k = 1$, we have

$$z^{\frac{1}{3}} = 2\left[\cos\left(\dfrac{2\pi}{9} + \dfrac{6\pi}{9}\right) + i\sin\left(\dfrac{2\pi}{9} + \dfrac{6\pi}{9}\right)\right] \qquad \text{Add } \dfrac{2(1)\pi}{3} \text{ to each angle.}$$

$$z^{\frac{1}{3}} = 2\left(\cos\left(\dfrac{8\pi}{9}\right) + i\sin\left(\dfrac{8\pi}{9}\right)\right)$$

When $k = 2$, we have

$$z^{\frac{1}{3}} = 2\left[\cos\left(\dfrac{2\pi}{9} + \dfrac{12\pi}{9}\right) + i\sin\left(\dfrac{2\pi}{9} + \dfrac{12\pi}{9}\right)\right] \qquad \text{Add } \dfrac{2(2)\pi}{3} \text{ to each angle.}$$

$$z^{\frac{1}{3}} = 2\left(\cos\left(\dfrac{14\pi}{9}\right) + i\sin\left(\dfrac{14\pi}{9}\right)\right)$$

Remember to find the common denominator to simplify fractions in situations like this one. For $k = 1$, the angle simplification is

$$\dfrac{\dfrac{2\pi}{3}}{3} + \dfrac{2(1)\pi}{3} = \dfrac{2\pi}{3}\left(\dfrac{1}{3}\right) + \dfrac{2(1)\pi}{3}\left(\dfrac{3}{3}\right)$$

$$= \dfrac{2\pi}{9} + \dfrac{6\pi}{9}$$

$$= \dfrac{8\pi}{9}$$

Try It #8

Find the four fourth roots of $16(\cos(120°) + i\sin(120°))$.

Access these online resources for additional instruction and practice with polar forms of complex numbers.

- The Product and Quotient of Complex Numbers in Trigonometric Form (http://openstaxcollege.org/l/prodquocomplex)
- De Moivre's Theorem (http://openstaxcollege.org/l/demoivre)

10.5   SECTION EXERCISES

VERBAL

1. A complex number is $a + bi$. Explain each part.

2. What does the absolute value of a complex number represent?

3. How is a complex number converted to polar form?

4. How do we find the product of two complex numbers?

5. What is De Moivre's Theorem and what is it used for?

ALGEBRAIC

For the following exercises, find the absolute value of the given complex number.

6. $5 + 3i$

7. $-7 + i$

8. $-3 - 3i$

9. $\sqrt{2} - 6i$

10. $2i$

11. $2.2 - 3.1i$

For the following exercises, write the complex number in polar form.

12. $2 + 2i$

13. $8 - 4i$

14. $-\dfrac{1}{2} - \dfrac{1}{2}i$

15. $\sqrt{3} + i$

16. $3i$

For the following exercises, convert the complex number from polar to rectangular form.

17. $z = 7\text{cis}\left(\dfrac{\pi}{6}\right)$

18. $z = 2\text{cis}\left(\dfrac{\pi}{3}\right)$

19. $z = 4\text{cis}\left(\dfrac{7\pi}{6}\right)$

20. $z = 7\text{cis}(25°)$

21. $z = 3\text{cis}(240°)$

22. $z = \sqrt{2}\text{cis}(100°)$

For the following exercises, find $z_1 z_2$ in polar form.

23. $z_1 = 2\sqrt{3}\text{cis}(116°); z_2 = 2\text{cis}(82°)$

24. $z_1 = \sqrt{2}\text{cis}(205°); z_2 = 2\sqrt{2}\text{cis}(118°)$

25. $z_1 = 3\text{cis}(120°); z_2 = \dfrac{1}{4}\text{cis}(60°)$

26. $z_1 = 3\text{cis}\left(\dfrac{\pi}{4}\right); z_2 = 5\text{cis}\left(\dfrac{\pi}{6}\right)$

27. $z_1 = \sqrt{5}\text{cis}\left(\dfrac{5\pi}{8}\right); z_2 = \sqrt{15}\,\text{cis}\left(\dfrac{\pi}{12}\right)$

28. $z_1 = 4\text{cis}\left(\dfrac{\pi}{2}\right); z_2 = 2\text{cis}\left(\dfrac{\pi}{4}\right)$

For the following exercises, find $\dfrac{z_1}{z_2}$ in polar form.

29. $z_1 = 21\text{cis}(135°); z_2 = 3\text{cis}(65°)$

30. $z_1 = \sqrt{2}\text{cis}(90°); z_2 = 2\text{cis}(60°)$

31. $z_1 = 15\text{cis}(120°); z_2 = 3\text{cis}(40°)$

32. $z_1 = 6\text{cis}\left(\dfrac{\pi}{3}\right); z_2 = 2\text{cis}\left(\dfrac{\pi}{4}\right)$

33. $z_1 = 5\sqrt{2}\text{cis}(\pi); z_2 = \sqrt{2}\text{cis}\left(\dfrac{2\pi}{3}\right)$

34. $z_1 = 2\text{cis}\left(\dfrac{3\pi}{5}\right); z_2 = 3\text{cis}\left(\dfrac{\pi}{4}\right)$

For the following exercises, find the powers of each complex number in polar form.

35. Find z^3 when $z = 5\text{cis}(45°)$.

36. Find z^4 when $z = 2\text{cis}(70°)$.

37. Find z^2 when $z = 3\text{cis}(120°)$.

38. Find z^2 when $z = 4\text{cis}\left(\dfrac{\pi}{4}\right)$.

39. Find z_4 when $z = \text{cis}\left(\dfrac{3\pi}{16}\right)$.

40. Find z^3 when $z = 3\text{cis}\left(\dfrac{5\pi}{3}\right)$.

For the following exercises, evaluate each root.

41. Evaluate the cube root of z when $z = 27\text{cis}(240°)$.

42. Evaluate the square root of z when $z = 16\text{cis}(100°)$.

43. Evaluate the cube root of z when $z = 32\text{cis}\left(\dfrac{2\pi}{3}\right)$.

44. Evaluate the square root of z when $z = 32\text{cis}(\pi)$.

45. Evaluate the cube root of z when $z = 8\text{cis}\left(\dfrac{7\pi}{4}\right)$.

GRAPHICAL

For the following exercises, plot the complex number in the complex plane.

46. $2 + 4i$

47. $-3 - 3i$

48. $5 - 4i$

49. $-1 - 5i$

50. $3 + 2i$

51. $2i$

52. -4

53. $6 - 2i$

54. $-2 + i$

55. $1 - 4i$

TECHNOLOGY

For the following exercises, find all answers rounded to the nearest hundredth.

56. Use the rectangular to polar feature on the graphing calculator to change $5 + 5i$ to polar form.

57. Use the rectangular to polar feature on the graphing calculator to change $3 - 2i$ to polar form.

58. Use the rectangular to polar feature on the graphing calculator to change $-3 - 8i$ to polar form.

59. Use the polar to rectangular feature on the graphing calculator to change $4\text{cis}(120°)$ to rectangular form.

60. Use the polar to rectangular feature on the graphing calculator to change $2\text{cis}(45°)$ to rectangular form.

61. Use the polar to rectangular feature on the graphing calculator to change $5\text{cis}(210°)$ to rectangular form.

LEARNING OBJECTIVES

In this section, you will:

- Parameterize a curve.
- Eliminate the parameter.
- Find a rectangular equation for a curve defined parametrically.
- Find parametric equations for curves defined by rectangular equations.

10.6   PARAMETRIC EQUATIONS

Consider the path a moon follows as it orbits a planet, which simultaneously rotates around the sun, as seen in **Figure 1**. At any moment, the moon is located at a particular spot relative to the planet. But how do we write and solve the equation for the position of the moon when the distance from the planet, the speed of the moon's orbit around the planet, and the speed of rotation around the sun are all unknowns? We can solve only for one variable at a time.

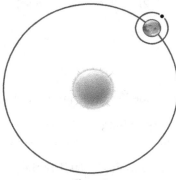

Figure 1

In this section, we will consider sets of equations given by $x(t)$ and $y(t)$ where t is the independent variable of time.

We can use these parametric equations in a number of applications when we are looking for not only a particular position but also the direction of the movement. As we trace out successive values of t, the orientation of the curve becomes clear.

This is one of the primary advantages of using parametric equations: we are able to trace the movement of an object along a path according to time. We begin this section with a look at the basic components of parametric equations and what it means to parameterize a curve. Then we will learn how to eliminate the parameter, translate the equations of a curve defined parametrically into rectangular equations, and find the parametric equations for curves defined by rectangular equations.

Parameterizing a Curve

When an object moves along a curve—or curvilinear path—in a given direction and in a given amount of time, the position of the object in the plane is given by the x-coordinate and the y-coordinate. However, both x and y vary over time and so are functions of time. For this reason, we add another variable, the **parameter**, upon which both x and y are dependent functions. In the example in the section opener, the parameter is time, t. The x position of the moon at time, t, is represented as the function $x(t)$, and the y position of the moon at time, t, is represented as the function $y(t)$. Together, $x(t)$ and $y(t)$ are called parametric equations, and generate an ordered pair $(x(t), y(t))$. Parametric equations primarily describe motion and direction.

When we parameterize a curve, we are translating a single equation in two variables, such as x and y, into an equivalent pair of equations in three variables, x, y, and t. One of the reasons we parameterize a curve is because the parametric equations yield more information: specifically, the direction of the object's motion over time.

When we graph parametric equations, we can observe the individual behaviors of x and of y. There are a number of shapes that cannot be represented in the form $y = f(x)$, meaning that they are not functions. For example, consider the graph of a circle, given as $r^2 = x^2 + y^2$. Solving for y gives $y = \pm \sqrt{r^2 - x^2}$, or two equations: $y_1 = \sqrt{r^2 - x^2}$ and $y_2 = -\sqrt{r^2 - x^2}$. If we graph y_1 and y_2 together, the graph will not pass the vertical line test, as shown in **Figure 2**. Thus, the equation for the graph of a circle is not a function.

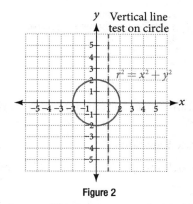

Figure 2

However, if we were to graph each equation on its own, each one would pass the vertical line test and therefore would represent a function. In some instances, the concept of breaking up the equation for a circle into two functions is similar to the concept of creating parametric equations, as we use two functions to produce a non-function. This will become clearer as we move forward.

> ### *parametric equations*
> Suppose t is a number on an interval, I. The set of ordered pairs, $(x(t), y(t))$, where $x = f(t)$ and $y = g(t)$, forms a plane curve based on the parameter t. The equations $x = f(t)$ and $y = g(t)$ are the parametric equations.

Example 1   **Parameterizing a Curve**

Parameterize the curve $y = x^2 - 1$ letting $x(t) = t$. Graph both equations.

Solution   If $x(t) = t$, then to find $y(t)$ we replace the variable x with the expression given in $x(t)$. In other words, $y(t) = t^2 - 1$. Make a table of values similar to **Table 1**, and sketch the graph.

t	$x(t)$	$y(t)$
−4	−4	$y(-4) = (-4)^2 - 1 = 15$
−3	−3	$y(-3) = (-3)^2 - 1 = 8$
−2	−2	$y(-2) = (-2)^2 - 1 = 3$
−1	−1	$y(-1) = (-1)^2 - 1 = 0$
0	0	$y(0) = (0)^2 - 1 = -1$
1	1	$y(1) = (1)^2 - 1 = 0$
2	2	$y(2) = (2)^2 - 1 = 3$
3	3	$y(3) = (3)^2 - 1 = 8$
4	4	$y(4) = (4)^2 - 1 = 15$

Table 1

See the graphs in **Figure 3**. It may be helpful to use the **TRACE** feature of a graphing calculator to see how the points are generated as t increases.

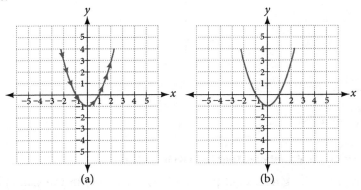

Figure 3 (a) Parametric $y(t) = t^2 - 1$ (b) Rectangular $y = x^2 - 1$

Analysis   The arrows indicate the direction in which the curve is generated. Notice the curve is identical to the curve of $y = x^2 - 1$.

Try It #1

Construct a table of values and plot the parametric equations: $x(t) = t - 3$, $y(t) = 2t + 4$; $-1 \le t \le 2$.

Example 2   **Finding a Pair of Parametric Equations**

Find a pair of parametric equations that models the graph of $y = 1 - x^2$, using the parameter $x(t) = t$. Plot some points and sketch the graph.

Solution   If $x(t) = t$ and we substitute t for x into the y equation, then $y(t) = 1 - t^2$. Our pair of parametric equations is

$$x(t) = t$$
$$y(t) = 1 - t^2$$

To graph the equations, first we construct a table of values like that in **Table 2**. We can choose values around $t = 0$, from $t = -3$ to $t = 3$. The values in the $x(t)$ column will be the same as those in the t column because $x(t) = t$. Calculate values for the column $y(t)$.

t	$x(t) = t$	$y(t) = 1 - t^2$
-3	-3	$y(-3) = 1 - (-3)^2 = -8$
-2	-2	$y(-2) = 1 - (-2)^2 = -3$
-1	-1	$y(-1) = 1 - (-1)^2 = 0$
0	0	$y(0) = 1 - 0 = 1$
1	1	$y(1) = 1 - (1)^2 = 0$
2	2	$y(2) = 1 - (2)^2 = -3$
3	3	$y(3) = 1 - (3)^2 = -8$

Table 2

The graph of $y = 1 - t^2$ is a parabola facing downward, as shown in **Figure 4**. We have mapped the curve over the interval $[-3, 3]$, shown as a solid line with arrows indicating the orientation of the curve according to t. Orientation refers to the path traced along the curve in terms of increasing values of t. As this parabola is symmetric with respect to the line $x = 0$, the values of x are reflected across the y-axis.

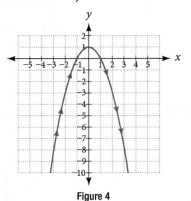

Figure 4

Try It #2

Parameterize the curve given by $x = y^3 - 2y$.

Example 3   **Finding Parametric Equations That Model Given Criteria**

An object travels at a steady rate along a straight path $(-5, 3)$ to $(3, -1)$ in the same plane in four seconds. The coordinates are measured in meters. Find parametric equations for the position of the object.

Solution   The parametric equations are simple linear expressions, but we need to view this problem in a step-by-step fashion. The x-value of the object starts at -5 meters and goes to 3 meters. This means the distance x has changed by 8 meters in 4 seconds, which is a rate of $\frac{8m}{4s}$, or 2 m/s. We can write the x-coordinate as a linear function with respect to time as $x(t) = 2t - 5$. In the linear function template $y = mx + b$, $2t = mx$ and $-5 = b$. Similarly, the y-value of the object starts at 3 and goes to -1, which is a change in the distance y of -4 meters in 4 seconds, which is a rate of $\frac{-4m}{4s}$, or -1 m/s. We can also write the y-coordinate as the linear function $y(t) = -t + 3$. Together, these are the parametric equations for the position of the object, where x and y are expressed in meters and t represents time:

$$x(t) = 2t - 5$$
$$y(t) = -t + 3$$

Using these equations, we can build a table of values for t, x, and y (see **Table 3**). In this example, we limited values of t to non-negative numbers. In general, any value of t can be used.

t	$x(t) = 2t - 5$	$y(t) = -t + 3$
0	$x = 2(0) - 5 = -5$	$y = -(0) + 3 = 3$
1	$x = 2(1) - 5 = -3$	$y = -(1) + 3 = 2$
2	$x = 2(2) - 5 = -1$	$y = -(2) + 3 = 1$
3	$x = 2(3) - 5 = 1$	$y = -(3) + 3 = 0$
4	$x = 2(4) - 5 = 3$	$y = -(4) + 3 = -1$

Table 3

From this table, we can create three graphs, as shown in **Figure 5**.

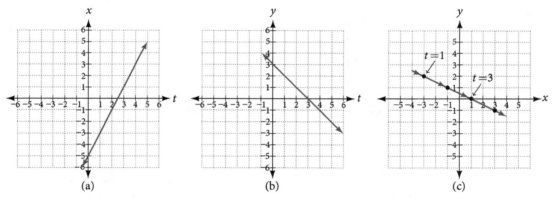

(a)   (b)   (c)

Figure 5   (a) A graph of x vs. t, representing the horizontal position over time. (b) A graph of y vs. t, representing the vertical position over time. (c) A graph of y vs. x, representing the position of the object in the plane at time t.

Analysis   Again, we see that, in **Figure 5(c)**, when the parameter represents time, we can indicate the movement of the object along the path with arrows.

Eliminating the Parameter

In many cases, we may have a pair of parametric equations but find that it is simpler to draw a curve if the equation involves only two variables, such as x and y. Eliminating the parameter is a method that may make graphing some curves easier.

However, if we are concerned with the mapping of the equation according to time, then it will be necessary to indicate the orientation of the curve as well. There are various methods for eliminating the parameter t from a set of parametric equations; not every method works for every type of equation. Here we will review the methods for the most common types of equations.

Eliminating the Parameter from Polynomial, Exponential, and Logarithmic Equations

For polynomial, exponential, or logarithmic equations expressed as two parametric equations, we choose the equation that is most easily manipulated and solve for t. We substitute the resulting expression for t into the second equation. This gives one equation in x and y.

Example 4   Eliminating the Parameter in Polynomials

Given $x(t) = t^2 + 1$ and $y(t) = 2 + t$, eliminate the parameter, and write the parametric equations as a Cartesian equation.

Solution   We will begin with the equation for y because the linear equation is easier to solve for t.

$$y = 2 + t$$
$$y - 2 = t$$

Next, substitute $y - 2$ for t in $x(t)$.

$$x = t^2 + 1$$
$$x = (y - 2)^2 + 1 \qquad \text{Substitute the expression for } t \text{ into } x.$$
$$x = y^2 - 4y + 4 + 1$$
$$x = y^2 - 4y + 5$$
$$x = y^2 - 4y + 5$$

The Cartesian form is $x = y^2 - 4y + 5$.

Analysis   *This is an equation for a parabola in which, in rectangular terms, x is dependent on y. From the curve's vertex at $(1, 2)$, the graph sweeps out to the right. See **Figure 6**. In this section, we consider sets of equations given by the functions $x(t)$ and $y(t)$, where t is the independent variable of time. Notice, both x and y are functions of time; so in general y is not a function of x.*

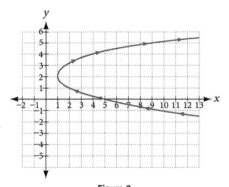

Figure 6

Try It #3

Given the equations below, eliminate the parameter and write as a rectangular equation for y as a function of x.

$$x(t) = 2t^2 + 6$$
$$y(t) = 5 - t$$

Example 5   Eliminating the Parameter in Exponential Equations

Eliminate the parameter and write as a Cartesian equation: $x(t) = e^{-t}$ and $y(t) = 3e^t, t > 0$.

Solution   Isolate e^t.

$$x = e^{-t}$$
$$e^t = \frac{1}{x}$$

Substitute the expression into $y(t)$.

$$y = 3e^t$$
$$y = 3\left(\frac{1}{x}\right)$$
$$y = \frac{3}{x}$$

The Cartesian form is $y = \dfrac{3}{x}$

Analysis   *The graph of the parametric equation is shown in **Figure 7(a)**. The domain is restricted to $t > 0$. The Cartesian equation, $y = 3x$ is shown in **Figure 7(b)** and has only one restriction on the domain, $x \neq 0$.*

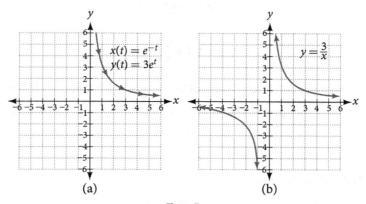

(a)   (b)

Figure 7

Example 6   **Eliminating the Parameter in Logarithmic Equations**

Eliminate the parameter and write as a Cartesian equation: $x(t) = \sqrt{t} + 2$ and $y(t) = \log(t)$.

Solution   Solve the first equation for t.

$$x = \sqrt{t} + 2$$
$$x - 2 = \sqrt{t}$$
$$(x - 2)^2 = t \qquad \text{Square both sides.}$$

Then, substitute the expression for t into the y equation.

$$y = \log(t)$$
$$y = \log(x - 2)^2$$

The Cartesian form is $y = \log(x - 2)^2$.

Analysis   *To be sure that the parametric equations are equivalent to the Cartesian equation, check the domains. The parametric equations restrict the domain on $x = \sqrt{t} + 2$ to $t > 0$; we restrict the domain on x to $x > 2$. The domain for the parametric equation $y = \log(t)$ is restricted to $t > 0$; we limit the domain on $y = \log(x - 2)^2$ to $x > 2$.*

Try It #4

Eliminate the parameter and write as a rectangular equation.

$$x(t) = t^2$$
$$y(t) = \ln(t) \qquad t > 0$$

Eliminating the Parameter from Trigonometric Equations

Eliminating the parameter from trigonometric equations is a straightforward substitution. We can use a few of the familiar trigonometric identities and the Pythagorean Theorem.

First, we use the identities:

$$x(t) = a\cos t$$
$$y(t) = b\sin t$$

Solving for $\cos t$ and $\sin t$, we have

$$\frac{x}{a} = \cos t$$
$$\frac{y}{a} = \sin t$$

Then, use the Pythagorean Theorem:

$$\cos^2 t + \sin^2 t = 1$$

Substituting gives

$$\cos^2 t + \sin^2 t = \left(\frac{x}{a}\right)^2 + \left(\frac{y}{b}\right)^2 = 1$$

Example 7   Eliminating the Parameter from a Pair of Trigonometric Parametric Equations

Eliminate the parameter from the given pair of trigonometric equations where $0 \le t \le 2\pi$ and sketch the graph.

$$x(t) = 4\cos t$$
$$y(t) = 3\sin t$$

Solution   Solving for $\cos t$ and $\sin t$, we have

$$x = 4\cos t$$
$$\frac{x}{4} = \cos t$$
$$y = 3\sin t$$
$$\frac{y}{3} = \sin t$$

Next, use the Pythagorean identity and make the substitutions.

$$\cos^2 t + \sin^2 t = 1$$
$$\left(\frac{x}{4}\right)^2 + \left(\frac{y}{3}\right)^2 = 1$$
$$\frac{x^2}{16} + \frac{y^2}{9} = 1$$

The graph for the equation is shown in **Figure 8**.

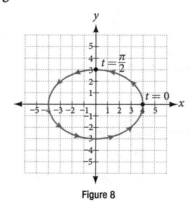

Figure 8

Analysis   *Applying the general equations for conic sections (introduced in **Analytic Geometry**, we can identify* $\frac{x^2}{16} + \frac{y^2}{9} = 1$ *as an ellipse centered at* (0, 0). *Notice that when* $t = 0$ *the coordinates are* (4, 0), *and when* $t = \frac{\pi}{2}$ *the coordinates are* (0, 3). *This shows the orientation of the curve with increasing values of t.*

Try It #5

Eliminate the parameter from the given pair of parametric equations and write as a Cartesian equation: $x(t) = 2\cos t$ and $y(t) = 3\sin t$.

Finding Cartesian Equations from Curves Defined Parametrically

When we are given a set of parametric equations and need to find an equivalent Cartesian equation, we are essentially "eliminating the parameter." However, there are various methods we can use to rewrite a set of parametric equations as a Cartesian equation. The simplest method is to set one equation equal to the parameter, such as $x(t) = t$. In this case, $y(t)$ can be any expression. For example, consider the following pair of equations.

$$x(t) = t$$
$$y(t) = t^2 - 3$$

Rewriting this set of parametric equations is a matter of substituting x for t. Thus, the Cartesian equation is $y = x^2 - 3$.

Example 8   Finding a Cartesian Equation Using Alternate Methods

Use two different methods to find the Cartesian equation equivalent to the given set of parametric equations.

$$x(t) = 3t - 2$$
$$y(t) = t + 1$$

Solution

Method 1. First, let's solve the x equation for t. Then we can substitute the result into the y equation.

$$x = 3t - 2$$
$$x + 2 = 3t$$
$$\frac{x + 2}{3} = t$$

Now substitute the expression for t into the y equation.

$$y = t + 1$$
$$y = \left(\frac{x + 2}{3}\right) + 1$$
$$y = \frac{x}{3} + \frac{2}{3} + 1$$
$$y = \frac{1}{3}x + \frac{5}{3}$$

Method 2. Solve the y equation for t and substitute this expression in the x equation.

$$y = t + 1$$
$$y - 1 = t$$

Make the substitution and then solve for y.

$$x = 3(y - 1) - 2$$
$$x = 3y - 3 - 2$$
$$x = 3y - 5$$
$$x + 5 = 3y$$
$$\frac{x + 5}{3} = y$$
$$y = \frac{1}{3}x + \frac{5}{3}$$

Try It #6

Write the given parametric equations as a Cartesian equation: $x(t) = t^3$ and $y(t) = t^6$.

Finding Parametric Equations for Curves Defined by Rectangular Equations

Although we have just shown that there is only one way to interpret a set of parametric equations as a rectangular equation, there are multiple ways to interpret a rectangular equation as a set of parametric equations. Any strategy we may use to find the parametric equations is valid if it produces equivalency. In other words, if we choose an expression to represent x, and then substitute it into the y equation, and it produces the same graph over the same domain as the rectangular equation, then the set of parametric equations is valid. If the domain becomes restricted in the set of parametric equations, and the function does not allow the same values for x as the domain of the rectangular equation, then the graphs will be different.

Example 9　**Finding a Set of Parametric Equations for Curves Defined by Rectangular Equations**

Find a set of equivalent parametric equations for $y = (x + 3)^2 + 1$.

Solution　An obvious choice would be to let $x(t) = t$. Then $y(t) = (t + 3)^2 + 1$. But let's try something more interesting. What if we let $x = t + 3$? Then we have

$$y = (x + 3)^2 + 1$$
$$y = ((t + 3) + 3)^2 + 1$$
$$y = (t + 6)^2 + 1$$

The set of parametric equations is

$$x(t) = t + 3$$
$$y(t) = (t + 6)^2 + 1$$

See **Figure 9**.

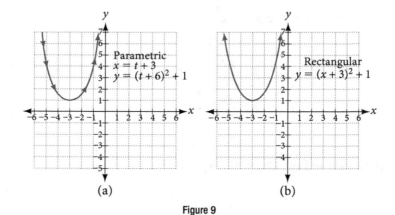

(a)　　　　　(b)

Figure 9

Access these online resources for additional instruction and practice with parametric equations.

- Introduction to Parametric Equations (http://openstaxcollege.org/l/introparametric)
- Converting Parametric Equations to Rectangular Form (http://openstaxcollege.org/l/convertpara)

10.6   SECTION EXERCISES

VERBAL

1. What is a system of parametric equations?

2. Some examples of a third parameter are time, length, speed, and scale. Explain when time is used as a parameter.

3. Explain how to eliminate a parameter given a set of parametric equations.

4. What is a benefit of writing a system of parametric equations as a Cartesian equation?

5. What is a benefit of using parametric equations?

6. Why are there many sets of parametric equations to represent on Cartesian function?

ALGEBRAIC

For the following exercises, eliminate the parameter t to rewrite the parametric equation as a Cartesian equation.

7. $\begin{cases} x(t) = 5 - t \\ y(t) = 8 - 2t \end{cases}$

8. $\begin{cases} x(t) = 6 - 3t \\ y(t) = 10 - t \end{cases}$

9. $\begin{cases} x(t) = 2t + 1 \\ y(t) = 3\sqrt{t} \end{cases}$

10. $\begin{cases} x(t) = 3t - 1 \\ y(t) = 2t^2 \end{cases}$

11. $\begin{cases} x(t) = 2e^t \\ y(t) = 1 - 5t \end{cases}$

12. $\begin{cases} x(t) = e^{-2t} \\ y(t) = 2e^{-t} \end{cases}$

13. $\begin{cases} x(t) = 4 \log (t) \\ y(t) = 3 + 2t \end{cases}$

14. $\begin{cases} x(t) = \log (2t) \\ y(t) = \sqrt{t - 1} \end{cases}$

15. $\begin{cases} x(t) = t^3 - t \\ y(t) = 2t \end{cases}$

16. $\begin{cases} x(t) = t - t^4 \\ y(t) = t + 2 \end{cases}$

17. $\begin{cases} x(t) = e^{2t} \\ y(t) = e^{6t} \end{cases}$

18. $\begin{cases} x(t) = t^5 \\ y(t) = t^{10} \end{cases}$

19. $\begin{cases} x(t) = 4 \cos t \\ y(t) = 5 \sin t \end{cases}$

20. $\begin{cases} x(t) = 3 \sin t \\ y(t) = 6 \cos t \end{cases}$

21. $\begin{cases} x(t) = 2 \cos^2 t \\ y(t) = -\sin t \end{cases}$

22. $\begin{cases} x(t) = \cos t + 4 \\ y(t) = 2 \sin^2 t \end{cases}$

23. $\begin{cases} x(t) = t - 1 \\ y(t) = t^2 \end{cases}$

24. $\begin{cases} x(t) = -t \\ y(t) = t^3 + 1 \end{cases}$

25. $\begin{cases} x(t) = 2t - 1 \\ y(t) = t^3 - 2 \end{cases}$

For the following exercises, rewrite the parametric equation as a Cartesian equation by building an x-y table.

26. $\begin{cases} x(t) = 2t - 1 \\ y(t) = t + 4 \end{cases}$

27. $\begin{cases} x(t) = 4 - t \\ y(t) = 3t + 2 \end{cases}$

28. $\begin{cases} x(t) = 2t - 1 \\ y(t) = 5t \end{cases}$

29. $\begin{cases} x(t) = 4t - 1 \\ y(t) = 4t + 2 \end{cases}$

For the following exercises, parameterize (write parametric equations for) each Cartesian equation by setting $x(t) = t$ or by setting $y(t) = t$.

30. $y(x) = 3x^2 + 3$

31. $y(x) = 2 \sin x + 1$

32. $x(y) = 3 \log (y) + y$

33. $x(y) = \sqrt{y} + 2y$

For the following exercises, parameterize (write parametric equations for) each Cartesian equation by using $x(t) = a \cos t$ and $y(t) = b \sin t$. Identify the curve.

34. $\dfrac{x^2}{4} + \dfrac{y^2}{9} = 1$

35. $\dfrac{x^2}{16} + \dfrac{y^2}{36} = 1$

36. $x^2 + y^2 = 16$

37. $x^2 + y^2 = 10$

38. Parameterize the line from $(3, 0)$ to $(-2, -5)$ so that the line is at $(3, 0)$ at $t = 0$, and at $(-2, -5)$ at $t = 1$.

39. Parameterize the line from $(-1, 0)$ to $(3, -2)$ so that the line is at $(-1, 0)$ at $t = 0$, and at $(3, -2)$ at $t = 1$.

40. Parameterize the line from $(-1, 5)$ to $(2, 3)$ so that the line is at $(-1, 5)$ at $t = 0$, and at $(2, 3)$ at $t = 1$.

41. Parameterize the line from $(4, 1)$ to $(6, -2)$ so that the line is at $(4, 1)$ at $t = 0$, and at $(6, -2)$ at $t = 1$.

TECHNOLOGY

For the following exercises, use the table feature in the graphing calculator to determine whether the graphs intersect.

42. $\begin{cases} x_1(t) = 3t \\ y_1(t) = 2t - 1 \end{cases}$ and $\begin{cases} x_2(t) = t + 3 \\ y_2(t) = 4t - 4 \end{cases}$

43. $\begin{cases} x_1(t) = t^2 \\ y_1(t) = 2t - 1 \end{cases}$ and $\begin{cases} x_2(t) = -t + 6 \\ y_2(t) = t + 1 \end{cases}$

For the following exercises, use a graphing calculator to complete the table of values for each set of parametric equations.

44. $\begin{cases} x_1(t) = 3t^2 - 3t + 7 \\ y_1(t) = 2t + 3 \end{cases}$

t	x	y
−1		
0		
1		

45. $\begin{cases} x_1(t) = t^2 - 4 \\ y_1(t) = 2t^2 - 1 \end{cases}$

t	x	y
1		
2		
3		

46. $\begin{cases} x_1(t) = t^4 \\ y_1(t) = t^3 + 4 \end{cases}$

t	x	y
−1		
0		
1		
2		

EXTENSIONS

47. Find two different sets of parametric equations for $y = (x + 1)^2$.

48. Find two different sets of parametric equations for $y = 3x - 2$.

49. Find two different sets of parametric equations for $y = x^2 - 4x + 4$.

LEARNING OBJECTIVES

In this section, you will:

- Graph plane curves described by parametric equations by plotting points.
- Graph parametric equations.

10.7 PARAMETRIC EQUATIONS: GRAPHS

It is the bottom of the ninth inning, with two outs and two men on base. The home team is losing by two runs. The batter swings and hits the baseball at 140 feet per second and at an angle of approximately 45° to the horizontal. How far will the ball travel? Will it clear the fence for a game-winning home run? The outcome may depend partly on other factors (for example, the wind), but mathematicians can model the path of a projectile and predict approximately how far it will travel using parametric equations. In this section, we'll discuss parametric equations and some common applications, such as projectile motion problems.

Figure 1 Parametric equations can model the path of a projectile. (credit: Paul Kreher, Flickr)

Graphing Parametric Equations by Plotting Points

In lieu of a graphing calculator or a computer graphing program, plotting points to represent the graph of an equation is the standard method. As long as we are careful in calculating the values, point-plotting is highly dependable.

How To...

Given a pair of parametric equations, sketch a graph by plotting points.

1. Construct a table with three columns: t, $x(t)$, and $y(t)$.
2. Evaluate x and y for values of t over the interval for which the functions are defined.
3. Plot the resulting pairs (x, y).

Example 1   **Sketching the Graph of a Pair of Parametric Equations by Plotting Points**

Sketch the graph of the parametric equations $x(t) = t^2 + 1, y(t) = 2 + t$.

Solution   Construct a table of values for t, $x(t)$, and $y(t)$, as in **Table 1**, and plot the points in a plane.

t	$x(t) = t^2 + 1$	$y(t) = 2 + t$
-5	26	-3
-4	17	-2
-3	10	-1
-2	5	0
-1	2	1
0	1	2
1	2	3
2	5	4
3	10	5
4	17	6
5	26	7

Table 1

The graph is a parabola with vertex at the point $(1, 2)$, opening to the right. See **Figure 2**.

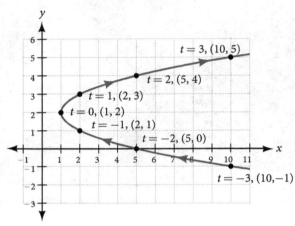

Figure 2

Analysis   *As values for t progress in a positive direction from 0 to 5, the plotted points trace out the top half of the parabola. As values of t become negative, they trace out the lower half of the parabola. There are no restrictions on the domain. The arrows indicate direction according to increasing values of t. The graph does not represent a function, as it will fail the vertical line test. The graph is drawn in two parts: the positive values for t, and the negative values for t.*

Try It #1

Sketch the graph of the parametric equations $x = \sqrt{t}, y = 2t + 3, 0 \le t \le 3$.

Example 2   **Sketching the Graph of Trigonometric Parametric Equations**

Construct a table of values for the given parametric equations and sketch the graph:

$$x = 2\cos t$$
$$y = 4\sin t$$

Solution   Construct a table like that in **Table 2** using angle measure in radians as inputs for t, and evaluating x and y. Using angles with known sine and cosine values for t makes calculations easier.

t	$x = 2\cos t$	$y = 4\sin t$
0	$x = 2\cos(0) = 2$	$y = 4\sin(0) = 0$
$\dfrac{\pi}{6}$	$x = 2\cos\left(\dfrac{\pi}{6}\right) = \sqrt{3}$	$y = 4\sin\left(\dfrac{\pi}{6}\right) = 2$
$\dfrac{\pi}{3}$	$x = 2\cos\left(\dfrac{\pi}{3}\right) = 1$	$y = 4\sin\left(\dfrac{\pi}{3}\right) = 2\sqrt{3}$
$\dfrac{\pi}{2}$	$x = 2\cos\left(\dfrac{\pi}{2}\right) = 0$	$y = 4\sin\left(\dfrac{\pi}{2}\right) = 4$
$\dfrac{2\pi}{3}$	$x = 2\cos\left(\dfrac{2\pi}{3}\right) = -1$	$y = 4\sin\left(\dfrac{2\pi}{3}\right) = -2\sqrt{3}$
$\dfrac{5\pi}{6}$	$x = 2\cos\left(\dfrac{5\pi}{6}\right) = -\sqrt{3}$	$y = 4\sin\left(\dfrac{5\pi}{6}\right) = 2$
π	$x = 2\cos(\pi) = -2$	$y = 4\sin(\pi) = 0$
$\dfrac{7\pi}{6}$	$x = 2\cos\left(\dfrac{7\pi}{6}\right) = -\sqrt{3}$	$y = 4\sin\left(\dfrac{7\pi}{6}\right) = -2$
$\dfrac{4\pi}{3}$	$x = 2\cos\left(\dfrac{4\pi}{3}\right) = -1$	$y = 4\sin\left(\dfrac{4\pi}{3}\right) = -2\sqrt{3}$
$\dfrac{3\pi}{2}$	$x = 2\cos\left(\dfrac{3\pi}{2}\right) = 0$	$y = 4\sin\left(\dfrac{3\pi}{2}\right) = -4$
$\dfrac{5\pi}{3}$	$x = 2\cos\left(\dfrac{5\pi}{3}\right) = 1$	$y = 4\sin\left(\dfrac{5\pi}{3}\right) = -2\sqrt{3}$
$\dfrac{11\pi}{6}$	$x = 2\cos\left(\dfrac{11\pi}{6}\right) = \sqrt{3}$	$y = 4\sin\left(\dfrac{11\pi}{6}\right) = -2$
2π	$x = 2\cos(2\pi) = 2$	$y = 4\sin(2\pi) = 0$

Table 2

Figure 3 shows the graph.

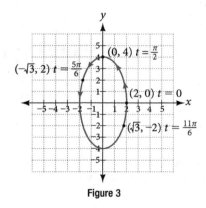

Figure 3

By the symmetry shown in the values of x and y, we see that the parametric equations represent an ellipse.

The ellipse is mapped in a counterclockwise direction as shown by the arrows indicating increasing t values.

Analysis We have seen that parametric equations can be graphed by plotting points. However, a graphing calculator will save some time and reveal nuances in a graph that may be too tedious to discover using only hand calculations.

*Make sure to change the mode on the calculator to parametric (**PAR**). To confirm, the **Y=** window should show*

$$X_{1T} =$$

$$Y_{1T} =$$

*instead of **Y₁ =**.*

Try It #2

Graph the parametric equations: $x = 5\cos t$, $y = 3\sin t$.

Example 3   Graphing Parametric Equations and Rectangular Form Together

Graph the parametric equations $x = 5\cos t$ and $y = 2\sin t$. First, construct the graph using data points generated from the parametric form. Then graph the rectangular form of the equation. Compare the two graphs.

Solution   Construct a table of values like that in **Table 3**.

t	$x = 5\cos t$	$y = 2\sin t$
0	$x = 5\cos(0) = 5$	$y = 2\sin(0) = 0$
1	$x = 5\cos(1) \approx 2.7$	$y = 2\sin(1) \approx 1.7$
2	$x = 5\cos(2) \approx -2.1$	$y = 2\sin(2) \approx 1.8$
3	$x = 5\cos(3) \approx -4.95$	$y = 2\sin(3) \approx 0.28$
4	$x = 5\cos(4) \approx -3.3$	$y = 2\sin(4) \approx -1.5$
5	$x = 5\cos(5) \approx 1.4$	$y = 2\sin(5) \approx -1.9$
−1	$x = 5\cos(-1) \approx 2.7$	$y = 2\sin(-1) \approx -1.7$
−2	$x = 5\cos(-2) \approx -2.1$	$y = 2\sin(-2) \approx -1.8$
−3	$x = 5\cos(-3) \approx -4.95$	$y = 2\sin(-3) \approx -0.28$
−4	$x = 5\cos(-4) \approx -3.3$	$y = 2\sin(-4) \approx 1.5$
−5	$x = 5\cos(-5) \approx 1.4$	$y = 2\sin(-5) \approx 1.9$

Table 3

Plot the (x, y) values from the table. See **Figure 4**.

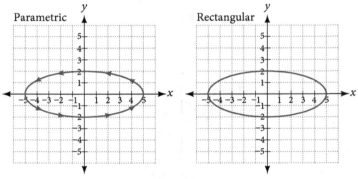

Figure 4

Next, translate the parametric equations to rectangular form. To do this, we solve for t in either $x(t)$ or $y(t)$, and then substitute the expression for t in the other equation. The result will be a function $y(x)$ if solving for t as a function of x, or $x(y)$ if solving for t as a function of y.

$$x = 5\cos t$$

$$\frac{x}{5} = \cos t \qquad \text{Solve for } \cos t.$$

$$y = 2\sin t \qquad \text{Solve for } \sin t.$$

$$\frac{y}{2} = \sin t$$

Then, use the Pythagorean Theorem.

$$\cos^2 t + \sin^2 t = 1$$

$$\left(\frac{x}{5}\right)^2 + \left(\frac{y}{2}\right)^2 = 1$$

$$\frac{x^2}{25} + \frac{y^2}{4} = 1$$

Analysis In **Figure 5**, the data from the parametric equations and the rectangular equation are plotted together. The parametric equations are plotted in blue; the graph for the rectangular equation is drawn on top of the parametric in a dashed style colored red. Clearly, both forms produce the same graph.

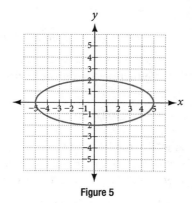

Figure 5

Example 4   **Graphing Parametric Equations and Rectangular Equations on the Coordinate System**

Graph the parametric equations $x = t + 1$ and $y = \sqrt{t}, t \geq 0$, and the rectangular equivalent $y = \sqrt{x-1}$ on the same coordinate system.

Solution   Construct a table of values for the parametric equations, as we did in the previous example, and graph $y = \sqrt{t}, t \geq 0$ on the same grid, as in **Figure 6**.

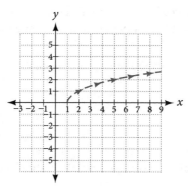

Figure 6

Analysis   With the domain on t restricted, we only plot positive values of t. The parametric data is graphed in blue and the graph of the rectangular equation is dashed in red. Once again, we see that the two forms overlap.

Try It #3

Sketch the graph of the parametric equations $x = 2\cos \theta$ and $y = 4\sin \theta$, along with the rectangular equation on the same grid.

Applications of Parametric Equations

Many of the advantages of parametric equations become obvious when applied to solving real-world problems. Although rectangular equations in x and y give an overall picture of an object's path, they do not reveal the position of an object at a specific time. Parametric equations, however, illustrate how the values of x and y change depending on t, as the location of a moving object at a particular time.

A common application of parametric equations is solving problems involving projectile motion. In this type of motion, an object is propelled forward in an upward direction forming an angle of θ to the horizontal, with an initial speed of v_0, and at a height h above the horizontal.

The path of an object propelled at an inclination of θ to the horizontal, with initial speed v_0, and at a height h above the horizontal, is given by

$$x = (v_0 \cos \theta)t$$

$$y = -\frac{1}{2}gt^2 + (v_0 \sin \theta)t + h$$

where g accounts for the effects of gravity and h is the initial height of the object. Depending on the units involved in the problem, use $g = 32$ ft/s^2 or $g = 9.8$ m/s^2. The equation for x gives horizontal distance, and the equation for y gives the vertical distance.

How To...

Given a projectile motion problem, use parametric equations to solve.

1. The horizontal distance is given by $x = (v_0 \cos \theta)t$. Substitute the initial speed of the object for v_0.
2. The expression $\cos \theta$ indicates the angle at which the object is propelled. Substitute that angle in degrees for $\cos \theta$.
3. The vertical distance is given by the formula $y = -\frac{1}{2}gt^2 + (v_0 \sin \theta)t + h$. The term $-\frac{1}{2}gt^2$ represents the effect of gravity. Depending on units involved, use $g = 32$ ft/s^2 or $g = 9.8$ m/s^2. Again, substitute the initial speed for v_0, and the height at which the object was propelled for h.
4. Proceed by calculating each term to solve for t.

Example 5   **Finding the Parametric Equations to Describe the Motion of a Baseball**

Solve the problem presented at the beginning of this section. Does the batter hit the game-winning home run? Assume that the ball is hit with an initial velocity of 140 feet per second at an angle of 45° to the horizontal, making contact 3 feet above the ground.

    a. Find the parametric equations to model the path of the baseball.
    b. Where is the ball after 2 seconds?
    c. How long is the ball in the air?
    d. Is it a home run?

Solution

    a. Use the formulas to set up the equations. The horizontal position is found using the parametric equation for x. Thus,

$$x = (v_0 \cos \theta)t$$
$$x = (140\cos(45°))t$$

    The vertical position is found using the parametric equation for y. Thus,

$$y = -16t^2 + (v_0 \sin \theta)t + h$$
$$y = -16t^2 + (140\sin(45°))t + 3$$

    b. Substitute 2 into the equations to find the horizontal and vertical positions of the ball.

$$x = (140\cos(45°))(2)$$
$$x = 198 \text{ feet}$$
$$y = -16(2)^2 + (140\sin(45°))(2) + 3$$
$$y = 137 \text{ feet}$$

After 2 seconds, the ball is 198 feet away from the batter's box and 137 feet above the ground.

c. To calculate how long the ball is in the air, we have to find out when it will hit ground, or when $y = 0$. Thus,

$$y = -16t^2 + (140\sin(45°))t + 3$$

$$y = 0 \qquad\qquad\qquad \text{Set } y(t) = 0 \text{ and solve the quadratic.}$$

$$t = 6.2173$$

When $t = 6.2173$ seconds, the ball has hit the ground. (The quadratic equation can be solved in various ways, but this problem was solved using a computer math program.)

d. We cannot confirm that the hit was a home run without considering the size of the outfield, which varies from field to field. However, for simplicity's sake, let's assume that the outfield wall is 400 feet from home plate in the deepest part of the park. Let's also assume that the wall is 10 feet high. In order to determine whether the ball clears the wall, we need to calculate how high the ball is when $x = 400$ feet. So we will set $x = 400$, solve for t, and input t into y.

$$x = (140\cos(45°))t$$

$$400 = (140\cos(45°))t$$

$$t = 4.04$$

$$y = -16(4.04)^2 + (140\sin(45°))(4.04) + 3$$

$$y = 141.8$$

The ball is 141.8 feet in the air when it soars out of the ballpark. It was indeed a home run. See **Figure 7**.

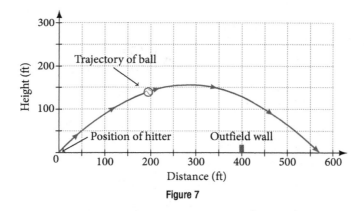

Figure 7

Access the following online resource for additional instruction and practice with graphs of parametric equations.

- Graphing Parametric Equations on the TI-84 (http://openstaxcollege.org/l/graphpara84)

10.7   SECTION EXERCISES

VERBAL

1. What are two methods used to graph parametric equations?

2. What is one difference in point-plotting parametric equations compared to Cartesian equations?

3. Why are some graphs drawn with arrows?

4. Name a few common types of graphs of parametric equations.

5. Why are parametric graphs important in understanding projectile motion?

GRAPHICAL

For the following exercises, graph each set of parametric equations by making a table of values. Include the orientation on the graph.

6. $\begin{cases} x(t) = t \\ y(t) = t^2 - 1 \end{cases}$

t	x	y
−3		
−2		
−1		
0		
1		
2		
3		

7. $\begin{cases} x(t) = t - 1 \\ y(t) = t^2 \end{cases}$

t	−3	−2	−1	0	1	2
x						
y						

8. $\begin{cases} x(t) = 2 + t \\ y(t) = 3 - 2t \end{cases}$

t	− 2	− 1	0	1	2	3
x						
y						

9. $\begin{cases} x(t) = -2 - 2t \\ y(t) = 3 + t \end{cases}$

t	− 3	− 2	− 1	0	1
x					
y					

10. $\begin{cases} x(t) = t^3 \\ y(t) = t + 2 \end{cases}$

t	− 2	− 1	0	1	2
x					
y					

11. $\begin{cases} x(t) = t^2 \\ y(t) = t + 3 \end{cases}$

t	− 2	− 1	0	1	2
x					
y					

For the following exercises, sketch the curve and include the orientation.

12. $\begin{cases} x(t) = t \\ y(t) = \sqrt{t} \end{cases}$

13. $\begin{cases} x(t) = -\sqrt{t} \\ y(t) = t \end{cases}$

14. $\begin{cases} x(t) = 5 - |t| \\ y(t) = t + 2 \end{cases}$

15. $\begin{cases} x(t) = -t + 2 \\ y(t) = 5 - |t| \end{cases}$

16. $\begin{cases} x(t) = 4\sin t \\ y(t) = 2\cos t \end{cases}$

17. $\begin{cases} x(t) = 2\sin t \\ y(t) = 4\cos t \end{cases}$

18. $\begin{cases} x(t) = 3\cos^2 t \\ y(t) = -3\sin t \end{cases}$

19. $\begin{cases} x(t) = 3\cos^2 t \\ y(t) = -3\sin^2 t \end{cases}$

20. $\begin{cases} x(t) = \sec t \\ y(t) = \tan t \end{cases}$

21. $\begin{cases} x(t) = \sec t \\ y(t) = \tan^2 t \end{cases}$

22. $\begin{cases} x(t) = \dfrac{1}{e^{2t}} \\ y(t) = e^{-t} \end{cases}$

For the following exercises, graph the equation and include the orientation. Then, write the Cartesian equation.

23. $\begin{cases} x(t) = t - 1 \\ y(t) = -t^2 \end{cases}$

24. $\begin{cases} x(t) = t^3 \\ y(t) = t + 3 \end{cases}$

25. $\begin{cases} x(t) = 2\cos t \\ y(t) = -\sin t \end{cases}$

26. $\begin{cases} x(t) = 7\cos t \\ y(t) = 7\sin t \end{cases}$ **27.** $\begin{cases} x(t) = e^{2t} \\ y(t) = -e^t \end{cases}$

For the following exercises, graph the equation and include the orientation.

28. $x = t^2, y = 3t, 0 \le t \le 5$ **29.** $x = 2t, y = t^2, -5 \le t \le 5$ **30.** $x = t, y = \sqrt{25 - t^2}, 0 < t \le 5$

31. $x(t) = -t, y(t) = \sqrt{t}, t \ge 5$ **32.** $x(t) = -2\cos t, y = 6\sin t \, 0 \le t \le \pi$ **33.** $x(t) = -\sec t, y = \tan t, -\dfrac{\pi}{2} < t < \dfrac{\pi}{2}$

For the following exercises, use the parametric equations for integers a and b:

$$x(t) = a\cos((a + b)t) \qquad y(t) = a\cos((a - b)t)$$

34. Graph on the domain $[-\pi, 0]$, where $a = 2$ and $b = 1$, and include the orientation.

35. Graph on the domain $[-\pi, 0]$, where $a = 3$ and $b = 2$, and include the orientation.

36. Graph on the domain $[-\pi, 0]$, where $a = 4$ and $b = 3$, and include the orientation.

37. Graph on the domain $[-\pi, 0]$, where $a = 5$ and $b = 4$, and include the orientation.

38. If a is 1 more than b, describe the effect the values of a and b have on the graph of the parametric equations.

39. Describe the graph if $a = 100$ and $b = 99$.

40. What happens if b is 1 more than a? Describe the graph.

41. If the parametric equations $x(t) = t^2$ and $y(t) = 6 - 3t$ have the graph of a horizontal parabola opening to the right, what would change the direction of the curve?

For the following exercises, describe the graph of the set of parametric equations.

42. $x(t) = -t^2$ and $y(t)$ is linear

43. $y(t) = t^2$ and $x(t)$ is linear

44. $y(t) = -t^2$ and $x(t)$ is linear

45. Write the parametric equations of a circle with center $(0, 0)$, radius 5, and a counterclockwise orientation.

46. Write the parametric equations of an ellipse with center $(0, 0)$, major axis of length 10, minor axis of length 6, and a counterclockwise orientation.

For the following exercises, use a graphing utility to graph on the window $[-3, 3]$ by $[-3, 3]$ on the domain $[0, 2\pi)$ for the following values of a and b, and include the orientation.

$$\begin{cases} x(t) = \sin(at) \\ y(t) = \sin(bt) \end{cases}$$

47. $a = 1, b = 2$ **48.** $a = 2, b = 1$ **49.** $a = 3, b = 3$

50. $a = 5, b = 5$ **51.** $a = 2, b = 5$ **52.** $a = 5, b = 2$

TECHNOLOGY

For the following exercises, look at the graphs that were created by parametric equations of the form $\begin{cases} x(t) = a\cos(bt) \\ y(t) = c\sin(dt) \end{cases}$
Use the parametric mode on the graphing calculator to find the values of $a, b, c,$ and d to achieve each graph.

53.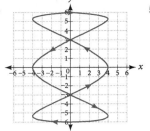

54.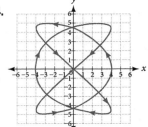

55.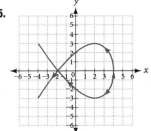

56.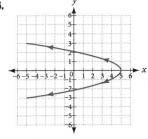

For the following exercises, use a graphing utility to graph the given parametric equations.

a. $\begin{cases} x(t) = \cos t - 1 \\ y(t) = \sin t + t \end{cases}$
b. $\begin{cases} x(t) = \cos t + t \\ y(t) = \sin t - 1 \end{cases}$
c. $\begin{cases} x(t) = t - \sin t \\ y(t) = \cos t - 1 \end{cases}$

57. Graph all three sets of parametric equations on the domain $[0, 2\pi]$.

58. Graph all three sets of parametric equations on the domain $[0, 4\pi]$.

59. Graph all three sets of parametric equations on the domain $[-4\pi, 6\pi]$.

60. The graph of each set of parametric equations appears to "creep" along one of the axes. What controls which axis the graph creeps along?

61. Explain the effect on the graph of the parametric equation when we switched $\sin t$ and $\cos t$.

62. Explain the effect on the graph of the parametric equation when we changed the domain.

EXTENSIONS

63. An object is thrown in the air with vertical velocity of 20 ft/s and horizontal velocity of 15 ft/s. The object's height can be described by the equation $y(t) = -16t^2 + 20t$, while the object moves horizontally with constant velocity 15 ft/s. Write parametric equations for the object's position, and then eliminate time to write height as a function of horizontal position.

64. A skateboarder riding on a level surface at a constant speed of 9 ft/s throws a ball in the air, the height of which can be described by the equation $y(t) = -16t^2 + 10t + 5$. Write parametric equations for the ball's position, and then eliminate time to write height as a function of horizontal position.

For the following exercises, use this scenario: A dart is thrown upward with an initial velocity of 65 ft/s at an angle of elevation of 52°. Consider the position of the dart at any time t. Neglect air resistance.

65. Find parametric equations that model the problem situation.

66. Find all possible values of x that represent the situation.

67. When will the dart hit the ground?

68. Find the maximum height of the dart.

69. At what time will the dart reach maximum height?

For the following exercises, look at the graphs of each of the four parametric equations. Although they look unusual and beautiful, they are so common that they have names, as indicated in each exercise. Use a graphing utility to graph each on the indicated domain.

70. An epicycloid: $\begin{cases} x(t) = 14\cos t - \cos(14t) \\ y(t) = 14\sin t + \sin(14t) \end{cases}$

on the domain $[0, 2\pi]$.

71. An hypocycloid: $\begin{cases} x(t) = 6\sin t + 2\sin(6t) \\ y(t) = 6\cos t - 2\cos(6t) \end{cases}$

on the domain $[0, 2\pi]$.

72. An hypotrochoid: $\begin{cases} x(t) = 2\sin t + 5\cos(6t) \\ y(t) = 5\cos t - 2\sin(6t) \end{cases}$

on the domain $[0, 2\pi]$.

73. A rose: $\begin{cases} x(t) = 5\sin(2t) \sin t \\ y(t) = 5\sin(2t) \cos t \end{cases}$

on the domain $[0, 2\pi]$.

LEARNING OBJECTIVES

In this section, you will:

- View vectors geometrically.
- Find magnitude and direction.
- Perform vector addition and scalar multiplication.
- Find the component form of a vector.
- Find the unit vector in the direction of *v*.
- Perform operations with vectors in terms of *i* and *j*.
- Find the dot product of two vectors.

10.8 VECTORS

An airplane is flying at an airspeed of 200 miles per hour headed on a SE bearing of 140°. A north wind (from north to south) is blowing at 16.2 miles per hour, as shown in **Figure 1**. What are the ground speed and actual bearing of the plane?

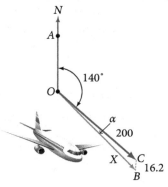

Figure 1

Ground speed refers to the speed of a plane relative to the ground. Airspeed refers to the speed a plane can travel relative to its surrounding air mass. These two quantities are not the same because of the effect of wind. In an earlier section, we used triangles to solve a similar problem involving the movement of boats. Later in this section, we will find the airplane's groundspeed and bearing, while investigating another approach to problems of this type. First, however, let's examine the basics of vectors.

A Geometric View of Vectors

A **vector** is a specific quantity drawn as a line segment with an arrowhead at one end. It has an **initial point**, where it begins, and a **terminal point**, where it ends. A vector is defined by its **magnitude**, or the length of the line, and its direction, indicated by an arrowhead at the terminal point. Thus, a vector is a directed line segment. There are various symbols that distinguish vectors from other quantities:

- Lower case, boldfaced type, with or without an arrow on top such as $v, u, w, \vec{v}, \vec{u}, \vec{w}$.
- Given initial point P and terminal point Q, a vector can be represented as $\overrightarrow{PQ}$. The arrowhead on top is what indicates that it is not just a line, but a directed line segment.
- Given an initial point of $(0, 0)$ and terminal point (a, b), a vector may be represented as $\langle a, b \rangle$.

This last symbol $\langle a, b \rangle$ has special significance. It is called the **standard position**. The position vector has an initial point $(0, 0)$ and a terminal point $\langle a, b \rangle$. To change any vector into the position vector, we think about the change in the x-coordinates and the change in the y-coordinates. Thus, if the initial point of a vector $\overrightarrow{CD}$ is $C(x_1, y_1)$ and the terminal point is $D(x_2, y_2)$, then the position vector is found by calculating

$$\overrightarrow{AB} = \langle x_2 - x_1, y_2 - y_1 \rangle$$
$$= \langle a, b \rangle$$

In **Figure 2**, we see the original vector $\overrightarrow{CD}$ and the position vector $\overrightarrow{AB}$.

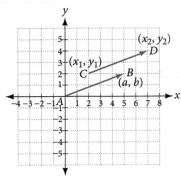

Figure 2

> *properties of vectors*
>
> A vector is a directed line segment with an initial point and a terminal point. Vectors are identified by magnitude, or the length of the line, and direction, represented by the arrowhead pointing toward the terminal point. The position vector has an initial point at $(0, 0)$ and is identified by its terminal point $\langle a, b \rangle$.

Example 1   **Find the Position Vector**

Consider the vector whose initial point is $P(2, 3)$ and terminal point is $Q(6, 4)$. Find the position vector.

Solution The position vector is found by subtracting one x-coordinate from the other x-coordinate, and one y-coordinate from the other y-coordinate. Thus

$$v = \langle 6 - 2, 4 - 3 \rangle$$
$$= \langle 4, 1 \rangle$$

The position vector begins at $(0, 0)$ and terminates at $(4, 1)$. The graphs of both vectors are shown in **Figure 3**.

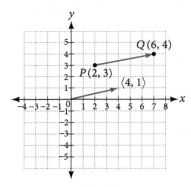

Figure 3

We see that the position vector is $\langle 4, 1 \rangle$.

Example 2   **Drawing a Vector with the Given Criteria and Its Equivalent Position Vector**

Find the position vector given that vector v has an initial point at $(-3, 2)$ and a terminal point at $(4, 5)$, then graph both vectors in the same plane.

Solution The position vector is found using the following calculation:

$$v = \langle 4 - (-3), 5 - 2 \rangle$$
$$= \langle 7, 3 \rangle$$

Thus, the position vector begins at $(0, 0)$ and terminates at $(7, 3)$. See **Figure 4**.

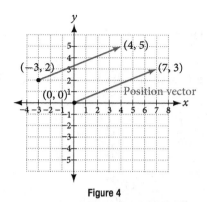

Figure 4

···

Try It #1

Draw a vector v that connects from the origin to the point (3, 5).

···

Finding Magnitude and Direction

To work with a vector, we need to be able to find its magnitude and its direction. We find its magnitude using the Pythagorean Theorem or the distance formula, and we find its direction using the inverse tangent function.

---

magnitude and direction of a vector

Given a position vector $v = \langle a, b \rangle$, the magnitude is found by $|v| = \sqrt{a^2 + b^2}$. The direction is equal to the angle formed with the x-axis, or with the y-axis, depending on the application. For a position vector, the direction is found by $\tan \theta = \left(\frac{b}{a}\right) \Rightarrow \theta = \tan^{-1}\left(\frac{b}{a}\right)$, as illustrated in **Figure 5.**

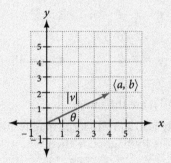

Figure 5

Two vectors v and u are considered equal if they have the same magnitude and the same direction. Additionally, if both vectors have the same position vector, they are equal.

Example 3   **Finding the Magnitude and Direction of a Vector**

Find the magnitude and direction of the vector with initial point $P(-8, 1)$ and terminal point $Q(-2, -5)$. Draw the vector.

Solution   First, find the position vector.

$$u = \langle -2, -(-8), -5-1 \rangle$$
$$= \langle 6, -6 \rangle$$

We use the Pythagorean Theorem to find the magnitude.

$$|u| = \sqrt{(6)^2 + (-6)^2}$$
$$= \sqrt{72}$$
$$= 6\sqrt{2}$$

The direction is given as

$$\tan \theta = \frac{-6}{6} = -1 \Rightarrow \theta = \tan^{-1}(-1)$$
$$= -45°$$

However, the angle terminates in the fourth quadrant, so we add 360° to obtain a positive angle. Thus, $-45° + 360° = 315°$. See **Figure 6**.

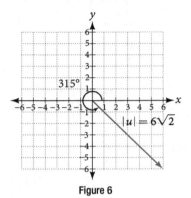

Figure 6

Example 4   Showing That Two Vectors Are Equal

Show that vector v with initial point at $(5, -3)$ and terminal point at $(-1, 2)$ is equal to vector u with initial point at $(-1, -3)$ and terminal point at $(-7, 2)$. Draw the position vector on the same grid as v and u. Next, find the magnitude and direction of each vector.

Solution   As shown in **Figure 7**, draw the vector v starting at initial $(5, -3)$ and terminal point $(-1, 2)$. Draw the vector u with initial point $(-1, -3)$ and terminal point $(-7, 2)$. Find the standard position for each.

Next, find and sketch the position vector for v and u. We have

$$v = \langle -1 - 5, 2 - (-3) \rangle$$
$$= \langle -6, 5 \rangle$$
$$u = \langle -7 - (-1), 2 - (-3) \rangle$$
$$= \langle -6, 5 \rangle$$

Since the position vectors are the same, v and u are the same.

An alternative way to check for vector equality is to show that the magnitude and direction are the same for both vectors. To show that the magnitudes are equal, use the Pythagorean Theorem.

$$|v| = \sqrt{(-1 - 5)^2 + (2 - (-3))^2}$$
$$= \sqrt{(-6)^2 + (5)^2}$$
$$= \sqrt{36 + 25}$$
$$= \sqrt{61}$$
$$|u| = \sqrt{(-7 - (-1))^2 + (2 - (-3))^2}$$
$$= \sqrt{(-6)^2 + (5)^2}$$
$$= \sqrt{36 + 25}$$
$$= \sqrt{61}$$

As the magnitudes are equal, we now need to verify the direction. Using the tangent function with the position vector gives

$$\tan \theta = -\frac{5}{6} \Rightarrow \theta = \tan^{-1}\left(-\frac{5}{6}\right)$$
$$= -39.8°$$

However, we can see that the position vector terminates in the second quadrant, so we add 180°. Thus, the direction is $-39.8° + 180° = 140.2°$.

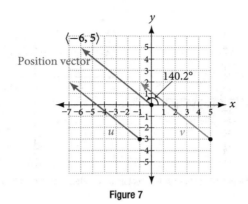

Figure 7

Performing Vector Addition and Scalar Multiplication

Now that we understand the properties of vectors, we can perform operations involving them. While it is convenient to think of the vector $u = \langle x, y \rangle$ as an arrow or directed line segment from the origin to the point (x, y), vectors can be situated anywhere in the plane. The sum of two vectors u and v, or **vector addition**, produces a third vector $u + v$, the **resultant** vector.

To find $u + v$, we first draw the vector u, and from the terminal end of u, we drawn the vector v. In other words, we have the initial point of v meet the terminal end of u. This position corresponds to the notion that we move along the first vector and then, from its terminal point, we move along the second vector. The sum $u + v$ is the resultant vector because it results from addition or subtraction of two vectors. The resultant vector travels directly from the beginning of u to the end of v in a straight path, as shown in **Figure 8**.

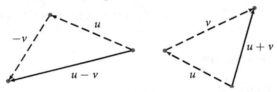

Figure 8

Vector subtraction is similar to vector addition. To find $u - v$, view it as $u + (-v)$. Adding $-v$ is reversing direction of v and adding it to the end of u. The new vector begins at the start of u and stops at the end point of $-v$. See **Figure 9** for a visual that compares vector addition and vector subtraction using parallelograms.

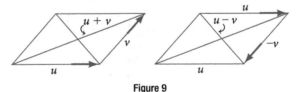

Figure 9

Example 5 Adding and Subtracting Vectors

Given $u = \langle 3, -2 \rangle$ and $v = \langle -1, 4 \rangle$, find two new vectors $u + v$, and $u - v$.

Solution   To find the sum of two vectors, we add the components. Thus,

$$u + v = \langle 3, -2 \rangle + \langle -1, 4 \rangle$$
$$= \langle 3 + (-1), -2 + 4 \rangle$$
$$= \langle 2, 2 \rangle$$

See **Figure 10(a)**.

To find the difference of two vectors, add the negative components of v to u. Thus,

$$u + (-v) = \langle 3, -2 \rangle + \langle 1, -4 \rangle$$
$$= \langle 3 + 1, -2 + (-4) \rangle$$
$$= \langle 4, -6 \rangle$$

See **Figure 10(b)**.

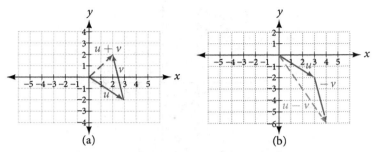

Figure 10 (a) Sum of two vectors (b) Difference of two vectors

Multiplying By a Scalar

While adding and subtracting vectors gives us a new vector with a different magnitude and direction, the process of multiplying a vector by a **scalar**, a constant, changes only the magnitude of the vector or the length of the line. Scalar multiplication has no effect on the direction unless the scalar is negative, in which case the direction of the resulting vector is opposite the direction of the original vector.

> **scalar multiplication**
>
> **Scalar multiplication** involves the product of a vector and a scalar. Each component of the vector is multiplied by the scalar. Thus, to multiply $v = \langle a, b \rangle$ by k, we have
>
> $$kv = \langle ka, kb \rangle$$
>
> Only the magnitude changes, unless k is negative, and then the vector reverses direction.

Example 6   **Performing Scalar Multiplication**

Given vector $v = \langle 3, 1 \rangle$, find $3v$, $\frac{1}{2}v$, and $-v$.

Solution   See **Figure 11** for a geometric interpretation. If $v = \langle 3, 1 \rangle$, then

$$3v = \langle 3 \cdot 3, 3 \cdot 1 \rangle$$
$$= \langle 9, 3 \rangle$$

$$\frac{1}{2}v = \left\langle \frac{1}{2} \cdot 3, \frac{1}{2} \cdot 1 \right\rangle$$

$$= \left\langle \frac{3}{2}, \frac{1}{2} \right\rangle$$

$$-v = \langle -3, -1 \rangle$$

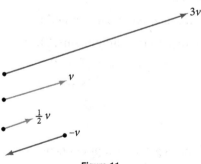

Figure 11

Analysis   Notice that the vector $3v$ is three times the length of v, $\frac{1}{2}v$ is half the length of v, and $-v$ is the same length of v, but in the opposite direction.

Try It #2

Find the scalar multiple $3u$ given $u = \langle 5, 4 \rangle$.

Example 7   **Using Vector Addition and Scalar Multiplication to Find a New Vector**

Given $u = \langle 3, -2 \rangle$ and $v = \langle -1, 4 \rangle$, find a new vector $w = 3u + 2v$.

Solution   First, we must multiply each vector by the scalar.

$$3u = 3 \langle 3, -2 \rangle$$
$$= \langle 9, -6 \rangle$$
$$2v = 2 \langle -1, 4 \rangle$$
$$= \langle -2, 8 \rangle$$

Then, add the two together.

$$w = 3u + 2v$$
$$= \langle 9, -6 \rangle + \langle -2, 8 \rangle$$
$$= \langle 9 - 2, -6 + 8 \rangle$$
$$= \langle 7, 2 \rangle$$

So, $w = \langle 7, 2 \rangle$.

Finding Component Form

In some applications involving vectors, it is helpful for us to be able to break a vector down into its components. Vectors are comprised of two components: the horizontal component is the x direction, and the vertical component is the y direction. For example, we can see in the graph in **Figure 12** that the position vector $\langle 2, 3 \rangle$ comes from adding the vectors v_1 and v_2. We have v_1 with initial point $(0, 0)$ and terminal point $(2, 0)$.

$$v_1 = \langle 2 - 0, 0 - 0 \rangle$$
$$= \langle 2, 0 \rangle$$

We also have v_2 with initial point $(0, 0)$ and terminal point $(0, 3)$.

$$v_2 = \langle 0 - 0, 3 - 0 \rangle$$
$$= \langle 0, 3 \rangle$$

Therefore, the position vector is

$$v = \langle 2 + 0, 3 + 0 \rangle$$
$$= \langle 2, 3 \rangle$$

Using the Pythagorean Theorem, the magnitude of v_1 is 2, and the magnitude of v_2 is 3. To find the magnitude of v, use the formula with the position vector.

$$|v| = \sqrt{|v_1|^2 + |v_2|^2}$$
$$= \sqrt{2^2 + 3^2}$$
$$= \sqrt{13}$$

The magnitude of v is $\sqrt{13}$. To find the direction, we use the tangent function $\tan \theta = \dfrac{y}{x}$.

$$\tan \theta = \frac{v_2}{v_1}$$

$$\tan \theta = \frac{3}{2}$$

$$\theta = \tan^{-1}\left(\frac{3}{2}\right) = 56.3°$$

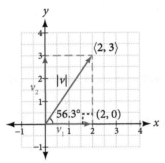

Figure 12

Thus, the magnitude of v is $\sqrt{13}$ and the direction is 56.3° off the horizontal.

Example 8   **Finding the Components of the Vector**

Find the components of the vector v with initial point (3, 2) and terminal point (7, 4).

Solution   First find the standard position.

$$v = \langle 7 - 3, 4 - 2 \rangle$$
$$= \langle 4, 2 \rangle$$

See the illustration in **Figure 13**.

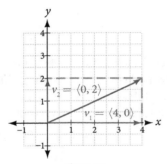

Figure 13

The horizontal component is $v_1 = \langle 4, 0 \rangle$ and the vertical component is $v_2 = \langle 0, 2 \rangle$.

Finding the Unit Vector in the Direction of v

In addition to finding a vector's components, it is also useful in solving problems to find a vector in the same direction as the given vector, but of magnitude 1. We call a vector with a magnitude of 1 a **unit vector**. We can then preserve the direction of the original vector while simplifying calculations.

Unit vectors are defined in terms of components. The horizontal unit vector is written as $i = \langle 1, 0 \rangle$ and is directed along the positive horizontal axis. The vertical unit vector is written as $j = \langle 0, 1 \rangle$ and is directed along the positive vertical axis. See **Figure 14**.

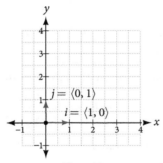

Figure 14

---

the unit vectors

If v is a nonzero vector, then $\dfrac{v}{|v|}$ is a unit vector in the direction of v. Any vector divided by its magnitude is a unit vector. Notice that magnitude is always a scalar, and dividing by a scalar is the same as multiplying by the reciprocal of the scalar.

Example 9   **Finding the Unit Vector in the Direction of *v***

Find a unit vector in the same direction as $v = \langle -5, 12 \rangle$.

Solution   First, we will find the magnitude.

$$|v| = \sqrt{(-5)^2 + (12)^2}$$
$$= \sqrt{25 + 144}$$
$$= \sqrt{169}$$
$$= 13$$

Then we divide each component by $|v|$, which gives a unit vector in the same direction as v:

$$\frac{v}{|v|} = -\frac{5}{13}i + \frac{12}{13}j$$

or, in component form

$$\frac{v}{|v|} = \left\langle -\frac{5}{13}, \frac{12}{13} \right\rangle$$

See **Figure 15**.

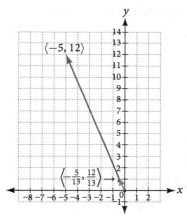

Figure 15

Verify that the magnitude of the unit vector equals 1. The magnitude of $-\dfrac{5}{13}i + \dfrac{12}{13}j$ is given as

$$\sqrt{\left(-\frac{5}{13}\right)^2 + \left(\frac{12}{13}\right)^2} = \sqrt{\frac{25}{169} + \frac{144}{169}}$$
$$= \sqrt{\frac{169}{169}}$$
$$= 1$$

The vector $u = \dfrac{5}{13}i + \dfrac{12}{13}j$ is the unit vector in the same direction as $v = \langle -5, 12 \rangle$.

Performing Operations with Vectors in Terms of *i* and *j*

So far, we have investigated the basics of vectors: magnitude and direction, vector addition and subtraction, scalar multiplication, the components of vectors, and the representation of vectors geometrically. Now that we are familiar with the general strategies used in working with vectors, we will represent vectors in rectangular coordinates in terms of *i* and *j*.

vectors in the rectangular plane

Given a vector v with initial point $P = (x_1, y_1)$ and terminal point $Q = (x_2, y_2)$, v is written as

$$v = (x_2 - x_1)i + (y_1 - y_2)j$$

The position vector from $(0, 0)$ to (a, b), where $(x_2 - x_1) = a$ and $(y_2 - y_1) = b$, is written as $v = ai + bj$. This vector sum is called a linear combination of the vectors i and j.

The magnitude of $v = ai + bj$ is given as $|v| = \sqrt{a^2 + b^2}$. See **Figure 16**.

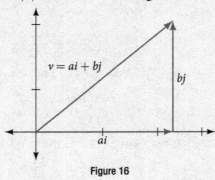

Figure 16

Example 10   Writing a Vector in Terms of *i* and *j*

Given a vector v with initial point $P = (2, -6)$ and terminal point $Q = (-6, 6)$, write the vector in terms of i and j.

Solution   Begin by writing the general form of the vector. Then replace the coordinates with the given values.

$$v = (x_2 - x_1)i + (y_2 - y_1)j$$
$$= (-6 - 2)i + (6 - (-6))j$$
$$= -8i + 12j$$

Example 11   Writing a Vector in Terms of *i* and *j* Using Initial and Terminal Points

Given initial point $P_1 = (-1, 3)$ and terminal point $P_2 = (2, 7)$, write the vector v in terms of i and j.

Solution   Begin by writing the general form of the vector. Then replace the coordinates with the given values.

$$v = (x_2 - x_1)i + (y_2 - y_1)j$$
$$v = (2 - (-1))i + (7 - 3)j$$
$$= 3i + 4j$$

Try It #3

Write the vector u with initial point $P = (-1, 6)$ and terminal point $Q = (7, -5)$ in terms of i and j.

Performing Operations on Vectors in Terms of *i* and *j*

When vectors are written in terms of i and j, we can carry out addition, subtraction, and scalar multiplication by performing operations on corresponding components.

adding and subtracting vectors in rectangular coordinates

Given $v = ai + bj$ and $u = ci + dj$, then

$$v + u = (a + c)i + (b + d)j$$
$$v - u = (a - c)i + (b - d)j$$

Example 12   **Finding the Sum of the Vectors**

Find the sum of $v_1 = 2i - 3j$ and $v_2 = 4i + 5j$.

Solution   According to the formula, we have

$$v_1 + v_2 = (2 + 4)i + (-3 + 5)j$$
$$= 6i + 2j$$

Calculating the Component Form of a Vector: Direction

We have seen how to draw vectors according to their initial and terminal points and how to find the position vector. We have also examined notation for vectors drawn specifically in the Cartesian coordinate plane using i and j. For any of these vectors, we can calculate the magnitude. Now, we want to combine the key points, and look further at the ideas of magnitude and direction.

Calculating direction follows the same straightforward process we used for polar coordinates. We find the direction of the vector by finding the angle to the horizontal. We do this by using the basic trigonometric identities, but with $|v|$ replacing r.

---

vector components in terms of magnitude and direction
Given a position vector $v = \langle x, y \rangle$ and a direction angle θ,

$$\cos \theta = \frac{x}{|v|} \quad \text{and} \quad \sin \theta = \frac{y}{|v|}$$

$$x = |v| \cos \theta \qquad y = |v| \sin \theta$$

Thus, $v = xi + yj = |v|\cos \theta i + |v|\sin \theta j$, and magnitude is expressed as $|v| = \sqrt{x^2 + y^2}$.

Example 13   **Writing a Vector in Terms of Magnitude and Direction**

Write a vector with length 7 at an angle of 135° to the positive x-axis in terms of magnitude and direction.

Solution   Using the conversion formulas $x = |v| \cos \theta i$ and $y = |v| \sin \theta j$, we find that

$$x = 7\cos(135°)i$$

$$= -\frac{7\sqrt{2}}{2}$$

$$y = 7\sin(135°)j$$

$$= \frac{7\sqrt{2}}{2}$$

This vector can be written as $v = 7\cos(135°)i + 7\sin(135°)j$ or simplified as

$$v = -\frac{7\sqrt{2}}{2}i + \frac{7\sqrt{2}}{2}j$$

Try It #4

A vector travels from the origin to the point (3, 5). Write the vector in terms of magnitude and direction.

Finding the Dot Product of Two Vectors

As we discussed earlier in the section, scalar multiplication involves multiplying a vector by a scalar, and the result is a vector. As we have seen, multiplying a vector by a number is called scalar multiplication. If we multiply a vector by a vector, there are two possibilities: the *dot product* and the *cross product*. We will only examine the dot product here; you may encounter the cross product in more advanced mathematics courses.

The dot product of two vectors involves multiplying two vectors together, and the result is a scalar.

> **dot product**
> The **dot product** of two vectors $v = \langle a, b \rangle$ and $u = \langle c, d \rangle$ is the sum of the product of the horizontal components and the product of the vertical components.
>
> $$v \cdot u = ac + bd$$
>
> To find the angle between the two vectors, use the formula below.
>
> $$\cos \theta = \frac{v}{|v|} \cdot \frac{u}{|u|}$$

Example 14   **Finding the Dot Product of Two Vectors**

Find the dot product of $v = \langle 5, 12 \rangle$ and $u = \langle -3, 4 \rangle$.

Solution   Using the formula, we have

$$\begin{aligned}
v \cdot u &= \langle 5, 12 \rangle \cdot \langle -3, 4 \rangle \\
&= 5 \cdot (-3) + 12 \cdot 4 \\
&= -15 + 48 \\
&= 33
\end{aligned}$$

Example 15   **Finding the Dot Product of Two Vectors and the Angle between Them**

Find the dot product of $v_1 = 5i + 2j$ and $v_2 = 3i + 7j$. Then, find the angle between the two vectors.

Solution   Finding the dot product, we multiply corresponding components.

$$\begin{aligned}
v_1 \cdot v_2 &= \langle 5, 2 \rangle \cdot \langle 3, 7 \rangle \\
&= 5 \cdot 3 + 2 \cdot 7 \\
&= 15 + 14 \\
&= 29
\end{aligned}$$

To find the angle between them, we use the formula $\cos \theta = \dfrac{v}{|v|} \cdot \dfrac{u}{|u|}$

$$\frac{v}{|v|} \cdot \frac{u}{|u|} = \left\langle \frac{5}{\sqrt{29}} + \frac{2}{\sqrt{29}} \right\rangle \cdot \left\langle \frac{3}{\sqrt{58}} + \frac{7}{\sqrt{58}} \right\rangle$$

$$= \frac{5}{\sqrt{29}} \cdot \frac{3}{\sqrt{58}} + \frac{2}{\sqrt{29}} \cdot \frac{7}{\sqrt{58}}$$

$$= \frac{15}{\sqrt{1682}} + \frac{14}{\sqrt{1682}} = \frac{29}{\sqrt{1682}}$$

$$= 0.707107$$

$$\cos^{-1}(0.707107) = 45°$$

See **Figure 17**.

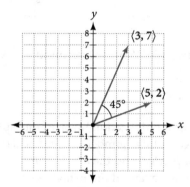

Figure 17

Example 16 **Finding the Angle between Two Vectors**

Find the angle between $u = \langle -3, 4 \rangle$ and $v = \langle 5, 12 \rangle$.

Solution Using the formula, we have

$$\theta = \cos^{-1}\left(\frac{u}{|u|} \cdot \frac{v}{|v|}\right)$$

$$\left(\frac{u}{|u|} \cdot \frac{v}{|v|}\right) = \frac{-3i + 4j}{5} \cdot \frac{5i + 12j}{13}$$

$$= \left(-\frac{3}{5} \cdot \frac{5}{13}\right) + \left(\frac{4}{5} \cdot \frac{12}{13}\right)$$

$$= -\frac{15}{65} + \frac{48}{65}$$

$$= \frac{33}{65}$$

$$\theta = \cos^{-1}\left(\frac{33}{65}\right)$$

$$= 59.5°$$

See **Figure 18**.

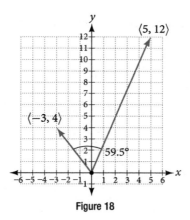

Figure 18

Example 17 **Finding Ground Speed and Bearing Using Vectors**

We now have the tools to solve the problem we introduced in the opening of the section.

An airplane is flying at an airspeed of 200 miles per hour headed on a SE bearing of 140°. A north wind (from north to south) is blowing at 16.2 miles per hour. What are the ground speed and actual bearing of the plane? See **Figure 19**.

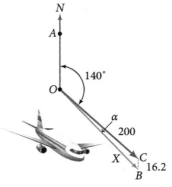

Figure 19

Solution The ground speed is represented by x in the diagram, and we need to find the angle α in order to calculate the adjusted bearing, which will be $140° + \alpha$.

Notice in **Figure 19**, that angle BCO must be equal to angle AOC by the rule of alternating interior angles, so angle BCO is 140°. We can find x by the Law of Cosines:

$$x^2 = (16.2)^2 + (200)^2 - 2(16.2)(200)\cos(140°)$$
$$x^2 = 45{,}226.41$$
$$x = \sqrt{45{,}226.41}$$
$$x = 212.7$$

The ground speed is approximately 213 miles per hour. Now we can calculate the bearing using the Law of Sines.

$$\frac{\sin\alpha}{16.2} = \frac{\sin(140°)}{212.7}$$
$$\sin\alpha = \frac{16.2\sin(140°)}{212.7}$$
$$= 0.04896$$
$$\sin^{-1}(0.04896) = 2.8°$$

Therefore, the plane has a SE bearing of $140° + 2.8° = 142.8°$. The ground speed is 212.7 miles per hour.

Access these online resources for additional instruction and practice with vectors.

- Introduction to Vectors (http://openstaxcollege.org/l/introvectors)
- Vector Operations (http://openstaxcollege.org/l/vectoroperation)
- The Unit Vector (http://openstaxcollege.org/l/unitvector)

10.8   SECTION EXERCISES

VERBAL

1. What are the characteristics of the letters that are commonly used to represent vectors?

2. How is a vector more specific than a line segment?

3. What are i and j, and what do they represent?

4. What is component form?

5. When a unit vector is expressed as $\langle a, b \rangle$, which letter is the coefficient of the i and which the j?

ALGEBRAIC

6. Given a vector with initial point $(5, 2)$ and terminal point $(-1, -3)$, find an equivalent vector whose initial point is $(0, 0)$. Write the vector in component form $\langle a, b \rangle$.

7. Given a vector with initial point $(-4, 2)$ and terminal point $(3, -3)$, find an equivalent vector whose initial point is $(0, 0)$. Write the vector in component form $\langle a, b \rangle$.

8. Given a vector with initial point $(7, -1)$ and terminal point $(-1, -7)$, find an equivalent vector whose initial point is $(0, 0)$. Write the vector in component form $\langle a, b \rangle$.

For the following exercises, determine whether the two vectors u and v are equal, where u has an initial point P_1 and a terminal point P_2 and v has an initial point P_3 and a terminal point P_4.

9. $P_1 = (5, 1), P_2 = (3, -2), P_3 = (-1, 3),$ and $P_4 = (9, -4)$

10. $P_1 = (2, -3), P_2 = (5, 1), P_3 = (6, -1),$ and $P_4 = (9, 3)$

11. $P_1 = (-1, -1), P_2 = (-4, 5), P_3 = (-10, 6),$ and $P_4 = (-13, 12)$

12. $P_1 = (3, 7), P_2 = (2, 1), P_3 = (1, 2),$ and $P_4 = (-1, -4)$

13. $P_1 = (8, 3), P_2 = (6, 5), P_3 = (11, 8),$ and $P_4 = (9, 10)$

14. Given initial point $P_1 = (-3, 1)$ and terminal point $P_2 = (5, 2)$, write the vector v in terms of i and j.

15. Given initial point $P_1 = (6, 0)$ and terminal point $P_2 = (-1, -3)$, write the vector v in terms of i and j.

For the following exercises, use the vectors $u = i + 5j$, $v = -2i - 3j$, and $w = 4i - j$.

16. Find $u + (v - w)$

17. Find $4v + 2u$

For the following exercises, use the given vectors to compute $u + v$, $u - v$, and $2u - 3v$.

18. $u = \langle 2, -3 \rangle$, $v = \langle 1, 5 \rangle$

19. $u = \langle -3, 4 \rangle$, $v = \langle -2, 1 \rangle$

20. Let $v = -4i + 3j$. Find a vector that is half the length and points in the same direction as v.

21. Let $v = 5i + 2j$. Find a vector that is twice the length and points in the opposite direction as v.

For the following exercises, find a unit vector in the same direction as the given vector.

22. $a = 3i + 4j$

23. $b = -2i + 5j$

24. $c = 10i - j$

25. $d = -\dfrac{1}{3}i + \dfrac{5}{2}j$

26. $u = 100i + 200j$

27. $u = -14i + 2j$

For the following exercises, find the magnitude and direction of the vector, $0 \le \theta < 2\pi$.

28. $\langle 0, 4 \rangle$

29. $\langle 6, 5 \rangle$

30. $\langle 2, -5 \rangle$

31. $\langle -4, -6 \rangle$

32. Given $u = 3i - 4j$ and $v = -2i + 3j$, calculate $u \cdot v$.

33. Given $u = -i - j$ and $v = i + 5j$, calculate $u \cdot v$.

34. Given $u = \langle -2, 4 \rangle$ and $v = \langle -3, 1 \rangle$, calculate $u \cdot v$.

35. Given $u = \langle -1, 6 \rangle$ and $v = \langle 6, -1 \rangle$, calculate $u \cdot v$.

GRAPHICAL

For the following exercises, given v, draw v, $3v$ and $\frac{1}{2}v$.

36. $\langle 2, -1 \rangle$ **37.** $\langle -1, 4 \rangle$ **38.** $\langle -3, -2 \rangle$

For the following exercises, use the vectors shown to sketch $u + v$, $u - v$, and $2u$.

39.

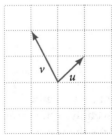

40.

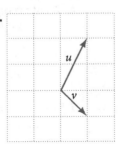

41.

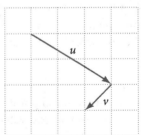

For the following exercises, use the vectors shown to sketch $2u + v$.

42.

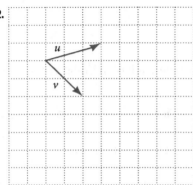

43.

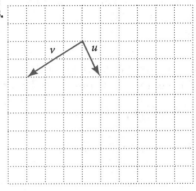

For the following exercises, use the vectors shown to sketch $u - 3v$.

44.

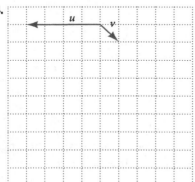

45.

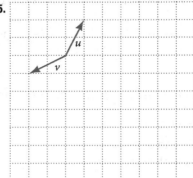

For the following exercises, write the vector shown in component form.

46.

47.

48. Given initial point $P_1 = (2, 1)$ and terminal point $P_2 = (-1, 2)$, write the vector v in terms of i and j, then draw the vector on the graph.

49. Given initial point $P_1 = (4, -1)$ and terminal point $P_2 = (-3, 2)$, write the vector v in terms of i and j. Draw the points and the vector on the graph.

50. Given initial point $P_1 = (3, 3)$ and terminal point $P_2 = (-3, 3)$, write the vector v in terms of i and j. Draw the points and the vector on the graph.

EXTENSIONS

For the following exercises, use the given magnitude and direction in standard position, write the vector in component form.

51. $|v| = 6, \theta = 45°$ **52.** $|v| = 8, \theta = 220°$ **53.** $|v| = 2, \theta = 300°$ **54.** $|v| = 5, \theta = 135°$

55. A 60-pound box is resting on a ramp that is inclined 12°. Rounding to the nearest tenth,
  a. Find the magnitude of the normal (perpendicular) component of the force.
  b. Find the magnitude of the component of the force that is parallel to the ramp.

56. A 25-pound box is resting on a ramp that is inclined 8°. Rounding to the nearest tenth,
  a. Find the magnitude of the normal (perpendicular) component of the force.
  b. Find the magnitude of the component of the force that is parallel to the ramp.

57. Find the magnitude of the horizontal and vertical components of a vector with magnitude 8 pounds pointed in a direction of 27° above the horizontal. Round to the nearest hundredth.

58. Find the magnitude of the horizontal and vertical components of the vector with magnitude 4 pounds pointed in a direction of 127° above the horizontal. Round to the nearest hundredth.

59. Find the magnitude of the horizontal and vertical components of a vector with magnitude 5 pounds pointed in a direction of 55° above the horizontal. Round to the nearest hundredth.

60. Find the magnitude of the horizontal and vertical components of the vector with magnitude 1 pound pointed in a direction of 8° above the horizontal. Round to the nearest hundredth.

REAL-WORLD APPLICATIONS

61. A woman leaves home and walks 3 miles west, then 2 miles southwest. How far from home is she, and in what direction must she walk to head directly home?

62. A boat leaves the marina and sails 6 miles north, then 2 miles northeast. How far from the marina is the boat, and in what direction must it sail to head directly back to the marina?

63. A man starts walking from home and walks 4 miles east, 2 miles southeast, 5 miles south, 4 miles southwest, and 2 miles east. How far has he walked? If he walked straight home, how far would he have to walk?

64. A woman starts walking from home and walks 4 miles east, 7 miles southeast, 6 miles south, 5 miles southwest, and 3 miles east. How far has she walked? If she walked straight home, how far would she have to walk?

65. A man starts walking from home and walks 3 miles at 20° north of west, then 5 miles at 10° west of south, then 4 miles at 15° north of east. If he walked straight home, how far would he have to the walk, and in what direction?

66. A woman starts walking from home and walks 6 miles at 40° north of east, then 2 miles at 15° east of south, then 5 miles at 30° south of west. If she walked straight home, how far would she have to walk, and in what direction?

67. An airplane is heading north at an airspeed of 600 km/hr, but there is a wind blowing from the southwest at 80 km/hr. How many degrees off course will the plane end up flying, and what is the plane's speed relative to the ground?

68. An airplane is heading north at an airspeed of 500 km/hr, but there is a wind blowing from the northwest at 50 km/hr. How many degrees off course will the plane end up flying, and what is the plane's speed relative to the ground?

69. An airplane needs to head due north, but there is a wind blowing from the southwest at 60 km/hr. The plane flies with an airspeed of 550 km/hr. To end up flying due north, how many degrees west of north will the pilot need to fly the plane?

70. An airplane needs to head due north, but there is a wind blowing from the northwest at 80 km/hr. The plane flies with an airspeed of 500 km/hr. To end up flying due north, how many degrees west of north will the pilot need to fly the plane?

71. As part of a video game, the point (5, 7) is rotated counterclockwise about the origin through an angle of 35°. Find the new coordinates of this point.

72. As part of a video game, the point (7, 3) is rotated counterclockwise about the origin through an angle of 40°. Find the new coordinates of this point.

73. Two children are throwing a ball back and forth straight across the back seat of a car. The ball is being thrown 10 mph relative to the car, and the car is traveling 25 mph down the road. If one child doesn't catch the ball, and it flies out the window, in what direction does the ball fly (ignoring wind resistance)?

74. Two children are throwing a ball back and forth straight across the back seat of a car. The ball is being thrown 8 mph relative to the car, and the car is traveling 45 mph down the road. If one child doesn't catch the ball, and it flies out the window, in what direction does the ball fly (ignoring wind resistance)?

75. A 50-pound object rests on a ramp that is inclined 19°. Find the magnitude of the components of the force parallel to and perpendicular to (normal) the ramp to the nearest tenth of a pound.

76. Suppose a body has a force of 10 pounds acting on it to the right, 25 pounds acting on it upward, and 5 pounds acting on it 45° from the horizontal. What single force is the resultant force acting on the body?

77. Suppose a body has a force of 10 pounds acting on it to the right, 25 pounds acting on it −135° from the horizontal, and 5 pounds acting on it directed 150° from the horizontal. What single force is the resultant force acting on the body?

78. The condition of equilibrium is when the sum of the forces acting on a body is the zero vector. Suppose a body has a force of 2 pounds acting on it to the right, 5 pounds acting on it upward, and 3 pounds acting on it 45° from the horizontal. What single force is needed to produce a state of equilibrium on the body?

79. Suppose a body has a force of 3 pounds acting on it to the left, 4 pounds acting on it upward, and 2 pounds acting on it 30° from the horizontal. What single force is needed to produce a state of equilibrium on the body? Draw the vector.

CHAPTER 10 REVIEW

Key Terms

altitude a perpendicular line from one vertex of a triangle to the opposite side, or in the case of an obtuse triangle, to the line containing the opposite side, forming two right triangles

ambiguous case a scenario in which more than one triangle is a valid solution for a given oblique SSA triangle

Archimedes' spiral a polar curve given by $r = \theta$. When multiplied by a constant, the equation appears as $r = a\theta$. As $r = \theta$, the curve continues to widen in a spiral path over the domain.

argument the angle associated with a complex number; the angle between the line from the origin to the point and the positive real axis

cardioid a member of the limaçon family of curves, named for its resemblance to a heart; its equation is given as $r = a \pm b\cos\theta$ and $r = a \pm b\sin\theta$, where $\frac{a}{b} = 1$

convex limaçon a type of one-loop limaçon represented by $r = a \pm b\cos\theta$ and $r = a \pm b\sin\theta$ such that $\frac{a}{b} \geq 2$

De Moivre's Theorem formula used to find the nth power or nth roots of a complex number; states that, for a positive integer n, z^n is found by raising the modulus to the nth power and multiplying the angles by n

dimpled limaçon a type of one-loop limaçon represented by $r = a \pm b\cos\theta$ and $r = a \pm b\sin\theta$ such that $1 < \frac{a}{b} < 2$

dot product given two vectors, the sum of the product of the horizontal components and the product of the vertical components

Generalized Pythagorean Theorem an extension of the Law of Cosines; relates the sides of an oblique triangle and is used for SAS and SSS triangles

initial point the origin of a vector

inner-loop limaçon a polar curve similar to the cardioid, but with an inner loop; passes through the pole twice; represented by $r = a \pm b\cos\theta$ and $r = a \pm b\sin\theta$ where $a < b$

Law of Cosines states that the square of any side of a triangle is equal to the sum of the squares of the other two sides minus twice the product of the other two sides and the cosine of the included angle

Law of Sines states that the ratio of the measurement of one angle of a triangle to the length of its opposite side is equal to the remaining two ratios of angle measure to opposite side; any pair of proportions may be used to solve for a missing angle or side

lemniscate a polar curve resembling a **Figure 8** and given by the equation $r^2 = a^2 \cos 2\theta$ and $r^2 = a^2 \sin 2\theta$, $a \neq 0$

magnitude the length of a vector; may represent a quantity such as speed, and is calculated using the Pythagorean Theorem

modulus the absolute value of a complex number, or the distance from the origin to the point (x, y); also called the amplitude

oblique triangle any triangle that is not a right triangle

one-loop limaçon a polar curve represented by $r = a \pm b\cos\theta$ and $r = a \pm b\sin\theta$ such that $a > 0$, $b > 0$, and $\frac{a}{b} > 1$; may be dimpled or convex; does not pass through the pole

parameter a variable, often representing time, upon which x and y are both dependent

polar axis on the polar grid, the equivalent of the positive x-axis on the rectangular grid

polar coordinates on the polar grid, the coordinates of a point labeled (r, θ), where θ indicates the angle of rotation from the polar axis and r represents the radius, or the distance of the point from the pole in the direction of θ

polar equation an equation describing a curve on the polar grid

polar form of a complex number a complex number expressed in terms of an angle θ and its distance from the origin r; can be found by using conversion formulas $x = r\cos\theta$, $y = r\sin\theta$, and $r = \sqrt{x^2 + y^2}$

pole the origin of the polar grid

resultant a vector that results from addition or subtraction of two vectors, or from scalar multiplication

rose curve a polar equation resembling a flower, given by the equations $r = a\cos n\theta$ and $r = a\sin n\theta$; when n is even there are $2n$ petals, and the curve is highly symmetrical; when n is odd there are n petals.

scalar a quantity associated with magnitude but not direction; a constant

scalar multiplication the product of a constant and each component of a vector

standard position the placement of a vector with the initial point at $(0, 0)$ and the terminal point (a, b), represented by the change in the x-coordinates and the change in the y-coordinates of the original vector

terminal point the end point of a vector, usually represented by an arrow indicating its direction

unit vector a vector that begins at the origin and has magnitude of 1; the horizontal unit vector runs along the x-axis and is defined as $v_1 = \langle 1, 0 \rangle$ the vertical unit vector runs along the y-axis and is defined as $v_2 = \langle 0, 1 \rangle$.

vector a quantity associated with both magnitude and direction, represented as a directed line segment with a starting point (initial point) and an end point (terminal point)

vector addition the sum of two vectors, found by adding corresponding components

Key Equations

Law of Sines

$$\frac{\sin \alpha}{a} = \frac{\sin \beta}{b} = \frac{\sin \gamma}{c}$$

$$\frac{a}{\sin \alpha} = \frac{b}{\sin \beta} = \frac{c}{\sin \gamma}$$

Area for oblique triangles

$$\text{Area} = \frac{1}{2}bc\sin \alpha$$

$$= \frac{1}{2}ac\sin \beta$$

$$= \frac{1}{2}ab\sin \gamma$$

Law of Cosines

$$a^2 = b^2 + c^2 - 2bc\cos \alpha$$

$$b^2 = a^2 + c^2 - 2ac\cos \beta$$

$$c^2 = a^2 + b^2 - 2ab\cos \gamma$$

Heron's formula

$$\text{Area} = \sqrt{s(s-a)(s-b)(s-c)} \text{ where } s = \frac{(a+b+c)}{2}$$

Conversion formulas

$$\cos \theta = \frac{x}{r} \rightarrow x = r\cos \theta$$

$$\sin \theta = \frac{y}{r} \rightarrow y = r\sin \theta$$

$$r^2 = x^2 + y^2$$

$$\tan \theta = \frac{y}{x}$$

Key Concepts

10.1 Non-right Triangles: Law of Sines

- The Law of Sines can be used to solve oblique triangles, which are non-right triangles.
- According to the Law of Sines, the ratio of the measurement of one of the angles to the length of its opposite side equals the other two ratios of angle measure to opposite side.

- There are three possible cases: ASA, AAS, SSA. Depending on the information given, we can choose the appropriate equation to find the requested solution. See **Example 1**.

- The ambiguous case arises when an oblique triangle can have different outcomes.

- There are three possible cases that arise from SSA arrangement—a single solution, two possible solutions, and no solution. See **Example 2** and **Example 3**.

- The Law of Sines can be used to solve triangles with given criteria. See **Example 4**.

- The general area formula for triangles translates to oblique triangles by first finding the appropriate height value. See **Example 5**.

- There are many trigonometric applications. They can often be solved by first drawing a diagram of the given information and then using the appropriate equation. See **Example 6**.

10.2 Non-right Triangles: Law of Cosines

- The Law of Cosines defines the relationship among angle measurements and lengths of sides in oblique triangles.

- The Generalized Pythagorean Theorem is the Law of Cosines for two cases of oblique triangles: SAS and SSS. Dropping an imaginary perpendicular splits the oblique triangle into two right triangles or forms one right triangle, which allows sides to be related and measurements to be calculated. See **Example 1** and **Example 2**.

- The Law of Cosines is useful for many types of applied problems. The first step in solving such problems is generally to draw a sketch of the problem presented. If the information given fits one of the three models (the three equations), then apply the Law of Cosines to find a solution. See **Example 3** and **Example 4**.

- Heron's formula allows the calculation of area in oblique triangles. All three sides must be known to apply Heron's formula. See **Example 5** and See **Example 6**.

10.3 Polar Coordinates

- The polar grid is represented as a series of concentric circles radiating out from the pole, or origin.

- To plot a point in the form (r, θ), $\theta > 0$, move in a counterclockwise direction from the polar axis by an angle of θ, and then extend a directed line segment from the pole the length of r in the direction of θ. If θ is negative, move in a clockwise direction, and extend a directed line segment the length of r in the direction of θ. See **Example 1**.

- If r is negative, extend the directed line segment in the opposite direction of θ. See **Example 2**.

- To convert from polar coordinates to rectangular coordinates, use the formulas $x = r\cos\theta$ and $y = r\sin\theta$. See **Example 3** and **Example 4**.

- To convert from rectangular coordinates to polar coordinates, use one or more of the formulas: $\cos\theta = \dfrac{x}{r}$, $\sin\theta = \dfrac{y}{r}$, $\tan\theta = \dfrac{y}{x}$, and $r = \sqrt{x^2 + y^2}$. See **Example 5**.

- Transforming equations between polar and rectangular forms means making the appropriate substitutions based on the available formulas, together with algebraic manipulations. See **Example 6**, **Example 7**, and **Example 8**.

- Using the appropriate substitutions makes it possible to rewrite a polar equation as a rectangular equation, and then graph it in the rectangular plane. See **Example 9**, **Example 10**, and **Example 11**.

10.4 Polar Coordinates: Graphs

- It is easier to graph polar equations if we can test the equations for symmetry with respect to the line $\theta = \dfrac{\pi}{2}$, the polar axis, or the pole.

- There are three symmetry tests that indicate whether the graph of a polar equation will exhibit symmetry. If an equation fails a symmetry test, the graph may or may not exhibit symmetry. See **Example 1**.

- Polar equations may be graphed by making a table of values for θ and r.

- The maximum value of a polar equation is found by substituting the value θ that leads to the maximum value of the trigonometric expression.

- The zeros of a polar equation are found by setting $r = 0$ and solving for θ. See **Example 2**.

- Some formulas that produce the graph of a circle in polar coordinates are given by $r = a\cos\theta$ and $r = a\sin\theta$. See **Example 3**.

- The formulas that produce the graphs of a cardioid are given by $r = a \pm b\cos\theta$ and $r = a \pm b\sin\theta$, for $a > 0$, $b > 0$, and $\dfrac{a}{b} = 1$. See **Example 4**.

- The formulas that produce the graphs of a one-loop limaçon are given by $r = a \pm b\cos\theta$ and $r = a \pm b\sin\theta$ for $1 < \frac{a}{b} < 2$. See **Example 5**.

- The formulas that produce the graphs of an inner-loop limaçon are given by $r = a \pm b\cos\theta$ and $r = a \pm b\sin\theta$ for $a > 0$, $b > 0$, and $a < b$. See **Example 6**.

- The formulas that produce the graphs of a lemniscates are given by $r^2 = a^2 \cos 2\theta$ and $r^2 = a^2 \sin 2\theta$, where $a \neq 0$. See **Example 7**.

- The formulas that produce the graphs of rose curves are given by $r = a\cos n\theta$ and $r = a\sin n\theta$, where $a \neq 0$; if n is even, there are $2n$ petals, and if n is odd, there are n petals. See **Example 8** and **Example 9**.

- The formula that produces the graph of an Archimedes' spiral is given by $r = \theta$, $\theta \geq 0$. See **Example 10**.

10.5 Polar Form of Complex Numbers

- Complex numbers in the form $a + bi$ are plotted in the complex plane similar to the way rectangular coordinates are plotted in the rectangular plane. Label the x-axis as the real axis and the y-axis as the imaginary axis. See **Example 1**.

- The absolute value of a complex number is the same as its magnitude. It is the distance from the origin to the point: $|z| = \sqrt{a^2 + b^2}$. See **Example 2** and **Example 3**.

- To write complex numbers in polar form, we use the formulas $x = r\cos\theta$, $y = r\sin\theta$, and $r = \sqrt{x^2 + y^2}$. Then, $z = r(\cos\theta + i\sin\theta)$. See **Example 4** and **Example 5**.

- To convert from polar form to rectangular form, first evaluate the trigonometric functions. Then, multiply through by r. See **Example 6** and **Example 7**.

- To find the product of two complex numbers, multiply the two moduli and add the two angles. Evaluate the trigonometric functions, and multiply using the distributive property. See **Example 8**.

- To find the quotient of two complex numbers in polar form, find the quotient of the two moduli and the difference of the two angles. See **Example 9**.

- To find the power of a complex number z^n, raise r to the power n, and multiply θ by n. See **Example 10**.

- Finding the roots of a complex number is the same as raising a complex number to a power, but using a rational exponent. See **Example 11**.

10.6 Parametric Equations

- Parameterizing a curve involves translating a rectangular equation in two variables, x and y, into two equations in three variables, x, y, and t. Often, more information is obtained from a set of parametric equations. See **Example 1**, **Example 2**, and **Example 3**.

- Sometimes equations are simpler to graph when written in rectangular form. By eliminating t, an equation in x and y is the result.

- To eliminate t, solve one of the equations for t, and substitute the expression into the second equation. See **Example 4**, **Example 5**, **Example 6**, and **Example 7**.

- Finding the rectangular equation for a curve defined parametrically is basically the same as eliminating the parameter. Solve for t in one of the equations, and substitute the expression into the second equation. See **Example 8**.

- There are an infinite number of ways to choose a set of parametric equations for a curve defined as a rectangular equation.

- Find an expression for x such that the domain of the set of parametric equations remains the same as the original rectangular equation. See **Example 9**.

10.7 Parametric Equations: Graphs

- When there is a third variable, a third parameter on which x and y depend, parametric equations can be used.

- To graph parametric equations by plotting points, make a table with three columns labeled t, $x(t)$, and $y(t)$. Choose values for t in increasing order. Plot the last two columns for x and y. See **Example 1** and **Example 2**.

- When graphing a parametric curve by plotting points, note the associated t-values and show arrows on the graph indicating the orientation of the curve. See **Example 3** and **Example 4**.

- Parametric equations allow the direction or the orientation of the curve to be shown on the graph. Equations that are not functions can be graphed and used in many applications involving motion. See **Example 5**.

- Projectile motion depends on two parametric equations: $x = (v_0 \cos \theta)t$ and $y = -16t^2 + (v_0 \sin \theta)t + h$. Initial velocity is symbolized as v_0. θ represents the initial angle of the object when thrown, and h represents the height at which the object is propelled.

10.8 Vectors

- The position vector has its initial point at the origin. See **Example 1**.

- If the position vector is the same for two vectors, they are equal. See **Example 2**. Vectors are defined by their magnitude and direction. See **Example 3**.

- If two vectors have the same magnitude and direction, they are equal. See **Example 4**.

- Vector addition and subtraction result in a new vector found by adding or subtracting corresponding elements. See **Example 5**.

- Scalar multiplication is multiplying a vector by a constant. Only the magnitude changes; the direction stays the same. See **Example 6** and **Example 7**.

- Vectors are comprised of two components: the horizontal component along the positive x-axis, and the vertical component along the positive y-axis. See **Example 8**.

- The unit vector in the same direction of any nonzero vector is found by dividing the vector by its magnitude.

- The magnitude of a vector in the rectangular coordinate system is $|v| = \sqrt{a^2 + b^2}$. See **Example 9**.

- In the rectangular coordinate system, unit vectors may be represented in terms of i and j where i represents the horizontal component and j represents the vertical component. Then, $v = ai + bj$ is a scalar multiple of v by real numbers a and b. See **Example 10** and **Example 11**.

- Adding and subtracting vectors in terms of i and j consists of adding or subtracting corresponding coefficients of i and corresponding coefficients of j. See **Example 12**.

- A vector $v = ai + bj$ is written in terms of magnitude and direction as $v = |v|\cos \theta i + |v|\sin \theta j$. See **Example 13**.

- The dot product of two vectors is the product of the i terms plus the product of the j terms. See **Example 14**.

- We can use the dot product to find the angle between two vectors. **Example 15** and **Example 16**.

- Dot products are useful for many types of physics applications. See **Example 17**.

CHAPTER 10 REVIEW EXERCISES

NON-RIGHT TRIANGLES: LAW OF SINES

For the following exercises, assume α is opposite side a, β is opposite side b, and γ is opposite side c. Solve each triangle, if possible. Round each answer to the nearest tenth.

1. $\beta = 50°$, $a = 105$, $b = 45$

2. $\alpha = 43.1°$, $a = 184.2$, $b = 242.8$

3. Solve the triangle.

4. Find the area of the triangle.

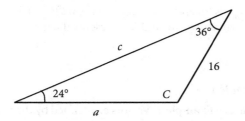

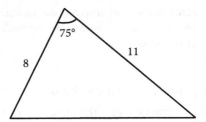

5. A pilot is flying over a straight highway. He determines the angles of depression to two mileposts, 2.1 km apart, to be 25° and 49°, as shown in **Figure 1**. Find the distance of the plane from point A and the elevation of the plane.

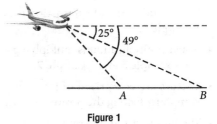

Figure 1

NON-RIGHT TRIANGLES: LAW OF COSINES

6. Solve the triangle, rounding to the nearest tenth, assuming α is opposite side a, β is opposite side b, and γ is opposite side c: $a = 4$, $b = 6$, $c = 8$.

7. Solve the triangle in **Figure 2**, rounding to the nearest tenth.

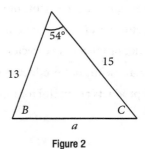

Figure 2

8. Find the area of a triangle with sides of length 8.3, 6.6, and 9.1.

9. To find the distance between two cities, a satellite calculates the distances and angle shown in **Figure 3** (not to scale). Find the distance between the cities. Round answers to the nearest tenth.

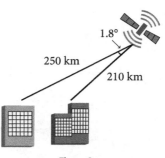

Figure 3

POLAR COORDINATES

10. Plot the point with polar coordinates $\left(3, \dfrac{\pi}{6}\right)$.

11. Plot the point with polar coordinates $\left(5, -\dfrac{2\pi}{3}\right)$

12. Convert $\left(6, -\dfrac{3\pi}{4}\right)$ to rectangular coordinates.

13. Convert $\left(-2, \dfrac{3\pi}{2}\right)$ to rectangular coordinates.

14. Convert $(7, -2)$ to polar coordinates.

15. Convert $(-9, -4)$ to polar coordinates.

For the following exercises, convert the given Cartesian equation to a polar equation.

16. $x = -2$

17. $x^2 + y^2 = 64$

18. $x^2 + y^2 = -2y$

For the following exercises, convert the given polar equation to a Cartesian equation.

19. $r = 7\cos\theta$

20. $r = \dfrac{-2}{4\cos\theta + \sin\theta}$

For the following exercises, convert to rectangular form and graph.

21. $\theta = \dfrac{3\pi}{4}$

22. $r = 5\sec\theta$

POLAR COORDINATES: GRAPHS

For the following exercises, test each equation for symmetry.

23. $r = 4 + 4\sin\theta$

24. $r = 7$

25. Sketch a graph of the polar equation $r = 1 - 5\sin\theta$. Label the axis intercepts.

26. Sketch a graph of the polar equation $r = 5\sin(7\theta)$.

27. Sketch a graph of the polar equation $r = 3 - 3\cos\theta$

POLAR FORM OF COMPLEX NUMBERS

For the following exercises, find the absolute value of each complex number.

28. $-2 + 6i$

29. $4 - 3i$

Write the complex number in polar form.

30. $5 + 9i$

31. $\dfrac{1}{2} - \dfrac{\sqrt{3}}{2}i$

For the following exercises, convert the complex number from polar to rectangular form.

32. $z = 5\text{cis}\left(\dfrac{5\pi}{6}\right)$

33. $z = 3\text{cis}(40°)$

For the following exercises, find the product $z_1 z_2$ in polar form.

34. $z_1 = 2\text{cis}(89°)$, $z_2 = 5\text{cis}(23°)$

35. $z_1 = 10\text{cis}\left(\dfrac{\pi}{6}\right)$, $z_2 = 6\text{cis}\left(\dfrac{\pi}{3}\right)$

For the following exercises, find the quotient $\dfrac{z_1}{z_2}$ in polar form.

36. $z_1 = 12\text{cis}(55°)$, $z_2 = 3\text{cis}(18°)$

37. $z_1 = 27\text{cis}\left(\dfrac{5\pi}{3}\right)$, $z_2 = 9\text{cis}\left(\dfrac{\pi}{3}\right)$

For the following exercises, find the powers of each complex number in polar form.

38. Find z^4 when $z = 2\text{cis}(70°)$

39. Find z^2 when $z = 5\text{cis}\left(\dfrac{3\pi}{4}\right)$

For the following exercises, evaluate each root.

40. Evaluate the cube root of z when $z = 64\text{cis}(210°)$.

41. Evaluate the square root of z when $z = 25\text{cis}\left(\dfrac{3\pi}{2}\right)$.

For the following exercises, plot the complex number in the complex plane.

42. $6 - 2i$

43. $-1 + 3i$

PARAMETRIC EQUATIONS

For the following exercises, eliminate the parameter t to rewrite the parametric equation as a Cartesian equation.

44. $\begin{cases} x(t) = 3t - 1 \\ y(t) = \sqrt{t} \end{cases}$

45. $\begin{cases} x(t) = -\cos t \\ y(t) = 2\sin^2 t \end{cases}$

46. Parameterize (write a parametric equation for) each Cartesian equation by using $x(t) = a\cos t$ and $y(t) = b\sin t$ for $\dfrac{x^2}{25} + \dfrac{y^2}{16} = 1$.

47. Parameterize the line from $(-2, 3)$ to $(4, 7)$ so that the line is at $(-2, 3)$ at $t = 0$ and $(4, 7)$ at $t = 1$.

PARAMETRIC EQUATIONS: GRAPHS

For the following exercises, make a table of values for each set of parametric equations, graph the equations, and include an orientation; then write the Cartesian equation.

48. $\begin{cases} x(t) = 3t^2 \\ y(t) = 2t - 1 \end{cases}$

49. $\begin{cases} x(t) = e^t \\ y(t) = -2e^{5t} \end{cases}$

50. $\begin{cases} x(t) = 3\cos t \\ y(t) = 2\sin t \end{cases}$

51. A ball is launched with an initial velocity of 80 feet per second at an angle of 40° to the horizontal. The ball is released at a height of 4 feet above the ground.

    a. Find the parametric equations to model the path of the ball.

    b. Where is the ball after 3 seconds?

    c. How long is the ball in the air?

VECTORS

For the following exercises, determine whether the two vectors, u and v, are equal, where u has an initial point P_1 and a terminal point P_2, and v has an initial point P_3 and a terminal point P_4.

52. $P_1 = (-1, 4)$, $P_2 = (3, 1)$, $P_3 = (5, 5)$ and $P_4 = (9, 2)$

53. $P_1 = (6, 11)$, $P_2 = (-2, 8)$, $P_3 = (0, -1)$ and $P_4 = (-8, 2)$

For the following exercises, use the vectors $u = 2i - j$, $v = 4i - 3j$, and $w = -2i + 5j$ to evaluate the expression.

54. $u - v$

55. $2v - u + w$

For the following exercises, find a unit vector in the same direction as the given vector.

56. $a = 8i - 6j$

57. $b = -3i - j$

For the following exercises, find the magnitude and direction of the vector.

58. $\langle 6, -2 \rangle$

59. $\langle -3, -3 \rangle$

For the following exercises, calculate $u \cdot v$.

60. $u = -2i + j$ and $v = 3i + 7j$

61. $u = i + 4j$ and $v = 4i + 3j$

62. Given $v = \langle -3, 4 \rangle$ draw v, $2v$, and $\dfrac{1}{2}v$.

63. Given the vectors shown in **Figure 4**, sketch $u + v$, $u - v$ and $3v$.

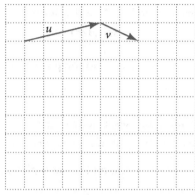

Figure 4

64. Given initial point $P_1 = (3, 2)$ and terminal point $P_2 = (-5, -1)$, write the vector v in terms of i and j. Draw the points and the vector on the graph.

CHAPTER 10 PRACTICE TEST

1. Assume α is opposite side a, β is opposite side b, and γ is opposite side c. Solve the triangle, if possible, and round each answer to the nearest tenth, given $\beta = 68°$, $b = 21, c = 16$.

2. Find the area of the triangle in **Figure 1**. Round each answer to the nearest tenth.

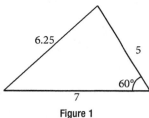

Figure 1

3. A pilot flies in a straight path for 2 hours. He then makes a course correction, heading 15° to the right of his original course, and flies 1 hour in the new direction. If he maintains a constant speed of 575 miles per hour, how far is he from his starting position?

4. Convert (2, 2) to polar coordinates, and then plot the point.

5. Convert $\left(2, \dfrac{\pi}{3} \right)$ to rectangular coordinates.

6. Convert the polar equation to a Cartesian equation: $x^2 + y^2 = 5y$.

7. Convert to rectangular form and graph: $r = -3\csc \theta$.

8. Test the equation for symmetry: $r = -4\sin(2\theta)$.

9. Graph $r = 3 + 3\cos \theta$.

10. Graph $r = 3 - 5\sin \theta$.

11. Find the absolute value of the complex number $5 - 9i$.

12. Write the complex number in polar form: $4 + i$.

13. Convert the complex number from polar to rectangular form: $z = 5\text{cis}\left(\dfrac{2\pi}{3} \right)$.

Given $z_1 = 8\text{cis}(36°)$ and $z_2 = 2\text{cis}(15°)$, evaluate each expression.

14. $z_1 z_2$

15. $\dfrac{z_1}{z_2}$

16. $(z_2)^3$

17. $\sqrt{z_1}$

18. Plot the complex number $-5 - i$ in the complex plane.

19. Eliminate the parameter t to rewrite the following parametric equations as a Cartesian equation:
$$\begin{cases} x(t) = t + 1 \\ y(t) = 2t^2 \end{cases}$$

20. Parameterize (write a parametric equation for) the following Cartesian equation by using $x(t) = a\cos t$ and $y(t) = b\sin t$: $\dfrac{x^2}{36} + \dfrac{y^2}{100} = 1$.

21. Graph the set of parametric equations and find the Cartesian equation:
$$\begin{cases} x(t) = -2\sin t \\ y(t) = 5\cos t \end{cases}$$

22. A ball is launched with an initial velocity of 95 feet per second at an angle of 52° to the horizontal. The ball is released at a height of 3.5 feet above the ground.
  a. Find the parametric equations to model the path of the ball.
  b. Where is the ball after 2 seconds?
  c. How long is the ball in the air?

For the following exercises, use the vectors $u = i - 3j$ and $v = 2i + 3j$.

23. Find $2u - 3v$.

24. Calculate $u \cdot v$.

25. Find a unit vector in the same direction as v.

26. Given vector v has an initial point $P_1 = (2, 2)$ and terminal point $P_2 = (-1, 0)$, write the vector v in terms of i and j. On the graph, draw v, and $-v$.

11

Systems of Equations and Inequalities

Figure 1 Enigma machines like this one, once owned by Italian dictator Benito Mussolini, were used by government and military officials for enciphering and deciphering top-secret communications during World War II. (credit: Dave Addey, Flickr)

CHAPTER OUTLINE

11.1 Systems of Linear Equations: Two Variables

11.2 Systems of Linear Equations: Three Variables

11.3 Systems of Nonlinear Equations and Inequalities: Two Variables

11.4 Partial Fractions

11.5 Matrices and Matrix Operations

11.6 Solving Systems with Gaussian Elimination

11.7 Solving Systems with Inverses

11.8 Solving Systems with Cramer's Rule

Introduction

By 1943, it was obvious to the Nazi regime that defeat was imminent unless it could build a weapon with unlimited destructive power, one that had never been seen before in the history of the world. In September, Adolf Hitler ordered German scientists to begin building an atomic bomb. Rumors and whispers began to spread from across the ocean. Refugees and diplomats told of the experiments happening in Norway. However, Franklin D. Roosevelt wasn't sold, and even doubted British Prime Minister Winston Churchill's warning. Roosevelt wanted undeniable proof. Fortunately, he soon received the proof he wanted when a group of mathematicians cracked the "Enigma" code, proving beyond a doubt that Hitler was building an atomic bomb. The next day, Roosevelt gave the order that the United States begin work on the same.

The Enigma is perhaps the most famous cryptographic device ever known. It stands as an example of the pivotal role cryptography has played in society. Now, technology has moved cryptanalysis to the digital world.

Many ciphers are designed using invertible matrices as the method of message transference, as finding the inverse of a matrix is generally part of the process of decoding. In addition to knowing the matrix and its inverse, the receiver must also know the key that, when used with the matrix inverse, will allow the message to be read.

In this chapter, we will investigate matrices and their inverses, and various ways to use matrices to solve systems of equations. First, however, we will study systems of equations on their own: linear and nonlinear, and then partial fractions. We will not be breaking any secret codes here, but we will lay the foundation for future courses.

LEARNING OBJECTIVES

In this section, you will:

- Solve systems of equations by graphing.
- Solve systems of equations by substitution.
- Solve systems of equations by addition.
- Identify inconsistent systems of equations containing two variables.
- Express the solution of a system of dependent equations containing two variables.

11.1　SYSTEMS OF LINEAR EQUATIONS: TWO VARIABLES

Figure 1 (credit: Thomas Sørenes)

A skateboard manufacturer introduces a new line of boards. The manufacturer tracks its costs, which is the amount it spends to produce the boards, and its revenue, which is the amount it earns through sales of its boards. How can the company determine if it is making a profit with its new line? How many skateboards must be produced and sold before a profit is possible? In this section, we will consider linear equations with two variables to answer these and similar questions.

Introduction to Systems of Equations

In order to investigate situations such as that of the skateboard manufacturer, we need to recognize that we are dealing with more than one variable and likely more than one equation. A **system of linear equations** consists of two or more linear equations made up of two or more variables such that all equations in the system are considered simultaneously. To find the unique solution to a system of linear equations, we must find a numerical value for each variable in the system that will satisfy all equations in the system at the same time. Some linear systems may not have a solution and others may have an infinite number of solutions. In order for a linear system to have a unique solution, there must be at least as many equations as there are variables. Even so, this does not guarantee a unique solution.

In this section, we will look at systems of linear equations in two variables, which consist of two equations that contain two different variables. For example, consider the following system of linear equations in two variables.

$$2x + y = 15$$
$$3x - y = 5$$

The *solution* to a system of linear equations in two variables is any ordered pair that satisfies each equation independently. In this example, the ordered pair (4, 7) is the solution to the system of linear equations. We can verify the solution by substituting the values into each equation to see if the ordered pair satisfies both equations. Shortly we will investigate methods of finding such a solution if it exists.

$$2(4) + (7) = 15　\text{True}$$
$$3(4) - (7) = 5　\text{True}$$

In addition to considering the number of equations and variables, we can categorize systems of linear equations by the number of solutions. A **consistent system** of equations has at least one solution. A consistent system is considered to be an **independent system** if it has a single solution, such as the example we just explored. The two lines have different slopes and intersect at one point in the plane. A consistent system is considered to be a **dependent system** if the equations have the same slope and the same y-intercepts. In other words, the lines coincide so the equations represent the same line. Every point on the line represents a coordinate pair that satisfies the system. Thus, there are an infinite number of solutions.

Another type of system of linear equations is an **inconsistent system**, which is one in which the equations represent two parallel lines. The lines have the same slope and different y-intercepts. There are no points common to both lines; hence, there is no solution to the system.

---

types of linear systems

There are three types of systems of linear equations in two variables, and three types of solutions.

- An **independent system** has exactly one solution pair (x, y). The point where the two lines intersect is the only solution.
- An **inconsistent system** has no solution. Notice that the two lines are parallel and will never intersect.
- A **dependent system** has infinitely many solutions. The lines are coincident. They are the same line, so every coordinate pair on the line is a solution to both equations.

Figure 2 compares graphical representations of each type of system.

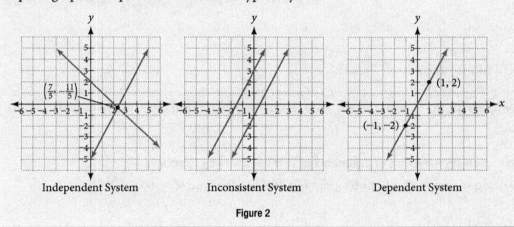

Independent System   Inconsistent System   Dependent System

Figure 2

How To...

Given a system of linear equations and an ordered pair, determine whether the ordered pair is a solution.

1. Substitute the ordered pair into each equation in the system.
2. Determine whether true statements result from the substitution in both equations; if so, the ordered pair is a solution.

Example 1   **Determining Whether an Ordered Pair Is a Solution to a System of Equations**

Determine whether the ordered pair $(5, 1)$ is a solution to the given system of equations.

$$x + 3y = 8$$
$$2x - 9 = y$$

Solution   Substitute the ordered pair $(5, 1)$ into both equations.

$$(5) + 3(1) = 8$$
$$8 = 8 \qquad \text{True}$$
$$2(5) - 9 = (1)$$
$$1 = 1 \qquad \text{True}$$

The ordered pair $(5, 1)$ satisfies both equations, so it is the solution to the system.

Analysis   *We can see the solution clearly by plotting the graph of each equation. Since the solution is an ordered pair that satisfies both equations, it is a point on both of the lines and thus the point of intersection of the two lines. See **Figure 3**.*

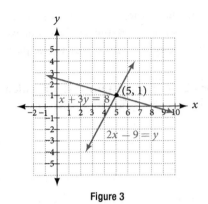

Figure 3

Try It #1

Determine whether the ordered pair (8, 5) is a solution to the following system.

$$5x - 4y = 20$$
$$2x + 1 = 3y$$

Solving Systems of Equations by Graphing

There are multiple methods of solving systems of linear equations. For a system of linear equations in two variables, we can determine both the type of system and the solution by graphing the system of equations on the same set of axes.

Example 2   **Solving a System of Equations in Two Variables by Graphing**

Solve the following system of equations by graphing. Identify the type of system.

$$2x + y = -8$$
$$x - y = -1$$

Solution   Solve the first equation for *y*.

$$2x + y = -8$$
$$y = -2x - 8$$

Solve the second equation for *y*.

$$x - y = -1$$
$$y = x + 1$$

Graph both equations on the same set of axes as in **Figure 4**.

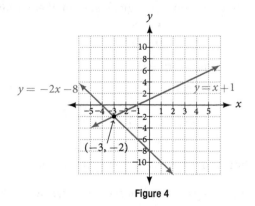

Figure 4

The lines appear to intersect at the point $(-3, -2)$. We can check to make sure that this is the solution to the system by substituting the ordered pair into both equations.

$$2(-3) + (-2) = -8$$
$$-8 = -8 \text{ True}$$
$$(-3) - (-2) = -1$$
$$-1 = -1 \text{ True}$$

The solution to the system is the ordered pair $(-3, -2)$, so the system is independent.

Try It #2

Solve the following system of equations by graphing.

$$2x - 5y = -25$$
$$-4x + 5y = 35$$

Q & A...

Can graphing be used if the system is inconsistent or dependent?

Yes, in both cases we can still graph the system to determine the type of system and solution. If the two lines are parallel, the system has no solution and is inconsistent. If the two lines are identical, the system has infinite solutions and is a dependent system.

Solving Systems of Equations by Substitution

Solving a linear system in two variables by graphing works well when the solution consists of integer values, but if our solution contains decimals or fractions, it is not the most precise method. We will consider two more methods of solving a system of linear equations that are more precise than graphing. One such method is solving a system of equations by the **substitution method**, in which we solve one of the equations for one variable and then substitute the result into the second equation to solve for the second variable. Recall that we can solve for only one variable at a time, which is the reason the substitution method is both valuable and practical.

How To...

Given a system of two equations in two variables, solve using the substitution method.

1. Solve one of the two equations for one of the variables in terms of the other.
2. Substitute the expression for this variable into the second equation, then solve for the remaining variable.
3. Substitute that solution into either of the original equations to find the value of the first variable. If possible, write the solution as an ordered pair.
4. Check the solution in both equations.

Example 3   Solving a System of Equations in Two Variables by Substitution

Solve the following system of equations by substitution.

$$-x + y = -5$$
$$2x - 5y = 1$$

Solution   First, we will solve the first equation for y.

$$-x + y = -5$$
$$y = x - 5$$

Now we can substitute the expression $x - 5$ for y in the second equation.

$$2x - 5y = 1$$
$$2x - 5(x - 5) = 1$$
$$2x - 5x + 25 = 1$$
$$-3x = -24$$
$$x = 8$$

Now, we substitute $x = 8$ into the first equation and solve for y.

$$-(8) + y = -5$$
$$y = 3$$

Our solution is $(8, 3)$.

Check the solution by substituting $(8, 3)$ into both equations.

$$-x + y = -5$$
$$-(8) + (3) = -5 \qquad \text{True}$$
$$2x - 5y = 1$$
$$2(8) - 5(3) = 1 \qquad \text{True}$$

Try It #3

Solve the following system of equations by substitution.

$$x = y + 3$$
$$4 = 3x - 2y$$

Q & A...

Can the substitution method be used to solve any linear system in two variables?

Yes, but the method works best if one of the equations contains a coefficient of 1 or -1 so that we do not have to deal with fractions.

Solving Systems of Equations in Two Variables by the Addition Method

A third method of solving systems of linear equations is the **addition method**. In this method, we add two terms with the same variable, but opposite coefficients, so that the sum is zero. Of course, not all systems are set up with the two terms of one variable having opposite coefficients. Often we must adjust one or both of the equations by multiplication so that one variable will be eliminated by addition.

How To...

Given a system of equations, solve using the addition method.

1. Write both equations with x- and y-variables on the left side of the equal sign and constants on the right.
2. Write one equation above the other, lining up corresponding variables. If one of the variables in the top equation has the opposite coefficient of the same variable in the bottom equation, add the equations together, eliminating one variable. If not, use multiplication by a nonzero number so that one of the variables in the top equation has the opposite coefficient of the same variable in the bottom equation, then add the equations to eliminate the variable.
3. Solve the resulting equation for the remaining variable.
4. Substitute that value into one of the original equations and solve for the second variable.
5. Check the solution by substituting the values into the other equation.

Example 4   **Solving a System by the Addition Method**

Solve the given system of equations by addition.

$$x + 2y = -1$$
$$-x + y = 3$$

Solution   Both equations are already set equal to a constant. Notice that the coefficient of x in the second equation, -1, is the opposite of the coefficient of x in the first equation, 1. We can add the two equations to eliminate x without needing to multiply by a constant.

$$x + 2y = -1$$
$$\underline{-x + y = 3}$$
$$3y = 2$$

Now that we have eliminated x, we can solve the resulting equation for y.

$$3y = 2$$
$$y = \frac{2}{3}$$

Then, we substitute this value for y into one of the original equations and solve for x.

$$-x + y = 3$$
$$-x + \frac{2}{3} = 3$$
$$-x = 3 - \frac{2}{3}$$
$$-x = \frac{7}{3}$$
$$x = -\frac{7}{3}$$

The solution to this system is $\left(-\frac{7}{3}, \frac{2}{3}\right)$.

Check the solution in the first equation.

$$x + 2y = -1$$
$$\left(-\frac{7}{3}\right) + 2\left(\frac{2}{3}\right) = -1$$
$$-\frac{7}{3} + \frac{4}{3} = -1$$
$$-\frac{3}{3} = -1$$
$$-1 = -1 \qquad \text{True}$$

Analysis   *We gain an important perspective on systems of equations by looking at the graphical representation. See* **Figure 5** *to find that the equations intersect at the solution. We do not need to ask whether there may be a second solution because observing the graph confirms that the system has exactly one solution.*

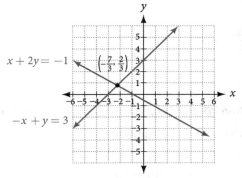

Figure 5

Example 5   **Using the Addition Method When Multiplication of One Equation Is Required**

Solve the given system of equations by the addition method.

$$3x + 5y = -11$$
$$x - 2y = 11$$

Solution Adding these equations as presented will not eliminate a variable. However, we see that the first equation has $3x$ in it and the second equation has x. So if we multiply the second equation by -3, the x-terms will add to zero.

$$x - 2y = 11$$
$$-3(x - 2y) = -3(11)$$ Multiply both sides by -3.
$$-3x + 6y = -33$$ Use the distributive property.

Now, let's add them.

$$3x + 5y = -11$$
$$\underline{-3x + 6y = -33}$$
$$11y = -44$$
$$y = -4$$

For the last step, we substitute $y = -4$ into one of the original equations and solve for x.

$$3x + 5y = -11$$
$$3x + 5(-4) = -11$$
$$3x - 20 = -11$$
$$3x = 9$$
$$x = 3$$

Our solution is the ordered pair $(3, -4)$. See **Figure 6**. Check the solution in the original second equation.

$$x - 2y = 11$$
$$(3) - 2(-4) = 3 + 8$$
$$11 = 11 \qquad \text{True}$$

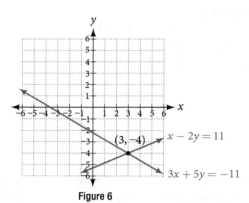

Figure 6

Try It #4

Solve the system of equations by addition.

$$2x - 7y = 2$$
$$3x + y = -20$$

Example 6   **Using the Addition Method When Multiplication of Both Equations Is Required**

Solve the given system of equations in two variables by addition.

$$2x + 3y = -16$$
$$5x - 10y = 30$$

Solution   One equation has $2x$ and the other has $5x$. The least common multiple is $10x$ so we will have to multiply both equations by a constant in order to eliminate one variable. Let's eliminate x by multiplying the first equation by -5 and the second equation by 2.

$$-5(2x + 3y) = -5(-16)$$
$$-10x - 15y = 80$$
$$2(5x - 10y) = 2(30)$$
$$10x - 20y = 60$$

Then, we add the two equations together.

$$-10x - 15y = 80$$
$$\underline{10x - 20y = 60}$$
$$-35y = 140$$
$$y = -4$$

Substitute $y = -4$ into the original first equation.

$$2x + 3(-4) = -16$$
$$2x - 12 = -16$$
$$2x = -4$$
$$x = -2$$

The solution is $(-2, -4)$. Check it in the other equation.

$$5x - 10y = 30$$
$$5(-2) - 10(-4) = 30$$
$$-10 + 40 = 30$$
$$30 = 30$$

See **Figure 7**.

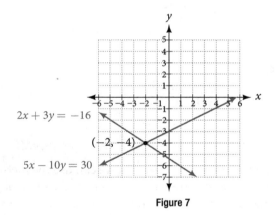

Figure 7

Example 7   **Using the Addition Method in Systems of Equations Containing Fractions**

Solve the given system of equations in two variables by addition.

$$\frac{x}{3} + \frac{y}{6} = 3$$

$$\frac{x}{2} - \frac{y}{4} = 1$$

Solution   First clear each equation of fractions by multiplying both sides of the equation by the least common denominator.

$$6\left(\frac{x}{3} + \frac{y}{6}\right) = 6(3)$$
$$2x + y = 18$$
$$4\left(\frac{x}{2} - \frac{y}{4}\right) = 4(1)$$
$$2x - y = 4$$

Now multiply the second equation by -1 so that we can eliminate the x-variable.

$$-1(2x - y) = -1(4)$$
$$-2x + y = -4$$

Add the two equations to eliminate the x-variable and solve the resulting equation.

$$2x + y = 18$$
$$\underline{-2x + y = -4}$$
$$2y = 14$$
$$y = 7$$

Substitute $y = 7$ into the first equation.

$$2x + (7) = 18$$
$$2x = 11$$
$$x = \frac{11}{2}$$
$$= 5.5$$

The solution is $\left(\frac{11}{2}, 7\right)$. Check it in the other equation.

$$\frac{x}{2} - \frac{y}{4} = 1$$
$$\frac{\frac{11}{2}}{2} - \frac{7}{4} = 1$$
$$\frac{11}{4} - \frac{7}{4} = 1$$
$$\frac{4}{4} = 1$$

Try It #5

Solve the system of equations by addition.

$$2x + 3y = 8$$
$$3x + 5y = 10$$

Identifying Inconsistent Systems of Equations Containing Two Variables

Now that we have several methods for solving systems of equations, we can use the methods to identify inconsistent systems. Recall that an inconsistent system consists of parallel lines that have the same slope but different y-intercepts. They will never intersect. When searching for a solution to an inconsistent system, we will come up with a false statement, such as $12 = 0$.

Example 8   **Solving an Inconsistent System of Equations**

Solve the following system of equations.

$$x = 9 - 2y$$
$$x + 2y = 13$$

Solution   We can approach this problem in two ways. Because one equation is already solved for x, the most obvious step is to use substitution.

$$x + 2y = 13$$
$$(9 - 2y) + 2y = 13$$
$$9 + 0y = 13$$
$$9 = 13$$

Clearly, this statement is a contradiction because $9 \neq 13$. Therefore, the system has no solution.

The second approach would be to first manipulate the equations so that they are both in slope-intercept form. We manipulate the first equation as follows.

$$x = 9 - 2y$$
$$2y = -x + 9$$
$$y = -\frac{1}{2}x + \frac{9}{2}$$

We then convert the second equation expressed to slope-intercept form.

$$x + 2y = 13$$
$$2y = -x + 13$$
$$y = -\frac{1}{2}x + \frac{13}{2}$$

Comparing the equations, we see that they have the same slope but different y-intercepts. Therefore, the lines are parallel and do not intersect.

$$y = -\frac{1}{2}x + \frac{9}{2}$$
$$y = -\frac{1}{2}x + \frac{13}{2}$$

Analysis *Writing the equations in slope-intercept form confirms that the system is inconsistent because all lines will intersect eventually unless they are parallel. Parallel lines will never intersect; thus, the two lines have no points in common. The graphs of the equations in this example are shown in* **Figure 8**.

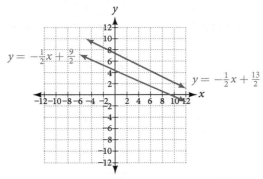

Figure 8

Try It #6

Solve the following system of equations in two variables.

$$2y - 2x = 2$$
$$2y - 2x = 6$$

Expressing the Solution of a System of Dependent Equations Containing Two Variables

Recall that a dependent system of equations in two variables is a system in which the two equations represent the same line. Dependent systems have an infinite number of solutions because all of the points on one line are also on the other line. After using substitution or addition, the resulting equation will be an identity, such as $0 = 0$.

Example 9 **Finding a Solution to a Dependent System of Linear Equations**

Find a solution to the system of equations using the addition method.

$$x + 3y = 2$$
$$3x + 9y = 6$$

Solution With the addition method, we want to eliminate one of the variables by adding the equations. In this case, let's focus on eliminating x. If we multiply both sides of the first equation by -3, then we will be able to eliminate the x-variable.

$$x + 3y = 2$$
$$(-3)(x + 3y) = (-3)(2)$$
$$-3x - 9y = -6$$

Now add the equations.

$$-3x - 9y = -6$$
$$+ \quad 3x + 9y = 6$$
$$\overline{ 0 = 0}$$

We can see that there will be an infinite number of solutions that satisfy both equations.

Analysis *If we rewrote both equations in the slope-intercept form, we might know what the solution would look like before adding. Let's look at what happens when we convert the system to slope-intercept form.*

$$x + 3y = 2$$
$$3y = -x + 2$$
$$y = -\frac{1}{3}x + \frac{2}{3}$$
$$3x + 9y = 6$$
$$9y = -3x + 6$$
$$y = -\frac{3}{9}x + \frac{6}{9}$$
$$y = -\frac{1}{3}x + \frac{2}{3}$$

See **Figure 9**. Notice the results are the same. The general solution to the system is $\left(x, -\frac{1}{3}x + \frac{2}{3} \right)$.

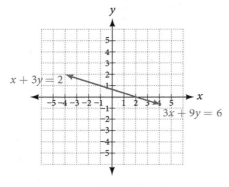

Figure 9

Try It #7

Solve the following system of equations in two variables.

$$y - 2x = 5$$
$$-3y + 6x = -15$$

Using Systems of Equations to Investigate Profits

Using what we have learned about systems of equations, we can return to the skateboard manufacturing problem at the beginning of the section. The skateboard manufacturer's **revenue function** is the function used to calculate the amount of money that comes into the business. It can be represented by the equation $R = xp$, where x = quantity and p = price. The revenue function is shown in orange in **Figure 10**.

The **cost function** is the function used to calculate the costs of doing business. It includes fixed costs, such as rent and salaries, and variable costs, such as utilities. The cost function is shown in blue in **Figure 10**. The x-axis represents quantity in hundreds of units. The y-axis represents either cost or revenue in hundreds of dollars.

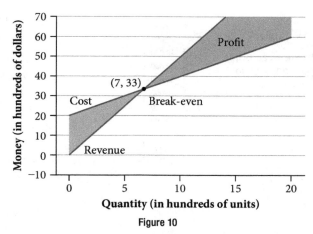

Figure 10

The point at which the two lines intersect is called the **break-even point**. We can see from the graph that if 700 units are produced, the cost is $3,300 and the revenue is also $3,300. In other words, the company breaks even if they produce and sell 700 units. They neither make money nor lose money.

The shaded region to the right of the break-even point represents quantities for which the company makes a profit. The shaded region to the left represents quantities for which the company suffers a loss. The **profit function** is the revenue function minus the cost function, written as $P(x) = R(x) - C(x)$. Clearly, knowing the quantity for which the cost equals the revenue is of great importance to businesses.

Example 10   **Finding the Break-Even Point and the Profit Function Using Substitution**

Given the cost function $C(x) = 0.85x + 35,000$ and the revenue function $R(x) = 1.55x$, find the break-even point and the profit function.

Solution   Write the system of equations using y to replace function notation.

$$y = 0.85x + 35,000$$
$$y = 1.55x$$

Substitute the expression $0.85x + 35,000$ from the first equation into the second equation and solve for x.

$$0.85x + 35,000 = 1.55x$$
$$35,000 = 0.7x$$
$$50,000 = x$$

Then, we substitute $x = 50,000$ into either the cost function or the revenue function.

$$1.55(50,000) = 77,500$$

The break-even point is (50,000, 77,500).

The profit function is found using the formula $P(x) = R(x) - C(x)$.

$$P(x) = 1.55x - (0.85x + 35,000)$$
$$= 0.7x - 35,000$$

The profit function is $P(x) = 0.7x - 35,000$.

Analysis   *The cost to produce 50,000 units is $77,500, and the revenue from the sales of 50,000 units is also $77,500. To make a profit, the business must produce and sell more than 50,000 units. See **Figure 11**.*

*We see from the graph in **Figure 12** that the profit function has a negative value until $x = 50,000$, when the graph crosses the x-axis. Then, the graph emerges into positive y-values and continues on this path as the profit function is a straight line. This illustrates that the break-even point for businesses occurs when the profit function is 0. The area to the left of the break-even point represents operating at a loss.*

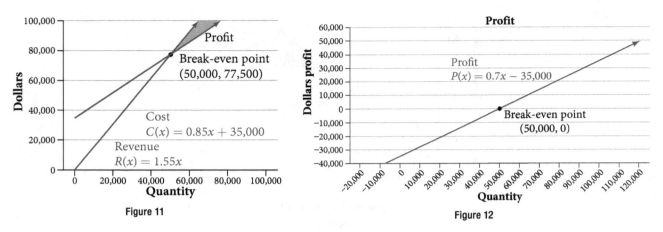

Figure 11

Figure 12

Example 11 Writing and Solving a System of Equations in Two Variables

The cost of a ticket to the circus is $25.00 for children and $50.00 for adults. On a certain day, attendance at the circus is 2,000 and the total gate revenue is $70,000. How many children and how many adults bought tickets?

Solution   Let c = the number of children and a = the number of adults in attendance.

The total number of people is 2,000. We can use this to write an equation for the number of people at the circus that day.

$$c + a = 2,000$$

The revenue from all children can be found by multiplying $25.00 by the number of children, $25c$. The revenue from all adults can be found by multiplying $50.00 by the number of adults, $50a$. The total revenue is $70,000.

We can use this to write an equation for the revenue.

$$25c + 50a = 70,000$$

We now have a system of linear equations in two variables.

$$c + a = 2,000$$
$$25c + 50a = 70,000$$

In the first equation, the coefficient of both variables is 1. We can quickly solve the first equation for either c or a. We will solve for a.

$$c + a = 2,000$$
$$a = 2,000 - c$$

Substitute the expression $2,000 - c$ in the second equation for a and solve for c.

$$25c + 50(2,000 - c) = 70,000$$
$$25c + 100,000 - 50c = 70,000$$
$$-25c = -30,000$$
$$c = 1,200$$

Substitute $c = 1,200$ into the first equation to solve for a.

$$1,200 + a = 2,000$$
$$a = 800$$

We find that 1,200 children and 800 adults bought tickets to the circus that day.

Try It #8

Meal tickets at the circus cost $4.00 for children and $12.00 for adults. If 1,650 meal tickets were bought for a total of $14,200, how many children and how many adults bought meal tickets?

Access these online resources for additional instruction and practice with systems of linear equations.

- Solving Systems of Equations Using Substitution (http://openstaxcollege.org/l/syssubst)
- Solving Systems of Equations Using Elimination (http://openstaxcollege.org/l/syselim)
- Applications of Systems of Equations (http://openstaxcollege.org/l/sysapp)

11.1   SECTION EXERCISES

VERBAL

1. Can a system of linear equations have exactly two solutions? Explain why or why not.

2. If you are performing a break-even analysis for a business and their cost and revenue equations are dependent, explain what this means for the company's profit margins.

3. If you are solving a break-even analysis and get a negative break-even point, explain what this signifies for the company?

4. If you are solving a break-even analysis and there is no break-even point, explain what this means for the company. How should they ensure there is a break-even point?

5. Given a system of equations, explain at least two different methods of solving that system.

ALGEBRAIC

For the following exercises, determine whether the given ordered pair is a solution to the system of equations.

6. $5x - y = 4$
$x + 6y = 2$ and $(4, 0)$

7. $-3x - 5y = 13$
$-x + 4y = 10$ and $(-6, 1)$

8. $3x + 7y = 1$
$2x + 4y = 0$ and $(2, 3)$

9. $-2x + 5y = 7$
$2x + 9y = 7$ and $(-1, 1)$

10. $x + 8y = 43$
$3x - 2y = -1$ and $(3, 5)$

For the following exercises, solve each system by substitution.

11. $x + 3y = 5$
$2x + 3y = 4$

12. $3x - 2y = 18$
$5x + 10y = -10$

13. $4x + 2y = -10$
$3x + 9y = 0$

14. $2x + 4y = -3.8$
$9x - 5y = 1.3$

15. $-2x + 3y = 1.2$
$-3x - 6y = 1.8$

16. $x - 0.2y = 1$
$-10x + 2y = 5$

17. $3 \ \ x + 5y = 9$
$30x + 50y = -90$

18. $-3x + y = 2$
$12x - 4y = -8$

19. $\frac{1}{2}x + \frac{1}{3}y = 16$
$\frac{1}{6}x + \frac{1}{4}y = 9$

20. $-\frac{1}{4}x + \frac{3}{2}y = 11$
$-\frac{1}{8}x + \frac{1}{3}y = 3$

For the following exercises, solve each system by addition.

21. $-2x + 5y = -42$
$7x + 2y = 30$

22. $6x - 5y = -34$
$2x + 6y = 4$

23. $5x - y = -2.6$
$-4x - 6y = 1.4$

24. $7x - 2y = 3$
$4x + 5y = 3.25$

25. $-x + 2y = -1$
$5x - 10y = 6$

26. $7x + 6y = 2$
$-28x - 24y = -8$

27. $\frac{5}{6}x + \frac{1}{4}y = 0$
$\frac{1}{8}x - \frac{1}{2}y = -\frac{43}{120}$

28. $\frac{1}{3}x + \frac{1}{9}y = \frac{2}{9}$
$-\frac{1}{2}x + \frac{4}{5}y = -\frac{1}{3}$

29. $-0.2x + 0.4y = 0.6$
$x - 2y = -3$

30. $-0.1x + 0.2y = 0.6$
$5x - 10y = 1$

For the following exercises, solve each system by any method.

31. $5x + 9y = 16$
$x + 2y = 4$

32. $6x - 8y = -0.6$
$3x + 2y = 0.9$

33. $5x - 2y = 2.25$
$7x - 4y = 3$

34. $x - \frac{5}{12}y = -\frac{55}{12}$
$-6x + \frac{5}{2}y = \frac{55}{2}$

35. $7x - 4y = \dfrac{7}{6}$

$2x + 4y = \dfrac{1}{3}$

36. $3x + 6y = 11$

$2x + 4y = 9$

37. $\dfrac{7}{3}x - \dfrac{1}{6}y = 2$

$-\dfrac{21}{6}x + \dfrac{3}{12}y = -3$

38. $\dfrac{1}{2}x + \dfrac{1}{3}y = \dfrac{1}{3}$

$\dfrac{3}{2}x + \dfrac{1}{4}y = -\dfrac{1}{8}$

39. $2.2x + 1.3y = -0.1$

$4.2x + 4.2y = 2.1$

40. $0.1x + 0.2y = 2$

$0.35x - 0.3y = 0$

GRAPHICAL

For the following exercises, graph the system of equations and state whether the system is consistent, inconsistent, or dependent and whether the system has one solution, no solution, or infinite solutions.

41. $3x - y = 0.6$

$x - 2y = 1.3$

42. $-x + 2y = 4$

$2x - 4y = 1$

43. $x + 2y = 7$

$2x + 6y = 12$

44. $3x - 5y = 7$

$x - 2y = 3$

45. $3x - 2y = 5$

$-9x + 6y = -15$

TECHNOLOGY

For the following exercises, use the intersect function on a graphing device to solve each system. Round all answers to the nearest hundredth.

46. $0.1x + 0.2y = 0.3$

$-0.3x + 0.5y = 1$

47. $-0.01x + 0.12y = 0.62$

$0.15x + 0.20y = 0.52$

48. $0.5x + 0.3y = 4$

$0.25x - 0.9y = 0.46$

49. $0.15x + 0.27y = 0.39$

$-0.34x + 0.56y = 1.8$

50. $-0.71x + 0.92y = 0.13$

$0.83x + 0.05y = 2.1$

EXTENSIONS

For the following exercises, solve each system in terms of A, B, C, D, E, and F where A – F are nonzero numbers. Note that $A \neq B$ and $AE \neq BD$.

51. $x + y = A$

$x - y = B$

52. $x + Ay = 1$

$x + By = 1$

53. $Ax + y = 0$

$Bx + y = 1$

54. $Ax + By = C$

$x + y = 1$

55. $Ax + By = C$

$Dx + Ey = F$

REAL-WORLD APPLICATIONS

For the following exercises, solve for the desired quantity.

56. A stuffed animal business has a total cost of production $C = 12x + 30$ and a revenue function $R = 20x$. Find the break-even point.

57. A fast-food restaurant has a cost of production $C(x) = 11x + 120$ and a revenue function $R(x) = 5x$. When does the company start to turn a profit?

58. A cell phone factory has a cost of production $C(x) = 150x + 10,000$ and a revenue function $R(x) = 200x$. What is the break-even point?

59. A musician charges $C(x) = 64x + 20,000$, where x is the total number of attendees at the concert. The venue charges $80 per ticket. After how many people buy tickets does the venue break even, and what is the value of the total tickets sold at that point?

60. A guitar factory has a cost of production $C(x) = 75x + 50,000$. If the company needs to break even after 150 units sold, at what price should they sell each guitar? Round up to the nearest dollar, and write the revenue function.

For the following exercises, use a system of linear equations with two variables and two equations to solve.

61. Find two numbers whose sum is 28 and difference is 13.

62. A number is 9 more than another number. Twice the sum of the two numbers is 10. Find the two numbers.

63. The startup cost for a restaurant is $120,000, and each meal costs $10 for the restaurant to make. If each meal is then sold for $15, after how many meals does the restaurant break even?

64. A moving company charges a flat rate of $150, and an additional $5 for each box. If a taxi service would charge $20 for each box, how many boxes would you need for it to be cheaper to use the moving company, and what would be the total cost?

65. A total of 1,595 first- and second-year college students gathered at a pep rally. The number of freshmen exceeded the number of sophomores by 15. How many freshmen and sophomores were in attendance?

66. 276 students enrolled in a freshman-level chemistry class. By the end of the semester, 5 times the number of students passed as failed. Find the number of students who passed, and the number of students who failed.

67. There were 130 faculty at a conference. If there were 18 more women than men attending, how many of each gender attended the conference?

68. A jeep and BMW enter a highway running east-west at the same exit heading in opposite directions. The jeep entered the highway 30 minutes before the BMW did, and traveled 7 mph slower than the BMW. After 2 hours from the time the BMW entered the highway, the cars were 306.5 miles apart. Find the speed of each car, assuming they were driven on cruise control.

69. If a scientist mixed 10% saline solution with 60% saline solution to get 25 gallons of 40% saline solution, how many gallons of 10% and 60% solutions were mixed?

70. An investor earned triple the profits of what she earned last year. If she made $500,000.48 total for both years, how much did she earn in profits each year?

71. An investor who dabbles in real estate invested 1.1 million dollars into two land investments. On the first investment, Swan Peak, her return was a 110% increase on the money she invested. On the second investment, Riverside Community, she earned 50% over what she invested. If she earned $1 million in profits, how much did she invest in each of the land deals?

72. If an investor invests a total of $25,000 into two bonds, one that pays 3% simple interest, and the other that pays $2\frac{7}{8}$ % interest, and the investor earns $737.50 annual interest, how much was invested in each account?

73. If an investor invests $23,000 into two bonds, one that pays 4% in simple interest, and the other paying 2% simple interest, and the investor earns $710.00 annual interest, how much was invested in each account?

74. CDs cost $5.96 more than DVDs at All Bets Are Off Electronics. How much would 6 CDs and 2 DVDs cost if 5 CDs and 2 DVDs cost $127.73?

75. A store clerk sold 60 pairs of sneakers. The high-tops sold for $98.99 and the low-tops sold for $129.99. If the receipts for the two types of sales totaled $6,404.40, how many of each type of sneaker were sold?

76. A concert manager counted 350 ticket receipts the day after a concert. The price for a student ticket was $12.50, and the price for an adult ticket was $16.00. The register confirms that $5,075 was taken in. How many student tickets and adult tickets were sold?

77. Admission into an amusement park for 4 children and 2 adults is $116.90. For 6 children and 3 adults, the admission is $175.35. Assuming a different price for children and adults, what is the price of the child's ticket and the price of the adult ticket?

LEARNING OBJECTIVES

In this section, you will:

- Solve systems of three equations in three variables.
- Identify inconsistent systems of equations containing three variables.
- Express the solution of a system of dependent equations containing three variables.

11.2   SYSTEMS OF LINEAR EQUATIONS: THREE VARIABLES

Figure 1 (credit: "Elembis," Wikimedia Commons)

John received an inheritance of $12,000 that he divided into three parts and invested in three ways: in a money-market fund paying 3% annual interest; in municipal bonds paying 4% annual interest; and in mutual funds paying 7% annual interest. John invested $4,000 more in municipal funds than in municipal bonds. He earned $670 in interest the first year. How much did John invest in each type of fund?

Understanding the correct approach to setting up problems such as this one makes finding a solution a matter of following a pattern. We will solve this and similar problems involving three equations and three variables in this section. Doing so uses similar techniques as those used to solve systems of two equations in two variables. However, finding solutions to systems of three equations requires a bit more organization and a touch of visual gymnastics.

Solving Systems of Three Equations in Three Variables

In order to solve systems of equations in three variables, known as three-by-three systems, the primary tool we will be using is called Gaussian elimination, named after the prolific German mathematician Karl Friedrich Gauss. While there is no definitive order in which operations are to be performed, there are specific guidelines as to what type of moves can be made. We may number the equations to keep track of the steps we apply. The goal is to eliminate one variable at a time to achieve upper triangular form, the ideal form for a three-by-three system because it allows for straightforward back-substitution to find a solution (x, y, z), which we call an ordered triple. A system in upper triangular form looks like the following:

$$Ax + By + Cz = D$$
$$Ey + Fz = G$$
$$Hz = K$$

The third equation can be solved for z, and then we back-substitute to find y and x. To write the system in upper triangular form, we can perform the following operations:

1. Interchange the order of any two equations.

2. Multiply both sides of an equation by a nonzero constant.

3. Add a nonzero multiple of one equation to another equation.

The **solution set** to a three-by-three system is an ordered triple $\{(x, y, z)\}$. Graphically, the ordered triple defines the point that is the intersection of three planes in space. You can visualize such an intersection by imagining any corner in a rectangular room. A corner is defined by three planes: two adjoining walls and the floor (or ceiling). Any point where two walls and the floor meet represents the intersection of three planes.

---

number of possible solutions

Figure 2 and **Figure 3** illustrate possible solution scenarios for three-by-three systems.

- Systems that have a single solution are those which, after elimination, result in a **solution set** consisting of an ordered triple $\{(x, y, z)\}$. Graphically, the ordered triple defines a point that is the intersection of three planes in space.

- Systems that have an infinite number of solutions are those which, after elimination, result in an expression that is always true, such as $0 = 0$. Graphically, an infinite number of solutions represents a line or coincident plane that serves as the intersection of three planes in space.

- Systems that have no solution are those that, after elimination, result in a statement that is a contradiction, such as $3 = 0$. Graphically, a system with no solution is represented by three planes with no point in common.

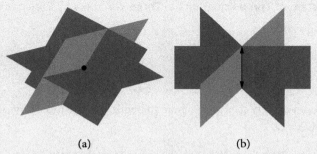

(a)   (b)

Figure 2 (a)Three planes intersect at a single point, representing a three-by-three system with a single solution.
(b) Three planes intersect in a line, representing a three-by-three system with infinite solutions.

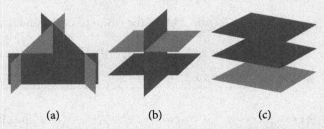

(a)   (b)   (c)

Figure 3 All three figures represent three-by-three systems with no solution. (a) The three planes intersect with each other, but not at a common point.
(b) Two of the planes are parallel and intersect with the third plane, but not with each other.
(c) All three planes are parallel, so there is no point of intersection.

Example 1   **Determining Whether an Ordered Triple Is a Solution to a System**

Determine whether the ordered triple $(3, -2, 1)$ is a solution to the system.

$$x + y + z = 2$$
$$6x - 4y + 5z = 31$$
$$5x + 2y + 2z = 13$$

Solution   We will check each equation by substituting in the values of the ordered triple for x, y, and z.

$$x + y + z = 2$$
$$(3) + (-2) + (1) = 2$$
True

$$6x - 4y + 5z = 31$$
$$6(3) - 4(-2) + 5(1) = 31$$
$$18 + 8 + 5 = 31$$
True

$$5x + 2y + 2z = 13$$
$$5(3) + 2(-2) + 2(1) = 13$$
$$15 - 4 + 2 = 13$$
$$\text{True}$$

The ordered triple $(3, -2, 1)$ is indeed a solution to the system.

How To...

Given a linear system of three equations, solve for three unknowns.

1. Pick any pair of equations and solve for one variable.
2. Pick another pair of equations and solve for the same variable.
3. You have created a system of two equations in two unknowns. Solve the resulting two-by-two system.
4. Back-substitute known variables into any one of the original equations and solve for the missing variable.

Example 2   **Solving a System of Three Equations in Three Variables by Elimination**

Find a solution to the following system:

$$x - 2y + 3z = 9 \qquad (1)$$
$$-x + 3y - z = -6 \qquad (2)$$
$$2x - 5y + 5z = 17 \qquad (3)$$

Solution   There will always be several choices as to where to begin, but the most obvious first step here is to eliminate x by adding equations (1) and (2).

$$x - 2y + 3z = 9 \qquad (1)$$
$$\underline{-x + 3y - z = -6 \qquad (2)}$$
$$y + 2z = 3 \qquad (3)$$

The second step is multiplying equation (1) by -2 and adding the result to equation (3). These two steps will eliminate the variable x.

$$-2x + 4y - 6z = -18 \qquad (1) \text{ multiplied by} - 2$$
$$\underline{2x - 5y + 5z = 17 \qquad (3)}$$
$$-y - z = -1 \qquad (5)$$

In equations (4) and (5), we have created a new two-by-two system. We can solve for z by adding the two equations.

$$y + 2z = 3 \qquad (4)$$
$$\underline{-y - z = -1 \qquad (5)}$$
$$z = 2 \qquad (6)$$

Choosing one equation from each new system, we obtain the upper triangular form:

$$x - 2y + 3z = 9 \qquad (1)$$
$$y + 2z = 3 \qquad (4)$$
$$z = 2 \qquad (6)$$

Next, we back-substitute $z = 2$ into equation (4) and solve for y.

$$y + 2(2) = 3$$
$$y + 4 = 3$$
$$y = -1$$

Finally, we can back-substitute $z = 2$ and $y = -1$ into equation (1). This will yield the solution for x.

$$x - 2(-1) + 3(2) = 9$$
$$x + 2 + 6 = 9$$
$$x = 1$$

The solution is the ordered triple $(1, -1, 2)$. See **Figure 4**.

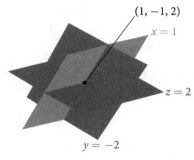

Figure 4

Example 3 **Solving a Real-World Problem Using a System of Three Equations in Three Variables**

In the problem posed at the beginning of the section, John invested his inheritance of $12,000 in three different funds: part in a money-market fund paying 3% interest annually; part in municipal bonds paying 4% annually; and the rest in mutual funds paying 7% annually. John invested $4,000 more in mutual funds than he invested in municipal bonds. The total interest earned in one year was $670. How much did he invest in each type of fund?

Solution To solve this problem, we use all of the information given and set up three equations. First, we assign a variable to each of the three investment amounts:

$$x = \text{amount invested in money-market fund}$$
$$y = \text{amount invested in municipal bonds}$$
$$z = \text{amount invested in mutual funds}$$

The first equation indicates that the sum of the three principal amounts is $12,000.

$$x + y + z = 12{,}000$$

We form the second equation according to the information that John invested $4,000 more in mutual funds than he invested in municipal bonds.

$$z = y + 4{,}000$$

The third equation shows that the total amount of interest earned from each fund equals $670.

$$0.03x + 0.04y + 0.07z = 670$$

Then, we write the three equations as a system.

$$x + y + z = 12{,}000$$
$$-y + z = 4{,}000$$
$$0.03x + 0.04y + 0.07z = 670$$

To make the calculations simpler, we can multiply the third equation by 100. Thus,

$$x + y + z = 12{,}000 \qquad (1)$$
$$-y + z = 4{,}000 \qquad (2)$$
$$3x + 4y + 7z = 67{,}000 \qquad (3)$$

Step 1. Interchange equation (2) and equation (3) so that the two equations with three variables will line up.

$$x + y + z = 12{,}000$$
$$3x + 4y + 7z = 67{,}000$$
$$-y + z = 4{,}000$$

Step 2. Multiply equation (1) by -3 and add to equation (2). Write the result as row 2.

$$x + y + z = 12{,}000$$
$$y + 4z = 31{,}000$$
$$-y + z = 4{,}000$$

Step 3. Add equation (2) to equation (3) and write the result as equation (3).

$$x + y + z = 12,000$$
$$y + 4z = 31,000$$
$$5z = 35,000$$

Step 4. Solve for z in equation (3). Back-substitute that value in equation (2) and solve for y. Then, back-substitute the values for z and y into equation (1) and solve for x.

$$5z = 35,000$$
$$z = 7,000$$
$$y + 4(7,000) = 31,000$$
$$y = 3,000$$
$$x + 3,000 + 7,000 = 12,000$$
$$x = 2,000$$

John invested $2,000 in a money-market fund, $3,000 in municipal bonds, and $7,000 in mutual funds.

Try It #1

Solve the system of equations in three variables.

$$2x + y - 2z = -1$$
$$3x - 3y - z = 5$$
$$x - 2y + 3z = 6$$

Identifying Inconsistent Systems of Equations Containing Three Variables

Just as with systems of equations in two variables, we may come across an inconsistent system of equations in three variables, which means that it does not have a solution that satisfies all three equations. The equations could represent three parallel planes, two parallel planes and one intersecting plane, or three planes that intersect the other two but not at the same location. The process of elimination will result in a false statement, such as $3 = 7$ or some other contradiction.

Example 4   **Solving an Inconsistent System of Three Equations in Three Variables**

Solve the following system.

$$x - 3y + z = 4 \qquad (1)$$
$$-x + 2y - 5z = 3 \qquad (2)$$
$$5x - 13y + 13z = 8 \qquad (3)$$

Solution   Looking at the coefficients of x, we can see that we can eliminate x by adding equation (1) to equation (2).

$$x - 3y + z = 4 \qquad (1)$$
$$\underline{-x + 2y - 5z = 3 \qquad (2)}$$
$$-y - 4z = 7 \qquad (4)$$

Next, we multiply equation (1) by -5 and add it to equation (3).

$$-5x + 15y - 5z = -20 \qquad \text{(1) multiplied by } -5$$
$$\underline{5x - 13y + 13z = 8 \qquad (3)}$$
$$2y + 8z = -12 \qquad (5)$$

Then, we multiply equation (4) by 2 and add it to equation (5).

$$-2y - 8z = 14 \qquad \text{(4) multiplied by 2}$$
$$\underline{2y + 8z = -12 \qquad (5)}$$
$$0 = 2$$

The final equation $0 = 2$ is a contradiction, so we conclude that the system of equations in inconsistent and, therefore, has no solution.

Analysis In this system, each plane intersects the other two, but not at the same location. Therefore, the system is inconsistent.

Try It #2

Solve the system of three equations in three variables.

$$x + y + z = 2$$
$$y - 3z = 1$$
$$2x + y + 5z = 0$$

Expressing the Solution of a System of Dependent Equations Containing Three Variables

We know from working with systems of equations in two variables that a dependent system of equations has an infinite number of solutions. The same is true for dependent systems of equations in three variables. An infinite number of solutions can result from several situations. The three planes could be the same, so that a solution to one equation will be the solution to the other two equations. All three equations could be different but they intersect on a line, which has infinite solutions. Or two of the equations could be the same and intersect the third on a line.

Example 5   **Finding the Solution to a Dependent System of Equations**

Find the solution to the given system of three equations in three variables.

$$2x + y - 3z = 0 \qquad (1)$$
$$4x + 2y - 6z = 0 \qquad (2)$$
$$x - y + z = 0 \qquad (3)$$

Solution   First, we can multiply equation (1) by -2 and add it to equation (2).

$$\begin{array}{ll} -4x - 2y + 6z = 0 & \text{equation (1) multiplied by } -2 \\ \underline{4x + 2y - 6z = 0} & (2) \\ \quad\quad\quad 0 = 0 & \end{array}$$

We do not need to proceed any further. The result we get is an identity, $0 = 0$, which tells us that this system has an infinite number of solutions. There are other ways to begin to solve this system, such as multiplying equation (3) by -2, and adding it to equation (1). We then perform the same steps as above and find the same result, $0 = 0$.

When a system is dependent, we can find general expressions for the solutions. Adding equations (1) and (3), we have

$$2x + y - 3z = 0$$
$$x - y + z = 0$$
$$3x - 2z = 0$$

We then solve the resulting equation for z.

$$3x - 2z = 0$$
$$z = \frac{3}{2}x$$

We back-substitute the expression for z into one of the equations and solve for y.

$$2x + y - 3\left(\frac{3}{2}x\right) = 0$$

$$2x + y - \frac{9}{2}x = 0$$

$$y = \frac{9}{2}x - 2x$$

$$y = \frac{5}{2}x$$

So the general solution is $\left(x, \frac{5}{2}x, \frac{3}{2}x\right)$. In this solution, x can be any real number. The values of y and z are dependent on the value selected for x.

Analysis As shown in **Figure 5**, *two of the planes are the same and they intersect the third plane on a line. The solution set is infinite, as all points along the intersection line will satisfy all three equations.*

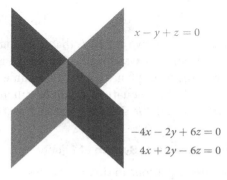

$x - y + z = 0$

$-4x - 2y + 6z = 0$

$4x + 2y - 6z = 0$

Figure 5

Q & A...

Does the generic solution to a dependent system always have to be written in terms of x?

No, you can write the generic solution in terms of any of the variables, but it is common to write it in terms of x and if needed x and y.

Try It #3

Solve the following system.

$$x + y + z = 7$$

$$3x - 2y - z = 4$$

$$x + 6y + 5z = 24$$

Access these online resources for additional instruction and practice with systems of equations in three variables.

- Ex 1: System of Three Equations with Three Unknowns Using Elimination (http://openstaxcollege.org/l/systhree)
- Ex. 2: System of Three Equations with Three Unknowns Using Elimination (http://openstaxcollege.org/l/systhelim)

11.2   SECTION EXERCISES

VERBAL

1. Can a linear system of three equations have exactly two solutions? Explain why or why not

2. If a given ordered triple solves the system of equations, is that solution unique? If so, explain why. If not, give an example where it is not unique.

3. If a given ordered triple does not solve the system of equations, is there no solution? If so, explain why. If not, give an example.

4. Using the method of addition, is there only one way to solve the system?

5. Can you explain whether there can be only one method to solve a linear system of equations? If yes, give an example of such a system of equations. If not, explain why not.

ALGEBRAIC

For the following exercises, determine whether the ordered triple given is the solution to the system of equations.

6. $2x - 6y + 6z = -12$
   $x + 4y + 5z = -1$ and $(0, 1, -1)$
   $-x + 2y + 3z = -1$

7. $6x - y + 3z = 6$
   $3x + 5y + 2z = 0$ and $(3, -3, -5)$
   $x + y = 0$

8. $6x - 7y + z = 2$
   $-x - y + 3z = 4$ and $(4, 2, -6)$
   $2x + y - z = 1$

9. $x - y = 0$
   $x - z = 5$ and $(4, 4, -1)$
   $x - y + z = -1$

10. $-x - y + 2z = 3$
    $5x + 8y - 3z = 4$ and $(4, 1, -7)$
    $-x + 3y - 5z = -5$

For the following exercises, solve each system by substitution.

11. $3x - 4y + 2z = -15$
    $2x + 4y + z = 16$
    $2x + 3y + 5z = 20$

12. $5x - 2y + 3z = 20$
    $2x - 4y - 3z = -9$
    $x + 6y - 8z = 21$

13. $5x + 2y + 4z = 9$
    $-3x + 2y + z = 10$
    $4x - 3y + 5z = -3$

14. $4x - 3y + 5z = 31$
    $-x + 2y + 4z = 20$
    $x + 5y - 2z = -29$

15. $5x - 2y + 3z = 4$
    $-4x + 6y - 7z = -1$
    $3x + 2y - z = 4$

16. $4x + 6y + 9z = 0$
    $-5x + 2y - 6z = 3$
    $7x - 4y + 3z = -3$

For the following exercises, solve each system by Gaussian elimination.

17. $2x - y + 3z = 17$
    $-5x + 4y - 2z = -46$
    $2y + 5z = -7$

18. $5x - 6y + 3z = 50$
    $-x + 4y = 10$
    $2x - z = 10$

19. $2x + 3y - 6z = 1$
    $-4x - 6y + 12z = -2$
    $x + 2y + 5z = 10$

20. $4x + 6y - 2z = 8$
    $6x + 9y - 3z = 12$
    $-2x - 3y + z = -4$

21. $2x + 3y - 4z = 5$
    $-3x + 2y + z = 11$
    $-x + 5y + 3z = 4$

22. $10x + 2y - 14z = 8$
    $-x - 2y - 4z = -1$
    $-12x - 6y + 6z = -12$

23. $x + y + z = 14$
    $2y + 3z = -14$
    $-16y - 24z = -112$

24. $5x - 3y + 4z = -1$
    $-4x + 2y - 3z = 0$
    $-x + 5y + 7z = -11$

25. $x + y + z = 0$
    $2x - y + 3z = 0$
    $x - z = 0$

26. $3x + 2y - 5z = 6$
$5x - 4y + 3z = -12$
$4x + 5y - 2z = 15$

27. $x + y + z = 0$
$2x - y + 3z = 0$
$x - z = 1$

28. $3x - \dfrac{1}{2}y - z = -\dfrac{1}{2}$
$4x + z = 3$
$-x + \dfrac{3}{2}y = \dfrac{5}{2}$

29. $6x - 5y + 6z = 38$
$\dfrac{1}{5}x - \dfrac{1}{2}y + \dfrac{3}{5}z = 1$
$-4x - \dfrac{3}{2}y - z = -74$

30. $\dfrac{1}{2}x - \dfrac{1}{5}y + \dfrac{2}{5}z = -\dfrac{13}{10}$
$\dfrac{1}{4}x - \dfrac{2}{5}y - \dfrac{1}{5}z = -\dfrac{7}{20}$
$-\dfrac{1}{2}x - \dfrac{3}{4}y - \dfrac{1}{2}z = -\dfrac{5}{4}$

31. $-\dfrac{1}{3}x - \dfrac{1}{2}y - \dfrac{1}{4}z = \dfrac{3}{4}$
$-\dfrac{1}{2}x - \dfrac{1}{4}y - \dfrac{1}{2}z = 2$
$-\dfrac{1}{4}x - \dfrac{3}{4}y - \dfrac{1}{2}z = -\dfrac{1}{2}$

32. $\dfrac{1}{2}x - \dfrac{1}{4}y + \dfrac{3}{4}z = 0$
$\dfrac{1}{4}x - \dfrac{1}{10}y + \dfrac{2}{5}z = -2$
$\dfrac{1}{8}x + \dfrac{1}{5}y - \dfrac{1}{8}z = 2$

33. $\dfrac{4}{5}x - \dfrac{7}{8}y + \dfrac{1}{2}z = 1$
$-\dfrac{4}{5}x - \dfrac{3}{4}y + \dfrac{1}{3}z = -8$
$-\dfrac{2}{5}x - \dfrac{7}{8}y + \dfrac{1}{2}z = -5$

34. $-\dfrac{1}{3}x - \dfrac{1}{8}y + \dfrac{1}{6}z = -\dfrac{4}{3}$
$-\dfrac{2}{3}x - \dfrac{7}{8}y + \dfrac{1}{3}z = -\dfrac{23}{3}$
$-\dfrac{1}{3}x - \dfrac{5}{8}y + \dfrac{5}{6}z = 0$

35. $-\dfrac{1}{4}x - \dfrac{5}{4}y + \dfrac{5}{2}z = -5$
$-\dfrac{1}{2}x - \dfrac{5}{3}y + \dfrac{5}{4}z = \dfrac{55}{12}$
$-\dfrac{1}{3}x - \dfrac{1}{3}y + \dfrac{1}{3}z = \dfrac{5}{3}$

36. $\dfrac{1}{40}x + \dfrac{1}{60}y + \dfrac{1}{80}z = \dfrac{1}{100}$
$-\dfrac{1}{2}x - \dfrac{1}{3}y - \dfrac{1}{4}z = -\dfrac{1}{5}$
$\dfrac{3}{8}x + \dfrac{3}{12}y + \dfrac{3}{16}z = \dfrac{3}{20}$

37. $0.1x - 0.2y + 0.3z = 2$
$0.5x - 0.1y + 0.4z = 8$
$0.7x - 0.2y + 0.3z = 8$

38. $0.2x + 0.1y - 0.3z = 0.2$
$0.8x + 0.4y - 1.2z = 0.1$
$1.6x + 0.8y - 2.4z = 0.2$

39. $1.1x + 0.7y - 3.1z = -1.79$
$2.1x + 0.5y - 1.6z = -0.13$
$0.5x + 0.4y - 0.5z = -0.07$

40. $0.5x - 0.5y + 0.5z = 10$
$0.2x - 0.2y + 0.2z = 4$
$0.1x - 0.1y + 0.1z = 2$

41. $0.1x + 0.2y + 0.3z = 0.37$
$0.1x - 0.2y - 0.3z = -0.27$
$0.5x - 0.1y - 0.3z = -0.03$

42. $0.5x - 0.5y - 0.3z = 0.13$
$0.4x - 0.1y - 0.3z = 0.11$
$0.2x - 0.8y - 0.9z = -0.32$

43. $0.5x + 0.2y - 0.3z = 1$
$0.4x - 0.6y + 0.7z = 0.8$
$0.3x - 0.1y - 0.9z = 0.6$

44. $0.3x + 0.3y + 0.5z = 0.6$
$0.4x + 0.4y + 0.4z = 1.8$
$0.4x + 0.2y + 0.1z = 1.6$

45. $0.8x + 0.8y + 0.8z = 2.4$
$0.3x - 0.5y + 0.2z = 0$
$0.1x + 0.2y + 0.3z = 0.6$

EXTENSIONS

For the following exercises, solve the system for x, y, and z.

46. $x + y + z = 3$
$\dfrac{x-1}{2} + \dfrac{y-3}{2} + \dfrac{z+1}{2} = 0$
$\dfrac{x-2}{3} + \dfrac{y+4}{3} + \dfrac{z-3}{3} = \dfrac{2}{3}$

47. $5x - 3y - \dfrac{z+1}{2} = \dfrac{1}{2}$
$6x + \dfrac{y-9}{2} + 2z = -3$
$\dfrac{x+8}{2} - 4y + z = 4$

48. $\dfrac{x+4}{7} - \dfrac{y-1}{6} + \dfrac{z+2}{3} = 1$
$\dfrac{x-2}{4} + \dfrac{y+1}{8} - \dfrac{z+8}{12} = 0$
$\dfrac{x+6}{3} - \dfrac{y+2}{3} + \dfrac{z+4}{2} = 3$

49. $\dfrac{x-3}{6} + \dfrac{y+2}{2} - \dfrac{z-3}{3} = 2$
$\dfrac{x+2}{4} + \dfrac{y-5}{2} + \dfrac{z+4}{2} = 1$
$\dfrac{x+6}{2} - \dfrac{y-3}{2} + z + 1 = 9$

50. $\dfrac{x-1}{3} + \dfrac{y+3}{4} + \dfrac{z+2}{6} = 1$
$4x + 3y - 2z = 11$
$0.02x + 0.015y - 0.01z = 0.065$

REAL-WORLD APPLICATIONS

51. Three even numbers sum up to 108. The smaller is half the larger and the middle number is $\frac{3}{4}$ the larger. What are the three numbers?

52. Three numbers sum up to 147. The smallest number is half the middle number, which is half the largest number. What are the three numbers?

53. At a family reunion, there were only blood relatives, consisting of children, parents, and grandparents, in attendance. There were 400 people total. There were twice as many parents as grandparents, and 50 more children than parents. How many children, parents, and grandparents were in attendance?

54. An animal shelter has a total of 350 animals comprised of cats, dogs, and rabbits. If the number of rabbits is 5 less than one-half the number of cats, and there are 20 more cats than dogs, how many of each animal are at the shelter?

55. Your roommate, Sarah, offered to buy groceries for you and your other roommate. The total bill was $82. She forgot to save the individual receipts but remembered that your groceries were $0.05 cheaper than half of her groceries, and that your other roommate's groceries were $2.10 more than your groceries. How much was each of your share of the groceries?

56. Your roommate, John, offered to buy household supplies for you and your other roommate. You live near the border of three states, each of which has a different sales tax. The total amount of money spent was $100.75. Your supplies were bought with 5% tax, John's with 8% tax, and your third roommate's with 9% sales tax. The total amount of money spent without taxes is $93.50. If your supplies before tax were $1 more than half of what your third roommate's supplies were before tax, how much did each of you spend? Give your answer both with and without taxes.

57. Three coworkers work for the same employer. Their jobs are warehouse manager, office manager, and truck driver. The sum of the annual salaries of the warehouse manager and office manager is $82,000. The office manager makes $4,000 more than the truck driver annually. The annual salaries of the warehouse manager and the truck driver total $78,000. What is the annual salary of each of the co-workers?

58. At a carnival, $2,914.25 in receipts were taken at the end of the day. The cost of a child's ticket was $20.50, an adult ticket was $29.75, and a senior citizen ticket was $15.25. There were twice as many senior citizens as adults in attendance, and 20 more children than senior citizens. How many children, adult, and senior citizen tickets were sold?

59. A local band sells out for their concert. They sell all 1,175 tickets for a total purse of $28,112.50. The tickets were priced at $20 for student tickets, $22.50 for children, and $29 for adult tickets. If the band sold twice as many adult as children tickets, how many of each type was sold?

60. In a bag, a child has 325 coins worth $19.50. There were three types of coins: pennies, nickels, and dimes. If the bag contained the same number of nickels as dimes, how many of each type of coin was in the bag?

61. Last year, at Haven's Pond Car Dealership, for a particular model of BMW, Jeep, and Toyota, one could purchase all three cars for a total of $140,000. This year, due to inflation, the same cars would cost $151,830. The cost of the BMW increased by 8%, the Jeep by 5%, and the Toyota by 12%. If the price of last year's Jeep was $7,000 less than the price of last year's BMW, what was the price of each of the three cars last year?

62. A recent college graduate took advantage of his business education and invested in three investments immediately after graduating. He invested $80,500 into three accounts, one that paid 4% simple interest, one that paid 4% simple interest, one that paid $3\frac{1}{8}$ % simple interest, and one that paid $2\frac{1}{2}$ % simple interest. He earned $2,670 interest at the end of one year. If the amount of the money invested in the second account was four times the amount invested in the third account, how much was invested in each account?

63. You inherit one million dollars. You invest it all in three accounts for one year. The first account pays 3% compounded annually, the second account pays 4% compounded annually, and the third account pays 2% compounded annually. After one year, you earn $34,000 in interest. If you invest four times the money into the account that pays 3% compared to 2%, how much did you invest in each account?

64. You inherit one hundred thousand dollars. You invest it all in three accounts for one year. The first account pays 4% compounded annually, the second account pays 3% compounded annually, and the third account pays 2% compounded annually. After one year, you earn $3,650 in interest. If you invest five times the money in the account that pays 4% compared to 3%, how much did you invest in each account?

65. The top three countries in oil consumption in a certain year are as follows: the United States, Japan, and China. In millions of barrels per day, the three top countries consumed 39.8% of the world's consumed oil. The United States consumed 0.7% more than four times China's consumption. The United States consumed 5% more than triple Japan's consumption. What percent of the world oil consumption did the United States, Japan, and China consume?[28]

66. The top three countries in oil production in the same year are Saudi Arabia, the United States, and Russia. In millions of barrels per day, the top three countries produced 31.4% of the world's produced oil. Saudi Arabia and the United States combined for 22.1% of the world's production, and Saudi Arabia produced 2% more oil than Russia. What percent of the world oil production did Saudi Arabia, the United States, and Russia produce?[29]

67. The top three sources of oil imports for the United States in the same year were Saudi Arabia, Mexico, and Canada. The three top countries accounted for 47% of oil imports. The United States imported 1.8% more from Saudi Arabia than they did from Mexico, and 1.7% more from Saudi Arabia than they did from Canada. What percent of the United States oil imports were from these three countries?[30]

68. The top three oil producers in the United States in a certain year are the Gulf of Mexico, Texas, and Alaska. The three regions were responsible for 64% of the United States oil production. The Gulf of Mexico and Texas combined for 47% of oil production. Texas produced 3% more than Alaska. What percent of United States oil production came from these regions?[31]

69. At one time, in the United States, 398 species of animals were on the endangered species list. The top groups were mammals, birds, and fish, which comprised 55% of the endangered species. Birds accounted for 0.7% more than fish, and fish accounted for 1.5% more than mammals. What percent of the endangered species came from mammals, birds, and fish?

70. Meat consumption in the United States can be broken into three categories: red meat, poultry, and fish. If fish makes up 4% less than one-quarter of poultry consumption, and red meat consumption is 18.2% higher than poultry consumption, what are the percentages of meat consumption?[32]

28 "Oil reserves, production and consumption in 2001," accessed April 6, 2014, http://scaruffi.com/politics/oil.html.
29 "Oil reserves, production and consumption in 2001," accessed April 6, 2014, http://scaruffi.com/politics/oil.html.
30 "Oil reserves, production and consumption in 2001," accessed April 6, 2014, http://scaruffi.com/politics/oil.html.
31 "USA: The coming global oil crisis," accessed April 6, 2014, http://www.oilcrisis.com/us/.
32 "The United States Meat Industry at a Glance," accessed April 6, 2014, http://www.meatami.com/ht/d/sp/i/47465/pid/ 47465.

LEARNING OBJECTIVES

In this section, you will:

- Solve a system of nonlinear equations using substitution.
- Solve a system of nonlinear equations using elimination.
- Graph a nonlinear inequality.
- Graph a system of nonlinear inequalities.

11.3 SYSTEMS OF NONLINEAR EQUATIONS AND INEQUALITIES: TWO VARIABLES

Halley's Comet (**Figure 1**) orbits the sun about once every 75 years. Its path can be considered to be a very elongated ellipse. Other comets follow similar paths in space. These orbital paths can be studied using systems of equations. These systems, however, are different from the ones we considered in the previous section because the equations are not linear.

Figure 1 Halley's Comet (credit: "NASA Blueshift"/Flickr)

In this section, we will consider the intersection of a parabola and a line, a circle and a line, and a circle and an ellipse. The methods for solving systems of nonlinear equations are similar to those for linear equations.

Solving a System of Nonlinear Equations Using Substitution

A **system of nonlinear equations** is a system of two or more equations in two or more variables containing at least one equation that is not linear. Recall that a linear equation can take the form $Ax + By + C = 0$. Any equation that cannot be written in this form in nonlinear. The substitution method we used for linear systems is the same method we will use for nonlinear systems. We solve one equation for one variable and then substitute the result into the second equation to solve for another variable, and so on. There is, however, a variation in the possible outcomes.

Intersection of a Parabola and a Line

There are three possible types of solutions for a system of nonlinear equations involving a parabola and a line.

---

possible types of solutions for points of intersection of a parabola and a line

Figure 2 illustrates possible solution sets for a system of equations involving a parabola and a line.

- No solution. The line will never intersect the parabola.
- One solution. The line is tangent to the parabola and intersects the parabola at exactly one point.
- Two solutions. The line crosses on the inside of the parabola and intersects the parabola at two points.

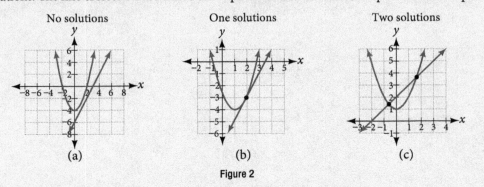

Figure 2

How To...

Given a system of equations containing a line and a parabola, find the solution.

1. Solve the linear equation for one of the variables.
2. Substitute the expression obtained in step one into the parabola equation.
3. Solve for the remaining variable.
4. Check your solutions in both equations.

Example 1 Solving a System of Nonlinear Equations Representing a Parabola and a Line

Solve the system of equations.

$$x - y = -1$$
$$y = x^2 + 1$$

Solution   Solve the first equation for x and then substitute the resulting expression into the second equation.

$$x - y = -1$$
$$x = y - 1 \qquad \text{Solve for } x.$$
$$y = x^2 + 1$$
$$y = (y - 1)^2 + 1 \qquad \text{Substitute expression for } x.$$

Expand the equation and set it equal to zero.

$$y = (y - 1)^2$$
$$= (y^2 - 2y + 1) + 1$$
$$= y^2 - 2y + 2$$
$$0 = y^2 - 3y + 2$$
$$= (y - 2)(y - 1)$$

Solving for y gives $y = 2$ and $y = 1$. Next, substitute each value for y into the first equation to solve for x. Always substitute the value into the linear equation to check for extraneous solutions.

$$x - y = -1$$
$$x - (2) = -1$$
$$x = 1$$
$$x - (1) = -1$$
$$x = 0$$

The solutions are (1, 2) and (0, 1), which can be verified by substituting these (x, y) values into both of the original equations. See **Figure 3**.

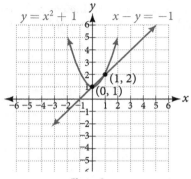

Figure 3

Q & A...

Could we have substituted values for *y* into the second equation to solve for *x* in Example 1?

Yes, but because *x* is squared in the second equation this could give us extraneous solutions for *x*.

For $y = 1$

$$y = x^2 + 1$$
$$1 = x^2 + 1$$
$$x^2 = 0$$
$$x = \pm\sqrt{0} = 0$$

This gives us the same value as in the solution.

For $y = 2$

$$y = x^2 + 1$$
$$2 = x^2 + 1$$
$$x^2 = 1$$
$$x = \pm\sqrt{1} = \pm 1$$

Notice that -1 is an extraneous solution.

Try It #1

Solve the given system of equations by substitution.

$$3x - y = -2$$
$$2x^2 - y = 0$$

Intersection of a Circle and a Line

Just as with a parabola and a line, there are three possible outcomes when solving a system of equations representing a circle and a line.

> **possible types of solutions for the points of intersection of a circle and a line**
>
> **Figure 4** illustrates possible solution sets for a system of equations involving a circle and a line.
> - No solution. The line does not intersect the circle.
> - One solution. The line is tangent to the circle and intersects the circle at exactly one point.
> - Two solutions. The line crosses the circle and intersects it at two points.
>
>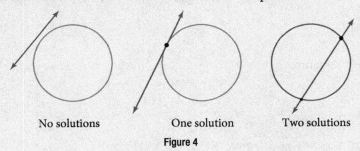
>
> No solutions   One solution   Two solutions
>
> **Figure 4**

How To...

Given a system of equations containing a line and a circle, find the solution.

1. Solve the linear equation for one of the variables.
2. Substitute the expression obtained in step one into the equation for the circle.
3. Solve for the remaining variable.
4. Check your solutions in both equations.

Example 2   **Finding the Intersection of a Circle and a Line by Substitution**

Find the intersection of the given circle and the given line by substitution.

$$x^2 + y^2 = 5$$
$$y = 3x - 5$$

Solution   One of the equations has already been solved for y. We will substitute $y = 3x - 5$ into the equation for the circle.

$$x^2 + (3x - 5)^2 = 5$$
$$x^2 + 9x^2 - 30x + 25 = 5$$
$$10x^2 - 30x + 20 = 0$$

Now, we factor and solve for x.

$$10(x^2 - 3x + 2) = 0$$
$$10(x - 2)(x - 1) = 0$$
$$x = 2$$
$$x = 1$$

Substitute the two x-values into the original linear equation to solve for y.

$$y = 3(2) - 5$$
$$= 1$$
$$y = 3(1) - 5$$
$$= -2$$

The line intersects the circle at $(2, 1)$ and $(1, -2)$, which can be verified by substituting these (x, y) values into both of the original equations. See **Figure 5**.

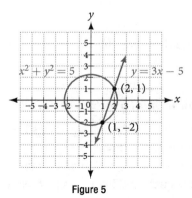

Figure 5

Try It #2

Solve the system of nonlinear equations.

$$x^2 + y^2 = 10$$
$$x - 3y = -10$$

Solving a System of Nonlinear Equations Using Elimination

We have seen that substitution is often the preferred method when a system of equations includes a linear equation and a nonlinear equation. However, when both equations in the system have like variables of the second degree, solving them using elimination by addition is often easier than substitution. Generally, elimination is a far simpler method when the system involves only two equations in two variables (a two-by-two system), rather than a three-by-three system, as there are fewer steps. As an example, we will investigate the possible types of solutions when solving a system of equations representing a circle and an ellipse.

possible types of solutions for the points of intersection of a circle and an ellipse

Figure 6 illustrates possible solution sets for a system of equations involving a circle and an ellipse.

- No solution. The circle and ellipse do not intersect. One shape is inside the other or the circle and the ellipse are a distance away from the other.
- One solution. The circle and ellipse are tangent to each other, and intersect at exactly one point.
- Two solutions. The circle and the ellipse intersect at two points.
- Three solutions. The circle and the ellipse intersect at three points.
- Four solutions. The circle and the ellipse intersect at four points.

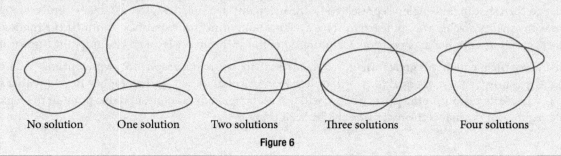

No solution One solution Two solutions Three solutions Four solutions

Figure 6

Example 3 **Solving a System of Nonlinear Equations Representing a Circle and an Ellipse**

Solve the system of nonlinear equations.

$$x^2 + y^2 = 26 \qquad (1)$$
$$3x^2 + 25y^2 = 100 \qquad (2)$$

Solution Let's begin by multiplying equation (1) by -3, and adding it to equation (2).

$$(-3)(x^2 + y^2) = (-3)(26)$$
$$-3x^2 - 3y^2 = -78$$
$$\underline{3x^2 + 25y^2 = 100}$$
$$22y^2 = 22$$

After we add the two equations together, we solve for y.

$$y^2 = 1$$
$$y = \pm \sqrt{1} = \pm 1$$

Substitute $y = \pm 1$ into one of the equations and solve for x.

$$x^2 + (1)^2 = 26 \qquad\qquad\qquad x^2 + (-1)^2 = 26$$
$$x^2 + 1 = 26 \qquad\qquad\qquad\quad x^2 + 1 = 26$$
$$x^2 = 25 \qquad\qquad\qquad\qquad x^2 = 25 = \pm 5$$
$$x = \pm \sqrt{25} = \pm 5$$

There are four solutions: $(5, 1)$, $(-5, 1)$, $(5, -1)$, and $(-5, -1)$. See **Figure 7**.

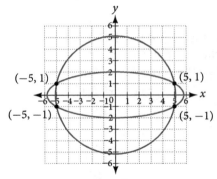

Figure 7

Try It #3

Find the solution set for the given system of nonlinear equations.
$$4x^2 + y^2 = 13$$
$$x^2 + y^2 = 10$$

Graphing a Nonlinear Inequality

All of the equations in the systems that we have encountered so far have involved equalities, but we may also encounter systems that involve inequalities. We have already learned to graph linear inequalities by graphing the corresponding equation, and then shading the region represented by the inequality symbol. Now, we will follow similar steps to graph a nonlinear inequality so that we can learn to solve systems of nonlinear inequalities. A **nonlinear inequality** is an inequality containing a nonlinear expression. Graphing a nonlinear inequality is much like graphing a linear inequality.

Recall that when the inequality is greater than, $y > a$, or less than, $y < a$, the graph is drawn with a dashed line. When the inequality is greater than or equal to, $y \geq a$, or less than or equal to, $y \leq a$, the graph is drawn with a solid line. The graphs will create regions in the plane, and we will test each region for a solution. If one point in the region works, the whole region works. That is the region we shade. See **Figure 8**.

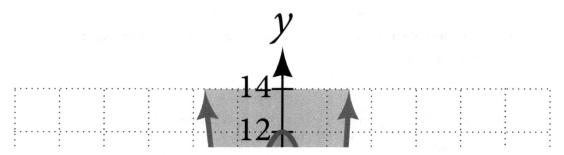

Figure 8 (a) an example of $y > a$; (b) an example of $y \geq a$; (c) an example of $y < a$; (d) an example of $y \leq a$

How To...

Given an inequality bounded by a parabola, sketch a graph.

1. Graph the parabola as if it were an equation. This is the boundary for the region that is the solution set.
2. If the boundary is included in the region (the operator is $\leq$ or $\geq$), the parabola is graphed as a solid line.
3. If the boundary is not included in the region (the operator is $<$ or $>$), the parabola is graphed as a dashed line.
4. Test a point in one of the regions to determine whether it satisfies the inequality statement. If the statement is true, the solution set is the region including the point. If the statement is false, the solution set is the region on the other side of the boundary line.
5. Shade the region representing the solution set.

Example 4   **Graphing an Inequality for a Parabola**

Graph the inequality $y > x^2 + 1$.

Solution   First, graph the corresponding equation $y = x^2 + 1$. Since $y > x^2 + 1$ has a greater than symbol, we draw the graph with a dashed line. Then we choose points to test both inside and outside the parabola. Let's test the points $(0, 2)$ and $(2, 0)$. One point is clearly inside the parabola and the other point is clearly outside.

$$y > x^2 + 1$$
$$2 > (0)^2 + 1$$
$$2 > 1 \quad \text{True}$$
$$0 > (2)^2 + 1$$
$$0 > 5 \quad \text{False}$$

The graph is shown in **Figure 9**. We can see that the solution set consists of all points inside the parabola, but not on the graph itself.

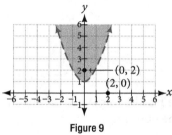

Figure 9

Graphing a System of Nonlinear Inequalities

Now that we have learned to graph nonlinear inequalities, we can learn how to graph systems of nonlinear inequalities. A **system of nonlinear inequalities** is a system of two or more inequalities in two or more variables containing at least one inequality that is not linear. Graphing a system of nonlinear inequalities is similar to graphing a system of linear inequalities. The difference is that our graph may result in more shaded regions that represent a solution than we find in a system of linear inequalities. The solution to a nonlinear system of inequalities is the region of the graph where the shaded regions of the graph of each inequality overlap, or where the regions intersect, called the **feasible region**.

How To...

Given a system of nonlinear inequalities, sketch a graph.

1. Find the intersection points by solving the corresponding system of nonlinear equations.
2. Graph the nonlinear equations.
3. Find the shaded regions of each inequality.
4. Identify the feasible region as the intersection of the shaded regions of each inequality or the set of points common to each inequality.

Example 5 **Graphing a System of Inequalities**

Graph the given system of inequalities.

$$x^2 - y \leq 0$$
$$2x^2 + y \leq 12$$

Solution   These two equations are clearly parabolas. We can find the points of intersection by the elimination process: Add both equations and the variable y will be eliminated. Then we solve for x.

$$x^2 - y = 0$$
$$\underline{2x^2 + y = 12}$$
$$3x^2 = 12$$
$$x^2 = 4$$
$$x = \pm 2$$

Substitute the x-values into one of the equations and solve for y.

$$x^2 - y = 0$$
$$(2)^2 - y = 0$$
$$4 - y = 0$$
$$y = 4$$
$$(-2)^2 - y = 0$$
$$4 - y = 0$$
$$y = 4$$

The two points of intersection are (2, 4) and (−2, 4). Notice that the equations can be rewritten as follows.

$$x^2 - y \leq 0$$
$$x^2 \leq y$$
$$y \geq x^2$$
$$2x^2 + y \leq 12$$
$$y \leq -2x^2 + 12$$

Graph each inequality. See **Figure 10**. The feasible region is the region between the two equations bounded by 2 $x^2 + y \leq 12$ on the top and $x^2 - y \leq 0$ on the bottom.

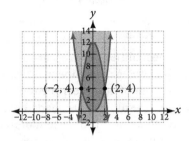

Figure 10

Try It #4

Graph the given system of inequalities.

$$y \geq x^2 - 1$$
$$x - y \geq -1$$

Access these online resources for additional instruction and practice with nonlinear equations.

- Solve a System of Nonlinear Equations Using Substitution (http://openstaxcollege.org/l/nonlinsub)
- Solve a System of Nonlinear Equations Using Elimination (http://openstaxcollege.org/l/nonlinelim)

11.3 SECTION EXERCISES

VERBAL

1. Explain whether a system of two nonlinear equations can have exactly two solutions. What about exactly three? If not, explain why not. If so, give an example of such a system, in graph form, and explain why your choice gives two or three answers.

2. When graphing an inequality, explain why we only need to test one point to determine whether an entire region is the solution?

3. When you graph a system of inequalities, will there always be a feasible region? If so, explain why. If not, give an example of a graph of inequalities that does not have a feasible region. Why does it not have a feasible region?

4. If you graph a revenue and cost function, explain how to determine in what regions there is profit.

5. If you perform your break-even analysis and there is more than one solution, explain how you would determine which x-values are profit and which are not.

ALGEBRAIC

For the following exercises, solve the system of nonlinear equations using substitution.

6. $x + y = 4$
   $x^2 + y^2 = 9$

7. $y = x - 3$
   $x^2 + y^2 = 9$

8. $y = x$
   $x^2 + y^2 = 9$

9. $y = -x$
   $x^2 + y^2 = 9$

10. $x = 2$
    $x^2 - y^2 = 9$

For the following exercises, solve the system of nonlinear equations using elimination.

11. $4x^2 - 9y^2 = 36$
    $4x^2 + 9y^2 = 36$

12. $x^2 + y^2 = 25$
    $x^2 - y^2 = 1$

13. $2x^2 + 4y^2 = 4$
    $2x^2 - 4y^2 = 25x - 10$

14. $y^2 - x^2 = 9$
    $3x^2 + 2y^2 = 8$

15. $x^2 + y^2 + \dfrac{1}{16} = 2500$
    $y = 2x^2$

For the following exercises, use any method to solve the system of nonlinear equations.

16. $-2x^2 + y = -5$
    $6x - y = 9$

17. $-x^2 + y = 2$
    $-x + y = 2$

18. $x^2 + y^2 = 1$
    $y = 20x^2 - 1$

19. $x^2 + y^2 = 1$
    $y = -x^2$

20. $2x^3 - x^2 = y$
    $y = \dfrac{1}{2} - x$

21. $9x^2 + 25y^2 = 225$
    $(x - 6)^2 + y^2 = 1$

22. $x^4 - x^2 = y$
    $x^2 + y = 0$

23. $2x^3 - x^2 = y$
    $x^2 + y = 0$

For the following exercises, use any method to solve the nonlinear system.

24. $x^2 + y^2 = 9$
    $y = 3 - x^2$

25. $x^2 - y^2 = 9$
    $x = 3$

26. $x^2 - y^2 = 9$
    $y = 3$

27. $x^2 - y^2 = 9$
    $x - y = 0$

28. $-x^2 + y = 2$
    $-4x + y = -1$

29. $-x^2 + y = 2$
    $2y = -x$

30. $x^2 + y^2 = 25$
    $x^2 - y^2 = 36$

31. $x^2 + y^2 = 1$
    $y^2 = x^2$

32. $16x^2 - 9y^2 + 144 = 0$
    $y^2 + x^2 = 16$

33.
$$3x^2 - y^2 = 12$$
$$(x-1)^2 + y^2 = 1$$

34.
$$3x^2 - y^2 = 12$$
$$(x-1)^2 + y^2 = 4$$

35. $3x^2 - y^2 = 12$
$$x^2 + y^2 = 16$$

36. $x^2 - y^2 - 6x - 4y - 11 = 0$
$$-x^2 + y^2 = 5$$

37. $x^2 + y^2 - 6y = 7$
$$x^2 + y = 1$$

38. $x^2 + y^2 = 6$
$$xy = 1$$

GRAPHICAL

For the following exercises, graph the inequality.

39. $x^2 + y < 9$

40. $x^2 + y^2 < 4$

For the following exercises, graph the system of inequalities. Label all points of intersection.

41. $x^2 + y < 1$
$$y > 2x$$

42. $x^2 + y < -5$
$$y > 5x + 10$$

43. $x^2 + y^2 < 25$
$$3x^2 - y^2 > 12$$

44. $x^2 - y^2 > -4$
$$x^2 + y^2 < 12$$

45. $x^2 + 3y^2 > 16$
$$3x^2 - y^2 < 1$$

EXTENSIONS

For the following exercises, graph the inequality.

46. $y \geq e^x$
$$y \leq \ln(x) + 5$$

47. $y \leq -\log(x)$
$$y \leq e^x$$

For the following exercises, find the solutions to the nonlinear equations with two variables.

48.
$$\frac{4}{x^2} + \frac{1}{y^2} = 24$$
$$\frac{5}{x^2} - \frac{2}{y^2} + 4 = 0$$

49.
$$\frac{6}{x^2} - \frac{1}{y^2} = 8$$
$$\frac{1}{x^2} - \frac{6}{y^2} = \frac{1}{8}$$

50. $x^2 - xy + y^2 - 2 = 0$
$$x + 3y = 4$$

51. $x^2 - xy - 2y^2 - 6 = 0$
$$x^2 + y^2 = 1$$

52. $x^2 + 4xy - 2y^2 - 6 = 0$
$$x = y + 2$$

TECHNOLOGY

For the following exercises, solve the system of inequalities. Use a calculator to graph the system to confirm the answer.

53. $xy < 1$
$$y > \sqrt{x}$$

54. $x^2 + y < 3$
$$y > 2x$$

REAL-WORLD APPLICATIONS

For the following exercises, construct a system of nonlinear equations to describe the given behavior, then solve for the requested solutions.

55. Two numbers add up to 300. One number is twice the square of the other number. What are the numbers?

56. The squares of two numbers add to 360. The second number is half the value of the first number squared. What are the numbers?

57. A laptop company has discovered their cost and revenue functions for each day: $C(x) = 3x^2 - 10x + 200$ and $R(x) = -2x^2 + 100x + 50$. If they want to make a profit, what is the range of laptops per day that they should produce? Round to the nearest number which would generate profit.

58. A cell phone company has the following cost and revenue functions: $C(x) = 8x^2 - 600x + 21,500$ and $R(x) = -3x^2 + 480x$. What is the range of cell phones they should produce each day so there is profit? round to the nearest number that generates profit.

LEARNING OBJECTIVES

In this section, you will:

- Decompose $P(x)Q(x)$, where $Q(x)$ has only nonrepeated linear factors.
- Decompose $P(x)Q(x)$, where $Q(x)$ has repeated linear factors.
- Decompose $P(x)Q(x)$, where $Q(x)$ has a nonrepeated irreducible quadratic factor.
- Decompose $P(x)Q(x)$, where $Q(x)$ has a repeated irreducible quadratic factor.

11.4   PARTIAL FRACTIONS

Earlier in this chapter, we studied systems of two equations in two variables, systems of three equations in three variables, and nonlinear systems. Here we introduce another way that systems of equations can be utilized—the decomposition of rational expressions.

Fractions can be complicated; adding a variable in the denominator makes them even more so. The methods studied in this section will help simplify the concept of a rational expression.

Decomposing $\dfrac{P(x)}{Q(x)}$ Where $Q(x)$ Has Only Nonrepeated Linear Factors

Recall the algebra regarding adding and subtracting rational expressions. These operations depend on finding a common denominator so that we can write the sum or difference as a single, simplified rational expression. In this section, we will look at partial fraction decomposition, which is the undoing of the procedure to add or subtract rational expressions. In other words, it is a return from the single simplified rational expression to the original expressions, called the **partial fractions**.

For example, suppose we add the following fractions:

$$\frac{2}{x-3} + \frac{-1}{x+2}$$

We would first need to find a common denominator, $(x+2)(x-3)$.

Next, we would write each expression with this common denominator and find the sum of the terms.

$$\frac{2}{x-3}\left(\frac{x+2}{x+2}\right) + \frac{-1}{x+2}\left(\frac{x-3}{x-3}\right) = \frac{2x+4-x+3}{(x+2)(x-3)} = \frac{x+7}{x^2-x-6}$$

Partial fraction decomposition is the reverse of this procedure. We would start with the solution and rewrite (decompose) it as the sum of two fractions.

$$\underset{\text{Simplified sum}}{\frac{x+7}{x^2-x-6}} = \underset{\text{Partial fraction decomposition}}{\frac{2}{x-3} + \frac{-1}{x+2}}$$

We will investigate rational expressions with linear factors and quadratic factors in the denominator where the degree of the numerator is less than the degree of the denominator. Regardless of the type of expression we are decomposing, the first and most important thing to do is factor the denominator.

When the denominator of the simplified expression contains distinct linear factors, it is likely that each of the original rational expressions, which were added or subtracted, had one of the linear factors as the denominator. In other words, using the example above, the factors of $x^2 - x - 6$ are $(x-3)(x+2)$, the denominators of the decomposed rational expression.

So we will rewrite the simplified form as the sum of individual fractions and use a variable for each numerator. Then, we will solve for each numerator using one of several methods available for partial fraction decomposition.

> ### *partial fraction decomposition of $\frac{P(x)}{Q(x)}$: Q(x) has nonrepeated linear factors*
>
> The partial fraction decomposition of $\frac{P(x)}{Q(x)}$ when $Q(x)$ has nonrepeated linear factors and the degree of $P(x)$ is less than the degree of $Q(x)$ is
>
> $$\frac{P(x)}{Q(x)} = \frac{A_1}{(a_1 x + b_1)} + \frac{A_2}{(a_2 x + b_2)} + \frac{A_3}{(a_3 x + b_3)} + \dots + \frac{A_n}{(a_n x + b_n)}.$$

How To...

Given a rational expression with distinct linear factors in the denominator, decompose it.

1. Use a variable for the original numerators, usually A, B, or C, depending on the number of factors, placing each variable over a single factor. For the purpose of this definition, we use A_n for each numerator

$$\frac{P(x)}{Q(x)} = \frac{A_1}{(a_1 x + b_1)} + \frac{A_2}{(a_2 x + b_2)} + \dots + \frac{A_n}{(a_n x + b_n)}.$$

2. Multiply both sides of the equation by the common denominator to eliminate fractions.
3. Expand the right side of the equation and collect like terms.
4. Set coefficients of like terms from the left side of the equation equal to those on the right side to create a system of equations to solve for the numerators.

Example 1   **Decomposing a Rational Function with Distinct Linear Factors**

Decompose the given rational expression with distinct linear factors.

$$\frac{3x}{(x + 2)(x - 1)}$$

Solution   We will separate the denominator factors and give each numerator a symbolic label, like A, B, or C.

$$\frac{3x}{(x + 2)(x - 1)} = \frac{A}{(x + 2)} + \frac{B}{(x - 1)}$$

Multiply both sides of the equation by the common denominator to eliminate the fractions:

$$(x + 2)(x - 1)\left[\frac{3x}{(x + 2)(x - 1)}\right] = \cancel{(x + 2)}(x - 1)\left[\frac{A}{\cancel{(x + 2)}}\right] + (x + 2)\cancel{(x - 1)}\left[\frac{B}{\cancel{(x - 1)}}\right]$$

The resulting equation is

$$3x = A(x - 1) + B(x + 2)$$

Expand the right side of the equation and collect like terms.

$$3x = Ax - A + Bx + 2B$$
$$3x = (A + B)x - A + 2B$$

Set up a system of equations associating corresponding coefficients.

$$3 = A + B$$
$$0 = -A + 2B$$

Add the two equations and solve for B.

$$
\begin{aligned}
3 &= A + B \\
0 &= -A + 2B \\
\hline
3 &= 0 + 3B \\
1 &= B
\end{aligned}
$$

Substitute $B = 1$ into one of the original equations in the system.

$$3 = A + 1$$
$$2 = A$$

Thus, the partial fraction decomposition is

$$\frac{3x}{(x + 2)(x - 1)} = \frac{2}{(x + 2)} + \frac{1}{(x - 1)}$$

Another method to use to solve for A or B is by considering the equation that resulted from eliminating the fractions and substituting a value for x that will make either the A- or B-term equal 0. If we let $x = 1$, the A-term becomes 0 and we can simply solve for B.

$$3x = A(x - 1) + B(x + 2)$$
$$3(1) = A[(1) - 1] + B[(1) + 2]$$
$$3 = 0 + 3B$$
$$1 = B$$

Next, either substitute $B = 1$ into the equation and solve for A, or make the B-term 0 by substituting $x = -2$ into the equation.

$$3x = A(x - 1) + B(x + 2)$$
$$3(-2) = A[(-2) - 1] + B[(-2) + 2]$$
$$-6 = -3A + 0$$
$$\frac{-6}{-3} = A$$
$$2 = A$$

We obtain the same values for A and B using either method, so the decompositions are the same using either method.

$$\frac{3x}{(x + 2)(x - 1)} = \frac{2}{(x + 2)} + \frac{1}{(x - 1)}$$

Although this method is not seen very often in textbooks, we present it here as an alternative that may make some partial fraction decompositions easier. It is known as the Heaviside method, named after Charles Heaviside, a pioneer in the study of electronics.

Try It #1

Find the partial fraction decomposition of the following expression.

$$\frac{x}{(x - 3)(x - 2)}$$

Decomposing $\frac{P(x)}{Q(x)}$ Where $Q(x)$ Has Repeated Linear Factors

Some fractions we may come across are special cases that we can decompose into partial fractions with repeated linear factors. We must remember that we account for repeated factors by writing each factor in increasing powers.

---

partial fraction decomposition of $\frac{P(x)}{Q(x)}$: Q(x) has repeated linear factors

The partial fraction decomposition of $\frac{P(x)}{Q(x)}$ when $Q(x)$ has repeated linear factor occurring n times and the degree of $P(x)$ is less than the degree of $Q(x)$, is

$$\frac{P(x)}{Q(x)} = \frac{A_1}{(ax + b)} + \frac{A_2}{(ax + b)^2} + \frac{A_3}{(ax + b)^3} + \cdots + \frac{A_n}{(ax + b)^n}$$

Write the denominator powers in increasing order.

How To...

Given a rational expression with repeated linear factors, decompose it.

1. Use a variable like A, B, or C for the numerators and account for increasing powers of the denominators.

$$\frac{P(x)}{Q(x)} = \frac{A_1}{(ax + b)} + \frac{A_2}{(ax + b)^2} + \cdots + \frac{A_n}{(ax + b)^n}$$

2. Multiply both sides of the equation by the common denominator to eliminate fractions.
3. Expand the right side of the equation and collect like terms.
4. Set coefficients of like terms from the left side of the equation equal to those on the right side to create a system of equations to solve for the numerators.

Example 2   **Decomposing with Repeated Linear Factors**

Decompose the given rational expression with repeated linear factors.

$$\frac{-x^2 + 2x + 4}{x^3 - 4x^2 + 4x}$$

Solution   The denominator factors are $x(x - 2)^2$. To allow for the repeated factor of $(x - 2)$, the decomposition will include three denominators: x, $(x - 2)$, and $(x - 2)^2$. Thus,

$$\frac{-x^2 + 2x + 4}{x^3 - 4x^2 + 4x} = \frac{A}{x} + \frac{B}{(x - 2)} + \frac{C}{(x - 2)^2}$$

Next, we multiply both sides by the common denominator.

$$x(x - 2)^2 \left[\frac{-x^2 + 2x + 4}{x(x - 2)^2} \right] = \left[\frac{A}{x} + \frac{B}{(x - 2)} + \frac{C}{(x - 2)^2} \right] x(x - 2)^2$$

$$-x^2 + 2x + 4 = A(x - 2)^2 + Bx(x - 2) + Cx$$

On the right side of the equation, we expand and collect like terms.

$$-x^2 + 2x + 4 = A(x^2 - 4x + 4) + B(x^2 - 2x) + Cx$$

$$= Ax^2 - 4Ax + 4A + Bx^2 - 2Bx + Cx$$

$$= (A + B)x^2 + (-4A - 2B + C)x + 4A$$

Next, we compare the coefficients of both sides. This will give the system of equations in three variables:

$$-x^2 + 2x + 4 = (A + B)x^2 + (-4A - 2B + C)x + 4A$$

$$A + B = -1 \qquad (1)$$

$$-4A - 2B + C = 2 \qquad (2)$$

$$4A = 4 \qquad (3)$$

Solving for A, we have

$$4A = 4$$

$$A = 1$$

Substitute $A = 1$ into equation (1).

$$A + B = -1$$

$$(1) + B = -1$$

$$B = -2$$

Then, to solve for C, substitute the values for A and B into equation (2).

$$-4A - 2B + C = 2$$

$$-4(1) - 2(-2) + C = 2$$

$$-4 + 4 + C = 2$$

$$C = 2$$

Thus,

$$\frac{-x^2 + 2x + 4}{x^3 - 4x^2 + 4x} = \frac{1}{x} - \frac{2}{(x - 2)} + \frac{2}{(x - 2)^2}$$

Try It #2

Find the partial fraction decomposition of the expression with repeated linear factors.

$$\frac{6x - 11}{(x - 1)^2}$$

Decomposing $\dfrac{P(x)}{Q(x)}$ Where $Q(x)$ Has a Nonrepeated Irreducible Quadratic Factor

So far, we have performed partial fraction decomposition with expressions that have had linear factors in the denominator, and we applied numerators A, B, or C representing constants. Now we will look at an example where one of the factors in the denominator is a quadratic expression that does not factor. This is referred to as an irreducible quadratic factor. In cases like this, we use a linear numerator such as $Ax + B$, $Bx + C$, etc.

---

decomposition of $\dfrac{P(x)}{Q(x)}$: $Q(x)$ has a nonrepeated irreducible quadratic factor

The partial fraction decomposition of $\dfrac{P(x)}{Q(x)}$ such that $Q(x)$ has a nonrepeated irreducible quadratic factor and the **degree of** $P(x)$ is less than the degree of $Q(x)$, is **written as**

$$\frac{P(x)}{Q(x)} = \frac{A_1 x + B_1}{(a_1 x^2 + b_1 x + c_1)} + \frac{A_2 x + B_2}{(a_2 x^2 + b_2 x + c_2)} + \cdots + \frac{A_n x + B_n}{(a_n x^2 + b_n x + c_n)}$$

The decomposition may contain more rational expressions if there are linear factors. Each linear factor will have a different constant numerator: A, B, C, and so on.

How To…

Given a rational expression where the factors of the denominator are distinct, irreducible quadratic factors, decompose it.

1. Use variables such as A, B, or C for the constant numerators over linear factors, and linear expressions such as $A_1 x + B_1$, $A_2 x + B_2$, etc., for the numerators of each quadratic factor in the denominator.

$$\frac{P(x)}{Q(x)} = \frac{A}{ax + b} + \frac{A_1 x + B_1}{(a_1 x^2 + b_1 x + c_1)} + \frac{A_2 x + B_2}{(a_2 x^2 + b_2 x + c_2)} + \cdots + \frac{A_n x + B_n}{(a_n x^2 + b_n x + c_n)}$$

2. Multiply both sides of the equation by the common denominator to eliminate fractions.
3. Expand the right side of the equation and collect like terms.
4. Set coefficients of like terms from the left side of the equation equal to those on the right side to create a system of equations to solve for the numerators.

Example 3   **Decomposing $\dfrac{P(x)}{Q(x)}$ When $Q(x)$ Contains a Nonrepeated Irreducible Quadratic Factor**

Find a partial fraction decomposition of the given expression.

$$\frac{8x^2 + 12x - 20}{(x + 3)(x^2 + x + 2)}$$

Solution   We have one linear factor and one irreducible quadratic factor in the denominator, so one numerator will be a constant and the other numerator will be a linear expression. Thus,

$$\frac{8x^2 + 12x - 20}{(x + 3)(x^2 + x + 2)} = \frac{A}{(x + 3)} + \frac{Bx + C}{(x^2 + x + 2)}$$

We follow the same steps as in previous problems. First, clear the fractions by multiplying both sides of the equation by the common denominator.

$$(x + 3)(x^2 + x + 2)\left[\frac{8x^2 + 12x - 20}{(x + 3)(x^2 + x + 2)}\right] = \left[\frac{A}{(x + 3)} + \frac{Bx + C}{(x^2 + x + 2)}\right](x + 3)(x^2 + x + 2)$$

$$8x^2 + 12x - 20 = A(x^2 + x + 2) + (Bx + C)(x + 3)$$

Notice we could easily solve for A by choosing a value for x that will make the $Bx + C$ term equal 0. Let $x = -3$ and substitute it into the equation.

$$8x^2 + 12x - 20 = A(x^2 + x + 2) + (Bx + C)(x + 3)$$
$$8(-3)^2 + 12(-3) - 20 = A((-3)^2 + (-3) + 2) + (B(-3) + C)((-3) + 3)$$
$$16 = 8A$$
$$A = 2$$

Now that we know the value of A, substitute it back into the equation. Then expand the right side and collect like terms.

$$8x^2 + 12x - 20 = 2(x^2 + x + 2) + (Bx + C)(x + 3)$$
$$8x^2 + 12x - 20 = 2x^2 + 2x + 4 + Bx^2 + 3B + Cx + 3C$$
$$8x^2 + 12x - 20 = (2 + B)x^2 + (2 + 3B + C)x + (4 + 3C)$$

Setting the coefficients of terms on the right side equal to the coefficients of terms on the left side gives the system of equations.

$$2 + B = 8 \qquad (1)$$
$$2 + 3B + C = 12 \qquad (2)$$
$$4 + 3C = -20 \qquad (3)$$

Solve for B using equation (1) and solve for C using equation (3).

$$2 + B = 8 \qquad (1)$$
$$B = 6$$
$$4 + 3C = -20 \qquad (3)$$
$$3C = -24$$
$$C = -8$$

Thus, the partial fraction decomposition of the expression is

$$\frac{8x^2 + 12x - 20}{(x + 3)(x^2 + x + 2)} = \frac{2}{(x + 3)} + \frac{6x - 8}{(x^2 + x + 2)}$$

Q & A...

Could we have just set up a system of equations to solve Example 3?

Yes, we could have solved it by setting up a system of equations without solving for A first. The expansion on the right would be:

$$8x^2 + 12x - 20 = Ax^2 + Ax + 2A + Bx^2 + 3B + Cx + 3C$$
$$8x^2 + 12x - 20 = (A + B)x^2 + (A + 3B + C)x + (2A + 3C)$$

So the system of equations would be:

$$A + B = 8$$
$$A + 3B + C = 12$$
$$2A + 3C = -20$$

Try It #3

Find the partial fraction decomposition of the expression with a nonrepeating irreducible quadratic factor.

$$\frac{5x^2 - 6x + 7}{(x - 1)(x^2 + 1)}$$

Decomposing $\frac{P(x)}{Q(x)}$ Where $Q(x)$ Has a Repeated Irreducible Quadratic Factor

Now that we can decompose a simplified rational expression with an irreducible quadratic factor, we will learn how to do partial fraction decomposition when the simplified rational expression has repeated irreducible quadratic factors. The decomposition will consist of partial fractions with linear numerators over each irreducible quadratic factor represented in increasing powers.

---

decomposition of $\frac{P(x)}{Q(x)}$: when $Q(x)$ has a repeated irreducible quadratic factor

The partial fraction decomposition of $\frac{P(x)}{Q(x)}$, when $Q(x)$ has a repeated irreducible quadratic factor and the degree of $P(x)$ is less than the degree of $Q(x)$, is

$$\frac{P(x)}{(ax^2 + bx + c)^n} = \frac{A_1x + B_1}{(ax^2 + bx + c)} + \frac{A_2x + B_2}{(ax^2 + bx + c)^2} + \frac{A_3x + B_3}{(ax^2 + bx + c)^3} + \dots + \frac{A_nx + B_n}{(ax^2 + bx + c)^n}$$

Write the denominators in increasing powers.

How To…

Given a rational expression that has a repeated irreducible factor, decompose it.

1. Use variables like A, B, or C for the constant numerators over linear factors, and linear expressions such as $A_1x + B_1$, $A_2x + B_2$, etc., for the numerators of each quadratic factor in the denominator written in increasing powers, such as

$$\frac{P(x)}{Q(x)} = \frac{A}{ax + b} + \frac{A_1x + B_1}{(ax^2 + bx + c)} + \frac{A_2x + B_2}{(ax^2 + bx + c)^2} + \dots + \frac{A_nx + B_n}{(ax^2 + bx + c)^n}$$

2. Multiply both sides of the equation by the common denominator to eliminate fractions.
3. Expand the right side of the equation and collect like terms.
4. Set coefficients of like terms from the left side of the equation equal to those on the right side to create a system of equations to solve for the numerators.

Example 4   **Decomposing a Rational Function with a Repeated Irreducible Quadratic Factor in the Denominator**

Decompose the given expression that has a repeated irreducible factor in the denominator.

$$\frac{x^4 + x^3 + x^2 - x + 1}{x(x^2 + 1)^2}$$

Solution   The factors of the denominator are x, $(x^2 + 1)$, and $(x^2 + 1)^2$. Recall that, when a factor in the denominator is a quadratic that includes at least two terms, the numerator must be of the linear form $Ax + B$. So, let's begin the decomposition.

$$\frac{x^4 + x^3 + x^2 - x + 1}{x(x^2 + 1)^2} = \frac{A}{x} + \frac{Bx + C}{(x^2 + 1)} + \frac{Dx + E}{(x^2 + 1)^2}$$

We eliminate the denominators by multiplying each term by $x(x^2 + 1)^2$. Thus,

$$x^4 + x^3 + x^2 - x + 1 = A(x^2 + 1)^2 + (Bx + C)(x)(x^2 + 1) + (Dx + E)(x)$$

Expand the right side.

$$x^4 + x^3 + x^2 - x + 1 = A(x^4 + 2x^2 + 1) + Bx^4 + Bx^2 + Cx^3 + Cx + Dx^2 + Ex$$
$$= Ax^4 + 2Ax^2 + A + Bx^4 + Bx^2 + Cx^3 + Cx + Dx^2 + Ex$$

Now we will collect like terms.

$$x^4 + x^3 + x^2 - x + 1 = (A + B)x^4 + (C)x^3 + (2A + B + D)x^2 + (C + E)x + A$$

Set up the system of equations matching corresponding coefficients on each side of the equal sign.

$$A + B = 1$$

$$C = 1$$

$$2A + B + D = 1$$

$$C + E = -1$$

$$A = 1$$

We can use substitution from this point. Substitute $A = 1$ into the first equation.

$$1 + B = 1$$

$$B = 0$$

Substitute $A = 1$ and $B = 0$ into the third equation.

$$2(1) + 0 + D = 1$$

$$D = -1$$

Substitute $C = 1$ into the fourth equation.

$$1 + E = -1$$

$$E = -2$$

Now we have solved for all of the unknowns on the right side of the equal sign. We have $A = 1, B = 0, C = 1, D = -1,$ and $E = -2$. We can write the decomposition as follows:

$$\frac{x^4 + x^3 + x^2 - x + 1}{x(x^2 + 1)^2} = \frac{1}{x} + \frac{1}{(x^2 + 1)} - \frac{x + 2}{(x^2 + 1)^2}$$

Try It #4

Find the partial fraction decomposition of the expression with a repeated irreducible quadratic factor.

$$\frac{x^3 - 4x^2 + 9x - 5}{(x^2 - 2x + 3)^2}$$

Access these online resources for additional instruction and practice with partial fractions.

- Partial Fraction Decomposition (http://openstaxcollege.org/l/partdecomp)
- Partial Fraction Decomposition With Repeated Linear Factors (http://openstaxcollege.org/l/partdecomprlf)
- Partial Fraction Decomposition With Linear and Quadratic Factors (http://openstaxcollege.org/l/partdecomlqu)

11.4 SECTION EXERCISES

VERBAL

1. Can any quotient of polynomials be decomposed into at least two partial fractions? If so, explain why, and if not, give an example of such a fraction

2. Can you explain why a partial fraction decomposition is unique? (Hint: Think about it as a system of equations.)

3. Can you explain how to verify a partial fraction decomposition graphically?

4. You are unsure if you correctly decomposed the partial fraction correctly. Explain how you could double check your answer.

5. Once you have a system of equations generated by the partial fraction decomposition, can you explain another method to solve it? For example if you had $\dfrac{7x + 13}{3x^2 + 8x + 15} = \dfrac{A}{x + 1} + \dfrac{B}{3x + 5}$, we eventually simplify to $7x + 13 = A(3x + 5) + B(x + 1)$. Explain how you could intelligently choose an x-value that will eliminate either A or B and solve for A and B.

ALGEBRAIC

For the following exercises, find the decomposition of the partial fraction for the nonrepeating linear factors.

6. $\dfrac{5x + 16}{x^2 + 10x + 24}$

7. $\dfrac{3x - 79}{x^2 - 5x - 24}$

8. $\dfrac{-x - 24}{x^2 - 2x - 24}$

9. $\dfrac{10x + 47}{x^2 + 7x + 10}$

10. $\dfrac{x}{6x^2 + 25x + 25}$

11. $\dfrac{32x - 11}{20x^2 - 13x + 2}$

12. $\dfrac{x + 1}{x^2 + 7x + 10}$

13. $\dfrac{5x}{x^2 - 9}$

14. $\dfrac{10x}{x^2 - 25}$

15. $\dfrac{6x}{x^2 - 4}$

16. $\dfrac{2x - 3}{x^2 - 6x + 5}$

17. $\dfrac{4x - 1}{x^2 - x - 6}$

18. $\dfrac{4x + 3}{x^2 + 8x + 15}$

19. $\dfrac{3x - 1}{x^2 - 5x + 6}$

For the following exercises, find the decomposition of the partial fraction for the repeating linear factors.

20. $\dfrac{-5x - 19}{(x + 4)^2}$

21. $\dfrac{x}{(x - 2)^2}$

22. $\dfrac{7x + 14}{(x + 3)^2}$

23. $\dfrac{-24x - 27}{(4x + 5)^2}$

24. $\dfrac{-24x - 27}{(6x - 7)^2}$

25. $\dfrac{5 - x}{(x - 7)^2}$

26. $\dfrac{5x + 14}{2x^2 + 12x + 18}$

27. $\dfrac{5x^2 + 20x + 8}{2x(x + 1)^2}$

28. $\dfrac{4x^2 + 55x + 25}{5x(3x + 5)^2}$

29. $\dfrac{54x^3 + 127x^2 + 80x + 16}{2x^2(3x + 2)^2}$

30. $\dfrac{x^3 - 5x^2 + 12x + 144}{x^2(x^2 + 12x + 36)}$

For the following exercises, find the decomposition of the partial fraction for the irreducible non repeating quadratic factor.

31. $\dfrac{4x^2 + 6x + 11}{(x + 2)(x^2 + x + 3)}$

32. $\dfrac{4x^2 + 9x + 23}{(x - 1)(x^2 + 6x + 11)}$

33. $\dfrac{-2x^2 + 10x + 4}{(x - 1)(x^2 + 3x + 8)}$

34. $\dfrac{x^2 + 3x + 1}{(x + 1)(x^2 + 5x - 2)}$

35. $\dfrac{4x^2 + 17x - 1}{(x + 3)(x^2 + 6x + 1)}$

36. $\dfrac{4x^2}{(x + 5)(x^2 + 7x - 5)}$

37. $\dfrac{4x^2 + 5x + 3}{x^3 - 1}$

38. $\dfrac{-5x^2 + 18x - 4}{x^3 + 8}$

39. $\dfrac{3x^2 - 7x + 33}{x^3 + 27}$

40. $\dfrac{x^2 + 2x + 40}{x^3 - 125}$

41. $\dfrac{4x^2 + 4x + 12}{8x^3 - 27}$

42. $\dfrac{-50x^2 + 5x - 3}{125x^3 - 1}$

43. $\dfrac{-2x^3 - 30x^2 + 36x + 216}{x^4 + 216x}$

For the following exercises, find the decomposition of the partial fraction for the irreducible repeating quadratic factor.

44. $\dfrac{3x^3 + 2x^2 + 14x + 15}{(x^2 + 4)^2}$

45. $\dfrac{x^3 + 6x^2 + 5x + 9}{(x^2 + 1)^2}$

46. $\dfrac{x^3 - x^2 + x - 1}{(x^2 - 3)^2}$

47. $\dfrac{x^2 + 5x + 5}{(x + 2)^2}$

48. $\dfrac{x^3 + 2x^2 + 4x}{(x^2 + 2x + 9)^2}$

49. $\dfrac{x^2 + 25}{(x^2 + 3x + 25)^2}$

50. $\dfrac{2x^3 + 11x + 7x + 70}{(2x^2 + x + 14)^2}$

51. $\dfrac{5x + 2}{x(x^2 + 4)^2}$

52. $\dfrac{x^4 + x^3 + 8x^2 + 6x + 36}{x(x^2 + 6)^2}$

53. $\dfrac{2x - 9}{(x^2 - x)^2}$

54. $\dfrac{5x^3 - 2x + 1}{(x^2 + 2x)^2}$

EXTENSIONS

For the following exercises, find the partial fraction expansion.

55. $\dfrac{x^2 + 4}{(x + 1)^3}$

56. $\dfrac{x^3 - 4x^2 + 5x + 4}{(x - 2)^3}$

For the following exercises, perform the operation and then find the partial fraction decomposition.

57. $\dfrac{7}{x + 8} + \dfrac{5}{x - 2} - \dfrac{x - 1}{x^2 - 6x - 16}$

58. $\dfrac{1}{x - 4} - \dfrac{3}{x + 6} - \dfrac{2x + 7}{x^2 + 2x - 24}$

59. $\dfrac{2x}{x^2 - 16} - \dfrac{1 - 2x}{x^2 + 6x + 8} - \dfrac{x - 5}{x^2 - 4x}$

LEARNING OBJECTIVES

In this section, you will:

- Find the sum and difference of two matrices.
- Find scalar multiples of a matrix.
- Find the product of two matrices.

11.5 MATRICES AND MATRIX OPERATIONS

Figure 1 (credit: "SD Dirk," Flickr)

Two club soccer teams, the Wildcats and the Mud Cats, are hoping to obtain new equipment for an upcoming season. **Table 1** shows the needs of both teams.

	Wildcats	**Mud Cats**
Goals	6	10
Balls	30	24
Jerseys	14	20

Table 1

A goal costs $300; a ball costs $10; and a jersey costs $30. How can we find the total cost for the equipment needed for each team? In this section, we discover a method in which the data in the soccer equipment table can be displayed and used for calculating other information. Then, we will be able to calculate the cost of the equipment.

Finding the Sum and Difference of Two Matrices

To solve a problem like the one described for the soccer teams, we can use a matrix, which is a rectangular array of numbers. A row in a matrix is a set of numbers that are aligned horizontally. A column in a matrix is a set of numbers that are aligned vertically. Each number is an entry, sometimes called an element, of the matrix. Matrices (plural) are enclosed in [ ] or ( ), and are usually named with capital letters. For example, three matrices named A, B, and C are shown below.

$$A = \begin{bmatrix} 1 & 2 \\ 3 & 4 \end{bmatrix}, B = \begin{bmatrix} 1 & 2 & 7 \\ 0 & -5 & 6 \\ 7 & 8 & 2 \end{bmatrix}, C = \begin{bmatrix} -1 & 3 \\ 0 & 2 \\ 3 & 1 \end{bmatrix}$$

Describing Matrices

A matrix is often referred to by its size or dimensions: $m \times n$ indicating m rows and n columns. Matrix entries are defined first by row and then by column. For example, to locate the entry in matrix A identified as a_{ij}, we look for the entry in row i, column j. In matrix A, shown below, the entry in row 2, column 3 is a_{23}.

$$A = \begin{bmatrix} a_{11} & a_{12} & a_{13} \\ a_{21} & a_{22} & a_{23} \\ a_{31} & a_{32} & a_{33} \end{bmatrix}$$

A square matrix is a matrix with dimensions $n \times n$, meaning that it has the same number of rows as columns. The 3×3 matrix above is an example of a square matrix.

A row matrix is a matrix consisting of one row with dimensions $1 \times n$.

$$\begin{bmatrix} a_{11} & a_{12} & a_{13} \end{bmatrix}$$

A column matrix is a matrix consisting of one column with dimensions $m \times 1$.

$$\begin{bmatrix} a_{11} \\ a_{12} \\ a_{13} \end{bmatrix}$$

A matrix may be used to represent a system of equations. In these cases, the numbers represent the coefficients of the variables in the system. Matrices often make solving systems of equations easier because they are not encumbered with variables. We will investigate this idea further in the next section, but first we will look at basic matrix operations.

---

matrices

A **matrix** is a rectangular array of numbers that is usually named by a capital letter: A, B, C, and so on. Each entry in a matrix is referred to as a_{ij}, such that i represents the row and j represents the column. Matrices are often referred to by their dimensions: $m \times n$ indicating m rows and n columns.

Example 1   **Finding the Dimensions of the Given Matrix and Locating Entries**

Given matrix A:

   a. What are the dimensions of matrix A?

   b. What are the entries at a_{31} and a_{22} ?

$$A = \begin{bmatrix} 2 & 1 & 0 \\ 2 & 4 & 7 \\ 3 & 1 & -2 \end{bmatrix}$$

Solution

   a. The dimensions are 3×3 because there are three rows and three columns.

   b. Entry a_{31} is the number at row 3, column 1, which is 3. The entry a_{22} is the number at row 2, column 2, which is 4. Remember, the row comes first, then the column.

Adding and Subtracting Matrices

We use matrices to list data or to represent systems. Because the entries are numbers, we can perform operations on matrices. We add or subtract matrices by adding or subtracting corresponding entries.

In order to do this, the entries must correspond. Therefore, *addition and subtraction of matrices is only possible when the matrices have the same dimensions*. We can add or subtract a 3×3 matrix and another 3×3 matrix, but we cannot add or subtract a 2×3 matrix and a 3×3 matrix because some entries in one matrix will not have a corresponding entry in the other matrix.

---

adding and subtracting matrices

Given matrices A and B of like dimensions, addition and subtraction of A and B will produce matrix C or matrix D of the same dimension.

$$A + B = C \text{ such that } a_{ij} + b_{ij} = c_{ij}$$
$$A - B = D \text{ such that } a_{ij} - b_{ij} = d_{ij}$$

Matrix addition is commutative.

$$A + B = B + A$$

It is also associative.

$$(A + B) + C = A + (B + C)$$

Example 2 **Finding the Sum of Matrices**

Find the sum of A and B, given

$$A = \begin{bmatrix} a & b \\ c & d \end{bmatrix} \text{ and } B = \begin{bmatrix} e & f \\ g & h \end{bmatrix}$$

Solution Add corresponding entries.

$$A + B = \begin{bmatrix} a & b \\ c & d \end{bmatrix} + \begin{bmatrix} e & f \\ g & h \end{bmatrix}$$

$$= \begin{bmatrix} a + e & b + f \\ c + g & d + h \end{bmatrix}$$

Example 3 **Adding Matrix *A* and Matrix *B***

Find the sum of A and B.

$$A = \begin{bmatrix} 4 & 1 \\ 3 & 2 \end{bmatrix} \text{ and } B = \begin{bmatrix} 5 & 9 \\ 0 & 7 \end{bmatrix}$$

Solution Add corresponding entries. Add the entry in row 1, column 1, a_{11}, of matrix A to the entry in row 1, column 1, b_{11}, of B. Continue the pattern until all entries have been added.

$$A + B = \begin{bmatrix} 4 & 1 \\ 3 & 2 \end{bmatrix} + \begin{bmatrix} 5 & 9 \\ 0 & 7 \end{bmatrix}$$

$$= \begin{bmatrix} 4 + 5 & 1 + 9 \\ 3 + 0 & 2 + 7 \end{bmatrix}$$

$$= \begin{bmatrix} 9 & 10 \\ 3 & 9 \end{bmatrix}$$

Example 4 **Finding the Difference of Two Matrices**

Find the difference of A and B.

$$A = \begin{bmatrix} -2 & 3 \\ 0 & 1 \end{bmatrix} \text{ and } B = \begin{bmatrix} 8 & 1 \\ 5 & 4 \end{bmatrix}$$

Solution We subtract the corresponding entries of each matrix.

$$A - B = \begin{bmatrix} -2 & 3 \\ 0 & 1 \end{bmatrix} - \begin{bmatrix} 8 & 1 \\ 5 & 4 \end{bmatrix}$$

$$= \begin{bmatrix} -2 - 8 & 3 - 1 \\ 0 - 5 & 1 - 4 \end{bmatrix}$$

$$= \begin{bmatrix} -10 & 2 \\ -5 & -3 \end{bmatrix}$$

Example 5   **Finding the Sum and Difference of Two 3 x 3 Matrices**

Given A and B :

    a. Find the sum.

    b. Find the difference.

$$A = \begin{bmatrix} 2 & -10 & -2 \\ 14 & 12 & 10 \\ 4 & -2 & 2 \end{bmatrix} \text{ and } B = \begin{bmatrix} 6 & 10 & -2 \\ 0 & -12 & -4 \\ -5 & 2 & -2 \end{bmatrix}$$

Solution

    a. Add the corresponding entries.

$$A + B = \begin{bmatrix} 2 & -10 & -2 \\ 14 & 12 & 10 \\ 4 & -2 & 2 \end{bmatrix} + \begin{bmatrix} 6 & 10 & -2 \\ 0 & -12 & -4 \\ -5 & 2 & -2 \end{bmatrix}$$

$$= \begin{bmatrix} 2+6 & -10+10 & -2-2 \\ 14+0 & 12-12 & 10-4 \\ 4-5 & -2+2 & 2-2 \end{bmatrix}$$

$$= \begin{bmatrix} 8 & 0 & -4 \\ 14 & 0 & 6 \\ -1 & 0 & 0 \end{bmatrix}$$

    b. Subtract the corresponding entries.

$$A - B = \begin{bmatrix} 2 & -10 & -2 \\ 14 & 12 & 10 \\ 4 & -2 & 2 \end{bmatrix} - \begin{bmatrix} 6 & 10 & -2 \\ 0 & -12 & -4 \\ -5 & 2 & -2 \end{bmatrix}$$

$$= \begin{bmatrix} 2-6 & -10-10 & -2+2 \\ 14-0 & 12+12 & 10+4 \\ 4+5 & -2-2 & 2+2 \end{bmatrix}$$

$$= \begin{bmatrix} -4 & -20 & 0 \\ 14 & 24 & 14 \\ 9 & -4 & 4 \end{bmatrix}$$

Try It #1

Add matrix A and matrix B.

$$A = \begin{bmatrix} 2 & 6 \\ 1 & 0 \\ 1 & -3 \end{bmatrix} \text{ and } B = \begin{bmatrix} 3 & -2 \\ 1 & 5 \\ -4 & 3 \end{bmatrix}$$

Finding Scalar Multiples of a Matrix

Besides adding and subtracting whole matrices, there are many situations in which we need to multiply a matrix by a constant called a scalar. Recall that a scalar is a real number quantity that has magnitude, but not direction. For example, time, temperature, and distance are scalar quantities. The process of scalar multiplication involves multiplying each entry in a matrix by a scalar. A **scalar multiple** is any entry of a matrix that results from scalar multiplication.

Consider a real-world scenario in which a university needs to add to its inventory of computers, computer tables, and chairs in two of the campus labs due to increased enrollment. They estimate that 15% more equipment is needed in both labs. The school's current inventory is displayed in **Table 2**.

	Lab A	**Lab B**
Computers	15	27
Computer Tables	16	34
Chairs	16	34

Table 2

Converting the data to a matrix, we have

$$C_{2013} = \begin{bmatrix} 15 & 27 \\ 16 & 34 \\ 16 & 34 \end{bmatrix}$$

To calculate how much computer equipment will be needed, we multiply all entries in matrix C by 0.15.

$$(0.15)C_{2013} = \begin{bmatrix} (0.15)15 & (0.15)27 \\ (0.15)16 & (0.15)34 \\ (0.15)16 & (0.15)34 \end{bmatrix} = \begin{bmatrix} 2.25 & 4.05 \\ 2.4 & 5.1 \\ 2.4 & 5.1 \end{bmatrix}$$

We must round up to the next integer, so the amount of new equipment needed is

$$\begin{bmatrix} 3 & 5 \\ 3 & 6 \\ 3 & 6 \end{bmatrix}$$

Adding the two matrices as shown below, we see the new inventory amounts.

$$\begin{bmatrix} 15 & 27 \\ 16 & 34 \\ 16 & 34 \end{bmatrix} + \begin{bmatrix} 3 & 5 \\ 3 & 6 \\ 3 & 6 \end{bmatrix} = \begin{bmatrix} 18 & 32 \\ 19 & 40 \\ 19 & 40 \end{bmatrix}$$

This means

$$C_{2014} = \begin{bmatrix} 18 & 32 \\ 19 & 40 \\ 19 & 40 \end{bmatrix}$$

Thus, Lab A will have 18 computers, 19 computer tables, and 19 chairs; Lab B will have 32 computers, 40 computer tables, and 40 chairs.

---

scalar multiplication

Scalar multiplication involves finding the product of a constant by each entry in the matrix. Given

$$A = \begin{bmatrix} a_{11} & a_{12} \\ a_{21} & a_{22} \end{bmatrix}$$

the scalar multiple cA is

$$cA = c\begin{bmatrix} a_{11} & a_{12} \\ a_{21} & a_{22} \end{bmatrix}$$

$$= \begin{bmatrix} ca_{11} & ca_{12} \\ ca_{21} & ca_{22} \end{bmatrix}$$

Scalar multiplication is distributive. For the matrices A, B, and C with scalars a and b,

$$a(A + B) = aA + aB$$
$$(a + b)A = aA + bA$$

Example 6   **Multiplying the Matrix by a Scalar**

Multiply matrix A by the scalar 3.

$$A = \begin{bmatrix} 8 & 1 \\ 5 & 4 \end{bmatrix}$$

Solution   Multiply each entry in A by the scalar 3.

$$3A = 3\begin{bmatrix} 8 & 1 \\ 5 & 4 \end{bmatrix}$$

$$= \begin{bmatrix} 3 \cdot 8 & 3 \cdot 1 \\ 3 \cdot 5 & 3 \cdot 4 \end{bmatrix}$$

$$= \begin{bmatrix} 24 & 3 \\ 15 & 12 \end{bmatrix}$$

Try It #2

Given matrix B, find $-2B$ where

$$A = \begin{bmatrix} 4 & 1 \\ 3 & 2 \end{bmatrix}$$

Example 7   **Finding the Sum of Scalar Multiples**

Find the sum $3A + 2B$.

$$A = \begin{bmatrix} 1 & -2 & 0 \\ 0 & -1 & 2 \\ 4 & 3 & -6 \end{bmatrix} \text{ and } B = \begin{bmatrix} -1 & 2 & 1 \\ 0 & -3 & 2 \\ 0 & 1 & -4 \end{bmatrix}$$

Solution   First, find $3A$, then $2B$.

$$3A = \begin{bmatrix} 3 \cdot 1 & 3(-2) & 3 \cdot 0 \\ 3 \cdot 0 & 3(-1) & 3 \cdot 2 \\ 3 \cdot 4 & 3 \cdot 3 & 3(-6) \end{bmatrix}$$

$$= \begin{bmatrix} 3 & -6 & 0 \\ 0 & -3 & 6 \\ 12 & 9 & -18 \end{bmatrix}$$

$$2B = \begin{bmatrix} 2(-1) & 2 \cdot 2 & 2 \cdot 1 \\ 2 \cdot 0 & 2(-3) & 2 \cdot 2 \\ 2 \cdot 0 & 2 \cdot 1 & 2(-4) \end{bmatrix}$$

$$= \begin{bmatrix} -2 & 4 & 2 \\ 0 & -6 & 4 \\ 0 & 2 & -8 \end{bmatrix}$$

Now, add $3A + 2B$.

$$3A + 2B = \begin{bmatrix} 3 & -6 & 0 \\ 0 & -3 & 6 \\ 12 & 9 & -18 \end{bmatrix} + \begin{bmatrix} -2 & 4 & 2 \\ 0 & -6 & 4 \\ 0 & 2 & -8 \end{bmatrix}$$

$$= \begin{bmatrix} 3-2 & -6+4 & 0+2 \\ 0+0 & -3-6 & 6+4 \\ 12+0 & 9+2 & -18-8 \end{bmatrix}$$

$$= \begin{bmatrix} 1 & -2 & 2 \\ 0 & -9 & 10 \\ 12 & 11 & -26 \end{bmatrix}$$

Finding the Product of Two Matrices

In addition to multiplying a matrix by a scalar, we can multiply two matrices. Finding the product of two matrices is only possible when the inner dimensions are the same, meaning that the number of columns of the first matrix is equal to the number of rows of the second matrix. If A is an $m \times r$ matrix and B is an $r \times n$ matrix, then the product matrix AB is an $m \times n$ matrix. For example, the product AB is possible because the number of columns in A is the same as the number of rows in B. If the inner dimensions do not match, the product is not defined.

$$\begin{array}{ccc} A & \cdot & B \\ 2 \times 3 & & 3 \times 3 \\ & \text{same} & \end{array}$$

We multiply entries of A with entries of B according to a specific pattern as outlined below. The process of matrix multiplication becomes clearer when working a problem with real numbers.

To obtain the entries in row i of AB, we multiply the entries in row i of A by column j in B and add. For example, given matrices A and B, where the dimensions of A are 2×3 and the dimensions of B are 3×3, the product of AB will be a 2×3 matrix.

$$A = \begin{bmatrix} a_{11} & a_{12} & a_{13} \\ a_{21} & a_{22} & a_{23} \end{bmatrix} \text{ and } B = \begin{bmatrix} b_{11} & b_{12} & b_{13} \\ b_{21} & b_{22} & b_{23} \\ b_{31} & b_{32} & b_{33} \end{bmatrix}$$

Multiply and add as follows to obtain the first entry of the product matrix AB.

1. To obtain the entry in row 1, column 1 of AB, multiply the first row in A by the first column in B, and add.

$$[a_{11} \quad a_{12} \quad a_{13}] \begin{bmatrix} b_{11} \\ b_{21} \\ b_{31} \end{bmatrix} = a_{11} \cdot b_{11} + a_{12} \cdot b_{21} + a_{13} \cdot b_{31}$$

2. To obtain the entry in row 1, column 2 of AB, multiply the first row of A by the second column in B, and add.

$$[a_{11} \quad a_{12} \quad a_{13}] \begin{bmatrix} b_{12} \\ b_{22} \\ b_{32} \end{bmatrix} = a_{11} \cdot b_{12} + a_{12} \cdot b_{22} + a_{13} \cdot b_{32}$$

3. To obtain the entry in row 1, column 3 of AB, multiply the first row of A by the third column in B, and add.

$$[a_{11} \quad a_{12} \quad a_{13}] \begin{bmatrix} b_{13} \\ b_{23} \\ b_{33} \end{bmatrix} = a_{11} \cdot b_{13} + a_{12} \cdot b_{23} + a_{13} \cdot b_{33}$$

We proceed the same way to obtain the second row of AB. In other words, row 2 of A times column 1 of B; row 2 of A times column 2 of B; row 2 of A times column 3 of B. When complete, the product matrix will be

$$AB = \begin{bmatrix} a_{11} \cdot b_{11} + a_{12} \cdot b_{21} + a_{13} \cdot b_{31} & a_{11} \cdot b_{12} + a_{12} \cdot b_{22} + a_{13} \cdot b_{32} & a_{11} \cdot b_{13} + a_{12} \cdot b_{23} + a_{13} \cdot b_{33} \\ a_{21} \cdot b_{11} + a_{22} \cdot b_{21} + a_{23} \cdot b_{31} & a_{21} \cdot b_{12} + a_{22} \cdot b_{22} + a_{23} \cdot b_{32} & a_{21} \cdot b_{13} + a_{22} \cdot b_{23} + a_{23} \cdot b_{33} \end{bmatrix}$$

---

properties of matrix multiplication

For the matrices A, B, and C the following properties hold.

- Matrix multiplication is associative: $(AB)C = A(BC)$.

$$C(A + B) = CA + CB,$$

- Matrix multiplication is distributive:

$$(A + B)C = AC + BC.$$

Note that matrix multiplication is not commutative.

Example 8 **Multiplying Two Matrices**

Multiply matrix A and matrix B.

$$A = \begin{bmatrix} 1 & 2 \\ 3 & 4 \end{bmatrix} \quad \text{and } B = \begin{bmatrix} 5 & 6 \\ 7 & 8 \end{bmatrix}$$

Solution First, we check the dimensions of the matrices. Matrix A has dimensions 2×2 and matrix B has dimensions 2×2. The inner dimensions are the same so we can perform the multiplication. The product will have the dimensions 2×2.

We perform the operations outlined previously.

$$AB = \begin{bmatrix} 1 & 2 \\ 3 & 4 \end{bmatrix} \begin{bmatrix} 5 & 6 \\ 7 & 8 \end{bmatrix}$$

$$= \begin{bmatrix} 1(5) + 2(7) & 1(6) + 2(8) \\ 3(5) + 4(7) & 3(6) + 4(8) \end{bmatrix}$$

$$= \begin{bmatrix} 19 & 22 \\ 43 & 50 \end{bmatrix}$$

Example 9 **Multiplying Two Matrices**

Given A and B :

    a. Find AB.   **b.** Find BA.

$$A = \begin{bmatrix} -1 & 2 & 3 \\ 4 & 0 & 5 \end{bmatrix} \quad \text{and } B = \begin{bmatrix} 5 & -1 \\ -4 & 0 \\ 2 & 3 \end{bmatrix}$$

Solution

a. As the dimensions of A are 2×3 and the dimensions of B are 3×2, these matrices can be multiplied together because the number of columns in A matches the number of rows in B. The resulting product will be a 2×2 matrix, the number of rows in A by the number of columns in B.

$$AB = \begin{bmatrix} -1 & 2 & 3 \\ 4 & 0 & 5 \end{bmatrix} \begin{bmatrix} 5 & -1 \\ -4 & 0 \\ 2 & 3 \end{bmatrix}$$
$$= \begin{bmatrix} -1(5) + 2(-4) + 3(2) & -1(-1) + 2(0) + 3(3) \\ 4(5) + 0(-4) + 5(2) & 4(-1) + 0(0) + 5(3) \end{bmatrix}$$
$$= \begin{bmatrix} -7 & 10 \\ 30 & 11 \end{bmatrix}$$

b. The dimensions of B are 3×2 and the dimensions of A are 2×3. The inner dimensions match so the product is defined and will be a 3×3 matrix.

$$BA = \begin{bmatrix} 5 & -1 \\ -4 & 0 \\ 2 & 3 \end{bmatrix} \begin{bmatrix} -1 & 2 & 3 \\ 4 & 0 & 5 \end{bmatrix}$$
$$= \begin{bmatrix} 5(-1) + -1(4) & 5(2) + -1(0) & 5(3) + -1(5) \\ -4(-1) + 0(4) & -4(2) + 0(0) & -4(3) + 0(5) \\ 2(-1) + 3(4) & 2(2) + 3(0) & 2(3) + 3(5) \end{bmatrix}$$
$$= \begin{bmatrix} -9 & 10 & 10 \\ 4 & -8 & -12 \\ 10 & 4 & 21 \end{bmatrix}$$

Analysis Notice that the products AB and BA are not equal.

$$AB = \begin{bmatrix} -7 & 10 \\ 30 & 11 \end{bmatrix} \neq \begin{bmatrix} -9 & 10 & 10 \\ 4 & -8 & -12 \\ 10 & 4 & 21 \end{bmatrix} = BA$$

This illustrates the fact that matrix multiplication is not commutative.

Q & A...

Is it possible for AB to be defined but not BA?

Yes, consider a matrix A with dimension 3×4 and matrix B with dimension 4×2. For the product AB the inner dimensions are 4 and the product is defined, but for the product BA the inner dimensions are 2 and 3 so the product is undefined.

Example 10   **Using Matrices in Real-World Problems**

Let's return to the problem presented at the opening of this section. We have **Table 3,** representing the equipment needs of two soccer teams.

	Wildcats	Mud Cats
Goals	6	10
Balls	30	24
Jerseys	14	20

Table 3

We are also given the prices of the equipment, as shown in **Table 4.**

Goals	$300
Balls	$10
Jerseys	$30

Table 4

We will convert the data to matrices. Thus, the equipment need matrix is written as

$$E = \begin{bmatrix} 6 & 10 \\ 30 & 24 \\ 14 & 20 \end{bmatrix}$$

The cost matrix is written as

$$C = \begin{bmatrix} 300 & 10 & 30 \end{bmatrix}$$

We perform matrix multiplication to obtain costs for the equipment.

$$CE = \begin{bmatrix} 300 & 10 & 30 \end{bmatrix} \begin{bmatrix} 6 & 10 \\ 30 & 24 \\ 14 & 20 \end{bmatrix}$$

$$= [300(6) + 10(30) + 30(14)\ 300(10) + 10(24) + 30(20)]$$

$$= [2{,}520\ 3{,}840]$$

The total cost for equipment for the Wildcats is \$2,520, and the total cost for equipment for the Mud Cats is \$3,840.

How To...

Given a matrix operation, evaluate using a calculator.

1. Save each matrix as a matrix variable $[A]$, $[B]$, $[C]$, ...
2. Enter the operation into the calculator, calling up each matrix variable as needed.
3. If the operation is defined, the calculator will present the solution matrix; if the operation is undefined, it will display an error message.

Example 11 **Using a Calculator to Perform Matrix Operations**

Find $AB - C$ given

$$A = \begin{bmatrix} -15 & 25 & 32 \\ 41 & -7 & -28 \\ 10 & 34 & -2 \end{bmatrix}, B = \begin{bmatrix} 45 & 21 & -37 \\ -24 & 52 & 19 \\ 6 & -48 & -31 \end{bmatrix}, \text{ and } C = \begin{bmatrix} -100 & -89 & -98 \\ 25 & -56 & 74 \\ -67 & 42 & -75 \end{bmatrix}.$$

Solution   On the matrix page of the calculator, we enter matrix A above as the matrix variable $[A]$, matrix B above as the matrix variable $[B]$, and matrix C above as the matrix variable $[C]$.

On the home screen of the calculator, we type in the problem and call up each matrix variable as needed.

$$[A] \times [B] - [C]$$

The calculator gives us the following matrix.

$$\begin{bmatrix} -983 & -462 & 136 \\ 1{,}820 & 1{,}897 & -856 \\ -311 & 2{,}032 & 413 \end{bmatrix}$$

Access these online resources for additional instruction and practice with matrices and matrix operations.

* Dimensions of a Matrix (http://openstaxcollege.org/l/matrixdimen)
* Matrix Addition and Subtraction (http://openstaxcollege.org/l/matrixaddsub)
* Matrix Operations (http://openstaxcollege.org/l/matrixoper)
* Matrix Multiplication (http://openstaxcollege.org/l/matrixmult)

11.5   SECTION EXERCISES

VERBAL

1. Can we add any two matrices together? If so, explain why; if not, explain why not and give an example of two matrices that cannot be added together.

2. Can we multiply any column matrix by any row matrix? Explain why or why not.

3. Can both the products AB and BA be defined? If so, explain how; if not, explain why.

4. Can any two matrices of the same size be multiplied? If so, explain why, and if not, explain why not and give an example of two matrices of the same size that cannot be multiplied together.

5. Does matrix multiplication commute? That is, does $AB = BA$? If so, prove why it does. If not, explain why it does not.

ALGEBRAIC

For the following exercises, use the matrices below and perform the matrix addition or subtraction. Indicate if the operation is undefined.

$$A = \begin{bmatrix} 1 & 3 \\ 0 & 7 \end{bmatrix}, B = \begin{bmatrix} 2 & 14 \\ 22 & 6 \end{bmatrix}, C = \begin{bmatrix} 1 & 5 \\ 8 & 92 \\ 12 & 6 \end{bmatrix}, D = \begin{bmatrix} 10 & 14 \\ 7 & 2 \\ 5 & 61 \end{bmatrix}, E = \begin{bmatrix} 6 & 12 \\ 14 & 5 \end{bmatrix}, F = \begin{bmatrix} 0 & 9 \\ 78 & 17 \\ 15 & 4 \end{bmatrix}$$

6. $A + B$
7. $C + D$
8. $A + C$
9. $B - E$
10. $C + F$
11. $D - B$

For the following exercises, use the matrices below to perform scalar multiplication.

$$A = \begin{bmatrix} 4 & 6 \\ 13 & 12 \end{bmatrix}, B = \begin{bmatrix} 3 & 9 \\ 21 & 12 \\ 0 & 64 \end{bmatrix}, C = \begin{bmatrix} 16 & 3 & 7 & 18 \\ 90 & 5 & 3 & 29 \end{bmatrix}, D = \begin{bmatrix} 18 & 12 & 13 \\ 8 & 14 & 6 \\ 7 & 4 & 21 \end{bmatrix}$$

12. $5A$
13. $3B$
14. $-2B$
15. $-4C$
16. $\frac{1}{2}C$
17. $100D$

For the following exercises, use the matrices below to perform matrix multiplication.

$$A = \begin{bmatrix} -1 & 5 \\ 3 & 2 \end{bmatrix}, B = \begin{bmatrix} 3 & 6 & 4 \\ -8 & 0 & 12 \end{bmatrix}, C = \begin{bmatrix} 4 & 10 \\ -2 & 6 \\ 5 & 9 \end{bmatrix}, D = \begin{bmatrix} 2 & -3 & 12 \\ 9 & 3 & 1 \\ 0 & 8 & -10 \end{bmatrix}$$

18. AB
19. BC
20. CA
21. BD
22. DC
23. CB

For the following exercises, use the matrices below to perform the indicated operation if possible. If not possible, explain why the operation cannot be performed.

$$A = \begin{bmatrix} 2 & -5 \\ 6 & 7 \end{bmatrix}, B = \begin{bmatrix} -9 & 6 \\ -4 & 2 \end{bmatrix}, C = \begin{bmatrix} 0 & 9 \\ 7 & 1 \end{bmatrix}, D = \begin{bmatrix} -8 & 7 & -5 \\ 4 & 3 & 2 \\ 0 & 9 & 2 \end{bmatrix}, E = \begin{bmatrix} 4 & 5 & 3 \\ 7 & -6 & -5 \\ 1 & 0 & 9 \end{bmatrix}$$

24. $A + B - C$
25. $4A + 5D$
26. $2C + B$
27. $3D + 4E$
28. $C - 0.5D$
29. $100D - 10E$

For the following exercises, use the matrices below to perform the indicated operation if possible. If not possible, explain why the operation cannot be performed. (Hint: $A^2 = A \cdot A$)

$$A = \begin{bmatrix} -10 & 20 \\ 5 & 25 \end{bmatrix}, B = \begin{bmatrix} 40 & 10 \\ -20 & 30 \end{bmatrix}, C = \begin{bmatrix} -1 & 0 \\ 0 & -1 \\ 1 & 0 \end{bmatrix}$$

30. AB **31.** BA **32.** CA **33.** BC **34.** A^2 **35.** B^2

36. C^2 **37.** B^2A^2 **38.** $A^2 B^2$ **39.** $(AB)^2$ **40.** $(BA)^2$

For the following exercises, use the matrices below to perform the indicated operation if possible. If not possible, explain why the operation cannot be performed. (Hint: $A^2 = A \cdot A$)

$$A = \begin{bmatrix} 1 & 0 \\ 2 & 3 \end{bmatrix}, B = \begin{bmatrix} -2 & 3 & 4 \\ -1 & 1 & -5 \end{bmatrix}, C = \begin{bmatrix} 0.5 & 0.1 \\ 1 & 0.2 \\ -0.5 & 0.3 \end{bmatrix}, D = \begin{bmatrix} 1 & 0 & -1 \\ -6 & 7 & 5 \\ 4 & 2 & 1 \end{bmatrix}$$

41. AB **42.** BA **43.** BD **44.** DC **45.** D^2 **46.** A^2

47. D^3 **48.** $(AB)C$ **49.** $A(BC)$

TECHNOLOGY

For the following exercises, use the matrices below to perform the indicated operation if possible. If not possible, explain why the operation cannot be performed. Use a calculator to verify your solution.

$$A = \begin{bmatrix} -2 & 0 & 9 \\ 1 & 8 & -3 \\ 0.5 & 4 & 5 \end{bmatrix}, B = \begin{bmatrix} 0.5 & 3 & 0 \\ -4 & 1 & 6 \\ 8 & 7 & 2 \end{bmatrix}, C = \begin{bmatrix} 1 & 0 & 1 \\ 0 & 1 & 0 \\ 1 & 0 & 1 \end{bmatrix}$$

50. AB **51.** BA **52.** CA **53.** BC **54.** ABC

EXTENSIONS

For the following exercises, use the matrix below to perform the indicated operation on the given matrix.

$$B = \begin{bmatrix} 1 & 0 & 0 \\ 0 & 0 & 1 \\ 0 & 1 & 0 \end{bmatrix}$$

55. B^2 **56.** B^3 **57.** B^4 **58.** B^5

59. Using the above questions, find a formula for B^n. Test the formula for B^{201} and B^{202}, using a calculator.

LEARNING OBJECTIVES

In this section, you will:

- Write the augmented matrix of a system of equations.
- Write the system of equations from an augmented matrix.
- Perform row operations on a matrix.
- Solve a system of linear equations using matrices.

11.6   SOLVING SYSTEMS WITH GAUSSIAN ELIMINATION

Figure 1 German mathematician Carl Friedrich Gauss (1777–1855).

Carl Friedrich Gauss lived during the late 18th century and early 19th century, but he is still considered one of the most prolific mathematicians in history. His contributions to the science of mathematics and physics span fields such as algebra, number theory, analysis, differential geometry, astronomy, and optics, among others. His discoveries regarding matrix theory changed the way mathematicians have worked for the last two centuries.

We first encountered Gaussian elimination in **Systems of Linear Equations: Two Variables**. In this section, we will revisit this technique for solving systems, this time using matrices.

Writing the Augmented Matrix of a System of Equations

A matrix can serve as a device for representing and solving a system of equations. To express a system in matrix form, we extract the coefficients of the variables and the constants, and these become the entries of the matrix. We use a vertical line to separate the coefficient entries from the constants, essentially replacing the equal signs. When a system is written in this form, we call it an **augmented matrix**.

For example, consider the following 2×2 system of equations.

$$3x + 4y = 7$$
$$4x - 2y = 5$$

We can write this system as an augmented matrix:

$$\left[\begin{array}{cc|c} 3 & 4 & 7 \\ 4 & -2 & 5 \end{array} \right]$$

We can also write a matrix containing just the coefficients. This is called the **coefficient matrix**.

$$\left[\begin{array}{cc} 3 & 4 \\ 4 & -2 \end{array} \right]$$

A three-by-three system of equations such as

$$3x - y - z = 0$$
$$x + y = 5$$
$$2x - 3z = 2$$

has a coefficient matrix

$$\begin{bmatrix} 3 & -1 & -1 \\ 1 & 1 & 0 \\ 2 & 0 & -3 \end{bmatrix}$$

and is represented by the augmented matrix

$$\left[\begin{array}{ccc|c} 3 & -1 & -1 & 0 \\ 1 & 1 & 0 & 5 \\ 2 & 0 & -3 & 2 \end{array}\right]$$

Notice that the matrix is written so that the variables line up in their own columns: x-terms go in the first column, y-terms in the second column, and z-terms in the third column. It is very important that each equation is written in standard form $ax + by + cz = d$ so that the variables line up. When there is a missing variable term in an equation, the coefficient is 0.

How To...

Given a system of equations, write an augmented matrix.

1. Write the coefficients of the x-terms as the numbers down the first column.
2. Write the coefficients of the y-terms as the numbers down the second column.
3. If there are z-terms, write the coefficients as the numbers down the third column.
4. Draw a vertical line and write the constants to the right of the line.

Example 1   **Writing the Augmented Matrix for a System of Equations**

Write the augmented matrix for the given system of equations.

$$x + 2y - z = 3$$
$$2x - y + 2z = 6$$
$$x - 3y + 3z = 4$$

Solution   The augmented matrix displays the coefficients of the variables, and an additional column for the constants.

$$\left[\begin{array}{ccc|c} 1 & 2 & -1 & 3 \\ 2 & -1 & 2 & 6 \\ 1 & -3 & 3 & 4 \end{array}\right]$$

Try It #1

Write the augmented matrix of the given system of equations.

$$4x - 3y = 11$$
$$3x + 2y = 4$$

Writing a System of Equations from an Augmented Matrix

We can use augmented matrices to help us solve systems of equations because they simplify operations when the systems are not encumbered by the variables. However, it is important to understand how to move back and forth between formats in order to make finding solutions smoother and more intuitive. Here, we will use the information in an augmented matrix to write the system of equations in standard form.

<u>Example 2</u>   **Writing a System of Equations from an Augmented Matrix Form**

Find the system of equations from the augmented matrix.

$$\begin{bmatrix} 1 & -3 & -5 & | & -2 \\ 2 & -5 & -4 & | & 5 \\ -3 & 5 & 4 & | & 6 \end{bmatrix}$$

Solution   When the columns represent the variables x, y, and z,

$$\begin{bmatrix} 1 & -3 & -5 & | & -2 \\ 2 & -5 & -4 & | & 5 \\ -3 & 5 & 4 & | & 6 \end{bmatrix} \rightarrow \begin{array}{c} x - 3y - 5z = -2 \\ 2x - 5y - 4z = 5 \\ -3x + 5y + 4z = 6 \end{array}$$

Try It #2

Write the system of equations from the augmented matrix.

$$\begin{bmatrix} 1 & -1 & 1 & | & 5 \\ 2 & -1 & 3 & | & 1 \\ 0 & 1 & 1 & | & -9 \end{bmatrix}$$

Performing Row Operations on a Matrix

Now that we can write systems of equations in augmented matrix form, we will examine the various **row operations** that can be performed on a matrix, such as addition, multiplication by a constant, and interchanging rows.

Performing row operations on a matrix is the method we use for solving a system of equations. In order to solve the system of equations, we want to convert the matrix to **row-echelon form**, in which there are ones down the **main diagonal** from the upper left corner to the lower right corner, and zeros in every position below the main diagonal as shown.

Row-echelon form
$$\begin{bmatrix} 1 & a & b \\ 0 & 1 & d \\ 0 & 0 & 1 \end{bmatrix}$$

We use row operations corresponding to equation operations to obtain a new matrix that is **row-equivalent** in a simpler form. Here are the guidelines to obtaining row-echelon form.

1. In any nonzero row, the first nonzero number is a 1. It is called a *leading* 1.

2. Any all-zero rows are placed at the bottom on the matrix.

3. Any leading 1 is below and to the right of a previous leading 1.

4. Any column containing a leading 1 has zeros in all other positions in the column.

To solve a system of equations we can perform the following row operations to convert the coefficient matrix to row-echelon form and do back-substitution to find the solution.

1. Interchange rows. (Notation: $R_i \leftrightarrow R_j$)

2. Multiply a row by a constant. (Notation: cR_i)

3. Add the product of a row multiplied by a constant to another row. (Notation: $R_i + cR_j$)

Each of the row operations corresponds to the operations we have already learned to solve systems of equations in three variables. With these operations, there are some key moves that will quickly achieve the goal of writing a matrix in row-echelon form. To obtain a matrix in row-echelon form for finding solutions, we use Gaussian elimination, a method that uses row operations to obtain a 1 as the first entry so that row 1 can be used to convert the remaining rows.

> ### Gaussian elimination
>
> The **Gaussian elimination** method refers to a strategy used to obtain the row-echelon form of a matrix. The goal is to write matrix A with the number 1 as the entry down the main diagonal and have all zeros below.
>
> $$A = \begin{bmatrix} a_{11} & a_{12} & a_{13} \\ a_{21} & a_{22} & a_{23} \\ a_{31} & a_{32} & a_{33} \end{bmatrix} \xrightarrow{\text{After Gaussian elimination}} A = \begin{bmatrix} 1 & b_{12} & b_{13} \\ 0 & 1 & b_{23} \\ 0 & 0 & 1 \end{bmatrix}$$
>
> The first step of the Gaussian strategy includes obtaining a 1 as the first entry, so that row 1 may be used to alter the rows below.

How To…

Given an augmented matrix, perform row operations to achieve row-echelon form.

1. The first equation should have a leading coefficient of 1. Interchange rows or multiply by a constant, if necessary.
2. Use row operations to obtain zeros down the first column below the first entry of 1.
3. Use row operations to obtain a 1 in row 2, column 2.
4. Use row operations to obtain zeros down column 2, below the entry of 1.
5. Use row operations to obtain a 1 in row 3, column 3.
6. Continue this process for all rows until there is a 1 in every entry down the main diagonal and there are only zeros below.
7. If any rows contain all zeros, place them at the bottom.

Example 3   **Solving a 2 × 2 System by Gaussian Elimination**

Solve the given system by Gaussian elimination.

$$2x + 3y = 6$$

$$x - y = \frac{1}{2}$$

Solution   First, we write this as an augmented matrix.

$$\begin{bmatrix} 2 & 3 & 6 \\ 1 & -1 & \frac{1}{2} \end{bmatrix}$$

We want a 1 in row 1, column 1. This can be accomplished by interchanging row 1 and row 2.

$$R_1 \leftrightarrow R_2 \rightarrow \begin{bmatrix} 1 & -1 & \frac{1}{2} \\ 2 & 3 & 6 \end{bmatrix}$$

We now have a 1 as the first entry in row 1, column 1. Now let's obtain a 0 in row 2, column 1. This can be accomplished by multiplying row 1 by -2, and then adding the result to row 2.

$$-2R_1 + R_2 = R_2 \rightarrow \begin{bmatrix} 1 & -1 & \frac{1}{2} \\ 0 & 5 & 5 \end{bmatrix}$$

We only have one more step, to multiply row 2 by $\frac{1}{5}$.

$$\frac{1}{5}R_2 = R_2 \rightarrow \begin{bmatrix} 1 & -1 & \frac{1}{2} \\ 0 & 1 & 1 \end{bmatrix}$$

Use back-substitution. The second row of the matrix represents $y = 1$. Back-substitute $y = 1$ into the first equation.

$$x - (1) = \frac{1}{2}$$

$$x = \frac{3}{2}$$

The solution is the point $\left(\frac{3}{2}, 1 \right)$.

Try It #3

Solve the given system by Gaussian elimination.

$$4x + 3y = 11$$
$$x - 3y = -1$$

Example 4   Using Gaussian Elimination to Solve a System of Equations

Use Gaussian elimination to solve the given 2×2 system of equations.

$$2x + y = 1$$
$$4x + 2y = 6$$

Solution   Write the system as an augmented matrix.

$$\begin{bmatrix} 2 & 1 & | & 1 \\ 4 & 2 & | & 6 \end{bmatrix}$$

Obtain a 1 in row 1, column 1. This can be accomplished by multiplying the first row by $\frac{1}{2}$.

$$\frac{1}{2}R_1 = R_1 \rightarrow \begin{bmatrix} 1 & \frac{1}{2} & | & \frac{1}{2} \\ 4 & 2 & | & 6 \end{bmatrix}$$

Next, we want a 0 in row 2, column 1. Multiply row 1 by -4 and add row 1 to row 2.

$$-4R_1 + R_2 = R_2 \rightarrow \begin{bmatrix} 1 & \frac{1}{2} & | & \frac{1}{2} \\ 0 & 0 & | & 4 \end{bmatrix}$$

The second row represents the equation $0 = 4$. Therefore, the system is inconsistent and has no solution.

Example 5   Solving a Dependent System

Solve the system of equations.

$$3x + 4y = 12$$
$$6x + 8y = 24$$

Solution   Perform row operations on the augmented matrix to try and achieve row-echelon form.

$$A = \begin{bmatrix} 3 & 4 & | & 12 \\ 6 & 8 & | & 24 \end{bmatrix}$$

$$-\frac{1}{2}R_2 + R_1 = R_1 \rightarrow \begin{bmatrix} 0 & 0 & | & 0 \\ 6 & 8 & | & 24 \end{bmatrix}$$

$$R_1 \leftrightarrow R_2 \rightarrow \begin{bmatrix} 6 & 8 & | & 24 \\ 0 & 0 & | & 0 \end{bmatrix}$$

The matrix ends up with all zeros in the last row: $0y = 0$. Thus, there are an infinite number of solutions and the system is classified as dependent. To find the generic solution, return to one of the original equations and solve for y.

$$3x + 4y = 12$$
$$4y = 12 - 3x$$
$$y = 3 - \frac{3}{4}x$$

So the solution to this system is $\left(x, 3 - \frac{3}{4}x \right)$.

Example 6   Performing Row Operations on a 3 × 3 Augmented Matrix to Obtain Row-Echelon Form

Perform row operations on the given matrix to obtain row-echelon form.

$$\begin{bmatrix} 1 & -3 & 4 & | & 3 \\ 2 & -5 & 6 & | & 6 \\ -3 & 3 & 4 & | & 6 \end{bmatrix}$$

Solution   The first row already has a 1 in row 1, column 1. The next step is to multiply row 1 by -2 and add it to row 2.

Then replace row 2 with the result.

$$-2R_1 + R_2 = R_2 \rightarrow \begin{bmatrix} 1 & -3 & 4 & | & 3 \\ 0 & 1 & -2 & | & 0 \\ -3 & 3 & 4 & | & 6 \end{bmatrix}$$

Next, obtain a zero in row 3, column 1.

$$3R_1 + R_3 = R_3 \rightarrow \begin{bmatrix} 1 & -3 & 4 & | & 3 \\ 0 & 1 & -2 & | & 0 \\ 0 & -6 & 16 & | & 15 \end{bmatrix}$$

Next, obtain a zero in row 3, column 2.

$$6R_2 + R_3 = R_3 \rightarrow \begin{bmatrix} 1 & -3 & 4 & | & 3 \\ 0 & 1 & -2 & | & 0 \\ 0 & 0 & 4 & | & 15 \end{bmatrix}$$

The last step is to obtain a 1 in row 3, column 3.

$$\frac{1}{2}R_3 = R_3 \rightarrow \begin{bmatrix} 1 & -3 & 4 & | & 3 \\ 0 & 1 & -2 & | & -6 \\ 0 & 0 & 1 & | & \frac{21}{2} \end{bmatrix}$$

Try It #4

Write the system of equations in row-echelon form.

$$x - 2y + 3z = 9$$
$$-x + 3y = -4$$
$$2x - 5y + 5z = 17$$

Solving a System of Linear Equations Using Matrices

We have seen how to write a system of equations with an augmented matrix, and then how to use row operations and back-substitution to obtain row-echelon form. Now, we will take row-echelon form a step farther to solve a 3 by 3 system of linear equations. The general idea is to eliminate all but one variable using row operations and then back-substitute to solve for the other variables.

Example 7 **Solving a System of Linear Equations Using Matrices**

Solve the system of linear equations using matrices.

$$x - y + z = 8$$
$$2x + 3y - z = -2$$
$$3x - 2y - 9z = 9$$

Solution First, we write the augmented matrix.

$$\begin{bmatrix} 1 & -1 & 1 & | & 8 \\ 2 & 3 & -1 & | & -2 \\ 3 & -2 & -9 & | & 9 \end{bmatrix}$$

Next, we perform row operations to obtain row-echelon form.

$$-2R_1 + R_2 = R_2 \rightarrow \begin{bmatrix} 1 & -1 & 1 & | & 8 \\ 0 & 5 & -3 & | & -18 \\ 3 & -2 & -9 & | & 9 \end{bmatrix} \qquad -3R_1 + R_3 = R_3 \rightarrow \begin{bmatrix} 1 & -1 & 1 & | & 8 \\ 0 & 5 & -3 & | & -18 \\ 0 & 1 & -12 & | & -15 \end{bmatrix}$$

The easiest way to obtain a 1 in row 2 of column 1 is to interchange R_2 and R_3.

$$\text{Interchange } R_2 \text{ and } R_3 \rightarrow \begin{bmatrix} 1 & -1 & 1 & | & 8 \\ 0 & 1 & -12 & | & -15 \\ 0 & 5 & -3 & | & -18 \end{bmatrix}$$

Then

$$-5R_2 + R_3 = R_3 \rightarrow \begin{bmatrix} 1 & -1 & 1 & | & 8 \\ 0 & 1 & -12 & | & -15 \\ 0 & 0 & 57 & | & 57 \end{bmatrix} \qquad -\frac{1}{57}R_3 = R_3 \rightarrow \begin{bmatrix} 1 & -1 & 1 & | & 8 \\ 0 & 1 & -12 & | & -15 \\ 0 & 0 & 1 & | & 1 \end{bmatrix}$$

The last matrix represents the equivalent system.

$$x - y + z = 8$$
$$y - 12z = -15$$
$$z = 1$$

Using back-substitution, we obtain the solution as $(4, -3, 1)$.

Example 8   Solving a Dependent System of Linear Equations Using Matrices

Solve the following system of linear equations using matrices.

$$-x - 2y + z = -1$$
$$2x + 3y = 2$$
$$y - 2z = 0$$

Solution   Write the augmented matrix.

$$\begin{bmatrix} -1 & -2 & 1 & | & -1 \\ 2 & 3 & 0 & | & 2 \\ 0 & 1 & -2 & | & 0 \end{bmatrix}$$

First, multiply row 1 by -1 to get a 1 in row 1, column 1. Then, perform row operations to obtain row-echelon form.

$$-R_1 \rightarrow \begin{bmatrix} -1 & -2 & 1 & | & -1 \\ 2 & 3 & 0 & | & 2 \\ 0 & 1 & -2 & | & 0 \end{bmatrix}$$

$$R_2 \leftrightarrow R_3 \rightarrow \begin{bmatrix} 1 & 2 & -1 & | & 1 \\ 0 & 1 & -2 & | & 0 \\ 2 & 3 & 0 & | & 2 \end{bmatrix}$$

$$-2R_1 + R_3 = R_3 \rightarrow \begin{bmatrix} 1 & 2 & -1 & | & 1 \\ 0 & 1 & -2 & | & 0 \\ 0 & -1 & 2 & | & 0 \end{bmatrix}$$

$$R_2 + R_3 = R_3 \rightarrow \begin{bmatrix} 1 & 2 & -1 & | & 2 \\ 0 & 1 & -2 & | & 1 \\ 0 & 0 & 0 & | & 0 \end{bmatrix}$$

The last matrix represents the following system.

$$x + 2y - z = 1$$
$$y - 2z = 0$$
$$0 = 0$$

We see by the identity $0 = 0$ that this is a dependent system with an infinite number of solutions. We then find the generic solution. By solving the second equation for y and substituting it into the first equation we can solve for z in terms of x.

$$x + 2y - z = 1$$
$$y = 2z$$
$$x + 2(2z) - z = 1$$
$$x + 3z = 1$$
$$z = \frac{1 - x}{3}$$

Now we substitute the expression for z into the second equation to solve for y in terms of x.

$$y - 2z = 0$$

$$z = \frac{1 - x}{3}$$

$$y - 2\left(\frac{1 - x}{3}\right) = 0$$

$$y = \frac{2 - 2x}{3}$$

The generic solution is $\left(x, \dfrac{2 - 2x}{3}, \dfrac{1 - x}{3}\right)$.

Try It #5

Solve the system using matrices.

$$x + 4y - z = 4$$
$$2x + 5y + 8z = 15$$
$$x + 3y - 3z = 1$$

Q & A...

Can any system of linear equations be solved by Gaussian elimination?

Yes, a system of linear equations of any size can be solved by Gaussian elimination.

How To...

Given a system of equations, solve with matrices using a calculator.

1. Save the augmented matrix as a matrix variable $[A]$, $[B]$, $[C]$, ...
2. Use the **ref(** function in the calculator, calling up each matrix variable as needed.

Example 9   **Solving Systems of Equations with Matrices Using a Calculator**

Solve the system of equations.

$$5x + 3y + 9z = -1$$
$$-2x + 3y - z = -2$$
$$-x - 4y + 5z = 1$$

Solution   Write the augmented matrix for the system of equations.

$$\begin{bmatrix} 5 & 3 & 9 & -1 \\ -2 & 3 & -1 & -2 \\ -1 & -4 & 5 & -1 \end{bmatrix}$$

On the matrix page of the calculator, enter the augmented matrix above as the matrix variable $[A]$.

$$[A] = \begin{bmatrix} 5 & 3 & 9 & -1 \\ -2 & 3 & -1 & -2 \\ -1 & -4 & 5 & 1 \end{bmatrix}$$

Use the **ref(** function in the calculator, calling up the matrix variable $[A]$.

$$\text{ref}([A])$$

Evaluate.

$$\begin{bmatrix} 1 & \frac{3}{5} & \frac{9}{5} & \frac{1}{5} \\ 0 & 1 & \frac{13}{21} & -\frac{4}{7} \\ 0 & 0 & 1 & -\frac{24}{187} \end{bmatrix} \rightarrow \begin{aligned} x + \tfrac{3}{5}y + \tfrac{9}{5}z &= -\tfrac{1}{5} \\ y + \tfrac{13}{21}z &= -\tfrac{4}{7} \\ z &= -\tfrac{24}{187} \end{aligned}$$

Using back-substitution, the solution is $\left(\dfrac{61}{187}, -\dfrac{92}{187}, -\dfrac{24}{187}\right)$.

Example 10   **Applying 2 × 2 Matrices to Finance**

Carolyn invests a total of $12,000 in two municipal bonds, one paying 10.5% interest and the other paying 12% interest. The annual interest earned on the two investments last year was $1,335. How much was invested at each rate?

Solution   We have a system of two equations in two variables. Let $x =$ the amount invested at 10.5% interest, and $y =$ the amount invested at 12% interest.

$$x + y = 12,000$$
$$0.105x + 0.12y = 1,335$$

As a matrix, we have

$$\begin{bmatrix} 1 & 1 & | & 12,000 \\ 0.105 & 0.12 & | & 1,335 \end{bmatrix}$$

Multiply row 1 by -0.105 and add the result to row 2.

$$\begin{bmatrix} 1 & 1 & | & 12,000 \\ 0 & 0.015 & | & 75 \end{bmatrix}$$

Then,

$$0.015y = 75$$
$$y = 5,000$$

So $12,000 - 5,000 = 7,000$.

Thus, $5,000 was invested at 12% interest and $7,000 at 10.5% interest.

Example 11   **Applying 3 × 3 Matrices to Finance**

Ava invests a total of $10,000 in three accounts, one paying 5% interest, another paying 8% interest, and the third paying 9% interest. The annual interest earned on the three investments last year was $770. The amount invested at 9% was twice the amount invested at 5%. How much was invested at each rate?

Solution   We have a system of three equations in three variables. Let x be the amount invested at 5% interest, let y be the amount invested at 8% interest, and let z be the amount invested at 9% interest. Thus,

$$x + y + z = 10,000$$
$$0.05x + 0.08y + 0.09z = 770$$
$$2x - z = 0$$

As a matrix, we have

$$\begin{bmatrix} 1 & 1 & 1 & | & 10,000 \\ 0.05 & 0.08 & 0.09 & | & 770 \\ 2 & 0 & -1 & | & 0 \end{bmatrix}$$

Now, we perform Gaussian elimination to achieve row-echelon form.

$$-0.05R_1 + R_2 = R_2 \rightarrow \begin{bmatrix} 1 & 1 & 1 & | & 10,000 \\ 0 & 0.03 & 0.04 & | & 270 \\ 2 & 0 & -1 & | & 0 \end{bmatrix}$$

$$-2R_1 + R_3 = R_3 \rightarrow \begin{bmatrix} 1 & 1 & 1 & | & 10,000 \\ 0 & 0.03 & 0.04 & | & 270 \\ 0 & -2 & -3 & | & -20,000 \end{bmatrix}$$

$$\frac{1}{0.03}R_2 = R_2 \rightarrow \begin{bmatrix} 0 & 1 & 1 & | & 10,000 \\ 0 & 1 & \frac{4}{3} & | & 9,000 \\ 0 & -2 & -3 & | & -20,000 \end{bmatrix}$$

$$2R_2 + R_3 = R_3 \rightarrow \begin{bmatrix} 1 & 1 & 1 & | & 10,000 \\ 0 & 1 & \frac{4}{3} & | & 9,000 \\ 0 & 0 & -\frac{1}{3} & | & -2,000 \end{bmatrix}$$

The third row tells us $-\frac{1}{3}z = -2,000$; thus $z = 6,000$.

The second row tells us $y + \frac{4}{3}z = 9,000$. Substituting $z = 6,000$, we get

$$y + \frac{4}{3}(6,000) = 9,000$$
$$y + 8,000 = 9,000$$
$$y = 1,000$$

The first row tells us $x + y + z = 10,000$. Substituting $y = 1,000$ and $z = 6,000$, we get

$$x + 1,000 + 6,000 = 10,000$$
$$x = 3,000$$

The answer is $3,000 invested at 5% interest, $1,000 invested at 8%, and $6,000 invested at 9% interest.

Try It #6

A small shoe company took out a loan of $1,500,000 to expand their inventory. Part of the money was borrowed at 7%, part was borrowed at 8%, and part was borrowed at 10%. The amount borrowed at 10% was four times the amount borrowed at 7%, and the annual interest on all three loans was $130,500. Use matrices to find the amount borrowed at each rate.

Access these online resources for additional instruction and practice with solving systems of linear equations using Gaussian elimination.

- Solve a System of Two Equations Using an Augmented Matrix (http://openstaxcollege.org/l/system2augmat)
- Solve a System of Three Equations Using an Augmented Matrix (http://openstaxcollege.org/l/system3augmat)
- Augmented Matrices on the Calculator (http://openstaxcollege.org/l/augmatcalc)

11.6 SECTION EXERCISES

VERBAL

1. Can any system of linear equations be written as an augmented matrix? Explain why or why not. Explain how to write that augmented matrix.

2. Can any matrix be written as a system of linear equations? Explain why or why not. Explain how to write that system of equations.

3. Is there only one correct method of using row operations on a matrix? Try to explain two different row operations possible to solve the augmented matrix
$$\begin{bmatrix} 9 & 3 & | & 0 \\ 1 & -2 & | & 6 \end{bmatrix}.$$

4. Can a matrix whose entry is 0 on the diagonal be solved? Explain why or why not. What would you do to remedy the situation?

5. Can a matrix that has 0 entries for an entire row have one solution? Explain why or why not.

ALGEBRAIC

For the following exercises, write the augmented matrix for the linear system.

6. $8x - 37y = 8$
$2x + 12y = 3$

7. $16y = 4$
$9x - y = 2$

8. $3x + 2y + 10z = 3$
$-6x + 2y + 5z = 13$
$4x + z = 18$

9. $x + 5y + 8z = 19$
$12x + 3y = 4$
$3x + 4y + 9z = -7$

10. $6x + 12y + 16z = 4$
$19x - 5y + 3z = -9$
$x + 2y = -8$

For the following exercises, write the linear system from the augmented matrix.

11. $\begin{bmatrix} -2 & 5 & | & 5 \\ 6 & -18 & | & 26 \end{bmatrix}$

12. $\begin{bmatrix} 3 & 4 & | & 10 \\ 10 & 17 & | & 439 \end{bmatrix}$

13. $\begin{bmatrix} 3 & 2 & 0 & | & 3 \\ -1 & -9 & 4 & | & -1 \\ 8 & 5 & 7 & | & 8 \end{bmatrix}$

14. $\begin{bmatrix} 8 & 29 & 1 & | & 43 \\ -1 & 7 & 5 & | & 38 \\ 0 & 0 & 3 & | & 10 \end{bmatrix}$

15. $\begin{bmatrix} 4 & 5 & -2 & | & 12 \\ 0 & 1 & 58 & | & 2 \\ 8 & 7 & -3 & | & -5 \end{bmatrix}$

For the following exercises, solve the system by Gaussian elimination.

16. $\begin{bmatrix} 1 & 0 & | & 3 \\ 0 & 0 & | & 0 \end{bmatrix}$

17. $\begin{bmatrix} 1 & 0 & | & 1 \\ 1 & 0 & | & 2 \end{bmatrix}$

18. $\begin{bmatrix} 1 & 2 & | & 3 \\ 4 & 5 & | & 6 \end{bmatrix}$

19. $\begin{bmatrix} -1 & 2 & | & -3 \\ 4 & -5 & | & 6 \end{bmatrix}$

20. $\begin{bmatrix} -2 & 0 & | & 1 \\ 0 & 2 & | & -1 \end{bmatrix}$

21. $2x - 3y = -9$
$5x + 4y = 58$

22. $6x + 2y = -4$
$3x + 4y = -17$

23. $2x + 3y = 12$
$4x + y = 14$

24. $-4x - 3y = -2$
$3x - 5y = -13$

25. $-5x + 8y = 3$
$10x + 6y = 5$

26. $3x + 4y = 12$
$-6x - 8y = -24$

27. $-60x + 45y = 12$
$20x - 15y = -4$

28. $11x + 10y = 43$
$15x + 20y = 65$

29. $2x - y = 2$
$3x + 2y = 17$

30. $-1.06x - 2.25y = 5.51$
$-5.03x - 1.08y = 5.40$

31. $\frac{3}{4}x - \frac{3}{5}y = 4$
$\frac{1}{4}x + \frac{2}{3}y = 1$

32. $\frac{1}{4}x - \frac{2}{3}y = -1$
$\frac{1}{2}x + \frac{1}{3}y = 3$

33. $\begin{bmatrix} 1 & 0 & 0 & | & 31 \\ 0 & 1 & 1 & | & 45 \\ 0 & 0 & 1 & | & 87 \end{bmatrix}$

34. $\begin{bmatrix} 1 & 0 & 1 & | & 50 \\ 1 & 1 & 0 & | & 20 \\ 0 & 1 & 1 & | & -90 \end{bmatrix}$

35. $\begin{bmatrix} 1 & 2 & 3 & | & 4 \\ 0 & 5 & 6 & | & 7 \\ 0 & 0 & 8 & | & 9 \end{bmatrix}$

36. $\begin{bmatrix} -0.1 & 0.3 & -0.1 & | & 0.2 \\ -0.4 & 0.2 & 0.1 & | & 0.8 \\ 0.6 & 0.1 & 0.7 & | & -0.8 \end{bmatrix}$

37. $-2x + 3y - 2z = 3$
$4x + 2y - z = 9$
$4x - 8y + 2z = -6$

38. $x + y - 4z = -4$
$5x - 3y - 2z = 0$
$2x + 6y + 7z = 30$

39. $2x + 3y + 2z = 1$
$-4x - 6y - 4z = -2$
$10x + 15y + 10z = 5$

40. $x + 2y - z = 1$
$-x - 2y + 2z = -2$
$3x + 6y - 3z = 5$

41. $x + 2y - z = 1$
$-x - 2y + 2z = -2$
$3x + 6y - 3z = 3$

42. $x + y = 2$
$x + z = 1$
$-y - z = -3$

43. $x + y + z = 100$
$x + 2z = 125$
$-y + 2z = 25$

44. $\frac{1}{4}x - \frac{2}{3}z = -\frac{1}{2}$
$\frac{1}{5}x + \frac{1}{3}y = \frac{4}{7}$
$\frac{1}{5}y - \frac{1}{3}z = \frac{2}{9}$

45. $-\frac{1}{2}x + \frac{1}{2}y + \frac{1}{7}z = -\frac{53}{14}$
$\frac{1}{2}x - \frac{1}{2}y + \frac{1}{4}z = 3$
$\frac{1}{4}x + \frac{1}{5}y + \frac{1}{3}z = \frac{23}{15}$

46. $-\frac{1}{2}x - \frac{1}{3}y + \frac{1}{4}z = -\frac{29}{6}$
$\frac{1}{5}x + \frac{1}{6}y - \frac{1}{7}z = \frac{431}{210}$
$-\frac{1}{8}x + \frac{1}{9}y + \frac{1}{10}z = -\frac{49}{45}$

EXTENSIONS

For the following exercises, use Gaussian elimination to solve the system.

47. $\frac{x-1}{7} + \frac{y-2}{8} + \frac{z-3}{4} = 0$
$x + y + z = 6$
$\frac{x+2}{3} + 2y + \frac{z-3}{3} = 5$

48. $\frac{x-1}{4} - \frac{y+1}{4} + 3z = -1$
$\frac{x+5}{2} + \frac{y+7}{4} - z = 4$
$x + y - \frac{z-2}{2} = 1$

49. $\frac{x-3}{4} - \frac{y-1}{3} + 2z = -1$
$\frac{x+5}{2} + \frac{y+5}{2} + \frac{z+5}{2} = 8$
$x + y + z = 1$

50. $\frac{x-3}{10} + \frac{y+3}{2} - 2z = 3$
$\frac{x+5}{4} - \frac{y-1}{8} + z = \frac{3}{2}$
$\frac{x-1}{4} + \frac{y+4}{2} + 3z = \frac{3}{2}$

51. $\frac{x-3}{4} - \frac{y-1}{3} + 2z = -1$
$\frac{x+5}{2} + \frac{y+5}{2} + \frac{z+5}{2} = 7$
$x + y + z = 1$

REAL-WORLD APPLICATIONS

For the following exercises, set up the augmented matrix that describes the situation, and solve for the desired solution.

52. Every day, a cupcake store sells 5,000 cupcakes in chocolate and vanilla flavors. If the chocolate flavor is 3 times as popular as the vanilla flavor, how many of each cupcake sell per day?

53. At a competing cupcake store, $4,520 worth of cupcakes are sold daily. The chocolate cupcakes cost $2.25 and the red velvet cupcakes cost $1.75. If the total number of cupcakes sold per day is 2,200, how many of each flavor are sold each day?

54. You invested $10,000 into two accounts: one that has simple 3% interest, the other with 2.5% interest. If your total interest payment after one year was $283.50, how much was in each account after the year passed?

55. You invested $2,300 into account 1, and $2,700 into account 2. If the total amount of interest after one year is $254, and account 2 has 1.5 times the interest rate of account 1, what are the interest rates? Assume simple interest rates.

56. Bikes'R'Us manufactures bikes, which sell for $250. It costs the manufacturer $180 per bike, plus a startup fee of $3,500. After how many bikes sold will the manufacturer break even?

57. A major appliance store is considering purchasing vacuums from a small manufacturer. The store would be able to purchase the vacuums for $86 each, with a delivery fee of $9,200, regardless of how many vacuums are sold. If the store needs to start seeing a profit after 230 units are sold, how much should they charge for the vacuums?

58. The three most popular ice cream flavors are chocolate, strawberry, and vanilla, comprising 83% of the flavors sold at an ice cream shop. If vanilla sells 1% more than twice strawberry, and chocolate sells 11% more than vanilla, how much of the total ice cream consumption are the vanilla, chocolate, and strawberry flavors?

59. At an ice cream shop, three flavors are increasing in demand. Last year, banana, pumpkin, and rocky road ice cream made up 12% of total ice cream sales. This year, the same three ice creams made up 16.9% of ice cream sales. The rocky road sales doubled, the banana sales increased by 50%, and the pumpkin sales increased by 20%. If the rocky road ice cream had one less percent of sales than the banana ice cream, find out the percentage of ice cream sales each individual ice cream made last year.

60. A bag of mixed nuts contains cashews, pistachios, and almonds. There are 1,000 total nuts in the bag, and there are 100 less almonds than pistachios. The cashews weigh 3 g, pistachios weigh 4 g, and almonds weigh 5 g. If the bag weighs 3.7 kg, find out how many of each type of nut is in the bag.

61. A bag of mixed nuts contains cashews, pistachios, and almonds. Originally there were 900 nuts in the bag. 30% of the almonds, 20% of the cashews, and 10% of the pistachios were eaten, and now there are 770 nuts left in the bag. Originally, there were 100 more cashews than almonds. Figure out how many of each type of nut was in the bag to begin with.

LEARNING OBJECTIVES

In this section, you will:

- Find the inverse of a matrix.
- Solve a system of linear equations using an inverse matrix.

11.7 SOLVING SYSTEMS WITH INVERSES

Nancy plans to invest $10,500 into two different bonds to spread out her risk. The first bond has an annual return of 10%, and the second bond has an annual return of 6%. In order to receive an 8.5% return from the two bonds, how much should Nancy invest in each bond? What is the best method to solve this problem?

There are several ways we can solve this problem. As we have seen in previous sections, systems of equations and matrices are useful in solving real-world problems involving finance. After studying this section, we will have the tools to solve the bond problem using the inverse of a matrix.

Finding the Inverse of a Matrix

We know that the multiplicative inverse of a real number a is a^{-1}, and $aa^{-1} = a^{-1}a = \left(\frac{1}{a}\right)a = 1$. For example, $2^{-1} = \frac{1}{2}$ and $\left(\frac{1}{2}\right)2 = 1$. The multiplicative inverse of a matrix is similar in concept, except that the product of matrix A and its inverse A^{-1} equals the identity matrix. The identity matrix is a square matrix containing ones down the main diagonal and zeros everywhere else. We identify identity matrices by I_n where n represents the dimension of the matrix. The following equations are the identity matrices for a 2×2 matrix and a 3×3 matrix, respectively.

$$I_2 = \begin{bmatrix} 1 & 0 \\ 0 & 1 \end{bmatrix}$$

$$I_3 = \begin{bmatrix} 1 & 0 & 0 \\ 0 & 1 & 0 \\ 0 & 0 & 1 \end{bmatrix}$$

The identity matrix acts as a 1 in matrix algebra. For example, $AI = IA = A$.

A matrix that has a multiplicative inverse has the properties

$$AA^{-1} = I$$
$$A^{-1}A = I$$

A matrix that has a multiplicative inverse is called an invertible matrix. Only a square matrix may have a multiplicative inverse, as the reversibility, $AA^{-1} = A^{-1}A = I$, is a requirement. Not all square matrices have an inverse, but if A is invertible, then A^{-1} is unique. We will look at two methods for finding the inverse of a 2×2 matrix and a third method that can be used on both 2×2 and 3×3 matrices.

---

the identity matrix and multiplicative inverse

The **identity matrix**, I_n, is a square matrix containing ones down the main diagonal and zeros everywhere else.

$$I_2 = \begin{bmatrix} 1 & 0 \\ 0 & 1 \end{bmatrix} \qquad I_3 = \begin{bmatrix} 1 & 0 & 0 \\ 0 & 1 & 0 \\ 0 & 0 & 1 \end{bmatrix}$$

$$2 \times 2 \qquad\qquad 3 \times 3$$

If A is an $n \times n$ matrix and B is an $n \times n$ matrix such that $AB = BA = I_n$, then $B = A^{-1}$, the **multiplicative inverse of a matrix** A.

Example 1   **Showing That the Identity Matrix Acts as a 1**

Given matrix A, show that $AI = IA = A$.

$$A = \begin{bmatrix} 3 & 4 \\ -2 & 5 \end{bmatrix}$$

Solution   Use matrix multiplication to show that the product of A and the identity is equal to the product of the identity and A.

$$AI = \begin{bmatrix} 3 & 4 \\ -2 & 5 \end{bmatrix} \begin{bmatrix} 1 & 0 \\ 0 & 1 \end{bmatrix} = \begin{bmatrix} 3 \cdot 1 + 4 \cdot 0 & 3 \cdot 0 + 4 \cdot 1 \\ -2 \cdot 1 + 5 \cdot 0 & -2 \cdot 0 + 5 \cdot 1 \end{bmatrix} = \begin{bmatrix} 3 & 4 \\ -2 & 5 \end{bmatrix}$$

$$AI = \begin{bmatrix} 1 & 0 \\ 0 & 1 \end{bmatrix} \begin{bmatrix} 3 & 4 \\ -2 & 5 \end{bmatrix} = \begin{bmatrix} 1 \cdot 3 + 0 \cdot (-2) & 1 \cdot 4 + 0 \cdot 5 \\ 0 \cdot 3 + 1 \cdot (-2) & 0 \cdot 4 + 1 \cdot 5 \end{bmatrix} = \begin{bmatrix} 3 & 4 \\ -2 & 5 \end{bmatrix}$$

How To...

Given two matrices, show that one is the multiplicative inverse of the other.

1. Given matrix A of order $n \times n$ and matrix B of order $n \times n$ multiply AB.
2. If $AB = I$, then find the product BA. If $BA = I$, then $B = A^{-1}$ and $A = B^{-1}$.

Example 2   **Showing That Matrix A Is the Multiplicative Inverse of Matrix B**

Show that the given matrices are multiplicative inverses of each other.

$$A = \begin{bmatrix} 1 & 5 \\ -2 & -9 \end{bmatrix}, B = \begin{bmatrix} -9 & -5 \\ 2 & 1 \end{bmatrix}$$

Solution   Multiply AB and BA. If both products equal the identity, then the two matrices are inverses of each other.

$$AB = \begin{bmatrix} 1 & 5 \\ -2 & -9 \end{bmatrix} \begin{bmatrix} -9 & -5 \\ 2 & 1 \end{bmatrix}$$

$$= \begin{bmatrix} 1(-9) + 5(2) & 1(-5) + 5(1) \\ -2(-9) - 9(2) & -2(-5) - 9(1) \end{bmatrix}$$

$$= \begin{bmatrix} 1 & 0 \\ 0 & 1 \end{bmatrix}$$

$$BA = \begin{bmatrix} -9 & -5 \\ 2 & 1 \end{bmatrix} \begin{bmatrix} 1 & 5 \\ -2 & -9 \end{bmatrix}$$

$$= \begin{bmatrix} -9(1) - 5(-2) & -9(5) - 5(-9) \\ 2(1) + 1(-2) & 2(-5) + 1(-9) \end{bmatrix}$$

$$= \begin{bmatrix} 1 & 0 \\ 0 & 1 \end{bmatrix}$$

A and B are inverses of each other.

Try It #1

Show that the following two matrices are inverses of each other.

$$A = \begin{bmatrix} 1 & 4 \\ -1 & -3 \end{bmatrix}, B = \begin{bmatrix} -3 & -4 \\ 1 & 1 \end{bmatrix}$$

Finding the Multiplicative Inverse Using Matrix Multiplication

We can now determine whether two matrices are inverses, but how would we find the inverse of a given matrix? Since we know that the product of a matrix and its inverse is the identity matrix, we can find the inverse of a matrix by setting up an equation using matrix multiplication.

Example 3   **Finding the Multiplicative Inverse Using Matrix Multiplication**

Use matrix multiplication to find the inverse of the given matrix.

$$A = \begin{bmatrix} 1 & -2 \\ 2 & -3 \end{bmatrix}$$

Solution   For this method, we multiply A by a matrix containing unknown constants and set it equal to the identity.

$$\begin{bmatrix} 1 & -2 \\ 2 & -3 \end{bmatrix} \begin{bmatrix} a & b \\ c & d \end{bmatrix} = \begin{bmatrix} 1 & 0 \\ 0 & 1 \end{bmatrix}$$

Find the product of the two matrices on the left side of the equal sign.

$$\begin{bmatrix} 1 & -2 \\ 2 & -3 \end{bmatrix} \begin{bmatrix} a & b \\ c & d \end{bmatrix} = \begin{bmatrix} 1a - 2c & 1b - 2d \\ 2a - 3c & 2b - 3d \end{bmatrix}$$

Next, set up a system of equations with the entry in row 1, column 1 of the new matrix equal to the first entry of the identity, 1. Set the entry in row 2, column 1 of the new matrix equal to the corresponding entry of the identity, which is 0.

$$\begin{aligned} 1a - 2c &= 1 & R_1 \\ 2a - 3c &= 0 & R_2 \end{aligned}$$

Using row operations, multiply and add as follows: $(-2)R_1 + R_2 \rightarrow R_2$. Add the equations, and solve for c.

$$\begin{aligned} 1a - 2c &= 1 \\ 0 + 1c &= -2 \\ c &= -2 \end{aligned}$$

Back-substitute to solve for a.

$$\begin{aligned} a - 2(-2) &= 1 \\ a + 4 &= 1 \\ a &= -3 \end{aligned}$$

Write another system of equations setting the entry in row 1, column 2 of the new matrix equal to the corresponding entry of the identity, 0. Set the entry in row 2, column 2 equal to the corresponding entry of the identity.

$$\begin{aligned} 1b - 2d &= 0 & R_1 \\ 2b - 3d &= 1 & R_2 \end{aligned}$$

Using row operations, multiply and add as follows: $(-2)R_1 + R_2 = R_2$. Add the two equations and solve for d.

$$\begin{aligned} 1b - 2d &= 0 \\ \underline{0 + 1d = 1} \\ d &= 1 \end{aligned}$$

Once more, back-substitute and solve for b.

$$\begin{aligned} b - 2(1) &= 0 \\ b - 2 &= 0 \\ b &= 2 \end{aligned}$$

$$A^{-1} = \begin{bmatrix} -3 & 2 \\ -2 & 1 \end{bmatrix}$$

Finding the Multiplicative Inverse by Augmenting with the Identity

Another way to find the multiplicative inverse is by augmenting with the identity. When matrix A is transformed into I, the augmented matrix I transforms into A^{-1}.

For example, given

$$A = \begin{bmatrix} 2 & 1 \\ 5 & 3 \end{bmatrix}$$

augment A with the identity

$$\begin{bmatrix} 2 & 1 & | & 1 & 0 \\ 5 & 3 & | & 0 & 1 \end{bmatrix}$$

Perform row operations with the goal of turning A into the identity.

1. Switch row 1 and row 2.

$$\begin{bmatrix} 5 & 3 & | & 0 & 1 \\ 2 & 1 & | & 1 & 0 \end{bmatrix}$$

2. Multiply row 2 by -2 and add to row 1.

$$\begin{bmatrix} 1 & 1 & | & -2 & 1 \\ 2 & 1 & | & 1 & 0 \end{bmatrix}$$

3. Multiply row 1 by -2 and add to row 2.

$$\begin{bmatrix} 1 & 1 & | & -2 & 1 \\ 0 & -1 & | & 5 & -2 \end{bmatrix}$$

4. Add row 2 to row 1.

$$\begin{bmatrix} 1 & 0 & | & 3 & -1 \\ 0 & -1 & | & 5 & -2 \end{bmatrix}$$

5. Multiply row 2 by -1.

$$\begin{bmatrix} 1 & 0 & | & 3 & -1 \\ 0 & 1 & | & -5 & 2 \end{bmatrix}$$

The matrix we have found is A^{-1}.

$$A^{-1} = \begin{bmatrix} 3 & -1 \\ -5 & 2 \end{bmatrix}$$

Finding the Multiplicative Inverse of 2 × 2 Matrices Using a Formula

When we need to find the multiplicative inverse of a 2×2 matrix, we can use a special formula instead of using matrix multiplication or augmenting with the identity.

If A is a 2×2 matrix, such as

$$A = \begin{bmatrix} a & b \\ c & d \end{bmatrix}$$

the multiplicative inverse of A is given by the formula

$$A^{-1} = \frac{1}{ad - bc} \begin{bmatrix} d & -b \\ -c & a \end{bmatrix}$$

where $ad - bc \neq 0$. If $ad - bc = 0$, then A has no inverse.

Example 4   **Using the Formula to Find the Multiplicative Inverse of Matrix A**

Use the formula to find the multiplicative inverse of

$$A = \begin{bmatrix} 1 & -2 \\ 2 & -3 \end{bmatrix}$$

Solution   Using the formula, we have

$$A^{-1} = \frac{1}{(1)(-3) - (-2)(2)} \begin{bmatrix} -3 & 2 \\ -2 & 1 \end{bmatrix}$$

$$= \frac{1}{-3 + 4} \begin{bmatrix} -3 & 2 \\ -2 & 1 \end{bmatrix}$$

$$= \begin{bmatrix} -3 & 2 \\ -2 & 1 \end{bmatrix}$$

Analysis   We can check that our formula works by using one of the other methods to calculate the inverse. Let's augment A with the identity.

$$\begin{bmatrix} 1 & -2 & | & 1 & 0 \\ 2 & -3 & | & 0 & 1 \end{bmatrix}$$

Perform row operations with the goal of turning A into the identity.

1. *Multiply row 1 by −2 and add to row 2.*

$$\left[\begin{array}{cc|cc} 1 & -2 & 1 & 0 \\ 0 & 1 & -2 & 1 \end{array}\right]$$

2. *Multiply row 1 by 2 and add to row 1.*

$$\left[\begin{array}{cc|cc} 1 & 0 & -3 & 2 \\ 0 & 1 & -2 & 1 \end{array}\right]$$

So, we have verified our original solution.

$$A^{-1} = \begin{bmatrix} -3 & 2 \\ -2 & 1 \end{bmatrix}$$

Try It #2

Use the formula to find the inverse of matrix A. Verify your answer by augmenting with the identity matrix.

$$A^{-1} = \begin{bmatrix} 1 & -1 \\ 2 & 3 \end{bmatrix}$$

Example 5   **Finding the Inverse of the Matrix, If It Exists**

Find the inverse, if it exists, of the given matrix.

$$A = \begin{bmatrix} 3 & 6 \\ 1 & 2 \end{bmatrix}$$

Solution   We will use the method of augmenting with the identity.

$$\left[\begin{array}{cc|cc} 3 & 6 & 1 & 0 \\ 1 & 3 & 0 & 1 \end{array}\right]$$

1. Switch row 1 and row 2.

$$\left[\begin{array}{cc|cc} 1 & 3 & 0 & 1 \\ 3 & 6 & 1 & 0 \end{array}\right]$$

2. Multiply row 1 by −3 and add it to row 2.

$$\left[\begin{array}{cc|cc} 1 & 2 & 1 & 0 \\ 0 & 0 & -3 & 1 \end{array}\right]$$

3. There is nothing further we can do. The zeros in row 2 indicate that this matrix has no inverse.

Finding the Multiplicative Inverse of 3 × 3 Matrices

Unfortunately, we do not have a formula similar to the one for a 2 × 2 matrix to find the inverse of a 3 × 3 matrix. Instead, we will augment the original matrix with the identity matrix and use row operations to obtain the inverse.

Given a 3 × 3 matrix

$$A = \begin{bmatrix} 2 & 3 & 1 \\ 3 & 3 & 1 \\ 2 & 4 & 1 \end{bmatrix}$$

augment A with the identity matrix

$$A \,\Big|\, I = \left[\begin{array}{ccc|ccc} 2 & 3 & 1 & 1 & 0 & 0 \\ 3 & 3 & 1 & 0 & 1 & 0 \\ 2 & 4 & 1 & 0 & 0 & 1 \end{array}\right]$$

To begin, we write the augmented matrix with the identity on the right and A on the left. Performing elementary row operations so that the identity matrix appears on the left, we will obtain the inverse matrix on the right. We will find the inverse of this matrix in the next example.

How To…

Given a 3 × 3 matrix, find the inverse

1. Write the original matrix augmented with the identity matrix on the right.
2. Use elementary row operations so that the identity appears on the left.
3. What is obtained on the right is the inverse of the original matrix.
4. Use matrix multiplication to show that $AA^{-1} = I$ and $A^{-1}A = I$.

Example 6   **Finding the Inverse of a 3 × 3 Matrix**

Given the 3×3 matrix A, find the inverse.

$$A = \begin{bmatrix} 2 & 3 & 1 \\ 3 & 3 & 1 \\ 2 & 4 & 1 \end{bmatrix}$$

Solution   Augment A with the identity matrix, and then begin row operations until the identity matrix replaces A. The matrix on the right will be the inverse of A.

$$\left[\begin{array}{ccc|ccc} 2 & 3 & 1 & 1 & 0 & 0 \\ 3 & 3 & 1 & 0 & 1 & 0 \\ 2 & 4 & 1 & 0 & 0 & 1 \end{array}\right] \xrightarrow{\text{Interchange } R_2 \text{ and } R_1} \left[\begin{array}{ccc|ccc} 3 & 3 & 1 & 0 & 1 & 0 \\ 2 & 3 & 1 & 1 & 0 & 0 \\ 2 & 4 & 1 & 0 & 0 & 1 \end{array}\right]$$

$$-R_2 + R_1 = R_1 \rightarrow \left[\begin{array}{ccc|ccc} 1 & 0 & 0 & -1 & 1 & 0 \\ 2 & 3 & 1 & 1 & 0 & 0 \\ 2 & 4 & 1 & 0 & 0 & 1 \end{array}\right]$$

$$-R_2 + R_3 = R_3 \rightarrow \left[\begin{array}{ccc|ccc} 1 & 0 & 0 & -1 & 1 & 0 \\ 2 & 3 & 1 & 1 & 0 & 0 \\ 0 & 1 & 0 & -1 & 0 & 1 \end{array}\right]$$

$$R_3 \leftrightarrow R_2 \rightarrow \left[\begin{array}{ccc|ccc} 1 & 0 & 0 & -1 & 1 & 0 \\ 0 & 1 & 0 & -1 & 0 & 1 \\ 2 & 3 & 1 & 1 & 0 & 0 \end{array}\right]$$

$$-2R_1 + R_3 = R_3 \rightarrow \left[\begin{array}{ccc|ccc} 1 & 0 & 0 & -1 & 1 & 0 \\ 0 & 1 & 0 & -1 & 0 & 1 \\ 0 & 3 & 1 & 3 & -2 & 0 \end{array}\right]$$

$$-3R_2 + R_3 = R_3 \rightarrow \left[\begin{array}{ccc|ccc} 1 & 0 & 0 & -1 & 1 & 0 \\ 0 & 1 & 0 & -1 & 0 & 1 \\ 0 & 0 & 1 & 6 & -2 & -3 \end{array}\right]$$

Thus,

$$A^{-1} = B = \begin{bmatrix} -1 & 1 & 0 \\ -1 & 0 & 1 \\ 6 & -2 & -3 \end{bmatrix}$$

Analysis   To prove that $B = A^{-1}$, let's multiply the two matrices together to see if the product equals the identity, if $AA^{-1} = I$ and $A^{-1}A = I$.

$$AA^{-1} = \begin{bmatrix} 2 & 3 & 1 \\ 3 & 3 & 1 \\ 2 & 4 & 1 \end{bmatrix} \begin{bmatrix} -1 & 1 & 0 \\ -1 & 0 & 1 \\ 6 & -2 & -3 \end{bmatrix}$$

$$= \begin{bmatrix} 2(-1) + 3(-1) + 1(6) & 2(1) + 3(0) + 1(-2) & 2(0) + 3(1) + 1(-3) \\ 3(-1) + 3(-1) + 1(6) & 3(1) + 3(0) + 1(-2) & 3(0) + 3(1) + 1(-3) \\ 2(-1) + 4(-1) + 1(6) & 2(1) + 4(0) + 1(-2) & 2(0) + 4(1) + 1(-3) \end{bmatrix}$$

$$= \begin{bmatrix} 1 & 0 & 0 \\ 0 & 1 & 0 \\ 0 & 0 & 1 \end{bmatrix}$$

$$A^{-1}A = \begin{bmatrix} -1 & 1 & 0 \\ -1 & 0 & 1 \\ 6 & -2 & -3 \end{bmatrix} \begin{bmatrix} 2 & 3 & 1 \\ 3 & 3 & 1 \\ 2 & 4 & 1 \end{bmatrix}$$

$$= \begin{bmatrix} -1(2) + 1(3) + 0(2) & -1(3) + 1(3) + 0(4) & -1(1) + 1(1) + 0(1) \\ -1(2) + 0(3) + 1(2) & -1(3) + 0(3) + 1(4) & -1(1) + 0(1) + 1(1) \\ 6(2) + -2(3) + -3(2) & 6(3) + -2(3) + -3(4) & 6(1) + -2(1) + -3(1) \end{bmatrix}$$

$$= \begin{bmatrix} 1 & 0 & 0 \\ 0 & 1 & 0 \\ 0 & 0 & 1 \end{bmatrix}$$

Try It #3

Find the inverse of the 3×3 matrix.

$$A = \begin{bmatrix} 2 & -17 & 11 \\ -1 & 11 & -7 \\ 0 & 3 & -2 \end{bmatrix}$$

Solving a System of Linear Equations Using the Inverse of a Matrix

Solving a system of linear equations using the inverse of a matrix requires the definition of two new matrices: X is the matrix representing the variables of the system, and B is the matrix representing the constants. Using matrix multiplication, we may define a system of equations with the same number of equations as variables as

$$AX = B$$

To solve a system of linear equations using an inverse matrix, let A be the coefficient matrix, let X be the variable matrix, and let B be the constant matrix. Thus, we want to solve a system $AX = B$. For example, look at the following system of equations.

$$a_1 x + b_1 y = c_1$$
$$a_2 x + b_2 y = c_2$$

From this system, the coefficient matrix is

$$A = \begin{bmatrix} a_1 & b_1 \\ a_2 & b_2 \end{bmatrix}$$

The variable matrix is

$$X = \begin{bmatrix} x \\ y \end{bmatrix}$$

And the constant matrix is

$$B = \begin{bmatrix} c_1 \\ c_2 \end{bmatrix}$$

Then $AX = B$ looks like

$$\begin{bmatrix} a_1 & b_1 \\ a_2 & b_2 \end{bmatrix} \begin{bmatrix} x \\ y \end{bmatrix} = \begin{bmatrix} c_1 \\ c_2 \end{bmatrix}$$

Recall the discussion earlier in this section regarding multiplying a real number by its inverse, $(2^{-1})\,2 = \left(\frac{1}{2}\right)2 = 1$. To solve a single linear equation $ax = b$ for x, we would simply multiply both sides of the equation by the multiplicative inverse (reciprocal) of a. Thus,

$$ax = b$$
$$\left(\frac{1}{a}\right)ax = \left(\frac{1}{a}\right)b$$
$$(a^{-1})ax = (a^{-1})b$$
$$[(a^{-1})a]x = (a^{-1})b$$
$$1x = (a^{-1})b$$
$$x = (a^{-1})b$$

The only difference between a solving a linear equation and a system of equations written in matrix form is that finding the inverse of a matrix is more complicated, and matrix multiplication is a longer process. However, the goal is the same—to isolate the variable.

We will investigate this idea in detail, but it is helpful to begin with a 2×2 system and then move on to a 3×3 system.

solving a system of equations using the inverse of a matrix
Given a system of equations, write the coefficient matrix A, the variable matrix X, and the constant matrix B. Then

$$AX = B$$

Multiply both sides by the inverse of A to obtain the solution.

$$(A^{-1})AX = (A^{-1})B$$
$$[(A^{-1})A]X = (A^{-1})B$$
$$IX = (A^{-1})B$$
$$X = (A^{-1})B$$

Q & A...

If the coefficient matrix does not have an inverse, does that mean the system has no solution?

No, if the coefficient matrix is not invertible, the system could be inconsistent and have no solution, or be dependent and have infinitely many solutions.

Example 7   **Solving a 2 × 2 System Using the Inverse of a Matrix**

Solve the given system of equations using the inverse of a matrix.

$$3x + 8y = 5$$
$$4x + 11y = 7$$

Solution   Write the system in terms of a coefficient matrix, a variable matrix, and a constant matrix.

$$A = \begin{bmatrix} 3 & 8 \\ 4 & 11 \end{bmatrix}, X = \begin{bmatrix} x \\ y \end{bmatrix}, B = \begin{bmatrix} 5 \\ 7 \end{bmatrix}$$

Then

$$\begin{bmatrix} 3 & 8 \\ 4 & 11 \end{bmatrix} \begin{bmatrix} x \\ y \end{bmatrix} = \begin{bmatrix} 5 \\ 7 \end{bmatrix}$$

First, we need to calculate A^{-1}. Using the formula to calculate the inverse of a 2 by 2 matrix, we have:

$$A^{-1} = \frac{1}{ad - bc} \begin{bmatrix} d & -b \\ -c & a \end{bmatrix}$$

$$= \frac{1}{3(11) - 8(4)} \begin{bmatrix} 11 & -8 \\ -4 & 3 \end{bmatrix}$$

$$= \frac{1}{1} \begin{bmatrix} 11 & -8 \\ -4 & 3 \end{bmatrix}$$

So,

$$A^{-1} = \begin{bmatrix} 11 & -8 \\ -4 & 3 \end{bmatrix}$$

Now we are ready to solve. Multiply both sides of the equation by A^{-1}.

$$(A^{-1})AX = (A^{-1})B$$

$$\begin{bmatrix} 11 & -8 \\ -4 & 3 \end{bmatrix} \begin{bmatrix} 3 & 8 \\ 4 & 11 \end{bmatrix} \begin{bmatrix} x \\ y \end{bmatrix} = \begin{bmatrix} 11 & -8 \\ -4 & 3 \end{bmatrix} \begin{bmatrix} 5 \\ 7 \end{bmatrix}$$

$$\begin{bmatrix} 1 & 0 \\ 0 & 1 \end{bmatrix} \begin{bmatrix} x \\ y \end{bmatrix} = \begin{bmatrix} 11(5) + (-8)7 \\ -4(5) + 3(7) \end{bmatrix}$$

$$\begin{bmatrix} x \\ y \end{bmatrix} = \begin{bmatrix} -1 \\ 1 \end{bmatrix}$$

The solution is $(-1, 1)$.

Q & A...
Can we solve for X by finding the product BA^{-1}?

No, recall that matrix multiplication is not commutative, so $A^{-1}B \neq BA^{-1}$. Consider our steps for solving the matrix equation.

$$(A^{-1})AX = (A^{-1})B$$
$$[(A^{-1})A]X = (A^{-1})B$$
$$IX = (A^{-1})B$$
$$X = (A^{-1})B$$

Notice in the first step we multiplied both sides of the equation by A^{-1}, but the A^{-1} was to the left of A on the left side and to the left of B on the right side. Because matrix multiplication is not commutative, order matters.

Example 8   **Solving a 3 × 3 System Using the Inverse of a Matrix**

Solve the following system using the inverse of a matrix.

$$5x + 15y + 56z = 35$$
$$-4x - 11y - 41z = -26$$
$$-x - 3y - 11z = -7$$

Solution   Write the equation $AX = B$.

$$\begin{bmatrix} 5 & 15 & 56 \\ -4 & -11 & -41 \\ -1 & -3 & -11 \end{bmatrix} \begin{bmatrix} x \\ y \\ z \end{bmatrix} = \begin{bmatrix} 35 \\ -26 \\ -7 \end{bmatrix}$$

First, we will find the inverse of A by augmenting with the identity.

$$\left[\begin{array}{ccc|ccc} 5 & 15 & 56 & 1 & 0 & 0 \\ -4 & -11 & -41 & 0 & 1 & 0 \\ -1 & -3 & -11 & 0 & 0 & 1 \end{array}\right]$$

Multiply row 1 by $\frac{1}{5}$.

$$\left[\begin{array}{ccc|ccc} 1 & 3 & \frac{56}{5} & \frac{1}{5} & 0 & 0 \\ -4 & -11 & -41 & 0 & 1 & 0 \\ -1 & -3 & -11 & 0 & 0 & 1 \end{array}\right]$$

Multiply row 1 by 4 and add to row 2.

$$\left[\begin{array}{ccc|ccc} 1 & 3 & \frac{56}{5} & \frac{1}{5} & 0 & 0 \\ 0 & 1 & \frac{19}{5} & \frac{4}{5} & 1 & 0 \\ -1 & -3 & -11 & 0 & 0 & 1 \end{array}\right]$$

Add row 1 to row 3.

$$\left[\begin{array}{ccc|ccc} 1 & 3 & \frac{56}{5} & \frac{1}{5} & 0 & 0 \\ 0 & 1 & \frac{19}{5} & \frac{4}{5} & 1 & 0 \\ 0 & 0 & \frac{1}{5} & \frac{1}{5} & 0 & 1 \end{array}\right]$$

Multiply row 2 by -3 and add to row 1.

$$\left[\begin{array}{ccc|ccc} 1 & 0 & -\frac{1}{5} & -\frac{11}{5} & -3 & 0 \\ 0 & 1 & \frac{19}{5} & \frac{4}{5} & 1 & 0 \\ 0 & 0 & \frac{1}{5} & \frac{1}{5} & 0 & 1 \end{array}\right]$$

Multiply row 3 by 5.

$$\left[\begin{array}{ccc|ccc} 1 & 0 & -\frac{1}{5} & -\frac{11}{5} & -3 & 0 \\ 0 & 1 & \frac{19}{5} & \frac{4}{5} & 1 & 0 \\ 0 & 0 & 1 & 1 & 0 & 5 \end{array}\right]$$

Multiply row 3 by $\frac{1}{5}$ and add to row 1.

$$\left[\begin{array}{ccc|ccc} 1 & 0 & 0 & -2 & -3 & 1 \\ 0 & 1 & \frac{19}{5} & \frac{4}{5} & 1 & 0 \\ 0 & 0 & 1 & 1 & 0 & 5 \end{array}\right]$$

Multiply row 3 by $-\frac{19}{5}$ and add to row 2.

$$\left[\begin{array}{ccc|ccc} 1 & 0 & 0 & -2 & -3 & 1 \\ 0 & 1 & 0 & -3 & 1 & -19 \\ 0 & 0 & 1 & 1 & 0 & 5 \end{array}\right]$$

So,

$$A^{-1} = \left[\begin{array}{ccc} -2 & -3 & 1 \\ -3 & 1 & -19 \\ 1 & 0 & 5 \end{array}\right]$$

Multiply both sides of the equation by A^{-1}. We want $A^{-1}AX = A^{-1}B$:

$$\left[\begin{array}{ccc} -2 & -3 & 1 \\ -3 & 1 & -19 \\ 1 & 0 & 5 \end{array}\right]\left[\begin{array}{ccc} 5 & 15 & 56 \\ -4 & -11 & -41 \\ -1 & -3 & -11 \end{array}\right]\left[\begin{array}{c} x \\ y \\ z \end{array}\right] = \left[\begin{array}{ccc} -2 & -3 & 1 \\ -3 & 1 & -19 \\ 1 & 0 & 5 \end{array}\right]\left[\begin{array}{c} 35 \\ -26 \\ -7 \end{array}\right]$$

Thus,

$$A^{-1}B = \left[\begin{array}{c} -70 + 78 - 7 \\ -105 - 26 + 133 \\ 35 + 0 - 35 \end{array}\right] = \left[\begin{array}{c} 1 \\ 2 \\ 0 \end{array}\right]$$

The solution is (1, 2, 0).

Try It #4

Solve the system using the inverse of the coefficient matrix.

$$2x - 17y + 11z = 0$$
$$-x + 11y - 7z = 8$$
$$3y - 2z = -2$$

How To...

Given a system of equations, solve with matrix inverses using a calculator.

1. Save the coefficient matrix and the constant matrix as matrix variables [A] and [B].
2. Enter the multiplication into the calculator, calling up each matrix variable as needed.
3. If the coefficient matrix is invertible, the calculator will present the solution matrix; if the coefficient matrix is not invertible, the calculator will present an error message.

Example 9   **Using a Calculator to Solve a System of Equations with Matrix Inverses**

Solve the system of equations with matrix inverses using a calculator

$$2x + 3y + z = 32$$
$$3x + 3y + z = -27$$
$$2x + 4y + z = -2$$

Solution   On the matrix page of the calculator, enter the coefficient matrix as the matrix variable [A], and enter the constant matrix as the matrix variable [B].

$$[A] = \left[\begin{array}{ccc} 2 & 3 & 1 \\ 3 & 3 & 1 \\ 2 & 4 & 1 \end{array}\right], \quad [B] = \left[\begin{array}{c} 32 \\ -27 \\ -2 \end{array}\right]$$

On the home screen of the calculator, type in the multiplication to solve for X, calling up each matrix variable as needed.

$$[A]^{-1} \times [B]$$

Evaluate the expression.

$$\begin{bmatrix} -59 \\ -34 \\ 252 \end{bmatrix}$$

Access these online resources for additional instruction and practice with solving systems with inverses.

- The Identity Matrix (http://openstaxcollege.org/l/identmatrix)
- Determining Inverse Matrices (http://openstaxcollege.org/l/inversematrix)
- Using a Matrix Equation to Solve a System of Equations (http://openstaxcollege.org/l/matrixsystem)

11.7   SECTION EXERCISES

VERBAL

1. In a previous section, we showed that matrix multiplication is not commutative, that is, $AB \neq BA$ in most cases. Can you explain why matrix multiplication is commutative for matrix inverses, that is, $A^{-1}A = AA^{-1}$?

2. Does every 2×2 matrix have an inverse? Explain why or why not. Explain what condition is necessary for an inverse to exist.

3. Can you explain whether a 2×2 matrix with an entire row of zeros can have an inverse?

4. Can a matrix with an entire column of zeros have an inverse? Explain why or why not.

5. Can a matrix with zeros on the diagonal have an inverse? If so, find an example. If not, prove why not. For simplicity, assume a 2×2 matrix.

ALGEBRAIC

In the following exercises, show that matrix A is the inverse of matrix B.

6. $A = \begin{bmatrix} 1 & 0 \\ -1 & 1 \end{bmatrix}, B = \begin{bmatrix} 1 & 0 \\ 1 & 1 \end{bmatrix}$

7. $A = \begin{bmatrix} 1 & 2 \\ 3 & 4 \end{bmatrix}, B = \begin{bmatrix} -2 & 1 \\ \frac{3}{2} & -\frac{1}{2} \end{bmatrix}$

8. $A = \begin{bmatrix} 4 & 5 \\ 7 & 0 \end{bmatrix}, B = \begin{bmatrix} 0 & \frac{1}{7} \\ \frac{1}{5} & -\frac{4}{35} \end{bmatrix}$

9. $A = \begin{bmatrix} -2 & \frac{1}{2} \\ 3 & -1 \end{bmatrix}, B = \begin{bmatrix} -2 & -1 \\ -6 & -4 \end{bmatrix}$

10. $A = \begin{bmatrix} 1 & 0 & 1 \\ 0 & 1 & -1 \\ 0 & 1 & 1 \end{bmatrix}, B = \frac{1}{2}\begin{bmatrix} 2 & 1 & -1 \\ 0 & 1 & 1 \\ 0 & -1 & 1 \end{bmatrix}$

11. $A = \begin{bmatrix} 1 & 2 & 3 \\ 4 & 0 & 2 \\ 1 & 6 & 9 \end{bmatrix}, B = \frac{1}{4}\begin{bmatrix} 6 & 0 & -2 \\ 17 & -3 & -5 \\ -12 & 2 & 4 \end{bmatrix}$

12. $A = \begin{bmatrix} 3 & 8 & 2 \\ 1 & 1 & 1 \\ 5 & 6 & 12 \end{bmatrix}, B = \frac{1}{36}\begin{bmatrix} -6 & 84 & -6 \\ 7 & -26 & 1 \\ -1 & -22 & 5 \end{bmatrix}$

For the following exercises, find the multiplicative inverse of each matrix, if it exists.

13. $\begin{bmatrix} 3 & -2 \\ 1 & 9 \end{bmatrix}$

14. $\begin{bmatrix} -2 & 2 \\ 3 & 1 \end{bmatrix}$

15. $\begin{bmatrix} -3 & 7 \\ 9 & 2 \end{bmatrix}$

16. $\begin{bmatrix} -4 & -3 \\ -5 & 8 \end{bmatrix}$

17. $\begin{bmatrix} 1 & 1 \\ 2 & 2 \end{bmatrix}$

18. $\begin{bmatrix} 0 & 1 \\ 1 & 0 \end{bmatrix}$

19. $\begin{bmatrix} 0.5 & 1.5 \\ 1 & -0.5 \end{bmatrix}$

20. $\begin{bmatrix} 1 & 0 & 6 \\ -2 & 1 & 7 \\ 3 & 0 & 2 \end{bmatrix}$

21. $\begin{bmatrix} 0 & 1 & -3 \\ 4 & 1 & 0 \\ 1 & 0 & 5 \end{bmatrix}$

22. $\begin{bmatrix} 1 & 2 & -1 \\ -3 & 4 & 1 \\ -2 & -4 & -5 \end{bmatrix}$

23. $\begin{bmatrix} 1 & 9 & -3 \\ 2 & 5 & 6 \\ 4 & -2 & 7 \end{bmatrix}$

24. $\begin{bmatrix} 1 & -2 & 3 \\ -4 & 8 & -12 \\ 1 & 4 & 2 \end{bmatrix}$

25. $\begin{bmatrix} \frac{1}{2} & \frac{1}{2} & \frac{1}{2} \\ \frac{1}{3} & \frac{1}{4} & \frac{1}{5} \\ \frac{1}{6} & \frac{1}{7} & \frac{1}{8} \end{bmatrix}$

26. $\begin{bmatrix} 1 & 2 & 3 \\ 4 & 5 & 6 \\ 7 & 8 & 9 \end{bmatrix}$

For the following exercises, solve the system using the inverse of a 2 × 2 matrix.

27. $5x - 6y = -61$
$4x + 3y = -2$

28. $8x + 4y = -100$
$3x - 4y = 1$

29. $3x - 2y = 6$
$-x + 5y = -2$

30. $5x - 4y = -5$
$4x + y = 2.3$

31. $-3x - 4y = 9$
$12x + 4y = -6$

32. $-2x + 3y = \dfrac{3}{10}$
$-x + 5y = \dfrac{1}{2}$

33. $\dfrac{8}{5}x - \dfrac{4}{5}y = \dfrac{2}{5}$
$-\dfrac{8}{5}x + \dfrac{1}{5}y = \dfrac{7}{10}$

34. $\dfrac{1}{2}x + \dfrac{1}{5}y = -\dfrac{1}{4}$
$\dfrac{1}{2}x - \dfrac{3}{5}y = -\dfrac{9}{4}$

For the following exercises, solve a system using the inverse of a 3 × 3 matrix.

35. $3x - 2y + 5z = 21$
$5x + 4y = 37$
$x - 2y - 5z = 5$

36. $4x + 4y + 4z = 40$
$2x - 3y + 4z = -12$
$-x + 3y + 4z = 9$

37. $6x - 5y - z = 31$
$-x + 2y + z = -6$
$3x + 3y + 2z = 13$

38. $6x - 5y + 2z = -4$
$2x + 5y - z = 12$
$2x + 5y + z = 12$

39. $4x - 2y + 3z = -12$
$2x + 2y - 9z = 33$
$6y - 4z = 1$

40. $\dfrac{1}{10}x - \dfrac{1}{5}y + 4z = -\dfrac{41}{2}$
$\dfrac{1}{5}x - 20y + \dfrac{2}{5}z = -101$
$\dfrac{3}{10}x + 4y - \dfrac{3}{10}z = 23$

41. $\dfrac{1}{2}x - \dfrac{1}{5}y + \dfrac{1}{5}z = \dfrac{31}{100}$
$-\dfrac{3}{4}x - \dfrac{1}{4}y + \dfrac{1}{2}z = \dfrac{7}{40}$
$-\dfrac{4}{5}x - \dfrac{1}{2}y + \dfrac{3}{2}z = 14$

42. $0.1x + 0.2y + 0.3z = -1.4$
$0.1x - 0.2y + 0.3z = 0.6$
$0.4y + 0.9z = -2$

TECHNOLOGY

For the following exercises, use a calculator to solve the system of equations with matrix inverses.

43. $2x - y = -3$
$-x + 2y = 2.3$

44. $-\dfrac{1}{2}x - \dfrac{3}{2}y = -\dfrac{43}{20}$
$\dfrac{5}{2}x + \dfrac{11}{5}y = \dfrac{31}{4}$

45. $12.3x - 2y - 2.5z = 2$
$36.9x + 7y - 7.5z = -7$
$8y - 5z = -10$

46. $0.5x - 3y + 6z = -0.8$
$0.7x - 2y = -0.06$
$0.5x + 4y + 5z = 0$

EXTENSIONS

For the following exercises, find the inverse of the given matrix.

47. $\begin{bmatrix} 1 & 0 & 1 & 0 \\ 0 & 1 & 0 & 1 \\ 0 & 1 & 1 & 0 \\ 0 & 0 & 1 & 1 \end{bmatrix}$

48. $\begin{bmatrix} -1 & 0 & 2 & 5 \\ 0 & 0 & 0 & 2 \\ 0 & 2 & -1 & 0 \\ 1 & -3 & 0 & 1 \end{bmatrix}$

49. $\begin{bmatrix} 1 & -2 & 3 & 0 \\ 0 & 1 & 0 & 2 \\ 1 & 4 & -2 & 3 \\ -5 & 0 & 1 & 1 \end{bmatrix}$

50. $\begin{bmatrix} 1 & 2 & 0 & 2 & 3 \\ 0 & 2 & 1 & 0 & 0 \\ 0 & 0 & 3 & 0 & 1 \\ 0 & 2 & 0 & 0 & 1 \\ 0 & 0 & 1 & 2 & 0 \end{bmatrix}$

51. $\begin{bmatrix} 1 & 0 & 0 & 0 & 0 & 0 \\ 0 & 1 & 0 & 0 & 0 & 0 \\ 0 & 0 & 1 & 0 & 0 & 0 \\ 0 & 0 & 0 & 1 & 0 & 0 \\ 0 & 0 & 0 & 0 & 1 & 0 \\ 1 & 1 & 1 & 1 & 1 & 1 \end{bmatrix}$

REAL-WORLD APPLICATIONS

For the following exercises, write a system of equations that represents the situation. Then, solve the system using the inverse of a matrix.

52. 2,400 tickets were sold for a basketball game. If the prices for floor 1 and floor 2 were different, and the total amount of money brought in is $64,000, how much was the price of each ticket?

53. In the previous exercise, if you were told there were 400 more tickets sold for floor 2 than floor 1, how much was the price of each ticket?

54. A food drive collected two different types of canned goods, green beans and kidney beans. The total number of collected cans was 350 and the total weight of all donated food was 348 lb, 12 oz. If the green bean cans weigh 2 oz less than the kidney bean cans, how many of each can was donated?

55. Students were asked to bring their favorite fruit to class. 95% of the fruits consisted of banana, apple, and oranges. If oranges were twice as popular as bananas, and apples were 5% less popular than bananas, what are the percentages of each individual fruit?

56. A sorority held a bake sale to raise money and sold brownies and chocolate chip cookies. They priced the brownies at $1 and the chocolate chip cookies at $0.75. They raised $700 and sold 850 items. How many brownies and how many cookies were sold?

57. A clothing store needs to order new inventory. It has three different types of hats for sale: straw hats, beanies, and cowboy hats. The straw hat is priced at $13.99, the beanie at $7.99, and the cowboy hat at $14.49. If 100 hats were sold this past quarter, $1,119 was taken in by sales, and the amount of beanies sold was 10 more than cowboy hats, how many of each should the clothing store order to replace those already sold?

58. Anna, Ashley, and Andrea weigh a combined 370 lb. If Andrea weighs 20 lb more than Ashley, and Anna weighs 1.5 times as much as Ashley, how much does each girl weigh?

59. Three roommates shared a package of 12 ice cream bars, but no one remembers who ate how many. If Tom ate twice as many ice cream bars as Joe, and Albert ate three less than Tom, how many ice cream bars did each roommate eat?

60. A farmer constructed a chicken coop out of chicken wire, wood, and plywood. The chicken wire cost $2 per square foot, the wood $10 per square foot, and the plywood $5 per square foot. The farmer spent a total of $51, and the total amount of materials used was 14 ft^2. He used 3 ft^2 more chicken wire than plywood. How much of each material in did the farmer use?

61. Jay has lemon, orange, and pomegranate trees in his backyard. An orange weighs 8 oz, a lemon 5 oz, and a pomegranate 11 oz. Jay picked 142 pieces of fruit weighing a total of 70 lb, 10 oz. He picked 15.5 times more oranges than pomegranates. How many of each fruit did Jay pick?

LEARNING OBJECTIVES

In this section, you will:
- Evaluate 2×2 determinants.
- Use Cramer's Rule to solve a system of equations in two variables.
- Evaluate 3×3 determinants.
- Use Cramer's Rule to solve a system of three equations in three variables.
- Know the properties of determinants.

11.8 SOLVING SYSTEMS WITH CRAMER'S RULE

We have learned how to solve systems of equations in two variables and three variables, and by multiple methods: substitution, addition, Gaussian elimination, using the inverse of a matrix, and graphing. Some of these methods are easier to apply than others and are more appropriate in certain situations. In this section, we will study two more strategies for solving systems of equations.

Evaluating the Determinant of a 2 × 2 Matrix

A determinant is a real number that can be very useful in mathematics because it has multiple applications, such as calculating area, volume, and other quantities. Here, we will use determinants to reveal whether a matrix is invertible by using the entries of a square matrix to determine whether there is a solution to the system of equations. Perhaps one of the more interesting applications, however, is their use in cryptography. Secure signals or messages are sometimes sent encoded in a matrix. The data can only be decrypted with an invertible matrix and the determinant. For our purposes, we focus on the determinant as an indication of the invertibility of the matrix. Calculating the determinant of a matrix involves following the specific patterns that are outlined in this section.

---

find the determinant of a 2 × 2 matrix
The **determinant** of a 2×2 matrix, given

$$A = \begin{bmatrix} a & b \\ c & d \end{bmatrix}$$

is defined as

$$\det(A) = \begin{vmatrix} a & b \\ c & d \end{vmatrix} = ad - cb$$

Notice the change in notation. There are several ways to indicate the determinant, including $\det(A)$ and replacing the brackets in a matrix with straight lines, $|A|$.

Example 1   **Finding the Determinant of a 2 × 2 Matrix**

Find the determinant of the given matrix.

$$A = \begin{bmatrix} 5 & 2 \\ -6 & 3 \end{bmatrix}$$

Solution

$$\det(A) = \begin{vmatrix} 5 & 2 \\ -6 & 3 \end{vmatrix}$$

$$= 5(3) - (-6)(2)$$

$$= 27$$

Using Cramer's Rule to Solve a System of Two Equations in Two Variables

We will now introduce a final method for solving systems of equations that uses determinants. Known as Cramer's Rule, this technique dates back to the middle of the 18th century and is named for its innovator, the Swiss mathematician Gabriel Cramer (1704-1752), who introduced it in 1750 in *Introduction à l'Analyse des lignes Courbes algébriques*. Cramer's Rule is a viable and efficient method for finding solutions to systems with an arbitrary number of unknowns, provided that we have the same number of equations as unknowns.

Cramer's Rule will give us the unique solution to a system of equations, if it exists. However, if the system has no solution or an infinite number of solutions, this will be indicated by a determinant of zero. To find out if the system is inconsistent or dependent, another method, such as elimination, will have to be used.

To understand Cramer's Rule, let's look closely at how we solve systems of linear equations using basic row operations. Consider a system of two equations in two variables.

$$a_1 x + b_1 y = c_1 \qquad (1)$$
$$a_2 x + b_2 y = c_2 \qquad (2)$$

We eliminate one variable using row operations and solve for the other. Say that we wish to solve for x. If equation (2) is multiplied by the opposite of the coefficient of y in equation (1), equation (1) is multiplied by the coefficient of y in equation (2), and we add the two equations, the variable y will be eliminated.

$$
\begin{array}{ll}
b_2\, a_1 x + b_2\, b_1 y = b_2 c_1 & \text{Multiply } R_1 \text{ by } b_2 \\
\underline{-b_1\, a_2 x - b_1 b_2 y = -b_1 c_2} & \text{Multiply } R_2 \text{ by } -b_1 \\
b_2\, a_1 x - b_1\, a_2 x = b_2 c_1 - b_1 c_2 &
\end{array}
$$

Now, solve for x.

$$b_2\, a_1 x - b_1\, a_2 x = b_2 c_1 - b_1 c_2$$
$$x(b_2\, a_1 - b_1\, a_2) = b_2 c_1 - b_1 c_2$$

$$x = \frac{b_2 c_1 - b_1 c_2}{b_2 a_1 - b_1 a_2} = \frac{\begin{bmatrix} c_1 & b_1 \\ c_2 & b_2 \end{bmatrix}}{\begin{bmatrix} a_1 & b_1 \\ a_2 & b_2 \end{bmatrix}}$$

Similarly, to solve for y, we will eliminate x.

$$
\begin{array}{ll}
a_2 a_1 x + a_2 b_1 y = a_2 c_1 & \text{Multiply } R_1 \text{ by } a_2 \\
\underline{-a_1 a_2 x - a_1 b_2 y = -a_1 c_2} & \text{Multiply } R_2 \text{ by } -a_1 \\
a_2 b_1 y - a_1 b_2 y = a_2 c_1 - a_1 c_2 &
\end{array}
$$

Solving for y gives

$$a_2 b_1 y - a_1 b_2 y = a_2 c_1 - a_1 c_2$$
$$y(a_2 b_1 - a_1 b_2) = a_2 c_1 - a_1 c_2$$

$$y = \frac{a_2 c_1 - a_1 c_2}{a_2 b_1 - a_1 b_2} = \frac{a_1 c_2 - a_2 c_1}{a_1 b_2 - a_2 b_1} = \frac{\begin{bmatrix} a_1 & c_1 \\ a_2 & c_2 \end{bmatrix}}{\begin{bmatrix} a_1 & b_1 \\ a_2 & b_2 \end{bmatrix}}$$

Notice that the denominator for both x and y is the determinant of the coefficient matrix.

We can use these formulas to solve for x and y, but Cramer's Rule also introduces new notation:

- D: determinant of the coefficient matrix
- D_x: determinant of the numerator in the solution of x

$$x = \frac{D_x}{D}$$

- D_y: determinant of the numerator in the solution of y

$$y = \frac{D_y}{D}$$

The key to Cramer's Rule is replacing the variable column of interest with the constant column and calculating the determinants. We can then express x and y as a quotient of two determinants.

Cramer's Rule for 2 × 2 systems

Cramer's Rule is a method that uses determinants to solve systems of equations that have the same number of equations as variables.

Consider a system of two linear equations in two variables.

$$a_1x + b_1y = c_1$$
$$a_2x + b_2y = c_2$$

The solution using Cramer's Rule is given as

$$x = \frac{D_x}{D} = \frac{\begin{bmatrix} c_1 & b_1 \\ c_2 & b_2 \end{bmatrix}}{\begin{bmatrix} a_1 & b_1 \\ a_2 & b_2 \end{bmatrix}}, D \neq 0; y = \frac{D_y}{D} = \frac{\begin{bmatrix} a_1 & c_1 \\ a_2 & c_2 \end{bmatrix}}{\begin{bmatrix} a_1 & b_1 \\ a_2 & b_2 \end{bmatrix}}, D \neq 0.$$

If we are solving for x, the x column is replaced with the constant column. If we are solving for y, the y column is replaced with the constant column.

Example 2   **Using Cramer's Rule to Solve a 2 × 2 System**

Solve the following 2 × 2 system using Cramer's Rule.

$$12x + 3y = 15$$
$$2x - 3y = 13$$

Solution   Solve for x.

$$x = \frac{D_x}{D} = \frac{\begin{vmatrix} 15 & 3 \\ 13 & -3 \end{vmatrix}}{\begin{vmatrix} 12 & 3 \\ 2 & -3 \end{vmatrix}} = \frac{-45 - 39}{-36 - 6} = \frac{-84}{-42} = 2$$

Solve for y.

$$y = \frac{D_y}{D} = \frac{\begin{vmatrix} 12 & 15 \\ 2 & 13 \end{vmatrix}}{\begin{vmatrix} 12 & 3 \\ 2 & -3 \end{vmatrix}} = \frac{156 - 30}{-36 - 6} = -\frac{126}{42} = -3$$

The solution is $(2, -3)$.

Try It #1

Use Cramer's Rule to solve the 2 × 2 system of equations.

$$x + 2y = -11$$
$$-2x + y = -13$$

Evaluating the Determinant of a 3 × 3 Matrix

Finding the determinant of a 2 × 2 matrix is straightforward, but finding the determinant of a 3 × 3 matrix is more complicated. One method is to augment the 3 × 3 matrix with a repetition of the first two columns, giving a 3 × 5 matrix. Then we calculate the sum of the products of entries *down* each of the three diagonals (upper left to lower right), and subtract the products of entries *up* each of the three diagonals (lower left to upper right). This is more easily understood with a visual and an example.

Find the determinant of the 3 × 3 matrix.

$$A = \begin{bmatrix} a_1 & b_1 & c_1 \\ a_2 & b_2 & c_2 \\ a_3 & b_3 & c_3 \end{bmatrix}$$

1. Augment A with the first two columns.

$$\det(A) = \begin{vmatrix} a_1 & b_1 & c_1 & a_1 & b_1 \\ a_2 & b_2 & c_2 & a_2 & b_2 \\ a_3 & b_3 & c_3 & a_3 & b_3 \end{vmatrix}$$

2. From upper left to lower right: Multiply the entries down the first diagonal. Add the result to the product of entries down the second diagonal. Add this result to the product of the entries down the third diagonal.

3. From lower left to upper right: Subtract the product of entries up the first diagonal. From this result subtract the product of entries up the second diagonal. From this result, subtract the product of entries up the third diagonal.

$$\det(A) = \begin{vmatrix} a_1 & b_1 & c_1 & a_1 & b_1 \\ a_2 & b_2 & c_2 & a_2 & b_2 \\ a_3 & b_3 & c_3 & a_3 & b_3 \end{vmatrix}$$

The algebra is as follows:

$$|A| = a_1 b_2 c_3 + b_1 c_2 a_3 + c_1 a_2 b_3 - a_3 b_2 c_1 - b_3 c_2 a_1 - c_3 a_2 b_1$$

Example 3   **Finding the Determinant of a 3 × 3 Matrix**

Find the determinant of the 3 × 3 matrix given

$$A = \begin{bmatrix} 0 & 2 & 1 \\ 3 & -1 & 1 \\ 4 & 0 & 1 \end{bmatrix}$$

Solution   Augment the matrix with the first two columns and then follow the formula. Thus,

$$|A| = \begin{vmatrix} 0 & 2 & 1 & 0 & 2 \\ 3 & -1 & 1 & 3 & -1 \\ 4 & 0 & 1 & 4 & 2 \end{vmatrix}$$

$$= 0(-1)(1) + 2(1)(4) + 1(3)(0) - 4(-1)(1) - 0(1)(0) - 1(3)(2)$$

$$= 0 + 8 + 0 + 4 - 0 - 6$$

$$= 6$$

Try It #2

Find the determinant of the 3 × 3 matrix.

$$\det(A) = \begin{vmatrix} 1 & -3 & 7 \\ 1 & 1 & 1 \\ 1 & -2 & 3 \end{vmatrix}$$

Q & A...

Can we use the same method to find the determinant of a larger matrix?

No, this method only works for 2 × 2 and 3 × 3 matrices. For larger matrices it is best to use a graphing utility or computer software.

Using Cramer's Rule to Solve a System of Three Equations in Three Variables

Now that we can find the determinant of a 3 × 3 matrix, we can apply Cramer's Rule to solve a system of three equations in three variables. Cramer's Rule is straightforward, following a pattern consistent with Cramer's Rule for 2 × 2 matrices. As the order of the matrix increases to 3 × 3, however, there are many more calculations required.

When we calculate the determinant to be zero, Cramer's Rule gives no indication as to whether the system has no solution or an infinite number of solutions. To find out, we have to perform elimination on the system.

Consider a 3×3 system of equations.

$$a_1x + b_1y + c_1z = d_1$$
$$a_2x + b_2y + c_2z = d_2$$
$$a_3x + b_3y + c_3z = d_3$$

$$x = \frac{D_x}{D}, y = \frac{D_y}{D}, z = \frac{D_z}{D}, D \neq 0$$

where

$$D = \begin{vmatrix} a_1 & b_1 & c_1 \\ a_2 & b_2 & c_2 \\ a_3 & b_3 & c_3 \end{vmatrix}, D_x = \begin{vmatrix} d_1 & b_1 & c_1 \\ d_2 & b_2 & c_2 \\ d_3 & b_3 & c_3 \end{vmatrix}, D_y = \begin{vmatrix} a_1 & d_1 & c_1 \\ a_2 & d_2 & c_2 \\ a_3 & d_3 & c_3 \end{vmatrix}, D_z = \begin{vmatrix} a_1 & b_1 & d_1 \\ a_2 & b_2 & d_2 \\ a_3 & b_3 & d_3 \end{vmatrix}$$

If we are writing the determinant D_x, we replace the x column with the constant column. If we are writing the determinant D_y, we replace the y column with the constant column. If we are writing the determinant D_z, we replace the z column with the constant column. Always check the answer.

Example 4   Solving a 3 × 3 System Using Cramer's Rule

Find the solution to the given 3×3 system using Cramer's Rule.

$$x + y - z = 6$$
$$3x - 2y + z = -5$$
$$x + 3y - 2z = 14$$

Solution   Use Cramer's Rule.

$$D = \begin{vmatrix} 1 & 1 & -1 \\ 3 & -2 & 1 \\ 1 & 3 & -2 \end{vmatrix}, D_x = \begin{vmatrix} 6 & 1 & -1 \\ -5 & -2 & 1 \\ 14 & 3 & -2 \end{vmatrix}, D_y = \begin{vmatrix} 1 & 6 & -1 \\ 3 & -5 & 1 \\ 1 & 14 & -2 \end{vmatrix}, D_z = \begin{vmatrix} 1 & 1 & 6 \\ 3 & -2 & -5 \\ 1 & 3 & 14 \end{vmatrix}$$

Then,

$$x = \frac{D_x}{D} = \frac{-3}{-3} = 1$$

$$y = \frac{D_y}{D} = \frac{-9}{-3} = 3$$

$$z = \frac{D_z}{D} = \frac{6}{-3} = -2$$

The solution is $(1, 3, -2)$.

Try It #3

Use Cramer's Rule to solve the 3×3 matrix.

$$x - 3y + 7z = 13$$
$$x + y + z = 1$$
$$x - 2y + 3z = 4$$

Example 5   Using Cramer's Rule to Solve an Inconsistent System

Solve the system of equations using Cramer's Rule.

$$3x - 2y = 4 \quad (1)$$
$$6x - 4y = 0 \quad (2)$$

Solution   We begin by finding the determinants D, D_x, and D_y.

$$D = \begin{vmatrix} 3 & -2 \\ 6 & -4 \end{vmatrix} = 3(-4) - 6(-2) = 0$$

We know that a determinant of zero means that either the system has no solution or it has an infinite number of solutions. To see which one, we use the process of elimination. Our goal is to eliminate one of the variables.

1. Multiply equation (1) by -2.

2. Add the result to equation (2).

$$-6x + 4y = -8$$
$$\underline{6x - 4y = 0}$$
$$0 = -8$$

We obtain the equation $0 = -8$, which is false. Therefore, the system has no solution. Graphing the system reveals two parallel lines. See **Figure 1**.

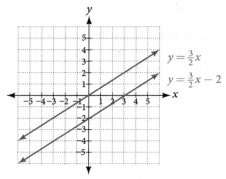

Figure 1

Example 6 Use Cramer's Rule to Solve a Dependent System

Solve the system with an infinite number of solutions.

$$x - 2y + 3z = 0 \qquad (1)$$
$$3x + y - 2z = 0 \qquad (2)$$
$$2x - 4y + 6z = 0 \qquad (3)$$

Solution Let's find the determinant first. Set up a matrix augmented by the first two columns.

$$\begin{vmatrix} 1 & -2 & 3 \\ 3 & 1 & -2 \\ 2 & -4 & 6 \end{vmatrix} \begin{matrix} 1 & -2 \\ 3 & 1 \\ 2 & -4 \end{matrix}$$

Then,

$$1(1)(6) + (-2)(-2)(2) + 3(3)(-4) - 2(1)(3) - (-4)(-2)(1) - 6(3)(-2) = 0$$

As the determinant equals zero, there is either no solution or an infinite number of solutions. We have to perform elimination to find out.

1. Multiply equation (1) by -2 and add the result to equation (3):

$$-2x + 4y - 6x = 0$$
$$\underline{2x - 4y + 6z = 0}$$
$$0 = 0$$

2. Obtaining an answer of $0 = 0$, a statement that is always true, means that the system has an infinite number of solutions. Graphing the system, we can see that two of the planes are the same and they both intersect the third plane on a line. See **Figure 2**.

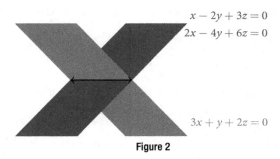

$$x - 2y + 3z = 0$$
$$2x - 4y + 6z = 0$$

$$3x + y + 2z = 0$$

Figure 2

Understanding Properties of Determinants

There are many properties of determinants. Listed here are some properties that may be helpful in calculating the determinant of a matrix.

> ### properties of determinants
> 1. If the matrix is in upper triangular form, the determinant equals the product of entries down the main diagonal.
> 2. When two rows are interchanged, the determinant changes sign.
> 3. If either two rows or two columns are identical, the determinant equals zero.
> 4. If a matrix contains either a row of zeros or a column of zeros, the determinant equals zero.
> 5. The determinant of an inverse matrix A^{-1} is the reciprocal of the determinant of the matrix A.
> 6. If any row or column is multiplied by a constant, the determinant is multiplied by the same factor.

Example 7   **Illustrating Properties of Determinants**

Illustrate each of the properties of determinants.

Solution   Property 1 states that if the matrix is in upper triangular form, the determinant is the product of the entries down the main diagonal.

$$A = \begin{bmatrix} 1 & 2 & 3 \\ 0 & 2 & 1 \\ 0 & 0 & -1 \end{bmatrix}$$

Augment A with the first two columns.

$$A = \begin{bmatrix} 1 & 2 & 3 & 1 & 2 \\ 0 & 2 & 1 & 0 & 2 \\ 0 & 0 & -1 & 0 & 0 \end{bmatrix}$$

Then

$$\det(A) = 1(2)(-1) + 2(1)(0) + 3(0)(0) - 0(2)(3) - 0(1)(1) + 1(0)(2)$$
$$= -2$$

Property 2 states that interchanging rows changes the sign. Given

$$A = \begin{bmatrix} -1 & 5 \\ 4 & -3 \end{bmatrix}, \det(A) = (-1)(-3) - (4)(5) = 3 - 20 = -17$$

$$B = \begin{bmatrix} 4 & -3 \\ -1 & 5 \end{bmatrix}, \det(B) = (4)(5) - (-1)(-3) = 20 - 3 = 17$$

Property 3 states that if two rows or two columns are identical, the determinant equals zero.

$$A = \begin{vmatrix} 1 & 2 & 2 \\ 2 & 2 & 2 \\ -1 & 2 & 2 \end{vmatrix} \begin{matrix} 1 & 2 \\ 2 & 2 \\ -1 & 2 \end{matrix}$$

$$\det(A) = 1(2)(2) + 2(2)(-1) + 2(2)(2) + 1(2)(2) - 2(2)(1) - 2(2)(2)$$

$$= 4 - 4 + 8 + 4 - 4 - 8 = 0$$

Property 4 states that if a row or column equals zero, the determinant equals zero. Thus,

$$A = \begin{bmatrix} 1 & 2 \\ 0 & 0 \end{bmatrix}, \det(A) = 1(0) - 2(0) = 0$$

Property 5 states that the determinant of an inverse matrix A^{-1} is the reciprocal of the determinant A. Thus,

$$A = \begin{bmatrix} 1 & 2 \\ 3 & 4 \end{bmatrix}, \det(A) = 1(4) - 3(2) = -2$$

$$A^{-1} = \begin{bmatrix} -2 & 1 \\ \frac{3}{2} & -\frac{1}{2} \end{bmatrix}, \det(A^{-1}) = -2\left(-\frac{1}{2}\right) - \left(\frac{3}{2}\right)(1) = -\frac{1}{2}$$

Property 6 states that if any row or column of a matrix is multiplied by a constant, the determinant is multiplied by the same factor. Thus,

$$A = \begin{bmatrix} 1 & 2 \\ 3 & 4 \end{bmatrix}, \det(A) = 1(4) - 2(3) = -2$$

$$B = \begin{bmatrix} 2(1) & 2(2) \\ 3 & 4 \end{bmatrix}, \det(B) = 2(4) - 3(4) = -4$$

Example 8   **Using Cramer's Rule and Determinant Properties to Solve a System**

Find the solution to the given 3×3 system.

$$2x + 4y + 4z = 2 \qquad (1)$$
$$3x + 7y + 7z = -5 \qquad (2)$$
$$x + 2y + 2z = 4 \qquad (3)$$

Solution   Using Cramer's Rule, we have

$$D = \begin{vmatrix} 2 & 4 & 4 \\ 3 & 7 & 7 \\ 1 & 2 & 2 \end{vmatrix}$$

Notice that the second and third columns are identical. According to Property 3, the determinant will be zero, so there is either no solution or an infinite number of solutions. We have to perform elimination to find out.

1. Multiply equation (3) by –2 and add the result to equation (1).

$$-2x - 4y - 4x = -8$$
$$\underline{2x + 4y + 4z = 2}$$
$$0 = -6$$

Obtaining a statement that is a contradiction means that the system has no solution.

Access these online resources for additional instruction and practice with Cramer's Rule.

- Solve a System of Two Equations Using Cramer's Rule (http://openstaxcollege.org/l/system2cramer)
- Solve a Systems of Three Equations using Cramer's Rule (http://openstaxcollege.org/l/system3cramer)

11.8 SECTION EXERCISES

VERBAL

1. Explain why we can always evaluate the determinant of a square matrix.

2. Examining Cramer's Rule, explain why there is no unique solution to the system when the determinant of your matrix is 0. For simplicity, use a 2×2 matrix.

3. Explain what it means in terms of an inverse for a matrix to have a 0 determinant.

4. The determinant of 2×2 matrix A is 3. If you switch the rows and multiply the first row by 6 and the second row by 2, explain how to find the determinant and provide the answer.

ALGEBRAIC

For the following exercises, find the determinant.

5. $\begin{vmatrix} 1 & 2 \\ 3 & 4 \end{vmatrix}$

6. $\begin{vmatrix} -1 & 2 \\ 3 & -4 \end{vmatrix}$

7. $\begin{vmatrix} 2 & -5 \\ -1 & 6 \end{vmatrix}$

8. $\begin{vmatrix} -8 & 4 \\ -1 & 5 \end{vmatrix}$

9. $\begin{vmatrix} 1 & 0 \\ 3 & -4 \end{vmatrix}$

10. $\begin{vmatrix} 10 & 20 \\ 0 & -10 \end{vmatrix}$

11. $\begin{vmatrix} 10 & 0.2 \\ 5 & 0.1 \end{vmatrix}$

12. $\begin{vmatrix} 6 & -3 \\ 8 & 4 \end{vmatrix}$

13. $\begin{vmatrix} -2 & -3 \\ 3.1 & 4{,}000 \end{vmatrix}$

14. $\begin{vmatrix} -1.1 & 0.6 \\ 7.2 & -0.5 \end{vmatrix}$

15. $\begin{vmatrix} -1 & 0 & 0 \\ 0 & 1 & 0 \\ 0 & 0 & -3 \end{vmatrix}$

16. $\begin{vmatrix} -1 & 4 & 0 \\ 0 & 2 & 3 \\ 0 & 0 & -3 \end{vmatrix}$

17. $\begin{vmatrix} 1 & 0 & 1 \\ 0 & 1 & 0 \\ 1 & 0 & 0 \end{vmatrix}$

18. $\begin{vmatrix} 2 & -3 & 1 \\ 3 & -4 & 1 \\ -5 & 6 & 1 \end{vmatrix}$

19. $\begin{vmatrix} -2 & 1 & 4 \\ -4 & 2 & -8 \\ 2 & -8 & -3 \end{vmatrix}$

20. $\begin{vmatrix} 6 & -1 & 2 \\ -4 & -3 & 5 \\ 1 & 9 & -1 \end{vmatrix}$

21. $\begin{vmatrix} 5 & 1 & -1 \\ 2 & 3 & 1 \\ 3 & -6 & -3 \end{vmatrix}$

22. $\begin{vmatrix} 1.1 & 2 & -1 \\ -4 & 0 & 0 \\ 4.1 & -0.4 & 2.5 \end{vmatrix}$

23. $\begin{vmatrix} 2 & -1.6 & 3.1 \\ 1.1 & 3 & -8 \\ -9.3 & 0 & 2 \end{vmatrix}$

24. $\begin{vmatrix} -\frac{1}{2} & \frac{1}{3} & \frac{1}{4} \\ \frac{1}{5} & -\frac{1}{6} & \frac{1}{7} \\ 0 & 0 & \frac{1}{8} \end{vmatrix}$

For the following exercises, solve the system of linear equations using Cramer's Rule.

25. $2x - 3y = -1$
$4x + 5y = 9$

26. $5x - 4y = 2$
$-4x + 7y = 6$

27. $6x - 3y = 2$
$-8x + 9y = -1$

28. $2x + 6y = 12$
$5x - 2y = 13$

29. $4x + 3y = 23$
$2x - y = -1$

30. $10x - 6y = 2$
$-5x + 8y = -1$

31. $4x - 3y = -3$
$2x + 6y = -4$

32. $4x - 5y = 7$
$-3x + 9y = 0$

33. $4x + 10y = 180$
$-3x - 5y = -105$

34. $8x - 2y = -3$
$-4x + 6y = 4$

For the following exercises, solve the system of linear equations using Cramer's Rule.

35. $x + 2y - 4z = -1$
$7x + 3y + 5z = 26$
$-2x - 6y + 7z = -6$

36. $-5x + 2y - 4z = -47$
$4x - 3y - z = -94$
$3x - 3y + 2z = 94$

37. $4x + 5y - z = -7$
$-2x - 9y + 2z = 8$
$5y + 7z = 21$

38. $4x - 3y + 4z = 10$
$5x - 2z = -2$
$3x + 2y - 5z = -9$

39. $4x - 2y + 3z = 6$
$-6x + y = -2$
$2x + 7y + 8z = 24$

40. $5x + 2y - z = 1$
$-7x - 8y + 3z = 1.5$
$6x - 12y + z = 7$

41. $13x - 17y + 16z = 73$
$-11x + 15y + 17z = 61$
$46x + 10y - 30z = -18$

42. $-4x - 3y - 8z = -7$
$2x - 9y + 5z = 0.5$
$5x - 6y - 5z = -2$

43.
$$4x - 6y + 8z = 10$$
$$-2x + 3y - 4z = -5$$
$$x + y + z = 1$$

44.
$$4x - 6y + 8z = 10$$
$$-2x + 3y - 4z = -5$$
$$12x + 18y - 24z = -30$$

TECHNOLOGY

For the following exercises, use the determinant function on a graphing utility.

45.
$$\begin{vmatrix} 1 & 0 & 8 & 9 \\ 0 & 2 & 1 & 0 \\ 1 & 0 & 3 & 0 \\ 0 & 2 & 4 & 3 \end{vmatrix}$$

46.
$$\begin{vmatrix} 1 & 0 & 2 & 1 \\ 0 & -9 & 1 & 3 \\ 3 & 0 & -2 & -1 \\ 0 & 1 & 1 & -2 \end{vmatrix}$$

47.
$$\begin{vmatrix} \frac{1}{2} & 1 & 7 & 4 \\ 0 & \frac{1}{2} & 100 & 5 \\ 0 & 0 & 2 & 2{,}000 \\ 0 & 0 & 0 & 2 \end{vmatrix}$$

48.
$$\begin{vmatrix} 1 & 0 & 0 & 0 \\ 2 & 3 & 0 & 0 \\ 4 & 5 & 6 & 0 \\ 7 & 8 & 9 & 0 \end{vmatrix}$$

REAL-WORLD APPLICATIONS

For the following exercises, create a system of linear equations to describe the behavior. Then, calculate the determinant. Will there be a unique solution? If so, find the unique solution.

49. Two numbers add up to 56. One number is 20 less than the other.

50. Two numbers add up to 104. If you add two times the first number plus two times the second number, your total is 208

51. Three numbers add up to 106. The first number is 3 less than the second number. The third number is 4 more than the first number.

52. Three numbers add to 216. The sum of the first two numbers is 112. The third number is 8 less than the first two numbers combined.

For the following exercises, create a system of linear equations to describe the behavior. Then, solve the system for all solutions using Cramer's Rule.

53. You invest $10,000 into two accounts, which receive 8% interest and 5% interest. At the end of a year, you had $10,710 in your combined accounts. How much was invested in each account?

54. You invest $80,000 into two accounts, $22,000 in one account, and $58,000 in the other account. At the end of one year, assuming simple interest, you have earned $2,470 in interest. The second account receives half a percent less than twice the interest on the first account. What are the interest rates for your accounts?

55. A movie theater needs to know how many adult tickets and children tickets were sold out of the 1,200 total tickets. If children's tickets are $5.95, adult tickets are $11.15, and the total amount of revenue was $12,756, how many children's tickets and adult tickets were sold?

56. A concert venue sells single tickets for $40 each and couple's tickets for $65. If the total revenue was $18,090 and the 321 tickets were sold, how many single tickets and how many couple's tickets were sold?

57. You decide to paint your kitchen green. You create the color of paint by mixing yellow and blue paints. You cannot remember how many gallons of each color went into your mix, but you know there were 10 gal total. Additionally, you kept your receipt, and know the total amount spent was $29.50. If each gallon of yellow costs $2.59, and each gallon of blue costs $3.19, how many gallons of each color go into your green mix?

58. You sold two types of scarves at a farmers' market and would like to know which one was more popular. The total number of scarves sold was 56, the yellow scarf cost $10, and the purple scarf cost $11. If you had total revenue of $583, how many yellow scarves and how many purple scarves were sold?

59. Your garden produced two types of tomatoes, one green and one red. The red weigh 10 oz, and the green weigh 4 oz. You have 30 tomatoes, and a total weight of 13 lb, 14 oz. How many of each type of tomato do you have?

60. At a market, the three most popular vegetables make up 53% of vegetable sales. Corn has 4% higher sales than broccoli, which has 5% more sales than onions. What percentage does each vegetable have in the market share?

61. At the same market, the three most popular fruits make up 37% of the total fruit sold. Strawberries sell twice as much as oranges, and kiwis sell one more percentage point than oranges. For each fruit, find the percentage of total fruit sold.

62. Three bands performed at a concert venue. The first band charged $15 per ticket, the second band charged $45 per ticket, and the final band charged $22 per ticket. There were 510 tickets sold, for a total of $12,700. If the first band had 40 more audience members than the second band, how many tickets were sold for each band?

63. A movie theatre sold tickets to three movies. The tickets to the first movie were $5, the tickets to the second movie were $11, and the third movie was $12. 100 tickets were sold to the first movie. The total number of tickets sold was 642, for a total revenue of $6,774. How many tickets for each movie were sold?

64. Men aged 20–29, 30–39, and 40–49 made up 78% of the population at a prison last year. This year, the same age groups made up 82.08% of the population. The 20–29 age group increased by 20%, the 30–39 age group increased by 2%, and the 40–49 age group decreased to $\frac{3}{4}$ of their previous population. Originally, the 30–39 age group had 2% more prisoners than the 20–29 age group. Determine the prison population percentage for each age group last year.

65. At a women's prison down the road, the total number of inmates aged 20–49 totaled 5,525. This year, the 20–29 age group increased by 10%, the 30–39 age group decreased by 20%, and the 40–49 age group doubled. There are now 6,040 prisoners. Originally, there were 500 more in the 30–39 age group than the 20–29 age group. Determine the prison population for each age group last year.

For the following exercises, use this scenario: A health-conscious company decides to make a trail mix out of almonds, dried cranberries, and chocolate-covered cashews. The nutritional information for these items is shown in **Table 1**.

	Fat (g)	Protein (g)	Carbohydrates (g)
Almonds (10)	6	2	3
Cranberries (10)	0.02	0	8
Cashews (10)	7	3.5	5.5

Table 1

66. For the special "low-carb" trail mix, there are 1,000 pieces of mix. The total number of carbohydrates is 425 g, and the total amount of fat is 570.2 g. If there are 200 more pieces of cashews than cranberries, how many of each item is in the trail mix?

67. For the "hiking" mix, there are 1,000 pieces in the mix, containing 390.8 g of fat, and 165 g of protein. If there is the same amount of almonds as cashews, how many of each item is in the trail mix?

68. For the "energy-booster" mix, there are 1,000 pieces in the mix, containing 145 g of protein and 625 g of carbohydrates. If the number of almonds and cashews summed together is equivalent to the amount of cranberries, how many of each item is in the trail mix?

CHAPTER 11 REVIEW

Key Terms

addition method an algebraic technique used to solve systems of linear equations in which the equations are added in a way that eliminates one variable, allowing the resulting equation to be solved for the remaining variable; substitution is then used to solve for the first variable

augmented matrix a coefficient matrix adjoined with the constant column separated by a vertical line within the matrix brackets

break-even point the point at which a cost function intersects a revenue function; where profit is zero

coefficient matrix a matrix that contains only the coefficients from a system of equations

column a set of numbers aligned vertically in a matrix

consistent system a system for which there is a single solution to all equations in the system and it is an independent system, or if there are an infinite number of solutions and it is a dependent system

cost function the function used to calculate the costs of doing business; it usually has two parts, fixed costs and variable costs

Cramer's Rule a method for solving systems of equations that have the same number of equations as variables using determinants

dependent system a system of linear equations in which the two equations represent the same line; there are an infinite number of solutions to a dependent system

determinant a number calculated using the entries of a square matrix that determines such information as whether there is a solution to a system of equations

entry an element, coefficient, or constant in a matrix

feasible region the solution to a system of nonlinear inequalities that is the region of the graph where the shaded regions of each inequality intersect

Gaussian elimination using elementary row operations to obtain a matrix in row-echelon form

identity matrix a square matrix containing ones down the main diagonal and zeros everywhere else; it acts as a 1 in matrix algebra

inconsistent system a system of linear equations with no common solution because they represent parallel lines, which have no point or line in common

independent system a system of linear equations with exactly one solution pair (x, y)

main diagonal entries from the upper left corner diagonally to the lower right corner of a square matrix

matrix a rectangular array of numbers

multiplicative inverse of a matrix a matrix that, when multiplied by the original, equals the identity matrix

nonlinear inequality an inequality containing a nonlinear expression

partial fraction decomposition the process of returning a simplified rational expression to its original form, a sum or difference of simpler rational expressions

partial fractions the individual fractions that make up the sum or difference of a rational expression before combining them into a simplified rational expression

profit function the profit function is written as $P(x) = R(x) - C(x)$, revenue minus cost

revenue function the function that is used to calculate revenue, simply written as $R = xp$, where $x =$ quantity and $p =$ price

row a set of numbers aligned horizontally in a matrix

row operations adding one row to another row, multiplying a row by a constant, interchanging rows, and so on, with the goal of achieving row-echelon form

row-echelon form after performing row operations, the matrix form that contains ones down the main diagonal and zeros at every space below the diagonal

row-equivalent two matrices A and B are row-equivalent if one can be obtained from the other by performing basic row operations

scalar multiple an entry of a matrix that has been multiplied by a scalar

solution set the set of all ordered pairs or triples that satisfy all equations in a system of equations

substitution method an algebraic technique used to solve systems of linear equations in which one of the two equations is solved for one variable and then substituted into the second equation to solve for the second variable

system of linear equations a set of two or more equations in two or more variables that must be considered simultaneously.

system of nonlinear equations a system of equations containing at least one equation that is of degree larger than one

system of nonlinear inequalities a system of two or more inequalities in two or more variables containing at least one inequality that is not linear

Key Equations

Identity matrix for a 2×2 matrix

$$I_2 = \begin{bmatrix} 1 & 0 \\ 0 & 1 \end{bmatrix}$$

Identity matrix for a 3×3 matrix

$$I_3 = \begin{bmatrix} 1 & 0 & 0 \\ 0 & 1 & 0 \\ 0 & 0 & 1 \end{bmatrix}$$

Multiplicative inverse of a 2×2 matrix

$$A^{-1} = \frac{1}{ad - bc} \begin{bmatrix} d & -b \\ -c & a \end{bmatrix}, \text{ where } ad - bc \neq 0$$

Key Concepts

11.1 Systems of Linear Equations: Two Variables

- A system of linear equations consists of two or more equations made up of two or more variables such that all equations in the system are considered simultaneously.
- The solution to a system of linear equations in two variables is any ordered pair that satisfies each equation independently. See **Example 1**.
- Systems of equations are classified as independent with one solution, dependent with an infinite number of solutions, or inconsistent with no solution.
- One method of solving a system of linear equations in two variables is by graphing. In this method, we graph the equations on the same set of axes. See **Example 2**.
- Another method of solving a system of linear equations is by substitution. In this method, we solve for one variable in one equation and substitute the result into the second equation. See **Example 3**.
- A third method of solving a system of linear equations is by addition, in which we can eliminate a variable by adding opposite coefficients of corresponding variables. See **Example 4**.
- It is often necessary to multiply one or both equations by a constant to facilitate elimination of a variable when adding the two equations together. See **Example 5**, **Example 6**, and **Example 7**.
- Either method of solving a system of equations results in a false statement for inconsistent systems because they are made up of parallel lines that never intersect. See **Example 8**.
- The solution to a system of dependent equations will always be true because both equations describe the same line. See **Example 9**.
- Systems of equations can be used to solve real-world problems that involve more than one variable, such as those relating to revenue, cost, and profit. See **Example 10** and **Example 11**.

11.2 Systems of Linear Equations: Three Variables

- A solution set is an ordered triple $\{(x, y, z)\}$ that represents the intersection of three planes in space. See **Example 1**.
- A system of three equations in three variables can be solved by using a series of steps that forces a variable to be eliminated. The steps include interchanging the order of equations, multiplying both sides of an equation by a nonzero constant, and adding a nonzero multiple of one equation to another equation. See **Example 2**.
- Systems of three equations in three variables are useful for solving many different types of real-world problems. See **Example 3**.
- A system of equations in three variables is inconsistent if no solution exists. After performing elimination operations, the result is a contradiction. See **Example 4**.
- Systems of equations in three variables that are inconsistent could result from three parallel planes, two parallel planes and one intersecting plane, or three planes that intersect the other two but not at the same location.

- A system of equations in three variables is dependent if it has an infinite number of solutions. After performing elimination operations, the result is an identity. See **Example 5**.

- Systems of equations in three variables that are dependent could result from three identical planes, three planes intersecting at a line, or two identical planes that intersect the third on a line.

11.3 Systems of Nonlinear Equations and Inequalities: Two Variables

- There are three possible types of solutions to a system of equations representing a line and a parabola: (1) no solution, the line does not intersect the parabola; (2) one solution, the line is tangent to the parabola; and (3) two solutions, the line intersects the parabola in two points. See **Example 1**.

- There are three possible types of solutions to a system of equations representing a circle and a line: (1) no solution, the line does not intersect the circle; (2) one solution, the line is tangent to the parabola; (3) two solutions, the line intersects the circle in two points. See **Example 2**.

- There are five possible types of solutions to the system of nonlinear equations representing an ellipse and a circle: (1) no solution, the circle and the ellipse do not intersect; (2) one solution, the circle and the ellipse are tangent to each other; (3) two solutions, the circle and the ellipse intersect in two points; (4) three solutions, the circle and ellipse intersect in three places; (5) four solutions, the circle and the ellipse intersect in four points. See **Example 3**.

- An inequality is graphed in much the same way as an equation, except for $>$ or $<$, we draw a dashed line and shade the region containing the solution set. See **Example 4**.

- Inequalities are solved the same way as equalities, but solutions to systems of inequalities must satisfy both inequalities. See **Example 5**.

11.4 Partial Fractions

- Decompose $\dfrac{P(x)}{Q(x)}$ by writing the partial fractions as $\dfrac{A}{a_1 x + b_1} + \dfrac{B}{a_2 x + b_2}$. Solve by clearing the fractions, expanding the right side, collecting like terms, and setting corresponding coefficients equal to each other, then setting up and solving a system of equations. See **Example 1**.

- The decomposition of $\dfrac{P(x)}{Q(x)}$ with repeated linear factors must account for the factors of the denominator in increasing powers. See **Example 2**.

- The decomposition of $\dfrac{P(x)}{Q(x)}$ with a nonrepeated irreducible quadratic factor needs a linear numerator over the quadratic factor, as in $\dfrac{A}{x} + \dfrac{Bx + C}{(ax^2 + bx + c)}$. See **Example 3**.

- In the decomposition of $\dfrac{P(x)}{Q(x)}$, where $Q(x)$ has a repeated irreducible quadratic factor, when the irreducible quadratic factors are repeated, powers of the denominator factors must be represented in increasing powers as

$$\frac{Ax + B}{(ax^2 + bx + c)} + \frac{A_2 x + B_2}{(ax^2 + bx + c)^2} + \ldots + \frac{A_n x + B_n}{(ax^2 + bx + c)^n}.$$ See **Example 4**.

11.5 Matrices and Matrix Operations

- A matrix is a rectangular array of numbers. Entries are arranged in rows and columns.

- The dimensions of a matrix refer to the number of rows and the number of columns. A 3×2 matrix has three rows and two columns. See **Example 1**.

- We add and subtract matrices of equal dimensions by adding and subtracting corresponding entries of each matrix. See **Example 2**, **Example 3**, **Example 4**, and **Example 5**.

- Scalar multiplication involves multiplying each entry in a matrix by a constant. See **Example 6**.

- Scalar multiplication is often required before addition or subtraction can occur. See **Example 7**.

- Multiplying matrices is possible when inner dimensions are the same—the number of columns in the first matrix must match the number of rows in the second.

- The product of two matrices, A and B, is obtained by multiplying each entry in row 1 of A by each entry in column 1 of B; then multiply each entry of row 1 of A by each entry in columns 2 of B, and so on. See **Example 8** and **Example 9**.

- Many real-world problems can often be solved using matrices. See **Example 10**.
- We can use a calculator to perform matrix operations after saving each matrix as a matrix variable. See **Example 11**.

11.6 Solving Systems with Gaussian Elimination

- An augmented matrix is one that contains the coefficients and constants of a system of equations. See **Example 1**.
- A matrix augmented with the constant column can be represented as the original system of equations. See **Example 2**.
- Row operations include multiplying a row by a constant, adding one row to another row, and interchanging rows.
- We can use Gaussian elimination to solve a system of equations. See **Example 3**, **Example 4**, and **Example 5**.
- Row operations are performed on matrices to obtain row-echelon form. See **Example 6**.
- To solve a system of equations, write it in augmented matrix form. Perform row operations to obtain row-echelon form. Back-substitute to find the solutions. See **Example 7** and **Example 8**.
- A calculator can be used to solve systems of equations using matrices. See **Example 9**.
- Many real-world problems can be solved using augmented matrices. See **Example 10** and **Example 11**.

11.7 Solving Systems with Inverses

- An identity matrix has the property $AI = IA = A$. See **Example 1**.
- An invertible matrix has the property $AA^{-1} = A^{-1}A = I$. See **Example 2**.
- Use matrix multiplication and the identity to find the inverse of a 2×2 matrix. See **Example 3**.
- The multiplicative inverse can be found using a formula. See **Example 4**.
- Another method of finding the inverse is by augmenting with the identity. See **Example 5**.
- We can augment a 3×3 matrix with the identity on the right and use row operations to turn the original matrix into the identity, and the matrix on the right becomes the inverse. See **Example 6**.
- Write the system of equations as $AX = B$, and multiply both sides by the inverse of A: $A^{-1}AX = A^{-1}B$. See **Example 7** and **Example 8**.
- We can also use a calculator to solve a system of equations with matrix inverses. See **Example 9**.

11.8 Solving Systems with Cramer's Rule

- The determinant for $\begin{bmatrix} a & b \\ c & d \end{bmatrix}$ is $ad - bc$. See **Example 1**.
- Cramer's Rule replaces a variable column with the constant column. Solutions are $x = \dfrac{D_x}{D}, y = \dfrac{D_y}{D}$. See **Example 2**.
- To find the determinant of a 3×3 matrix, augment with the first two columns. Add the three diagonal entries (upper left to lower right) and subtract the three diagonal entries (lower left to upper right). See **Example 3**.
- To solve a system of three equations in three variables using Cramer's Rule, replace a variable column with the constant column for each desired solution: $x = \dfrac{D_x}{D}, y = \dfrac{D_y}{D}, z = \dfrac{D_z}{D}$. See **Example 4**.
- Cramer's Rule is also useful for finding the solution of a system of equations with no solution or infinite solutions. See **Example 5** and **Example 6**.
- Certain properties of determinants are useful for solving problems. For example:
  - If the matrix is in upper triangular form, the determinant equals the product of entries down the main diagonal.
  - When two rows are interchanged, the determinant changes sign.
  - If either two rows or two columns are identical, the determinant equals zero.
  - If a matrix contains either a row of zeros or a column of zeros, the determinant equals zero.
  - The determinant of an inverse matrix A^{-1} is the reciprocal of the determinant of the matrix A.
  - If any row or column is multiplied by a constant, the determinant is multiplied by the same factor. See **Example 7** and **Example 8**.

CHAPTER 11 REVIEW EXERCISES

SYSTEMS OF LINEAR EQUATIONS: TWO VARIABLES

For the following exercises, determine whether the ordered pair is a solution to the system of equations.

1. $3x - y = 4$
$x + 4y = -3$ and $(-1, 1)$

2. $6x - 2y = 24$
$-3x + 3y = 18$ and $(9, 15)$

For the following exercises, use substitution to solve the system of equations.

3. $10x + 5y = -5$
$3x - 2y = -12$

4. $\frac{4}{7}x + \frac{1}{5}y = \frac{43}{70}$
$\frac{5}{6}x - \frac{1}{3}y = -\frac{2}{3}$

5. $5x + 6y = 14$
$4x + 8y = 8$

For the following exercises, use addition to solve the system of equations.

6. $3x + 2y = -7$
$2x + 4y = 6$

7. $3x + 4y = 2$
$9x + 12y = 3$

8. $8x + 4y = 2$
$6x - 5y = 0.7$

For the following exercises, write a system of equations to solve each problem. Solve the system of equations.

9. A factory has a cost of production $C(x) = 150x + 15{,}000$ and a revenue function $R(x) = 200x$. What is the break-even point?

10. A performer charges $C(x) = 50x + 10{,}000$, where x is the total number of attendees at a show. The venue charges $75 per ticket. After how many people buy tickets does the venue break even, and what is the value of the total tickets sold at that point?

SYSTEMS OF LINEAR EQUATIONS: THREE VARIABLES

For the following exercises, solve the system of three equations using substitution or addition.

11. $0.5x - 0.5y = 10$
$-0.2y + 0.2x = 4$
$0.1x + 0.1z = 2$

12. $5x + 3y - z = 5$
$3x - 2y + 4z = 13$
$4x + 3y + 5z = 22$

13. $x + y + z = 1$
$2x + 2y + 2z = 1$
$3x + 3y = 2$

14. $2x - 3y + z = -1$
$x + y + z = -4$
$4x + 2y - 3z = 33$

15. $3x + 2y - z = -10$
$x - y + 2z = 7$
$-x + 3y + z = -2$

16. $3x + 4z = -11$
$x - 2y = 5$
$4y - z = -10$

17. $2x - 3y + z = 0$
$2x + 4y - 3z = 0$
$6x - 2y - z = 0$

18. $6x - 4y - 2z = 2$
$3x + 2y - 5z = 4$
$6y - 7z = 5$

For the following exercises, write a system of equations to solve each problem. Solve the system of equations.

19. Three odd numbers sum up to 61. The smaller is one-third the larger and the middle number is 16 less than the larger. What are the three numbers?

20. A local theatre sells out for their show. They sell all 500 tickets for a total purse of $8,070.00. The tickets were priced at $15 for students, $12 for children, and $18 for adults. If the band sold three times as many adult tickets as children's tickets, how many of each type was sold?

SYSTEMS OF NONLINEAR EQUATIONS AND INEQUALITIES: TWO VARIABLES

For the following exercises, solve the system of nonlinear equations.

21. $y = x^2 - 7$
$y = 5x - 13$

22. $y = x^2 - 4$
$y = 5x + 10$

23. $x^2 + y^2 = 16$
$y = x - 8$

24. $x^2 + y^2 = 25$
$y = x^2 + 5$

25. $x^2 + y^2 = 4$
$y - x^2 = 3$

For the following exercises, graph the inequality.

26. $y > x^2 - 1$

27. $\frac{1}{4}x^2 + y^2 < 4$

For the following exercises, graph the system of inequalities.

28. $x^2 + y^2 + 2x < 3$
$y > -x^2 - 3$

29. $x^2 - 2x + y^2 - 4x < 4$
$y < -x + 4$

30. $x^2 + y^2 < 1$
$y^2 < x$

PARTIAL FRACTIONS

For the following exercises, decompose into partial fractions.

31. $\dfrac{-2x + 6}{x^2 + 3x + 2}$

32. $\dfrac{10x + 2}{4x^2 + 4x + 1}$

33. $\dfrac{7x + 20}{x^2 + 10x + 25}$

34. $\dfrac{x - 18}{x^2 - 12x + 36}$

35. $\dfrac{-x^2 + 36x + 70}{x^3 - 125}$

36. $\dfrac{-5x^2 + 6x - 2}{x^3 + 27}$

37. $\dfrac{x^3 - 4x^2 + 3x + 11}{(x^2 - 2)^2}$

38. $\dfrac{4x^4 - 2x^3 + 22x^2 - 6x + 48}{x(x^2 + 4)^2}$

MATRICES AND MATRIX OPERATIONS

For the following exercises, perform the requested operations on the given matrices.

$$A = \begin{bmatrix} 4 & -2 \\ 1 & 3 \end{bmatrix}, B = \begin{bmatrix} 6 & 7 & -3 \\ 11 & -2 & 4 \end{bmatrix}, C = \begin{bmatrix} 6 & 7 \\ 11 & -2 \\ 14 & 0 \end{bmatrix}, D = \begin{bmatrix} 1 & -4 & 9 \\ 10 & 5 & -7 \\ 2 & 8 & 5 \end{bmatrix}, E = \begin{bmatrix} 7 & -14 & 3 \\ 2 & -1 & 3 \\ 0 & 1 & 9 \end{bmatrix}$$

39. $-4A$

40. $10D - 6E$

41. $B + C$

42. AB

43. BA

44. BC

45. CB

46. DE

47. ED

48. EC

49. CE

50. A^3

SOLVING SYSTEMS WITH GAUSSIAN ELIMINATION

For the following exercises, write the system of linear equations from the augmented matrix. Indicate whether there will be a unique solution.

51. $\begin{bmatrix} 1 & 0 & -3 & | & 7 \\ 0 & 1 & 2 & | & -5 \\ 0 & 0 & 0 & | & 0 \end{bmatrix}$

52. $\begin{bmatrix} 1 & 0 & 5 & | & -9 \\ 0 & 1 & -2 & | & 4 \\ 0 & 0 & 0 & | & 3 \end{bmatrix}$

For the following exercises, write the augmented matrix from the system of linear equations.

53. $-2x + 2y + z = 7$
$2x - 8y + 5z = 0$
$19x - 10y + 22z = 3$

54. $4x + 2y - 3z = 14$
$-12x + 3y + z = 100$
$9x - 6y + 2z = 31$

55. $x + 3z = 12$
$-x + 4y = 0$
$y + 2z = -7$

For the following exercises, solve the system of linear equations using Gaussian elimination.

56. $3x - 4y = -7$
$-6x + 8y = 14$

57. $3x - 4y = 1$
$-6x + 8y = 6$

58. $-1.1x - 2.3y = 6.2$
$-5.2x - 4.1y = 4.3$

59. $2x + 3y + 2z = 1$
$-4x - 6y - 4z = -2$
$10x + 15y + 10z = 0$

60. $-x + 2y - 4z = 8$
$3y + 8z = -4$
$-7x + y + 2z = 1$

SOLVING SYSTEMS WITH INVERSES

For the following exercises, find the inverse of the matrix.

61. $\begin{bmatrix} -0.2 & 1.4 \\ 1.2 & -0.4 \end{bmatrix}$

62. $\begin{bmatrix} \dfrac{1}{2} & -\dfrac{1}{2} \\ -\dfrac{1}{4} & \dfrac{3}{4} \end{bmatrix}$

63. $\begin{bmatrix} 12 & 9 & -6 \\ -1 & 3 & 2 \\ -4 & -3 & 2 \end{bmatrix}$

64. $\begin{bmatrix} 2 & 1 & 3 \\ 1 & 2 & 3 \\ 3 & 2 & 1 \end{bmatrix}$

For the following exercises, find the solutions by computing the inverse of the matrix.

65. $0.3x - 0.1y = -10$
$-0.1x + 0.3y = 14$

66. $0.4x - 0.2y = -0.6$
$-0.1x + 0.05y = 0.3$

67. $4x + 3y - 3z = -4.3$
$5x - 4y - z = -6.1$
$x + z = -0.7$

68. $-2x - 3y + 2z = 3$
$-x + 2y + 4z = -5$
$-2y + 5z = -3$

For the following exercises, write a system of equations to solve each problem. Solve the system of equations.

69. Students were asked to bring their favorite fruit to class. 90% of the fruits consisted of banana, apple, and oranges. If oranges were half as popular as bananas and apples were 5% more popular than bananas, what are the percentages of each individual fruit?

70. A sorority held a bake sale to raise money and sold brownies and chocolate chip cookies. They priced the brownies at $2 and the chocolate chip cookies at $1. They raised $250 and sold 175 items. How many brownies and how many cookies were sold?

SOLVING SYSTEMS WITH CRAMER'S RULE

For the following exercises, find the determinant.

71. $\begin{bmatrix} 100 & 0 \\ 0 & 0 \end{bmatrix}$

72. $\begin{bmatrix} 0.2 & -0.6 \\ 0.7 & -1.1 \end{bmatrix}$

73. $\begin{bmatrix} -1 & 4 & 3 \\ 0 & 2 & 3 \\ 0 & 0 & -3 \end{bmatrix}$

74. $\begin{bmatrix} \sqrt{2} & 0 & 0 \\ 0 & \sqrt{2} & 0 \\ 0 & 0 & \sqrt{2} \end{bmatrix}$

For the following exercises, use Cramer's Rule to solve the linear systems of equations.

75. $4x - 2y = 23$
$-5x - 10y = -35$

76. $0.2x - 0.1y = 0$
$-0.3x + 0.3y = 2.5$

77. $-0.5x + 0.1y = 0.3$
$-0.25x + 0.05y = 0.15$

78. $x + 6y + 3z = 4$
$2x + y + 2z = 3$
$3x - 2y + z = 0$

79. $4x - 3y + 5z = -\dfrac{5}{2}$
$7x - 9y - 3z = \dfrac{3}{2}$
$x - 5y - 5z = \dfrac{5}{2}$

80. $\dfrac{3}{10}x - \dfrac{1}{5}y - \dfrac{3}{10}z = -\dfrac{1}{50}$
$\dfrac{1}{10}x - \dfrac{1}{10}y - \dfrac{1}{2}z = -\dfrac{9}{50}$
$\dfrac{2}{5}x - \dfrac{1}{2}y - \dfrac{3}{5}z = -\dfrac{1}{5}$

CHAPTER 11 PRACTICE TEST

Is the following ordered pair a solution to the system of equations?

1. $-5x - y = 12$
$x + 4y = 9$ with $(-3, 3)$

For the following exercises, solve the systems of linear and nonlinear equations using substitution or elimination. Indicate if no solution exists.

2. $\frac{1}{2}x - \frac{1}{3}y = 4$

$\frac{3}{2}x - y = 0$

3. $-\frac{1}{2}x - 4y = 4$

$2x + 16y = 2$

4. $5x - y = 1$
$-10x + 2y = -2$

5. $4x - 6y - 2z = \frac{1}{10}$

$x - 7y + 5z = -\frac{1}{4}$

$3x + 6y - 9z = \frac{6}{5}$

6. $x + z = 20$
$x + y + z = 20$
$x + 2y + z = 10$

7. $5x - 4y - 3z = 0$
$2x + y + 2z = 0$
$x - 6y - 7z = 0$

8. $y = x^2 + 2x - 3$
$y = x - 1$

9. $y^2 + x^2 = 25$
$y^2 - 2x^2 = 1$

For the following exercises, graph the following inequalities.

10. $y < x^2 + 9$

11. $x^2 + y^2 > 4$
$y < x^2 + 1$

For the following exercises, write the partial fraction decomposition.

12. $\dfrac{-8x - 30}{x^2 + 10x + 25}$

13. $\dfrac{13x + 2}{(3x + 1)^2}$

14. $\dfrac{x^4 - x^3 + 2x - 1}{x(x^2 + 1)^2}$

For the following exercises, perform the given matrix operations.

15. $5\begin{bmatrix} 4 & 9 \\ -2 & 3 \end{bmatrix} + \frac{1}{2}\begin{bmatrix} -6 & 12 \\ 4 & -8 \end{bmatrix}$

16. $\begin{bmatrix} 1 & 4 & -7 \\ -2 & 9 & 5 \\ 12 & 0 & -4 \end{bmatrix}\begin{bmatrix} 3 & -4 \\ 1 & 3 \\ 5 & 10 \end{bmatrix}$

17. $\begin{bmatrix} \frac{1}{2} & \frac{1}{3} \\ \frac{1}{4} & \frac{1}{5} \end{bmatrix}^{-1}$

18. $\det\begin{vmatrix} 0 & 0 \\ 400 & 4{,}000 \end{vmatrix}$

19. $\det\begin{vmatrix} \frac{1}{2} & -\frac{1}{2} & 0 \\ -\frac{1}{2} & 0 & \frac{1}{2} \\ 0 & \frac{1}{2} & 0 \end{vmatrix}$

20. If $\det(A) = -6$, what would be the determinant if you switched rows 1 and 3, multiplied the second row by 12, and took the inverse?

21. Rewrite the system of linear equations as an augmented matrix.
$14x - 2y + 13z = 140$
$-2x + 3y - 6z = -1$
$x - 5y + 12z = 11$

22. Rewrite the augmented matrix as a system of linear equations.
$$\begin{bmatrix} 1 & 0 & 3 & | & 12 \\ -2 & 4 & 9 & | & -5 \\ -6 & 1 & 2 & | & 8 \end{bmatrix}$$

For the following exercises, use Gaussian elimination to solve the systems of equations.

23. $\begin{aligned} x - 6y &= 4 \\ 2x - 12y &= 0 \end{aligned}$

24. $\begin{aligned} 2x + y + z &= -3 \\ x - 2y + 3z &= 6 \\ x - y - z &= 6 \end{aligned}$

For the following exercises, use the inverse of a matrix to solve the systems of equations.

25. $\begin{aligned} 4x - 5y &= -50 \\ -x + 2y &= 80 \end{aligned}$

26. $\begin{aligned} \frac{1}{100}x - \frac{3}{100}y + \frac{1}{20}z &= -49 \\ \frac{3}{100}x - \frac{7}{100}y - \frac{1}{100}z &= 13 \\ \frac{9}{100}x - \frac{9}{100}y - \frac{9}{100}z &= 99 \end{aligned}$

For the following exercises, use Cramer's Rule to solve the systems of equations.

27. $\begin{aligned} 200x - 300y &= 2 \\ 400x + 715y &= 4 \end{aligned}$

28. $\begin{aligned} 0.1x + 0.1y - 0.1z &= -1.2 \\ 0.1x - 0.2y + 0.4z &= -1.2 \\ 0.5x - 0.3y + 0.8z &= -5.9 \end{aligned}$

For the following exercises, solve using a system of linear equations.

29. A factory producing cell phones has the following cost and revenue functions: $C(x) = x^2 + 75x + 2{,}688$ and $R(x) = x^2 + 160x$. What is the range of cell phones they should produce each day so there is profit? Round to the nearest number that generates profit.

30. A small fair charges $1.50 for students, $1 for children, and $2 for adults. In one day, three times as many children as adults attended. A total of 800 tickets were sold for a total revenue of $1,050. How many of each type of ticket was sold?

12

Analytic Geometry

a

b

Figure 1 (a) Greek philosopher Aristotle (384–322 BCE) (b) German mathematician and astronomer Johannes Kepler (1571–1630)

CHAPTER OUTLINE

12.1 The Ellipse

12.2 The Hyperbola

12.3 The Parabola

12.4 Rotation of Axes

12.5 Conic Sections in Polar Coordinates

Introduction

The Greek mathematician Menaechmus (c. 380–c. 320 BCE) is generally credited with discovering the shapes formed by the intersection of a plane and a right circular cone. Depending on how he tilted the plane when it intersected the cone, he formed different shapes at the intersection—beautiful shapes with near-perfect symmetry.

It was also said that Aristotle may have had an intuitive understanding of these shapes, as he observed the orbit of the planet to be circular. He presumed that the planets moved in circular orbits around Earth, and for nearly 2000 years this was the commonly held belief.

It was not until the Renaissance movement that Johannes Kepler noticed that the orbits of the planet were not circular in nature. His published law of planetary motion in the 1600s changed our view of the solar system forever. He claimed that the sun was at one end of the orbits, and the planets revolved around the sun in an oval-shaped path.

In this chapter, we will investigate the two-dimensional figures that are formed when a right circular cone is intersected by a plane. We will begin by studying each of three figures created in this manner. We will develop defining equations for each figure and then learn how to use these equations to solve a variety of problems.

LEARNING OBJECTIVES

In this section, you will:

- Write equations of ellipses in standard form.
- Graph ellipses centered at the origin.
- Graph ellipses not centered at the origin.
- Solve applied problems involving ellipses.

12.1   THE ELLIPSE

Figure 1   The National Statuary Hall in Washington, D.C. (credit: Greg Palmer, Flickr)

Can you imagine standing at one end of a large room and still being able to hear a whisper from a person standing at the other end? The National Statuary Hall in Washington, D.C., shown in **Figure 1**, is such a room.[33] It is an oval-shaped room called a *whispering chamber* because the shape makes it possible for sound to travel along the walls. In this section, we will investigate the shape of this room and its real-world applications, including how far apart two people in Statuary Hall can stand and still hear each other whisper.

Writing Equations of Ellipses in Standard Form

A conic section, or **conic**, is a shape resulting from intersecting a right circular cone with a plane. The angle at which the plane intersects the cone determines the shape, as shown in **Figure 2**.

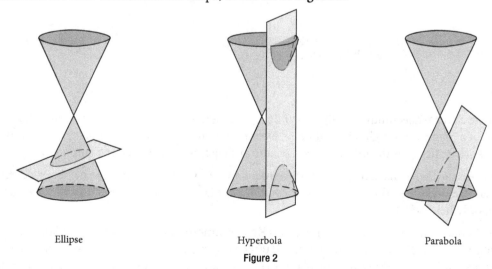

Ellipse   Hyperbola   Parabola

Figure 2

Conic sections can also be described by a set of points in the coordinate plane. Later in this chapter, we will see that the graph of any quadratic equation in two variables is a conic section. The signs of the equations and the coefficients of the variable terms determine the shape. This section focuses on the four variations of the standard form of the equation for the ellipse. An **ellipse** is the set of all points (x, y) in a plane such that the sum of their distances from two fixed points is a constant. Each fixed point is called a **focus** (plural: **foci**).

We can draw an ellipse using a piece of cardboard, two thumbtacks, a pencil, and string. Place the thumbtacks in the cardboard to form the foci of the ellipse. Cut a piece of string longer than the distance between the two thumbtacks (the length of the string represents the constant in the definition). Tack each end of the string to the cardboard, and trace a curve with a pencil held taut against the string. The result is an ellipse. See **Figure 3**.

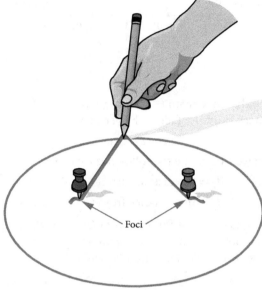

Figure 3

Every ellipse has two axes of symmetry. The longer axis is called the **major axis**, and the shorter axis is called the **minor axis**. Each endpoint of the major axis is the **vertex** of the ellipse (plural: **vertices**), and each endpoint of the minor axis is a co-vertex of the ellipse. The **center of an ellipse** is the midpoint of both the major and minor axes. The axes are perpendicular at the center. The foci always lie on the major axis, and the sum of the distances from the foci to any point on the ellipse (the constant sum) is greater than the distance between the foci. See **Figure 4**.

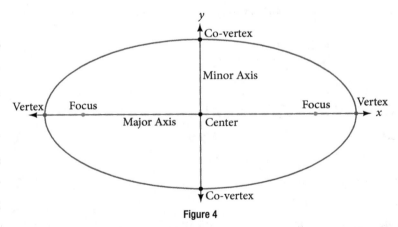

Figure 4

In this section, we restrict ellipses to those that are positioned vertically or horizontally in the coordinate plane. That is, the axes will either lie on or be parallel to the x- and y-axes. Later in the chapter, we will see ellipses that are rotated in the coordinate plane.

To work with horizontal and vertical ellipses in the coordinate plane, we consider two cases: those that are centered at the origin and those that are centered at a point other than the origin. First we will learn to derive the equations of ellipses, and then we will learn how to write the equations of ellipses in standard form. Later we will use what we learn to draw the graphs.

Deriving the Equation of an Ellipse Centered at the Origin

To derive the equation of an ellipse centered at the origin, we begin with the foci $(-c, 0)$ and $(c, 0)$. The ellipse is the set of all points (x, y) such that the sum of the distances from (x, y) to the foci is constant, as shown in **Figure 5**.

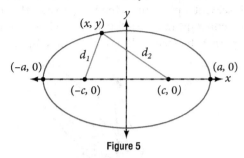

Figure 5

If $(a, 0)$ is a vertex of the ellipse, the distance from $(-c, 0)$ to $(a, 0)$ is $a - (-c) = a + c$. The distance from $(c, 0)$ to $(a, 0)$ is $a - c$. The sum of the distances from the foci to the vertex is

$$(a + c) + (a - c) = 2a$$

If (x, y) is a point on the ellipse, then we can define the following variables:

$$d_1 = \text{the distance from } (-c, 0) \text{ to } (x, y)$$
$$d_2 = \text{the distance from } (c, 0) \text{ to } (x, y)$$

By the definition of an ellipse, $d_1 + d_2$ is constant for any point (x, y) on the ellipse. We know that the sum of these distances is $2a$ for the vertex $(a, 0)$. It follows that $d_1 + d_2 = 2a$ for any point on the ellipse. We will begin the derivation by applying the distance formula. The rest of the derivation is algebraic.

$$d_1 + d_2 = \sqrt{(x - (-c))^2 + (y - 0)^2} + \sqrt{(x - c)^2 + (y - 0)^2} = 2a \quad \text{Distance formula}$$

$\sqrt{(x + c)^2 + y^2} + \sqrt{(x - c)^2 + y^2} = 2a$	Simplify expressions.
$\sqrt{(x + c)^2 + y^2} = 2a - \sqrt{(x - c)^2 + y^2}$	Move radical to opposite side.
$(x + c)^2 + y^2 = \left[2a - \sqrt{(x - c)^2 + y^2}\right]^2$	Square both sides.
$x^2 + 2cx + c^2 + y^2 = 4a^2 - 4a\sqrt{(x - c)^2 + y^2} + (x - c)^2 + y^2$	Expand the squares.
$x^2 + 2cx + c^2 + y^2 = 4a^2 - 4a\sqrt{(x - c)^2 + y^2} + x^2 - 2cx + c^2 + y^2$	Expand remaining squares.
$2cx = 4a^2 - 4a\sqrt{(x - c)^2 + y^2} - 2cx$	Combine like terms.
$4cx - 4a^2 = -4a\sqrt{(x - c)^2 + y^2}$	Isolate the radical.
$cx - a^2 = -a\sqrt{(x - c)^2 + y^2}$	Divide by 4.
$\left[cx - a^2\right]^2 = a^2\left[\sqrt{(x - c)^2 + y^2}\right]^2$	Square both sides.
$c^2 x^2 - 2a^2 cx + a^4 = a^2(x^2 - 2cx + c^2 + y^2)$	Expand the squares.
$c^2 x^2 - 2a^2 cx + a^4 = a^2 x^2 - 2a^2 cx + a^2 c^2 + a^2 y^2$	Distribute a^2.
$a^2 x^2 - c^2 x^2 + a^2 y^2 = a^4 - a^2 c^2$	Rewrite.
$x^2(a^2 - c^2) + a^2 y^2 = a^2(a^2 - c^2)$	Factor common terms.
$x^2 b^2 + a^2 y^2 = a^2 b^2$	Set $b^2 = a^2 - c^2$.
$\dfrac{x^2 b^2}{a^2 b^2} + \dfrac{a^2 y^2}{a^2 b^2} = \dfrac{a^2 b^2}{a^2 b^2}$	Divide both sides by $a^2 b^2$.
$\dfrac{x^2}{a^2} + \dfrac{y^2}{b^2} = 1$	Simplify.

Thus, the standard equation of an ellipse is $\dfrac{x^2}{a^2} + \dfrac{y^2}{b^2} = 1$. This equation defines an ellipse centered at the origin.

If $a > b$, the ellipse is stretched further in the horizontal direction, and if $b > a$, the ellipse is stretched further in the vertical direction.

Writing Equations of Ellipses Centered at the Origin in Standard Form

Standard forms of equations tell us about key features of graphs. Take a moment to recall some of the standard forms of equations we've worked with in the past: linear, quadratic, cubic, exponential, logarithmic, and so on. By learning to interpret standard forms of equations, we are bridging the relationship between algebraic and geometric representations of mathematical phenomena.

The key features of the ellipse are its center, vertices, co-vertices, foci, and lengths and positions of the major and minor axes. Just as with other equations, we can identify all of these features just by looking at the standard form of the equation. There are four variations of the standard form of the ellipse. These variations are categorized first by the location of the center (the origin or not the origin), and then by the position (horizontal or vertical). Each is presented along with a description of how the parts of the equation relate to the graph. Interpreting these parts allows us to form a mental picture of the ellipse.

---

standard forms of the equation of an ellipse with center (0, 0)

The standard form of the equation of an ellipse with center (0, 0) and major axis on the x-axis is

$$\frac{x^2}{a^2} + \frac{y^2}{b^2} = 1$$

where

- $a > b$
- the length of the major axis is $2a$
- the coordinates of the vertices are $(\pm a, 0)$
- the length of the minor axis is $2b$
- the coordinates of the co-vertices are $(0, \pm b)$
- the coordinates of the foci are $(\pm c, 0)$, where $c^2 = a^2 - b^2$. See **Figure 6a.**

The standard form of the equation of an ellipse with center (0, 0) and major axis on the y-axis is

$$\frac{x^2}{b^2} + \frac{y^2}{a^2} = 1$$

where

- $a > b$
- the length of the major axis is $2a$
- the coordinates of the vertices are $(0, \pm a)$
- the length of the minor axis is $2b$
- the coordinates of the co-vertices are $(\pm b, 0)$
- the coordinates of the foci are $(0, \pm c)$, where $c^2 = a^2 - b^2$. See **Figure 6b.**

Note that the vertices, co-vertices, and foci are related by the equation $c^2 = a^2 - b^2$. When we are given the coordinates of the foci and vertices of an ellipse, we can use this relationship to find the equation of the ellipse in standard form.

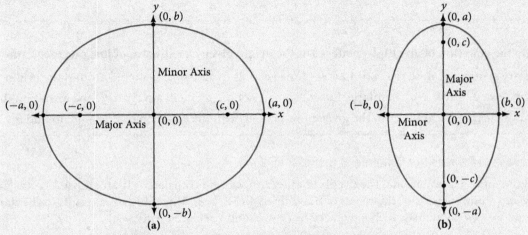

Figure 6 (a) Horizontal ellipse with center (0, 0) (b) Vertical ellipse with center (0, 0)

How To...

Given the vertices and foci of an ellipse centered at the origin, write its equation in standard form.

1. Determine whether the major axis lies on the *x*- or *y*-axis.

   a. If the given coordinates of the vertices and foci have the form $(\pm a, 0)$ and $(\pm c, 0)$ respectively, then the major axis is the *x*-axis. Use the standard form $\dfrac{x^2}{a^2} + \dfrac{y^2}{b^2} = 1$.

   b. If the given coordinates of the vertices and foci have the form $(0, \pm a)$ and $(\pm c, 0)$, respectively, then the major axis is the *y*-axis. Use the standard form $\dfrac{x^2}{b^2} + \dfrac{y^2}{a^2} = 1$.

2. Use the equation $c^2 = a^2 - b^2$, along with the given coordinates of the vertices and foci, to solve for b^2.

3. Substitute the values for a^2 and b^2 into the standard form of the equation determined in Step 1.

Example 1   **Writing the Equation of an Ellipse Centered at the Origin in Standard Form**

What is the standard form equation of the ellipse that has vertices $(\pm 8, 0)$ and foci $(\pm 5, 0)$?

Solution   The foci are on the *x*-axis, so the major axis is the *x*-axis. Thus, the equation will have the form

$$\frac{x^2}{a^2} + \frac{y^2}{b^2} = 1$$

The vertices are $(\pm 8, 0)$, so $a = 8$ and $a^2 = 64$.

The foci are $(\pm 5, 0)$, so $c = 5$ and $c^2 = 25$.

We know that the vertices and foci are related by the equation $c^2 = a^2 - b^2$. Solving for b^2, we have:

$$c^2 = a^2 - b^2$$
$$25 = 64 - b^2 \qquad \text{Substitute for } c^2 \text{ and } a^2.$$
$$b^2 = 39 \qquad \text{Solve for } b^2.$$

Now we need only substitute $a^2 = 64$ and $b^2 = 39$ into the standard form of the equation. The equation of the ellipse is $\dfrac{x^2}{64} + \dfrac{y^2}{39} = 1$.

Try It #1

What is the standard form equation of the ellipse that has vertices $(0, \pm 4)$ and foci $(0, \pm \sqrt{15})$?

Q & A...

Can we write the equation of an ellipse centered at the origin given coordinates of just one focus and vertex?

Yes. Ellipses are symmetrical, so the coordinates of the vertices of an ellipse centered around the origin will always have the form $(\pm a, 0)$ or $(0, \pm a)$. Similarly, the coordinates of the foci will always have the form $(\pm c, 0)$ or $(0, \pm c)$. Knowing this, we can use a and c from the given points, along with the equation $c^2 = a^2 - b^2$, to find b^2.

Writing Equations of Ellipses Not Centered at the Origin

Like the graphs of other equations, the graph of an ellipse can be translated. If an ellipse is translated *h* units horizontally and *k* units vertically, the center of the ellipse will be (h, k). This translation results in the standard form of the equation we saw previously, with *x* replaced by $(x - h)$ and *y* replaced by $(y - k)$.

standard forms of the equation of an ellipse with center (h, k)

The standard form of the equation of an ellipse with center (h, k) and major axis parallel to the x-axis is

$$\frac{(x - h)^2}{a^2} + \frac{(y - k)^2}{b^2} = 1$$

where

- $a > b$
- the length of the major axis is $2a$
- the coordinates of the vertices are $(h \pm a, k)$
- the length of the minor axis is $2b$
- the coordinates of the co-vertices are $(h, k \pm b)$
- the coordinates of the foci are $(h \pm c, k)$, where $c^2 = a^2 - b^2$. See **Figure 7a**.

The standard form of the equation of an ellipse with center (h, k) and major axis parallel to the y-axis is

$$\frac{(x - h)^2}{b^2} + \frac{(y - k)^2}{a^2} = 1$$

where

- $a > b$
- the length of the major axis is $2a$
- the coordinates of the vertices are $(h, k \pm a)$
- the length of the minor axis is $2b$
- the coordinates of the co-vertices are $(h \pm b, k)$
- the coordinates of the foci are $(h, k \pm c)$, where $c^2 = a^2 - b^2$. See **Figure 7b**.

Just as with ellipses centered at the origin, ellipses that are centered at a point (h, k) have vertices, co-vertices, and foci that are related by the equation $c^2 = a^2 - b^2$. We can use this relationship along with the midpoint and distance formulas to find the equation of the ellipse in standard form when the vertices and foci are given.

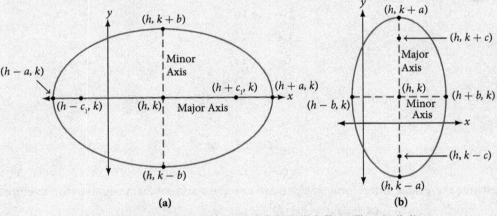

Figure 7 (a) Horizontal ellipse with center (h, k) (b) Vertical ellipse with center (h, k)

How To...

Given the vertices and foci of an ellipse not centered at the origin, write its equation in standard form.

1. Determine whether the major axis is parallel to the x- or y-axis.
   a. If the y-coordinates of the given vertices and foci are the same, then the major axis is parallel to the x-axis. Use the standard form $\dfrac{(x - h)^2}{a^2} + \dfrac{(y - k)^2}{b^2} = 1$.
   b. If the x-coordinates of the given vertices and foci are the same, then the major axis is parallel to the y-axis. Use the standard form $\dfrac{(x - h)^2}{b^2} + \dfrac{(y - k)^2}{a^2} = 1$.

2. Identify the center of the ellipse (h, k) using the midpoint formula and the given coordinates for the vertices.
3. Find a^2 by solving for the length of the major axis, $2a$, which is the distance between the given vertices.
4. Find c^2 using h and k, found in Step 2, along with the given coordinates for the foci.
5. Solve for b^2 using the equation $c^2 = a^2 - b^2$.
6. Substitute the values for h, k, a^2, and b^2 into the standard form of the equation determined in Step 1.

Example 2   **Writing the Equation of an Ellipse Centered at a Point Other Than the Origin**

What is the standard form equation of the ellipse that has vertices $(-2, -8)$ and $(-2, 2)$ and foci $(-2, -7)$ and $(-2, 1)$?

Solution   The x-coordinates of the vertices and foci are the same, so the major axis is parallel to the y-axis. Thus, the equation of the ellipse will have the form

$$\frac{(x - h)^2}{b^2} + \frac{(y - k)^2}{a^2} = 1$$

First, we identify the center, (h, k). The center is halfway between the vertices, $(-2, -8)$ and $(-2, 2)$.

Applying the midpoint formula, we have:

$$(h, k) = \left(\frac{-2 + (-2)}{2}, \frac{-8 + 2}{2} \right)$$
$$= (-2, -3)$$

Next, we find a^2. The length of the major axis, $2a$, is bounded by the vertices. We solve for a by finding the distance between the y-coordinates of the vertices.

$$2a = 2 - (-8)$$
$$2a = 10$$
$$a = 5$$

So $a^2 = 25$.

Now we find c^2. The foci are given by $(h, k \pm c)$. So, $(h, k - c) = (-2, -7)$ and $(h, k + c) = (-2, 1)$. We substitute $k = -3$ using either of these points to solve for c.

$$k + c = 1$$
$$-3 + c = 1$$
$$c = 4$$

So $c^2 = 16$.

Next, we solve for b^2 using the equation $c^2 = a^2 - b^2$.

$$c^2 = a^2 - b^2$$
$$16 = 25 - b^2$$
$$b^2 = 9$$

Finally, we substitute the values found for h, k, a^2, and b^2 into the standard form equation for an ellipse:

$$\frac{(x + 2)^2}{9} + \frac{(y + 3)^2}{25} = 1$$

Try It #2

What is the standard form equation of the ellipse that has vertices $(-3, 3)$ and $(5, 3)$ and foci $(1 - 2\sqrt{3}, 3)$ and $(1 + 2\sqrt{3}, 3)$?

Graphing Ellipses Centered at the Origin

Just as we can write the equation for an ellipse given its graph, we can graph an ellipse given its equation. To graph ellipses centered at the origin, we use the standard form $\frac{x^2}{a^2} + \frac{y^2}{b^2} = 1$, $a > b$ for horizontal ellipses and $\frac{x^2}{b^2} + \frac{y^2}{a^2} = 1$, $a > b$ for vertical ellipses.

How To...

Given the standard form of an equation for an ellipse centered at $(0, 0)$, sketch the graph.

1. Use the standard forms of the equations of an ellipse to determine the major axis, vertices, co-vertices, and foci.

   a. If the equation is in the form $\dfrac{x^2}{a^2} + \dfrac{y^2}{b^2} = 1$, where $a > b$, then

   - the major axis is the x-axis
   - the coordinates of the vertices are $(\pm a, 0)$
   - the coordinates of the co-vertices are $(0, \pm b)$
   - the coordinates of the foci are $(\pm c, 0)$

   b. If the equation is in the form $\dfrac{x^2}{b^2} + \dfrac{y^2}{a^2} = 1$, where $a > b$, then

   - the major axis is the y-axis
   - the coordinates of the vertices are $(0, \pm a)$
   - the coordinates of the co-vertices are $(\pm b, 0)$
   - the coordinates of the foci are $(0, \pm c)$

2. Solve for c using the equation $c^2 = a^2 - b^2$.
3. Plot the center, vertices, co-vertices, and foci in the coordinate plane, and draw a smooth curve to form the ellipse.

Example 3   **Graphing an Ellipse Centered at the Origin**

Graph the ellipse given by the equation, $\dfrac{x^2}{9} + \dfrac{y^2}{25} = 1$. Identify and label the center, vertices, co-vertices, and foci.

Solution   First, we determine the position of the major axis. Because $25 > 9$, the major axis is on the y-axis. Therefore, the equation is in the form $\dfrac{x^2}{b^2} + \dfrac{y^2}{a^2} = 1$, where $b^2 = 9$ and $a^2 = 25$. It follows that:

- the center of the ellipse is $(0, 0)$
- the coordinates of the vertices are $(0, \pm a) = \left(0, \pm \sqrt{25}\right) = (0, \pm 5)$
- the coordinates of the co-vertices are $(\pm b, 0) = \left(\pm \sqrt{9}, 0\right) = (\pm 3, 0)$
- the coordinates of the foci are $(0, \pm c)$, where $c^2 = a^2 - b^2$ Solving for c, we have:

$$c = \pm \sqrt{a^2 - b^2}$$
$$= \pm \sqrt{25 - 9}$$
$$= \pm \sqrt{16}$$
$$= \pm 4$$

Therefore, the coordinates of the foci are $(0, \pm 4)$.

Next, we plot and label the center, vertices, co-vertices, and foci, and draw a smooth curve to form the ellipse. See **Figure 8**.

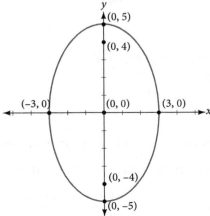

Figure 8

Try It #3

Graph the ellipse given by the equation $\frac{x^2}{36} + \frac{y^2}{4} = 1$. Identify and label the center, vertices, co-vertices, and foci.

Example 4   **Graphing an Ellipse Centered at the Origin from an Equation Not in Standard Form**

Graph the ellipse given by the equation $4x^2 + 25y^2 = 100$. Rewrite the equation in standard form. Then identify and label the center, vertices, co-vertices, and foci.

Solution   First, use algebra to rewrite the equation in standard form.

$$4x^2 + 25y^2 = 100$$
$$\frac{4x^2}{100} + \frac{25y^2}{100} = \frac{100}{100}$$
$$\frac{x^2}{25} + \frac{y^2}{4} = 1$$

Next, we determine the position of the major axis. Because $25 > 4$, the major axis is on the x-axis. Therefore, the equation is in the form $\frac{x^2}{a^2} + \frac{y^2}{b^2} = 1$, where $a^2 = 25$ and $b^2 = 4$. It follows that:

- the center of the ellipse is $(0, 0)$
- the coordinates of the vertices are $(\pm a, 0) = (\pm\sqrt{25}, 0) = (\pm 5, 0)$
- the coordinates of the co-vertices are $(0, \pm b) = (0, \pm\sqrt{4}) = (0, \pm 2)$
- the coordinates of the foci are $(\pm c, 0)$, where $c^2 = a^2 - b^2$. Solving for c, we have:

$$c = \pm\sqrt{a^2 - b^2}$$
$$= \pm\sqrt{25 - 4}$$
$$= \pm\sqrt{21}$$

Therefore the coordinates of the foci are $(\pm\sqrt{21}, 0)$.

Next, we plot and label the center, vertices, co-vertices, and foci, and draw a smooth curve to form the ellipse. See **Figure 9**.

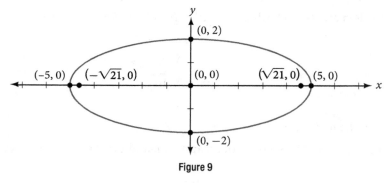

Figure 9

Try It #4

Graph the ellipse given by the equation $49x^2 + 16y^2 = 784$. Rewrite the equation in standard form. Then identify and label the center, vertices, co-vertices, and foci.

Graphing Ellipses Not Centered at the Origin

When an ellipse is not centered at the origin, we can still use the standard forms to find the key features of the graph.

When the ellipse is centered at some point, (h, k), we use the standard forms $\frac{(x - h)^2}{a^2} + \frac{(y - k)^2}{b^2} = 1, a > b$ for horizontal ellipses and $\frac{(x - h)^2}{b^2} + \frac{(y - k)^2}{a^2} = 1, a > b$ for vertical ellipses. From these standard equations, we can easily determine the center, vertices, co-vertices, foci, and positions of the major and minor axes.

How To...

Given the standard form of an equation for an ellipse centered at (h, k), sketch the graph.

1. Use the standard forms of the equations of an ellipse to determine the center, position of the major axis, vertices, co-vertices, and foci.

    a. If the equation is in the form $\dfrac{(x-h)^2}{a^2} + \dfrac{(y-k)^2}{b^2} = 1$, where $a > b$, then
    - the center is (h, k)
    - the major axis is parallel to the x-axis
    - the coordinates of the vertices are $(h \pm a, k)$
    - the coordinates of the co-vertices are $(h, k \pm b)$
    - the coordinates of the foci are $(h \pm c, k)$

    b. If the equation is in the form $\dfrac{(x-h)^2}{b^2} + \dfrac{(y-k)^2}{a^2} = 1$, where $a > b$, then
    - the center is (h, k)
    - the major axis is parallel to the y-axis
    - the coordinates of the vertices are $(h, k \pm a)$
    - the coordinates of the co-vertices are $(h \pm b, k)$
    - the coordinates of the foci are $(h, k \pm c)$

2. Solve for c using the equation $c^2 = a^2 - b^2$.
3. Plot the center, vertices, co-vertices, and foci in the coordinate plane, and draw a smooth curve to form the ellipse.

Example 5   **Graphing an Ellipse Centered at (*h, k*)**

Graph the ellipse given by the equation, $\dfrac{(x+2)^2}{4} + \dfrac{(y-5)^2}{9} = 1$. Identify and label the center, vertices, covertices, and foci.

Solution   First, we determine the position of the major axis. Because $9 > 4$, the major axis is parallel to the y-axis.

Therefore, the equation is in the form $\dfrac{(x-h)^2}{b^2} + \dfrac{(y-k)^2}{a^2} = 1$, where $b^2 = 4$ and $a^2 = 9$. It follows that:

- the center of the ellipse is $(h, k) = (-2, 5)$
- the coordinates of the vertices are $(h, k \pm a) = \left(-2, 5 \pm \sqrt{9}\right) = (-2, 5 \pm 3)$, or $(-2, 2)$ and $(-2, 8)$
- the coordinates of the co-vertices are $(h \pm b, k) = \left(-2 \pm \sqrt{4}, 5\right) = (-2 \pm 2, 5)$, or $(-4, 5)$ and $(0, 5)$
- the coordinates of the foci are $(h, k \pm c)$, where $c^2 = a^2 - b^2$. Solving for c, we have:

$$c = \pm \sqrt{a^2 - b^2}$$
$$= \pm \sqrt{9 - 4}$$
$$= \pm \sqrt{5}$$

Therefore, the coordinates of the foci are $\left(-2, 5 - \sqrt{5}\right)$ and $\left(-2, 5 + \sqrt{5}\right)$.

Next, we plot and label the center, vertices, co-vertices, and foci, and draw a smooth curve to form the ellipse.

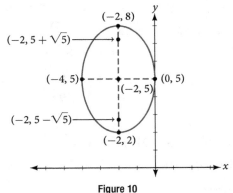

Figure 10

Try It #5

Graph the ellipse given by the equation $\dfrac{(x-4)^2}{36} + \dfrac{(y-2)^2}{20} = 1$. Identify and label the center, vertices, co-vertices, and foci.

How To...

Given the general form of an equation for an ellipse centered at (h, k), express the equation in standard form.

1. Recognize that an ellipse described by an equation in the form $ax^2 + by^2 + cx + dy + e = 0$ is in general form.
2. Rearrange the equation by grouping terms that contain the same variable. Move the constant term to the opposite side of the equation.
3. Factor out the coefficients of the x^2 and y^2 terms in preparation for completing the square.
4. Complete the square for each variable to rewrite the equation in the form of the sum of multiples of two binomials squared set equal to a constant, $m_1 (x - h)^2 + m_2(y - k)^2 = m_3$, where m_1, m_2, and m_3 are constants.
5. Divide both sides of the equation by the constant term to express the equation in standard form.

Example 6   **Graphing an Ellipse Centered at (h, k) by First Writing It in Standard Form**

Graph the ellipse given by the equation $4x^2 + 9y^2 - 40x + 36y + 100 = 0$. Identify and label the center, vertices, co-vertices, and foci.

Solution   We must begin by rewriting the equation in standard form.

$$4x^2 + 9y^2 - 40x + 36y + 100 = 0$$

Group terms that contain the same variable, and move the constant to the opposite side of the equation.

$$(4x^2 - 40x) + (9y^2 + 36y) = -100$$

Factor out the coefficients of the squared terms.

$$4(x^2 - 10x) + 9(y^2 + 4y) = -100$$

Complete the square twice. Remember to balance the equation by adding the same constants to each side.

$$4(x^2 - 10x + 25) + 9(y^2 + 4y + 4) = -100 + 100 + 36$$

Rewrite as perfect squares.

$$4(x - 5)^2 + 9(y + 2)^2 = 36$$

Divide both sides by the constant term to place the equation in standard form.

$$\frac{(x - 5)^2}{9} + \frac{(y + 2)^2}{4} = 1$$

Now that the equation is in standard form, we can determine the position of the major axis. Because $9 > 4$, the major axis is parallel to the x-axis. Therefore, the equation is in the form $\dfrac{(x - h)^2}{a^2} + \dfrac{(y - k)^2}{b^2} = 1$, where $a^2 = 9$ and $b^2 = 4$. It follows that:

- the center of the ellipse is $(h, k) = (5, -2)$
- the coordinates of the vertices are $(h \pm a, k) = \left(5 \pm \sqrt{9}, -2\right) = (5 \pm 3, -2)$, or $(2, -2)$ and $(8, -2)$
- the coordinates of the co-vertices are $(h, k \pm b) = \left(5, -2 \pm \sqrt{4}\right) = (5, -2 \pm 2)$, or $(5, -4)$ and $(5, 0)$
- the coordinates of the foci are $(h \pm c, k)$, where $c^2 = a^2 - b^2$. Solving for c, we have:

$$c = \pm \sqrt{a^2 - b^2}$$
$$= \pm \sqrt{9 - 4}$$
$$= \pm \sqrt{5}$$

Therefore, the coordinates of the foci are $\left(5 - \sqrt{5}, -2\right)$ and $\left(5 + \sqrt{5}, -2\right)$.

Next we plot and label the center, vertices, co-vertices, and foci, and draw a smooth curve to form the ellipse as shown in **Figure 11.**

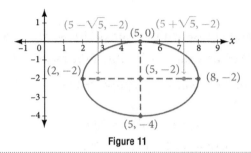

Figure 11

Try It #6

Express the equation of the ellipse given in standard form. Identify the center, vertices, co-vertices, and foci of the ellipse.

$$4x^2 + y^2 - 24x + 2y + 21 = 0$$

Solving Applied Problems Involving Ellipses

Many real-world situations can be represented by ellipses, including orbits of planets, satellites, moons and comets, and shapes of boat keels, rudders, and some airplane wings. A medical device called a lithotripter uses elliptical reflectors to break up kidney stones by generating sound waves. Some buildings, called whispering chambers, are designed with elliptical domes so that a person whispering at one focus can easily be heard by someone standing at the other focus. This occurs because of the acoustic properties of an ellipse. When a sound wave originates at one focus of a whispering chamber, the sound wave will be reflected off the elliptical dome and back to the other focus. See **Figure 12**. In the whisper chamber at the Museum of Science and Industry in Chicago, two people standing at the foci—about 43 feet apart—can hear each other whisper.

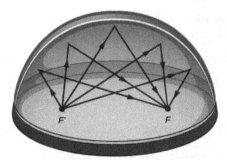

Figure 12 Sound waves are reflected between foci in an elliptical room, called a whispering chamber.

Example 7   **Locating the Foci of a Whispering Chamber**

The Statuary Hall in the Capitol Building in Washington, D.C. is a whispering chamber. Its dimensions are 46 feet wide by 96 feet long as shown in **Figure 13**.

  a. What is the standard form of the equation of the ellipse representing the outline of the room? Hint: assume a horizontal ellipse, and let the center of the room be the point $(0, 0)$.

  b. If two senators standing at the foci of this room can hear each other whisper, how far apart are the senators? Round to the nearest foot.

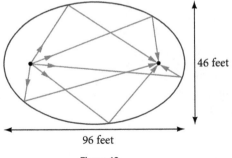

96 feet

46 feet

Figure 13

Solution

a. We are assuming a horizontal ellipse with center $(0, 0)$, so we need to find an equation of the form $\frac{x^2}{a^2} + \frac{y^2}{b^2} = 1$, where $a > b$. We know that the length of the major axis, $2a$, is longer than the length of the minor axis, $2b$. So the length of the room, 96, is represented by the major axis, and the width of the room, 46, is represented by the minor axis.

- Solving for a, we have $2a = 96$, so $a = 48$, and $a^2 = 2304$.
- Solving for b, we have $2b = 46$, so $b = 23$, and $b^2 = 529$.

    Therefore, the equation of the ellipse is $\frac{x^2}{2304} + \frac{y^2}{529} = 1$.

b. To find the distance between the senators, we must find the distance between the foci, $(\pm c, 0)$, where $c^2 = a^2 - b^2$. Solving for c, we have:

$$c^2 = a^2 - b^2$$
$$c^2 = 2304 - 529 \qquad \text{Substitute using the values found in part (a).}$$
$$c = \pm \sqrt{2304 - 529} \qquad \text{Take the square root of both sides.}$$
$$c = \pm \sqrt{1775} \qquad \text{Subtract.}$$
$$c \approx \pm 42 \qquad \text{Round to the nearest foot.}$$

The points $(\pm 42, 0)$ represent the foci. Thus, the distance between the senators is $2(42) = 84$ feet.

Try It #7

Suppose a whispering chamber is 480 feet long and 320 feet wide.

a. What is the standard form of the equation of the ellipse representing the room? Hint: assume a horizontal ellipse, and let the center of the room be the point $(0, 0)$.

b. If two people are standing at the foci of this room and can hear each other whisper, how far apart are the people? Round to the nearest foot.

Access these online resources for additional instruction and practice with ellipses.

- Conic Sections: The Ellipse (http://openstaxcollege.org/l/conicellipse)
- Graph an Ellipse with Center at the Origin (http://openstaxcollege.org/l/grphellorigin)
- Graph an Ellipse with Center Not at the Origin (http://openstaxcollege.org/l/grphellnot)

12.1 SECTION EXERCISES

VERBAL

1. Define an ellipse in terms of its foci.

2. Where must the foci of an ellipse lie?

3. What special case of the ellipse do we have when the major and minor axis are of the same length?

4. For the special case mentioned in the previous question, what would be true about the foci of that ellipse?

5. What can be said about the symmetry of the graph of an ellipse with center at the origin and foci along the y-axis?

ALGEBRAIC

For the following exercises, determine whether the given equations represent ellipses. If yes, write in standard form.

6. $2x^2 + y = 4$

7. $4x^2 + 9y^2 = 36$

8. $4x^2 - y^2 = 4$

9. $4x^2 + 9y^2 = 1$

10. $4x^2 - 8x + 9y^2 - 72y + 112 = 0$

For the following exercises, write the equation of an ellipse in standard form, and identify the end points of the major and minor axes as well as the foci.

11. $\dfrac{x^2}{4} + \dfrac{y^2}{49} = 1$

12. $\dfrac{x^2}{100} + \dfrac{y^2}{64} = 1$

13. $x^2 + 9y^2 = 1$

14. $4x^2 + 16y^2 = 1$

15. $\dfrac{(x-2)^2}{49} + \dfrac{(y-4)^2}{25} = 1$

16. $\dfrac{(x-2)^2}{81} + \dfrac{(y+1)^2}{16} = 1$

17. $\dfrac{(x+5)^2}{4} + \dfrac{(y-7)^2}{9} = 1$

18. $\dfrac{(x-7)^2}{49} + \dfrac{(y-7)^2}{49} = 1$

19. $4x^2 - 8x + 9y^2 - 72y + 112 = 0$

20. $9x^2 - 54x + 9y^2 - 54y + 81 = 0$

21. $4x^2 - 24x + 36y^2 - 360y + 864 = 0$

22. $4x^2 + 24x + 16y^2 - 128y + 228 = 0$

23. $4x^2 + 40x + 25y^2 - 100y + 100 = 0$

24. $x^2 + 2x + 100y^2 - 1000y + 2401 = 0$

25. $4x^2 + 24x + 25y^2 + 200y + 336 = 0$

26. $9x^2 + 72x + 16y^2 + 16y + 4 = 0$

For the following exercises, find the foci for the given ellipses.

27. $\dfrac{(x+3)^2}{25} + \dfrac{(y+1)^2}{36} = 1$

28. $\dfrac{(x+1)^2}{100} + \dfrac{(y-2)^2}{4} = 1$

29. $x^2 + y^2 = 1$

30. $x^2 + 4y^2 + 4x + 8y = 1$

31. $10x^2 + y^2 + 200x = 0$

GRAPHICAL

For the following exercises, graph the given ellipses, noting center, vertices, and foci.

32. $\dfrac{x^2}{25} + \dfrac{y^2}{36} = 1$

33. $\dfrac{x^2}{16} + \dfrac{y^2}{9} = 1$

34. $4x^2 + 9y^2 = 1$

35. $81x^2 + 49y^2 = 1$

36. $\dfrac{(x-2)^2}{64} + \dfrac{(y-4)^2}{16} = 1$

37. $\dfrac{(x+3)^2}{9} + \dfrac{(y-3)^2}{9} = 1$

38. $\dfrac{x^2}{2} + \dfrac{(y+1)^2}{5} = 1$

39. $4x^2 - 8x + 16y^2 - 32y - 44 = 0$

40. $x^2 - 8x + 25y^2 - 100y + 91 = 0$

41. $x^2 + 8x + 4y^2 - 40y + 112 = 0$

42. $64x^2 + 128x + 9y^2 - 72y - 368 = 0$

43. $16x^2 + 64x + 4y^2 - 8y + 4 = 0$

44. $100x^2 + 1000x + y^2 - 10y + 2425 = 0$

45. $4x^2 + 16x + 4y^2 + 16y + 16 = 0$

For the following exercises, use the given information about the graph of each ellipse to determine its equation.

46. Center at the origin, symmetric with respect to the x- and y-axes, focus at $(4, 0)$, and point on graph $(0, 3)$.

47. Center at the origin, symmetric with respect to the x- and y-axes, focus at $(0, -2)$, and point on graph $(5, 0)$.

48. Center at the origin, symmetric with respect to the x- and y-axes, focus at $(3, 0)$, and major axis is twice as long as minor axis.

49. Center $(4, 2)$; vertex $(9, 2)$; one focus: $\left(4 + 2\sqrt{6}, 2\right)$.

50. Center $(3, 5)$; vertex $(3, 11)$; one focus: $\left(3, 5 + 4\sqrt{2}\right)$

51. Center $(-3, 4)$; vertex $(1, 4)$; one focus: $\left(-3 + 2\sqrt{3}, 4\right)$

For the following exercises, given the graph of the ellipse, determine its equation.

52.

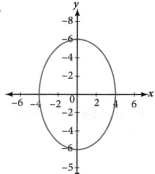

53.

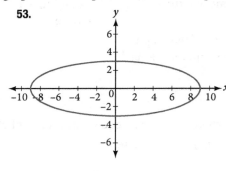

54.

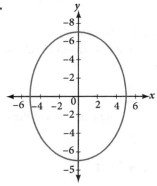

55.

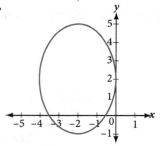

56.

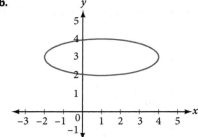

EXTENSIONS

For the following exercises, find the area of the ellipse. The area of an ellipse is given by the formula Area $= a \cdot b \cdot \pi$.

57. $\dfrac{(x-3)^2}{9} + \dfrac{(y-3)^2}{16} = 1$

58. $\dfrac{(x+6)^2}{16} + \dfrac{(y-6)^2}{36} = 1$

59. $\dfrac{(x+1)^2}{4} + \dfrac{(y-2)^2}{5} = 1$

60. $4x^2 - 8x + 9y^2 - 72y + 112 = 0$

61. $9x^2 - 54x + 9y^2 - 54y + 81 = 0$

REAL-WORLD APPLICATIONS

62. Find the equation of the ellipse that will just fit inside a box that is 8 units wide and 4 units high.

63. Find the equation of the ellipse that will just fit inside a box that is four times as wide as it is high. Express in terms of h, the height.

64. An arch has the shape of a semi-ellipse (the top half of an ellipse). The arch has a height of 8 feet and a span of 20 feet. Find an equation for the ellipse, and use that to find the height to the nearest 0.01 foot of the arch at a distance of 4 feet from the center.

65. An arch has the shape of a semi-ellipse. The arch has a height of 12 feet and a span of 40 feet. Find an equation for the ellipse, and use that to find distance from the center to a point at which the height is 6 feet. Round to the nearest hundredth.

66. A bridge is to be built in the shape of a semi-elliptical arch and is to have a span of 120 feet. The height of the arch at a distance of 40 feet from the center is to be 8 feet. Find the height of the arch at its center.

67. A person in a whispering gallery standing at one focus of the ellipse can whisper and be heard by a person standing at the other focus because all the sound waves that reach the ceiling are reflected to the other person. If a whispering gallery has a length of 120 feet, and the foci are located 30 feet from the center, find the height of the ceiling at the center.

68. A person is standing 8 feet from the nearest wall in a whispering gallery. If that person is at one focus, and the other focus is 80 feet away, what is the length and height at the center of the gallery?

LEARNING OBJECTIVES

In this section, you will:

- Locate a hyperbola's vertices and foci.
- Write equations of hyperbolas in standard form.
- Graph hyperbolas centered at the origin.
- Graph hyperbolas not centered at the origin.
- Solve applied problems involving hyperbolas.

12.2   THE HYPERBOLA

What do paths of comets, supersonic booms, ancient Grecian pillars, and natural draft cooling towers have in common? They can all be modeled by the same type of conic. For instance, when something moves faster than the speed of sound, a shock wave in the form of a cone is created. A portion of a conic is formed when the wave intersects the ground, resulting in a sonic boom. See **Figure 1**.

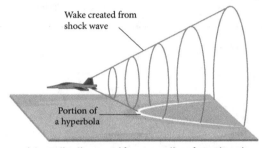

Figure 1   A shock wave intersecting the ground forms a portion of a conic and results in a sonic boom.

Most people are familiar with the sonic boom created by supersonic aircraft, but humans were breaking the sound barrier long before the first supersonic flight. The crack of a whip occurs because the tip is exceeding the speed of sound. The bullets shot from many firearms also break the sound barrier, although the bang of the gun usually supersedes the sound of the sonic boom.

Locating the Vertices and Foci of a Hyperbola

In analytic geometry, a **hyperbola** is a conic section formed by intersecting a right circular cone with a plane at an angle such that both halves of the cone are intersected. This intersection produces two separate unbounded curves that are mirror images of each other. See **Figure 2**.

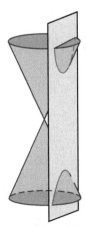

Figure 2   A hyperbola

Like the ellipse, the hyperbola can also be defined as a set of points in the coordinate plane. A hyperbola is the set of all points (x, y) in a plane such that the difference of the distances between (x, y) and the foci is a positive constant.

Notice that the definition of a hyperbola is very similar to that of an ellipse. The distinction is that the hyperbola is defined in terms of the *difference* of two distances, whereas the ellipse is defined in terms of the *sum* of two distances.

As with the ellipse, every hyperbola has two axes of symmetry. The **transverse axis** is a line segment that passes through the center of the hyperbola and has vertices as its endpoints. The foci lie on the line that contains the transverse axis. The **conjugate axis** is perpendicular to the transverse axis and has the co-vertices as its endpoints. The **center of a hyperbola** is the midpoint of both the transverse and conjugate axes, where they intersect. Every hyperbola also has two **asymptotes** that pass through its center. As a hyperbola recedes from the center, its branches approach these asymptotes. The **central rectangle** of the hyperbola is centered at the origin with sides that pass through each vertex and co-vertex; it is a useful tool for graphing the hyperbola and its asymptotes. To sketch the asymptotes of the hyperbola, simply sketch and extend the diagonals of the central rectangle. See **Figure 3**.

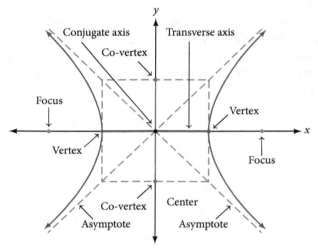

Figure 3 Key features of the hyperbola

In this section, we will limit our discussion to hyperbolas that are positioned vertically or horizontally in the coordinate plane; the axes will either lie on or be parallel to the x- and y-axes. We will consider two cases: those that are centered at the origin, and those that are centered at a point other than the origin.

Deriving the Equation of an Ellipse Centered at the Origin

Let $(-c, 0)$ and $(c, 0)$ be the foci of a hyperbola centered at the origin. The hyperbola is the set of all points (x, y) such that the difference of the distances from (x, y) to the foci is constant. See **Figure 4**.

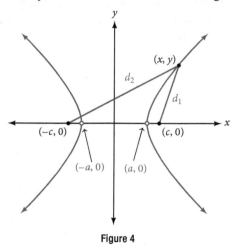

Figure 4

If $(a, 0)$ is a vertex of the hyperbola, the distance from $(-c, 0)$ to $(a, 0)$ is $a - (-c) = a + c$. The distance from $(c, 0)$ to $(a, 0)$ is $c - a$. The sum of the distances from the foci to the vertex is

$$(a + c) - (c - a) = 2a$$

If (x, y) is a point on the hyperbola, we can define the following variables:

$$d_2 = \text{the distance from } (-c, 0) \text{ to } (x, y)$$
$$d_1 = \text{the distance from } (c, 0) \text{ to } (x, y)$$

By definition of a hyperbola, $d_2 - d_1$ is constant for any point (x, y) on the hyperbola. We know that the difference of these distances is $2a$ for the vertex $(a, 0)$. It follows that $d_2 - d_1 = 2a$ for any point on the hyperbola. As with the derivation of the equation of an ellipse, we will begin by applying the distance formula. The rest of the derivation is algebraic. Compare this derivation with the one from the previous section for ellipses.

$d_2 - d_1 = \sqrt{(x-(-c))^2 + (y-0)^2} - \sqrt{(x-c)^2 + (y-0)^2} = 2a$	Distance formula
$\sqrt{(x+c)^2 + y^2} - \sqrt{(x-c)^2 + y^2} = 2a$	Simplify expressions.
$\sqrt{(x+c)^2 + y^2} = 2a + \sqrt{(x-c)^2 + y^2}$	Move radical to opposite side.
$(x+c)^2 + y^2 = \left(2a + \sqrt{(x-c)^2 + y^2}\right)^2$	Square both sides.
$x^2 + 2cx + c^2 + y^2 = 4a^2 + 4a\sqrt{(x-c)^2 + y^2} + (x-c)^2 + y^2$	Expand the squares.
$x^2 + 2cx + c^2 + y^2 = 4a^2 + 4a\sqrt{(x-c)^2 + y^2} + x^2 - 2cx + c^2 + y^2$	Expand remaining square.
$2cx = 4a^2 + 4a\sqrt{(x-c)^2 + y^2} - 2cx$	Combine like terms.
$4cx - 4a^2 = 4a\sqrt{(x-c)^2 + y^2}$	Isolate the radical.
$cx - a^2 = a\sqrt{(x-c)^2 + y^2}$	Divide by 4.
$(cx - a^2)^2 = a^2\left(\sqrt{(x-c)^2 + y^2}\right)^2$	Square both sides.
$c^2x^2 - 2a^2cx + a^4 = a^2(x^2 - 2cx + c^2 + y^2)$	Expand the squares.
$c^2x^2 - 2a^2cx + a^4 = a^2x^2 - 2a^2cx + a^2c^2 + a^2y^2$	Distribute a^2.
$a^4 + c^2x^2 = a^2x^2 + a^2c^2 + a^2y^2$	Combine like terms.
$c^2x^2 - a^2x^2 - a^2y^2 = a^2c^2 - a^4$	Rearrange terms.
$x^2(c^2 - a^2) - a^2y^2 = a^2(c^2 - a^2)$	Factor common terms
$x^2b^2 - a^2y^2 = a^2b^2$	Set $b^2 = c^2 - a^2$.
$\dfrac{x^2b^2}{a^2b^2} - \dfrac{a^2y^2}{a^2b^2} = \dfrac{a^2b^2}{a^2b^2}$	Divide both sides by a^2b^2.
$\dfrac{x^2}{a^2} - \dfrac{y^2}{b^2} = 1$	

This equation defines a hyperbola centered at the origin with vertices $(\pm a, 0)$ and co-vertices $(0 \pm b)$.

---

standard forms of the equation of a hyperbola with center $(0, 0)$

The standard form of the equation of a hyperbola with center $(0, 0)$ and major axis on the x-axis is

$$\frac{x^2}{a^2} - \frac{y^2}{b^2} = 1$$

where

- the length of the transverse axis is $2a$
- the coordinates of the vertices are $(\pm a, 0)$
- the length of the conjugate axis is $2b$
- the coordinates of the co-vertices are $(0, \pm b)$
- the distance between the foci is $2c$, where $c^2 = a^2 + b^2$
- the coordinates of the foci are $(\pm c, 0)$
- the equations of the asymptotes are $y = \pm\dfrac{b}{a}x$

See **Figure 5a.**

The standard form of the equation of a hyperbola with center $(0, 0)$ and transverse axis on the y-axis is

$$\frac{y^2}{a^2} - \frac{x^2}{b^2} = 1$$

where

- the length of the transverse axis is $2a$
- the coordinates of the vertices are $(0, \pm a)$
- the length of the conjugate axis is $2b$
- the coordinates of the co-vertices are $(\pm b, 0)$
- the distance between the foci is $2c$, where $c^2 = a^2 + b^2$
- the coordinates of the foci are $(0, \pm c)$
- the equations of the asymptotes are $y = \pm \frac{a}{b} x$

See **Figure 5b.**

Note that the vertices, co-vertices, and foci are related by the equation $c^2 = a^2 + b^2$. When we are given the equation of a hyperbola, we can use this relationship to identify its vertices and foci.

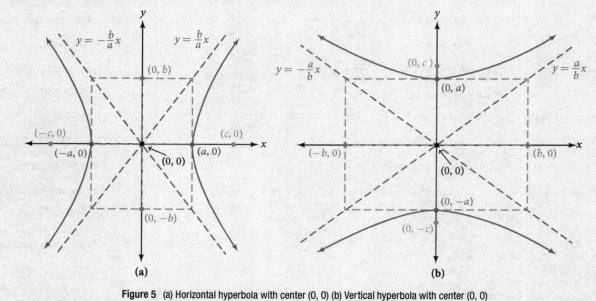

Figure 5   (a) Horizontal hyperbola with center $(0, 0)$ (b) Vertical hyperbola with center $(0, 0)$

How To...

Given the equation of a hyperbola in standard form, locate its vertices and foci.

1. Determine whether the transverse axis lies on the x- or y-axis. Notice that a^2 is always under the variable with the positive coefficient. So, if you set the other variable equal to zero, you can easily find the intercepts. In the case where the hyperbola is centered at the origin, the intercepts coincide with the vertices.

   a. If the equation has the form $\dfrac{x^2}{a^2} - \dfrac{y^2}{b^2} = 1$, then the transverse axis lies on the x-axis. The vertices are located at $(\pm a, 0)$, and the foci are located at $(\pm c, 0)$.

   b. If the equation has the form $\dfrac{y^2}{a^2} - \dfrac{x^2}{b^2} = 1$, then the transverse axis lies on the y-axis. The vertices are located at $(0, \pm a)$, and the foci are located at $(0, \pm c)$.

2. Solve for a using the equation $a = \sqrt{a^2}$.

3. Solve for c using the equation $c = \sqrt{a^2 + b^2}$.

Example 1   Locating a Hyperbola's Vertices and Foci

Identify the vertices and foci of the hyperbola with equation $\dfrac{y^2}{49} - \dfrac{x^2}{32} = 1$.

Solution   The equation has the form $\dfrac{y^2}{a^2} - \dfrac{x^2}{b^2} = 1$, so the transverse axis lies on the y-axis. The hyperbola is centered at the origin, so the vertices serve as the y-intercepts of the graph. To find the vertices, set $x = 0$, and solve for y.

$$1 = \frac{y^2}{49} - \frac{x^2}{32}$$

$$1 = \frac{y^2}{49} - \frac{0^2}{32}$$

$$1 = \frac{y^2}{49}$$

$$y^2 = 49$$

$$y = \pm\sqrt{49} = \pm 7$$

The foci are located at $(0, \pm c)$. Solving for c,

$$c = \sqrt{a^2 + b^2} = \sqrt{49 + 32} = \sqrt{81} = 9$$

Therefore, the vertices are located at $(0, \pm 7)$, and the foci are located at $(0, 9)$.

Try It #1

Identify the vertices and foci of the hyperbola with equation $\dfrac{x^2}{9} - \dfrac{y^2}{25} = 1$.

Writing Equations of Hyperbolas in Standard Form

Just as with ellipses, writing the equation for a hyperbola in standard form allows us to calculate the key features: its center, vertices, co-vertices, foci, asymptotes, and the lengths and positions of the transverse and conjugate axes. Conversely, an equation for a hyperbola can be found given its key features. We begin by finding standard equations for hyperbolas centered at the origin. Then we will turn our attention to finding standard equations for hyperbolas centered at some point other than the origin.

Hyperbolas Centered at the Origin

Reviewing the standard forms given for hyperbolas centered at $(0, 0)$, we see that the vertices, co-vertices, and foci are related by the equation $c^2 = a^2 + b^2$. Note that this equation can also be rewritten as $b^2 = c^2 - a^2$. This relationship is used to write the equation for a hyperbola when given the coordinates of its foci and vertices.

How To...

Given the vertices and foci of a hyperbola centered at $(0, 0)$, write its equation in standard form.

1. Determine whether the transverse axis lies on the x- or y-axis.
   a. If the given coordinates of the vertices and foci have the form $(\pm a, 0)$ and $(\pm c, 0)$, respectively, then the transverse axis is the x-axis. Use the standard form $\dfrac{x^2}{a^2} - \dfrac{y^2}{b^2} = 1$.
   b. If the given coordinates of the vertices and foci have the form $(0, \pm a)$ and $(0, \pm c)$, respectively, then the transverse axis is the y-axis. Use the standard form $\dfrac{y^2}{a^2} - \dfrac{x^2}{b^2} = 1$.
2. Find b^2 using the equation $b^2 = c^2 - a^2$.
3. Substitute the values for a^2 and b^2 into the standard form of the equation determined in Step 1.

Example 2   **Finding the Equation of a Hyperbola Centered at (0, 0) Given its Foci and Vertices**

What is the standard form equation of the hyperbola that has vertices $(\pm 6, 0)$ and foci $\left(\pm 2\sqrt{10}, 0\right)$?

Solution   The vertices and foci are on the x-axis. Thus, the equation for the hyperbola will have the form $\dfrac{x^2}{a^2} - \dfrac{y^2}{b^2} = 1$.

The vertices are $(\pm 6, 0)$, so $a = 6$ and $a^2 = 36$.

The foci are $\left(\pm 2\sqrt{10}, 0\right)$, so $c = 2\sqrt{10}$ and $c^2 = 40$.

Solving for b^2, we have

$$b^2 = c^2 - a^2$$
$$b^2 = 40 - 36 \qquad \text{Substitute for } c^2 \text{ and } a^2.$$
$$b^2 = 4 \qquad \text{Subtract.}$$

Finally, we substitute $a^2 = 36$ and $b^2 = 4$ into the standard form of the equation, $\dfrac{x^2}{a^2} - \dfrac{y^2}{b^2} = 1$. The equation of the hyperbola is $\dfrac{x^2}{36} - \dfrac{y^2}{4} = 1$, as shown in **Figure 6**.

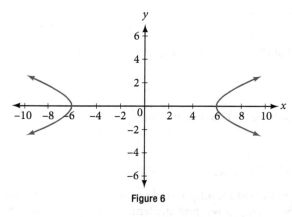

Figure 6

Try It #2

What is the standard form equation of the hyperbola that has vertices $(0, \pm 2)$ and foci $\left(0, \pm 2\sqrt{5}\right)$?

Hyperbolas Not Centered at the Origin

Like the graphs for other equations, the graph of a hyperbola can be translated. If a hyperbola is translated h units horizontally and k units vertically, the center of the hyperbola will be (h, k). This translation results in the standard form of the equation we saw previously, with x replaced by $(x - h)$ and y replaced by $(y - k)$.

> ***standard forms of the equation of a hyperbola with center (h, k)***
>
> The standard form of the equation of a hyperbola with center (h, k) and transverse axis parallel to the x-axis is
>
> $$\frac{(x - h)^2}{a^2} - \frac{(y - k)^2}{b^2} = 1$$
>
> where
> - the length of the transverse axis is $2a$
> - the coordinates of the vertices are $(h \pm a, k)$
> - the length of the conjugate axis is $2b$
> - the coordinates of the co-vertices are $(h, k \pm b)$
> - the distance between the foci is $2c$, where $c^2 = a^2 + b^2$
> - the coordinates of the foci are $(h \pm c, k)$

The asymptotes of the hyperbola coincide with the diagonals of the central rectangle. The length of the rectangle is $2a$ and its width is $2b$. The slopes of the diagonals are $\pm\dfrac{b}{a}$, and each diagonal passes through the center (h, k).

Using the **point-slope formula**, it is simple to show that the equations of the asymptotes are $y = \pm\dfrac{b}{a}(x - h) + k$. See **Figure 7a.**

The standard form of the equation of a hyperbola with center (h, k) and transverse axis parallel to the y-axis is

$$\frac{(y - k)^2}{a^2} - \frac{(x - h)^2}{b^2} = 1$$

where

- the length of the transverse axis is $2a$
- the coordinates of the vertices are $(h, k \pm a)$
- the length of the conjugate axis is $2b$
- the coordinates of the co-vertices are $(h \pm b, k)$
- the distance between the foci is $2c$, where $c^2 = a^2 + b^2$
- the coordinates of the foci are $(h, k \pm c)$

Using the reasoning above, the equations of the asymptotes are $y = \pm\dfrac{a}{b}(x - h) + k$. See **Figure 7b.**

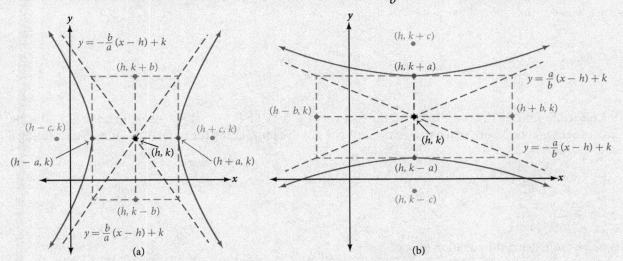

Figure 7 (a) Horizontal hyperbola with center (h, k) (b) Vertical hyperbola with center (h, k)

Like hyperbolas centered at the origin, hyperbolas centered at a point (h, k) have vertices, co-vertices, and foci that are related by the equation $c^2 = a^2 + b^2$. We can use this relationship along with the midpoint and distance formulas to find the standard equation of a hyperbola when the vertices and foci are given.

How To...

Given the vertices and foci of a hyperbola centered at (h, k), write its equation in standard form.

1. Determine whether the transverse axis is parallel to the x- or y-axis.

    a. If the y-coordinates of the given vertices and foci are the same, then the transverse axis is parallel to the x-axis. Use the standard form $\dfrac{(x - h)^2}{a^2} - \dfrac{(y - k)^2}{b^2} = 1.$

    b. If the x-coordinates of the given vertices and foci are the same, then the transverse axis is parallel to the y-axis. Use the standard form $\dfrac{(y - k)^2}{a^2} - \dfrac{(x - h)^2}{b^2} = 1.$

2. Identify the center of the hyperbola, (h, k), using the midpoint formula and the given coordinates for the vertices.

3. Find a^2 by solving for the length of the transverse axis, $2a$, which is the distance between the given vertices.
4. Find c^2 using h and k found in Step 2 along with the given coordinates for the foci.
5. Solve for b^2 using the equation $b^2 = c^2 - a^2$.
6. Substitute the values for h, k, a^2, and b^2 into the standard form of the equation determined in Step 1.

Example 3　Finding the Equation of a Hyperbola Centered at (h, k) Given its Foci and Vertices

What is the standard form equation of the hyperbola that has vertices at $(0, -2)$ and $(6, -2)$ and foci at $(-2, -2)$ and $(8, -2)$?

Solution　The y-coordinates of the vertices and foci are the same, so the transverse axis is parallel to the x-axis. Thus, the equation of the hyperbola will have the form

$$\frac{(x - h)^2}{a^2} - \frac{(y - k)^2}{b^2} = 1$$

First, we identify the center, (h, k). The center is halfway between the vertices $(0, -2)$ and $(6, -2)$. Applying the midpoint formula, we have

$$(h, k) = \left(\frac{0 + 6}{2}, \frac{-2 + (-2)}{2} \right) = (3, -2)$$

Next, we find a^2. The length of the transverse axis, $2a$, is bounded by the vertices. So, we can find a^2 by finding the distance between the x-coordinates of the vertices.

$$2a = |0 - 6|$$
$$2a = 6$$
$$a = 3$$
$$a^2 = 9$$

Now we need to find c^2. The coordinates of the foci are $(h \pm c, k)$. So $(h - c, k) = (-2, -2)$ and $(h + c, k) = (8, -2)$. We can use the x-coordinate from either of these points to solve for c. Using the point $(8, -2)$, and substituting $h = 3$,

$$h + c = 8$$
$$3 + c = 8$$
$$c = 5$$
$$c^2 = 25$$

Next, solve for b^2 using the equation $b^2 = c^2 - a^2$:

$$b^2 = c^2 - a^2$$
$$= 25 - 9$$
$$= 16$$

Finally, substitute the values found for h, k, a^2, and b^2 into the standard form of the equation.

$$\frac{(x - 3)^2}{9} - \frac{(y + 2)^2}{16} = 1$$

Try It #3

What is the standard form equation of the hyperbola that has vertices $(1, -2)$ and $(1, 8)$ and foci $(1, -10)$ and $(1, 16)$?

Graphing Hyperbolas Centered at the Origin

When we have an equation in standard form for a hyperbola centered at the origin, we can interpret its parts to identify the key features of its graph: the center, vertices, co-vertices, asymptotes, foci, and lengths and positions of the transverse and conjugate axes. To graph hyperbolas centered at the origin, we use the standard form $\frac{x^2}{a^2} - \frac{y^2}{b^2} = 1$ for horizontal hyperbolas and the standard form $\frac{y^2}{a^2} - \frac{x^2}{b^2} = 1$ for vertical hyperbolas.

How To...

Given a standard form equation for a hyperbola centered at (0, 0), sketch the graph.

1. Determine which of the standard forms applies to the given equation.

2. Use the standard form identified in Step 1 to determine the position of the transverse axis; coordinates for the vertices, co-vertices, and foci; and the equations for the asymptotes.

   a. If the equation is in the form $\frac{x^2}{a^2} - \frac{y^2}{b^2} = 1$, then

   - the transverse axis is on the x-axis
   - the coordinates of the vertices are $(\pm a, 0)$
   - the coordinates of the co-vertices are $(0, \pm b)$
   - the coordinates of the foci are $(\pm c, 0)$
   - the equations of the asymptotes are $y = \pm \frac{b}{a} x$

   b. If the equation is in the form $\frac{y^2}{a^2} - \frac{x^2}{b^2} = 1$, then

   - the transverse axis is on the y-axis
   - the coordinates of the vertices are $(0, \pm a)$
   - the coordinates of the co-vertices are $(\pm b, 0)$
   - the coordinates of the foci are $(0, \pm c)$
   - the equations of the asymptotes are $y = \pm \frac{a}{b} x$

3. Solve for the coordinates of the foci using the equation $c = \pm \sqrt{a^2 + b^2}$.

4. Plot the vertices, co-vertices, foci, and asymptotes in the coordinate plane, and draw a smooth curve to form the hyperbola.

Example 4   **Graphing a Hyperbola Centered at (0, 0) Given an Equation in Standard Form**

Graph the hyperbola given by the equation $\frac{y^2}{64} - \frac{x^2}{36} = 1$. Identify and label the vertices, co-vertices, foci, and asymptotes.

Solution   The standard form that applies to the given equation is $\frac{y^2}{a^2} - \frac{x^2}{b^2} = 1$. Thus, the transverse axis is on the y-axis

The coordinates of the vertices are $(0, \pm a) = (0, \pm \sqrt{64}) = (0, \pm 8)$

The coordinates of the co-vertices are $(\pm b, 0) = (\pm \sqrt{36}, 0) = (\pm 6, 0)$

The coordinates of the foci are $(0, \pm c)$, where $c = \pm \sqrt{a^2 + b^2}$. Solving for c, we have

$$c = \pm \sqrt{a^2 + b^2} = \pm \sqrt{64 + 36} = \pm \sqrt{100} = \pm 10$$

Therefore, the coordinates of the foci are $(0, \pm 10)$

The equations of the asymptotes are $y = \pm \frac{a}{b} x = \pm \frac{8}{6} x = \pm \frac{4}{3} x$

Plot and label the vertices and co-vertices, and then sketch the central rectangle. Sides of the rectangle are parallel to the axes and pass through the vertices and co-vertices. Sketch and extend the diagonals of the central rectangle to show the asymptotes. The central rectangle and asymptotes provide the framework needed to sketch an accurate graph of the hyperbola. Label the foci and asymptotes, and draw a smooth curve to form the hyperbola, as shown in **Figure 8**.

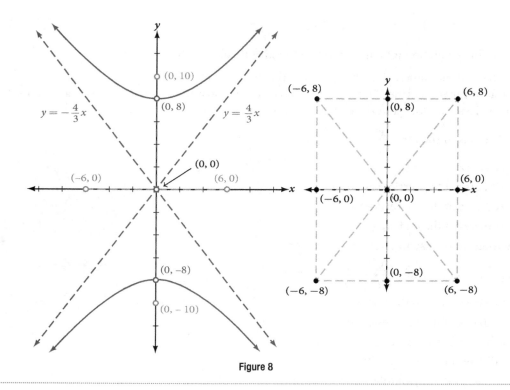

Figure 8

Try It #4

Graph the hyperbola given by the equation $\dfrac{x^2}{144} - \dfrac{y^2}{81} = 1$. Identify and label the vertices, co-vertices, foci, and asymptotes.

Graphing Hyperbolas Not Centered at the Origin

Graphing hyperbolas centered at a point (h, k) other than the origin is similar to graphing ellipses centered at a point other than the origin. We use the standard forms $\dfrac{(x - h)^2}{a^2} - \dfrac{(y - k)^2}{b^2} = 1$ for horizontal hyperbolas, and $\dfrac{(y - k)^2}{a^2} - \dfrac{(x - h)^2}{b^2} = 1$ for vertical hyperbolas. From these standard form equations we can easily calculate and plot key features of the graph: the coordinates of its center, vertices, co-vertices, and foci; the equations of its asymptotes; and the positions of the transverse and conjugate axes.

How To…

Given a general form for a hyperbola centered at (h, k), sketch the graph.

1. Determine which of the standard forms applies to the given equation. Convert the general form to that standard form.
2. Use the standard form identified in Step 1 to determine the position of the transverse axis; coordinates for the center, vertices, co-vertices, foci; and equations for the asymptotes.

   a. If the equation is in the form $\dfrac{(x - h)^2}{a^2} - \dfrac{(y - k)^2}{b^2} = 1$, then
      - the transverse axis is parallel to the x-axis
      - the center is (h, k)
      - the coordinates of the vertices are $(h \pm a, k)$
      - the coordinates of the co-vertices are $(h, k \pm b)$
      - the coordinates of the foci are $(h \pm c, k)$
      - the equations of the asymptotes are $y = \pm \dfrac{b}{a}(x - h) + k$

b. If the equation is in the form $\dfrac{(y-k)^2}{a^2} - \dfrac{(x-h)^2}{b^2} = 1$, then

- the transverse axis is parallel to the y-axis
- the center is (h, k)
- the coordinates of the vertices are $(h, k \pm a)$
- the coordinates of the co-vertices are $(h \pm b, k)$
- the coordinates of the foci are $(h, k \pm c)$
- the equations of the asymptotes are $y = \pm \dfrac{a}{b}(x - h) + k$

3. Solve for the coordinates of the foci using the equation $c = \pm \sqrt{a^2 + b^2}$.

4. Plot the center, vertices, co-vertices, foci, and asymptotes in the coordinate plane and draw a smooth curve to form the hyperbola.

Example 5   **Graphing a Hyperbola Centered at (h, k) Given an Equation in General Form**

Graph the hyperbola given by the equation $9x^2 - 4y^2 - 36x - 40y - 388 = 0$. Identify and label the center, vertices, co-vertices, foci, and asymptotes.

Solution   Start by expressing the equation in standard form. Group terms that contain the same variable, and move the constant to the opposite side of the equation.

$$(9x^2 - 36x) - (4y^2 + 40y) = 388$$

Factor the leading coefficient of each expression.

$$9(x^2 - 4x) - 4(y^2 + 10y) = 388$$

Complete the square twice. Remember to balance the equation by adding the same constants to each side.

$$9(x^2 - 4x + 4) - 4(y^2 + 10y + 25) = 388 + 36 - 100$$

Rewrite as perfect squares.

$$9(x - 2)^2 - 4(y + 5)^2 = 324$$

Divide both sides by the constant term to place the equation in standard form.

$$\frac{(x - 2)^2}{36} - \frac{(y + 5)^2}{81} = 1$$

The standard form that applies to the given equation is $\dfrac{(x - h)^2}{a^2} - \dfrac{(y - k)^2}{b^2} = 1$, where $a^2 = 36$ and $b^2 = 81$, or $a = 6$ and $b = 9$. Thus, the transverse axis is parallel to the x-axis. It follows that:

- the center of the ellipse is $(h, k) = (2, -5)$
- the coordinates of the vertices are $(h \pm a, k) = (2 \pm 6, -5)$, or $(-4, -5)$ and $(8, -5)$
- the coordinates of the co-vertices are $(h, k \pm b) = (2, -5 \pm 9)$, or $(2, -14)$ and $(2, 4)$
- the coordinates of the foci are $(h \pm c, k)$, where $c = \pm \sqrt{a^2 + b^2}$. Solving for c, we have

$$c = \pm \sqrt{36 + 81} = \pm \sqrt{117} = \pm 3\sqrt{13}$$

Therefore, the coordinates of the foci are $(2 - 3\sqrt{13}, -5)$ and $(2 + 3\sqrt{13}, -5)$.

The equations of the asymptotes are $y = \pm \dfrac{b}{a}(x - h) + k = \pm \dfrac{3}{2}(x - 2) - 5$.

Next, we plot and label the center, vertices, co-vertices, foci, and asymptotes and draw smooth curves to form the hyperbola, as shown in **Figure 9**.

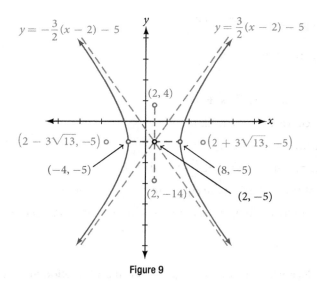

Figure 9

Try It #5

Graph the hyperbola given by the standard form of an equation $\dfrac{(y+4)^2}{100} - \dfrac{(x-3)^2}{64} = 1$. Identify and label the center, vertices, co-vertices, foci, and asymptotes.

Solving Applied Problems Involving Hyperbolas

As we discussed at the beginning of this section, hyperbolas have real-world applications in many fields, such as astronomy, physics, engineering, and architecture. The design efficiency of hyperbolic cooling towers is particularly interesting. Cooling towers are used to transfer waste heat to the atmosphere and are often touted for their ability to generate power efficiently. Because of their hyperbolic form, these structures are able to withstand extreme winds while requiring less material than any other forms of their size and strength. See **Figure 10**. For example, a 500-foot tower can be made of a reinforced concrete shell only 6 or 8 inches wide!

Figure 10 Cooling towers at the Drax power station in North Yorkshire, United Kingdom (credit: Les Haines, Flickr)

The first hyperbolic towers were designed in 1914 and were 35 meters high. Today, the tallest cooling towers are in France, standing a remarkable 170 meters tall. In **Example 6** we will use the design layout of a cooling tower to find a hyperbolic equation that models its sides.

Example 6   **Solving Applied Problems Involving Hyperbolas**

The design layout of a cooling tower is shown in **Figure 11**. The tower stands 179.6 meters tall. The diameter of the top is 72 meters. At their closest, the sides of the tower are 60 meters apart.

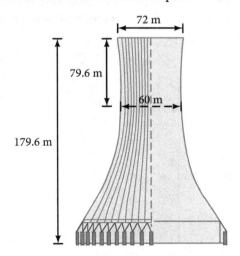

Figure 11 Project design for a natural draft cooling tower

Find the equation of the hyperbola that models the sides of the cooling tower. Assume that the center of the hyperbola—indicated by the intersection of dashed perpendicular lines in the figure—is the origin of the coordinate plane. Round final values to four decimal places.

Solution   We are assuming the center of the tower is at the origin, so we can use the standard form of a horizontal hyperbola centered at the origin: $\dfrac{x^2}{a^2} - \dfrac{y^2}{b^2} = 1$, where the branches of the hyperbola form the sides of the cooling tower. We must find the values of a^2 and b^2 to complete the model.

First, we find a^2. Recall that the length of the transverse axis of a hyperbola is $2a$. This length is represented by the distance where the sides are closest, which is given as 65.3 meters. So, $2a = 60$. Therefore, $a = 30$ and $a^2 = 900$.

To solve for b^2, we need to substitute for x and y in our equation using a known point. To do this, we can use the dimensions of the tower to find some point (x, y) that lies on the hyperbola. We will use the top right corner of the tower to represent that point. Since the y-axis bisects the tower, our x-value can be represented by the radius of the top, or 36 meters. The y-value is represented by the distance from the origin to the top, which is given as 79.6 meters. Therefore,

$$\frac{x^2}{a^2} - \frac{y^2}{b^2} = 1 \qquad\qquad \text{Standard form of horizontal hyperbola.}$$

$$b^2 = \frac{y^2}{\dfrac{x^2}{a^2} - 1} \qquad\qquad \text{Isolate } b^2$$

$$= \frac{(79.6)^2}{\dfrac{(36)^2}{900} - 1} \qquad\qquad \text{Substitute for } a^2, x, \text{ and } y$$

$$\approx 14400.3636 \qquad\qquad \text{Round to four decimal places}$$

The sides of the tower can be modeled by the hyperbolic equation

$$\frac{x^2}{900} - \frac{y^2}{14400.3636} = 1, \text{ or } \frac{x^2}{30^2} - \frac{y^2}{120.0015^2} = 1$$

Try It #6

A design for a cooling tower project is shown in **Figure 12**. Find the equation of the hyperbola that models the sides of the cooling tower. Assume that the center of the hyperbola—indicated by the intersection of dashed perpendicular lines in the figure—is the origin of the coordinate plane. Round final values to four decimal places.

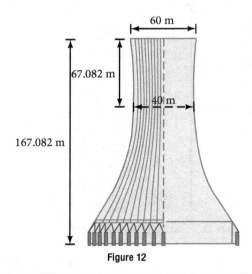

Figure 12

Access these online resources for additional instruction and practice with hyperbolas.

- Conic Sections: The Hyperbola Part 1 of 2 (http://openstaxcollege.org/l/hyperbola1)
- Conic Sections: The Hyperbola Part 2 of 2 (http://openstaxcollege.org/l/hyperbola2)
- Graph a Hyperbola with Center at Origin (http://openstaxcollege.org/l/hyperbolaorigin)
- Graph a Hyperbola with Center not at Origin (http://openstaxcollege.org/l/hbnotorigin)

12.2 SECTION EXERCISES

VERBAL

1. Define a hyperbola in terms of its foci.

2. What can we conclude about a hyperbola if its asymptotes intersect at the origin?

3. What must be true of the foci of a hyperbola?

4. If the transverse axis of a hyperbola is vertical, what do we know about the graph?

5. Where must the center of hyperbola be relative to its foci?

ALGEBRAIC

For the following exercises, determine whether the following equations represent hyperbolas. If so, write in standard form.

6. $3y^2 + 2x = 6$

7. $\dfrac{x^2}{36} - \dfrac{y^2}{9} = 1$

8. $5y^2 + 4x^2 = 6x$

9. $25x^2 - 16y^2 = 400$

10. $-9x^2 + 18x + y^2 + 4y - 14 = 0$

For the following exercises, write the equation for the hyperbola in standard form if it is not already, and identify the vertices and foci, and write equations of asymptotes.

11. $\dfrac{x^2}{25} - \dfrac{y^2}{36} = 1$

12. $\dfrac{x^2}{100} - \dfrac{y^2}{9} = 1$

13. $\dfrac{y^2}{4} - \dfrac{x^2}{81} = 1$

14. $9y^2 - 4x^2 = 1$

15. $\dfrac{(x-1)^2}{9} - \dfrac{(y-2)^2}{16} = 1$

16. $\dfrac{(y-6)^2}{36} - \dfrac{(x+1)^2}{16} = 1$

17. $\dfrac{(x-2)^2}{49} - \dfrac{(y+7)^2}{49} = 1$

18. $4x^2 - 8x - 9y^2 - 72y + 112 = 0$

19. $-9x^2 - 54x + 9y^2 - 54y + 81 = 0$

20. $4x^2 - 24x - 36y^2 - 360y + 864 = 0$

21. $-4x^2 + 24x + 16y^2 - 128y + 156 = 0$

22. $-4x^2 + 40x + 25y^2 - 100y + 100 = 0$

23. $x^2 + 2x - 100y^2 - 1000y + 2401 = 0$

24. $-9x^2 + 72x + 16y^2 + 16y + 4 = 0$

25. $4x^2 + 24x - 25y^2 + 200y - 464 = 0$

For the following exercises, find the equations of the asymptotes for each hyperbola.

26. $\dfrac{y^2}{3^2} - \dfrac{x^2}{3^2} = 1$

27. $\dfrac{(x-3)^2}{5^2} - \dfrac{(y+4)^2}{2^2} = 1$

28. $\dfrac{(y-3)^2}{3^2} - \dfrac{(x+5)^2}{6^2} = 1$

29. $9x^2 - 18x - 16y^2 + 32y - 151 = 0$

30. $16y^2 + 96y - 4x^2 + 16x + 112 = 0$

GRAPHICAL

For the following exercises, sketch a graph of the hyperbola, labeling vertices and foci.

31. $\dfrac{x^2}{49} - \dfrac{y^2}{16} = 1$

32. $\dfrac{x^2}{64} - \dfrac{y^2}{4} = 1$

33. $\dfrac{y^2}{9} - \dfrac{x^2}{25} = 1$

34. $81x^2 - 9y^2 = 1$

35. $\dfrac{(y+5)^2}{9} - \dfrac{(x-4)^2}{25} = 1$

36. $\dfrac{(x-2)^2}{8} - \dfrac{(y+3)^2}{27} = 1$

37. $\dfrac{(y-3)^2}{9} - \dfrac{(x-3)^2}{9} = 1$

38. $-4x^2 - 8x + 16y^2 - 32y - 52 = 0$

39. $x^2 - 8x - 25y^2 - 100y - 109 = 0$

40. $-x^2 + 8x + 4y^2 - 40y + 88 = 0$

41. $64x^2 + 128x - 9y^2 - 72y - 656 = 0$

42. $16x^2 + 64x - 4y^2 - 8y - 4 = 0$

43. $-100x^2 + 1000x + y^2 - 10y - 2575 = 0$

44. $4x^2 + 16x - 4y^2 + 16y + 16 = 0$

For the following exercises, given information about the graph of the hyperbola, find its equation.

45. Vertices at $(3, 0)$ and $(-3, 0)$ and one focus at $(5, 0)$.

46. Vertices at $(0, 6)$ and $(0, -6)$ and one focus at $(0, -8)$.

47. Vertices at $(1, 1)$ and $(11, 1)$ and one focus at $(12, 1)$.

48. Center: $(0, 0)$; vertex: $(0, -13)$; one focus: $(0, \sqrt{313})$.

49. Center: $(4, 2)$; vertex: $(9, 2)$; one focus: $(4 + \sqrt{26}, 2)$.

50. Center: $(3, 5)$; vertex: $(3, 11)$; one focus: $(3, 5 + 2\sqrt{10})$.

For the following exercises, given the graph of the hyperbola, find its equation.

51.

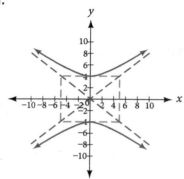

52.

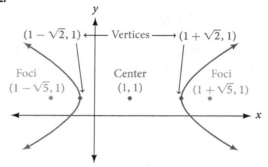

53.

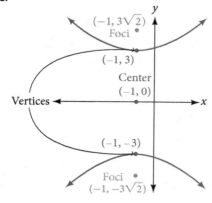

54.

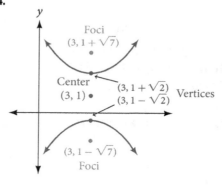

55.

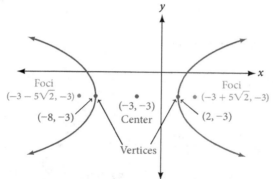

EXTENSIONS

For the following exercises, express the equation for the hyperbola as two functions, with y as a function of x. Express as simply as possible. Use a graphing calculator to sketch the graph of the two functions on the same axes.

56. $\dfrac{x^2}{4} - \dfrac{y^2}{9} = 1$

57. $\dfrac{y^2}{9} - \dfrac{x^2}{1} = 1$

58. $\dfrac{(x-2)^2}{16} - \dfrac{(y+3)^2}{25} = 1$

59. $-4x^2 - 16x + y^2 - 2y - 19 = 0$ **60.** $4x^2 - 24x - y^2 - 4y + 16 = 0$

REAL-WORLD APPLICATIONS

For the following exercises, a hedge is to be constructed in the shape of a hyperbola near a fountain at the center of the yard. Find the equation of the hyperbola and sketch the graph.

61. The hedge will follow the asymptotes $y = x$ and $y = -x$, and its closest distance to the center fountain is 5 yards.

62. The hedge will follow the asymptotes $y = 2x$ and $y = -2x$, and its closest distance to the center fountain is 6 yards.

63. The hedge will follow the asymptotes $y = \dfrac{1}{2}x$ and $y = -\dfrac{1}{2}x$, and its closest distance to the center fountain is 10 yards.

64. The hedge will follow the asymptotes $y = \dfrac{2}{3}x$ and $y = -\dfrac{2}{3}x$, and its closest distance to the center fountain is 12 yards.

65. The hedge will follow the asymptotes $y = \dfrac{3}{4}x$ and $y = -\dfrac{3}{4}x$, and its closest distance to the center fountain is 20 yards.

For the following exercises, assume an object enters our solar system and we want to graph its path on a coordinate system with the sun at the origin and the x-axis as the axis of symmetry for the object's path. Give the equation of the flight path of each object using the given information.

66. The object enters along a path approximated by the line $y = x - 2$ and passes within 1 au (astronomical unit) of the sun at its closest approach, so that the sun is one focus of the hyperbola. It then departs the solar system along a path approximated by the line $y = -x + 2$.

67. The object enters along a path approximated by the line $y = 2x - 2$ and passes within 0.5 au of the sun at its closest approach, so the sun is one focus of the hyperbola. It then departs the solar system along a path approximated by the line $y = -2x + 2$.

68. The object enters along a path approximated by the line $y = 0.5x + 2$ and passes within 1 au of the sun at its closest approach, so the sun is one focus of the hyperbola. It then departs the solar system along a path approximated by the line $y = -0.5x - 2$.

69. The object enters along a path approximated by the line $y = \dfrac{1}{3}x - 1$ and passes within 1 au of the sun at its closest approach, so the sun is one focus of the hyperbola. It then departs the solar system along a path approximated by the line $y = -\dfrac{1}{3}x + 1$.

70. The object enters along a path approximated by the line $y = 3x - 9$ and passes within 1 au of the sun at its closest approach, so the sun is one focus of the hyperbola. It then departs the solar system along a path approximated by the line $y = -3x + 9$.

LEARNING OBJECTIVES

In this section, you will:

- Graph parabolas with vertices at the origin.
- Write equations of parabolas in standard form.
- Graph parabolas with vertices not at the origin.
- Solve applied problems involving parabolas.

12.3   THE PARABOLA

Figure 1 The Olympic torch concludes its journey around the world when it is used to light the Olympic cauldron during the opening ceremony. (credit: Ken Hackman, U.S. Air Force)

Did you know that the Olympic torch is lit several months before the start of the games? The ceremonial method for lighting the flame is the same as in ancient times. The ceremony takes place at the Temple of Hera in Olympia, Greece, and is rooted in Greek mythology, paying tribute to Prometheus, who stole fire from Zeus to give to all humans. One of eleven acting priestesses places the torch at the focus of a parabolic mirror (see **Figure 1**), which focuses light rays from the sun to ignite the flame.

Parabolic mirrors (or reflectors) are able to capture energy and focus it to a single point. The advantages of this property are evidenced by the vast list of parabolic objects we use every day: satellite dishes, suspension bridges, telescopes, microphones, spotlights, and car headlights, to name a few. Parabolic reflectors are also used in alternative energy devices, such as solar cookers and water heaters, because they are inexpensive to manufacture and need little maintenance. In this section we will explore the parabola and its uses, including low-cost, energy-efficient solar designs.

Graphing Parabolas with Vertices at the Origin

In **The Ellipse,** we saw that an ellipse is formed when a plane cuts through a right circular cone. If the plane is parallel to the edge of the cone, an unbounded curve is formed. This curve is a **parabola**. See **Figure 2**.

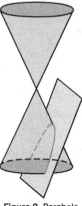

Figure 2 Parabola

Like the ellipse and hyperbola, the parabola can also be defined by a set of points in the coordinate plane. A parabola is the set of all points (x, y) in a plane that are the same distance from a fixed line, called the **directrix**, and a fixed point (the **focus**) not on the directrix.

In **Quadratic Functions**, we learned about a parabola's vertex and axis of symmetry. Now we extend the discussion to include other key features of the parabola. See **Figure 3**. Notice that the axis of symmetry passes through the focus and vertex and is perpendicular to the directrix. The vertex is the midpoint between the directrix and the focus.

The line segment that passes through the focus and is parallel to the directrix is called the **latus rectum**. The endpoints of the latus rectum lie on the curve. By definition, the distance d from the focus to any point P on the parabola is equal to the distance from P to the directrix.

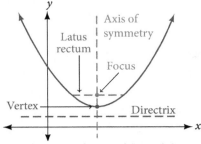

Figure 3 Key features of the parabola

To work with parabolas in the coordinate plane, we consider two cases: those with a vertex at the origin and those with a vertex at a point other than the origin. We begin with the former.

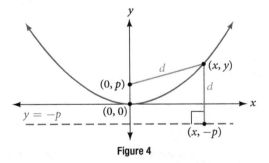

Figure 4

Let (x, y) be a point on the parabola with vertex $(0, 0)$, focus $(0, p)$, and directrix $y = -p$ as shown in **Figure 4**. The distance d from point (x, y) to point $(x, -p)$ on the directrix is the difference of the y-values: $d = y + p$. The distance from the focus $(0, p)$ to the point (x, y) is also equal to d and can be expressed using the distance formula.

$$d = \sqrt{(x - 0)^2 + (y - p)^2}$$
$$= \sqrt{x^2 + (y - p)^2}$$

Set the two expressions for d equal to each other and solve for y to derive the equation of the parabola. We do this because the distance from (x, y) to $(0, p)$ equals the distance from (x, y) to $(x, -p)$.

$$\sqrt{x^2 + (y - p)^2} = y + p$$

We then square both sides of the equation, expand the squared terms, and simplify by combining like terms.

$$x^2 + (y - p)^2 = (y + p)^2$$
$$x^2 + y^2 - 2py + p^2 = y^2 + 2py + p^2$$
$$x^2 - 2py = 2py$$
$$x^2 = 4py$$

The equations of parabolas with vertex $(0, 0)$ are $y^2 = 4px$ when the x-axis is the axis of symmetry and $x^2 = 4py$ when the y-axis is the axis of symmetry. These standard forms are given below, along with their general graphs and key features.

standard forms of parabolas with vertex **(0, 0)**

Table 1 and **Figure 5** summarize the standard features of parabolas with a vertex at the origin.

Axis of Symmetry	Equation	Focus	Directrix	Endpoints of Latus Rectum
x-axis	$y^2 = 4px$	$(p, 0)$	$x = -p$	$(p, \pm 2p)$
y-axis	$x^2 = 4py$	$(0, p)$	$y = -p$	$(\pm 2p, p)$

Table 1

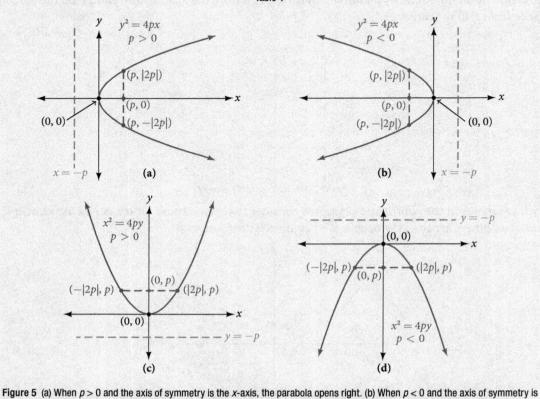

Figure 5 (a) When $p > 0$ and the axis of symmetry is the x-axis, the parabola opens right. (b) When $p < 0$ and the axis of symmetry is the x-axis, the parabola opens left. (c) When $p < 0$ and the axis of symmetry is the y-axis, the parabola opens up. (d) When $p < 0$ and the axis of symmetry is the y-axis, the parabola opens down.

The key features of a parabola are its vertex, axis of symmetry, focus, directrix, and latus rectum. See **Figure 5**. When given a standard equation for a parabola centered at the origin, we can easily identify the key features to graph the parabola.

A line is said to be tangent to a curve if it intersects the curve at exactly one point. If we sketch lines tangent to the parabola at the endpoints of the latus rectum, these lines intersect on the axis of symmetry, as shown in **Figure 6**.

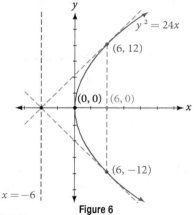

Figure 6

How To...

Given a standard form equation for a parabola centered at (0, 0), sketch the graph.

1. Determine which of the standard forms applies to the given equation: $y^2 = 4px$ or $x^2 = 4py$.
2. Use the standard form identified in Step 1 to determine the axis of symmetry, focus, equation of the directrix, and endpoints of the latus rectum.

   a. If the equation is in the form $y^2 = 4px$, then
      - the axis of symmetry is the x-axis, $y = 0$
      - set $4p$ equal to the coefficient of x in the given equation to solve for p. If $p > 0$, the parabola opens right. If $p < 0$, the parabola opens left.
      - use p to find the coordinates of the focus, $(p, 0)$
      - use p to find the equation of the directrix, $x = -p$
      - use p to find the endpoints of the latus rectum, $(p, \pm 2p)$. Alternately, substitute $x = p$ into the original equation.

   b. If the equation is in the form $x^2 = 4py$, then
      - the axis of symmetry is the y-axis, $x = 0$
      - set $4p$ equal to the coefficient of y in the given equation to solve for p. If $p > 0$, the parabola opens up. If $p < 0$, the parabola opens down.
      - use p to find the coordinates of the focus, $(0, p)$
      - use p to find equation of the directrix, $y = -p$
      - use p to find the endpoints of the latus rectum, $(\pm 2p, p)$

3. Plot the focus, directrix, and latus rectum, and draw a smooth curve to form the parabola.

Example 1   **Graphing a Parabola with Vertex (0, 0) and the x-axis as the Axis of Symmetry**

Graph $y^2 = 24x$. Identify and label the focus, directrix, and endpoints of the latus rectum.

Solution   The standard form that applies to the given equation is $y^2 = 4px$. Thus, the axis of symmetry is the x-axis. It follows that:

- $24 = 4p$, so $p = 6$. Since $p > 0$, the parabola opens right
- the coordinates of the focus are $(p, 0) = (6, 0)$
- the equation of the directrix is $x = -p = -6$
- the endpoints of the latus rectum have the same x-coordinate at the focus. To find the endpoints, substitute $x = 6$ into the original equation: $(6, \pm 12)$

Next we plot the focus, directrix, and latus rectum, and draw a smooth curve to form the parabola. See **Figure 7**.

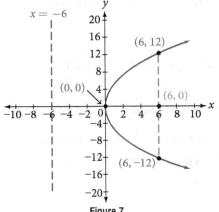

Figure 7

Try It #1

Graph $y^2 = -16x$. Identify and label the focus, directrix, and endpoints of the latus rectum.

Example 2 **Graphing a Parabola with Vertex (0, 0) and the y-axis as the Axis of Symmetry**

Graph $x^2 = -6y$. Identify and label the focus, directrix, and endpoints of the latus rectum.

Solution The standard form that applies to the given equation is $x^2 = 4py$. Thus, the axis of symmetry is the y-axis. It follows that:

- $-6 = 4p$, so $p = -\frac{3}{2}$. Since $p < 0$, the parabola opens down.
- the coordinates of the focus are $(0, p) = \left(0, -\frac{3}{2}\right)$
- the equation of the directrix is $y = -p = \frac{3}{2}$
- the endpoints of the latus rectum can be found by substituting $y = \frac{3}{2}$ into the original equation, $\left(\pm 3, -\frac{3}{2}\right)$

Next we plot the focus, directrix, and latus rectum, and draw a smooth curve to form the parabola.

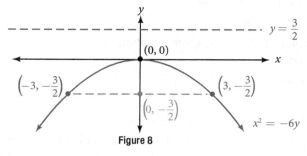

Figure 8

Try It #2

Graph $x^2 = 8y$. Identify and label the focus, directrix, and endpoints of the latus rectum.

Writing Equations of Parabolas in Standard Form

In the previous examples, we used the standard form equation of a parabola to calculate the locations of its key features. We can also use the calculations in reverse to write an equation for a parabola when given its key features.

How To...

Given its focus and directrix, write the equation for a parabola in standard form.

1. Determine whether the axis of symmetry is the x- or y-axis.

   a. If the given coordinates of the focus have the form $(p, 0)$, then the axis of symmetry is the x-axis.
      Use the standard form $y^2 = 4px$.

   b. If the given coordinates of the focus have the form $(0, p)$, then the axis of symmetry is the y-axis.
      Use the standard form $x^2 = 4py$.

2. Multiply $4p$.

3. Substitute the value from Step 2 into the equation determined in Step 1.

Example 3 **Writing the Equation of a Parabola in Standard Form Given its Focus and Directrix**

What is the equation for the parabola with focus $\left(-\frac{1}{2}, 0\right)$ and directrix $x = \frac{1}{2}$?

Solution The focus has the form $(p, 0)$, so the equation will have the form $y^2 = 4px$.

- Multiplying $4p$, we have $4p = 4\left(-\frac{1}{2}\right) = -2$.
- Substituting for $4p$, we have $y^2 = 4px = -2x$.

Therefore, the equation for the parabola is $y^2 = -2x$.

Try It #3

What is the equation for the parabola with focus $\left(0, \frac{7}{2}\right)$ and directrix $y = -\frac{7}{2}$?

Graphing Parabolas with Vertices Not at the Origin

Like other graphs we've worked with, the graph of a parabola can be translated. If a parabola is translated h units horizontally and k units vertically, the vertex will be (h, k). This translation results in the standard form of the equation we saw previously with x replaced by $(x - h)$ and y replaced by $(y - k)$.

To graph parabolas with a vertex (h, k) other than the origin, we use the standard form $(y - k)^2 = 4p(x - h)$ for parabolas that have an axis of symmetry parallel to the x-axis, and $(x - h)^2 = 4p(y - k)$ for parabolas that have an axis of symmetry parallel to the y-axis. These standard forms are given below, along with their general graphs and key features.

standard forms of parabolas with vertex (h, k)

Table 2 and **Figure 9** summarize the standard features of parabolas with a vertex at a point (h, k).

Axis of Symmetry	Equation	Focus	Directrix	Endpoints of Latus Rectum
$y = k$	$(y - k)^2 = 4p(x - h)$	$(h + p, k)$	$x = h - p$	$(h + p, k \pm 2p)$
$x = h$	$(x - h)^2 = 4p(y - k)$	$(h, k + p)$	$y = k - p$	$(h \pm 2p, k + p)$

Table 2

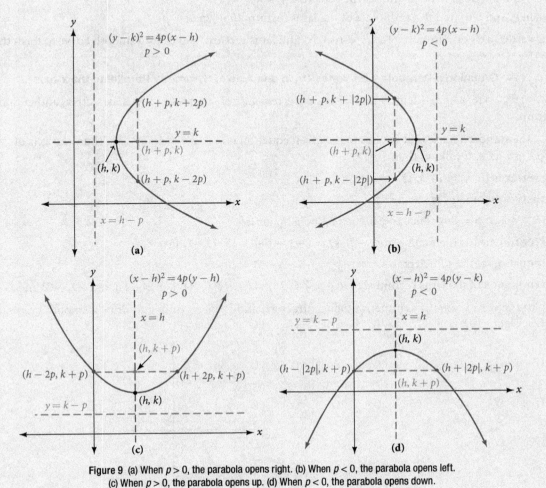

Figure 9 (a) When $p > 0$, the parabola opens right. (b) When $p < 0$, the parabola opens left.
(c) When $p > 0$, the parabola opens up. (d) When $p < 0$, the parabola opens down.

How To...

Given a standard form equation for a parabola centered at (h, k), sketch the graph.

1. Determine which of the standard forms applies to the given equation: $(y - k)^2 = 4p(x - h)$ or $(x - h)^2 = 4p(y - k)$.
2. Use the standard form identified in Step 1 to determine the vertex, axis of symmetry, focus, equation of the directrix, and endpoints of the latus rectum.
   a. If the equation is in the form $(y - k)^2 = 4p(x - h)$, then:
      - use the given equation to identify h and k for the vertex, (h, k)
      - use the value of k to determine the axis of symmetry, $y = k$
      - set $4p$ equal to the coefficient of $(x - h)$ in the given equation to solve for p. If $p > 0$, the parabola opens right. If $p < 0$, the parabola opens left.
      - use h, k, and p to find the coordinates of the focus, $(h + p, k)$
      - use h and p to find the equation of the directrix, $x = h - p$
      - use h, k, and p to find the endpoints of the latus rectum, $(h + p, k \pm 2p)$
   b. If the equation is in the form $(x - h)^2 = 4p(y - k)$, then:
      - use the given equation to identify h and k for the vertex, (h, k)
      - use the value of h to determine the axis of symmetry, $x = h$
      - set $4p$ equal to the coefficient of $(y - k)$ in the given equation to solve for p. If $p > 0$, the parabola opens up. If $p < 0$, the parabola opens down.
      - use h, k, and p to find the coordinates of the focus, $(h, k + p)$
      - use k and p to find the equation of the directrix, $y = k - p$
      - use h, k, and p to find the endpoints of the latus rectum, $(h \pm 2p, k + p)$
3. Plot the vertex, axis of symmetry, focus, directrix, and latus rectum, and draw a smooth curve to form the parabola.

Example 4   **Graphing a Parabola with Vertex (h, k) and Axis of Symmetry Parallel to the x-axis**

Graph $(y - 1)^2 = -16(x + 3)$. Identify and label the vertex, axis of symmetry, focus, directrix, and endpoints of the latus rectum.

Solution   The standard form that applies to the given equation is $(y - k)^2 = 4p(x - h)$. Thus, the axis of symmetry is parallel to the x-axis. It follows that:

- the vertex is $(h, k) = (-3, 1)$
- the axis of symmetry is $y = k = 1$
- $-16 = 4p$, so $p = -4$. Since $p < 0$, the parabola opens left.
- the coordinates of the focus are $(h + p, k) = (-3 + (-4), 1) = (-7, 1)$
- the equation of the directrix is $x = h - p = -3 - (-4) = 1$
- the endpoints of the latus rectum are $(h + p, k \pm 2p) = (-3 + (-4), 1 \pm 2(-4))$, or $(-7, -7)$ and $(-7, 9)$

Next we plot the vertex, axis of symmetry, focus, directrix, and latus rectum, and draw a smooth curve to form the parabola. See **Figure 10**.

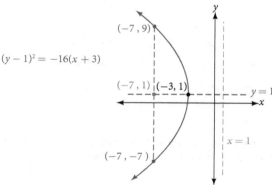

Figure 10

Try It #4

Graph $(y + 1)^2 = 4(x - 8)$. Identify and label the vertex, axis of symmetry, focus, directrix, and endpoints of the latus rectum.

Example 5   **Graphing a Parabola from an Equation Given in General Form**

Graph $x^2 - 8x - 28y - 208 = 0$. Identify and label the vertex, axis of symmetry, focus, directrix, and endpoints of the latus rectum.

Solution   Start by writing the equation of the parabola in standard form. The standard form that applies to the given equation is $(x - h)^2 = 4p(y - k)$. Thus, the axis of symmetry is parallel to the y-axis. To express the equation of the parabola in this form, we begin by isolating the terms that contain the variable x in order to complete the square.

$$x^2 - 8x - 28y - 208 = 0$$
$$x^2 - 8x = 28y + 208$$
$$x^2 - 8x + 16 = 28y + 208 + 16$$
$$(x - 4)^2 = 28y + 224$$
$$(x - 4)^2 = 28(y + 8)$$
$$(x - 4)^2 = 4 \cdot 7 \cdot (y + 8)$$

It follows that:

- the vertex is $(h, k) = (4, -8)$
- the axis of symmetry is $x = h = 4$
- since $p = 7, p > 0$ and so the parabola opens up
- the coordinates of the focus are $(h, k + p) = (4, -8 + 7) = (4, -1)$
- the equation of the directrix is $y = k - p = -8 - 7 = -15$
- the endpoints of the latus rectum are $(h \pm 2p, k + p) = (4 \pm 2(7), -8 + 7)$, or $(-10, -1)$ and $(18, -1)$

Next we plot the vertex, axis of symmetry, focus, directrix, and latus rectum, and draw a smooth curve to form the parabola. See **Figure 11**.

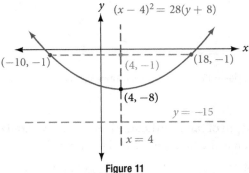

Figure 11

Try It #5

Graph $(x + 2)^2 = -20(y - 3)$. Identify and label the vertex, axis of symmetry, focus, directrix, and endpoints of the latus rectum.

Solving Applied Problems Involving Parabolas

As we mentioned at the beginning of the section, parabolas are used to design many objects we use every day, such as telescopes, suspension bridges, microphones, and radar equipment. Parabolic mirrors, such as the one used to light the Olympic torch, have a very unique reflecting property. When rays of light parallel to the parabola's axis of symmetry are directed toward any surface of the mirror, the light is reflected directly to the focus. See **Figure 12**. This is why the Olympic torch is ignited when it is held at the focus of the parabolic mirror.

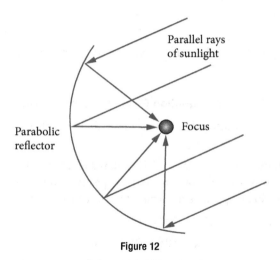

Figure 12

Parabolic mirrors have the ability to focus the sun's energy to a single point, raising the temperature hundreds of degrees in a matter of seconds. Thus, parabolic mirrors are featured in many low-cost, energy efficient solar products, such as solar cookers, solar heaters, and even travel-sized fire starters.

Example 6   **Solving Applied Problems Involving Parabolas**

A cross-section of a design for a travel-sized solar fire starter is shown in **Figure 13**. The sun's rays reflect off the parabolic mirror toward an object attached to the igniter. Because the igniter is located at the focus of the parabola, the reflected rays cause the object to burn in just seconds.

    a. Find the equation of the parabola that models the fire starter. Assume that the vertex of the parabolic mirror is the origin of the coordinate plane.

    b. Use the equation found in part (a) to find the depth of the fire starter.

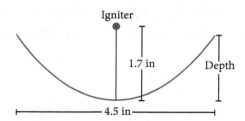

Figure 13 Cross-section of a travel-sized solar fire starter

Solution

    a. The vertex of the dish is the origin of the coordinate plane, so the parabola will take the standard form $x^2 = 4py$, where $p > 0$. The igniter, which is the focus, is 1.7 inches above the vertex of the dish. Thus we have $p = 1.7$.

$$x^2 = 4py \qquad \text{Standard form of upward-facing parabola with vertex } (0, 0)$$

$$x^2 = 4(1.7)y \qquad \text{Substitute 1.7 for } p.$$

$$x^2 = 6.8y \qquad \text{Multiply.}$$

    b. The dish extends $\dfrac{4.5}{2} = 2.25$ inches on either side of the origin. We can substitute 2.25 for x in the equation from part (a) to find the depth of the dish.

$$x^2 = 6.8y \qquad \text{Equation found in part (a).}$$

$$(2.25)^2 = 6.8y \qquad \text{Substitute 2.25 for } x.$$

$$y \approx 0.74 \qquad \text{Solve for } y.$$

The dish is about 0.74 inches deep.

Try It #6

Balcony-sized solar cookers have been designed for families living in India. The top of a dish has a diameter of 1,600 mm. The sun's rays reflect off the parabolic mirror toward the "cooker," which is placed 320 mm from the base.

a. Find an equation that models a cross-section of the solar cooker. Assume that the vertex of the parabolic mirror is the origin of the coordinate plane, and that the parabola opens to the right (i.e., has the *x*-axis as its axis of symmetry).

b. Use the equation found in part (a) to find the depth of the cooker.

Access these online resources for additional instruction and practice with parabolas.

- Conic Sections: The Parabola Part 1 of 2 (http://openstaxcollege.org/l/parabola1)
- Conic Sections: The Parabola Part 2 of 2 (http://openstaxcollege.org/l/parabola2)
- Parabola with Vertical Axis (http://openstaxcollege.org/l/parabolavertcal)
- Parabola with Horizontal Axis (http://openstaxcollege.org/l/parabolahoriz)

12.3   SECTION EXERCISES

VERBAL

1. Define a parabola in terms of its focus and directrix.

2. If the equation of a parabola is written in standard form and p is positive and the directrix is a vertical line, then what can we conclude about its graph?

3. If the equation of a parabola is written in standard form and p is negative and the directrix is a horizontal line, then what can we conclude about its graph?

4. What is the effect on the graph of a parabola if its equation in standard form has increasing values of p?

5. As the graph of a parabola becomes wider, what will happen to the distance between the focus and directrix?

ALGEBRAIC

For the following exercises, determine whether the given equation is a parabola. If so, rewrite the equation in standard form.

6. $y^2 = 4 - x^2$

7. $y = 4x^2$

8. $3x^2 - 6y^2 = 12$

9. $(y - 3)^2 = 8(x - 2)$

10. $y^2 + 12x - 6y - 51 = 0$

For the following exercises, rewrite the given equation in standard form, and then determine the vertex (V), focus (F), and directrix (d) of the parabola.

11. $x = 8y^2$

12. $y = \frac{1}{4}x^2$

13. $y = -4x^2$

14. $x = \frac{1}{8}y^2$

15. $x = 36y^2$

16. $x = \frac{1}{36}y^2$

17. $(x - 1)^2 = 4(y - 1)$

18. $(y - 2)^2 = \frac{4}{5}(x + 4)$

19. $(y - 4)^2 = 2(x + 3)$

20. $(x + 1)^2 = 2(y + 4)$

21. $(x + 4)^2 = 24(y + 1)$

22. $(y + 4)^2 = 16(x + 4)$

23. $y^2 + 12x - 6y + 21 = 0$

24. $x^2 - 4x - 24y + 28 = 0$

25. $5x^2 - 50x - 4y + 113 = 0$

26. $y^2 - 24x + 4y - 68 = 0$

27. $x^2 - 4x + 2y - 6 = 0$

28. $y^2 - 6y + 12x - 3 = 0$

29. $3y^2 - 4x - 6y + 23 = 0$

30. $x^2 + 4x + 8y - 4 = 0$

GRAPHICAL

For the following exercises, graph the parabola, labeling the focus and the directrix.

31. $x = \frac{1}{8}y^2$

32. $y = 36x^2$

33. $y = \frac{1}{36}x^2$

34. $y = -9x^2$

35. $(y - 2)^2 = -\frac{4}{3}(x + 2)$

36. $-5(x + 5)^2 = 4(y + 5)$

37. $-6(y + 5)^2 = 4(x - 4)$

38. $y^2 - 6y - 8x + 1 = 0$

39. $x^2 + 8x + 4y + 20 = 0$

40. $3x^2 + 30x - 4y + 95 = 0$

41. $y^2 - 8x + 10y + 9 = 0$

42. $x^2 + 4x + 2y + 2 = 0$

43. $y^2 + 2y - 12x + 61 = 0$

44. $-2x^2 + 8x - 4y - 24 = 0$

For the following exercises, find the equation of the parabola given information about its graph.

45. Vertex is $(0, 0)$; directrix is $y = 4$, focus is $(0, -4)$.

46. Vertex is $(0, 0)$; directrix is $x = 4$, focus is $(-4, 0)$.

47. Vertex is $(2, 2)$; directrix is $x = 2 - \sqrt{2}$, focus is $(2 + \sqrt{2}, 2)$.

48. Vertex is $(-2, 3)$; directrix is $x = -\frac{7}{2}$, focus is $\left(-\frac{1}{2}, 3\right)$.

49. Vertex is $(\sqrt{2}, -\sqrt{3})$; directrix is $x = 2\sqrt{2}$, focus is $(0, -\sqrt{3})$.

50. Vertex is $(1, 2)$; directrix is $y = \frac{11}{3}$, focus is $\left(1, \frac{1}{3}\right)$.

For the following exercises, determine the equation for the parabola from its graph.

51.

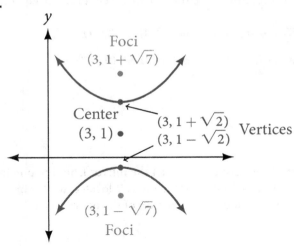

52.

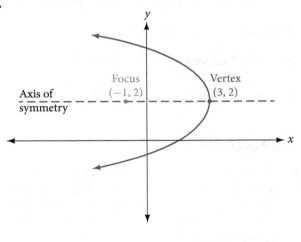

53.

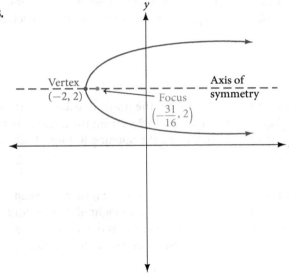

54.

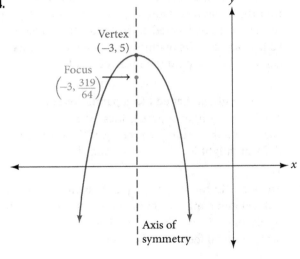

55.

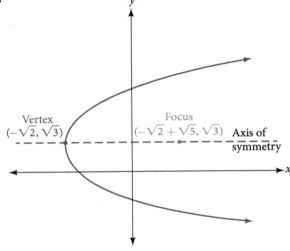

EXTENSIONS

For the following exercises, the vertex and endpoints of the latus rectum of a parabola are given. Find the equation.

56. $V(0, 0)$, Endpoints $(2, 1)$, $(-2, 1)$

57. $V(0, 0)$, Endpoints $(-2, 4)$, $(-2, -4)$

58. $V(1, 2)$, Endpoints $(-5, 5)$, $(7, 5)$

59. $V(-3, -1)$, Endpoints $(0, 5)$, $(0, -7)$

60. $V(4, -3)$, Endpoints $\left(5, -\dfrac{7}{2}\right)$, $\left(3, -\dfrac{7}{2}\right)$

REAL-WORLD APPLICATIONS

61. The mirror in an automobile headlight has a parabolic cross-section with the light bulb at the focus. On a schematic, the equation of the parabola is given as $x^2 = 4y$. At what coordinates should you place the light bulb?

62. If we want to construct the mirror from the previous exercise such that the focus is located at $(0, 0.25)$, what should the equation of the parabola be?

63. A satellite dish is shaped like a paraboloid of revolution. This means that it can be formed by rotating a parabola around its axis of symmetry. The receiver is to be located at the focus. If the dish is 12 feet across at its opening and 4 feet deep at its center, where should the receiver be placed?

64. Consider the satellite dish from the previous exercise. If the dish is 8 feet across at the opening and 2 feet deep, where should we place the receiver?

65. A searchlight is shaped like a paraboloid of revolution. A light source is located 1 foot from the base along the axis of symmetry. If the opening of the searchlight is 3 feet across, find the depth.

66. If the searchlight from the previous exercise has the light source located 6 inches from the base along the axis of symmetry and the opening is 4 feet, find the depth.

67. An arch is in the shape of a parabola. It has a span of 100 feet and a maximum height of 20 feet. Find the equation of the parabola, and determine the height of the arch 40 feet from the center.

68. If the arch from the previous exercise has a span of 160 feet and a maximum height of 40 feet, find the equation of the parabola, and determine the distance from the center at which the height is 20 feet.

69. An object is projected so as to follow a parabolic path given by $y = -x^2 + 96x$, where x is the horizontal distance traveled in feet and y is the height. Determine the maximum height the object reaches.

70. For the object from the previous exercise, assume the path followed is given by $y = -0.5x^2 + 80x$. Determine how far along the horizontal the object traveled to reach maximum height.

LEARNING OBJECTIVES

In this section, you will:

- Identify nondegenerate conic sections given their general form equations.
- Use rotation of axes formulas.
- Write equations of rotated conics in standard form.
- Identify conics without rotating axes.

12.4 ROTATION OF AXIS

As we have seen, conic sections are formed when a plane intersects two right circular cones aligned tip to tip and extending infinitely far in opposite directions, which we also call a cone. The way in which we slice the cone will determine the type of conic section formed at the intersection. A circle is formed by slicing a cone with a plane perpendicular to the axis of symmetry of the cone. An ellipse is formed by slicing a single cone with a slanted plane not perpendicular to the axis of symmetry. A parabola is formed by slicing the plane through the top or bottom of the double-cone, whereas a hyperbola is formed when the plane slices both the top and bottom of the cone. See **Figure 1**.

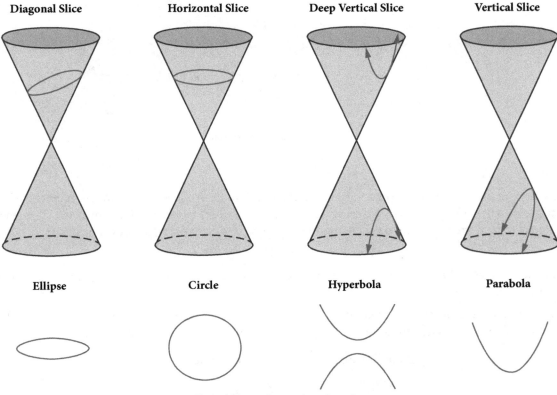

Figure 1 The nondegenerate conic sections

Ellipses, circles, hyperbolas, and parabolas are sometimes called the **nondegenerate conic sections**, in contrast to the **degenerate conic sections**, which are shown in **Figure 2**. A degenerate conic results when a plane intersects the double cone and passes through the apex. Depending on the angle of the plane, three types of degenerate conic sections are possible: a point, a line, or two intersecting lines.

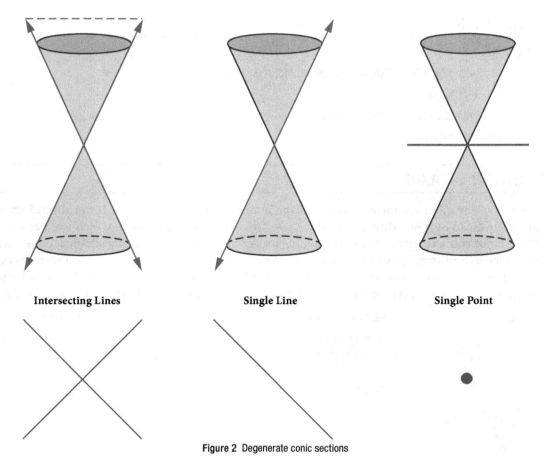

Figure 2 Degenerate conic sections

Identifying Nondegenerate Conics in General Form

In previous sections of this chapter, we have focused on the standard form equations for nondegenerate conic sections. In this section, we will shift our focus to the general form equation, which can be used for any conic. The general form is set equal to zero, and the terms and coefficients are given in a particular order, as shown below.

$$Ax^2 + Bxy + Cy^2 + Dx + Ey + F = 0$$

where A, B, and C are not all zero. We can use the values of the coefficients to identify which type conic is represented by a given equation.

You may notice that the general form equation has an xy term that we have not seen in any of the standard form equations. As we will discuss later, the xy term rotates the conic whenever B is not equal to zero.

Conic Sections	Example
ellipse	$4x^2 + 9y^2 = 1$
circle	$4x^2 + 4y^2 = 1$
hyperbola	$4x^2 - 9y^2 = 1$
parabola	$4x^2 = 9y$ or $4y^2 = 9x$
one line	$4x + 9y = 1$
intersecting lines	$(x - 4)(y + 4) = 0$
parallel lines	$(x - 4)(x - 9) = 0$
a point	$4x^2 + 4y^2 = 0$
no graph	$4x^2 + 4y^2 = -1$

Table 1

general form of conic sections

A **nondegenerate conic section** has the general form

$$Ax^2 + Bxy + Cy^2 + Dx + Ey + F = 0$$

where A, B, and C are not all zero.

Table 2 summarizes the different conic sections where $B = 0$, and A and C are nonzero real numbers. This indicates that the conic has not been rotated.

Conic Sections	Example
ellipse	$Ax^2 + Cy^2 + Dx + Ey + F = 0$, $A \neq C$ and $AC > 0$
circle	$Ax^2 + Cy^2 + Dx + Ey + F = 0$, $A = C$
hyperbola	$Ax^2 - Cy^2 + Dx + Ey + F = 0$ or $-Ax^2 + Cy^2 + Dx + Ey + F = 0$, where A and C are positive
parabola	$Ax^2 + Dx + Ey + F = 0$ or $Cy^2 + Dx + Ey + F = 0$

Table 2

How To...

Given the equation of a conic, identify the type of conic.

1. Rewrite the equation in the general form, $Ax^2 + Bxy + Cy^2 + Dx + Ey + F = 0$.
2. Identify the values of A and C from the general form.
   a. If A and C are nonzero, have the same sign, and are not equal to each other, then the graph is an ellipse.
   b. If A and C are equal and nonzero and have the same sign, then the graph is a circle.
   c. If A and C are nonzero and have opposite signs, then the graph is a hyperbola.
   d. If either A or C is zero, then the graph is a parabola.

Example 1   **Identifying a Conic from Its General Form**

Identify the graph of each of the following nondegenerate conic sections.

   a. $4x^2 - 9y^2 + 36x + 36y - 125 = 0$
   b. $9y^2 + 16x + 36y - 10 = 0$
   c. $3x^2 + 3y^2 - 2x - 6y - 4 = 0$
   d. $-25x^2 - 4y^2 + 100x + 16y + 20 = 0$

Solution

   a. Rewriting the general form, we have

$$Ax^2 + Bxy + Cy^2 + Dx + Ey + F = 0$$

$$4x^2 + 0xy + (-9)y^2 + 36x + 36y + (-125) = 0$$

$A = 4$ and $C = -9$, so we observe that A and C have opposite signs. The graph of this equation is a hyperbola.

   b. Rewriting the general form, we have

$$Ax^2 + Bxy + Cy^2 + Dx + Ey + F = 0$$

$$0x^2 + 0xy + 9y^2 + 16x + 36y + (-10) = 0$$

$A = 0$ and $C = 9$. We can determine that the equation is a parabola, since A is zero.

c. Rewriting the general form, we have

$$Ax^2 + Bxy + Cy^2 + Dx + Ey + F = 0$$

$$3x^2 + 0xy + 3y^2 + (-2)x + (-6)y + (-4) = 0$$

$A = 3$ and $C = 3$. Because $A = C$, the graph of this equation is a circle.

d. Rewriting the general form, we have

$$Ax^2 + Bxy + Cy^2 + Dx + Ey + F = 0$$

$$(-25)x^2 + 0xy + (-4)y^2 + 100x + 16y + 20 = 0$$

$A = -25$ and $C = -4$. Because $AC > 0$ and $A \neq C$, the graph of this equation is an ellipse.

Try It #1

Identify the graph of each of the following nondegenerate conic sections.

a. $16y^2 - x^2 + x - 4y - 9 = 0$ **b.** $16x^2 + 4y^2 + 16x + 49y - 81 = 0$

Finding a New Representation of the Given Equation after Rotating through a Given Angle

Until now, we have looked at equations of conic sections without an xy term, which aligns the graphs with the x- and y- axes. When we add an xy term, we are rotating the conic about the origin. If the x- and y-axes are rotated through an angle, say θ, then every point on the plane may be thought of as having two representations: (x, y) on the Cartesian plane with the original x-axis and y-axis, and (x', y') on the new plane defined by the new, rotated axes, called the x'-axis and y'-axis. See **Figure 3**.

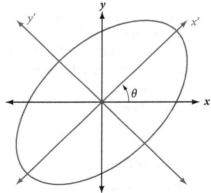

Figure 3 The graph of the rotated ellipse

$$x^2 + y^2 - xy - 15 = 0$$

We will find the relationships between x and y on the Cartesian plane with x' and y' on the new rotated plane. See **Figure 4**.

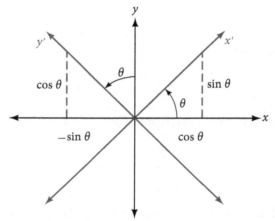

Figure 4 The Cartesian plane with x- and y-axes and the resulting x'- and y'-axes formed by a rotation by an angle θ.

The original coordinate x- and y-axes have unit vectors i and j. The rotated coordinate axes have unit vectors i' and j'. The angle θ is known as the **angle of rotation**. See **Figure 5**. We may write the new unit vectors in terms of the original ones.

$$i' = \cos\theta i + \sin\theta j$$

$$j' = -\sin\theta i + \cos\theta j$$

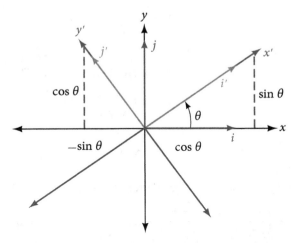

Figure 5 Relationship between the old and new coordinate planes.

Consider a vector u in the new coordinate plane. It may be represented in terms of its coordinate axes.

$u = x'i' + y'j'$

$u = x'(i\cos\theta + j\sin\theta) + y'(-i\sin\theta + j\cos\theta)$ Substitute.

$u = ix'\cos\theta + jx'\sin\theta - iy'\sin\theta + jy'\cos\theta$ Distribute.

$u = ix'\cos\theta - iy'\sin\theta + jx'\sin\theta + jy'\cos\theta$ Apply commutative property.

$u = (x'\cos\theta - y'\sin\theta)i + (x'\sin\theta + y'\cos\theta)j$ Factor by grouping.

Because $u = x'i' + y'j'$, we have representations of x and y in terms of the new coordinate system.

$$x = x'\cos\theta - y'\sin\theta \qquad \text{and} \qquad y = x'\sin\theta + y'\cos\theta$$

---

equations of rotation

If a point (x, y) on the Cartesian plane is represented on a new coordinate plane where the axes of rotation are formed by rotating an angle θ from the positive x-axis, then the coordinates of the point with respect to the new axes are (x', y'). We can use the following equations of rotation to define the relationship between (x, y) and (x', y'):

$$x = x'\cos\theta - y'\sin\theta \qquad \text{and} \qquad y = x'\sin\theta + y'\cos\theta$$

How To...

Given the equation of a conic, find a new representation after rotating through an angle.

1. Find x and y where $x = x'\cos\theta - y'\sin\theta$ and $y = x'\sin\theta + y'\cos\theta$.
2. Substitute the expression for x and y into in the given equation, then simplify.
3. Write the equations with x' and y' in standard form.

Example 2   **Finding a New Representation of an Equation after Rotating through a Given Angle**

Find a new representation of the equation $2x^2 - xy + 2y^2 - 30 = 0$ after rotating through an angle of $\theta = 45°$.

Solution   Find x and y, where $x = x'\cos\theta - y'\sin\theta$ and $y = x'\sin\theta + y'\cos\theta$.

Because $\theta = 45°$,

$$x = x' \cos(45°) - y' \sin(45°)$$

$$x = x' \left(\frac{1}{\sqrt{2}} \right) - y' \left(\frac{1}{\sqrt{2}} \right)$$

$$x = \frac{x' - y'}{\sqrt{2}}$$

and

$$y = x' \sin(45°) + y' \cos(45°)$$

$$y = x' \left(\frac{1}{\sqrt{2}} \right) + y' \left(\frac{1}{\sqrt{2}} \right)$$

$$y = \frac{x' + y'}{\sqrt{2}}$$

Substitute $x = x' \cos\theta - y' \sin\theta$ and $y = x' \sin\theta + y' \cos\theta$ into $2x^2 - xy + 2y^2 - 30 = 0$.

$$2 \left(\frac{x' - y'}{\sqrt{2}} \right)^2 - \left(\frac{x' - y'}{\sqrt{2}} \right) \left(\frac{x' + y'}{\sqrt{2}} \right) + 2 \left(\frac{x' + y'}{\sqrt{2}} \right)^2 - 30 = 0$$

Simplify.

$$\cancel{2} \frac{(x' - y')(x' - y')}{\cancel{2}} - \frac{(x' - y')(x' + y')}{2} + \cancel{2} \frac{(x' + y')(x' + y')}{\cancel{2}} - 30 = 0 \qquad \text{FOIL method}$$

$$x'^2 \cancel{- 2x'y'} + y'^2 - \frac{(x'^2 - y'^2)}{2} + x'^2 \cancel{+ 2x'y'} + y'^2 - 30 = 0 \qquad \text{Combine like terms.}$$

$$2x'^2 + 2y'^2 - \frac{(x'^2 - y'^2)}{2} = 30 \qquad \text{Combine like terms.}$$

$$2 \left(2x'^2 + 2y'^2 - \frac{(x'^2 - y'^2)}{2} \right) = 2(30) \qquad \text{Multiply both sides by 2.}$$

$$4x'^2 + 4y'^2 - (x'^2 - y'^2) = 60 \qquad \text{Simplify.}$$

$$4x'^2 + 4y'^2 - x'^2 + y'^2 = 60 \qquad \text{Distribute.}$$

$$\frac{3x'^2}{60} + \frac{5y'^2}{60} = \frac{60}{60} \qquad \text{Set equal to 1.}$$

Write the equations with x' and y' in the standard form.

$$\frac{x'^2}{20} + \frac{y'^2}{12} = 1$$

This equation is an ellipse. **Figure 6** shows the graph.

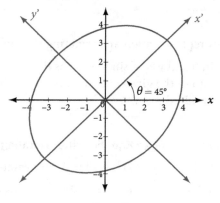

Figure 6

Writing Equations of Rotated Conics in Standard Form

Now that we can find the standard form of a conic when we are given an angle of rotation, we will learn how to transform the equation of a conic given in the form $Ax^2 + Bxy + Cy^2 + Dx + Ey + F = 0$. into standard form by rotating the axes. To do so, we will rewrite the general form as an equation in the x' and y' coordinate system without the $x'y'$ term, by rotating the axes by a measure of θ that satisfies

$$\cot(2\theta) = \frac{A - C}{B}$$

We have learned already that any conic may be represented by the second degree equation

$$Ax^2 + Bxy + Cy^2 + Dx + Ey + F = 0.$$

where A, B, and C are not all zero. However, if $B \neq 0$, then we have an xy term that prevents us from rewriting the equation in standard form. To eliminate it, we can rotate the axes by an acute angle θ where $\cot(2\theta) = \dfrac{A - C}{B}$.

- If $\cot(2\theta) > 0$, then 2θ is in the first quadrant, and θ is between $(0°, 45°)$.
- If $\cot(2\theta) < 0$, then 2θ is in the second quadrant, and θ is between $(45°, 90°)$.
- If $A = C$, then $\theta = 45°$.

How To...

Given an equation for a conic in the $x'y'$ system, rewrite the equation without the $x'y'$ term in terms of x' and y', where the x' and y' axes are rotations of the standard axes by θ degrees.

1. Find $\cot(2\theta)$.
2. Find $\sin\theta$ and $\cos\theta$.
3. Substitute $\sin\theta$ and $\cos\theta$ into $x = x'\cos\theta - y'\sin\theta$ and $y = x'\sin\theta + y'\cos\theta$.
4. Substitute the expression for x and y into in the given equation, and then simplify.
5. Write the equations with x' and y' in the standard form with respect to the rotated axes.

<u>Example 3</u>   **Rewriting an Equation with respect to the x′ and y′ axes without the x′y′ Term**

Rewrite the equation $8x^2 - 12xy + 17y^2 = 20$ in the $x'y'$ system without an $x'y'$ term.

Solution   First, we find $\cot(2\theta)$. See **Figure 7**.

$$8x^2 - 12xy + 17y^2 = 20 \Rightarrow A = 8, B = -12 \text{ and } C = 17$$

$$\cot(2\theta) = \frac{A - C}{B} = \frac{8 - 17}{-12}$$

$$\cot(2\theta) = \frac{-9}{-12} = \frac{3}{4}$$

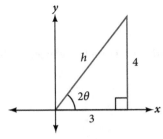

Figure 7

$$\cot(2\theta) = \frac{3}{4} = \frac{\text{adjacent}}{\text{opposite}}$$

So the hypotenuse is

$$3^2 + 4^2 = h^2$$

$$9 + 16 = h^2$$

$$25 = h^2$$

$$h = 5$$

Next, we find $\sin\theta$ and $\cos\theta$.

$$\sin\theta = \sqrt{\frac{1-\cos(2\theta)}{2}} = \sqrt{\frac{1-\frac{3}{5}}{2}} = \sqrt{\frac{\frac{5}{5}-\frac{3}{5}}{2}} = \sqrt{\frac{5-3}{5}\cdot\frac{1}{2}} = \sqrt{\frac{2}{10}} = \sqrt{\frac{1}{5}}$$

$$\sin\theta = \frac{1}{\sqrt{5}}$$

$$\cos\theta = \sqrt{\frac{1+\cos(2\theta)}{2}} = \sqrt{\frac{1+\frac{3}{5}}{2}} = \sqrt{\frac{\frac{5}{5}+\frac{3}{5}}{2}} = \sqrt{\frac{5+3}{5}\cdot\frac{1}{2}} = \sqrt{\frac{8}{10}} = \sqrt{\frac{4}{5}}$$

$$\cos\theta = \frac{2}{\sqrt{5}}$$

Substitute the values of $\sin\theta$ and $\cos\theta$ into $x = x'\cos\theta - y'\sin\theta$ and $y = x'\sin\theta + y'\cos\theta$.

$$x = x'\cos\theta - y'\sin\theta$$

$$x = x'\left(\frac{2}{\sqrt{5}}\right) - y'\left(\frac{1}{\sqrt{5}}\right)$$

$$x = \frac{2x'-y'}{\sqrt{5}}$$

and

$$y = x'\sin\theta + y'\cos\theta$$

$$y = x'\left(\frac{1}{\sqrt{5}}\right) + y'\left(\frac{2}{\sqrt{5}}\right)$$

$$y = \frac{x'+2y'}{\sqrt{5}}$$

Substitute the expressions for x and y into in the given equation, and then simplify.

$$8\left(\frac{2x'-y'}{\sqrt{5}}\right)^2 - 12\left(\frac{2x'-y'}{\sqrt{5}}\right)\left(\frac{x'+2y'}{\sqrt{5}}\right) + 17\left(\frac{x'+2y'}{\sqrt{5}}\right)^2 = 20$$

$$8\left(\frac{(2x'-y')(2x'-y')}{5}\right) - 12\left(\frac{(2x'-y')(x'+2y')}{5}\right) + 17\left(\frac{(x'+2y')(x'+2y')}{5}\right) = 20$$

$$8(4x'^2 - 4x'y' + y'^2) - 12(2x'^2 + 3x'y' - 2y'^2) + 17(x'^2 + 4x'y' + 4y'^2) = 100$$

$$32x'^2 - 32x'y' + 8y'^2 - 24x'^2 - 36x'y' + 24y'^2 + 17x'^2 + 68x'y' + 68y'^2 = 100$$

$$25x'^2 + 100y'^2 = 100$$

$$\frac{25}{100}x'^2 + \frac{100}{100}y'^2 = \frac{100}{100}$$

Write the equations with x' and y' in the standard form with respect to the new coordinate system.

$$\frac{x'^2}{4} + \frac{y'^2}{1} = 1$$

Figure 8 shows the graph of the ellipse.

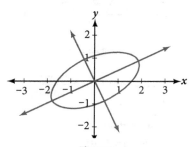

Figure 8

Try It #2

Rewrite the $13x^2 - 6\sqrt{3}xy + 7y^2 = 16$ in the $x'y'$ system without the $x'y'$ term.

Example 4 **Graphing an Equation That Has No $x'y'$ Terms**

Graph the following equation relative to the $x'y'$ system:

$$x^2 + 12xy - 4y^2 = 30$$

Solution First, we find $\cot(2\theta)$.

$$x^2 + 12xy - 4y^2 = 20 \Rightarrow A = 1, B = 12, \text{ and } C = -4$$

$$\cot(2\theta) = \frac{A - C}{B}$$

$$\cot(2\theta) = \frac{1 - (-4)}{12}$$

$$\cot(2\theta) = \frac{5}{12}$$

Because $\cot(2\theta) = \dfrac{5}{12}$, we can draw a reference triangle as in **Figure 9**.

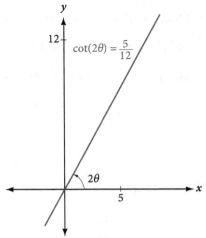

Figure 9

$$\cot(2\theta) = \frac{5}{12} = \frac{\text{adjacent}}{\text{opposite}}$$

Thus, the hypotenuse is

$$5^2 + 12^2 = h^2$$

$$25 + 144 = h^2$$

$$169 = h^2$$

$$h = 13$$

Next, we find $\sin\theta$ and $\cos\theta$. We will use half-angle identities.

$$\sin\theta = \sqrt{\frac{1 - \cos(2\theta)}{2}} = \sqrt{\frac{1 - \frac{5}{13}}{2}} = \sqrt{\frac{\frac{13}{13} - \frac{5}{13}}{2}} = \sqrt{\frac{8}{13} \cdot \frac{1}{2}} = \frac{2}{\sqrt{13}}$$

$$\cos\theta = \sqrt{\frac{1 + \cos(2\theta)}{2}} = \sqrt{\frac{1 + \frac{5}{13}}{2}} = \sqrt{\frac{\frac{13}{13} + \frac{5}{13}}{2}} = \sqrt{\frac{18}{13} \cdot \frac{1}{2}} = \frac{3}{\sqrt{13}}$$

Now we find x and y.

$$x = x'\cos\theta - y'\sin\theta$$

$$x = x'\left(\frac{3}{\sqrt{13}}\right) - y'\left(\frac{2}{\sqrt{13}}\right)$$

$$x = \frac{3x' - 2y'}{\sqrt{13}}$$

and

$$y = x' \sin\theta + y' \cos\theta$$

$$y = x'\left(\frac{2}{\sqrt{13}}\right) + y'\left(\frac{3}{\sqrt{13}}\right)$$

$$y = \frac{2x' + 3y'}{\sqrt{13}}$$

Now we substitute $x = \dfrac{3x' - 2y'}{\sqrt{13}}$ and $y = \dfrac{2x' + 3y'}{\sqrt{13}}$ into $x^2 + 12xy - 4y^2 = 30$.

$$\left(\frac{3x' - 2y'}{\sqrt{13}}\right)^2 + 12\left(\frac{3x' - 2y'}{\sqrt{13}}\right)\left(\frac{2x' + 3y'}{\sqrt{13}}\right) - 4\left(\frac{2x' + 3y'}{\sqrt{13}}\right)^2 = 30$$

$$\left(\frac{1}{13}\right)\left[(3x' - 2y')^2 + 12(3x' - 2y')(2x' + 3y') - 4\,(2x' + 3y')^2\right] = 30 \qquad \text{Factor.}$$

$$\left(\frac{1}{13}\right)\left[9x'^2 - 12x'y' + 4y'^2 + 12\,(6x'^2 + 5x'y' - 6y'^2) - 4\,(4x'^2 + 12x'y' + 9y'^2)\right] = 30 \qquad \text{Multiply.}$$

$$\left(\frac{1}{13}\right)\left[9x'^2 - 12x'y' + 4y'^2 + 72x'^2 + 60x'y' - 72y'^2 - 16x'^2 - 48x'y' - 36y'^2\right] = 30 \qquad \text{Distribute.}$$

$$\left(\frac{1}{13}\right)\left[65x'^2 - 104y'^2\right] = 30 \qquad \text{Combine like terms.}$$

$$65x'^2 - 104y'^2 = 390 \qquad \text{Multiply.}$$

$$\frac{x'^2}{6} - \frac{4y'^2}{15} = 1 \qquad \text{Divide by 390.}$$

Figure 10 shows the graph of the hyperbola $\dfrac{x'^2}{6} - \dfrac{4y'^2}{15} = 1$.

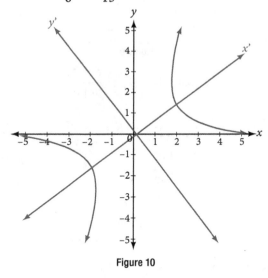

Figure 10

Identifying Conics without Rotating Axes

Now we have come full circle. How do we identify the type of conic described by an equation? What happens when the axes are rotated? Recall, the general form of a conic is

$$Ax^2 + Bxy + Cy^2 + Dx + Ey + F = 0$$

If we apply the rotation formulas to this equation we get the form

$$A'x'^2 + B'x'y' + C'y'^2 + D'x' + E'y' + F' = 0$$

It may be shown that $B^2 - 4AC = B'^2 - 4A'C'$. The expression does not vary after rotation, so we call the expression invariant. The discriminant, $B^2 - 4AC$, is invariant and remains unchanged after rotation. Because the discriminant remains unchanged, observing the discriminant enables us to identify the conic section.

---

using the discriminant to identify a conic

If the equation $Ax^2 + Bxy + Cy^2 + Dx + Ey + F = 0$ is transformed by rotating axes into the equation $A'x'^2 + B'x'y' + C'y'^2 + D'x' + E'y' + F' = 0$, then $B^2 - 4AC = B'^2 - 4A'C'$.

The equation $Ax^2 + Bxy + Cy^2 + Dx + Ey + F = 0$ is an ellipse, a parabola, or a hyperbola, or a degenerate case of one of these.

If the discriminant, $B^2 - 4AC$, is

- < 0, the conic section is an ellipse
- $= 0$, the conic section is a parabola
- > 0, the conic section is a hyperbola

Example 5   **Identifying the Conic without Rotating Axes**

Identify the conic for each of the following without rotating axes.

    a. $5x^2 + 2\sqrt{3}xy + 2y^2 - 5 = 0$

    b. $5x^2 + 2\sqrt{3}xy + 12y^2 - 5 = 0$

Solution

    a. Let's begin by determining A, B, and C.

$$\underset{A}{5x^2} + \underset{B}{2\sqrt{3}xy} + \underset{C}{2y^2} - 5 = 0$$

Now, we find the discriminant.

$$B^2 - 4AC = \left(2\sqrt{3}\right)^2 - 4(5)(2)$$
$$= 4(3) - 40$$
$$= 12 - 40$$
$$= -28 < 0$$

Therefore, $5x^2 + 2\sqrt{3}xy + 2y^2 - 5 = 0$ represents an ellipse.

    b. Again, let's begin by determining A, B, and C.

$$\underset{A}{5x^2} + \underset{B}{2\sqrt{3}xy} + \underset{C}{12y^2} - 5 = 0$$

Now, we find the discriminant.

$$B^2 - 4AC = \left(2\sqrt{3}\right)^2 - 4(5)(12)$$
$$= 4(3) - 240$$
$$= 12 - 240$$
$$= -228 < 0$$

Therefore, $5x^2 + 2\sqrt{3}xy + 12y^2 - 5 = 0$ represents an ellipse.

Try It #3

Identify the conic for each of the following without rotating axes.

a. $x^2 - 9xy + 3y^2 - 12 = 0$

b. $10x^2 - 9xy + 4y^2 - 4 = 0$

Access this online resource for additional instruction and practice with conic sections and rotation of axes.

- Introduction to Conic Sections (http://openstaxcollege.org/l/introconic)

12.4   SECTION EXERCISES

VERBAL

1. What effect does the xy term have on the graph of a conic section?

2. If the equation of a conic section is written in the form $Ax^2 + By^2 + Cx + Dy + E = 0$ and $AB = 0$, what can we conclude?

3. If the equation of a conic section is written in the form $Ax^2 + Bxy + Cy^2 + Dx + Ey + F = 0$, and $B^2 - 4AC > 0$, what can we conclude?

4. Given the equation $ax^2 + 4x + 3y^2 - 12 = 0$, what can we conclude if $a > 0$?

5. For the equation $Ax^2 + Bxy + Cy^2 + Dx + Ey + F = 0$, the value of θ that satisfies $\cot(2\theta) = \dfrac{A - C}{B}$ gives us what information?

ALGEBRAIC

For the following exercises, determine which conic section is represented based on the given equation.

6. $9x^2 + 4y^2 + 72x + 36y - 500 = 0$

7. $x^2 - 10x + 4y - 10 = 0$

8. $2x^2 - 2y^2 + 4x - 6y - 2 = 0$

9. $4x^2 - y^2 + 8x - 1 = 0$

10. $4y^2 - 5x + 9y + 1 = 0$

11. $2x^2 + 3y^2 - 8x - 12y + 2 = 0$

12. $4x^2 + 9xy + 4y^2 - 36y - 125 = 0$

13. $3x^2 + 6xy + 3y^2 - 36y - 125 = 0$

14. $-3x^2 + 3\sqrt{3}xy - 4y^2 + 9 = 0$

15. $2x^2 + 4\sqrt{3}xy + 6y^2 - 6x - 3 = 0$

16. $-x^2 + 4\sqrt{2}xy + 2y^2 - 2y + 1 = 0$

17. $8x^2 + 4\sqrt{2}xy + 4y^2 - 10x + 1 = 0$

For the following exercises, find a new representation of the given equation after rotating through the given angle.

18. $3x^2 + xy + 3y^2 - 5 = 0, \theta = 45°$

19. $4x^2 - xy + 4y^2 - 2 = 0, \theta = 45°$

20. $2x^2 + 8xy - 1 = 0, \theta = 30°$

21. $-2x^2 + 8xy + 1 = 0, \theta = 45°$

22. $4x^2 + \sqrt{2}xy + 4y^2 + y + 2 = 0, \theta = 45°$

For the following exercises, determine the angle θ that will eliminate the xy term and write the corresponding equation without the xy term.

23. $x^2 + 3\sqrt{3}xy + 4y^2 + y - 2 = 0$

24. $4x^2 + 2\sqrt{3}xy + 6y^2 + y - 2 = 0$

25. $9x^2 - 3\sqrt{3}xy + 6y^2 + 4y - 3 = 0$

26. $-3x^2 - \sqrt{3}xy - 2y^2 - x = 0$

27. $16x^2 + 24xy + 9y^2 + 6x - 6y + 2 = 0$

28. $x^2 + 4xy + 4y^2 + 3x - 2 = 0$

29. $x^2 + 4xy + y^2 - 2x + 1 = 0$

30. $4x^2 - 2\sqrt{3}xy + 6y^2 - 1 = 0$

GRAPHICAL

For the following exercises, rotate through the given angle based on the given equation. Give the new equation and graph the original and rotated equation.

31. $y = -x^2, \theta = -45°$

32. $x = y^2, \theta = 45°$

33. $\dfrac{x^2}{4} + \dfrac{y^2}{1} = 1, \theta = 45°$

34. $\dfrac{y^2}{16} + \dfrac{x^2}{9} = 1, \theta = 45°$

35. $y^2 - x^2 = 1, \theta = 45°$

36. $y = \dfrac{x^2}{2}, \theta = 30°$

37. $x = (y - 1)^2, \theta = 30°$

38. $\dfrac{x^2}{9} + \dfrac{y^2}{4} = 1, \theta = 30°$

For the following exercises, graph the equation relative to the $x'y'$ system in which the equation has no $x'y'$ term.

39. $xy = 9$

40. $x^2 + 10xy + y^2 - 6 = 0$

41. $x^2 - 10xy + y^2 - 24 = 0$

42. $4x^2 - 3\sqrt{3}xy + y^2 - 22 = 0$

43. $6x^2 + 2\sqrt{3}xy + 4y^2 - 21 = 0$

44. $11x^2 + 10\sqrt{3}xy + y^2 - 64 = 0$

45. $21x^2 + 2\sqrt{3}xy + 19y^2 - 18 = 0$

46. $16x^2 + 24xy + 9y^2 - 130x + 90y = 0$

47. $16x^2 + 24xy + 9y^2 - 60x + 80y = 0$

48. $13x^2 - 6\sqrt{3}xy + 7y^2 - 16 = 0$

49. $4x^2 - 4xy + y^2 - 8\sqrt{5}x - 16\sqrt{5}y = 0$

For the following exercises, determine the angle of rotation in order to eliminate the xy term. Then graph the new set of axes.

50. $6x^2 - 5\sqrt{3}xy + y^2 + 10x - 12y = 0$

51. $6x^2 - 5xy + 6y^2 + 20x - y = 0$

52. $6x^2 - 8\sqrt{3}xy + 14y^2 + 10x - 3y = 0$

53. $4x^2 + 6\sqrt{3}xy + 10y^2 + 20x - 40y = 0$

54. $8x^2 + 3xy + 4y^2 + 2x - 4 = 0$

55. $16x^2 + 24xy + 9y^2 + 20x - 44y = 0$

For the following exercises, determine the value of k based on the given equation.

56. Given $4x^2 + kxy + 16y^2 + 8x + 24y - 48 = 0$, find k for the graph to be a parabola.

57. Given $2x^2 + kxy + 12y^2 + 10x - 16y + 28 = 0$, find k for the graph to be an ellipse.

58. Given $3x^2 + kxy + 4y^2 - 6x + 20y + 128 = 0$, find k for the graph to be a hyperbola.

59. Given $kx^2 + 8xy + 8y^2 - 12x + 16y + 18 = 0$, find k for the graph to be a parabola.

60. Given $6x^2 + 12xy + ky^2 + 16x + 10y + 4 = 0$, find k for the graph to be an ellipse.

LEARNING OBJECTIVES

In this section, you will:

- Identify a conic in polar form.
- Graph the polar equations of conics.
- Define conics in terms of a focus and a directrix.

12.5   CONIC SECTIONS IN POLAR COORDINATES

Figure 1 Planets orbiting the sun follow elliptical paths. (credit: NASA Blueshift, Flickr)

Most of us are familiar with orbital motion, such as the motion of a planet around the sun or an electron around an atomic nucleus. Within the planetary system, orbits of planets, asteroids, and comets around a larger celestial body are often elliptical. Comets, however, may take on a parabolic or hyperbolic orbit instead. And, in reality, the characteristics of the planets' orbits may vary over time. Each orbit is tied to the location of the celestial body being orbited and the distance and direction of the planet or other object from that body. As a result, we tend to use polar coordinates to represent these orbits.

In an elliptical orbit, the periapsis is the point at which the two objects are closest, and the apoapsis is the point at which they are farthest apart. Generally, the velocity of the orbiting body tends to increase as it approaches the periapsis and decrease as it approaches the apoapsis. Some objects reach an escape velocity, which results in an infinite orbit. These bodies exhibit either a parabolic or a hyperbolic orbit about a body; the orbiting body breaks free of the celestial body's gravitational pull and fires off into space. Each of these orbits can be modeled by a conic section in the polar coordinate system.

Identifying a Conic in Polar Form

Any conic may be determined by three characteristics: a single focus, a fixed line called the directrix, and the ratio of the distances of each to a point on the graph. Consider the parabola $x = 2 + y^2$ shown in **Figure 2**.

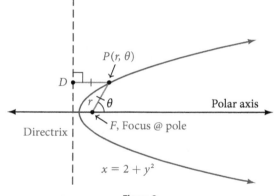

Figure 2

In **The Parabola**, we learned how a parabola is defined by the focus (a fixed point) and the directrix (a fixed line). In this section, we will learn how to define any conic in the polar coordinate system in terms of a fixed point, the focus $P(r, \theta)$ at the pole, and a line, the directrix, which is perpendicular to the polar axis.

If F is a fixed point, the focus, and D is a fixed line, the directrix, then we can let e be a fixed positive number, called the **eccentricity**, which we can define as the ratio of the distances from a point on the graph to the focus and the point on the graph to the directrix. Then the set of all points P such that $e = \dfrac{PF}{PD}$ is a conic. In other words, we can define a conic as the set of all points P with the property that the ratio of the distance from P to F to the distance from P to D is equal to the constant e.

For a conic with eccentricity e,

- if $0 \le e < 1$, the conic is an ellipse
- if $e = 1$, the conic is a parabola
- if $e > 1$, the conic is an hyperbola

With this definition, we may now define a conic in terms of the directrix, $x = \pm p$, the eccentricity e, and the angle θ. Thus, each conic may be written as a **polar equation**, an equation written in terms of r and θ.

---

the polar equation for a conic

For a conic with a focus at the origin, if the directrix is $x = \pm p$, where p is a positive real number, and the **eccentricity** is a positive real number e, the conic has a **polar equation.**

$$r = \frac{ep}{1 \pm e \cos \theta}$$

For a conic with a focus at the origin, if the directrix is $y = \pm p$, where p is a positive real number, and the eccentricity is a positive real number e, the conic has a polar equation.

$$r = \frac{ep}{1 \pm e \sin \theta}$$

How To...

Given the polar equation for a conic, identify the type of conic, the directrix, and the eccentricity.

1. Multiply the numerator and denominator by the reciprocal of the constant in the denominator to rewrite the equation in standard form.
2. Identify the eccentricity e as the coefficient of the trigonometric function in the denominator.
3. Compare e with 1 to determine the shape of the conic.
4. Determine the directrix as $x = p$ if cosine is in the denominator and $y = p$ if sine is in the denominator. Set ep equal to the numerator in standard form to solve for x or y.

Example 1   **Identifying a Conic Given the Polar Form**

For each of the following equations, identify the conic with focus at the origin, the directrix, and the eccentricity.

a. $r = \dfrac{6}{3 + 2 \sin \theta}$ **b.** $r = \dfrac{12}{4 + 5 \cos \theta}$ **c.** $r = \dfrac{7}{2 - 2 \sin \theta}$

Solution   For each of the three conics, we will rewrite the equation in standard form. Standard form has a 1 as the constant in the denominator. Therefore, in all three parts, the first step will be to multiply the numerator and denominator by the reciprocal of the constant of the original equation, $\dfrac{1}{c}$, where c is that constant.

a. Multiply the numerator and denominator by $\dfrac{1}{3}$.

$$r = \frac{6}{3 + 2\sin \theta} \cdot \frac{\left(\dfrac{1}{3}\right)}{\left(\dfrac{1}{3}\right)} = \frac{6\left(\dfrac{1}{3}\right)}{3\left(\dfrac{1}{3}\right) + 2\left(\dfrac{1}{3}\right)\sin \theta} = \frac{2}{1 + \dfrac{2}{3}\sin \theta}$$

Because $\sin \theta$ is in the denominator, the directrix is $y = p$. Comparing to standard form, note that $e = \dfrac{2}{3}$. Therefore, from the numerator,

$$2 = ep$$
$$2 = \frac{2}{3}p$$
$$\left(\frac{3}{2}\right)2 = \left(\frac{3}{2}\right)\frac{2}{3}p$$
$$3 = p$$

Since $e < 1$, the conic is an ellipse. The eccentricity is $e = \dfrac{2}{3}$ and the directrix is $y = 3$.

b. Multiply the numerator and denominator by $\dfrac{1}{4}$.

$$r = \frac{12}{4 + 5\cos \theta} \cdot \frac{\left(\frac{1}{4}\right)}{\left(\frac{1}{4}\right)}$$

$$r = \frac{12\left(\frac{1}{4}\right)}{4\left(\frac{1}{4}\right) + 5\left(\frac{1}{4}\right)\cos \theta}$$

$$r = \frac{3}{1 + \frac{5}{4}\cos \theta}$$

Because $\cos \theta$ is in the denominator, the directrix is $x = p$. Comparing to standard form, $e = \dfrac{5}{4}$. Therefore, from the numerator,

$$3 = ep$$
$$3 = \frac{5}{4}p$$
$$\left(\frac{4}{5}\right)3 = \left(\frac{4}{5}\right)\frac{5}{4}p$$
$$\frac{12}{5} = p$$

Since $e > 1$, the conic is a hyperbola. The eccentricity is $e = \dfrac{5}{4}$ and the directrix is $x = \dfrac{12}{5} = 2.4$.

c. Multiply the numerator and denominator by $\dfrac{1}{2}$.

$$r = \frac{7}{2 - 2\sin \theta} \cdot \frac{\left(\frac{1}{2}\right)}{\left(\frac{1}{2}\right)}$$

$$r = \frac{7\left(\frac{1}{2}\right)}{2\left(\frac{1}{2}\right) - 2\left(\frac{1}{2}\right)\sin \theta}$$

$$r = \frac{\frac{7}{2}}{1 - \sin \theta}$$

Because sine is in the denominator, the directrix is $y = -p$. Comparing to standard form, $e = 1$. Therefore, from the numerator,

$$\frac{7}{2} = ep$$
$$\frac{7}{2} = (1)p$$
$$\frac{7}{2} = p$$

Because $e = 1$, the conic is a parabola. The eccentricity is $e = 1$ and the directrix is $y = -\dfrac{7}{2} = -3.5$.

Try It #1

Identify the conic with focus at the origin, the directrix, and the eccentricity for $r = \dfrac{2}{3 - \cos \theta}$.

Graphing the Polar Equations of Conics

When graphing in Cartesian coordinates, each conic section has a unique equation. This is not the case when graphing in polar coordinates. We must use the eccentricity of a conic section to determine which type of curve to graph, and then determine its specific characteristics. The first step is to rewrite the conic in standard form as we have done in the previous example. In other words, we need to rewrite the equation so that the denominator begins with 1. This enables us to determine e and, therefore, the shape of the curve. The next step is to substitute values for θ and solve for r to plot a few key points. Setting θ equal to 0, $\dfrac{\pi}{2}$, π, and $\dfrac{3\pi}{2}$ provides the vertices so we can create a rough sketch of the graph.

Example 2 **Graphing a Parabola in Polar Form**

Graph $r = \dfrac{5}{3 + 3\cos \theta}$.

Solution First, we rewrite the conic in standard form by multiplying the numerator and denominator by the reciprocal of 3, which is $\dfrac{1}{3}$.

$$r = \dfrac{5}{3 + 3\cos\theta} = \dfrac{5\left(\dfrac{1}{3}\right)}{3\left(\dfrac{1}{3}\right) + 3\left(\dfrac{1}{3}\right)\cos\theta}$$

$$r = \dfrac{\dfrac{5}{3}}{1 + \cos\theta}$$

Because $e = 1$, we will graph a parabola with a focus at the origin. The function has a $\cos\theta$, and there is an addition sign in the denominator, so the directrix is $x = p$.

$$\dfrac{5}{3} = ep$$

$$\dfrac{5}{3} = (1)p$$

$$\dfrac{5}{3} = p$$

The directrix is $x = \dfrac{5}{3}$.

Plotting a few key points as in **Table 1** will enable us to see the vertices. See **Figure 3**.

		A	B	C	D
θ		0	$\dfrac{\pi}{2}$	π	$\dfrac{3\pi}{2}$
$r = \dfrac{5}{3 + 3\cos\theta}$		$\dfrac{5}{6} \approx 0.83$	$\dfrac{5}{3} \approx 1.67$	undefined	$\dfrac{5}{3} \approx 1.67$

Table 1

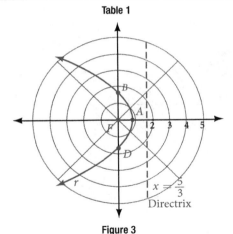

Figure 3

Analysis We can check our result with a graphing utility. See **Figure 4**.

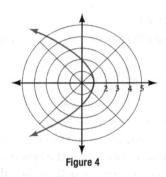

Figure 4

Example 3   **Graphing a Hyperbola in Polar Form**

Graph $r = \dfrac{8}{2 - 3\sin\theta}$.

Solution   First, we rewrite the conic in standard form by multiplying the numerator and denominator by the reciprocal of 2, which is $\dfrac{1}{2}$.

$$r = \frac{8}{2 - 3\sin\theta} = \frac{8\left(\frac{1}{2}\right)}{2\left(\frac{1}{2}\right) - 3\left(\frac{1}{2}\right)\sin\theta}$$

$$r = \frac{4}{1 - \frac{3}{2}\cos\theta}$$

Because $e = \dfrac{3}{2}$, $e > 1$, so we will graph a hyperbola with a focus at the origin. The function has a $\sin\theta$ term and there is a subtraction sign in the denominator, so the directrix is $y = -p$.

$$4 = ep$$

$$4 = \left(\frac{3}{2}\right)p$$

$$4\left(\frac{2}{3}\right) = p$$

$$\frac{8}{3} = p$$

The directrix is $y = -\dfrac{8}{3}$.

Plotting a few key points as in **Table 2** will enable us to see the vertices. See **Figure 5**.

	A	**B**	**C**	**D**
θ	0	$\dfrac{\pi}{2}$	π	$\dfrac{3\pi}{2}$
$r = \dfrac{8}{2 - 3\sin\theta}$	4	-8	4	$\dfrac{8}{5} = 1.6$

Table 2

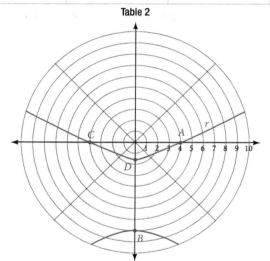

Figure 5

Example 4   **Graphing an Ellipse in Polar Form**

Graph $r = \dfrac{10}{5 - 4 \cos \theta}$.

Solution   First, we rewrite the conic in standard form by multiplying the numerator and denominator by the reciprocal of 5, which is $\dfrac{1}{5}$.

$$r = \frac{10}{5 - 4 \cos \theta} = \frac{10\left(\dfrac{1}{5}\right)}{5\left(\dfrac{1}{5}\right) - 4\left(\dfrac{1}{5}\right) \cos \theta}$$

$$r = \frac{2}{1 - \dfrac{4}{5} \sin \theta}$$

Because $e = \dfrac{4}{5}$, $e < 1$, so we will graph an ellipse with a focus at the origin. The function has a cos θ, and there is a subtraction sign in the denominator, so the directrix is $x = -p$.

$$2 = ep$$
$$2 = \left(\frac{4}{5}\right)p$$
$$2\left(\frac{5}{4}\right) = p$$
$$\frac{5}{2} = p$$

The directrix is $x = -\dfrac{5}{2}$.

Plotting a few key points as in **Table 3** will enable us to see the vertices. See **Figure 6**.

	A	**B**	**C**	**D**
θ	0	$\dfrac{\pi}{2}$	π	$\dfrac{3\pi}{2}$
$r = \dfrac{10}{5 - 4 \cos \theta}$	10	2	$\dfrac{10}{9} \approx 1.1$	2

Table 3

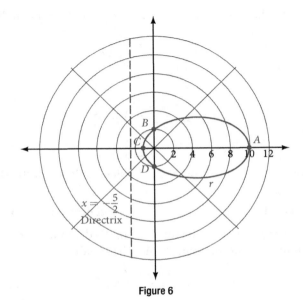

Figure 6

Analysis   We can check our result with a graphing utility.
See **Figure 7**.

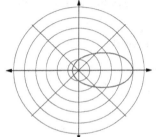

Figure 7 $r = \dfrac{10}{5 - 4\cos\theta}$ graphed on a viewing window
of $[-3, 12, 1]$ by $[-4, 4, 1]$, θ min $= 0$ and θ max $= 2\pi$.

Try It #2

Graph $r = \dfrac{2}{4 - \cos\theta}$.

Defining Conics in Terms of a Focus and a Directrix

So far we have been using polar equations of conics to describe and graph the curve. Now we will work in reverse; we will use information about the origin, eccentricity, and directrix to determine the polar equation.

How To...

Given the focus, eccentricity, and directrix of a conic, determine the polar equation.

1. Determine whether the directrix is horizontal or vertical. If the directrix is given in terms of y, we use the general polar form in terms of sine. If the directrix is given in terms of x, we use the general polar form in terms of cosine.
2. Determine the sign in the denominator. If $p < 0$, use subtraction. If $p > 0$, use addition.
3. Write the coefficient of the trigonometric function as the given eccentricity.
4. Write the absolute value of p in the numerator, and simplify the equation.

Example 5   Finding the Polar Form of a Vertical Conic Given a Focus at the Origin and the Eccentricity and Directrix

Find the polar form of the conic given a focus at the origin, $e = 3$ and directrix $y = -2$.

Solution   The directrix is $y = -p$, so we know the trigonometric function in the denominator is sine.

Because $y = -2$, $-2 < 0$, so we know there is a subtraction sign in the denominator. We use the standard form of

$$r = \frac{ep}{1 - e\sin\theta}$$

and $e = 3$ and $|-2| = 2 = p$.

Therefore,

$$r = \frac{(3)(2)}{1 - 3\sin\theta}$$

$$r = \frac{6}{1 - 3\sin\theta}$$

Example 6   Finding the Polar Form of a Horizontal Conic Given a Focus at the Origin and the Eccentricity and Directrix

Find the polar form of a conic given a focus at the origin, $e = \dfrac{3}{5}$, and directrix $x = 4$.

Solution   Because the directrix is $x = p$, we know the function in the denominator is cosine. Because $x = 4$, $4 > 0$, so we know there is an addition sign in the denominator. We use the standard form of

$$r = \frac{ep}{1 + e\cos\theta}$$

and $e = \dfrac{3}{5}$ and $|4| = 4 = p$.

Therefore,

$$r = \frac{\left(\frac{3}{5}\right)(4)}{1 + \frac{3}{5}\cos\theta}$$

$$r = \frac{\frac{12}{5}}{1 + \frac{3}{5}\cos\theta}$$

$$r = \frac{\frac{12}{5}}{1\left(\frac{5}{5}\right) + \frac{3}{5}\cos\theta}$$

$$r = \frac{\frac{12}{5}}{\frac{5}{5} + \frac{3}{5}\cos\theta}$$

$$r = \frac{12}{5} \cdot \frac{5}{5 + 3\cos\theta}$$

$$r = \frac{12}{5 + 3\cos\theta}$$

Try It #3

Find the polar form of the conic given a focus at the origin, $e = 1$, and directrix $x = -1$.

Example 7   Converting a Conic in Polar Form to Rectangular Form

Convert the conic $r = \dfrac{1}{5 - 5\sin\theta}$ to rectangular form.

Solution   We will rearrange the formula to use the identities $r = \sqrt{x^2 + y^2}$, $x = r\cos\theta$, and $y = r\sin\theta$.

$$r = \frac{1}{5 - 5\sin\theta}$$

$$r \cdot (5 - 5\sin\theta) = \frac{1}{5 - 5\sin\theta} \cdot (5 - 5\sin\theta) \qquad \text{Eliminate the fraction.}$$

$$5r - 5r\sin\theta = 1 \qquad\qquad\qquad\qquad \text{Distribute.}$$

$$5r = 1 + 5r\sin\theta \qquad\qquad\qquad \text{Isolate } 5r.$$

$$25r^2 = (1 + 5r\sin\theta)^2 \qquad\qquad \text{Square both sides.}$$

$$25(x^2 + y^2) = (1 + 5y)^2 \qquad\qquad \text{Substitute } r = \sqrt{x^2 + y^2} \text{ and } y = r\sin\theta.$$

$$25x^2 + 25y^2 = 1 + 10y + 25y^2 \qquad \text{Distribute and use FOIL.}$$

$$25x^2 - 10y = 1 \qquad\qquad\qquad \text{Rearrange terms and set equal to 1.}$$

Try It #4

Convert the conic $r = \dfrac{2}{1 + 2\cos\theta}$ to rectangular form.

Access these online resources for additional instruction and practice with conics in polar coordinates.

- Polar Equations of Conic Sections (http://openstaxcollege.org/l/determineconic)
- Graphing Polar Equations of Conics - 1 (http://openstaxcollege.org/l/graphconic1)
- Graphing Polar Equations of Conics - 2 (http://openstaxcollege.org/l/graphconic2)

12.5   SECTION EXERCISES

VERBAL

1. Explain how eccentricity determines which conic section is given.

2. If a conic section is written as a polar equation, what must be true of the denominator?

3. If a conic section is written as a polar equation, and the denominator involves $\sin\theta$, what conclusion can be drawn about the directrix?

4. If the directrix of a conic section is perpendicular to the polar axis, what do we know about the equation of the graph?

5. What do we know about the focus/foci of a conic section if it is written as a polar equation?

ALGEBRAIC

For the following exercises, identify the conic with a focus at the origin, and then give the directrix and eccentricity.

6. $r = \dfrac{6}{1 - 2\cos\theta}$

7. $r = \dfrac{3}{4 - 4\sin\theta}$

8. $r = \dfrac{8}{4 - 3\cos\theta}$

9. $r = \dfrac{5}{1 + 2\sin\theta}$

10. $r = \dfrac{16}{4 + 3\cos\theta}$

11. $r = \dfrac{3}{10 + 10\cos\theta}$

12. $r = \dfrac{2}{1 - \cos\theta}$

13. $r = \dfrac{4}{7 + 2\cos\theta}$

14. $r(1 - \cos\theta) = 3$

15. $r(3 + 5\sin\theta) = 11$

16. $r(4 - 5\sin\theta) = 1$

17. $r(7 + 8\cos\theta) = 7$

For the following exercises, convert the polar equation of a conic section to a rectangular equation.

18. $r = \dfrac{4}{1 + 3\sin\theta}$

19. $r = \dfrac{2}{5 - 3\sin\theta}$

20. $r = \dfrac{8}{3 - 2\cos\theta}$

21. $r = \dfrac{3}{2 + 5\cos\theta}$

22. $r = \dfrac{4}{2 + 2\sin\theta}$

23. $r = \dfrac{3}{8 - 8\cos\theta}$

24. $r = \dfrac{2}{6 + 7\cos\theta}$

25. $r = \dfrac{5}{5 - 11\sin\theta}$

26. $r(5 + 2\cos\theta) = 6$

27. $r(2 - \cos\theta) = 1$

28. $r(2.5 - 2.5\sin\theta) = 5$

29. $r = \dfrac{6\sec\theta}{-2 + 3\sec\theta}$

30. $r = \dfrac{6\csc\theta}{3 + 2\csc\theta}$

For the following exercises, graph the given conic section. If it is a parabola, label the vertex, focus, and directrix. If it is an ellipse, label the vertices and foci. If it is a hyperbola, label the vertices and foci.

31. $r = \dfrac{5}{2 + \cos\theta}$

32. $r = \dfrac{2}{3 + 3\sin\theta}$

33. $r = \dfrac{10}{5 - 4\sin\theta}$

34. $r = \dfrac{3}{1 + 2\cos\theta}$

35. $r = \dfrac{8}{4 - 5\cos\theta}$

36. $r = \dfrac{3}{4 - 4\cos\theta}$

37. $r = \dfrac{2}{1 - \sin\theta}$

38. $r = \dfrac{6}{3 + 2\sin\theta}$

39. $r(1 + \cos\theta) = 5$

40. $r(3 - 4\sin\theta) = 9$

41. $r(3 - 2\sin\theta) = 6$

42. $r(6 - 4\cos\theta) = 5$

For the following exercises, find the polar equation of the conic with focus at the origin and the given eccentricity and directrix.

43. Directrix: $x = 4$; $e = \dfrac{1}{5}$

44. Directrix: $x = -4$; $e = 5$

45. Directrix: $y = 2$; $e = 2$

46. Directrix: $y = -2$; $e = \dfrac{1}{2}$

47. Directrix: $x = 1$; $e = 1$

48. Directrix: $x = -1$; $e = 1$

49. Directrix: $x = -\dfrac{1}{4}$; $e = \dfrac{7}{2}$

50. Directrix: $y = \dfrac{2}{5}$; $e = \dfrac{7}{2}$

51. Directrix: $y = 4$; $e = \dfrac{3}{2}$

52. Directrix: $x = -2$; $e = \dfrac{8}{3}$

53. Directrix: $x = -5$; $e = \dfrac{3}{4}$

54. Directrix: $y = 2$; $e = 2.5$

55. Directrix: $x = -3$; $e = \dfrac{1}{3}$

EXTENSIONS

Recall from **Rotation of Axes** that equations of conics with an xy term have rotated graphs. For the following exercises, express each equation in polar form with r as a function of θ.

56. $xy = 2$

57. $x^2 + xy + y^2 = 4$

58. $2x^2 + 4xy + 2y^2 = 9$

59. $16x^2 + 24xy + 9y^2 = 1$

CHAPTER 12 REVIEW

Key Terms

angle of rotation an acute angle formed by a set of axes rotated from the Cartesian plane where, if $\cot(2\theta) > 0$, then θ is between $(0°, 45°)$; if $\cot(2\theta) < 0$, then θ is between $(45°, 90°)$; and if $\cot(2\theta) = 0$, then $\theta = 45°$

center of a hyperbola the midpoint of both the transverse and conjugate axes of a hyperbola

center of an ellipse the midpoint of both the major and minor axes

conic section any shape resulting from the intersection of a right circular cone with a plane

conjugate axis the axis of a hyperbola that is perpendicular to the transverse axis and has the co-vertices as its endpoints

degenerate conic sections any of the possible shapes formed when a plane intersects a double cone through the apex. Types of degenerate conic sections include a point, a line, and intersecting lines.

directrix a line perpendicular to the axis of symmetry of a parabola; a line such that the ratio of the distance between the points on the conic and the focus to the distance to the directrix is constant

eccentricity the ratio of the distances from a point P on the graph to the focus F and to the directrix D represented by $e = \dfrac{PF}{PD}$, where e is a positive real number

ellipse the set of all points (x, y) in a plane such that the sum of their distances from two fixed points is a constant

foci plural of focus

focus (of a parabola) a fixed point in the interior of a parabola that lies on the axis of symmetry

focus (of an ellipse) one of the two fixed points on the major axis of an ellipse such that the sum of the distances from these points to any point (x, y) on the ellipse is a constant

hyperbola the set of all points (x, y) in a plane such that the difference of the distances between (x, y) and the foci is a positive constant

latus rectum the line segment that passes through the focus of a parabola parallel to the directrix, with endpoints on the parabola

major axis the longer of the two axes of an ellipse

minor axis the shorter of the two axes of an ellipse

nondegenerate conic section a shape formed by the intersection of a plane with a double right cone such that the plane does not pass through the apex; nondegenerate conics include circles, ellipses, hyperbolas, and parabolas

parabola the set of all points (x, y) in a plane that are the same distance from a fixed line, called the directrix, and a fixed point (the focus) not on the directrix

polar equation an equation of a curve in polar coordinates r and θ

transverse axis the axis of a hyperbola that includes the foci and has the vertices as its endpoints

Key Equations

Horizontal ellipse, center at origin	$\dfrac{x^2}{a^2} + \dfrac{y^2}{b^2} = 1, a > b$
Vertical ellipse, center at origin	$\dfrac{x^2}{b^2} + \dfrac{y^2}{a^2} = 1, a > b$
Horizontal ellipse, center (h, k)	$\dfrac{(x - h)^2}{a^2} + \dfrac{(y - k)^2}{b^2} = 1, a > b$
Vertical ellipse, center (h, k)	$\dfrac{(x - h)^2}{b^2} + \dfrac{(y - k)^2}{a^2} = 1, a > b$
Hyperbola, center at origin, transverse axis on x-axis	$\dfrac{x^2}{a^2} - \dfrac{y^2}{b^2} = 1$
Hyperbola, center at origin, transverse axis on y-axis	$\dfrac{y^2}{a^2} - \dfrac{x^2}{b^2} = 1$

Hyperbola, center at *(h, k)*, transverse axis parallel to *x*-axis	$\dfrac{(x-h)^2}{a^2} - \dfrac{(y-k)^2}{b^2} = 1$
Hyperbola, center at *(h, k)*, transverse axis parallel to *y*-axis	$\dfrac{(y-k)^2}{a^2} - \dfrac{(x-h)^2}{b^2} = 1$
Parabola, vertex at origin, axis of symmetry on *x*-axis	$y^2 = 4px$
Parabola, vertex at origin, axis of symmetry on *y*-axis	$x^2 = 4py$
Parabola, vertex at *(h, k)*, axis of symmetry on *x*-axis	$(y-k)^2 = 4p(x-h)$
Parabola, vertex at *(h, k)*, axis of symmetry on *y*-axis	$(x-h)^2 = 4p(y-k)$
General Form equation of a conic section	$Ax^2 + Bxy + Cy^2 + Dx + Ey + F = 0$
Rotation of a conic section	$x = x'\cos\theta - y'\sin\theta$ $y = x'\sin\theta + y'\cos\theta$
Angle of rotation	θ, where $\cot(2\theta) = \dfrac{A-C}{B}$

Key Concepts

12.1 The Ellipse

- An ellipse is the set of all points (x, y) in a plane such that the sum of their distances from two fixed points is a constant. Each fixed point is called a focus (plural: foci).
- When given the coordinates of the foci and vertices of an ellipse, we can write the equation of the ellipse in standard form. See **Example 1** and **Example 2**.
- When given an equation for an ellipse centered at the origin in standard form, we can identify its vertices, covertices, foci, and the lengths and positions of the major and minor axes in order to graph the ellipse. See **Example 3** and **Example 4**.
- When given the equation for an ellipse centered at some point other than the origin, we can identify its key features and graph the ellipse. See **Example 5** and **Example 6**.
- Real-world situations can be modeled using the standard equations of ellipses and then evaluated to find key features, such as lengths of axes and distance between foci. See **Example 7**.

12.2 The Hyperbola

- A hyperbola is the set of all points (x, y) in a plane such that the difference of the distances between (x, y) and the foci is a positive constant.
- The standard form of a hyperbola can be used to locate its vertices and foci. See **Example 1**.
- When given the coordinates of the foci and vertices of a hyperbola, we can write the equation of the hyperbola in standard form. See **Example 2** and **Example 3**.
- When given an equation for a hyperbola, we can identify its vertices, co-vertices, foci, asymptotes, and lengths and positions of the transverse and conjugate axes in order to graph the hyperbola. See **Example 4** and **Example 5**.
- Real-world situations can be modeled using the standard equations of hyperbolas. For instance, given the dimensions of a natural draft cooling tower, we can find a hyperbolic equation that models its sides. See **Example 6**.

12.3 The Parabola

- A parabola is the set of all points (x, y) in a plane that are the same distance from a fixed line, called the directrix, and a fixed point (the focus) not on the directrix.

- The standard form of a parabola with vertex $(0, 0)$ and the x-axis as its axis of symmetry can be used to graph the parabola. If $p > 0$, the parabola opens right. If $p < 0$, the parabola opens left. See **Example 1**.

- The standard form of a parabola with vertex $(0, 0)$ and the y-axis as its axis of symmetry can be used to graph the parabola. If $p > 0$, the parabola opens up. If $p < 0$, the parabola opens down. See **Example 2**.

- When given the focus and directrix of a parabola, we can write its equation in standard form. See **Example 3**.

- The standard form of a parabola with vertex (h, k) and axis of symmetry parallel to the x-axis can be used to graph the parabola. If $p > 0$, the parabola opens right. If $p < 0$, the parabola opens left. See **Example 4**.

- The standard form of a parabola with vertex (h, k) and axis of symmetry parallel to the y-axis can be used to graph the parabola. If $p > 0$, the parabola opens up. If $p < 0$, the parabola opens down. See **Example 5**.

- Real-world situations can be modeled using the standard equations of parabolas. For instance, given the diameter and focus of a cross-section of a parabolic reflector, we can find an equation that models its sides. See **Example 6**.

12.4 Rotation of Axes

- Four basic shapes can result from the intersection of a plane with a pair of right circular cones connected tail to tail. They include an ellipse, a circle, a hyperbola, and a parabola.

- A nondegenerate conic section has the general form $Ax^2 + Bxy + Cy^2 + Dx + Ey + F = 0$ where A, B and C are not all zero. The values of A, B, and C determine the type of conic. See **Example 1**.

- Equations of conic sections with an xy term have been rotated about the origin. See **Example 2**.

- The general form can be transformed into an equation in the x' and y' coordinate system without the $x'y'$ term. See **Example 3** and **Example 4**.

- An expression is described as invariant if it remains unchanged after rotating. Because the discriminant is invariant, observing it enables us to identify the conic section. See **Example 5**.

12.5 Conic Sections in Polar Coordinates

- Any conic may be determined by a single focus, the corresponding eccentricity, and the directrix. We can also define a conic in terms of a fixed point, the focus $P(r, \theta)$ at the pole, and a line, the directrix, which is perpendicular to the polar axis.

- A conic is the set of all points $e = \dfrac{PF}{PD}$, where eccentricity e is a positive real number. Each conic may be written in terms of its polar equation. See **Example 1**.

- The polar equations of conics can be graphed. See **Example 2**, **Example 3**, and **Example 4**.

- Conics can be defined in terms of a focus, a directrix, and eccentricity. See **Example 5** and **Example 6**.

- We can use the identities $r = \sqrt{x^2 + y^2}$, $x = r\cos\theta$, and $y = r\sin\theta$ to convert the equation for a conic from polar to rectangular form. See **Example 7**.

CHAPTER 12 REVIEW EXERCISES

THE ELLIPSE

For the following exercises, write the equation of the ellipse in standard form. Then identify the center, vertices, and foci.

1. $\dfrac{x^2}{25} + \dfrac{y^2}{64} = 1$

2. $\dfrac{(x-2)^2}{100} + \dfrac{(y+3)^2}{36} = 1$

3. $9x^2 + y^2 + 54x - 4y + 76 = 0$

4. $9x^2 + 36y^2 - 36x + 72y + 36 = 0$

For the following exercises, graph the ellipse, noting center, vertices, and foci.

5. $\dfrac{x^2}{36} + \dfrac{y^2}{9} = 1$

6. $\dfrac{(x-4)^2}{25} + \dfrac{(y+3)^2}{49} = 1$

7. $4x^2 + y^2 + 16x + 4y - 44 = 0$

8. $2x^2 + 3y^2 - 20x + 12y + 38 = 0$

For the following exercises, use the given information to find the equation for the ellipse.

9. Center at $(0, 0)$, focus at $(3, 0)$, vertex at $(-5, 0)$

10. Center at $(2, -2)$, vertex at $(7, -2)$, focus at $(4, -2)$

11. A whispering gallery is to be constructed such that the foci are located 35 feet from the center. If the length of the gallery is to be 100 feet, what should the height of the ceiling be?

THE HYPERBOLA

For the following exercises, write the equation of the hyperbola in standard form. Then give the center, vertices, and foci.

12. $\dfrac{x^2}{81} - \dfrac{y^2}{9} = 1$

13. $\dfrac{(y+1)^2}{16} - \dfrac{(x-4)^2}{36} = 1$

14. $9y^2 - 4x^2 + 54y - 16x + 29 = 0$

15. $3x^2 - y^2 - 12x - 6y - 9 = 0$

For the following exercises, graph the hyperbola, labeling vertices and foci.

16. $\dfrac{x^2}{9} - \dfrac{y^2}{16} = 1$

17. $\dfrac{(y-1)^2}{49} - \dfrac{(x+1)^2}{4} = 1$

18. $x^2 - 4y^2 + 6x + 32y - 91 = 0$

19. $2y^2 - x^2 - 12y - 6 = 0$

For the following exercises, find the equation of the hyperbola.

20. Center at $(0, 0)$, vertex at $(0, 4)$, focus at $(0, -6)$

21. Foci at $(3, 7)$ and $(7, 7)$, vertex at $(6, 7)$

THE PARABOLA

For the following exercises, write the equation of the parabola in standard form. Then give the vertex, focus, and directrix.

22. $y^2 = 12x$

23. $(x+2)^2 = \dfrac{1}{2}(y-1)$

24. $y^2 - 6y - 6x - 3 = 0$

25. $x^2 + 10x - y + 23 = 0$

For the following exercises, graph the parabola, labeling vertex, focus, and directrix.

26. $x^2 + 4y = 0$

27. $(y-1)^2 = \dfrac{1}{2}(x+3)$

28. $x^2 - 8x - 10y + 46 = 0$

29. $2y^2 + 12y + 6x + 15 = 0$

For the following exercises, write the equation of the parabola using the given information.

30. Focus at $(-4, 0)$; directrix is $x = 4$

31. Focus at $\left(2, \dfrac{9}{8}\right)$; directrix is $y = \dfrac{7}{8}$

32. A cable TV receiving dish is the shape of a paraboloid of revolution. Find the location of the receiver, which is placed at the focus, if the dish is 5 feet across at its opening and 1.5 feet deep.

ROTATION OF AXES

For the following exercises, determine which of the conic sections is represented.

33. $16x^2 + 24xy + 9y^2 + 24x - 60y - 60 = 0$

34. $4x^2 + 14xy + 5y^2 + 18x - 6y + 30 = 0$

35. $4x^2 + xy + 2y^2 + 8x - 26y + 9 = 0$

For the following exercises, determine the angle θ that will eliminate the xy term, and write the corresponding equation without the xy term.

36. $x^2 + 4xy - 2y^2 - 6 = 0$

37. $x^2 - xy + y^2 - 6 = 0$

For the following exercises, graph the equation relative to the $x'y'$ system in which the equation has no $x'y'$ term.

38. $9x^2 - 24xy + 16y^2 - 80x - 60y + 100 = 0$

39. $x^2 - xy + y^2 - 2 = 0$

40. $6x^2 + 24xy - y^2 - 12x + 26y + 11 = 0$

CONIC SECTIONS IN POLAR COORDINATES

For the following exercises, given the polar equation of the conic with focus at the origin, identify the eccentricity and directrix.

41. $r = \dfrac{10}{1 - 5\cos\theta}$

42. $r = \dfrac{6}{3 + 2\cos\theta}$

43. $r = \dfrac{1}{4 + 3\sin\theta}$

44. $r = \dfrac{3}{5 - 5\sin\theta}$

For the following exercises, graph the conic given in polar form. If it is a parabola, label the vertex, focus, and directrix. If it is an ellipse or a hyperbola, label the vertices and foci.

45. $r = \dfrac{3}{1 - \sin\theta}$

46. $r = \dfrac{8}{4 + 3\sin\theta}$

47. $r = \dfrac{10}{4 + 5\cos\theta}$

48. $r = \dfrac{9}{3 - 6\cos\theta}$

For the following exercises, given information about the graph of a conic with focus at the origin, find the equation in polar form.

49. Directrix is $x = 3$ and eccentricity $e = 1$

50. Directrix is $y = -2$ and eccentricity $e = 4$

CHAPTER 12 PRACTICE TEST

For the following exercises, write the equation in standard form and state the center, vertices, and foci.

1. $\dfrac{x^2}{9} + \dfrac{y^2}{4} = 1$

2. $9y^2 + 16x^2 - 36y + 32x - 92 = 0$

For the following exercises, sketch the graph, identifying the center, vertices, and foci.

3. $\dfrac{(x-3)^2}{64} + \dfrac{(y-2)^2}{36} = 1$

4. $2x^2 + y^2 + 8x - 6y - 7 = 0$

5. Write the standard form equation of an ellipse with a center at $(1, 2)$, vertex at $(7, 2)$, and focus at $(4, 2)$.

6. A whispering gallery is to be constructed with a length of 150 feet. If the foci are to be located 20 feet away from the wall, how high should the ceiling be?

For the following exercises, write the equation of the hyperbola in standard form, and give the center, vertices, foci, and asymptotes.

7. $\dfrac{x^2}{49} - \dfrac{y^2}{81} = 1$

8. $16y^2 - 9x^2 + 128y + 112 = 0$

For the following exercises, graph the hyperbola, noting its center, vertices, and foci. State the equations of the asymptotes.

9. $\dfrac{(x-3)^2}{25} - \dfrac{(y+3)^2}{1} = 1$

10. $y^2 - x^2 + 4y - 4x - 18 = 0$

11. Write the standard form equation of a hyperbola with foci at $(1, 0)$ and $(1, 6)$, and a vertex at $(1, 2)$.

For the following exercises, write the equation of the parabola in standard form, and give the vertex, focus, and equation of the directrix.

12. $y^2 + 10x = 0$

13. $3x^2 - 12x - y + 11 = 0$

For the following exercises, graph the parabola, labeling the vertex, focus, and directrix.

14. $(x-1)^2 = -4(y+3)$

15. $y^2 + 8x - 8y + 40 = 0$

16. Write the equation of a parabola with a focus at $(2, 3)$ and directrix $y = -1$.

17. A searchlight is shaped like a paraboloid of revolution. If the light source is located 1.5 feet from the base along the axis of symmetry, and the depth of the searchlight is 3 feet, what should the width of the opening be?

For the following exercises, determine which conic section is represented by the given equation, and then determine the angle θ that will eliminate the xy term.

18. $3x^2 - 2xy + 3y^2 = 4$

19. $x^2 + 4xy + 4y^2 + 6x - 8y = 0$

For the following exercises, rewrite in the $x'y'$ system without the $x'y'$ term, and graph the rotated graph.

20. $11x^2 + 10\sqrt{3}xy + y^2 = 4$

21. $16x^2 + 24xy + 9y^2 - 125x = 0$

For the following exercises, identify the conic with focus at the origin, and then give the directrix and eccentricity.

22. $r = \dfrac{3}{2 - \sin\theta}$

23. $r = \dfrac{5}{4 + 6\cos\theta}$

For the following exercises, graph the given conic section. If it is a parabola, label vertex, focus, and directrix. If it is an ellipse or a hyperbola, label vertices and foci.

24. $r = \dfrac{12}{4 - 8\sin\theta}$

25. $r = \dfrac{2}{4 + 4\sin\theta}$

26. Find a polar equation of the conic with focus at the origin, eccentricity of $e = 2$, and directrix: $x = 3$.

13

Sequences, Probability and Counting Theory

Figure 1 (credit: Robert S. Donovan, Flickr.)

CHAPTER OUTLINE

13.1 Sequences and Their Notations

13.2 Arithmetic Sequences

13.3 Geometric Sequences

13.4 Series and Their Notations

13.5 Counting Principles

13.6 Binomial Theorem

13.7 Probability

Introduction

A lottery winner has some big decisions to make regarding what to do with the winnings. Buy a villa in Saint Barthélemy? A luxury convertible? A cruise around the world?

The likelihood of winning the lottery is slim, but we all love to fantasize about what we could buy with the winnings. One of the first things a lottery winner has to decide is whether to take the winnings in the form of a lump sum or as a series of regular payments, called an annuity, over the next 30 years or so.

This decision is often based on many factors, such as tax implications, interest rates, and investment strategies. There are also personal reasons to consider when making the choice, and one can make many arguments for either decision. However, most lottery winners opt for the lump sum.

In this chapter, we will explore the mathematics behind situations such as these. We will take an in-depth look at annuities. We will also look at the branch of mathematics that would allow us to calculate the number of ways to choose lottery numbers and the probability of winning.

LEARNING OBJECTIVES

In this section, you will:

- Write the terms of a sequence defined by an explicit formula.
- Write the terms of a sequence defined by a recursive formula.
- Use factorial notation.

13.1   SEQUENCES AND THEIR NOTATIONS

A video game company launches an exciting new advertising campaign. They predict the number of online visits to their website, or hits, will double each day. The model they are using shows 2 hits the first day, 4 hits the second day, 8 hits the third day, and so on. See **Table 1**.

Day	1	2	3	4	5	...
Hits	2	4	8	16	32	...

Table 1

If their model continues, how many hits will there be at the end of the month? To answer this question, we'll first need to know how to determine a list of numbers written in a specific order. In this section, we will explore these kinds of ordered lists.

Writing the Terms of a Sequence Defined by an Explicit Formula

One way to describe an ordered list of numbers is as a **sequence**. A sequence is a function whose domain is a subset of the counting numbers. The sequence established by the number of hits on the website is

$$\{2, 4, 8, 16, 32, ...\}.$$

The ellipsis (...) indicates that the sequence continues indefinitely. Each number in the sequence is called a **term**. The first five terms of this sequence are 2, 4, 8, 16, and 32.

Listing all of the terms for a sequence can be cumbersome. For example, finding the number of hits on the website at the end of the month would require listing out as many as 31 terms. A more efficient way to determine a specific term is by writing a formula to define the sequence.

One type of formula is an explicit formula, which defines the terms of a sequence using their position in the sequence. Explicit formulas are helpful if we want to find a specific term of a sequence without finding all of the previous terms. We can use the formula to find the nth term of the sequence, where n is any positive number. In our example, each number in the sequence is double the previous number, so we can use powers of 2 to write a formula for the nth term.

$$\{2, \quad 4, \quad 8, \quad 16, \quad 22, \quad ..., \quad ?, \quad ...\}$$
$$\downarrow \quad \downarrow \quad \downarrow \quad \downarrow \quad \downarrow \qquad \downarrow$$
$$\{2^1, 2^2, 2^3, 2^4, \quad 2^5, \quad ..., \quad 2^n, \quad ...\}$$

The first term of the sequence is $2^1 = 2$, the second term is $2^2 = 4$, the third term is $2^3 = 8$, and so on. The nth term of the sequence can be found by raising 2 to the nth power. An explicit formula for a sequence is named by a lower case letter a, b, c... with the subscript n. The explicit formula for this sequence is

$$a_n = 2^n.$$

Now that we have a formula for the nth term of the sequence, we can answer the question posed at the beginning of this section. We were asked to find the number of hits at the end of the month, which we will take to be 31 days. To find the number of hits on the last day of the month, we need to find the 31st term of the sequence. We will substitute 31 for n in the formula.

$$a_{31} = 2^{31}$$

$$= 2,147,483,648$$

If the doubling trend continues, the company will get 2,147,483,648 hits on the last day of the month. That is over 2.1 billion hits! The huge number is probably a little unrealistic because it does not take consumer interest and competition into account. It does, however, give the company a starting point from which to consider business decisions.

Another way to represent the sequence is by using a table. The first five terms of the sequence and the nth term of the sequence are shown in **Table 2**.

n	1	2	3	4	5	n
nth term of the sequence, a_n	2	4	8	16	32	2^n

Table 2

Graphing provides a visual representation of the sequence as a set of distinct points. We can see from the graph in **Figure 1** that the number of hits is rising at an exponential rate. This particular sequence forms an exponential function.

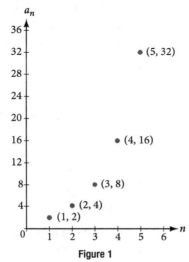

Figure 1

Lastly, we can write this particular sequence as

$$\{2, 4, 8, 16, 32, \ldots, 2^n, \ldots\}$$

A sequence that continues indefinitely is called an **infinite sequence**. The domain of an infinite sequence is the set of counting numbers. If we consider only the first 10 terms of the sequence, we could write

$$\{2, 4, 8, 16, 32, \ldots, 2^n, \ldots, 1024\}.$$

This sequence is called a **finite sequence** because it does not continue indefinitely.

---

sequence

A **sequence** is a function whose domain is the set of positive integers. A **finite sequence** is a sequence whose domain consists of only the first n positive integers. The numbers in a sequence are called **terms**. The variable a with a number subscript is used to represent the terms in a sequence and to indicate the position of the term in the sequence.

$$a_1, a_2, a_3, \ldots, a_n, \ldots$$

We call a_1 the first term of the sequence, a_2 the second term of the sequence, a_3 the third term of the sequence, and so on. The term an is called the **nth term of the sequence**, or the general term of the sequence. An **explicit formula** defines the nth term of a sequence using the position of the term. A sequence that continues indefinitely is an **infinite sequence**.

Q & A...

Does a sequence always have to begin with a_1?

No. In certain problems, it may be useful to define the initial term as a_0 instead of a_1. In these problems, the domain of the function includes 0.

How To...

Given an explicit formula, write the first n terms of a sequence.

1. Substitute each value of n into the formula. Begin with $n = 1$ to find the first term, a_1.
2. To find the second term, a_2, use $n = 2$.
3. Continue in the same manner until you have identified all n terms.

Example 1   **Writing the Terms of a Sequence Defined by an Explicit Formula**

Write the first five terms of the sequence defined by the explicit formula $a_n = -3n + 8$.

Solution   Substitute $n = 1$ into the formula. Repeat with values 2 through 5 for n.

$$n = 1 \quad a_1 = -3(1) + 8 = 5$$
$$n = 2 \quad a_2 = -3(2) + 8 = 2$$
$$n = 3 \quad a_3 = -3(3) + 8 = -1$$
$$n = 4 \quad a_4 = -3(4) + 8 = -4$$
$$n = 5 \quad a_5 = -3(5) + 8 = -7$$

The first five terms are $\{5, 2, -1, -4, -7\}$.

Analysis   *The sequence values can be listed in a table. A table, such as **Table 3**, is a convenient way to input the function into a graphing utility.*

n	1	2	3	4	5
a_n	5	2	-1	-4	-7

Table 3

A graph can be made from this table of values. From the graph in **Figure 2**, we can see that this sequence represents a linear function, but notice the graph is not continuous because the domain is over the positive integers only.

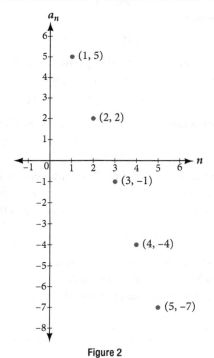

Figure 2

Try It #1

Write the first five terms of the sequence defined by the explicit formula $t_n = 5n - 4$.

Investigating Alternating Sequences

Sometimes sequences have terms that are alternate. In fact, the terms may actually alternate in sign. The steps to finding terms of the sequence are the same as if the signs did not alternate. However, the resulting terms will not show increase or decrease as n increases. Let's take a look at the following sequence.

$$\{2, -4, 6, -8\}$$

Notice the first term is greater than the second term, the second term is less than the third term, and the third term is greater than the fourth term. This trend continues forever. Do not rearrange the terms in numerical order to interpret the sequence.

How To...

Given an explicit formula with alternating terms, write the first n terms of a sequence.

1. Substitute each value of n into the formula. Begin with $n = 1$ to find the first term, a_1. The sign of the term is given by the $(-1)^n$ in the explicit formula.
2. To find the second term, a_2, use $n = 2$.
3. Continue in the same manner until you have identified all n terms.

Example 2   Writing the Terms of an Alternating Sequence Defined by an Explicit Formula

Write the first five terms of the sequence.

$$a_n = \frac{(-1)^n n^2}{n + 1}$$

Solution   Substitute $n = 1$, $n = 2$, and so on in the formula.

$$n = 1 \quad a_1 = \frac{(-1)^1 1^1}{1 + 1} = -\frac{1}{2}$$

$$n = 2 \quad a_2 = \frac{(-1)^2 2^2}{2 + 1} = \frac{4}{3}$$

$$n = 3 \quad a_3 = \frac{(-1)^3 3^2}{3 + 1} = -\frac{9}{4}$$

$$n = 4 \quad a_4 = \frac{(-1)^4 4^2}{4 + 1} = \frac{16}{5}$$

$$n = 5 \quad a_5 = \frac{(-1)^5 5^2}{5 + 1} = -\frac{25}{6}$$

The first five terms are $\left\{ -\frac{1}{2}, \frac{4}{3}, -\frac{9}{4}, \frac{16}{5}, -\frac{25}{6} \right\}$

Analysis   *The graph of this function, shown in **Figure 3**, looks different from the ones we have seen previously in this section because the terms of the sequence alternate between positive and negative values.*

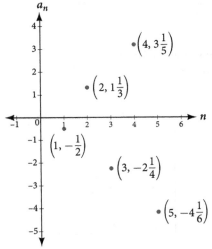

Figure 3

Q & A...

In Example 2, does the (−1) to the power of n account for the oscillations of signs?

Yes, the power might be n, $n + 1$, $n − 1$, and so on, but any odd powers will result in a negative term, and any even power will result in a positive term.

Try It #2

Write the first five terms of the sequence. $a_n = \dfrac{4n}{(-2)^n}$

Investigating Piecewise Explicit Formulas

We've learned that sequences are functions whose domain is over the positive integers. This is true for other types of functions, including some piecewise functions. Recall that a piecewise function is a function defined by multiple subsections. A different formula might represent each individual subsection.

How To...

Given an explicit formula for a piecewise function, write the first n terms of a sequence
1. Identify the formula to which $n = 1$ applies.
2. To find the first term, a_1, use $n = 1$ in the appropriate formula.
3. Identify the formula to which $n = 2$ applies.
4. To find the second term, a_2, use $n = 2$ in the appropriate formula.
5. Continue in the same manner until you have identified all n terms.

Example 3   **Writing the Terms of a Sequence Defined by a Piecewise Explicit Formula**

Write the first six terms of the sequence.

$$a_n = \begin{cases} n^2 \text{ if } n \text{ is not divisible by 3} \\ \dfrac{n}{3} \text{ if } n \text{ is divisible by 3} \end{cases}$$

Solution   Substitute $n = 1$, $n = 2$, and so on in the appropriate formula. Use n^2 when n is not a multiple of 3. Use $\dfrac{n}{3}$ when n is a multiple of 3.

$$a_1 = 1^2 = 1 \qquad \text{1 is not a multiple of 3. Use } n^2.$$
$$a_2 = 2^2 = 4 \qquad \text{2 is not a multiple of 3. Use } n^2.$$
$$a_3 = \frac{3}{3} = 1 \qquad \text{3 is a multiple of 3. Use } \frac{n}{3}.$$
$$a_4 = 4^2 = 16 \qquad \text{4 is not a multiple of 3. Use } n^2.$$
$$a_5 = 5^2 = 25 \qquad \text{5 is not a multiple of 3. Use } n^2.$$
$$a_6 = \frac{6}{3} = 2 \qquad \text{6 is a multiple of 3. Use } \frac{n}{3}.$$

The first six terms are {1, 4, 1, 16, 25, 2}.

Analysis   Every third point on the graph shown in **Figure 4** stands out from the two nearby points. This occurs because the sequence was defined by a piecewise function.

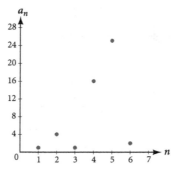

Figure 4

Try It #3

Write the first six terms of the sequence.
$$a_n = \begin{cases} 2n^3 & \text{if } n \text{ is odd} \\ \dfrac{5n}{2} & \text{if } n \text{ is even} \end{cases}$$

Finding an Explicit Formula

Thus far, we have been given the explicit formula and asked to find a number of terms of the sequence. Sometimes, the explicit formula for the nth term of a sequence is not given. Instead, we are given several terms from the sequence. When this happens, we can work in reverse to find an explicit formula from the first few terms of a sequence. The key to finding an explicit formula is to look for a pattern in the terms. Keep in mind that the pattern may involve alternating terms, formulas for numerators, formulas for denominators, exponents, or bases.

How To…

Given the first few terms of a sequence, find an explicit formula for the sequence.

1. Look for a pattern among the terms.
2. If the terms are fractions, look for a separate pattern among the numerators and denominators.
3. Look for a pattern among the signs of the terms.
4. Write a formula for a_n in terms of n. Test your formula for $n = 1$, $n = 2$, and $n = 3$.

Example 4   **Writing an Explicit Formula for the *n*th Term of a Sequence**

Write an explicit formula for the nth term of each sequence.

a. $\left\{ -\dfrac{2}{11}, \dfrac{3}{13}, -\dfrac{4}{15}, \dfrac{5}{17}, -\dfrac{6}{19}, \dots \right\}$

b. $\left\{ -\dfrac{2}{25}, -\dfrac{2}{125}, -\dfrac{2}{625}, -\dfrac{2}{3,125}, -\dfrac{2}{15,625}, \dots \right\}$

c. $\{e^4, e^5, e^6, e^7, e^8, \dots\}$

Solution   Look for the pattern in each sequence.

a. The terms alternate between positive and negative. We can use $(-1)^n$ to make the terms alternate. The numerator can be represented by $n + 1$. The denominator can be represented by $2n + 9$.
$$a_n = \frac{(-1)^n (n + 1)}{2n + 9}$$

b. The terms are all negative.

$\left\{ -\dfrac{2}{25}, -\dfrac{2}{125}, -\dfrac{2}{625}, -\dfrac{2}{3,125}, -\dfrac{2}{15,625}, \dots \right\}$ The numerator is 2

$\left\{ -\dfrac{2}{5^2}, -\dfrac{2}{5^3}, -\dfrac{2}{5^4}, -\dfrac{2}{5^5}, -\dfrac{2}{5^6}, -\dfrac{2}{5^7}, \dots -\dfrac{2}{5^n} \right\}$ The denominators are increasing powers of 5

So we know that the fraction is negative, the numerator is 2, and the denominator can be represented by 5^{n+1}.
$$a_n = -\frac{2}{5^{n+1}}$$

c. The terms are powers of e. For $n = 1$, the first term is e^4 so the exponent must be $n + 3$.
$$a_n = e^{n+3}$$

Try It #4

Write an explicit formula for the nth term of the sequence.

$$\{9, -81, 729, -6{,}561, 59{,}049, \dots\}$$

Try It #5

Write an explicit formula for the nth term of the sequence.

$$\left\{-\frac{3}{4}, -\frac{9}{8}, -\frac{27}{12}, -\frac{81}{16}, -\frac{243}{20}, \ldots\right\}$$

Try It #6

Write an explicit formula for the nth term of the sequence.

$$\left\{\frac{1}{e^2}, \frac{1}{e}, 1, e, e^2, \ldots\right\}$$

Writing the Terms of a Sequence Defined by a Recursive Formula

Sequences occur naturally in the growth patterns of nautilus shells, pinecones, tree branches, and many other natural structures. We may see the sequence in the leaf or branch arrangement, the number of petals of a flower, or the pattern of the chambers in a nautilus shell. Their growth follows the Fibonacci sequence, a famous sequence in which each term can be found by adding the preceding two terms. The numbers in the sequence are 1, 1, 2, 3, 5, 8, 13, 21, 34,.... Other examples from the natural world that exhibit the Fibonacci sequence are the Calla Lily, which has just one petal, the Black-Eyed Susan with 13 petals, and different varieties of daisies that may have 21 or 34 petals.

Each term of the Fibonacci sequence depends on the terms that come before it. The Fibonacci sequence cannot easily be written using an explicit formula. Instead, we describe the sequence using a **recursive formula**, a formula that defines the terms of a sequence using previous terms.

A recursive formula always has two parts: the value of an initial term (or terms), and an equation defining a_n in terms of preceding terms. For example, suppose we know the following:

$$a_1 = 3$$
$$a_n = 2a_{n-1} - 1, \text{ for } n \geq 2$$

We can find the subsequent terms of the sequence using the first term.

$$a_1 = 3$$
$$a_2 = 2a_1 - 1 = 2(3) - 1 = 5$$
$$a_3 = 2a_2 - 1 = 2(5) - 1 = 9$$
$$a_4 = 2a_3 - 1 = 2(9) - 1 = 17$$

So the first four terms of the sequence are $\{3, 5, 9, 17\}$.

The recursive formula for the Fibonacci sequence states the first two terms and defines each successive term as the sum of the preceding two terms.

$$a_1 = 1$$
$$a_2 = 1$$
$$a_n = a_{n-1} + a_{n-2} \text{ for } n \geq 3$$

To find the tenth term of the sequence, for example, we would need to add the eighth and ninth terms. We were told previously that the eighth and ninth terms are 21 and 34, so

$$a_{10} = a_9 + a_8 = 34 + 21 = 55$$

recursive formula

A **recursive formula** is a formula that defines each term of a sequence using preceding term(s). Recursive formulas must always state the initial term, or terms, of the sequence.

Q & A...

Must the first two terms always be given in a recursive formula?

No. The Fibonacci sequence defines each term using the two preceding terms, but many recursive formulas define each term using only one preceding term. These sequences need only the first term to be defined.

How To...

Given a recursive formula with only the first term provided, write the first n terms of a sequence.

1. Identify the initial term, a_1, which is given as part of the formula. This is the first term.
2. To find the second term, a_2, substitute the initial term into the formula for a_{n-1}. Solve.
3. To find the third term, a_3, substitute the second term into the formula. Solve.
4. Repeat until you have solved for the nth term.

Example 5   **Writing the Terms of a Sequence Defined by a Recursive Formula**

Write the first five terms of the sequence defined by the recursive formula.

$$a_1 = 9$$
$$a_n = 3a_{n-1} - 20, \text{ for } n \geq 2$$

Solution   The first term is given in the formula. For each subsequent term, we replace a_{n-1} with the value of the preceding term.

$$n = 1 \quad a_1 = 9$$
$$n = 2 \quad a_2 = 3a_1 - 20 = 3(9) - 20 = 27 - 20 = 7$$
$$n = 3 \quad a_3 = 3a_2 - 20 = 3(7) - 20 = 21 - 20 = 1$$
$$n = 4 \quad a_4 = 3a_3 - 20 = 3(1) - 20 = 3 - 20 = -17$$
$$n = 5 \quad a_5 = 3a_4 - 20 = 3(-17) - 20 = -51 - 20 = -71$$

The first five terms are $\{9, 7, 1, -17, -71\}$. See **Figure 5.**

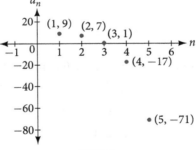

Figure 5

Try It #7

Write the first five terms of the sequence defined by the recursive formula.

$$a_1 = 2$$
$$a_n = 2a_{n-1} + 1, \text{ for } n \geq 2$$

How To...

Given a recursive formula with two initial terms, write the first n terms of a sequence.

1. Identify the initial term, a_1, which is given as part of the formula.
2. Identify the second term, a_2, which is given as part of the formula.
3. To find the third term, substitute the initial term and the second term into the formula. Evaluate.
4. Repeat until you have evaluated the nth term.

Example 6   **Writing the Terms of a Sequence Defined by a Recursive Formula**

Write the first six terms of the sequence defined by the recursive formula.

$$a_1 = 1$$
$$a_2 = 2$$
$$a_n = 3a_{n-1} + 4a_{n-2}, \text{ for } n \geq 3$$

Solution   The first two terms are given. For each subsequent term, we replace a_{n-1} and a_{n-2} with the values of the two preceding terms.

$$n = 3 \qquad a_3 = 3a_2 + 4a_1 = 3(2) + 4(1) = 10$$
$$n = 4 \qquad a_4 = 3a_3 + 4a_2 = 3(10) + 4(2) = 38$$
$$n = 5 \qquad a_5 = 3a_4 + 4a_3 = 3(38) + 4(10) = 154$$
$$n = 6 \qquad a_6 = 3a_5 + 4a_4 = 3(154) + 4(38) = 614$$

The first six terms are {1, 2, 10, 38, 154, 614}. See **Figure 6**.

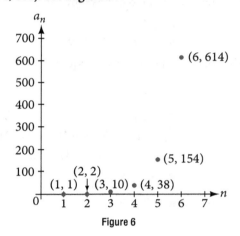

Figure 6

....

Try It #8

Write the first 8 terms of the sequence defined by the recursive formula.

$$a_1 = 0$$
$$a_2 = 1$$
$$a_3 = 1$$
$$a_n = \frac{a_{n-1}}{a_{n-2}} + a_{n-3}, \text{ for } n \geq 4$$

....

Using Factorial Notation

The formulas for some sequences include products of consecutive positive integers. *n* **factorial**, written as *n*!, is the product of the positive integers from 1 to *n*. For example,

$$4! = 4 \cdot 3 \cdot 2 \cdot 1 = 24$$
$$5! = 5 \cdot 4 \cdot 3 \cdot 2 \cdot 1 = 120$$

An example of formula containing a factorial is $a_n = (n + 1)!$. The sixth term of the sequence can be found by substituting 6 for *n*.

$$a_6 = (6 + 1)! = 7! = 7 \cdot 6 \cdot 5 \cdot 4 \cdot 3 \cdot 2 \cdot 1 = 5{,}040$$

The factorial of any whole number *n* is $n(n - 1)!$ We can therefore also think of 5! as $5 \cdot 4!$.

> **factorial**
>
> **n factorial** is a mathematical operation that can be defined using a recursive formula. The factorial of n, denoted $n!$, is defined for a positive integer n as:
>
> $$0! = 1$$
> $$1! = 1$$
> $$n! = n(n-1)(n-2) \cdots (2)(1), \text{ for } n \geq 2$$
>
> The special case 0! is defined as $0! = 1$.

Q & A...

Can factorials always be found using a calculator?

No. Factorials get large very quickly—faster than even exponential functions! When the output gets too large for the calculator, it will not be able to calculate the factorial.

Example 7   **Writing the Terms of a Sequence Using Factorials**

Write the first five terms of the sequence defined by the explicit formula $a_n = \dfrac{5n}{(n+2)!}$.

Solution   Substitute $n = 1$, $n = 2$, and so on in the formula.

$$n = 1 \qquad a_1 = \frac{5(1)}{(1+2)!} = \frac{5}{3!} = \frac{5}{3 \cdot 2 \cdot 1} = \frac{5}{6}$$

$$n = 2 \qquad a_2 = \frac{5(2)}{(2+2)!} = \frac{10}{4!} = \frac{10}{4 \cdot 3 \cdot 2 \cdot 1} = \frac{5}{12}$$

$$n = 3 \qquad a_3 = \frac{5(3)}{(3+2)!} = \frac{15}{5!} = \frac{15}{5 \cdot 4 \cdot 3 \cdot 2 \cdot 1} = \frac{1}{8}$$

$$n = 4 \qquad a_4 = \frac{5(4)}{(4+2)!} = \frac{20}{6!} = \frac{20}{6 \cdot 5 \cdot 4 \cdot 3 \cdot 2 \cdot 1} = \frac{1}{36}$$

$$n = 5 \qquad a_5 = \frac{5(5)}{(5+2)!} = \frac{25}{7!} = \frac{25}{7 \cdot 6 \cdot 5 \cdot 4 \cdot 3 \cdot 2 \cdot 1} = \frac{5}{1,008}$$

The first five terms are $\left\{ \dfrac{5}{6}, \dfrac{5}{12}, \dfrac{1}{8}, \dfrac{1}{36}, \dfrac{5}{1,008} \right\}$.

Analysis   **Figure 7** *shows the graph of the sequence. Notice that, since factorials grow very quickly, the presence of the factorial term in the denominator results in the denominator becoming much larger than the numerator as n increases. This means the quotient gets smaller and, as the plot of the terms shows, the terms are decreasing and nearing zero.*

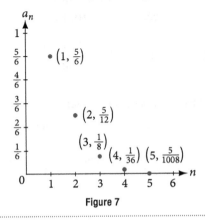

Figure 7

Try It #9

Write the first five terms of the sequence defined by the explicit formula $a_n = \dfrac{(n+1)!}{2n}$.

Access this online resource for additional instruction and practice with sequences.

• Finding Terms in a Sequence (http://openstaxcollege.org/l/findingterms)

13.1   SECTION EXERCISES

VERBAL

1. Discuss the meaning of a sequence. If a finite sequence is defined by a formula, what is its domain? What about an infinite sequence?

2. Describe three ways that a sequence can be defined.

3. Is the ordered set of even numbers an infinite sequence? What about the ordered set of odd numbers? Explain why or why not.

4. What happens to the terms a_n of a sequence when there is a negative factor in the formula that is raised to a power that includes n? What is the term used to describe this phenomenon?

5. What is a factorial, and how is it denoted? Use an example to illustrate how factorial notation can be beneficial.

ALGEBRAIC

For the following exercises, write the first four terms of the sequence.

6. $a_n = 2^n - 2$

7. $a_n = -\dfrac{16}{n+1}$

8. $a_n = -(-5)^{n-1}$

9. $a_n = \dfrac{2^n}{n^3}$

10. $a_n = \dfrac{2n+1}{n^3}$

11. $a_n = 1.25 \cdot (-4)^{n-1}$

12. $a_n = -4 \cdot (-6)^{n-1}$

13. $a_n = \dfrac{n^2}{2n+1}$

14. $a_n = (-10)^n + 1$

15. $a_n = -\left(\dfrac{4 \cdot (-5)^{n-1}}{5} \right)$

For the following exercises, write the first eight terms of the piecewise sequence.

16. $a_n = \begin{cases} (-2)^n - 2 & \text{if } n \text{ is even} \\ (3)^{n-1} & \text{if } n \text{ is odd} \end{cases}$

17. $a_n = \begin{cases} \dfrac{n^2}{2n+1} & \text{if } n \leq 5 \\ n^2 - 5 & \text{if } n > 5 \end{cases}$

18. $a_n = \begin{cases} (2n+1)^2 & \text{if } n \text{ is divisible by } 4 \\ \dfrac{2}{n} & \text{if } n \text{ is not divisible by } 4 \end{cases}$

19. $a_n = \begin{cases} -0.6 \cdot 5^{n-1} & \text{if } n \text{ is prime or } 1 \\ 2.5 \cdot (-2)^{n-1} & \text{if } n \text{ is composite} \end{cases}$

20. $a_n = \begin{cases} 4(n^2 - 2) & \text{if } n \leq 3 \text{ or } n > 6 \\ \dfrac{n^2 - 2}{4} & \text{if } 3 < n \leq 6 \end{cases}$

For the following exercises, write an explicit formula for each sequence.

21. $4, 7, 12, 19, 28, \ldots$

22. $-4, 2, -10, 14, -34, \ldots$

23. $1, 1, \dfrac{4}{3}, 2, \dfrac{16}{5}, \ldots$

24. $0, \dfrac{1-e^1}{1+e^2}, \dfrac{1-e^2}{1+e^3}, \dfrac{1-e^3}{1+e^4}, \dfrac{1-e^4}{1+e^5}, \ldots$

25. $1, -\dfrac{1}{2}, \dfrac{1}{4}, -\dfrac{1}{8}, \dfrac{1}{16}, \ldots$

For the following exercises, write the first five terms of the sequence.

26. $a_1 = 9, a_n = a_{n-1} + n$

27. $a_1 = 3, a_n = (-3)a_{n-1}$

28. $a_1 = -4, a_n = \dfrac{a_{n-1} + 2n}{a_{n-1} - 1}$

29. $a_1 = -1, a_n = \dfrac{(-3)^{n-1}}{a_{n-1} - 2}$

30. $a_1 = -30, a_n = \left(2 + a_{n-1}\right)\left(\dfrac{1}{2}\right)^n$

For the following exercises, write the first eight terms of the sequence.

31. $a_1 = \dfrac{1}{24}, a_2 = 1, a_n = \left(2a_{n-2}\right)\left(3a_{n-1}\right)$

32. $a_1 = -1, a_2 = 5, a_n = a_{n-2}\left(3 - a_{n-1}\right)$

33. $a_1 = 2, a_2 = 10, a_n = \dfrac{2\left(a_{n-1} + 2\right)}{a_{n-2}}$

For the following exercises, write a recursive formula for each sequence.

34. $-2.5, -5, -10, -20, -40, \ldots$ **35.** $-8, -6, -3, 1, 6, \ldots$ **36.** $2, 4, 12, 48, 240, \ldots$

37. $35, 38, 41, 44, 47, \ldots$ **38.** $15, 3, \dfrac{3}{5}, \dfrac{3}{25}, \dfrac{3}{125}, \ldots$

For the following exercises, evaluate the factorial.

39. $6!$ **40.** $\left(\dfrac{12}{6}\right)!$ **41.** $\dfrac{12!}{6!}$ **42.** $\dfrac{100!}{99!}$

For the following exercises, write the first four terms of the sequence.

43. $a_n = \dfrac{n!}{n^2}$ **44.** $a_n = \dfrac{3 \cdot n!}{4 \cdot n!}$ **45.** $a_n = \dfrac{n!}{n^2 - n - 1}$ **46.** $a_n = \dfrac{100 \cdot n}{n(n-1)!}$

GRAPHICAL

For the following exercises, graph the first five terms of the indicated sequence

47. $a_n = \dfrac{(-1)^n}{n} + n$

48. $a_n = \begin{cases} \dfrac{4+n}{2n} & \text{if } n \text{ in even} \\ 3+n & \text{if } n \text{ is odd} \end{cases}$

49. $a_1 = 2, a_n = (-a_{n-1} + 1)^2$

50. $a_n = 1, a_n = a_{n-1} + 8$

51. $a_n = \dfrac{(n+1)!}{(n-1)!}$

For the following exercises, write an explicit formula for the sequence using the first five points shown on the graph.

52.
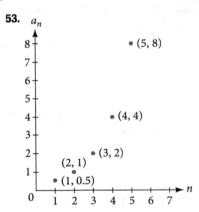

53.

54.
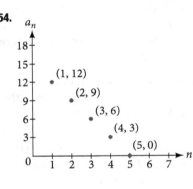

For the following exercises, write a recursive formula for the sequence using the first five points shown on the graph.

55.
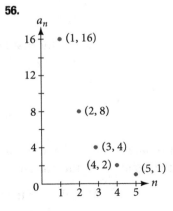

56.

TECHNOLOGY

Follow these steps to evaluate a sequence defined recursively using a graphing calculator:

- On the home screen, key in the value for the initial term a_1 and press [**ENTER**].
- Enter the recursive formula by keying in all numerical values given in the formula, along with the key strokes [**2ND**] **ANS** for the previous term a_{n-1}. Press [**ENTER**].
- Continue pressing [**ENTER**] to calculate the values for each successive term.

For the following exercises, use the steps above to find the indicated term or terms for the sequence.

57. Find the first five terms of the sequence $a_1 = \dfrac{87}{111}$, $a_n = \dfrac{4}{3}a_{n-1} + \dfrac{12}{37}$. Use the >**Frac** feature to give fractional results.

58. Find the 15th term of the sequence $a_1 = 625$, $a_n = 0.8a_{n-1} + 18$.

59. Find the first five terms of the sequence $a_1 = 2$, $a_n = 2^{[(a_{n-1})-1]} + 1$.

60. Find the first ten terms of the sequence $a_1 = 8$, $a_n = \dfrac{(a_{n-1}+1)!}{a_{n-1}!}$.

61. Find the tenth term of the sequence $a_1 = 2$, $a_n = na_{n-1}$

Follow these steps to evaluate a finite sequence defined by an explicit formula.

Using a TI-84, do the following.

- In the home screen, press [**2ND**] **LIST**.
- Scroll over to **OPS** and choose "**seq(**" from the dropdown list. Press [**ENTER**].
- In the line headed "**Expr:**" type in the explicit formula, using the [**X,T, θ, n**] button for n
- In the line headed "**Variable:**" type in the variable used on the previous step.
- In the line headed "**start:**" key in the value of n that begins the sequence.
- In the line headed "**end:**" key in the value of n that ends the sequence.
- Press [**ENTER**] 3 times to return to the home screen. You will see the sequence syntax on the screen. Press [**ENTER**] to see the list of terms for the finite sequence defined. Use the right arrow key to scroll through the list of terms.

Using a TI-83, do the following.

- In the home screen, press [**2ND**] **LIST**.
- Scroll over to **OPS** and choose "**seq(**" from the dropdown list. Press [**ENTER**].
- Enter the items in the order "**Expr**", "**Variable**", "**start**", "**end**" separated by commas. See the instructions above for the description of each item.
- Press [**ENTER**] to see the list of terms for the finite sequence defined. Use the right arrow key to scroll through the list of terms.

For the following exercises, use the steps above to find the indicated terms for the sequence. Round to the nearest thousandth when necessary.

62. List the first five terms of the sequence. $a_n = -\dfrac{28}{9}n + \dfrac{5}{3}$

63. List the first six terms of the sequence. $a_n = \dfrac{n^3 - 3.5n^2 + 4.1n - 1.5}{2.4n}$

64. List the first five terms of the sequence. $a_n = \dfrac{15n \cdot (-2)^{n-1}}{47}$

65. List the first four terms of the sequence. $a_n = 5.7^n + 0.275(n-1)!$

66. List the first six terms of the sequence $a_n = \dfrac{n!}{n}$.

EXTENSIONS

67. Consider the sequence defined by $a_n = -6 - 8n$. Is $a_n = -421$ a term in the sequence? Verify the result.

68. What term in the sequence $a_n = \dfrac{n^2 + 4n + 4}{2(n+2)}$ has the value 41? Verify the result.

69. Find a recursive formula for the sequence 1, 0, −1, −1, 0, 1, 1, 0, −1, −1, 0, 1, 1, ... (Hint: find a pattern for an based on the first two terms.)

70. Calculate the first eight terms of the sequences $a_n = \dfrac{(n+2)!}{(n-1)!}$ and $b_n = n^3 + 3n^2 + 2n$, and then make a conjecture about the relationship between these two sequences.

71. Prove the conjecture made in the preceding exercise.

LEARNING OBJECTIVES

In this section, you will:

- Find the common difference for an arithmetic sequence.
- Write terms of an arithmetic sequence.
- Use a recursive formula for an arithmetic sequence.
- Use an explicit formula for an arithmetic sequence.

13.2 ARITHMETIC SEQUENCES

Companies often make large purchases, such as computers and vehicles, for business use. The book-value of these supplies decreases each year for tax purposes. This decrease in value is called depreciation. One method of calculating depreciation is straight-line depreciation, in which the value of the asset decreases by the same amount each year.

As an example, consider a woman who starts a small contracting business. She purchases a new truck for $25,000. After five years, she estimates that she will be able to sell the truck for $8,000. The loss in value of the truck will therefore be $17,000, which is $3,400 per year for five years. The truck will be worth $21,600 after the first year; $18,200 after two years; $14,800 after three years; $11,400 after four years; and $8,000 at the end of five years. In this section, we will consider specific kinds of sequences that will allow us to calculate depreciation, such as the truck's value.

Finding Common Differences

The values of the truck in the example are said to form an **arithmetic sequence** because they change by a constant amount each year. Each term increases or decreases by the same constant value called the **common difference** of the sequence. For this sequence, the common difference is −3,400.

$$-3{,}400 \quad -3{,}400 \quad -3{,}400 \quad -3{,}400 \quad -3{,}400$$

$$\{25000, \quad 21600, \quad 18200, \quad 14800, \quad 11400, \quad 8000\}$$

The sequence below is another example of an arithmetic sequence. In this case, the constant difference is 3. You can choose any term of the sequence, and add 3 to find the subsequent term.

$$+3 \quad +3 \quad +3 \quad +3$$

$$\{3, \quad 6, \quad 9, \quad 12, \quad 15, ...\}$$

> **arithmetic sequence**
> An **arithmetic sequence** is a sequence that has the property that the difference between any two consecutive terms is a constant. This constant is called the **common difference**. If a_1 is the first term of an arithmetic sequence and d is the common difference, the sequence will be:
> $$\{a_n\} = \{a_1, a_1 + d, a_1 + 2d, a_1 + 3d,...\}$$

Example 1   **Finding Common Differences**

Is each sequence arithmetic? If so, find the common difference.

a. $\{1, 2, 4, 8, 16, ...\}$ **b.** $\{-3, 1, 5, 9, 13, ...\}$

Solution   Subtract each term from the subsequent term to determine whether a common difference exists.

a. The sequence is not arithmetic because there is no common difference.

$$2 - 1 = 1 \qquad 4 - 2 = 2 \qquad 8 - 4 = 4 \qquad 16 - 8 = 8$$

b. The sequence is arithmetic because there is a common difference. The common difference is 4.

$$1 - (-3) = 4 \qquad 5 - 1 = 4 \qquad 9 - 5 = 4 \qquad 13 - 9 = 4$$

Analysis   The graph of each of these sequences is shown in **Figure 1**. *We can see from the graphs that, although both sequences show growth, a is not linear whereas b is linear. Arithmetic sequences have a constant rate of change so their graphs will always be points on a line.*

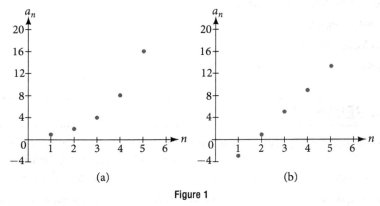

(a)   (b)

Figure 1

Q & A...

If we are told that a sequence is arithmetic, do we have to subtract every term from the following term to find the common difference?

No. If we know that the sequence is arithmetic, we can choose any one term in the sequence, and subtract it from the subsequent term to find the common difference.

Try It #1

Is the given sequence arithmetic? If so, find the common difference.

$$\{18, 16, 14, 12, 10, \dots \}$$

Try It #2

Is the given sequence arithmetic? If so, find the common difference.

$$\{1, 3, 6, 10, 15, \dots \}$$

Writing Terms of Arithmetic Sequences

Now that we can recognize an arithmetic sequence, we will find the terms if we are given the first term and the common difference. The terms can be found by beginning with the first term and adding the common difference repeatedly. In addition, any term can also be found by plugging in the values of n and d into formula below.

$$a_n = a_1 + (n - 1)d$$

How To...

Given the first term and the common difference of an arithmetic sequence, find the first several terms.

1. Add the common difference to the first term to find the second term.
2. Add the common difference to the second term to find the third term.
3. Continue until all of the desired terms are identified.
4. Write the terms separated by commas within brackets.

Example 2   Writing Terms of Arithmetic Sequences

Write the first five terms of the arithmetic sequence with $a_1 = 17$ and $d = -3$.

Solution   Adding -3 is the same as subtracting 3. Beginning with the first term, subtract 3 from each term to find the next term.

The first five terms are $\{17, 14, 11, 8, 5\}$

Analysis As expected, the graph of the sequence consists of points on a line as shown in **Figure 2**.

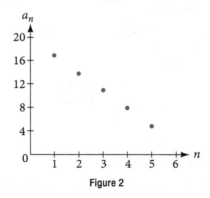

Figure 2

Try It #3

List the first five terms of the arithmetic sequence with $a_1 = 1$ and $d = 5$.

How To...

Given any first term and any other term in an arithmetic sequence, find a given term.

1. Substitute the values given for a_1, a_n, n into the formula $a_n = a_1 + (n - 1)d$ to solve for d.
2. Find a given term by substituting the appropriate values for a_1, n, and d into the formula $a_n = a_1 + (n - 1)d$.

Example 3   **Writing Terms of Arithmetic Sequences**

Given $a_1 = 8$ and $a_4 = 14$, find a_5.

Solution The sequence can be written in terms of the initial term 8 and the common difference d.

$$\{8, 8 + d, 8 + 2d, 8 + 3d\}$$

We know the fourth term equals 14; we know the fourth term has the form $a_1 + 3d = 8 + 3d$.

We can find the common difference d.

$$a_n = a_1 + (n - 1)d$$
$$a_4 = a_1 + 3d$$
$$a_4 = 8 + 3d \qquad \text{Write the fourth term of the sequence in terms of } a_1 \text{ and } d.$$
$$14 = 8 + 3d \qquad \text{Substitute 14 for } a_4.$$
$$d = 2 \qquad \text{Solve for the common difference.}$$

Find the fifth term by adding the common difference to the fourth term.

$$a_5 = a_4 + 2 = 16$$

Analysis Notice that the common difference is added to the first term once to find the second term, twice to find the third term, three times to find the fourth term, and so on. The tenth term could be found by adding the common difference to the first term nine times or by using the equation $a_n = a_1 + (n - 1)d$.

Try It #4

Given $a_3 = 7$ and $a_5 = 17$, find a_2.

Using Recursive Formulas for Arithmetic Sequences

Some arithmetic sequences are defined in terms of the previous term using a recursive formula. The formula provides an algebraic rule for determining the terms of the sequence. A recursive formula allows us to find any term of an arithmetic sequence using a function of the preceding term. Each term is the sum of the previous term and the common difference. For example, if the common difference is 5, then each term is the previous term plus 5. As with any recursive formula, the first term must be given.

$$a_n = a_{n-1} + d \quad n \geq 2$$

recursive formula for an arithmetic sequence
The recursive formula for an arithmetic sequence with common difference d is:
$$a_n = a_{n-1} + d \quad n \geq 2$$

How To...

Given an arithmetic sequence, write its recursive formula.

1. Subtract any term from the subsequent term to find the common difference.
2. State the initial term and substitute the common difference into the recursive formula for arithmetic sequences.

Example 4   **Writing a Recursive Formula for an Arithmetic Sequence**

Write a recursive formula for the arithmetic sequence.

$$\{ -18, -7, 4, 15, 26, \ldots \}$$

Solution   The first term is given as -18. The common difference can be found by subtracting the first term from the second term.

$$d = -7 - (-18) = 11$$

Substitute the initial term and the common difference into the recursive formula for arithmetic sequences.

$$a_1 = -18$$
$$a_n = a_{n-1} + 11, \text{ for } n \geq 2$$

Analysis   *We see that the common difference is the slope of the line formed when we graph the terms of the sequence, as shown in Figure 3. The growth pattern of the sequence shows the constant difference of 11 units.*

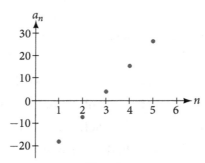

Figure 3

Q & A...

Do we have to subtract the first term from the second term to find the common difference?

No. We can subtract any term in the sequence from the subsequent term. It is, however, most common to subtract the first term from the second term because it is often the easiest method of finding the common difference.

Try It #5

Write a recursive formula for the arithmetic sequence.

$$\{25, 37, 49, 61, \ldots \}$$

Using Explicit Formulas for Arithmetic Sequences

We can think of an arithmetic sequence as a function on the domain of the natural numbers; it is a linear function because it has a constant rate of change. The common difference is the constant rate of change, or the slope of the function. We can construct the linear function if we know the slope and the vertical intercept.

$$a_n = a_1 + d(n-1)$$

To find the y-intercept of the function, we can subtract the common difference from the first term of the sequence. Consider the following sequence.

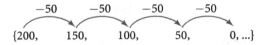

The common difference is -50, so the sequence represents a linear function with a slope of -50. To find the y-intercept, we subtract -50 from 200: $200 - (-50) = 200 + 50 = 250$. You can also find the y-intercept by graphing the function and determining where a line that connects the points would intersect the vertical axis. The graph is shown in **Figure 4**.

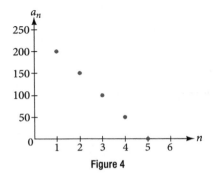

Figure 4

Recall the slope-intercept form of a line is $y = mx + b$. When dealing with sequences, we use a_n in place of y and n in place of x. If we know the slope and vertical intercept of the function, we can substitute them for m and b in the slope-intercept form of a line. Substituting -50 for the slope and 250 for the vertical intercept, we get the following equation:

$$a_n = -50n + 250$$

We do not need to find the vertical intercept to write an explicit formula for an arithmetic sequence. Another explicit formula for this sequence is $a_n = 200 - 50(n-1)$, which simplifies to $a_n = -50n + 250$.

> ### *explicit formula for an arithmetic sequence*
> An explicit formula for the nth term of an arithmetic sequence is given by
> $$a_n = a_1 + d(n-1)$$

How To...

Given the first several terms for an arithmetic sequence, write an explicit formula.

1. Find the common difference, $a_2 - a_1$.
2. Substitute the common difference and the first term into $a_n = a_1 + d(n-1)$.

Example 5   **Writing the *n*th Term Explicit Formula for an Arithmetic Sequence**

Write an explicit formula for the arithmetic sequence.

$$\{2, 12, 22, 32, 42, \dots\}$$

Solution   The common difference can be found by subtracting the first term from the second term.

$$d = a_2 - a_1$$
$$= 12 - 2$$
$$= 10$$

The common difference is 10. Substitute the common difference and the first term of the sequence into the formula and simplify.

$$a_n = 2 + 10(n - 1)$$
$$a_n = 10n - 8$$

Analysis   The graph of this sequence, represented in **Figure 5**, shows a slope of 10 and a vertical intercept of −8.

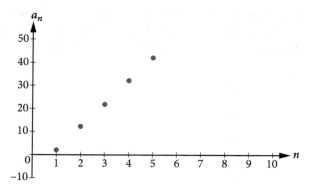

Figure 5

Try It #6

Write an explicit formula for the following arithmetic sequence.

$$\{50, 47, 44, 41, \ldots\}$$

Finding the Number of Terms in a Finite Arithmetic Sequence

Explicit formulas can be used to determine the number of terms in a finite arithmetic sequence. We need to find the common difference, and then determine how many times the common difference must be added to the first term to obtain the final term of the sequence.

How To...

Given the first three terms and the last term of a finite arithmetic sequence, find the total number of terms.

1. Find the common difference d.
2. Substitute the common difference and the first term into $a_n = a_1 + d(n - 1)$.
3. Substitute the last term for a_n and solve for n.

Example 6   **Finding the Number of Terms in a Finite Arithmetic Sequence**

Find the number of terms in the finite arithmetic sequence.

$$\{8, 1, -6, \ldots, -41\}$$

Solution   The common difference can be found by subtracting the first term from the second term.

$$1 - 8 = -7$$

The common difference is -7. Substitute the common difference and the initial term of the sequence into the nth term formula and simplify.

$$a_n = a_1 + d(n-1)$$
$$a_n = 8 + (-7)(n-1)$$
$$a_n = 15 - 7n$$

Substitute -41 for a_n and solve for n

$$-41 = 15 - 7n$$
$$8 = n$$

There are eight terms in the sequence.

Try It #7

Find the number of terms in the finite arithmetic sequence.

$$\{6, 11, 16, \dots, 56\}$$

Solving Application Problems with Arithmetic Sequences

In many application problems, it often makes sense to use an initial term of a_0 instead of a_1. In these problems, we alter the explicit formula slightly to account for the difference in initial terms. We use the following formula:

$$a_n = a_0 + dn$$

Example 7   **Solving Application Problems with Arithmetic Sequences**

A five-year old child receives an allowance of \$1 each week. His parents promise him an annual increase of \$2 per week.

    a. Write a formula for the child's weekly allowance in a given year.

    b. What will the child's allowance be when he is 16 years old?

Solution

    a. The situation can be modeled by an arithmetic sequence with an initial term of 1 and a common difference of 2.

    Let A be the amount of the allowance and n be the number of years after age 5. Using the altered explicit formula for an arithmetic sequence we get:

$$A_n = 1 + 2n$$

    b. We can find the number of years since age 5 by subtracting.

$$16 - 5 = 11$$

    We are looking for the child's allowance after 11 years. Substitute 11 into the formula to find the child's allowance at age 16.

$$A_{11} = 1 + 2(11) = 23$$

    The child's allowance at age 16 will be \$23 per week.

Try It #8

A woman decides to go for a 10-minute run every day this week and plans to increase the time of her daily run by 4 minutes each week. Write a formula for the time of her run after n weeks. How long will her daily run be 8 weeks from today?

Access this online resource for additional instruction and practice with arithmetic sequences.

- Arithmetic Sequences (http://openstaxcollege.org/l/arithmeticseq)

13.2 SECTION EXERCISES

VERBAL

1. What is an arithmetic sequence?

2. How is the common difference of an arithmetic sequence found?

3. How do we determine whether a sequence is arithmetic?

4. What are the main differences between using a recursive formula and using an explicit formula to describe an arithmetic sequence?

5. Describe how linear functions and arithmetic sequences are similar. How are they different?

ALGEBRAIC

For the following exercises, find the common difference for the arithmetic sequence provided.

6. $\{5, 11, 17, 23, 29, ...\}$

7. $\left\{0, \frac{1}{2}, 1, \frac{3}{2}, 2, ...\right\}$

For the following exercises, determine whether the sequence is arithmetic. If so find the common difference.

8. $\{11.4, 9.3, 7.2, 5.1, 3, ...\}$

9. $\{4, 16, 64, 256, 1024, ...\}$

For the following exercises, write the first five terms of the arithmetic sequence given the first term and common difference.

10. $a_1 = -25, d = -9$

11. $a_1 = 0, d = \frac{2}{3}$

For the following exercises, write the first five terms of the arithmetic series given two terms.

12. $a_1 = 17, a_7 = -31$

13. $a_{13} = -60, a_{33} = -160$

For the following exercises, find the specified term for the arithmetic sequence given the first term and common difference.

14. First term is 3, common difference is 4, find the 5th term.

15. First term is 4, common difference is 5, find the 4th term.

16. First term is 5, common difference is 6, find the 8th term.

17. First term is 6, common difference is 7, find the 6th term.

18. First term is 7, common difference is 8, find the 7th term.

For the following exercises, find the first term given two terms from an arithmetic sequence.

19. Find the first term or a_1 of an arithmetic sequence if $a_6 = 12$ and $a_{14} = 28$.

20. Find the first term or a_1 of an arithmetic sequence if $a_7 = 21$ and $a_{15} = 42$.

21. Find the first term or a_1 of an arithmetic sequence if $a_8 = 40$ and $a_{23} = 115$.

22. Find the first term or a_1 of an arithmetic sequence if $a_9 = 54$ and $a_{17} = 102$.

23. Find the first term or a_1 of an arithmetic sequence if $a_{11} = 11$ and $a_{21} = 16$.

For the following exercises, find the specified term given two terms from an arithmetic sequence.

24. $a_1 = 33$ and $a_7 = -15$. Find a_4.

25. $a_3 = -17.1$ and $a_{10} = -15.7$. Find a_{21}.

For the following exercises, use the recursive formula to write the first five terms of the arithmetic sequence.

26. $a_1 = 39; a_n = a_{n-1} - 3$

27. $a_1 = -19; a_n = a_{n-1} - 1.4$

For the following exercises, write a recursive formula for each arithmetic sequence.

28. $a = \{40, 60, 80, \ldots\}$

29. $a = \{17, 26, 35, \ldots\}$

30. $a = \{-1, 2, 5, \ldots\}$

31. $a = \{12, 17, 22, \ldots\}$

32. $a = \{-15, -7, 1, \ldots\}$

33. $a = \{8.9, 10.3, 11.7, \ldots\}$

34. $a = \{-0.52, -1.02, -1.52, \ldots\}$

35. $a = \left\{\dfrac{1}{5}, \dfrac{9}{20}, \dfrac{7}{10}, \ldots\right\}$

36. $a = \left\{-\dfrac{1}{2}, -\dfrac{5}{4}, -2, \ldots\right\}$

37. $a = \left\{\dfrac{1}{6}, -\dfrac{11}{12}, -2, \ldots\right\}$

For the following exercises, use the recursive formula to write the first five terms of the arithmetic sequence.

38. $a = \{7, 4, 1, \ldots\}$; Find the 17th term.

39. $a = \{4, 11, 18, \ldots\}$; Find the 14th term.

40. $a = \{2, 6, 10, \ldots\}$; Find the 12th term.

For the following exercises, use the recursive formula to write the first five terms of the arithmetic sequence.

41. $a = 24 - 4n$

42. $a = \dfrac{1}{2}n - \dfrac{1}{2}$

For the following exercises, write an explicit formula for each arithmetic sequence.

43. $a = \{3, 5, 7, \ldots\}$

44. $a = \{32, 24, 16, \ldots\}$

45. $a = \{-5, 95, 195, \ldots\}$

46. $a = \{-17, -217, -417, \ldots\}$

47. $a = \{1.8, 3.6, 5.4, \ldots\}$

48. $a = \{-18.1, -16.2, -14.3, \ldots\}$

49. $a = \{15.8, 18.5, 21.2, \ldots\}$

50. $a = \left\{\dfrac{1}{3}, -\dfrac{4}{3}, -3, \ldots\right\}$

51. $a = \left\{0, \dfrac{1}{3}, \dfrac{2}{3}, \ldots\right\}$

52. $a = \left\{-5, -\dfrac{10}{3}, -\dfrac{5}{3}, \ldots\right\}$

For the following exercises, find the number of terms in the given finite arithmetic sequence.

53. $a = \{3, -4, -11, \ldots, -60\}$

54. $a = \{1.2, 1.4, 1.6, \ldots, 3.8\}$

55. $a = \left\{\dfrac{1}{2}, 2, \dfrac{7}{2}, \ldots, 8\right\}$

GRAPHICAL

For the following exercises, determine whether the graph shown represents an arithmetic sequence.

56.

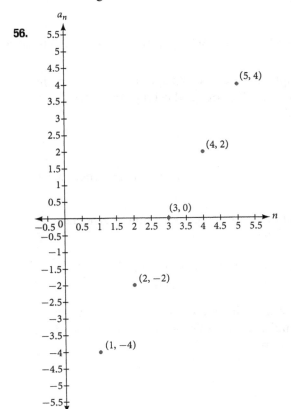

57.

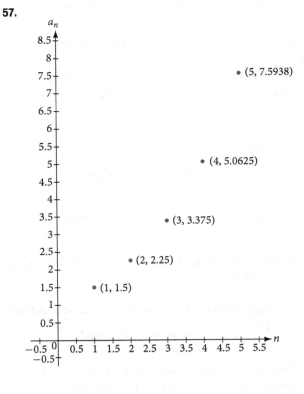

For the following exercises, use the information provided to graph the first 5 terms of the arithmetic sequence.

58. $a_1 = 0, d = 4$

59. $a_1 = 9; a_n = a_{n-1} - 10$

60. $a_n = -12 + 5n$

TECHNOLOGY

For the following exercises, follow the steps to work with the arithmetic sequence $a_n = 3n - 2$ using a graphing calculator:

- Press [**MODE**]
  › Select [**SEQ**] in the fourth line
  › Select [**DOT**] in the fifth line
  › Press [**ENTER**]
- Press [**Y=**]
  › nMin is the first counting number for the sequence. Set nMin $= 1$
  › $u(n)$ is the pattern for the sequence. Set $u(n) = 3n - 2$
  › $u(n$Min$)$ is the first number in the sequence. Set $u(n$Min$) = 1$
- Press [**2ND**] then [**WINDOW**] to go to **TBLSET**
  › Set TblStart $= 1$
  › Set ΔTbl $= 1$
  › Set Indpnt: Auto and Depend: Auto
- Press [**2ND**] then [**GRAPH**] to go to the [**TABLE**]

61. What are the first seven terms shown in the column with the heading $u(n)$?

62. Use the scroll-down arrow to scroll to $n = 50$. What value is given for $u(n)$?

63. Press [**WINDOW**]. Set nMin $= 1$, nMax $= 5$, xMin $= 0$, xMax $= 6$, yMin $= -1$, and yMax $= 14$. Then press [**GRAPH**]. Graph the sequence as it appears on the graphing calculator.

For the following exercises, follow the steps given above to work with the arithmetic sequence $a_n = \frac{1}{2}n + 5$ using a graphing calculator.

64. What are the first seven terms shown in the column with the heading $u(n)$ in the [**TABLE**] feature?

65. Graph the sequence as it appears on the graphing calculator. Be sure to adjust the [**WINDOW**] settings as needed.

EXTENSIONS

66. Give two examples of arithmetic sequences whose 4th terms are 9.

67. Give two examples of arithmetic sequences whose 10th terms are 206.

68. Find the 5th term of the arithmetic sequence $\{9b, 5b, b, \dots\}$.

69. Find the 11th term of the arithmetic sequence $\{3a - 2b, a + 2b, -a + 6b, \dots\}$.

70. At which term does the sequence $\{5.4, 14.5, 23.6, \dots\}$ exceed 151?

71. At which term does the sequence $\left\{\frac{17}{3}, \frac{31}{6}, \frac{14}{3}, \dots\right\}$ begin to have negative values?

72. For which terms does the finite arithmetic sequence $\left\{\frac{5}{2}, \frac{19}{8}, \frac{9}{4}, \dots, \frac{1}{8}\right\}$ have integer values?

73. Write an arithmetic sequence using a recursive formula. Show the first 4 terms, and then find the 31st term.

74. Write an arithmetic sequence using an explicit formula. Show the first 4 terms, and then find the 28th term.

LEARNING OBJECTIVES

In this section, you will:

- Find the common ratio for a geometric sequence.
- List the terms of a geometric sequence.
- Use a recursive formula for a geometric sequence.
- Use an explicit formula for a geometric sequence.

13.3   GEOMETRIC SEQUENCES

Many jobs offer an annual cost-of-living increase to keep salaries consistent with inflation. Suppose, for example, a recent college graduate finds a position as a sales manager earning an annual salary of $26,000. He is promised a 2% cost of living increase each year. His annual salary in any given year can be found by multiplying his salary from the previous year by 102%. His salary will be $26,520 after one year; $27,050.40 after two years; $27,591.41 after three years; and so on. When a salary increases by a constant rate each year, the salary grows by a constant factor. In this section, we will review sequences that grow in this way.

Finding Common Ratios

The yearly salary values described form a **geometric sequence** because they change by a constant factor each year. Each term of a geometric sequence increases or decreases by a constant factor called the **common ratio**. The sequence below is an example of a geometric sequence because each term increases by a constant factor of 6. Multiplying any term of the sequence by the common ratio 6 generates the subsequent term.

a_n

16 (1 16)

> **definition of a geometric sequence**
> A **geometric sequence** is one in which any term divided by the previous term is a constant. This constant is called the **common ratio** of the sequence. The common ratio can be found by dividing any term in the sequence by the previous term. If a_1 is the initial term of a geometric sequence and r is the common ratio, the sequence will be
> $$\{a_1, a_1 r, a_1 r^2, a_1 r^3, \dots\}.$$

How To...

Given a set of numbers, determine if they represent a geometric sequence.

1. Divide each term by the previous term.
2. Compare the quotients. If they are the same, a common ratio exists and the sequence is geometric.

Example 1   **Finding Common Ratios**

Is the sequence geometric? If so, find the common ratio.

    a. 1, 2, 4, 8, 16, ...   **b.** 48, 12, 4, 2,...

Solution   Divide each term by the previous term to determine whether a common ratio exists.

    a. $\dfrac{2}{1} = 2$ $\dfrac{4}{2} = 2$ $\dfrac{8}{4} = 2$ $\dfrac{16}{8} = 2$

        The sequence is geometric because there is a common ratio. The common ratio is 2.

    b. $\dfrac{12}{48} = \dfrac{1}{4}$ $\dfrac{4}{12} = \dfrac{1}{3}$ $\dfrac{2}{4} = \dfrac{1}{2}$

        The sequence is not geometric because there is not a common ratio.

Analysis The graph of each sequence is shown in **Figure 1**. It seems from the graphs that both (a) and (b) appear have the form of the graph of an exponential function in this viewing window. However, we know that (a) is geometric and so this interpretation holds, but (b) is not.

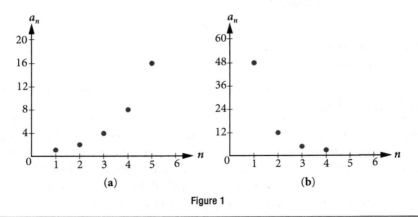

Figure 1

Q & A...

If you are told that a sequence is geometric, do you have to divide every term by the previous term to find the common ratio?

No. If you know that the sequence is geometric, you can choose any one term in the sequence and divide it by the previous term to find the common ratio.

Try It #1

Is the sequence geometric? If so, find the common ratio.

$$5, 10, 15, 20, ...$$

Try It #2

Is the sequence geometric? If so, find the common ratio.

$$100, 20, 4, \frac{4}{5}, ...$$

Writing Terms of Geometric Sequences

Now that we can identify a geometric sequence, we will learn how to find the terms of a geometric sequence if we are given the first term and the common ratio. The terms of a geometric sequence can be found by beginning with the first term and multiplying by the common ratio repeatedly. For instance, if the first term of a geometric sequence is $a_1 = -2$ and the common ratio is $r = 4$, we can find subsequent terms by multiplying $-2 \cdot 4$ to get -8 then multiplying the result $-8 \cdot 4$ to get -32 and so on.

$$a_1 = -2$$
$$a_2 = (-2 \cdot 4) = -8$$
$$a_3 = (-8 \cdot 4) = -32$$
$$a_4 = (-32 \cdot 4) = -128$$

The first four terms are $\{-2, -8, -32, -128\}$.

How To...

Given the first term and the common factor, find the first four terms of a geometric sequence.

1. Multiply the initial term, a_1, by the common ratio to find the next term, a_2.
2. Repeat the process, using $a_n = a_2$ to find a_3 and then a_3 to find a_4, until all four terms have been identified.
3. Write the terms separated by commons within brackets.

Example 2   **Writing the Terms of a Geometric Sequence**

List the first four terms of the geometric sequence with $a_1 = 5$ and $r = -2$.

Solution   Multiply a_1 by -2 to find a_2. Repeat the process, using a_2 to find a_3, and so on.

$$a_1 = 5$$
$$a_2 = -2a_1 = -10$$
$$a_3 = -2a_2 = 20$$
$$a_4 = -2a_3 = -40$$

The first four terms are $\{5, -10, 20, -40\}$.

Try It #3

List the first five terms of the geometric sequence with $a_1 = 18$ and $r = \dfrac{1}{3}$.

Using Recursive Formulas for Geometric Sequences

A recursive formula allows us to find any term of a geometric sequence by using the previous term. Each term is the product of the common ratio and the previous term. For example, suppose the common ratio is 9. Then each term is nine times the previous term. As with any recursive formula, the initial term must be given.

> **recursive formula for a geometric sequence**
> The recursive formula for a geometric sequence with common ratio r and first term a_1 is
> $$a_n = ra_{n-1}, n \geq 2$$

How To...

Given the first several terms of a geometric sequence, write its recursive formula.

1. State the initial term.
2. Find the common ratio by dividing any term by the preceding term.
3. Substitute the common ratio into the recursive formula for a geometric sequence.

Example 3   **Using Recursive Formulas for Geometric Sequences**

Write a recursive formula for the following geometric sequence.

$$\{6, 9, 13.5, 20.25, ... \}$$

Solution   The first term is given as 6. The common ratio can be found by dividing the second term by the first term.

$$r = \frac{9}{6} = 1.5$$

Substitute the common ratio into the recursive formula for geometric sequences and define a_1.

$$a_n = ra_{n-1}$$
$$a_n = 1.5a_{n-1} \text{ for } n \geq 2$$
$$a_1 = 6$$

Analysis   *The sequence of data points follows an exponential pattern. The common ratio is also the base of an exponential function as shown in* **Figure 2**.

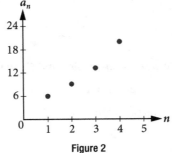

Figure 2

Q & A...

Do we have to divide the second term by the first term to find the common ratio?

No. We can divide any term in the sequence by the previous term. It is, however, most common to divide the second term by the first term because it is often the easiest method of finding the common ratio.

Try It #4

Write a recursive formula for the following geometric sequence.

$$\left\{2, \frac{4}{3}, \frac{8}{9}, \frac{16}{27}, ...\right\}$$

Using Explicit Formulas for Geometric Sequences

Because a geometric sequence is an exponential function whose domain is the set of positive integers, and the common ratio is the base of the function, we can write explicit formulas that allow us to find particular terms.

$$a_n = a_1 r^{n-1}$$

Let's take a look at the sequence {18, 36, 72, 144, 288,...}. This is a geometric sequence with a common ratio of 2 and an exponential function with a base of 2. An explicit formula for this sequence is

$$a_n = 18 \cdot 2^{n-1}$$

The graph of the sequence is shown in **Figure 3**.

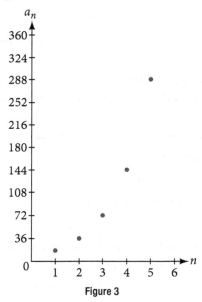

Figure 3

---

explicit formula for a geometric sequence
The nth term of a geometric sequence is given by the explicit formula:

$$a_n = a_1 r^{n-1}$$

Example 4   **Writing Terms of Geometric Sequences Using the Explicit Formula**

Given a geometric sequence with $a_1 = 3$ and $a_4 = 24$, find a_2.

Solution   The sequence can be written in terms of the initial term and the common ratio r.

$$3, 3r, 3r^2, 3r^3,...$$

Find the common ratio using the given fourth term.

$$a_n = a_1 r^{n-1}$$

$$a_4 = 3r^3 \qquad \text{Write the fourth term of sequence in terms of } a_1 \text{ and } r$$

$$24 = 3r^3 \qquad \text{Substitute 24 for } a_4$$

$$8 = r^3 \qquad \text{Divide}$$

$$r = 2 \qquad \text{Solve for the common ratio}$$

Find the second term by multiplying the first term by the common ratio.

$$a_2 = 2a_1$$

$$= 2(3)$$

$$= 6$$

Analysis *The common ratio is multiplied by the first term once to find the second term, twice to find the third term, three times to find the fourth term, and so on. The tenth term could be found by multiplying the first term by the common ratio nine times or by multiplying by the common ratio raised to the ninth power.*

Try It #5

Given a geometric sequence with $a_2 = 4$ and $a_3 = 32$, find a_6.

Example 5   **Writing an Explicit Formula for the *n*th Term of a Geometric Sequence**

Write an explicit formula for the *n*th term of the following geometric sequence.

$$\{2, 10, 50, 250,...\}$$

Solution   The first term is 2. The common ratio can be found by dividing the second term by the first term.

$$\frac{10}{2} = 5$$

The common ratio is 5. Substitute the common ratio and the first term of the sequence into the formula.

$$a_n = a_1 r^{(n-1)}$$

$$a_n = 2 \cdot 5^{n-1}$$

The graph of this sequence in **Figure 4** shows an exponential pattern.

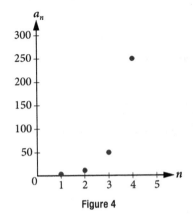

Figure 4

Try It #6

Write an explicit formula for the following geometric sequence.

$$\{-1, 3, -9, 27, ...\}$$

Solving Application Problems with Geometric Sequences

In real-world scenarios involving arithmetic sequences, we may need to use an initial term of a_0 instead of a_1. In these problems, we can alter the explicit formula slightly by using the following formula:

$$a_n = a_0 r^n$$

Example 6   Solving Application Problems with Geometric Sequences

In 2013, the number of students in a small school is 284. It is estimated that the student population will increase by 4% each year.

    a. Write a formula for the student population.

    b. Estimate the student population in 2020.

Solution

    a. The situation can be modeled by a geometric sequence with an initial term of 284. The student population will be 104% of the prior year, so the common ratio is 1.04.

    Let P be the student population and n be the number of years after 2013. Using the explicit formula for a geometric sequence we get

$$P_n = 284 \cdot 1.04^n$$

    b. We can find the number of years since 2013 by subtracting.

$$2020 - 2013 = 7$$

    We are looking for the population after 7 years. We can substitute 7 for n to estimate the population in 2020.

$$P_7 = 284 \cdot 1.04^7 \approx 374$$

    The student population will be about 374 in 2020.

Try It #7

A business starts a new website. Initially the number of hits is 293 due to the curiosity factor. The business estimates the number of hits will increase by 2.6% per week.

a. Write a formula for the number of hits.

b. Estimate the number of hits in 5 weeks.

Access these online resources for additional instruction and practice with geometric sequences.

- Geometric Sequences (http://openstaxcollege.org/l/geometricseq)
- Determine the Type of Sequence (http://openstaxcollege.org/l/sequencetype)
- Find the Formula for a Sequence (http://openstaxcollege.org/l/sequenceformula)

13.3   SECTION EXERCISES

VERBAL

1. What is a geometric sequence?

2. How is the common ratio of a geometric sequence found?

3. What is the procedure for determining whether a sequence is geometric?

4. What is the difference between an arithmetic sequence and a geometric sequence?

5. Describe how exponential functions and geometric sequences are similar. How are they different?

ALGEBRAIC

For the following exercises, find the common ratio for the geometric sequence.

6. $1, 3, 9, 27, 81, ...$

7. $-0.125, 0.25, -0.5, 1, -2, ...$

8. $-2, -\dfrac{1}{2}, -\dfrac{1}{8}, -\dfrac{1}{32}, -\dfrac{1}{128}, ...$

For the following exercises, determine whether the sequence is geometric. If so, find the common ratio.

9. $-6, -12, -24, -48, -96, ...$

10. $5, 5.2, 5.4, 5.6, 5.8, ...$

11. $-1, \dfrac{1}{2}, -\dfrac{1}{4}, \dfrac{1}{8}, -\dfrac{1}{16}, ...$

12. $6, 8, 11, 15, 20, ...$

13. $0.8, 4, 20, 100, 500, ...$

For the following exercises, write the first five terms of the geometric sequence, given the first term and common ratio.

14. $a_1 = 8, r = 0.3$

15. $a_1 = 5, r = \dfrac{1}{5}$

For the following exercises, write the first five terms of the geometric sequence, given any two terms.

16. $a_7 = 64, a_{10} = 512$

17. $a_6 = 25, a_8 = 6.25$

For the following exercises, find the specified term for the geometric sequence, given the first term and common ratio.

18. The first term is 2, and the common ratio is 3. Find the 5th term.

19. The first term is 16 and the common ratio is $-\dfrac{1}{3}$. Find the 4th term.

For the following exercises, find the specified term for the geometric sequence, given the first four terms.

20. $a_n = \{-1, 2, -4, 8, ...\}$. Find a_{12}.

21. $a_n = \left\{-2, \dfrac{2}{3}, -\dfrac{2}{9}, \dfrac{2}{27}, ...\right\}$ Find a_7.

For the following exercises, write the first five terms of the geometric sequence.

22. $a_1 = -486, a_n = -\dfrac{1}{3}a_{n-1}$

23. $a_1 = 7, a_n = 0.2a_{n-1}$

For the following exercises, write a recursive formula for each geometric sequence.

24. $a_n = \{-1, 5, -25, 125, ...\}$

25. $a_n = \{-32, -16, -8, -4, ...\}$

26. $a_n = \{14, 56, 224, 896, ...\}$

27. $a_n = \{10, -3, 0.9, -0.27, ...\}$

28. $a_n = \{0.61, 1.83, 5.49, 16.47, ...\}$

29. $a_n = \left\{\dfrac{3}{5}, \dfrac{1}{10}, \dfrac{1}{60}, \dfrac{1}{360}, ...\right\}$

30. $a_n = \left\{-2, \dfrac{4}{3}, -\dfrac{8}{9}, \dfrac{16}{27}, ...\right\}$

31. $a_n = \left\{\dfrac{1}{512}, -\dfrac{1}{128}, \dfrac{1}{32}, -\dfrac{1}{8}, ...\right\}$

For the following exercises, write the first five terms of the geometric sequence.

32. $a_n = -4 \cdot 5^{n-1}$

33. $a_n = 12 \cdot \left(-\dfrac{1}{2}\right)^{n-1}$

For the following exercises, write an explicit formula for each geometric sequence.

34. $a_n = \{-2, -4, -8, -16, \ldots\}$

35. $a_n = \{1, 3, 9, 27, \ldots\}$

36. $a_n = \{-4, -12, -36, -108, \ldots\}$

37. $a_n = \{0.8, -4, 20, -100, \ldots\}$

38. $a_n = \{-1.25, -5, -20, -80, \ldots\}$

39. $a_n = \left\{-1, -\dfrac{4}{5}, -\dfrac{16}{25}, -\dfrac{64}{125}, \ldots\right\}$

40. $a_n = \left\{2, \dfrac{1}{3}, \dfrac{1}{18}, \dfrac{1}{108}, \ldots\right\}$

41. $a_n = \left\{3, -1, \dfrac{1}{3}, -\dfrac{1}{9}, \ldots\right\}$

For the following exercises, find the specified term for the geometric sequence given.

42. Let $a_1 = 4$, $a_n = -3a_{n-1}$. Find a_8.

43. Let $a_n = -\left(-\dfrac{1}{3}\right)^{n-1}$. Find a_{12}.

For the following exercises, find the number of terms in the given finite geometric sequence.

44. $a_n = \{-1, 3, -9, \ldots, 2187\}$

45. $a_n = \left\{2, 1, \dfrac{1}{2}, \ldots, \dfrac{1}{1024}\right\}$

GRAPHICAL

For the following exercises, determine whether the graph shown represents a geometric sequence.

46.

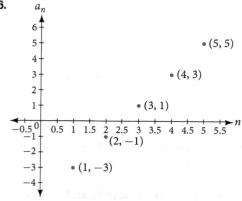

47.

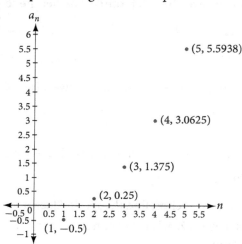

For the following exercises, use the information provided to graph the first five terms of the geometric sequence.

48. $a_1 = 1$, $r = \dfrac{1}{2}$

49. $a_1 = 3$, $a_n = 2a_{n-1}$

50. $a_n = 27 \cdot 0.3^{n-1}$

EXTENSIONS

51. Use recursive formulas to give two examples of geometric sequences whose 3rd terms are 200.

52. Use explicit formulas to give two examples of geometric sequences whose 7th terms are 1024.

53. Find the 5th term of the geometric sequence $\{b, 4b, 16b, \ldots\}$.

54. Find the 7th term of the geometric sequence $\{64a(-b), 32a(-3b), 16a(-9b), \ldots\}$.

55. At which term does the sequence $\{10, 12, 14.4, 17.28, \ldots\}$ exceed 100?

56. At which term does the sequence $\left\{\dfrac{1}{2187}, \dfrac{1}{729}, \dfrac{1}{243}, \dfrac{1}{81} \ldots\right\}$ begin to have integer values?

57. For which term does the geometric sequence $a_n = -36\left(\dfrac{2}{3}\right)^{n-1}$ first have a non-integer value?

58. Use the recursive formula to write a geometric sequence whose common ratio is an integer. Show the first four terms, and then find the 10th term.

59. Use the explicit formula to write a geometric sequence whose common ratio is a decimal number between 0 and 1. Show the first 4 terms, and then find the 8th term.

60. Is it possible for a sequence to be both arithmetic and geometric? If so, give an example.

LEARNING OBJECTIVES

In this section, you will:

- Use summation notation.
- Use the formula for the sum of the first n terms of an arithmetic series.
- Use the formula for the sum of the first n terms of a geometric series.
- Use the formula for the sum of an infinite geometric series.
- Solve annuity problems.

13.4 SERIES AND THEIR NOTATIONS

A couple decides to start a college fund for their daughter. They plan to invest $50 in the fund each month. The fund pays 6% annual interest, compounded monthly. How much money will they have saved when their daughter is ready to start college in 6 years? In this section, we will learn how to answer this question. To do so, we need to consider the amount of money invested and the amount of interest earned.

Using Summation Notation

To find the total amount of money in the college fund and the sum of the amounts deposited, we need to add the amounts deposited each month and the amounts earned monthly. The sum of the terms of a sequence is called a **series**. Consider, for example, the following series.

$$3 + 7 + 11 + 15 + 19 + \dots$$

The **nth partial sum** of a series is the sum of a finite number of consecutive terms beginning with the first term. The notation S_n represents the partial sum.

$$S_1 = 3$$
$$S_2 = 3 + 7 = 10$$
$$S_3 = 3 + 7 + 11 = 21$$
$$S_4 = 3 + 7 + 11 + 15 = 36$$

Summation notation is used to represent series. Summation notation is often known as sigma notation because it uses the Greek capital letter sigma, Σ, to represent the sum. Summation notation includes an explicit formula and specifies the first and last terms in the series. An explicit formula for each term of the series is given to the right of the sigma. A variable called the **index of summation** is written below the sigma. The index of summation is set equal to the **lower limit of summation**, which is the number used to generate the first term in the series. The number above the sigma, called the **upper limit of summation**, is the number used to generate the last term in a series.

Upper limit of summation $\longrightarrow$ $\displaystyle\sum_{k=1}^{5} 2k$ $\longleftarrow$ Explicit formula for kth term of series

Index of summation $\longrightarrow$ $\quad\longleftarrow$ Lower limit of summation

If we interpret the given notation, we see that it asks us to find the sum of the terms in the series $a_k = 2k$ for $k = 1$ through $k = 5$. We can begin by substituting the terms for k and listing out the terms of this series.

$$a_1 = 2(1) = 2$$
$$a_2 = 2(2) = 4$$
$$a_3 = 2(3) = 6$$
$$a_4 = 2(4) = 8$$
$$a_5 = 2(5) = 10$$

We can find the sum of the series by adding the terms:

$$\sum_{k=1}^{5} 2k = 2 + 4 + 6 + 8 + 10 = 30$$

---

summation notation

The sum of the first n terms of a **series** can be expressed in **summation notation** as follows:

$$\sum_{k=1}^{n} a_k$$

This notation tells us to find the sum of a_k from $k = 1$ to $k = n$.

k is called the **index of summation**, 1 is the **lower limit of summation**, and n is the **upper limit of summation**.

Q & A...

Does the lower limit of summation have to be 1?

No. The lower limit of summation can be any number, but 1 is frequently used. We will look at examples with lower limits of summation other than 1.

How To...

Given summation notation for a series, evaluate the value.

1. Identify the lower limit of summation.
2. Identify the upper limit of summation.
3. Substitute each value of k from the lower limit to the upper limit into the formula.
4. Add to find the sum.

Example 1   **Using Summation Notation**

Evaluate $\sum_{k=3}^{7} k^2$.

Solution   According to the notation, the lower limit of summation is 3 and the upper limit is 7. So we need to find the sum of k^2 from $k = 3$ to $k = 7$. We find the terms of the series by substituting $k = 3, 4, 5, 6,$ and 7 into the function k^2. We add the terms to find the sum.

$$\sum_{k=3}^{7} k^2 = 3^2 + 4^2 + 5^2 + 6^2 + 7^2$$
$$= 9 + 16 + 25 + 36 + 49$$
$$= 135$$

Try It #1

Evaluate $\sum_{k=2}^{5} (3k - 1)$.

Using the Formula for Arithmetic Series

Just as we studied special types of sequences, we will look at special types of series. Recall that an arithmetic sequence is a sequence in which the difference between any two consecutive terms is the common difference, d. The sum of the terms of an **arithmetic sequence** is called an arithmetic series. We can write the sum of the first n terms of an arithmetic series as:

$$S_n = a_1 + (a_1 + d) + (a_1 + 2d) + \ldots + (a_n - d) + a_n.$$

We can also reverse the order of the terms and write the sum as

$$S_n = a_n + (a_n - d) + (a_n - 2d) + \ldots + (a_1 + d) + a_1.$$

If we add these two expressions for the sum of the first n terms of an arithmetic series, we can derive a formula for the sum of the first n terms of any arithmetic series.

$$S_n = a_1 + (a_1 + d) + (a_1 + 2d) + \ldots + (a_n - d) + a_n$$

$$+ S_n = a_n + (a_n - d) + (a_n - 2d) + \ldots + (a_1 + d) + a_1$$

$$2S_n = (a_1 + a_n) + (a_1 + a_n) + \ldots + (a_1 + a_n)$$

Because there are n terms in the series, we can simplify this sum to

$$2S_n = n(a_1 + a_n).$$

We divide by 2 to find the formula for the sum of the first n terms of an arithmetic series.

$$S_n = \frac{n(a_1 + a_n)}{2}$$

> **formula for the sum of the first n terms of an arithmetic series**
> An **arithmetic series** is the sum of the terms of an arithmetic sequence. The formula for the sum of the first n terms of an arithmetic sequence is
> $$S_n = \frac{n(a_1 + a_n)}{2}.$$

How To...

Given terms of an arithmetic series, find the sum of the first n terms.

1. Identify a_1 and a_n.
2. Determine n.
3. Substitute values for a_1, a_n, and n into the formula $S_n = \frac{n(a_1 + a_n)}{2}$.
4. Simplify to find S_n.

Example 2   **Finding the First *n* Terms of an Arithmetic Series**

Find the sum of each arithmetic series.

    a. $5 + 8 + 11 + 14 + 17 + 20 + 23 + 26 + 29 + 32$
    b. $20 + 15 + 10 + \ldots + -50$
    c. $\displaystyle\sum_{k=1}^{12} 3k - 8$

Solution

    a. We are given $a_1 = 5$ and $a_n = 32$.
       Count the number of terms in the sequence to find $n = 10$.
       Substitute values for a_1, a_n, and n into the formula and simplify.

$$S_n = \frac{n(a_1 + a_n)}{2}$$

$$S_{10} = \frac{10(5 + 32)}{2} = 185$$

    b. We are given $a_1 = 20$ and $a_n = -50$.
       Use the formula for the general term of an arithmetic sequence to find n.

$$a_n = a_1 + (n-1)d$$

$$-50 = 20 + (n-1)(-5)$$

$$-70 = (n-1)(-5)$$

$$14 = n - 1$$

$$15 = n$$

Substitute values for a_1, a_n, n into the formula and simplify.

$$S_n = \frac{n(a_1 + a_n)}{2}$$

$$S_{15} = \frac{15(20 - 50)}{2} = -225$$

c. To find a_1, substitute $k = 1$ into the given explicit formula.

$$a_k = 3k - 8$$
$$a_1 = 3(1) - 8 = -5$$

We are given that $n = 12$. To find a_{12}, substitute $k = 12$ into the given explicit formula.

$$a_k = 3k - 8$$
$$a_{12} = 3(12) - 8 = 28$$

Substitute values for a_1, a_n, and n into the formula and simplify.

$$S_n = \frac{n(a_1 + a_n)}{2}$$

$$S_{12} = \frac{12(-5 + 28)}{2} = 138$$

Try It #2

Use the formula to find the sum of the arithmetic series.

$$1.4 + 1.6 + 1.8 + 2.0 + 2.2 + 2.4 + 2.6 + 2.8 + 3.0 + 3.2 + 3.4$$

Try It #3

Use the formula to find the sum of the arithmetic series.

$$13 + 21 + 29 + \dots + 69$$

Try It #4

Use the formula to find the sum of the arithmetic series.

$$\sum_{k=1}^{10} 5 - 6k$$

Example 3   **Solving Application Problems with Arithmetic Series**

On the Sunday after a minor surgery, a woman is able to walk a half-mile. Each Sunday, she walks an additional quarter-mile. After 8 weeks, what will be the total number of miles she has walked?

Solution   This problem can be modeled by an arithmetic series with $a_1 = \frac{1}{2}$ and $d = \frac{1}{4}$. We are looking for the total number of miles walked after 8 weeks, so we know that $n = 8$, and we are looking for S_8. To find a_8, we can use the explicit formula for an arithmetic sequence.

$$a_n = a_1 + d(n - 1)$$
$$a_8 = \frac{1}{2} + \frac{1}{4}(8 - 1) = \frac{9}{4}$$

We can now use the formula for arithmetic series.

$$S_n = \frac{n(a_1 + a_n)}{2}$$

$$S_8 = \frac{8\left(\frac{1}{2} + \frac{9}{4}\right)}{2} = 11$$

She will have walked a total of 11 miles.

Try It #5

A man earns \$100 in the first week of June. Each week, he earns \$12.50 more than the previous week. After 12 weeks, how much has he earned?

Using the Formula for Geometric Series

Just as the sum of the terms of an arithmetic sequence is called an arithmetic series, the sum of the terms in a geometric sequence is called a **geometric series**. Recall that a geometric sequence is a sequence in which the ratio of any two consecutive terms is the common ratio, r. We can write the sum of the first n terms of a geometric series as

$$S_n = a_1 + ra_1 + r^2a_1 + \ldots + r^{n-1}a_1.$$

Just as with arithmetic series, we can do some algebraic manipulation to derive a formula for the sum of the first n terms of a geometric series. We will begin by multiplying both sides of the equation by r.

$$rS_n = ra_1 + r^2a_1 + r^3a_1 + \ldots + r^na_1$$

Next, we subtract this equation from the original equation.

$$S_n = a_1 + ra_1 + r^2a_1 + \ldots + r^{n-1}a_1.$$
$$\underline{-rS_n = -(ra_1 + r^2a_1 + r^3a_1 + \ldots + r^na_1)}$$
$$(1-r)S_n = a_1 - r^n a_1$$

Notice that when we subtract, all but the first term of the top equation and the last term of the bottom equation cancel out. To obtain a formula for S_n, divide both sides by $(1-r)$.

$$S_n = \frac{a_1(1-r^n)}{1-r} \quad r \neq 1$$

> **formula for the sum of the first n terms of a geometric series**
> A **geometric series** is the sum of the terms in a geometric sequence. The formula for the sum of the first n terms of a geometric sequence is represented as
>
> $$S_n = \frac{a_1(1-r^n)}{1-r} \quad r \neq 1$$

How To…

Given a geometric series, find the sum of the first n terms.

1. Identify a_1, r, and n.
2. Substitute values for a_1, r, and n into the formula $S_n = \dfrac{a_1(1-r^n)}{1-r}$.
3. Simplify to find S_n.

Example 4 **Finding the First n Terms of a Geometric Series**

Use the formula to find the indicated partial sum of each geometric series.

    a. S_{11} for the series $8 + (-4) + 2 + \ldots$

    b. $\displaystyle\sum_{k=1}^{6} 3 \cdot 2^k$

Solution

    a. $a_1 = 8$, and we are given that $n = 11$.

        We can find r by dividing the second term of the series by the first.

$$r = \frac{-4}{8} = -\frac{1}{2}$$

    Substitute values for a_1, r, and n into the formula and simplify.

$$S_n = \frac{a_1(1-r^n)}{1-r}$$

$$S_{11} = \frac{8\left(1 - \left(-\frac{1}{2}\right)^{11}\right)}{1 - \left(-\frac{1}{2}\right)} \approx 5.336$$

b. Find a_1 by substituting $k = 1$ into the given explicit formula.

$$a_1 = 3 \cdot 2^1 = 6$$

We can see from the given explicit formula that $r = 2$. The upper limit of summation is 6, so $n = 6$.

Substitute values for a_1, r, and n into the formula, and simplify.

$$S_n = \frac{a_1(1 - r^n)}{1 - r}$$

$$S_6 = \frac{6(1 - 2^6)}{1 - 2} = 378$$

Try It #6

Use the formula to find the indicated partial sum of each geometric series.

S_{20} for the series $1{,}000 + 500 + 250 + \ldots$

Try It #7

Use the formula to find the indicated partial sum of each geometric series.

$$\sum_{k=1}^{8} 3k$$

Example 5   **Solving an Application Problem with a Geometric Series**

At a new job, an employee's starting salary is $26,750. He receives a 1.6% annual raise. Find his total earnings at the end of 5 years.

Solution   The problem can be represented by a geometric series with $a_1 = 26{,}750$; $n = 5$; and $r = 1.016$. Substitute values for a_1, r, and n into the formula and simplify to find the total amount earned at the end of 5 years.

$$S_n = \frac{a_1(1 - r^n)}{1 - r}$$

$$S_5 = \frac{26{,}750(1 - 1.016^5)}{1 - 1.016} \approx 138{,}099.03$$

He will have earned a total of $138,099.03 by the end of 5 years.

Try It #8

At a new job, an employee's starting salary is $32,100. She receives a 2% annual raise. How much will she have earned by the end of 8 years?

Using the Formula for the Sum of an Infinite Geometric Series

Thus far, we have looked only at finite series. Sometimes, however, we are interested in the sum of the terms of an infinite sequence rather than the sum of only the first n terms. An **infinite series** is the sum of the terms of an infinite sequence. An example of an infinite series is $2 + 4 + 6 + 8 + \ldots$

This series can also be written in summation notation as $\sum_{k=1}^{\infty} 2k$, where the upper limit of summation is infinity. Because the terms are not tending to zero, the sum of the series increases without bound as we add more terms. Therefore, the sum of this infinite series is not defined. When the sum is not a real number, we say the series **diverges**.

Determining Whether the Sum of an Infinite Geometric Series is Defined

If the terms of an infinite geometric series approach 0, the sum of an infinite geometric series can be defined. The terms in this series approach 0:

$$1 + 0.2 + 0.04 + 0.008 + 0.0016 + \ldots$$

The common ratio $r = 0.2$. As n gets very large, the values of r^n get very small and approach 0. Each successive term affects the sum less than the preceding term. As each succeeding term gets closer to 0, the sum of the terms approaches a finite value. The terms of any infinite geometric series with $-1 < r < 1$ approach 0; the sum of a geometric series is defined when $-1 < r < 1$.

> ***determining whether the sum of an infinite geometric series is defined***
> The sum of an infinite series is defined if the series is geometric and $-1 < r < 1$.

How To...

Given the first several terms of an infinite series, determine if the sum of the series exists.

1. Find the ratio of the second term to the first term.
2. Find the ratio of the third term to the second term.
3. Continue this process to ensure the ratio of a term to the preceding term is constant throughout. If so, the series is geometric.
4. If a common ratio, r, was found in step 3, check to see if $-1 < r < 1$. If so, the sum is defined. If not, the sum is not defined.

Example 6   **Determining Whether the Sum of an Infinite Series is Defined**

Determine whether the sum of each infinite series is defined.

    a. $12 + 8 + 4 + ...$ **b.** $\dfrac{3}{4} + \dfrac{1}{2} + \dfrac{1}{3} + ...$ **c.** $\displaystyle\sum_{k=1}^{\infty} 27 \cdot \left(\dfrac{1}{3}\right)^k$ **d.** $\displaystyle\sum_{k=1}^{\infty} 5k$

Solution

    a. The ratio of the second term to the first is $\dfrac{2}{3}$, which is not the same as the ratio of the third term to the second, $\dfrac{1}{2}$. The series is not geometric.

    b. The ratio of the second term to the first is the same as the ratio of the third term to the second. The series is geometric with a common ratio of $\dfrac{2}{3}$. The sum of the infinite series is defined.

    c. The given formula is exponential with a base of $\dfrac{1}{3}$; the series is geometric with a common ratio of $\dfrac{1}{3}$. The sum of the infinite series is defined.

    d. The given formula is not exponential; the series is not geometric because the terms are increasing, and so cannot yield a finite sum.

Try It #9

Determine whether the sum of the infinite series is defined.

$$\frac{1}{3} + \frac{1}{2} + \frac{3}{4} + \frac{9}{8} + ...$$

Try It #10

Determine whether the sum of the infinite series is defined.

$$24 + (-12) + 6 + (-3) + ...$$

Try It #11

Determine whether the sum of the infinite series is defined.

$$\sum_{k=1}^{\infty} 15 \cdot (-0.3)^k$$

Finding Sums of Infinite Series

When the sum of an infinite geometric series exists, we can calculate the sum. The formula for the sum of an infinite series is related to the formula for the sum of the first n terms of a geometric series.

$$S_n = \frac{a_1(1 - r^n)}{1 - r}$$

We will examine an infinite series with $r = \frac{1}{2}$. What happens to r^n as n increases?

$$\left(\frac{1}{2}\right)^2 = \frac{1}{4}$$

$$\left(\frac{1}{2}\right)^3 = \frac{1}{8}$$

$$\left(\frac{1}{2}\right)^4 = \frac{1}{16}$$

The value of r^n decreases rapidly. What happens for greater values of n?

$$\left(\frac{1}{2}\right)^{10} = \frac{1}{1,024}$$

$$\left(\frac{1}{2}\right)^{20} = \frac{1}{1,048,576}$$

$$\left(\frac{1}{2}\right)^{30} = \frac{1}{1,073,741,824}$$

As n gets very large, r^n gets very small. We say that, as n increases without bound, r^n approaches 0. As r^n approaches 0, $1 - r^n$ approaches 1. When this happens, the numerator approaches a_1. This give us a formula for the sum of an infinite geometric series.

---

formula for the sum of an infinite geometric series

The formula for the sum of an infinite geometric series with $-1 < r < 1$ is

$$S = \frac{a_1}{1 - r}$$

How To…

Given an infinite geometric series, find its sum.

1. Identify a_1 and r.
2. Confirm that $-1 < r < 1$.
3. Substitute values for a_1 and r into the formula, $S = \dfrac{a_1}{1 - r}$.
4. Simplify to find S.

Example 7   **Finding the Sum of an Infinite Geometric Series**

Find the sum, if it exists, for the following:

    a. $10 + 9 + 8 + 7 + \dots$ **b.** $248.6 + 99.44 + 39.776 + \dots$ **c.** $\sum\limits_{k=1}^{\infty} 4{,}374 \cdot \left(-\frac{1}{3}\right)^{k-1}$ **d.** $\sum\limits_{k=1}^{\infty} \frac{1}{9} \cdot \left(\frac{4}{3}\right)^{k}$

Solution

    a. There is not a constant ratio; the series is not geometric.

    b. There is a constant ratio; the series is geometric. $a_1 = 248.6$ and $r = \dfrac{99.44}{248.6} = 0.4$, so the sum exists.

        Substitute $a_1 = 248.6$ and $r = 0.4$ into the formula and simplify to find the sum:

$$S = \frac{a_1}{1 - r}$$

$$S = \frac{248.6}{1 - 0.4} = 414.\overline{3}$$

    c. The formula is exponential, so the series is geometric with $r = -\dfrac{1}{3}$. Find a_1 by substituting $k = 1$ into the given explicit formula:

$$a_1 = 4{,}374 \cdot \left(-\frac{1}{3}\right)^{1-1} = 4{,}374$$

Substitute $a_1 = 4{,}374$ and $r = -\frac{1}{3}$ into the formula, and simplify to find the sum:

$$S = \frac{a_1}{1 - r}$$

$$S = \frac{4{,}374}{1 - \left(-\frac{1}{3}\right)} = 3{,}280.5$$

d. The formula is exponential, so the series is geometric, but $r > 1$. The sum does not exist.

Example 8   **Finding an Equivalent Fraction for a Repeating Decimal**

Find an equivalent fraction for the repeating decimal $0.\overline{3}$

Solution   We notice the repeating decimal $0.\overline{3} = 0.333...$ so we can rewrite the repeating decimal as a sum of terms.

$$0.\overline{3} = 0.3 + 0.03 + 0.003 + ...$$

Looking for a pattern, we rewrite the sum, noticing that we see the first term multiplied to 0.1 in the second term, and the second term multiplied to 0.1 in the third term.

$$0.\overline{3} = 0.3 + (0.1)\underbrace{(0.3)}_{\text{First Term}} + (0.1)\underbrace{(0.1)(0.3)}_{\text{Second Term}}$$

Notice the pattern; we multiply each consecutive term by a common ratio of 0.1 starting with the first term of 0.3. So, substituting into our formula for an infinite geometric sum, we have

$$S = \frac{a_1}{1 - r} = \frac{0.3}{1 - 0.1} = \frac{0.3}{0.9} = \frac{1}{3}.$$

Try It #12

Find the sum, if it exists.

$$2 + \frac{2}{3} + \frac{2}{9} + ...$$

Try It #13

Find the sum, if it exists.

$$\sum_{k=1}^{\infty} 0.76k + 1$$

Try It #14

Find the sum, if it exists.

$$\sum_{k=1}^{\infty} \left(-\frac{3}{8}\right)^k$$

Solving Annuity Problems

At the beginning of the section, we looked at a problem in which a couple invested a set amount of money each month into a college fund for six years. An **annuity** is an investment in which the purchaser makes a sequence of periodic, equal payments. To find the amount of an annuity, we need to find the sum of all the payments and the interest earned. In the example, the couple invests \$50 each month. This is the value of the initial deposit. The account paid 6% annual interest, compounded monthly. To find the interest rate per payment period, we need to divide the 6% annual percentage interest (APR) rate by 12. So the monthly interest rate is 0.5%. We can multiply the amount in the account each month by 100.5% to find the value of the account after interest has been added.

We can find the value of the annuity right after the last deposit by using a geometric series with $a_1 = 50$ and $r = 100.5\% = 1.005$. After the first deposit, the value of the annuity will be \$50. Let us see if we can determine the amount in the college fund and the interest earned.

We can find the value of the annuity after n deposits using the formula for the sum of the first n terms of a geometric series. In 6 years, there are 72 months, so $n = 72$. We can substitute $a_1 = 50$, $r = 1.005$, and $n = 72$ into the formula, and simplify to find the value of the annuity after 6 years.

$$S_{72} = \frac{50(1 - 1.005^{72})}{1 - 1.005} \approx 4{,}320.44$$

After the last deposit, the couple will have a total of \$4,320.44 in the account. Notice, the couple made 72 payments of \$50 each for a total of $72(50) = \$3{,}600$. This means that because of the annuity, the couple earned \$720.44 interest in their college fund.

How To...

Given an initial deposit and an interest rate, find the value of an annuity.

1. Determine a_1, the value of the initial deposit.
2. Determine n, the number of deposits.
3. Determine r.
   a. Divide the annual interest rate by the number of times per year that interest is compounded.
   b. Add 1 to this amount to find r.
4. Substitute values for a_1, r, and n into the formula for the sum of the first n terms of a geometric series,

$$S_n = \frac{a_1(1 - r^n)}{1 - r} .$$

5. Simplify to find S_n, the value of the annuity after n deposits.

Example 9   **Solving an Annuity Problem**

A deposit of \$100 is placed into a college fund at the beginning of every month for 10 years. The fund earns 9% annual interest, compounded monthly, and paid at the end of the month. How much is in the account right after the last deposit?

Solution   The value of the initial deposit is \$100, so $a_1 = 100$. A total of 120 monthly deposits are made in the 10 years, so $n = 120$. To find r, divide the annual interest rate by 12 to find the monthly interest rate and add 1 to represent the new monthly deposit.

$$r = 1 + \frac{0.09}{12} = 1.0075$$

Substitute $a_1 = 100$, $r = 1.0075$, and $n = 120$ into the formula for the sum of the first n terms of a geometric series, and simplify to find the value of the annuity.

$$S_{120} = \frac{100(1 - 1.0075^{120})}{1 - 1.0075} \approx 19{,}351.43$$

So the account has \$19,351.43 after the last deposit is made.

Try It #15

At the beginning of each month, \$200 is deposited into a retirement fund. The fund earns 6% annual interest, compounded monthly, and paid into the account at the end of the month. How much is in the account if deposits are made for 10 years?

Access these online resources for additional instruction and practice with series.

- Arithmetic Series (http://openstaxcollege.org/l/arithmeticser)
- Geometric Series (http://openstaxcollege.org/l/geometricser)
- Summation Notation (http://openstaxcollege.org/l/sumnotation)

13.4 SECTION EXERCISES

VERBAL

1. What is an nth partial sum?

2. What is the difference between an arithmetic sequence and an arithmetic series?

3. What is a geometric series?

4. How is finding the sum of an infinite geometric series different from finding the nth partial sum?

5. What is an annuity?

ALGEBRAIC

For the following exercises, express each description of a sum using summation notation.

6. The sum of terms $m^2 + 3m$ from $m = 1$ to $m = 5$

7. The sum from of $n = 0$ to $n = 4$ of $5n$

8. The sum of $6k - 5$ from $k = -2$ to $k = 1$

9. The sum that results from adding the number 4 five times

For the following exercises, express each arithmetic sum using summation notation.

10. $5 + 10 + 15 + 20 + 25 + 30 + 35 + 40 + 45 + 50$

11. $10 + 18 + 26 + \dots + 162$

12. $\dfrac{1}{2} + 1 + \dfrac{3}{2} + 2 + \dots + 4$

For the following exercises, use the formula for the sum of the first n terms of each arithmetic sequence.

13. $\dfrac{3}{2} + 2 + \dfrac{5}{2} + 3 + \dfrac{7}{2}$

14. $19 + 25 + 31 + \dots + 73$

15. $3.2 + 3.4 + 3.6 + \dots + 5.6$

For the following exercises, express each geometric sum using summation notation.

16. $1 + 3 + 9 + 27 + 81 + 243 + 729 + 2187$

17. $8 + 4 + 2 + \dots + 0.125$

18. $-\dfrac{1}{6} + \dfrac{1}{12} - \dfrac{1}{24} + \dots + \dfrac{1}{768}$

For the following exercises, use the formula for the sum of the first n terms of each geometric sequence, and then state the indicated sum.

19. $9 + 3 + 1 + \dfrac{1}{3} + \dfrac{1}{9}$

20. $\displaystyle\sum_{n=1}^{9} 5 \cdot 2^{n-1}$

21. $\displaystyle\sum_{a=1}^{11} 64 \cdot 0.2^{a-1}$

For the following exercises, determine whether the infinite series has a sum. If so, write the formula for the sum. If not, state the reason.

22. $12 + 18 + 24 + 30 + \dots$

23. $2 + 1.6 + 1.28 + 1.024 + \dots$

24. $\displaystyle\sum_{m=1}^{\infty} 4^{m-1}$

25. $\displaystyle\sum_{k=1}^{\infty} -\left(-\dfrac{1}{2}\right)^{k-1}$

GRAPHICAL

For the following exercises, use the following scenario. Javier makes monthly deposits into a savings account. He opened the account with an initial deposit of $50. Each month thereafter he increased the previous deposit amount by $20.

26. Graph the arithmetic sequence showing one year of Javier's deposits.

27. Graph the arithmetic series showing the monthly sums of one year of Javier's deposits.

For the following exercises, use the geometric series $\displaystyle\sum_{k=1}^{\infty} \left(\frac{1}{2}\right)^k$.

28. Graph the first 7 partial sums of the series.

29. What number does S_n seem to be approaching in the graph? Find the sum to explain why this makes sense.

NUMERIC

For the following exercises, find the indicated sum.

30. $\displaystyle\sum_{a=1}^{14} a$

31. $\displaystyle\sum_{n=1}^{6} n(n-2)$

32. $\displaystyle\sum_{k=1}^{17} k^2$

33. $\displaystyle\sum_{k=1}^{7} 2^k$

For the following exercises, use the formula for the sum of the first n terms of an arithmetic series to find the sum.

34. $-1.7 + -0.4 + 0.9 + 2.2 + 3.5 + 4.8$

35. $6 + \dfrac{15}{2} + 9 + \dfrac{21}{2} + 12 + \dfrac{27}{2} + 15$

36. $-1 + 3 + 7 + \ldots + 31$

37. $\displaystyle\sum_{k=1}^{11} \left(\frac{k}{2} - \frac{1}{2}\right)$

For the following exercises, use the formula for the sum of the first n terms of a geometric series to find the partial sum.

38. S_6 for the series $-2 - 10 - 50 - 250 \ldots$

39. S_7 for the series $0.4 - 2 + 10 - 50 \ldots$

40. $\displaystyle\sum_{k=1}^{9} 2^{k-1}$

41. $\displaystyle\sum_{n=1}^{10} -2 \cdot \left(\frac{1}{2}\right)^{n-1}$

For the following exercises, find the sum of the infinite geometric series.

42. $4 + 2 + 1 + \dfrac{1}{2} \ldots$

43. $-1 - \dfrac{1}{4} - \dfrac{1}{16} - \dfrac{1}{64} \ldots$

44. $\displaystyle\sum_{\infty}^{k=1} 3 \cdot \left(\frac{1}{4}\right)^{k-1}$

45. $\displaystyle\sum_{n=1}^{\infty} 4.6 \cdot 0.5^{n-1}$

For the following exercises, determine the value of the annuity for the indicated monthly deposit amount, the number of deposits, and the interest rate.

46. Deposit amount: $50; total deposits: 60; interest rate: 5%, compounded monthly

47. Deposit amount: $150; total deposits: 24; interest rate: 3%, compounded monthly

48. Deposit amount: $450; total deposits: 60; interest rate: 4.5%, compounded quarterly

49. Deposit amount: $100; total deposits: 120; interest rate: 10%, compounded semi-annually

EXTENSIONS

50. The sum of terms $50 - k^2$ from $k = x$ through 7 is 115. What is x?

51. Write an explicit formula for a_k such that $\displaystyle\sum_{k=0}^{6} a_k = 189$. Assume this is an arithmetic series.

52. Find the smallest value of n such that $\displaystyle\sum_{k=1}^{n} (3k - 5) > 100$.

53. How many terms must be added before the series $-1 - 3 - 5 - 7\ldots$ has a sum less than -75?

54. Write $0.\overline{65}$ as an infinite geometric series using summation notation. Then use the formula for finding the sum of an infinite geometric series to convert 0.65 to a fraction.

55. The sum of an infinite geometric series is five times the value of the first term. What is the common ratio of the series?

56. To get the best loan rates available, the Riches want to save enough money to place 20% down on a $160,000 home. They plan to make monthly deposits of $125 in an investment account that offers 8.5% annual interest compounded semi-annually. Will the Riches have enough for a 20% down payment after five years of saving? How much money will they have saved?

57. Karl has two years to save $10,000 to buy a used car when he graduates. To the nearest dollar, what would his monthly deposits need to be if he invests in an account offering a 4.2% annual interest rate that compounds monthly?

REAL-WORLD APPLICATIONS

58. Keisha devised a week-long study plan to prepare for finals. On the first day, she plans to study for 1 hour, and each successive day she will increase her study time by 30 minutes. How many hours will Keisha have studied after one week?

59. A boulder rolled down a mountain, traveling 6 feet in the first second. Each successive second, its distance increased by 8 feet. How far did the boulder travel after 10 seconds?

60. A scientist places 50 cells in a petri dish. Every hour, the population increases by 1.5%. What will the cell count be after 1 day?

61. A pendulum travels a distance of 3 feet on its first swing. On each successive swing, it travels $\frac{3}{4}$ the distance of the previous swing. What is the total distance traveled by the pendulum when it stops swinging?

62. Rachael deposits $1,500 into a retirement fund each year. The fund earns 8.2% annual interest, compounded monthly. If she opened her account when she was 19 years old, how much will she have by the time she is 55? How much of that amount will be interest earned?

LEARNING OBJECTIVES

In this section, you will:

- Solve counting problems using the Addition Principle.
- Solve counting problems using the Multiplication Principle.
- Solve counting problems using permutations involving n distinct objects.
- Solve counting problems using combinations.
- Find the number of subsets of a given set.
- Solve counting problems using permutations involving n non-distinct objects.

13.5   COUNTING PRINCIPLES

A new company sells customizable cases for tablets and smartphones. Each case comes in a variety of colors and can be personalized for an additional fee with images or a monogram. A customer can choose not to personalize or could choose to have one, two, or three images or a monogram. The customer can choose the order of the images and the letters in the monogram. The company is working with an agency to develop a marketing campaign with a focus on the huge number of options they offer. Counting the possibilities is challenging!

We encounter a wide variety of counting problems every day. There is a branch of mathematics devoted to the study of counting problems such as this one. Other applications of counting include secure passwords, horse racing outcomes, and college scheduling choices. We will examine this type of mathematics in this section.

Using the Addition Principle

The company that sells customizable cases offers cases for tablets and smartphones. There are 3 supported tablet models and 5 supported smartphone models. The **Addition Principle** tells us that we can add the number of tablet options to the number of smartphone options to find the total number of options. By the Addition Principle, there are 8 total options, as we can see in **Figure 1**.

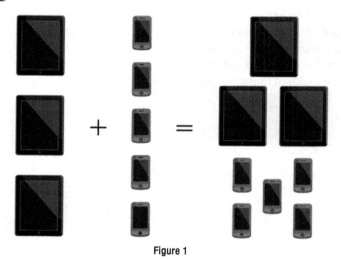

Figure 1

> **the Addition Principle**
> According to the **Addition Principle**, if one event can occur in m ways and a second event with no common outcomes can occur in n ways, then the first or second event can occur in $m + n$ ways.

Example 1   Using the Addition Principle

There are 2 vegetarian entrée options and 5 meat entrée options on a dinner menu. What is the total number of entrée options?

Solution   We can add the number of vegetarian options to the number of meat options to find the total number of entrée options.

Vegetarian	+	Vegetarian	+	Meat	+	Meat	+	Meat	+	Meat	+	Meat
↓		↓		↓		↓		↓		↓		↓
Option 1	+	Option 2	+	Option 3	+	Option 4	+	Option 5	+	Option 6	+	Option 7

There are 7 total options.

Try It #1

A student is shopping for a new computer. He is deciding among 3 desktop computers and 4 laptop computers. What is the total number of computer options?

Using the Multiplication Principle

The **Multiplication Principle** applies when we are making more than one selection. Suppose we are choosing an appetizer, an entrée, and a dessert. If there are 2 appetizer options, 3 entrée options, and 2 dessert options on a fixed-price dinner menu, there are a total of 12 possible choices of one each as shown in the tree diagram in **Figure 2**.

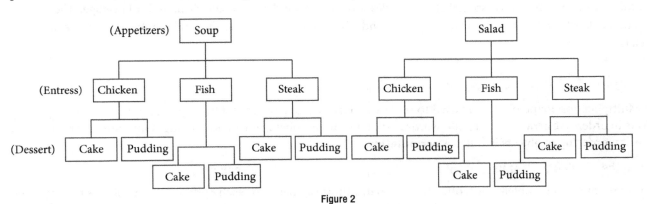

Figure 2

The possible choices are:

1. soup, chicken, cake
2. soup, chicken, pudding
3. soup, fish, cake
4. soup, fish, pudding
5. soup, steak, cake
6. soup, steak, pudding
7. salad, chicken, cake
8. salad, chicken, pudding
9. salad, fish, cake
10. salad, fish, pudding
11. salad, steak, cake
12. salad, steak, pudding

We can also find the total number of possible dinners by multiplying.

We could also conclude that there are 12 possible dinner choices simply by applying the Multiplication Principle.

# of appetizer options × # of entree options × # of dessert options

$$2 \quad \times \quad 3 \quad \times \quad 2 \quad = 12$$

> **the Multiplication Principle**
>
> According to the **Multiplication Principle**, if one event can occur in m ways and a second event can occur in n ways after the first event has occurred, then the two events can occur in $m \times n$ ways. This is also known as the **Fundamental Counting Principle**.

Example 2   **Using the Multiplication Principle**

Diane packed 2 skirts, 4 blouses, and a sweater for her business trip. She will need to choose a skirt and a blouse for each outfit and decide whether to wear the sweater. Use the Multiplication Principle to find the total number of possible outfits.

Solution   To find the total number of outfits, find the product of the number of skirt options, the number of blouse options, and the number of sweater options.

$$\text{\# of skirt options} \times \text{\# of blouse options} \times \text{\# of sweater options}$$
$$2 \quad \times \quad 4 \quad \times \quad 2 \quad = 16$$

There are 16 possible outfits.

Try It #2

A restaurant offers a breakfast special that includes a breakfast sandwich, a side dish, and a beverage. There are 3 types of breakfast sandwiches, 4 side dish options, and 5 beverage choices. Find the total number of possible breakfast specials.

Finding the Number of Permutations of *n* Distinct Objects

The Multiplication Principle can be used to solve a variety of problem types. One type of problem involves placing objects in order. We arrange letters into words and digits into numbers, line up for photographs, decorate rooms, and more. An ordering of objects is called a **permutation**.

Finding the Number of Permutations of *n* Distinct Objects Using the Multiplication Principle

To solve permutation problems, it is often helpful to draw line segments for each option. That enables us to determine the number of each option so we can multiply. For instance, suppose we have four paintings, and we want to find the number of ways we can hang three of the paintings in order on the wall. We can draw three lines to represent the three places on the wall.

$$\underline{\hspace{2cm}} \times \underline{\hspace{2cm}} \times \underline{\hspace{2cm}}$$

There are four options for the first place, so we write a 4 on the first line.

$$\underline{\hspace{1cm} 4 \hspace{1cm}} \times \underline{\hspace{2cm}} \times \underline{\hspace{2cm}}$$

After the first place has been filled, there are three options for the second place so we write a 3 on the second line.

$$\underline{\hspace{1cm} 4 \hspace{1cm}} \times \underline{\hspace{1cm} 3 \hspace{1cm}} \times \underline{\hspace{2cm}}$$

After the second place has been filled, there are two options for the third place so we write a 2 on the third line. Finally, we find the product.

$$\underline{\hspace{1cm} 4 \hspace{1cm}} \times \underline{\hspace{1cm} 3 \hspace{1cm}} \times \underline{\hspace{1cm} 2 \hspace{1cm}} = 24$$

There are 24 possible permutations of the paintings.

How To...

Given n distinct options, determine how many permutations there are.

1. Determine how many options there are for the first situation.
2. Determine how many options are left for the second situation.
3. Continue until all of the spots are filled.
4. Multiply the numbers together.

Example 3   **Finding the Number of Permutations Using the Multiplication Principle**

At a swimming competition, nine swimmers compete in a race.

a. How many ways can they place first, second, and third?

b. How many ways can they place first, second, and third if a swimmer named Ariel wins first place? (Assume there is only one contestant named Ariel.)

c. How many ways can all nine swimmers line up for a photo?

Solution

a. Draw lines for each place.

<u> options for 1st place </u> × <u> options for 2nd place </u> × <u> options for 3rd place </u>

There are 9 options for first place. Once someone has won first place, there are 8 remaining options for second place. Once first and second place have been won, there are 7 remaining options for third place.

$$\underline{\quad 9 \quad} \times \underline{\quad 8 \quad} \times \underline{\quad 7 \quad} = 504$$

Multiply to find that there are 504 ways for the swimmers to place.

b. Draw lines for describing each place.

<u> options for 1st place </u> × <u> options for 2nd place </u> × <u> options for 3rd place </u>

We know Ariel must win first place, so there is only 1 option for first place. There are 8 remaining options for second place, and then 7 remaining options for third place.

$$\underline{\quad 1 \quad} \times \underline{\quad 8 \quad} \times \underline{\quad 7 \quad} = 56$$

Multiply to find that there are 56 ways for the swimmers to place if Ariel wins first.

c. Draw lines for describing each place in the photo.

<u>   </u> × <u>   </u> × <u>   </u> × <u>   </u> × <u>   </u> × <u>   </u> × <u>   </u> × <u>   </u> × <u>   </u>

There are 9 choices for the first spot, then 8 for the second, 7 for the third, 6 for the fourth, and so on until only 1 person remains for the last spot.

$$\underline{\quad 9 \quad} \times \underline{\quad 8 \quad} \times \underline{\quad 7 \quad} \times \underline{\quad 6 \quad} \times \underline{\quad 5 \quad} \times \underline{\quad 4 \quad} \times \underline{\quad 3 \quad} \times \underline{\quad 2 \quad} \times \underline{\quad 1 \quad} = 362{,}880$$

There are 362,880 possible permutations for the swimmers to line up.

Analysis   *Note that in part c, we found there were 9! ways for 9 people to line up. The number of permutations of n distinct objects can always be found by n!.*

Try It #3

A family of five is having portraits taken. Use the Multiplication Principle to find how many ways the family can line up for the portrait.

Try It #4

A family of five is having portraits taken. Use the Multiplication Principle to find how many ways the photographer can line up 3 of the family members.

Try It #5

A family of five is having portraits taken. Use the Multiplication Principle to find how many ways the family can line up for the portrait if the parents are required to stand on each end.

Finding the Number of Permutations of n Distinct Objects Using a Formula

For some permutation problems, it is inconvenient to use the Multiplication Principle because there are so many numbers to multiply. Fortunately, we can solve these problems using a formula. Before we learn the formula, let's look at two common notations for permutations. If we have a set of n objects and we want to choose r objects from the set in order, we write $P(n, r)$. Another way to write this is $_nP_r$, a notation commonly seen on computers and calculators. To calculate $P(n, r)$, we begin by finding $n!$, the number of ways to line up all n objects. We then divide by $(n - r)!$ to cancel out the $(n - r)$ items that we do not wish to line up.

Let's see how this works with a simple example. Imagine a club of six people. They need to elect a president, a vice president, and a treasurer. Six people can be elected president, any one of the five remaining people can be elected vice president, and any of the remaining four people could be elected treasurer. The number of ways this may be done is $6 \times 5 \times 4 = 120$. Using factorials, we get the same result.

$$\frac{6!}{3!} = \frac{6 \cdot 5 \cdot 4 \cdot 3!}{3!} = 6 \cdot 5 \cdot 4 = 120$$

There are 120 ways to select 3 officers in order from a club with 6 members. We refer to this as a permutation of 6 taken 3 at a time. The general formula is as follows.

$$P(n, r) = \frac{n!}{(n - r)!}$$

Note that the formula stills works if we are choosing all n objects and placing them in order. In that case we would be dividing by $(n - n)!$ or $0!$, which we said earlier is equal to 1. So the number of permutations of n objects taken n at a time is $\frac{n!}{1}$ or just $n!$.

> **formula for permutations of n distinct objects**
> Given n distinct objects, the number of ways to select r objects from the set in order is
> $$P(n, r) = \frac{n!}{(n - r)!}$$

How To...

Given a word problem, evaluate the possible permutations.

1. Identify n from the given information.
2. Identify r from the given information.
3. Replace n and r in the formula with the given values.
4. Evaluate.

Example 4   **Finding the Number of Permutations Using the Formula**

A professor is creating an exam of 9 questions from a test bank of 12 questions. How many ways can she select and arrange the questions?

Solution   Substitute $n = 12$ and $r = 9$ into the permutation formula and simplify.

$$P(n, r) = \frac{n!}{(n - r)!}$$

$$P(12, 9) = \frac{12!}{(12 - 9)!} = \frac{12!}{3!} = 79{,}833{,}600$$

There are 79,833,600 possible permutations of exam questions!

Analysis We can also use a calculator to find permutations. For this problem, we would enter 15, press the [$_nP_r$ function], enter [12], and then press the equal sign. The [$_nP_r$ function] may be located under the [MATH] menu with probability commands.

Q & A...

Could we have solved Example 4 using the Multiplication Principle?

Yes. We could have multiplied $15 \cdot 14 \cdot 13 \cdot 12 \cdot 11 \cdot 10 \cdot 9 \cdot 8 \cdot 7 \cdot 6 \cdot 5 \cdot 4$ to find the same answer.

Try It #6

A play has a cast of 7 actors preparing to make their curtain call. Use the permutation formula to find how many ways the 7 actors can line up.

Try It #7

A play has a cast of 7 actors preparing to make their curtain call. Use the permutation formula to find how many ways 5 of the 7 actors can be chosen to line up.

Find the Number of Combinations Using the Formula

So far, we have looked at problems asking us to put objects in order. There are many problems in which we want to select a few objects from a group of objects, but we do not care about the order. When we are selecting objects and the order does not matter, we are dealing with **combinations**. A selection of r objects from a set of n objects where the order does not matter can be written as $C(n, r)$. Just as with permutations, $C(n, r)$ can also be written as $_nC_r$. In this case, the general formula is as follows.

$$C(n, r) = \frac{n!}{r!(n-r)!}$$

An earlier problem considered choosing 3 of 4 possible paintings to hang on a wall. We found that there were 24 ways to select 3 of the 4 paintings in order. But what if we did not care about the order? We would expect a smaller number because selecting paintings 1, 2, 3 would be the same as selecting paintings 2, 3, 1. To find the number of ways to select 3 of the 4 paintings, disregarding the order of the paintings, divide the number of permutations by the number of ways to order 3 paintings. There are $3! = 3 \cdot 2 \cdot 1 = 6$ ways to order 3 paintings. There are $\frac{24}{6}$, or 4 ways to select 3 of the 4 paintings.

This number makes sense because every time we are selecting 3 paintings, we are *not* selecting 1 painting. There are 4 paintings we could choose not to select, so there are 4 ways to select 3 of the 4 paintings.

> **formula for combinations of n distinct objects**
> Given n distinct objects, the number of ways to select r objects from the set is
> $$C(n, r) = \frac{n!}{r!(n-r)!}$$

How To...

Given a number of options, determine the possible number of combinations.

1. Identify n from the given information.
2. Identify r from the given information.
3. Replace n and r in the formula with the given values.
4. Evaluate.

Example 5   **Finding the Number of Combinations Using the Formula**

A fast food restaurant offers five side dish options. Your meal comes with two side dishes.

    a. How many ways can you select your side dishes?
    b. How many ways can you select 3 side dishes?

Solution

    a. We want to choose 2 side dishes from 5 options.

$$C(5, 2) = \frac{5!}{2!(5-2)!} = 10$$

    b. We want to choose 3 side dishes from 5 options.

$$C(5, 3) = \frac{5!}{3!(5-3)!} = 10$$

Analysis   We can also use a graphing calculator to find combinations. Enter **5**, then press $_nC_r$, enter **3**, and then press the equal sign. The $_nC_r$ *function* may be located under the **MATH** menu with probability commands.

Q & A...

Is it a coincidence that parts (a) and (b) in Example 5 have the same answers?

No. When we choose r objects from n objects, we are **not** choosing $(n - r)$ objects. Therefore, $C(n, r) = C(n, n - r)$.

Try It #8

An ice cream shop offers 10 flavors of ice cream. How many ways are there to choose 3 flavors for a banana split?

Finding the Number of Subsets of a Set

We have looked only at combination problems in which we chose exactly r objects. In some problems, we want to consider choosing every possible number of objects. Consider, for example, a pizza restaurant that offers 5 toppings. Any number of toppings can be ordered. How many different pizzas are possible?

To answer this question, we need to consider pizzas with any number of toppings. There is $C(5, 0) = 1$ way to order a pizza with no toppings. There are $C(5, 1) = 5$ ways to order a pizza with exactly one topping. If we continue this process, we get

$$C(5, 0) + C(5, 1) + C(5, 2) + C(5, 3) + C(5, 4) + C(5, 5) = 32$$

There are 32 possible pizzas. This result is equal to 2^5.

We are presented with a sequence of choices. For each of the n objects we have two choices: include it in the subset or not. So for the whole subset we have made n choices, each with two options. So there are a total of $2 \cdot 2 \cdot 2 \cdot ... \cdot 2$ possible resulting subsets, all the way from the empty subset, which we obtain when we say "no" each time, to the original set itself, which we obtain when we say "yes" each time.

> **formula for the number of subsets of a set**
> A set containing n distinct objects has 2^n subsets.

Example 6   Finding the Number of Subsets of a Set

A restaurant offers butter, cheese, chives, and sour cream as toppings for a baked potato. How many different ways are there to order a potato?

Solution   We are looking for the number of subsets of a set with 4 objects. Substitute $n = 4$ into the formula.

$$2^n = 2^4$$
$$= 16$$

There are 16 possible ways to order a potato.

Try It #9

A sundae bar at a wedding has 6 toppings to choose from. Any number of toppings can be chosen. How many different sundaes are possible?

Finding the Number of Permutations of n Non-Distinct Objects

We have studied permutations where all of the objects involved were distinct. What happens if some of the objects are indistinguishable? For example, suppose there is a sheet of 12 stickers. If all of the stickers were distinct, there would be 12! ways to order the stickers. However, 4 of the stickers are identical stars, and 3 are identical moons. Because all of the objects are not distinct, many of the 12! permutations we counted are duplicates. The general formula for this situation is as follows.

$$\frac{n!}{r_1!\, r_2! \dots r_k!}$$

In this example, we need to divide by the number of ways to order the 4 stars and the ways to order the 3 moons to find the number of unique permutations of the stickers. There are 4! ways to order the stars and 3! ways to order the moon.

$$\frac{12!}{4!3!} = 3{,}326{,}400$$

There are 3,326,400 ways to order the sheet of stickers.

---

formula for finding the number of permutations of n non-distinct objects

If there are n elements in a set and r_1 are alike, r_2 are alike, r_3 are alike, and so on through r_k, the number of permutations can be found by

$$\frac{n!}{r_1!\, r_2! \dots r_k!}$$

Example 7   **Finding the Number of Permutations of *n* Non-Distinct Objects**

Find the number of rearrangements of the letters in the word DISTINCT.

Solution   There are 8 letters. Both I and T are repeated 2 times. Substitute $n = 8$, $r_1 = 2$, and $r_2 = 2$ into the formula.

$$\frac{8!}{2!2!} = 10{,}080$$

There are 10,080 arrangements.

Try It #10

Find the number of rearrangements of the letters in the word CARRIER.

Access these online resources for additional instruction and practice with combinations and permutations.

- Combinations (http://openstaxcollege.org/l/combinations)
- Permutations (http://openstaxcollege.org/l/permutations)

13.5 SECTION EXERCISES

VERBAL

For the following exercises, assume that there are n ways an event A can happen, m ways an event B can happen, and that A and B are non-overlapping.

1. Use the Addition Principle of counting to explain how many ways event A or B can occur.

2. Use the Multiplication Principle of counting to explain how many ways event A and B can occur.

Answer the following questions.

3. When given two separate events, how do we know whether to apply the Addition Principle or the Multiplication Principle when calculating possible outcomes? What conjunctions may help to determine which operations to use?

4. Describe how the permutation of n objects differs from the permutation of choosing r objects from a set of n objects. Include how each is calculated.

5. What is the term for the arrangement that selects r objects from a set of n objects when the order of the r objects is not important? What is the formula for calculating the number of possible outcomes for this type of arrangement?

NUMERIC

For the following exercises, determine whether to use the Addition Principle or the Multiplication Principle. Then perform the calculations.

6. Let the set $A = \{-5, -3, -1, 2, 3, 4, 5, 6\}$. How many ways are there to choose a negative or an even number from A?

7. Let the set $B = \{-23, -16, -7, -2, 20, 36, 48, 72\}$. How many ways are there to choose a positive or an odd number from A?

8. How many ways are there to pick a red ace or a club from a standard card playing deck?

9. How many ways are there to pick a paint color from 5 shades of green, 4 shades of blue, or 7 shades of yellow?

10. How many outcomes are possible from tossing a pair of coins?

11. How many outcomes are possible from tossing a coin and rolling a 6-sided die?

12. How many two-letter strings—the first letter from A and the second letter from B—can be formed from the sets $A = \{b, c, d\}$ and $B = \{a, e, i, o, u\}$?

13. How many ways are there to construct a string of 3 digits if numbers can be repeated?

14. How many ways are there to construct a string of 3 digits if numbers cannot be repeated?

For the following exercises, compute the value of the expression.

15. $P(5, 2)$ **16.** $P(8, 4)$ **17.** $P(3, 3)$ **18.** $P(9, 6)$ **19.** $P(11, 5)$

20. $C(8, 5)$ **21.** $C(12, 4)$ **22.** $C(26, 3)$ **23.** $C(7, 6)$ **24.** $C(10, 3)$

For the following exercises, find the number of subsets in each given set.

25. $\{1, 2, 3, 4, 5, 6, 7, 8, 9, 10\}$

26. $\{a, b, c, \ldots, z\}$

27. A set containing 5 distinct numbers, 4 distinct letters, and 3 distinct symbols

28. The set of even numbers from 2 to 28

29. The set of two-digit numbers between 1 and 100 containing the digit 0

For the following exercises, find the distinct number of arrangements.

30. The letters in the word "juggernaut"

31. The letters in the word "academia"

32. The letters in the word "academia" that begin and end in "a"

33. The symbols in the string #,#,#,@,@,$,$,$,%,%,%,%

34. The symbols in the string #,#,#,@,@,$,$,$,%,%,%,% that begin and end with "%"

EXTENSIONS

35. The set, *S* consists of 900,000,000 whole numbers, each being the same number of digits long. How many digits long is a number from *S*? (*Hint:* use the fact that a whole number cannot start with the digit 0.)

36. The number of 5-element subsets from a set containing *n* elements is equal to the number of 6-element subsets from the same set. What is the value of *n*? (Hint: the order in which the elements for the subsets are chosen is not important.)

37. Can $C(n, r)$ ever equal $P(n, r)$? Explain.

38. Suppose a set *A* has 2,048 subsets. How many distinct objects are contained in *A*?

39. How many arrangements can be made from the letters of the word "mountains" if all the vowels must form a string?

REAL-WORLD APPLICATIONS

40. A family consisting of 2 parents and 3 children is to pose for a picture with 2 family members in the front and 3 in the back.

   a. How many arrangements are possible with no restrictions?

   b. How many arrangements are possible if the parents must sit in the front?

   c. How many arrangements are possible if the parents must be next to each other?

41. A cell phone company offers 6 different voice packages and 8 different data packages. Of those, 3 packages include both voice and data. How many ways are there to choose either voice or data, but not both?

42. In horse racing, a "trifecta" occurs when a bettor wins by selecting the first three finishers in the exact order (1st place, 2nd place, and 3rd place). How many different trifectas are possible if there are 14 horses in a race?

43. A wholesale T-shirt company offers sizes small, medium, large, and extra-large in organic or non-organic cotton and colors white, black, gray, blue, and red. How many different T-shirts are there to choose from?

44. Hector wants to place billboard advertisements throughout the county for his new business. How many ways can Hector choose 15 neighborhoods to advertise in if there are 30 neighborhoods in the county?

45. An art store has 4 brands of paint pens in 12 different colors and 3 types of ink. How many paint pens are there to choose from?

46. How many ways can a committee of 3 freshmen and 4 juniors be formed from a group of 8 freshmen and 11 juniors?

47. How many ways can a baseball coach arrange the order of 9 batters if there are 15 players on the team?

48. A conductor needs 5 cellists and 5 violinists to play at a diplomatic event. To do this, he ranks the orchestra's 10 cellists and 16 violinists in order of musical proficiency. What is the ratio of the total cellist rankings possible to the total violinist rankings possible?

49. A motorcycle shop has 10 choppers, 6 bobbers, and 5 café racers—different types of vintage motorcycles. How many ways can the shop choose 3 choppers, 5 bobbers, and 2 café racers for a weekend showcase?

50. A skateboard shop stocks 10 types of board decks, 3 types of trucks, and 4 types of wheels. How many different skateboards can be constructed?

51. Just-For-Kicks Sneaker Company offers an online customizing service. How many ways are there to design a custom pair of Just-For-Kicks sneakers if a customer can choose from a basic shoe up to 11 customizable options?

52. A car wash offers the following optional services to the basic wash: clear coat wax, triple foam polish, undercarriage wash, rust inhibitor, wheel brightener, air freshener, and interior shampoo. How many washes are possible if any number of options can be added to the basic wash?

53. Susan bought 20 plants to arrange along the border of her garden. How many distinct arrangements can she make if the plants are comprised of 6 tulips, 6 roses, and 8 daisies?

54. How many unique ways can a string of Christmas lights be arranged from 9 red, 10 green, 6 white, and 12 gold color bulbs?

LEARNING OBJECTIVES

In this section, you will:

- Apply the Binomial Theorem.

13.6   BINOMIAL THEOREM

A polynomial with two terms is called a binomial. We have already learned to multiply binomials and to raise binomials to powers, but raising a binomial to a high power can be tedious and time-consuming. In this section, we will discuss a shortcut that will allow us to find $(x + y)^n$ without multiplying the binomial by itself n times.

Identifying Binomial Coefficients

In **Counting Principles**, we studied combinations. In the shortcut to finding $(x + y)^n$, we will need to use combinations to find the coefficients that will appear in the expansion of the binomial. In this case, we use the notation $\binom{n}{r}$ instead of $C(n, r)$, but it can be calculated in the same way. So

$$\binom{n}{r} = C(n, r) = \frac{n!}{r!(n-r)!}$$

The combination $\binom{n}{r}$ is called a **binomial coefficient**. An example of a binomial coefficient is $\binom{5}{2} = C(5, 2) = 10$.

---

binomial coefficients

If n and r are integers greater than or equal to 0 with $n \geq r$, then the **binomial coefficient** is

$$\binom{n}{r} = C(n, r) = \frac{n!}{r!(n-r)!}$$

Q & A...

Is a binomial coefficient always a whole number?

Yes. Just as the number of combinations must always be a whole number, a binomial coefficient will always be a whole number.

Example 1   **Finding Binomial Coefficients**

Find each binomial coefficient.

   a. $\binom{5}{3}$ b. $\binom{9}{2}$ c. $\binom{9}{7}$

Solution

Use the formula to calculate each binomial coefficient. You can also use the $_nC_r$ function on your calculator.

$$\binom{n}{r} = C(n, r) = \frac{n!}{r!(n-r)!}$$

   a. $\binom{5}{3} = \frac{5!}{3!(5-3)!} = \frac{5 \cdot 4 \cdot 3!}{3!2!} = 10$

   b. $\binom{9}{2} = \frac{9!}{2!(9-2)!} = \frac{9 \cdot 8 \cdot 7!}{2!7!} = 36$

   c. $\binom{9}{7} = \frac{9!}{7!(9-7)!} = \frac{9 \cdot 8 \cdot 7!}{7!2!} = 36$

Analysis   Notice that we obtained the same result for parts (b) and (c). If you look closely at the solution for these two parts, you will see that you end up with the same two factorials in the denominator, but the order is reversed, just as with combinations.

$$\binom{n}{r} = \binom{n}{n-r}$$

Try It #1

Find each binomial coefficient.

a. $\binom{7}{3}$ b. $\binom{11}{4}$

Using the Binomial Theorem

When we expand $(x + y)^n$ by multiplying, the result is called a **binomial expansion**, and it includes binomial coefficients. If we wanted to expand $(x + y)^{52}$, we might multiply $(x + y)$ by itself fifty-two times. This could take hours! If we examine some simple binomial expansions, we can find patterns that will lead us to a shortcut for finding more complicated binomial expansions.

$$(x + y)^2 = x^2 + 2xy + y^2$$
$$(x + y)^3 = x^3 + 3x^2y + 3xy^2 + y^3$$
$$(x + y)^4 = x^4 + 4x^3y + 6x^2y^2 + 4xy^3 + y^4$$

First, let's examine the exponents. With each successive term, the exponent for x decreases and the exponent for y increases. The sum of the two exponents is n for each term.

Next, let's examine the coefficients. Notice that the coefficients increase and then decrease in a symmetrical pattern. The coefficients follow a pattern:

$$\binom{n}{0}, \binom{n}{1}, \binom{n}{2}, ..., \binom{n}{n}.$$

These patterns lead us to the **Binomial Theorem**, which can be used to expand any binomial.

$$(x + y)^n = \sum_{k=0}^{n}\binom{n}{k}x^{n-k}y^k$$
$$= x^n + \binom{n}{1}x^{n-1}y + \binom{n}{2}x^{n-2}y^2 + ... + \binom{n}{n-1}xy^{n-1} + y^n$$

Another way to see the coefficients is to examine the expansion of a binomial in general form, $x + y$, to successive powers 1, 2, 3, and 4.

$$(x + y)^1 = x + y$$
$$(x + y)^2 = x^2 + 2xy + y^2$$
$$(x + y)^3 = x^3 + 3x^2y + 3xy^2 + y^3$$
$$(x + y)^4 = x^4 + 4x^3y + 6x^2y^2 + 4xy^3 + y^4$$

Can you guess the next expansion for the binomial $(x + y)^5$?

Pascal's Triangle

	Exponent	Pattern	# of Terms
$(x + y)^{①} = x + y$	1	$1 + 1$	2
$(x + y)^{②} = x^2 + 2xy + y^2$	2	$2 + 1$	3
$(x + y)^{③} = x^3 + 3x^2y + 3xy^2 + y^3$	3	$3 + 1$	4
$(x + y)^{④} = x^4 + 4x^3y + 6x^2y^2 + 4xy^3 + y^4$	4	$4 + 1$	5
	n	$n + 1$	$n + 1$

Exponent sum: $\overset{4+0}{xy}$ $\overset{3+1}{xy}$ $\overset{2+2}{xy}$ $\overset{1+3}{xy}$ $\overset{0+4}{xy}$
Exponents on x: 4   3   2   1   0
Exponents on y: 0   1   2   3   4

Figure 1

See **Figure 1**, which illustrates the following:
- There are $n + 1$ terms in the expansion of $(x + y)^n$.
- The degree (or sum of the exponents) for each term is n.
- The powers on x begin with n and decrease to 0.
- The powers on y begin with 0 and increase to n.
- The coefficients are symmetric.

To determine the expansion on $(x + y)^5$, we see $n = 5$, thus, there will be $5 + 1 = 6$ terms. Each term has a combined degree of 5. In descending order for powers of x, the pattern is as follows:
- Introduce x^5, and then for each successive term reduce the exponent on x by 1 until $x^0 = 1$ is reached.
- Introduce $y^0 = 1$, and then increase the exponent on y by 1 until y^5 is reached.

$$x^5, \, x^4y, \, x^3y^2, \, x^2y^3, \, xy^4, \, y^5$$

The next expansion would be

$$(x + y)^5 = x^5 + 5x^4y + 10x^3y^2 + 10x^2y^3 + 5xy^4 + y^5.$$

But where do those coefficients come from? The binomial coefficients are symmetric. We can see these coefficients in an array known as Pascal's Triangle, shown in **Figure 2**.

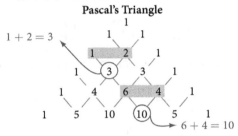

Figure 2

To generate Pascal's Triangle, we start by writing a 1. In the row below, row 2, we write two 1's. In the 3rd row, flank the ends of the rows with 1's, and add $1 + 1$ to find the middle number, 2. In the nth row, flank the ends of the row with 1's. Each element in the triangle is the sum of the two elements immediately above it.

To see the connection between Pascal's Triangle and binomial coefficients, let us revisit the expansion of the binomials in general form.

$$1 \longrightarrow (x + y)^0 = 1$$
$$1 \quad 1 \longrightarrow (x + y)^1 = x + y$$
$$1 \quad 2 \quad 1 \longrightarrow (x + y)^2 = x^2 + 2xy + y^2$$
$$1 \quad 3 \quad 3 \quad 1 \longrightarrow (x + y)^3 = x^3 + 3x^2y + 3xy^2 + y^3$$
$$1 \quad 4 \quad 6 \quad 4 \quad 1 \longrightarrow (x + y)^4 = x^4 + 4x^3y + 6x^2y^2 + 4xy^3 + y^4$$
$$1 \quad 5 \quad 10 \quad 10 \quad 5 \quad 1 \longrightarrow (x + y)^5 = x^5 + 5x^4y + 10x^3y^2 + 10x^2y^3 + 5xy^4 + y^5$$

the Binomial Theorem
The **Binomial Theorem** is a formula that can be used to expand any binomial.

$$(x + y)^n = \sum_{k=0}^{n} \binom{n}{k} x^{n-k}y^k$$

$$= x^n + \binom{n}{1}x^{n-1}y + \binom{n}{2}x^{n-2}y^2 + \dots + \binom{n}{n-1}xy^{n-1} + y^n$$

How To...

Given a binomial, write it in expanded form.

1. Determine the value of n according to the exponent.
2. Evaluate the $k = 0$ through $k = n$ using the Binomial Theorem formula.
3. Simplify.

Example 2 **Expanding a Binomial**

Write in expanded form.

    a. $(x + y)^5$

    b. $(3x - y)^4$

Solution

    a. Substitute $n = 5$ into the formula. Evaluate the $k = 0$ through $k = 5$ terms. Simplify.

$$(x + y)^5 = \binom{5}{0}x^5y^0 + \binom{5}{1}x^4y^1 + \binom{5}{2}x^3y^2 + \binom{5}{3}x^2y^3 + \binom{5}{4}x^1y^4 + \binom{5}{5}x^0y^5$$

$$(x + y)^5 = x^5 + 5x^4y + 10x^3y^2 + 10x^2y^3 + 5xy^4 + y^5$$

    b. Substitute $n = 4$ into the formula. Evaluate the $k = 0$ through $k = 4$ terms. Notice that $3x$ is in the place that was occupied by x and that $-y$ is in the place that was occupied by y. So we substitute them. Simplify.

$$(3x - y)^4 = \binom{4}{0}(3x)^4(-y)^0 + \binom{4}{1}(3x)^3(-y)^1 + \binom{4}{2}(3x)^2(-y)^2 + \binom{4}{3}(3x)^1(-y)^3 + \binom{4}{4}(3x)^0(-y)^4$$

$$(3x - y)^4 = 81x^4 - 108x^3y + 54x^2y^2 - 12xy^3 + y^4$$

Analysis *Notice the alternating signs in part b. This happens because* $(-y)$ *raised to odd powers is negative, but* $(-y)$ *raised to even powers is positive. This will occur whenever the binomial contains a subtraction sign.*

Try It #2

Write in expanded form.

a. $(x - y)^5$ **b.** $(2x + 5y)^3$

Using the Binomial Theorem to Find a Single Term

Expanding a binomial with a high exponent such as $(x + 2y)^{16}$ can be a lengthy process.

Sometimes we are interested only in a certain term of a binomial expansion. We do not need to fully expand a binomial to find a single specific term.

Note the pattern of coefficients in the expansion of $(x + y)^5$.

$$(x + y)^5 = x^5 + \binom{5}{1}x^4y + \binom{5}{2}x^3y^2 + \binom{5}{3}x^2y^3 + \binom{5}{4}xy^4 + y^5$$

The second term is $\binom{5}{1}x^4y$. The third term is $\binom{5}{2}x^3y^2$. We can generalize this result.

$$\binom{n}{r}x^{n-r}y^r$$

---

the $(r + 1)$th term of a binomial expansion

The $(r + 1)$th term of the binomial expansion of $(x + y)^n$ is:

$$\binom{n}{r}x^{n-r}y^r$$

How To...

Given a binomial, write a specific term without fully expanding.

1. Determine the value of n according to the exponent.
2. Determine $(r + 1)$.
3. Determine r.
4. Replace r in the formula for the $(r + 1)$th term of the binomial expansion.

Example 3   **Writing a Given Term of a Binomial Expansion**

Find the tenth term of $(x + 2y)^{16}$ without fully expanding the binomial.

Solution   Because we are looking for the tenth term, $r + 1 = 10$, we will use $r = 9$ in our calculations.

$$\binom{n}{r} x^{n-r} y^{r}$$

$$\binom{16}{9} x^{16-9} (2y)^{9} = 5{,}857{,}280 x^{7} y^{9}$$

Try It #3

Find the sixth term of $(3x - y)^{9}$ without fully expanding the binomial.

Access these online resources for additional instruction and practice with binomial expansion.

- The Binomial Theorem (http://openstaxcollege.org/l/binomialtheorem)
- Binomial Theorem Example (http://openstaxcollege.org/l/btexample)

13.6 SECTION EXERCISES

VERBAL

1. What is a binomial coefficient, and how it is calculated?

2. What role do binomial coefficients play in a binomial expansion? Are they restricted to any type of number?

3. What is the Binomial Theorem and what is its use?

4. When is it an advantage to use the Binomial Theorem? Explain.

ALGEBRAIC

For the following exercises, evaluate the binomial coefficient.

5. $\binom{6}{2}$

6. $\binom{5}{3}$

7. $\binom{7}{4}$

8. $\binom{9}{7}$

9. $\binom{10}{9}$

10. $\binom{25}{11}$

11. $\binom{17}{6}$

12. $\binom{200}{199}$

For the following exercises, use the Binomial Theorem to expand each binomial.

13. $(4a - b)^3$

14. $(5a + 2)^3$

15. $(3a + 2b)^3$

16. $(2x + 3y)^4$

17. $(4x + 2y)^5$

18. $(3x - 2y)^4$

19. $(4x - 3y)^5$

20. $\left(\frac{1}{x} + 3y\right)^5$

21. $(x^{-1} + 2y^{-1})^4$

22. $(\sqrt{x} - \sqrt{y})^5$

For the following exercises, use the Binomial Theorem to write the first three terms of each binomial.

23. $(a + b)^{17}$

24. $(x - 1)^{18}$

25. $(a - 2b)^{15}$

26. $(x - 2y)^8$

27. $(3a + b)^{20}$

28. $(2a + 4b)^7$

29. $(x^3 - \sqrt{y})^8$

For the following exercises, find the indicated term of each binomial without fully expanding the binomial.

30. The fourth term of $(2x - 3y)^4$

31. The fourth term of $(3x - 2y)^5$

32. The third term of $(6x - 3y)^7$

33. The eighth term of $(7 + 5y)^{14}$

34. The seventh term of $(a + b)^{11}$

35. The fifth term of $(x - y)^7$

36. The tenth term of $(x - 1)^{12}$

37. The ninth term of $(a - 3b^2)^{11}$

38. The fourth term of $\left(x^3 - \frac{1}{2}\right)^{10}$

39. The eighth term of $\left(\frac{y}{2} + \frac{2}{x}\right)^9$

GRAPHICAL

For the following exercises, use the Binomial Theorem to expand the binomial $f(x) = (x + 3)^4$. Then find and graph each indicated sum on one set of axes.

40. Find and graph $f_1(x)$, such that $f_1(x)$ is the first term of the expansion.

41. Find and graph $f_2(x)$, such that $f_2(x)$ is the sum of the first two terms of the expansion.

42. Find and graph $f_3(x)$, such that $f_3(x)$ is the sum of the first three terms of the expansion.

43. Find and graph $f_4(x)$, such that $f_4(x)$ is the sum of the first four terms of the expansion.

44. Find and graph $f_5(x)$, such that $f_5(x)$ is the sum of the first five terms of the expansion.

EXTENSIONS

45. In the expansion of $(5x + 3y)^n$, each term has the form $\binom{n}{k} a^{n-k} b^k$, where k successively takes on the value 0, 1, 2, ..., n. If $\binom{n}{k} = \binom{7}{2}$, what is the corresponding term?

46. In the expansion of $(a + b)^n$, the coefficient of $a^{n-k} b^k$ is the same as the coefficient of which other term?

47. Consider the expansion of $(x + b)^{40}$. What is the exponent of b in the kth term?

48. Find $\binom{n}{k-1} + \binom{n}{k}$ and write the answer as a binomial coefficient in the form $\binom{n}{k}$. Prove it. Hint: Use the fact that, for any integer p, such that $p \geq 1$, $p! = p(p-1)!$.

49. Which expression cannot be expanded using the Binomial Theorem? Explain.
  a. $(x^2 - 2x + 1)$
  b. $(\sqrt{a} + 4\sqrt{a} - 5)^8$
  c. $(x^3 + 2y^2 - z)^5$
  d. $(3x^2 - \sqrt{2y^3})^{12}$

LEARNING OBJECTIVES

In this section, you will:

- Construct probability models.
- Compute probabilities of equally likely outcomes.
- Compute probabilities of the union of two events.
- Use the complement rule to find probabilities.
- Compute probability using counting theory.

13.7 PROBABILITY

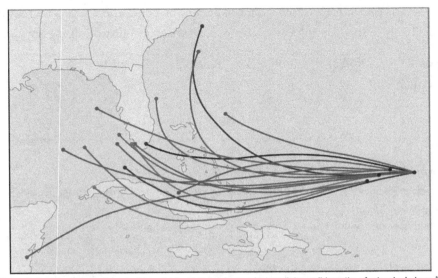

Figure 1 An example of a "spaghetti model," which can be used to predict possible paths of a tropical storm.[34]

Residents of the Southeastern United States are all too familiar with charts, known as spaghetti models, such as the one in **Figure 1**. They combine a collection of weather data to predict the most likely path of a hurricane. Each colored line represents one possible path. The group of squiggly lines can begin to resemble strands of spaghetti, hence the name. In this section, we will investigate methods for making these types of predictions.

Constructing Probability Models

Suppose we roll a six-sided number cube. Rolling a number cube is an example of an **experiment**, or an activity with an observable result. The numbers on the cube are possible results, or **outcomes**, of this experiment. The set of all possible outcomes of an experiment is called the **sample space** of the experiment. The sample space for this experiment is {1, 2, 3, 4, 5, 6}. An **event** is any subset of a sample space.

The likelihood of an event is known as **probability**. The probability of an event p is a number that always satisfies $0 \leq p \leq 1$, where 0 indicates an impossible event and 1 indicates a certain event. A **probability model** is a mathematical description of an experiment listing all possible outcomes and their associated probabilities. For instance, if there is a 1% chance of winning a raffle and a 99% chance of losing the raffle, a probability model would look much like **Table 1**.

Outcome	Probability
Winning the raffle	1%
Losing the raffle	99%

Table 1

The sum of the probabilities listed in a probability model must equal 1, or 100%.

34 The figure is for illustrative purposes only and does not model any particular storm.

How To...

Given a probability event where each event is equally likely, construct a probability model.

1. Identify every outcome.
2. Determine the total number of possible outcomes.
3. Compare each outcome to the total number of possible outcomes.

Example 1   **Constructing a Probability Model**

Construct a probability model for rolling a single, fair die, with the event being the number shown on the die.

Solution   Begin by making a list of all possible outcomes for the experiment. The possible outcomes are the numbers that can be rolled: 1, 2, 3, 4, 5, and 6. There are six possible outcomes that make up the sample space.

Assign probabilities to each outcome in the sample space by determining a ratio of the outcome to the number of possible outcomes. There is one of each of the six numbers on the cube, and there is no reason to think that any particular face is more likely to show up than any other one, so the probability of rolling any number is $\frac{1}{6}$.

Outcome	Roll of 1	Roll of 2	Roll of 3	Roll of 4	Roll of 5	Roll of 6
Probability	$\frac{1}{6}$	$\frac{1}{6}$	$\frac{1}{6}$	$\frac{1}{6}$	$\frac{1}{6}$	$\frac{1}{6}$

Table 2

Q & A...

Do probabilities always have to be expressed as fractions?

No. Probabilities can be expressed as fractions, decimals, or percents. Probability must always be a number between 0 and 1, inclusive of 0 and 1.

Try It #1

Construct a probability model for tossing a fair coin.

Computing Probabilities of Equally Likely Outcomes

Let S be a sample space for an experiment. When investigating probability, an event is any subset of S. When the outcomes of an experiment are all equally likely, we can find the probability of an event by dividing the number of outcomes in the event by the total number of outcomes in S. Suppose a number cube is rolled, and we are interested in finding the probability of the event "rolling a number less than or equal to 4." There are 4 possible outcomes in the event and 6 possible outcomes in S, so the probability of the event is $\frac{4}{6} = \frac{2}{3}$.

computing the probability of an event with equally likely outcomes

The probability of an event E in an experiment with sample space S with equally likely outcomes is given by

$$P(E) = \frac{\text{number of elements in } E}{\text{number of elements in } S} = \frac{n(E)}{n(S)}$$

E is a subset of S, so it is always true that $0 \leq P(E) \leq 1$.

Example 2   **Computing the Probability of an Event with Equally Likely Outcomes**

A six-sided number cube is rolled. Find the probability of rolling an odd number.

Solution   The event "rolling an odd number" contains three outcomes. There are 6 equally likely outcomes in the sample space. Divide to find the probability of the event.

$$P(E) = \frac{3}{6} = \frac{1}{2}$$

Try It #2

A six-sided number cube is rolled. Find the probability of rolling a number greater than 2.

Computing the Probability of the Union of Two Events

We are often interested in finding the probability that one of multiple events occurs. Suppose we are playing a card game, and we will win if the next card drawn is either a heart or a king. We would be interested in finding the probability of the next card being a heart or a king. The **union of two events** E and F, written $E \cup F$, is the event that occurs if either or both events occur.

$$P(E \cup F) = P(E) + P(F) - P(E \cap F)$$

Suppose the spinner in **Figure 2** is spun. We want to find the probability of spinning orange or spinning a b.

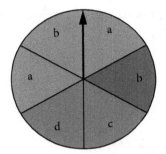

Figure 2

There are a total of 6 sections, and 3 of them are orange. So the probability of spinning orange is $\frac{3}{6} = \frac{1}{2}$. There are a total of 6 sections, and 2 of them have a b. So the probability of spinning a b is $\frac{2}{6} = \frac{1}{3}$. If we added these two probabilities, we would be counting the sector that is both orange and a b twice. To find the probability of spinning an orange or a b, we need to subtract the probability that the sector is both orange and has a b.

$$\frac{1}{2} + \frac{1}{3} - \frac{1}{6} = \frac{2}{3}$$

The probability of spinning orange or a b is $\frac{2}{3}$.

> ***probability of the union of two events***
>
> The probability of the union of two events E and F (written $E \cup F$) equals the sum of the probability of E and the probability of F minus the probability of E and F occurring together (which is called the intersection of E and F and is written as $E \cap F$).
>
> $$P(E \cup F) = P(E) + P(F) - P(E \cap F)$$

Example 3   **Computing the Probability of the Union of Two Events**

A card is drawn from a standard deck. Find the probability of drawing a heart or a 7.

Solution   A standard deck contains an equal number of hearts, diamonds, clubs, and spades. So the probability of drawing a heart is $\frac{1}{4}$. There are four 7s in a standard deck, and there are a total of 52 cards. So the probability of drawing a 7 is $\frac{1}{13}$.

The only card in the deck that is both a heart and a 7 is the 7 of hearts, so the probability of drawing both a heart and a 7 is $\frac{1}{52}$. Substitute $P(H) = \frac{1}{4}$, $P(7) = \frac{1}{13}$, and $P(H \cap 7) = \frac{1}{52}$ into the formula.

$$P(E \cup F) = P(E) + P(F) - P(E \cap F)$$

$$= \frac{1}{4} + \frac{1}{13} - \frac{1}{52}$$

$$= \frac{4}{13}$$

The probability of drawing a heart or a 7 is $\frac{4}{13}$.

Try It #3

A card is drawn from a standard deck. Find the probability of drawing a red card or an ace.

Computing the Probability of Mutually Exclusive Events

Suppose the spinner in **Figure 2** is spun again, but this time we are interested in the probability of spinning an orange or a *d*. There are no sectors that are both orange and contain a *d*, so these two events have no outcomes in common. Events are said to be **mutually exclusive events** when they have no outcomes in common. Because there is no overlap, there is nothing to subtract, so the general formula is

$$P(E \cup F) = P(E) + P(F)$$

Notice that with mutually exclusive events, the intersection of *E* and *F* is the empty set. The probability of spinning an orange is $\frac{3}{6} = \frac{1}{2}$ and the probability of spinning a *d* is $\frac{1}{6}$. We can find the probability of spinning an orange or a *d* simply by adding the two probabilities.

$$P(E \cup F) = P(E) + P(F)$$
$$= \frac{1}{2} + \frac{1}{6}$$
$$= \frac{2}{3}$$

The probability of spinning an orange or a *d* is $\frac{2}{3}$.

---

probability of the union of mutually exclusive events

The probability of the union of two mutually exclusive events *E* and *F* is given by

$$P(E \cup F) = P(E) + P(F)$$

How To...

Given a set of events, compute the probability of the union of mutually exclusive events.

1. Determine the total number of outcomes for the first event.
2. Find the probability of the first event.
3. Determine the total number of outcomes for the second event.
4. Find the probability of the second event.
5. Add the probabilities.

Example 4   **Computing the Probability of the Union of Mutually Exclusive Events**

A card is drawn from a standard deck. Find the probability of drawing a heart or a spade.

Solution   The events "drawing a heart" and "drawing a spade" are mutually exclusive because they cannot occur at the same time. The probability of drawing a heart is $\frac{1}{4}$, and the probability of drawing a spade is also $\frac{1}{4}$, so the probability of drawing a heart or a spade is

$$\frac{1}{4} + \frac{1}{4} = \frac{1}{2}$$

Try It #4

A card is drawn from a standard deck. Find the probability of drawing an ace or a king. Using the

Complement Rule to Compute Probabilities

We have discussed how to calculate the probability that an event will happen. Sometimes, we are interested in finding the probability that an event will not happen. The **complement of an event** E, denoted E', is the set of outcomes in the sample space that are not in E. For example, suppose we are interested in the probability that a horse will lose a race. If event W is the horse winning the race, then the complement of event W is the horse losing the race.

To find the probability that the horse loses the race, we need to use the fact that the sum of all probabilities in a probability model must be 1.

$$P(E') = 1 - P(E)$$

The probability of the horse winning added to the probability of the horse losing must be equal to 1. Therefore, if the probability of the horse winning the race is $\frac{1}{9}$, the probability of the horse losing the race is simply

$$1 - \frac{1}{9} = \frac{8}{9}$$

---

the complement rule

The probability that the **complement of an event** will occur is given by

$$P(E') = 1 - P(E)$$

Example 5   **Using the Complement Rule to Calculate Probabilities**

Two six-sided number cubes are rolled.

   a. Find the probability that the sum of the numbers rolled is less than or equal to 3.

   b. Find the probability that the sum of the numbers rolled is greater than 3.

Solution   The first step is to identify the sample space, which consists of all the possible outcomes. There are two number cubes, and each number cube has six possible outcomes. Using the Multiplication Principle, we find that there are 6×6, or 36 total possible outcomes. So, for example, 1-1 represents a 1 rolled on each number cube.

1-1	1-2	1-3	1-4	1-5	1-6
2-1	2-2	2-3	2-4	2-5	2-6
3-1	3-2	3-3	3-4	3-5	3-6
4-1	4-2	4-3	4-4	4-5	4-6
5-1	5-2	5-3	5-4	5-5	5-6
6-1	6-2	6-3	6-4	6-5	6-6

Table 3

   a. We need to count the number of ways to roll a sum of 3 or less. These would include the following outcomes: 1-1, 1-2, and 2-1. So there are only three ways to roll a sum of 3 or less. The probability is

$$\frac{3}{36} = \frac{1}{12}$$

   b. Rather than listing all the possibilities, we can use the Complement Rule. Because we have already found the probability of the complement of this event, we can simply subtract that probability from 1 to find the probability that the sum of the numbers rolled is greater than 3.

$$P(E') = 1 - P(E)$$
$$= 1 - \frac{1}{12}$$
$$= \frac{11}{12}$$

Try It #5

Two number cubes are rolled. Use the Complement Rule to find the probability that the sum is less than 10.

Computing Probability Using Counting Theory

Many interesting probability problems involve counting principles, permutations, and combinations. In these problems, we will use permutations and combinations to find the number of elements in events and sample spaces. These problems can be complicated, but they can be made easier by breaking them down into smaller counting problems.

Assume, for example, that a store has 8 cellular phones and that 3 of those are defective. We might want to find the probability that a couple purchasing 2 phones receives 2 phones that are not defective. To solve this problem, we need to calculate all of the ways to select 2 phones that are not defective as well as all of the ways to select 2 phones. There are 5 phones that are not defective, so there are $C(5, 2)$ ways to select 2 phones that are not defective. There are 8 phones, so there are $C(8, 2)$ ways to select 2 phones. The probability of selecting 2 phones that are not defective is:

$$\frac{\text{ways to select 2 phones that are not defective}}{\text{ways to select 2 phones}} = \frac{C(5, 2)}{C(8, 2)}$$

$$= \frac{10}{28}$$

$$= \frac{5}{14}$$

Example 6   Computing Probability Using Counting Theory

A child randomly selects 5 toys from a bin containing 3 bunnies, 5 dogs, and 6 bears.

    a. Find the probability that only bears are chosen.

    b. Find the probability that 2 bears and 3 dogs are chosen.

    c. Find the probability that at least 2 dogs are chosen.

Solution

    a. We need to count the number of ways to choose only bears and the total number of possible ways to select 5 toys. There are 6 bears, so there are $C(6, 5)$ ways to choose 5 bears. There are 14 toys, so there are $C(14, 5)$ ways to choose any 5 toys.

$$\frac{C(6, 5)}{C(14, 5)} = \frac{6}{2{,}002} = \frac{3}{1{,}001}$$

    b. We need to count the number of ways to choose 2 bears and 3 dogs and the total number of possible ways to select 5 toys. There are 6 bears, so there are $C(6, 2)$ ways to choose 2 bears. There are 5 dogs, so there are $C(5, 3)$ ways to choose 3 dogs. Since we are choosing both bears and dogs at the same time, we will use the Multiplication Principle. There are $C(6, 2) \cdot C(5, 3)$ ways to choose 2 bears and 3 dogs. We can use this result to find the probability.

$$\frac{C(6, 2)C(5, 3)}{C(14, 5)} = \frac{15 \cdot 10}{2{,}002} = \frac{75}{1{,}001}$$

    c. It is often easiest to solve "at least" problems using the Complement Rule. We will begin by finding the probability that fewer than 2 dogs are chosen. If less than 2 dogs are chosen, then either no dogs could be chosen, or 1 dog could be chosen.

    When no dogs are chosen, all 5 toys come from the 9 toys that are not dogs. There are $C(9, 5)$ ways to choose toys from the 9 toys that are not dogs. Since there are 14 toys, there are $C(14, 5)$ ways to choose the 5 toys from all of the toys.

$$\frac{C(9, 5)}{C(14, 5)} = \frac{63}{1{,}001}$$

    If there is 1 dog chosen, then 4 toys must come from the 9 toys that are not dogs, and 1 must come from the 5 dogs. Since we are choosing both dogs and other toys at the same time, we will use the Multiplication Principle. There are $C(5, 1) \cdot C(9, 4)$ ways to choose 1 dog and 1 other toy.

$$\frac{C(5, 1)C(9, 4)}{C(14, 5)} = \frac{5 \cdot 126}{2{,}002} = \frac{315}{1{,}001}$$

Because these events would not occur together and are therefore mutually exclusive, we add the probabilities to find the probability that fewer than 2 dogs are chosen.

$$\frac{63}{1,001} + \frac{315}{1,001} = \frac{378}{1,001}$$

We then subtract that probability from 1 to find the probability that at least 2 dogs are chosen.

$$1 - \frac{378}{1,001} = \frac{623}{1,001}$$

Try It #6

A child randomly selects 3 gumballs from a container holding 4 purple gumballs, 8 yellow gumballs, and 2 green gumballs.

a. Find the probability that all 3 gumballs selected are purple.

b. Find the probability that no yellow gumballs are selected.

c. Find the probability that at least 1 yellow gumball is selected.

Access these online resources for additional instruction and practice with probability.

- Introduction to Probability (http://openstaxcollege.org/l/introprob)
- Determining Probability (http://openstaxcollege.org/l/determineprob)

13.7 SECTION EXERCISES

VERBAL

1. What term is used to express the likelihood of an event occurring? Are there restrictions on its values? If so, what are they? If not, explain.

2. What is a sample space?

3. What is an experiment?

4. What is the difference between events and outcomes? Give an example of both using the sample space of tossing a coin 50 times.

5. The *union of two sets* is defined as a set of elements that are present in at least one of the sets. How is this similar to the definition used for the *union of two events* from a probability model? How is it different?

NUMERIC

For the following exercises, use the spinner shown in **Figure 3** to find the probabilities indicated.

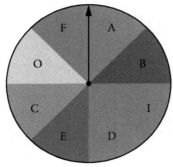

Figure 3

6. Landing on red

7. Landing on a vowel

8. Not landing on blue

9. Landing on purple or a vowel

10. Landing on blue or a vowel

11. Landing on green or blue

12. Landing on yellow or a consonant

13. Not landing on yellow or a consonant

For the following exercises, two coins are tossed.

14. What is the sample space?

15. Find the probability of tossing two heads.

16. Find the probability of tossing exactly one tail.

17. Find the probability of tossing at least one tail.

For the following exercises, four coins are tossed.

18. What is the sample space?

19. Find the probability of tossing exactly two heads.

20. Find the probability of tossing exactly three heads.

21. Find the probability of tossing four heads or four tails.

22. Find the probability of tossing all tails.

23. Find the probability of tossing not all tails.

24. Find the probability of tossing exactly two heads or at least two tails.

25. Find the probability of tossing either two heads or three heads.

For the following exercises, one card is drawn from a standard deck of 52 cards. Find the probability of drawing the following:

26. A club

27. A two

28. Six or seven

29. Red six

30. An ace or a diamond

31. A non-ace

32. A heart or a non-jack

For the following exercises, two dice are rolled, and the results are summed.

33. Construct a table showing the sample space of outcomes and sums.

34. Find the probability of rolling a sum of 3.

35. Find the probability of rolling at least one four or a sum of 8.

36. Find the probability of rolling an odd sum less than 9.

37. Find the probability of rolling a sum greater than or equal to 15.

38. Find the probability of rolling a sum less than 15.

39. Find the probability of rolling a sum less than 6 or greater than 9.

40. Find the probability of rolling a sum between 6 and 9, inclusive.

41. Find the probability of rolling a sum of 5 or 6.

42. Find the probability of rolling any sum other than 5 or 6.

For the following exercises, a coin is tossed, and a card is pulled from a standard deck. Find the probability of the following:

43. A head on the coin or a club

44. A tail on the coin or red ace

45. A head on the coin or a face card

46. No aces

For the following exercises, use this scenario: a bag of M&Ms contains 12 blue, 6 brown, 10 orange, 8 yellow, 8 red, and 4 green M&Ms. Reaching into the bag, a person grabs 5 M&Ms.

47. What is the probability of getting all blue M&Ms?

48. What is the probability of getting 4 blue M&Ms?

49. What is the probability of getting 3 blue M&Ms?

50. What is the probability of getting no brown M&Ms?

EXTENSIONS

Use the following scenario for the exercises that follow: In the game of Keno, a player starts by selecting 20 numbers from the numbers 1 to 80. After the player makes his selections, 20 winning numbers are randomly selected from numbers 1 to 80. A win occurs if the player has correctly selected 3, 4, or 5 of the 20 winning numbers. (Round all answers to the nearest hundredth of a percent.)

51. What is the percent chance that a player selects exactly 3 winning numbers?

52. What is the percent chance that a player selects exactly 4 winning numbers?

53. What is the percent chance that a player selects all 5 winning numbers?

54. What is the percent chance of winning?

55. How much less is a player's chance of selecting 3 winning numbers than the chance of selecting either 4 or 5 winning numbers?

REAL-WORLD APPLICATIONS

Use this data for the exercises that follow: In 2013, there were roughly 317 million citizens in the United States, and about 40 million were elderly (aged 65 and over).[35]

56. If you meet a U.S. citizen, what is the percent chance that the person is elderly? (Round to the nearest tenth of a percent.)

57. If you meet five U.S. citizens, what is the percent chance that exactly one is elderly? (Round to the nearest tenth of a percent.)

58. If you meet five U.S. citizens, what is the percent chance that three are elderly? (Round to the nearest tenth of a percent.)

59. If you meet five U.S. citizens, what is the percent chance that four are elderly? (Round to the nearest thousandth of a percent.)

60. It is predicted that by 2030, one in five U.S. citizens will be elderly. How much greater will the chances of meeting an elderly person be at that time? What policy changes do you foresee if these statistics hold true?

35 United States Census Bureau. http://www.census.gov

CHAPTER 13 REVIEW

Key Terms

Addition Principle if one event can occur in m ways and a second event with no common outcomes can occur in n ways, then the first or second event can occur in $m + n$ ways

annuity an investment in which the purchaser makes a sequence of periodic, equal payments

arithmetic sequence a sequence in which the difference between any two consecutive terms is a constant

arithmetic series the sum of the terms in an arithmetic sequence

binomial coefficient the number of ways to choose r objects from n objects where order does not matter; equivalent to $C(n, r)$, denoted $\binom{n}{r}$

binomial expansion the result of expanding $(x + y)^n$ by multiplying

Binomial Theorem a formula that can be used to expand any binomial

combination a selection of objects in which order does not matter

common difference the difference between any two consecutive terms in an arithmetic sequence

common ratio the ratio between any two consecutive terms in a geometric sequence

complement of an event the set of outcomes in the sample space that are not in the event E

diverge a series is said to diverge if the sum is not a real number

event any subset of a sample space

experiment an activity with an observable result

explicit formula a formula that defines each term of a sequence in terms of its position in the sequence

finite sequence a function whose domain consists of a finite subset of the positive integers $\{1, 2, \dots n\}$ for some positive integer n

Fundamental Counting Principle if one event can occur in m ways and a second event can occur in n ways after the first event has occurred, then the two events can occur in $m \times n$ ways; also known as the Multiplication Principle

geometric sequence a sequence in which the ratio of a term to a previous term is a constant

geometric series the sum of the terms in a geometric sequence

index of summation in summation notation, the variable used in the explicit formula for the terms of a series and written below the sigma with the lower limit of summation

infinite sequence a function whose domain is the set of positive integers

infinite series the sum of the terms in an infinite sequence

lower limit of summation the number used in the explicit formula to find the first term in a series

Multiplication Principle if one event can occur in m ways and a second event can occur in n ways after the first event has occurred, then the two events can occur in $m \times n$ ways; also known as the Fundamental Counting Principle

mutually exclusive events events that have no outcomes in common

n factorial the product of all the positive integers from 1 to n

nth partial sum the sum of the first n terms of a sequence

nth term of a sequence a formula for the general term of a sequence

outcomes the possible results of an experiment

permutation a selection of objects in which order matters

probability a number from 0 to 1 indicating the likelihood of an event

probability model a mathematical description of an experiment listing all possible outcomes and their associated probabilities

recursive formula a formula that defines each term of a sequence using previous term(s)

sample space the set of all possible outcomes of an experiment

sequence a function whose domain is a subset of the positive integers

series the sum of the terms in a sequence

summation notation a notation for series using the Greek letter sigma; it includes an explicit formula and specifies the first and last terms in the series

term a number in a sequence

union of two events the event that occurs if either or both events occur

upper limit of summation the number used in the explicit formula to find the last term in a series

Key Equations

Formula for a factorial	$0! = 1$ $1! = 1$ $n! = n(n-1)(n-2) \cdots (2)(1)$, for $n \geq 2$
recursive formula for nth term of an arithmetic sequence	$a_n = a_{n-1} + d; n \geq 2$
explicit formula for nth term of an arithmetic sequence	$a_n = a_1 + d(n-1)$
recursive formula for nth term of a geometric sequence	$a_n = ra_{n-1}, n \geq 2$
explicit formula for nth term of a geometric sequence	$a_n = a_1 r^{n-1}$
sum of the first n terms of an arithmetic series	$S_n = \dfrac{n(a_1 + a_n)}{2}$
sum of the first n terms of a geometric series	$S_n = \dfrac{a_1(1 - r^n)}{1 - r}, r \neq 1$
sum of an infinite geometric series with $-1 < r < 1$	$S_n = \dfrac{a_1}{1 - r}, r \neq 1$
number of permutations of n distinct objects taken r at a time	$P(n, r) = \dfrac{n!}{(n-r)!}$
number of combinations of n distinct objects taken r at a time	$C(n, r) = \dfrac{n!}{r!(n-r)!}$
number of permutations of n non-distinct objects	$\dfrac{n!}{r_1! r_2! \dots r_k!}$
Binomial Theorem	$(x+y)^n = \displaystyle\sum_{k-0}^{n} \binom{n}{k} x^{n-k} y^k$
$(r+1)^{\text{th}}$ term of a binomial expansion	$\binom{n}{r} x^{n-r} y^r$
probability of an event with equally likely outcomes	$P(E) = \dfrac{n(E)}{n(S)}$
probability of the union of two events	$P(E \cup F) = P(E) + P(F) - P(E \cap F)$
probability of the union of mutually exclusive events	$P(E \cup F) = P(E) + P(F)$
probability of the complement of an event	$P(E') = 1 - P(E)$

Key Concepts

13.1 Sequences and Their Notations

- A sequence is a list of numbers, called terms, written in a specific order.
- Explicit formulas define each term of a sequence using the position of the term. See **Example 1**, **Example 2**, and **Example 3**.
- An explicit formula for the nth term of a sequence can be written by analyzing the pattern of several terms. See **Example 4**.
- Recursive formulas define each term of a sequence using previous terms.
- Recursive formulas must state the initial term, or terms, of a sequence.
- A set of terms can be written by using a recursive formula. See **Example 5** and **Example 6**.
- A factorial is a mathematical operation that can be defined recursively.
- The factorial of n is the product of all integers from 1 to n See **Example 7**.

13.2 Arithmetic Sequences

- An arithmetic sequence is a sequence where the difference between any two consecutive terms is a constant.
- The constant between two consecutive terms is called the common difference.
- The common difference is the number added to any one term of an arithmetic sequence that generates the subsequent term. See **Example 1**.
- The terms of an arithmetic sequence can be found by beginning with the initial term and adding the common difference repeatedly. See **Example 2** and **Example 3**.
- A recursive formula for an arithmetic sequence with common difference d is given by $a_n = a_{n-1} + d$, $n \geq 2$. See **Example 4**.
- As with any recursive formula, the initial term of the sequence must be given.
- An explicit formula for an arithmetic sequence with common difference d is given by $a_n = a_1 + d(n-1)$. See **Example 5**.
- An explicit formula can be used to find the number of terms in a sequence. See **Example 6**.
- In application problems, we sometimes alter the explicit formula slightly to $a_n = a_0 + dn$. See **Example 7**.

13.3 Geometric Sequences

- A geometric sequence is a sequence in which the ratio between any two consecutive terms is a constant.
- The constant ratio between two consecutive terms is called the common ratio.
- The common ratio can be found by dividing any term in the sequence by the previous term. See **Example 1**.
- The terms of a geometric sequence can be found by beginning with the first term and multiplying by the common ratio repeatedly. See **Example 2** and **Example 4**.
- A recursive formula for a geometric sequence with common ratio r is given by $a_n = ra_{n-1}$ for $n \geq 2$.
- As with any recursive formula, the initial term of the sequence must be given. See **Example 3**.
- An explicit formula for a geometric sequence with common ratio r is given by $a_n = a_1 r^{n-1}$. See **Example 5**.
- In application problems, we sometimes alter the explicit formula slightly to $a_n = a_0 r^n$. See **Example 6**.

13.4 Series and Their Notations

- The sum of the terms in a sequence is called a series.
- A common notation for series is called summation notation, which uses the Greek letter sigma to represent the sum. See **Example 1**.
- The sum of the terms in an arithmetic sequence is called an arithmetic series.
- The sum of the first n terms of an arithmetic series can be found using a formula. See **Example 2** and **Example 3**.
- The sum of the terms in a geometric sequence is called a geometric series.
- The sum of the first n terms of a geometric series can be found using a formula. See **Example 4** and **Example 5**.
- The sum of an infinite series exists if the series is geometric with $-1 < r < 1$.

- If the sum of an infinite series exists, it can be found using a formula. See **Example 6**, **Example 7**, and **Example 8**.

- An annuity is an account into which the investor makes a series of regularly scheduled payments. The value of an annuity can be found using geometric series. See **Example 9**.

13.5 Counting Principles

- If one event can occur in m ways and a second event with no common outcomes can occur in n ways, then the first or second event can occur in $m + n$ ways. See **Example 1**.

- If one event can occur in m ways and a second event can occur in n ways after the first event has occurred, then the two events can occur in $m \times n$ ways. See **Example 2**.

- A permutation is an ordering of n objects.

- If we have a set of n objects and we want to choose r objects from the set in order, we write $P(n, r)$.

- Permutation problems can be solved using the Multiplication Principle or the formula for $P(n, r)$. See **Example 3** and **Example 4**.

- A selection of objects where the order does not matter is a combination.

- Given n distinct objects, the number of ways to select r objects from the set is $C(n, r)$ and can be found using a formula. See **Example 5**.

- A set containing n distinct objects has 2^n subsets. See **Example 6**.

- For counting problems involving non-distinct objects, we need to divide to avoid counting duplicate permutations. See **Example 7**.

13.6 Binomial Theorem

- $\binom{n}{r}$ is called a binomial coefficient and is equal to $C(n, r)$. See **Example 1**.

- The Binomial Theorem allows us to expand binomials without multiplying. See **Example 2**.

- We can find a given term of a binomial expansion without fully expanding the binomial. See **Example 3**.

13.7 Probability

- Probability is always a number between 0 and 1, where 0 means an event is impossible and 1 means an event is certain.

- The probabilities in a probability model must sum to 1. See **Example 1**.

- When the outcomes of an experiment are all equally likely, we can find the probability of an event by dividing the number of outcomes in the event by the total number of outcomes in the sample space for the experiment. See **Example 2**.

- To find the probability of the union of two events, we add the probabilities of the two events and subtract the probability that both events occur simultaneously. See **Example 3**.

- To find the probability of the union of two mutually exclusive events, we add the probabilities of each of the events. See **Example 4**.

- The probability of the complement of an event is the difference between 1 and the probability that the event occurs. See **Example 5**.

- In some probability problems, we need to use permutations and combinations to find the number of elements in events and sample spaces. See **Example 6**.

CHAPTER 13 REVIEW EXERCISES

SEQUENCES AND THEIR NOTATION

1. Write the first four terms of the sequence defined by the recursive formula $a_1 = 2$, $a_n = a_{n-1} + n$.

2. Evaluate $\dfrac{6!}{(5-3)!3!}$.

3. Write the first four terms of the sequence defined by the explicit formula $a_n = 10^n + 3$.

4. Write the first four terms of the sequence defined by the explicit formula $a_n = \dfrac{n!}{n(n+1)}$.

ARITHMETIC SEQUENCES

5. Is the sequence $\dfrac{4}{7}, \dfrac{47}{21}, \dfrac{82}{21}, \dfrac{39}{7}, \dots$ arithmetic? If so, find the common difference.

6. Is the sequence 2, 4, 8, 16, ... arithmetic? If so, find the common difference.

7. An arithmetic sequence has the first term $a_1 = 18$ and common difference $d = -8$. What are the first five terms?

8. An arithmetic sequence has terms $a_3 = 11.7$ and $a_8 = -14.6$. What is the first term?

9. Write a recursive formula for the arithmetic sequence $-20, -10, 0, 10, \dots$

10. Write a recursive formula for the arithmetic sequence $0, -\dfrac{1}{2}, -1, -\dfrac{3}{2}, \dots$, and then find the 31st term.

11. Write an explicit formula for the arithmetic sequence $\dfrac{7}{8}, \dfrac{29}{24}, \dfrac{37}{24}, \dfrac{15}{8}, \dots$

12. How many terms are in the finite arithmetic sequence 12, 20, 28, ... , 172?

GEOMETRIC SEQUENCES

13. Find the common ratio for the geometric sequence 2.5, 5, 10, 20, ...

14. Is the sequence 4, 16, 28, 40, ... geometric? If so find the common ratio. If not, explain why.

15. A geometric sequence has terms $a_7 = 16{,}384$ and $a_9 = 262{,}144$. What are the first five terms?

16. A geometric sequence has the first term $a_1 = -3$ and common ratio $r = \dfrac{1}{2}$. What is the 8th term?

17. What are the first five terms of the geometric sequence $a_1 = 3$, $a_n = 4 \cdot a_{n-1}$?

18. Write a recursive formula for the geometric sequence $1, \dfrac{1}{3}, \dfrac{1}{9}, \dfrac{1}{27}, \dots$

19. Write an explicit formula for the geometric sequence $-\dfrac{1}{5}, -\dfrac{1}{15}, -\dfrac{1}{45}, -\dfrac{1}{135}, \dots$

20. How many terms are in the finite geometric sequence $-5, -\dfrac{5}{3}, -\dfrac{5}{9}, \dots, -\dfrac{5}{59{,}049}$?

SERIES AND THEIR NOTATION

21. Use summation notation to write the sum of terms $\dfrac{1}{2}m + 5$ from $m = 0$ to $m = 5$.

22. Use summation notation to write the sum that results from adding the number 13 twenty times.

23. Use the formula for the sum of the first n terms of an arithmetic series to find the sum of the first eleven terms of the arithmetic series 2.5, 4, 5.5, ...

24. A ladder has 15 tapered rungs, the lengths of which increase by a common difference. The first rung is 5 inches long, and the last rung is 20 inches long. What is the sum of the lengths of the rungs?

25. Use the formula for the sum of the first n terms of a geometric series to find S_9 for the series $12, 6, 3, \frac{3}{2}, \ldots$

26. The fees for the first three years of a hunting club membership are given in **Table 1**. If fees continue to rise at the same rate, how much will the total cost be for the first ten years of membership?

Year	Membership Fees
1	$1500
2	$1950
3	$2535

Table 1

27. Find the sum of the infinite geometric series $\sum_{k-1}^{\infty} 45 \cdot \left(-\frac{1}{3}\right)^{k=1}$.

28. A ball has a bounce-back ratio $\frac{3}{5}$ of the height of the previous bounce. Write a series representing the total distance traveled by the ball, assuming it was initially dropped from a height of 5 feet. What is the total distance? (Hint: the total distance the ball travels on each bounce is the sum of the heights of the rise and the fall.)

29. Alejandro deposits $80 of his monthly earnings into an annuity that earns 6.25% annual interest, compounded monthly. How much money will he have saved after 5 years?

30. The twins Sarah and Scott both opened retirement accounts on their 21st birthday. Sarah deposits $4,800.00 each year, earning 5.5% annual interest, compounded monthly. Scott deposits $3,600.00 each year, earning 8.5% annual interest, compounded monthly. Which twin will earn the most interest by the time they are 55 years old? How much more?

COUNTING PRINCIPLES

31. How many ways are there to choose a number from the set $\{-10, -6, 4, 10, 12, 18, 24, 32\}$ that is divisible by either 4 or 6?

32. In a group of 20 musicians, 12 play piano, 7 play trumpet, and 2 play both piano and trumpet. How many musicians play either piano or trumpet?

33. How many ways are there to construct a 4-digit code if numbers can be repeated?

34. A palette of water color paints has 3 shades of green, 3 shades of blue, 2 shades of red, 2 shades of yellow, and 1 shade of black. How many ways are there to choose one shade of each color?

35. Calculate $P(18, 4)$.

36. In a group of 5 freshman, 10 sophomores, 3 juniors, and 2 seniors, how many ways can a president, vice president, and treasurer be elected?

37. Calculate $C(15, 6)$.

38. A coffee shop has 7 Guatemalan roasts, 4 Cuban roasts, and 10 Costa Rican roasts. How many ways can the shop choose 2 Guatemalan, 2 Cuban, and 3 Costa Rican roasts for a coffee tasting event?

39. How many subsets does the set $\{1, 3, 5, \ldots, 99\}$ have?

40. A day spa charges a basic day rate that includes use of a sauna, pool, and showers. For an extra charge, guests can choose from the following additional services: massage, body scrub, manicure, pedicure, facial, and straight-razor shave. How many ways are there to order additional services at the day spa?

41. How many distinct ways can the word DEADWOOD be arranged?

42. How many distinct rearrangements of the letters of the word DEADWOOD are there if the arrangement must begin and end with the letter D?

BINOMIAL THEOREM

43. Evaluate the binomial coefficient $\begin{pmatrix} 23 \\ 8 \end{pmatrix}$.

44. Use the Binomial Theorem to expand $\left(3x + \frac{1}{2}y\right)^6$.

45. Use the Binomial Theorem to write the first three terms of $(2a + b)^{17}$.

46. Find the fourth term of $(3a^2 - 2b)^{11}$ without fully expanding the binomial.

PROBABILITY

For the following exercises, assume two die are rolled.

47. Construct a table showing the sample space.

48. What is the probability that a roll includes a 2?

49. What is the probability of rolling a pair?

50. What is the probability that a roll includes a 2 or results in a pair?

51. What is the probability that a roll doesn't include a 2 or result in a pair?

52. What is the probability of rolling a 5 or a 6?

53. What is the probability that a roll includes neither a 5 nor a 6?

For the following exercises, use the following data: An elementary school survey found that 350 of the 500 students preferred soda to milk. Suppose 8 children from the school are attending a birthday party. (Show calculations and round to the nearest tenth of a percent.)

54. What is the percent chance that all the children attending the party prefer soda?

55. What is the percent chance that at least one of the children attending the party prefers milk?

56. What is the percent chance that exactly 3 of the children attending the party prefer soda?

57. What is the percent chance that exactly 3 of the children attending the party prefer milk?

CHAPTER 13 PRACTICE TEST

1. Write the first four terms of the sequence defined by the recursive formula $a = -14$, $a_n = \dfrac{2 + a_{n-1}}{2}$.

2. Write the first four terms of the sequence defined by the explicit formula $a_n = \dfrac{n^2 - n - 1}{n!}$.

3. Is the sequence 0.3, 1.2, 2.1, 3, ... arithmetic? If so find the common difference.

4. An arithmetic sequence has the first term $a_1 = -4$ and common difference $d = -\dfrac{4}{3}$. What is the 6th term?

5. Write a recursive formula for the arithmetic sequence $-2, -\dfrac{7}{2}, -5, -\dfrac{13}{2}, \ldots$ and then find the 22nd term.

6. Write an explicit formula for the arithmetic sequence 15.6, 15, 14.4, 13.8, ... and then find the 32nd term.

7. Is the sequence $-2, -1, -\dfrac{1}{2}, -\dfrac{1}{4}, \ldots$ geometric? If so find the common ratio. If not, explain why.

8. What is the 11th term of the geometric sequence $-1.5, -3, -6, -12, \ldots$?

9. Write a recursive formula for the geometric sequence $1, -\dfrac{1}{2}, \dfrac{1}{4}, -\dfrac{1}{8}, \ldots$

10. Write an explicit formula for the geometric sequence $4, -\dfrac{4}{3}, \dfrac{4}{9}, -\dfrac{4}{27}, \ldots$

11. Use summation notation to write the sum of terms $3k^2 - \dfrac{5}{6}k$ from $k = -3$ to $k = 15$.

12. A community baseball stadium has 10 seats in the first row, 13 seats in the second row, 16 seats in the third row, and so on. There are 56 rows in all. What is the seating capacity of the stadium?

13. Use the formula for the sum of the first n terms of a geometric series to find $\displaystyle\sum_{k=1}^{7} -0.2 \cdot (-5)^{k-1}$.

14. Find the sum of the infinite geometric series. $\displaystyle\sum_{k=1}^{\infty} \dfrac{1}{3} \cdot \left(-\dfrac{1}{5}\right)^{k-1}$

15. Rachael deposits $3,600 into a retirement fund each year. The fund earns 7.5% annual interest, compounded monthly. If she opened her account when she was 20 years old, how much will she have by the time she's 55? How much of that amount was interest earned?

16. In a competition of 50 professional ballroom dancers, 22 compete in the fox-trot competition, 18 compete in the tango competition, and 6 compete in both the fox-trot and tango competitions. How many dancers compete in the foxtrot or tango competitions?

17. A buyer of a new sedan can custom order the car by choosing from 5 different exterior colors, 3 different interior colors, 2 sound systems, 3 motor designs, and either manual or automatic transmission. How many choices does the buyer have?

18. To allocate annual bonuses, a manager must choose his top four employees and rank them first to fourth. In how many ways can he create the "Top-Four" list out of the 32 employees?

19. A rock group needs to choose 3 songs to play at the annual Battle of the Bands. How many ways can they choose their set if have 15 songs to pick from?

20. A self-serve frozen yogurt shop has 8 candy toppings and 4 fruit toppings to choose from. How many ways are there to top a frozen yogurt?

21. How many distinct ways can the word EVANESCENCE be arranged if the anagram must end with the letter E?

22. Use the Binomial Theorem to expand $\left(\dfrac{3}{2}x - \dfrac{1}{2}y\right)^5$.

23. Find the seventh term of $\left(x^2 - \dfrac{1}{2}\right)^{13}$ without fully expanding the binomial.

For the following exercises, use the spinner in **Figure 1**.

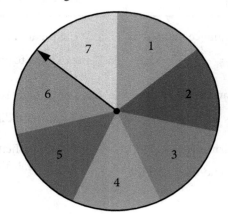

Figure 1

24. Construct a probability model showing each possible outcome and its associated probability. (Use the first letter for colors.)

25. What is the probability of landing on an odd number?

26. What is the probability of landing on blue?

27. What is the probability of landing on blue or an odd number?

28. What is the probability of landing on anything other than blue or an odd number?

29. A bowl of candy holds 16 peppermint, 14 butterscotch, and 10 strawberry flavored candies. Suppose a person grabs a handful of 7 candies. What is the percent chance that exactly 3 are butterscotch? (Show calculations and round to the nearest tenth of a percent.)

Proofs, Identities, and Toolkit Functions

A1 Graphs of the Parent Functions

Identity

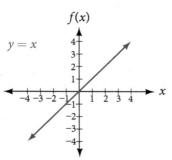

$y = x$

Domain: $(-\infty, \infty)$
Range: $(-\infty, \infty)$

Square

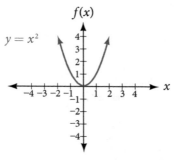

$y = x^2$

Domain: $(-\infty, \infty)$
Range: $[0, \infty)$

Square Root

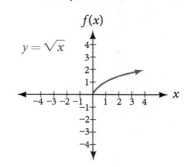

$y = \sqrt{x}$

Domain: $[0, \infty)$
Range: $[0, \infty)$

Figure A1

Cubic

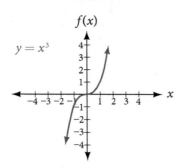

$y = x^3$

Domain: $(-\infty, \infty)$
Range: $(-\infty, \infty)$

Cube Root

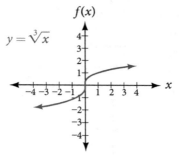

$y = \sqrt[3]{x}$

Domain: $(-\infty, \infty)$
Range: $(-\infty, \infty)$

Reciprocal

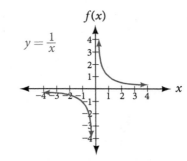

$y = \dfrac{1}{x}$

Domain: $(-\infty, 0) \cup (0, \infty)$
Range: $(-\infty, 0) \cup (0, \infty)$

Figure A2

Absolute Value

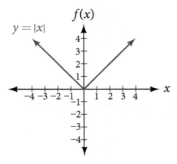

$y = |x|$

Domain: $(-\infty, \infty)$
Range: $[0, \infty)$

Exponential

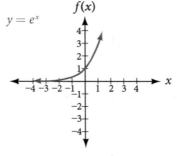

$y = e^x$

Domain: $(-\infty, \infty)$
Range: $[0, \infty)$

Natural Logarithm

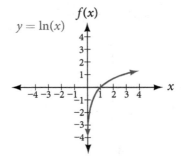

$y = \ln(x)$

Domain: $(0, \infty)$
Range: $(-\infty, \infty)$

Figure A3

A2 Graphs of the Trigonometric Functions

Sine

$y = \sin x$

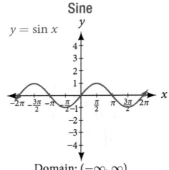

Domain: $(-\infty, \infty)$
Range: $(-1, 1)$

Cosine

$y = \cos x$

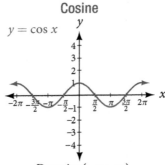

Domain: $(-\infty, \infty)$
Range: $(-1, 1)$

Figure A4

Tangent

$y = \tan x$

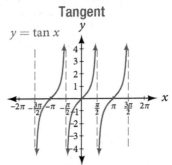

Domain: $x \neq \frac{\pi}{2}k$ where k is an odd integer
Range: $(-\infty, -1] \cup [1, \infty)$

Cosecant

$y = \csc x$

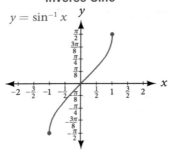

Domain: $x \neq \pi k$ where k is an integer
Range: $(-\infty, -1] \cup [1, \infty)$

Secant

$y = \sec x$

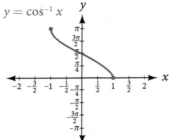

Domain: $x \neq \frac{\pi}{2}k$ where k is an odd integer
Range: $(-\infty, -1] \cup [1, \infty)$

Figure A5

Cotangent

$y = \cot x$

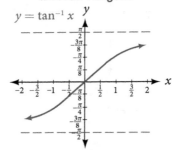

Domain: $x \neq \pi k$ where k is an integer
Range: $(-\infty, \infty)$

Inverse Sine

$y = \sin^{-1} x$

Domain: $[-1, 1]$

Range: $\left[-\frac{\pi}{2}, \frac{\pi}{2} \right]$

Inverse Cosine

$y = \cos^{-1} x$

Domain: $[-1, 1]$
Range: $[0, \pi)$

Figure A6

Inverse Tangent

$y = \tan^{-1} x$

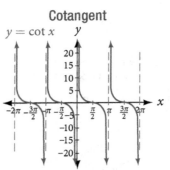

Domain: $(-\infty, \infty)$

Range: $\left(-\frac{\pi}{2}, \frac{\pi}{2} \right)$

Inverse Cosecant

$y = \csc^{-1} x$

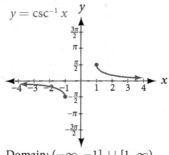

Domain: $(-\infty, -1] \cup [1, \infty)$

Range: $\left[-\frac{\pi}{2}, 0 \right) \cup \left(0, \frac{\pi}{2} \right]$

Inverse Secant

$y = \sec^{-1} x$

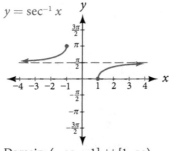

Domain: $(-\infty, -1] \cup [1, \infty)$

Range: $\left[0, \frac{\pi}{2} \right) \cup \left(\frac{\pi}{2}, \pi \right]$

Figure A7

Inverse Cotangent

$y = \cot^{-1} x$

Domain: $(-\infty, \infty)$

Range: $\left[-\frac{\pi}{2}, 0 \right) \cup \left(0, \frac{\pi}{2} \right]$

A3 Trigonometric Identities

Identities	Equations
Pythagorean Identities	$\sin^2\theta + \cos^2\theta = 1$ $1 + \tan^2\theta = \sec^2\theta$ $1 + \cot^2\theta = \csc^2\theta$
Even-odd Identities	$\cos(-\theta) = \cos\theta$ $\sec(-\theta) = \sec\theta$ $\sin(-\theta) = -\sin\theta$ $\tan(-\theta) = -\tan\theta$ $\csc(-\theta) = -\csc\theta$ $\cot(-\theta) = -\cot\theta$
Cofunction identities	$\sin\theta = \cos\left(\dfrac{\pi}{2} - \theta\right)$ $\cos\theta = \sin\left(\dfrac{\pi}{2} - \theta\right)$ $\tan\theta = \cot\left(\dfrac{\pi}{2} - \theta\right)$ $\cot\theta = \tan\left(\dfrac{\pi}{2} - \theta\right)$ $\sec\theta = \csc\left(\dfrac{\pi}{2} - \theta\right)$ $\csc\theta = \sec\left(\dfrac{\pi}{2} - \theta\right)$
Fundamental Identities	$\tan\theta = \dfrac{\sin\theta}{\cos\theta}$ $\sec\theta = \dfrac{1}{\cos\theta}$ $\csc\theta = \dfrac{1}{\sin\theta}$ $\cot\theta = \dfrac{1}{\tan\theta} = \dfrac{\cos\theta}{\sin\theta}$
Sum and Difference Identities	$\cos(\alpha + \beta) = \cos\alpha\cos\beta - \sin\alpha\sin\beta$ $\cos(\alpha - \beta) = \cos\alpha\cos\beta + \sin\alpha\sin\beta$ $\sin(\alpha + \beta) = \sin\alpha\cos\beta + \cos\alpha\sin\beta$ $\sin(\alpha - \beta) = \sin\alpha\cos\beta - \cos\alpha\sin\beta$ $\tan(\alpha + \beta) = \dfrac{\tan\alpha + \tan\beta}{1 - \tan\alpha\tan\beta}$ $\tan(\alpha - \beta) = \dfrac{\tan\alpha - \tan\beta}{1 + \tan\alpha\tan\beta}$
Double-Angle Formulas	$\sin(2\theta) = 2\sin\theta\cos\theta$ $\cos(2\theta) = \cos^2\theta - \sin^2\theta$ $\cos(2\theta) = 1 - 2\sin^2\theta$ $\cos(2\theta) = 2\cos^2\theta - 1$ $\tan(2\theta) = \dfrac{2\tan\theta}{1 - \tan^2\theta}$

Table A1

Identities	Equations
Half-Angle formulas	$\sin\frac{\alpha}{2} = \pm\sqrt{\frac{1-\cos\alpha}{2}}$ $\cos\frac{\alpha}{2} = \pm\sqrt{\frac{1+\cos\alpha}{2}}$ $\tan\frac{\alpha}{2} = \pm\sqrt{\frac{1-\cos\alpha}{1+\cos\alpha}}$ $= \frac{\sin\alpha}{1-\cos\alpha}$ $= \frac{1-\cos\alpha}{\sin\alpha}$
Reduction Formulas	$\sin^2\theta = \frac{1-\cos(2\theta)}{2}$ $\cos^2\theta = \frac{1+\cos(2\theta)}{2}$ $\tan^2\theta = \frac{1-\cos(2\theta)}{1+\cos(2\theta)}$
Product-to-Sum Formulas	$\cos\alpha\cos\beta = \frac{1}{2}\left[\cos(\alpha-\beta)+\cos(\alpha+\beta)\right]$ $\sin\alpha\cos\beta = \frac{1}{2}\left[\sin(\alpha+\beta)+\sin(\alpha-\beta)\right]$ $\sin\alpha\sin\beta = \frac{1}{2}\left[\cos(\alpha-\beta)-\cos(\alpha+\beta)\right]$ $\cos\alpha\sin\beta = \frac{1}{2}\left[\sin(\alpha+\beta)-\sin(\alpha-\beta)\right]$
Sum-to-Product Formulas	$\sin\alpha+\sin\beta = 2\sin\left(\frac{\alpha+\beta}{2}\right)\cos\left(\frac{\alpha-\beta}{2}\right)$ $\sin\alpha-\sin\beta = 2\sin\left(\frac{\alpha-\beta}{2}\right)\cos\left(\frac{\alpha+\beta}{2}\right)$ $\cos\alpha-\cos\beta = -2\sin\left(\frac{\alpha+\beta}{2}\right)\sin\left(\frac{\alpha-\beta}{2}\right)$ $\cos\alpha+\cos\beta = 2\cos\left(\frac{\alpha+\beta}{2}\right)\cos\left(\frac{\alpha-\beta}{2}\right)$
Law of Sines	$\frac{\sin\alpha}{a} = \frac{\sin\beta}{b} = \frac{\sin\gamma}{c}$ $\frac{\sin a}{\alpha} = \frac{\sin b}{\beta} = \frac{\sin c}{\gamma}$
Law of Cosines	$a^2 = b^2 + c^2 - 2bc\cos\alpha$ $b^2 = a^2 + c^2 - 2ac\cos\beta$ $c^2 = a^2 + b^2 - 2aa\cos\gamma$

Table A1

TRY IT ANSWERS FOR CHAPTERS 8–13

Chapter 8

Section 8.1

1. 6π **2.** $\frac{1}{2}$ compressed   **3.** $\frac{\pi}{2}$; right

4. 2 units up   **5.** Midline: $y = 0$; Amplitude: $|A| = \frac{1}{2}$;

Period: $P = \dfrac{2\pi}{|B|} = 6\pi$; Phase shift: $\dfrac{C}{B} = \pi$ **6.** $f(x) = \sin(x) + 2$

7. Two possibilities: $y = 4\sin\left(\dfrac{\pi}{5}x - \dfrac{\pi}{5}\right) + 4$ or

$y = -4\sin\left(\dfrac{\pi}{5}x + \dfrac{4\pi}{5}\right) + 4$

8.

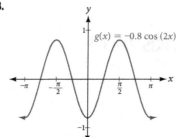

Midline: $y = 0$;

Amplitude: $|A| = 0.8$;

Period: $P = \dfrac{2\pi}{|B|} = \pi$;

Phase shift: $\dfrac{C}{B} = 0$ or none

9.

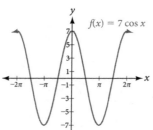

Midline: $y = 0$;

Amplitude: $|A| = 2$;

Period: $P = \dfrac{2\pi}{|B|} = 6$;

Phase shift: $\dfrac{C}{B} = -\dfrac{1}{2}$

10.

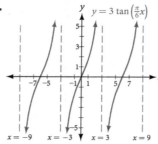

7

11.

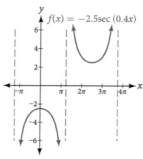

$3\cos(x) - 4$

Section 8.2

1.

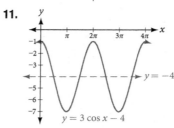

2. It would be reflected across the line $y = -1$, becoming an increasing function.

3. $g(x) = 4\tan(2x)$

4.

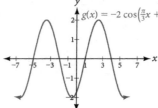

This is a vertical reflection of the preceding graph because A is negative.

5.

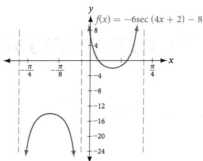

6.

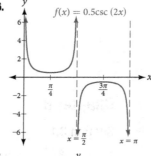

7.

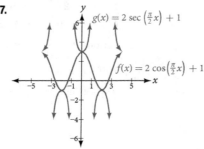

Section 8.3

1. $\arccos(0.8776) \approx 0.5$ **2. a.** $-\dfrac{\pi}{2}$ **b.** $-\dfrac{\pi}{4}$ **c.** π **d.** $\dfrac{\pi}{3}$

3. 1.9823 or $113.578°$ **4.** $\sin^{-1}(0.6) = 36.87° = 0.6435$ radians

5. $\dfrac{\pi}{8}; \dfrac{2\pi}{9}$ **6.** $\dfrac{3\pi}{4}$ **7.** $\dfrac{12}{13}$ **8.** $\dfrac{4\sqrt{2}}{9}$ **9.** $\dfrac{4x}{\sqrt{16x^2 + 1}}$

Chapter 9

Section 9.1

1. $\csc\theta\cos\theta\tan\theta = \left(\dfrac{1}{\sin\theta}\right)\cos\theta\left(\dfrac{\sin\theta}{\cos\theta}\right)$

$\qquad = \dfrac{\cos\theta}{\sin\theta}\left(\dfrac{\sin\theta}{\cos\theta}\right)$

$\qquad = \dfrac{\sin\theta\cos\theta}{\sin\theta\cos\theta}$

$\qquad = 1$

2. $\dfrac{\cot\theta}{\csc\theta} = \dfrac{\dfrac{\cos\theta}{\sin\theta}}{\dfrac{1}{\sin\theta}} = \dfrac{\cos\theta}{\sin\theta}\cdot\dfrac{\sin\theta}{1} = \cos\theta$

3. $\dfrac{\sin^2\theta - 1}{\tan\theta\sin\theta - \tan\theta} = \dfrac{(\sin\theta + 1)(\sin\theta - 1)}{\tan\theta(\sin\theta - 1)} = \dfrac{\sin\theta + 1}{\tan\theta}$

4. This is a difference of squares formula:
$25 - 9\sin^2\theta = (5 - 3\sin\theta)(5 + 3\sin\theta)$.

5. $\dfrac{\cos\theta}{1+\sin\theta}\left(\dfrac{1-\sin\theta}{1-\sin\theta}\right)=\dfrac{\cos\theta(1-\sin\theta)}{1-\sin^2\theta}$

$\qquad\qquad\qquad\quad = \dfrac{\cos\theta(1-\sin\theta)}{\cos^2\theta}$

$\qquad\qquad\qquad\quad = \dfrac{1-\sin\theta}{\cos\theta}$

Section 9.2

1. $\dfrac{\sqrt{2}+\sqrt{6}}{4}$ **2.** $\dfrac{\sqrt{2}-\sqrt{6}}{4}$ **3.** $\dfrac{1-\sqrt{3}}{1+\sqrt{3}}$ **4.** $\cos\left(\dfrac{5\pi}{14}\right)$

5. $\tan(\pi-\theta)=\dfrac{\tan(\pi)-\tan\theta}{1+\tan(\pi)\tan\theta}$

$\qquad\qquad\quad = \dfrac{0-\tan\theta}{1+0\cdot\tan\theta}$

$\qquad\qquad\quad = -\tan\theta$

Section 9.3

1. $\cos(2\alpha)=\dfrac{7}{32}$

2. $\cos^4\theta-\sin^4\theta=\left(\cos^2\theta+\sin^2\theta\right)\left(\cos^2\theta-\sin^2\theta\right)=\cos(2\theta)$

3. $\cos(2\theta)\cos\theta=(\cos^2\theta-\sin^2\theta)\cos\theta=\cos^3\theta-\cos\theta\sin^2\theta$

4. $10\cos^4 x = 10(\cos^2 x)^2$

$\qquad = 10\left[\dfrac{1+\cos(2x)}{2}\right]^2$ Substitute reduction formula for $\cos^2 x$.

$\qquad = \dfrac{10}{4}\left[1+2\cos(2x)+\cos^2(2x)\right]$

$\qquad = \dfrac{10}{4}+\dfrac{10}{2}\cos(2x)+\dfrac{10}{4}\left(\dfrac{1+\cos^2(2x)}{2}\right)$ Substitute reduction formula for $\cos^2 x$.

$\qquad = \dfrac{10}{4}+\dfrac{10}{2}\cos(2x)+\dfrac{10}{8}+\dfrac{10}{8}\cos(4x)$

$\qquad = \dfrac{30}{8}+5\cos(2x)+\dfrac{10}{8}\cos(4x)$

$\qquad = \dfrac{15}{4}+5\cos(2x)+\dfrac{5}{4}\cos(4x)$

5. $-\dfrac{2}{\sqrt{5}}$

Section 9.4

1. $\dfrac{1}{2}(\cos 6\theta+\cos 2\theta)$ **2.** $\dfrac{1}{2}(\sin 2x+\sin 2y)$ **3.** $\dfrac{-2-\sqrt{3}}{4}$

4. $2\sin(2\theta)\cos(\theta)$

5. $\tan\theta\cot\theta-\cos^2\theta=\left(\dfrac{\sin\theta}{\cos\theta}\right)\left(\dfrac{\cos\theta}{\sin\theta}\right)-\cos^2\theta$

$\qquad\qquad\qquad\qquad = 1-\cos^2\theta$

$\qquad\qquad\qquad\qquad = \sin^2\theta$

Section 9.5

1. $x=\dfrac{7\pi}{6},\dfrac{11\pi}{6}$ **2.** $\dfrac{\pi}{3}\pm\pi k$ **3.** $\theta\approx 1.7722\pm 2\pi k$ and

$\theta\approx 4.5110\pm 2\pi k$ **4.** $\cos\theta=-1,\theta=\pi$ **5.** $\dfrac{\pi}{2},\dfrac{2\pi}{3},\dfrac{4\pi}{3},\dfrac{3\pi}{2}$

Chapter 10

Section 10.1

1. $\alpha=98°, a=34.6; \beta=39°, b=22; \gamma=43°, c=23.8$

2. Solution 1 $\alpha=80°, a=120; \beta\approx 83.2°, b=121; \gamma\approx 16.8°, c\approx 35.2$

     Solution 2 $\alpha'=80°, a'=120; \beta'\approx 96.8°, b'=121; \gamma'\approx 3.2°, c'\approx 6.8$

3. $\beta\approx 5.7°, \gamma\approx 94.3°, c\approx 101.3$ **4.** Two

5. About 8.2 square feet   **6.** 161.9 yd.

Section 10.2

1. $a\approx 14.9, \beta\approx 23.8°, \gamma\approx 126.2°$ **2.** $\alpha\approx 27.7°, \beta\approx 40.5°, \gamma\approx 111.8°$

3. Area $= 552$ square feet   **4.** About 8.15 square feet

Section 10.3

1. 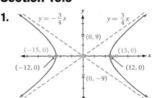   **2.**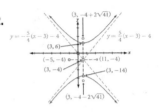

3. $(x,y)=\left(\dfrac{1}{2},-\dfrac{\sqrt{3}}{2}\right)$ **4.** $r=\sqrt{3}$ **5.** $x^2+y^2=2y$ or, in the standard form for a circle, $x^2+(y-1)^2=1$

Section 10.4

1. The equation fails the symmetry test with respect to the line $\theta=\dfrac{\pi}{2}$ and with respect to the pole. It passes the polar axis symmetry test.   **2.** Tests will reveal symmetry about the polar axis. The zero is $\left(\theta,\dfrac{\pi}{2}\right)$, and the maximum value is $(3,0)$.

3.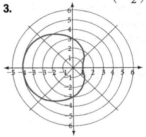

4. The graph is a rose curve, n even

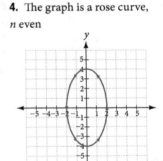

5. The graph is a rose curve, n odd

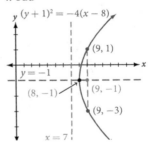

6.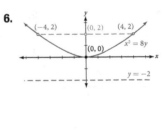

Section 10.5

1. 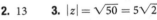   **2.** 13   **3.** $|z|=\sqrt{50}=5\sqrt{2}$

4. $z=3\left(\cos\left(\dfrac{\pi}{2}\right)+i\sin\left(\dfrac{\pi}{2}\right)\right)$

5. $z=2\left(\cos\left(\dfrac{\pi}{6}\right)+i\sin\left(\dfrac{\pi}{6}\right)\right)$

6. $z=2\sqrt{3}-2i$

7. $z_1 z_2=-4\sqrt{3}; \dfrac{z_1}{z_2}=-\dfrac{\sqrt{3}}{2}+\dfrac{3}{2}i$

8. $z_0=2(\cos(30°)+i\sin(30°)), z_1=2(\cos(120°)+i\sin(120°))$

     $z_2=2(\cos(210°)+i\sin(210°)), z_3=2(\cos(300°)+i\sin(300°))$

Section 10.6

1.

t	$x(t)$	$y(t)$
-1	-4	2
0	-3	4
1	-2	6
2	-1	8

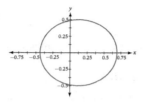

2. $x(t) = t^3 - 2t,\ y(t) = t$ **3.** $y = 5 - \sqrt{\dfrac{1}{2}x - 3}$

4. $y = \ln(\sqrt{x})$ **5.** $\dfrac{x^2}{4} + \dfrac{y^2}{9} = 1$ **6.** $y = x^2$

Section 10.7

1. 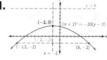   **2.**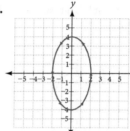

3.   The graph of the parametric equations is in red and the graph of the rectangular equation is drawn in blue dots on top of the parametric equations.

Section 10.8

1.

2. $3u = \langle 15, 12 \rangle$

3. $u = 8i - 11j$

4. $v = \sqrt{34}\cos(59°)i + \sqrt{34}\sin(59°)j$

Magnitude $= \sqrt{34}$

$\theta = \tan^{-1}\left(\dfrac{5}{3}\right) = 59.04°$

Chapter 11

Section 11.1

1. Not a solution

2. The solution to the system is the ordered pair $(-5, 3)$.

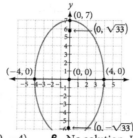

3. $(-2, -5)$ **4.** $(-6, -2)$ **5.** $(10, -4)$ **6.** No solution. It is an inconsistent system.

7. The system is dependent so there are infinite solutions of the form $(x, 2x + 5)$.   **8.** 700 children, 950 adults

Section 11.2

1. $(1, -1, 1)$ **2.** No solution   **3.** Infinite number of solutions of the form $(x, 4x - 11, -5x + 18)$

Section 11.3

1. $\left(-\dfrac{1}{2}, \dfrac{1}{2}\right)$ and $(2, 8)$ **2.** $(-1, 3)$ **3.** $\{(1, 3),(1, -3),(-1, 3),(-1, -3)\}$

4.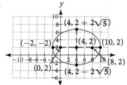

Section 11.4

1. $\dfrac{3}{x - 3} - \dfrac{2}{x - 2}$ **2.** $\dfrac{6}{x - 1} - \dfrac{5}{(x - 1)^2}$ **3.** $\dfrac{3}{x - 1} + \dfrac{2x - 4}{x^2 + 1}$

4. $\dfrac{x - 2}{x^2 - 2x + 3} + \dfrac{2x + 1}{(x^2 - 2x + 3)^2}$

Section 11.5

1. $A + B = \begin{bmatrix} 2 & 6 \\ 1 & 0 \\ 1 & -3 \end{bmatrix} + \begin{bmatrix} 3 & -2 \\ 1 & 5 \\ -4 & 3 \end{bmatrix} = \begin{bmatrix} 2 + 3 & 6 + (-2) \\ 1 + 1 & 0 + 5 \\ 1 + (-4) & -3 + 3 \end{bmatrix} = \begin{bmatrix} 5 & 4 \\ 2 & 5 \\ -3 & 0 \end{bmatrix}$

2. $-2B = \begin{bmatrix} -8 & -2 \\ -6 & -4 \end{bmatrix}$

Section 11.6

1. $\begin{bmatrix} 4 & -3 & | & 11 \\ 3 & 2 & | & 4 \end{bmatrix}$ **2.** $\begin{aligned} x - y + z &= 5 \\ 2x - y + 3z &= 1 \\ y + z &= -9 \end{aligned}$ **3.** $(2, 1)$

4. $\begin{bmatrix} 1 & -\frac{5}{2} & \frac{5}{2} & | & \frac{17}{2} \\ 0 & 1 & 5 & | & 9 \\ 0 & 0 & 1 & | & 2 \end{bmatrix}$ **5.** $(1, 1, 1)$

6. $150,000 at 7%, $750,000 at 8%, $600,000 at 10%

Section 11.7

1. $AB = \begin{bmatrix} 1 & 4 \\ -1 & -3 \end{bmatrix}\begin{bmatrix} -3 & -4 \\ 1 & 1 \end{bmatrix} = \begin{bmatrix} 1(-3) + 4(1) & 1(-4) + 4(1) \\ -1(-3) + -3(1) & -1(-4) + -3(1) \end{bmatrix}$
$= \begin{bmatrix} 1 & 0 \\ 0 & 1 \end{bmatrix}$

$BA = \begin{bmatrix} -3 & -4 \\ 1 & 1 \end{bmatrix}\begin{bmatrix} 1 & 4 \\ -1 & -3 \end{bmatrix} = \begin{bmatrix} -3(1) + -4(-1) & -3(4) + -4(-3) \\ 1(1) + 1(-1) & 1(4) + 1(-3) \end{bmatrix}$
$= \begin{bmatrix} 1 & 0 \\ 0 & 1 \end{bmatrix}$

2. $A^{-1} = \begin{bmatrix} \frac{3}{5} & \frac{1}{5} \\ -\frac{2}{5} & \frac{1}{5} \end{bmatrix}$ **3.** $A^{-1} = \begin{bmatrix} 1 & 1 & 2 \\ 2 & 4 & -3 \\ 3 & 6 & -5 \end{bmatrix}$ **4.** $X = \begin{bmatrix} 4 \\ 38 \\ 58 \end{bmatrix}$

Section 11.8

1. $(3, -7)$ **2.** -10 **3.** $\left(-2, \dfrac{3}{5}, \dfrac{12}{5}\right)$

Chapter 12

Section 12.1

1. $x^2 + \dfrac{y^2}{16} = 1$ **2.** $\dfrac{(x-1)^2}{16} + \dfrac{(y-3)^2}{4} = 1$

3. Center: $(0, 0)$;
vertices: $(\pm 6, 0)$;
co-vertices: $(0, \pm 2)$;
foci: $(\pm 4\sqrt{2}, 0)$

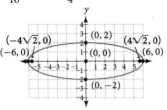

4. Standard form: $\dfrac{x^2}{16} + \dfrac{y^2}{49} = 1$;
center: $(0, 0)$;
vertices: $(0, \pm 7)$;
co-vertices: $(\pm 4, 0)$
foci: $(0, \pm\sqrt{33})$

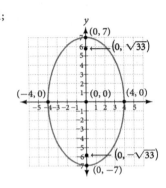

5. Center: $(4, 2)$;
vertices: $(-2, 2)$ and $(10, 2)$;
co-vertices: $(4, 2 - 2\sqrt{5})$
and $(4, 2 + 2\sqrt{5})$;
foci: $(0, 2)$ and $(8, 2)$

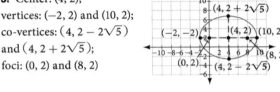

6. $\dfrac{(x-3)^2}{4} + \dfrac{(y+1)^2}{16} = 1$; center: $(3, -1)$; vertices: $(3, -5)$ and $(3, 3)$; co-vertices: $(1, -1)$ and $(5, -1)$; foci: $(3, -1 - 2\sqrt{3})$ and $(3, -1 + 2\sqrt{3})$ **7. a.** $\dfrac{x^2}{57{,}600} + \dfrac{y^2}{25{,}600} = 1$; **b.** The people are standing 358 feet apart.

Section 12.2

1. Vertices: $(\pm 3, 0)$; Foci: $(\pm\sqrt{34}, 0)$ **2.** $\dfrac{y^2}{4} - \dfrac{x^2}{16} = 1$

3. $\dfrac{(y-3)^2}{25} + \dfrac{(x-1)^2}{144} = 1$
4. Vertices: $(\pm 12, 0)$;
co-vertices: $(0, \pm 9)$;
foci: $(\pm 15, 0)$;
asymptotes: $y = \pm\dfrac{3}{4}x$

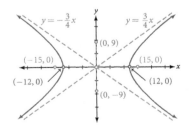

5. Center: $(3, -4)$; vertices: $(3, -14)$ and $(3, 6)$; co-vertices: $(-5, -4)$ and $(11, -4)$; foci: $(3, -4 - 2\sqrt{41})$ and $(3, -4 + 2\sqrt{41})$; Asyaptotes: $y = \pm\dfrac{5}{4}(x - 3) - 4$

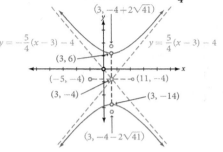

6. The sides of the tower can be modeled by the hyperbolic equation. $\dfrac{x^2}{400} - \dfrac{y^2}{3600} = 1$ or $\dfrac{x^2}{20^2} - \dfrac{y^2}{60^2} = 1$.

Section 12.3

1. Focus: $(-4, 0)$;
directrix: $x = 4$;
endpoints of the latus
rectum: $(-4, \pm 8)$

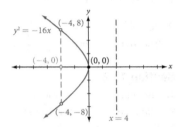

2. Focus: $(0, 2)$;
sirectrix: $y = -2$;
endpoints of the latus
rectum: $(\pm 4, 2)$

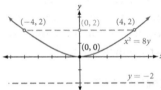

3. $x^2 = 14y$

4. Vertex: $(8, -1)$;
axis of symmetry: $y = -1$;
focus: $(9, -1)$;
directrix: $x = 7$;
endpoints of the latus rectum:
$(9, -3)$ and $(9, 1)$.

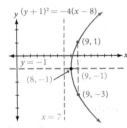

5. Vertex: $(-2, 3)$;
axis of symmetry: $x = -2$;
focus: $(-2, -2)$;
directrix: $y = 8$;
endpoints of the latus
rectum: $(-12, -2)$ and
$(8, -2)$.

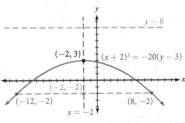

6. a. $y^2 = 1{,}280x$ **b.** The depth of the cooker is 500 mm.

Section 12.4

1. a. Hyperbola   **b.** Ellipse   **2.** $\dfrac{x'^2}{4} + \dfrac{y'^2}{1} = 1$
3. a. Hyperbola   **b.** Ellipse

Section 12.5

1. Ellipse; $e = \frac{1}{3}$; $x = -2$

2.

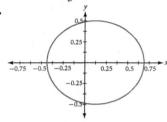

3. $r = \dfrac{1}{1 - \cos\theta}$

4. $4 - 8x + 3x^2 - y^2 = 0$

Section 13.7

1.

Outcome	Probability
Roll of 1	
Roll of 2	
Roll of 3	
Roll of 4	
Roll of 5	
Roll of 6	

2. $\frac{2}{3}$ **3.** $\frac{7}{13}$ **4.** $\frac{2}{13}$

5. $\frac{5}{6}$ **6. a.** $\frac{1}{91}$ **b.** $\frac{5}{91}$ **c.** $\frac{86}{91}$

Chapter 13

Section 13.1

1. The first five terms are $\{1, 6, 11, 16, 21\}$. **2.** The first five terms are $\left\{-2, 2, -\frac{3}{2}, 1, -\frac{5}{8}\right\}$. **3.** The first six terms are $\{2, 5, 54, 10, 250, 15\}$. **4.** $a_n = (-1)^{n+1} 9^n$ **5.** $a_n = -\frac{3n}{4n}$

6. $a_n = e^{n-3}$ **7.** $\{2, 5, 11, 23, 47\}$ **8.** $\left\{0, 1, 1, 1, 2, 3, \frac{5}{2}, \frac{17}{6}\right\}$
9. The first five terms are $\left\{1, \frac{3}{2}, 4, 15, 72\right\}$.

Section 13.2

1. The sequence is arithmetic. The common difference is -2.
2. The sequence is not arithmetic because $3 - 1 \neq 6 - 3$.
3. $\{1, 6, 11, 16, 21\}$ **4.** $a_2 = 2$ **5.** $a_1 = 25$; $a_n = a_{n-1} + 12$, for $n \geq 2$ **6.** $a_n = 53 - 3n$ **7.** There are 11 terms in the sequence. **8.** The formula is $T_n = 10 + 4n$, and it will take her 42 minutes.

Section 13.3

1. The sequence is not geometric because $\frac{10}{5} \neq \frac{15}{10}$.
2. The sequence is geometric. The common ratio is $\frac{1}{5}$.
3. $\left\{18, 6, 2, \frac{2}{3}, \frac{2}{9}\right\}$ **4.** $a_1 = 2$; $a_n = \frac{2}{3}a_{n-1}$ for $n \geq 2$
5. $a_6 = 16{,}384$ **6.** $a_n = -(-3)^{n-1}$ **7. a.** $P_n = 293 \cdot 1.026a^n$
b. The number of hits will be about 333.

Section 13.4

1. 38 **2.** 26.4 **3.** 328 **4.** -280 **5.** \$2,025
6. $\approx 2{,}000.00$ **7.** 9,840 **8.** \$275,513.31 **9.** The sum is defined. It is geometric. **10.** The sum of the infinite series is defined. **11.** The sum of the infinite series is defined. **12.** 3 **13.** The series is not geometric.
14. $-\frac{3}{11}$ **15.** \$92,408.18

Section 13.5

1. 7 **2.** There are 60 possible breakfast specials. **3.** 120
4. 60 **5.** 12 **6.** $P(7, 7) = 5{,}040$ **7.** $P(7, 5) = 2{,}520$
8. $C(10, 3) = 120$ **9.** 64 sundaes **10.** 840

Section 13.6

1. a. 35 **b.** 330 **2. a.** $x^5 - 5x^4y + 10x^3y^2 - 10x^2y^3 + 5xy^4 - y^5$
b. $8x^3 + 60x^2y + 150xy^2 + 125y^3$ **3.** $-10{,}206x^4y^5$

CHAPTER 8

Section 8.1

1. The sine and cosine functions have the property that $f(x + P) = f(x)$ for a certain P. This means that the function values repeat for every P units on the x-axis.   **3.** The absolute value of the constant A (amplitude) increases the total range and the constant D (vertical shift) shifts the graph vertically.

5. At the point where the terminal side of t intersects the unit circle, you can determine that the $\sin t$ equals the y-coordinate of the point.

7. Amplitude: $\frac{2}{3}$; period: 2π; midline: $y = 0$; maximum: $y = \frac{2}{3}$ occurs at $x = 0$; minimum: $y = -\frac{2}{3}$ occurs at $x = \pi$; for one period, the graph starts at 0 and ends at 2π.

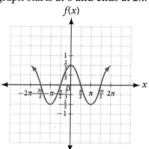

9. Amplitude: 4; period: 2π; midline: $y = 0$; maximum: $y = 4$ occurs at $x = \frac{\pi}{2}$; minimum: $y = -4$ occurs at $x = \frac{3\pi}{2}$; for one period, the graph starts at 0 and ends at 2π.

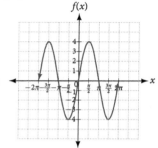

11. Amplitude: 1; period: π; midline: $y = 0$; maximum: $y = 1$ occurs at $x = \pi$; minimum: $y = -1$ occurs at $x = \frac{\pi}{2}$; for one period, the graph starts at 0 and ends at π.

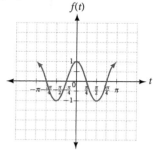

13. Amplitude: 4; period: 2; midline: $y = 0$; maximum: $y = 4$ occurs at $x = 0$; minimum: $y = -4$ occurs at $x = 1$; for one period, the graph starts at 0 and ends at π.

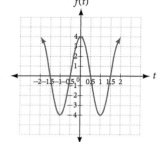

15. Amplitude: 3; period: $\frac{\pi}{4}$; midline: $y = 5$; maximum: $y = 8$ occurs at $x = 0.12$; minimum: $y = 2$ occurs at $x = 0.516$; horizontal shift: -4; vertical translation: 5; for one period, the graph starts at 0 and ends at $\frac{\pi}{4}$.

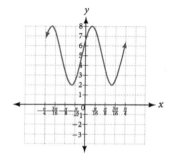

17. Amplitude: 5; period: $\frac{2\pi}{5}$; midline: $y = -2$; maximum: $y = 3$ occurs at $x = 0.08$; minimum: $y = -7$ occurs at $x = 0.71$; phase shift: -4; vertical translation: -2; for one period, the graph starts at 0 and ends at $\frac{2\pi}{5}$.

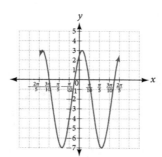

19. Amplitude: 1; period: 2π; midline: $y = 1$; maximum: $y = 2$ occurs at $t = 2.09$; minimum: $y = 0$ occurs at $t = 5.24$; phase shift: $-\frac{\pi}{3}$; vertical translation: 1; for one period, the graph starts at 0 and ends at 2π.

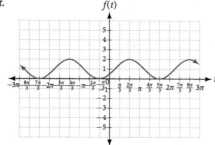

21. Amplitude: 1; period: 4π; midline: $y = 0$; maximum: $y = 1$ occurs at $t = 11.52$; minimum: $y = -1$ occurs at $t = 5.24$; phase shift: $-\frac{10\pi}{3}$; vertical shift: 0; for one period, the graph starts at 0 and ends at 4π.

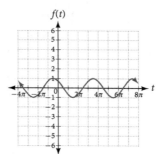

23. Amplitude: 2, midline: $y = -3$; period: 4; equation: $f(x) = 2\sin\left(\frac{\pi}{2}x\right) - 3$ **25.** Amplitude: 2, midline: $y = 3$; period: 5; equation: $f(x) = -2\cos\left(\frac{2\pi}{5}x\right) + 3$

27. Amplitude: 4, midline: $y = 0$; period: 2; equation: $f(x) = -4\cos\left(\pi\left(x - \frac{\pi}{2}\right)\right)$ **29.** Amplitude: 2, midline: $y = 1$; period: 2; equation: $f(x) = 2\cos(\pi x) + 1$ **31.** $0, \pi$

33. $\sin\left(\frac{\pi}{2}\right) = 1$ **35.** $\frac{\pi}{2}$ **37.** $f(x) = \sin x$ is symmetric with respect to the origin. **39.** $\frac{\pi}{3}, \frac{5\pi}{3}$

41. Maximum: 1 at $x = 0$; minimum: -1 at $x = \pi$

43. A linear function is added to a periodic sine function. The graph does not have an amplitude because as the linear function increases without bound the combined function $h(x) = x + \sin x$ will increase without bound as well. The graph is bounded between the graphs of $y = x + 1$ and $y = x - 1$ because sine oscillates between -1 and 1.

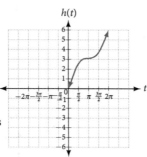

45. There is no amplitude because the function is not bounded.

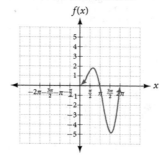

47. The graph is symmetric with respect to the y-axis and there is no amplitude because the function's bounds decrease as $|x|$ grows. There appears to be a horizontal asymptote at $y = 0$.

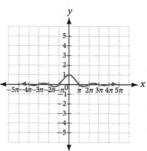

Section 8.2

1. Since $y = \csc x$ is the reciprocal function of $y = \sin x$, you can plot the reciprocal of the coordinates on the graph of $y = \sin x$ to obtain the y-coordinates of $y = \csc x$. The x-intercepts of the graph $y = \sin x$ are the vertical asymptotes for the graph of $y = \csc x$. **3.** Answers will vary. Using the unit circle, one can show that $\tan(x + \pi) = \tan x$. **5.** The period is the same: 2π **7.** IV **9.** III **11.** Period: 8; horizontal shift: 1 unit to the left **13.** 1.5 **15.** 5 **17.** $-\cot x \cos x - \sin x$

19. Stretching factor: 2; period: $\frac{\pi}{4}$; asymptotes: $x = \frac{1}{4}\left(\frac{\pi}{2} + \pi k\right) + 8$, where k is an integer

21. Stretching factor: 6; period: 6; asymptotes: $x = 3k$, where k is an integer

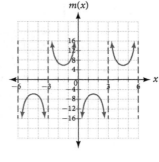

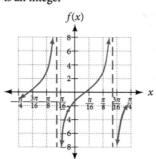

23. Stretching factor: 1; period: π; asymptotes: $x = \pi k$, where k is an integer

25. Stretching factor: 1; period: π; asymptotes: $x = \frac{\pi}{4} + \pi k$, where k is an integer

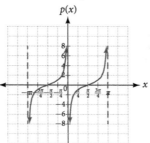

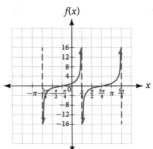

27. Stretching factor: 2; period: 2π; asymptotes: $x = \pi k$, where k is an integer

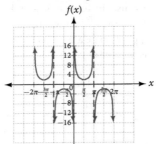

29. Stretching factor: 4; period: $\frac{2\pi}{3}$; asymptotes: $x = \frac{\pi}{6}k$, where k is an integer

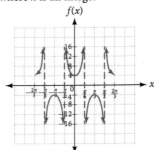

31. Stretching factor: 7; period: $\frac{2\pi}{5}$; asymptotes: $x = \frac{\pi}{10}k$, where k is an integer

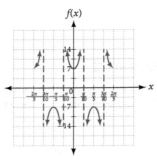

33. Stretching factor: 2; period: 2π; asymptotes: $x = -\frac{\pi}{4} + \pi k$, where k is an integer

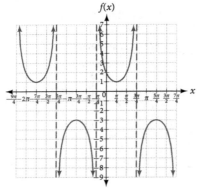

35. Stretching factor: $\frac{7}{5}$; period: 2π; asymptotes: $x = \frac{\pi}{4} + \pi k$, where k is an integer

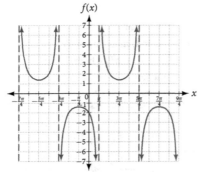

37. $y = \left(\tan 3\left(x - \frac{\pi}{4}\right)\right) + 2$

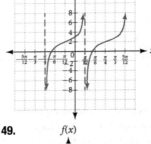

39. $f(x) = \csc(2x)$
41. $f(x) = \csc(4x)$
43. $f(x) = 2\csc x$
45. $f(x) = \frac{1}{2}\tan(100\pi x)$

47.

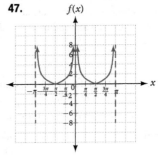

49.

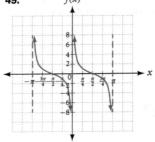

51.

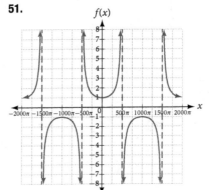

53.

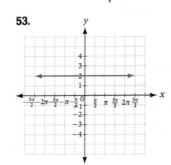

55. a. $\left(-\frac{\pi}{2}, \frac{\pi}{2}\right)$;
b.

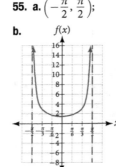

c. $x = -\frac{\pi}{2}$ and $x = \frac{\pi}{2}$; the distance grows without bound as $|x|$ approaches $\frac{\pi}{2}$ –i.e., at right angles to the line representing due north, the boat would be so far away, the fisherman could not see it **d.** 3; when $x = -\frac{\pi}{3}$, the boat is 3 km away **e.** 1.73; when $x = \frac{\pi}{6}$, the boat is about 1.73 km away **f.** 1.5 km; when $x = 0$

57. a. $h(x) = 2\tan\left(\dfrac{\pi}{120}x\right)$

b. $f(x)$

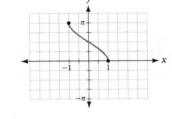

c. $h(0) = 0$: after 0 seconds, the rocket is 0 mi above the ground; $h(30) = 2$: after 30 seconds, the rockets is 2 mi high;   **d.** As x approaches 60 seconds, the values of $h(x)$ grow increasingly large. As $x \to 60$ the model breaks down, since it assumes that the angle of elevation continues to increase with x. In fact, the angle is bounded at 90 degrees.

Section 8.3

1. The function $y = \sin x$ is one-to-one on $\left[-\dfrac{\pi}{2}, \dfrac{\pi}{2}\right]$; thus, this interval is the range of the inverse function of $y = \sin x$, $f(x) = \sin^{-1} x$. The function $y = \cos x$ is one-to-one on $[0, \pi]$; thus, this interval is the range of the inverse function of $y = \cos x$, $f(x) = \cos^{-1} x$.   **3.** $\dfrac{\pi}{6}$ is the radian measure of an angle between $-\dfrac{\pi}{2}$ and $\dfrac{\pi}{2}$ whose sine is 0.5.   **5.** In order for any function to have an inverse, the function must be one-to-one and must pass the horizontal line test. The regular sine function is not one-to-one unless its domain is restricted in some way. Mathematicians have agreed to restrict the sine function to the interval $\left[-\dfrac{\pi}{2}, \dfrac{\pi}{2}\right]$ so that it is one-to-one and possesses an inverse.   **7.** True. The angle, θ_1 that equals arccos $(-x)$, $x > 0$, will be a second quadrant angle with reference angle, θ_2, where θ_2 equals arccos x, $x > 0$. Since θ_2 is the reference angle for θ_1, $\theta_1 = \pi - \theta_1$ and $\arccos(-x) = \pi - \arccos x$ **9.** $-\dfrac{\pi}{6}$

11. $\dfrac{3\pi}{4}$ **13.** $-\dfrac{\pi}{3}$ **15.** $\dfrac{\pi}{3}$ **17.** 1.98   **19.** 0.93

21. 1.41   **23.** 0.56 radians   **25.** 0   **27.** 0.71 radians

29. -0.71 radians   **31.** $-\dfrac{\pi}{4}$ radians   **33.** $\dfrac{4}{5}$ **35.** $\dfrac{5}{13}$

37. $\dfrac{x-1}{\sqrt{-x^2+2x}}$ **39.** $\dfrac{\sqrt{x^2-1}}{x}$ **41.** $\dfrac{x+0.5}{\sqrt{-x^2-x+\frac{3}{4}}}$

43. $\dfrac{\sqrt{2x+1}}{x+1}$ **45.** $\dfrac{\sqrt{2x+1}}{x}$ **47.** t

49. Domain: $[-1, 1]$; range: $[0, \pi]$ **51.** $x = 0$
53. 0.395 radians
55. 1.11 radians
57. 1.25 radians
59. 0.405 radians
61. No. The angle the ladder makes with the horizontal is 60 degrees.

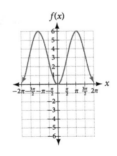

Chapter 8 Review Exercises

1. Amplitude: 3; period: is 2π; midline: $y = 3$; no asymptotes

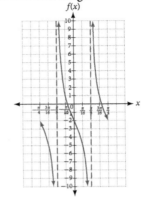

3. Amplitude: 3; period: is 2π; midline: $y = 0$; no asymptotes

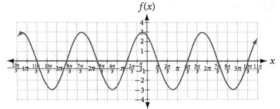

5. Amplitude: 3; period: is 2π; midline: $y = -4$; no asymptotes

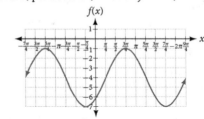

7. Amplitude: 6; period: is $\dfrac{2\pi}{3}$; midline: $y = -1$; no asymptotes

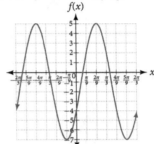

9. Stretching factor: none; period: π; midline: $y = -4$; asymptotes: $x = \dfrac{\pi}{2} + \pi k$, where k is an integer

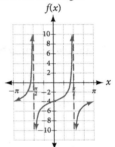

11. Stretching factor: 3; period: $\dfrac{\pi}{4}$; midline: $y = -2$; asymptotes: $x = \dfrac{\pi}{8} + \dfrac{\pi}{4}k$, where k is an integer

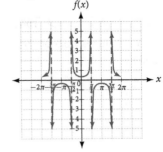

13. Amplitude: none; period: 2π; no phase shift; asymptotes: $x = \dfrac{\pi}{2}k$, where k is an odd integer

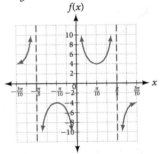

15. Amplitude: none; period: $\dfrac{2\pi}{5}$; no phase shift; asymptotes: $x = \dfrac{\pi}{5}k$, where k is an integer

17. Amplitude: none; period: 4π; no phase shift; asymptotes: $x = 2\pi k$, where k is an integer

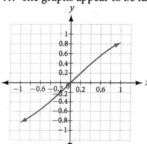

19. Largest: 20,000; smallest: 4,000

21. Amplitude: 8,000; period: 10; phase shift: 0

23. In 2007, the predicted population is 4,413. In 2010, the population will be 11,924.

25. 5 in.   **27.** 10 seconds

29. $\dfrac{\pi}{6}$ **31.** $\dfrac{\pi}{4}$ **33.** $\dfrac{\pi}{3}$

35. No solution   **37.** $\dfrac{12}{5}$

7. Amplitude: 3; period: 6π; midline: $y = 0$

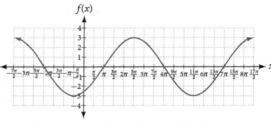

9. Amplitude: none; period: π; midline: $y = 0$; asymptotes: $x = \dfrac{2\pi}{3} + \pi k$, where k is some integer

11. Amplitude: none; period: $\dfrac{2\pi}{3}$; midline: $y = 0$; asymptotes: $x = \dfrac{\pi}{3}k$, where k is some integer

39. The graphs are not symmetrical with respect to the line $y = x$. They are symmetrical with respect to the y-axis.

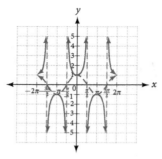

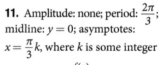

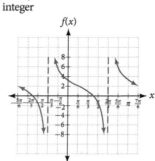

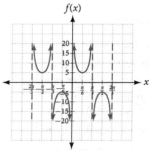

13. Amplitude: none; period: 2π; midline: $y = -3$

15. Amplitude; 2; period: 2; midline: $y = 0$; $f(x) = 2\sin(\pi(x - 1))$

17. Amplitude; 1; period: 12; phase shift: -6; midline: $y = -3$

19. $D(t) = 68 - 12\sin\left(\dfrac{\pi}{12}x\right)$

21. Period: $\dfrac{\pi}{6}$; horizontal shift: -7

23. $f(x) = \sec(\pi x)$; period: 2; phase shift: 0

25. 4

41. The graphs appear to be identical.

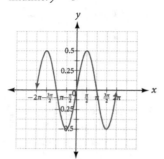

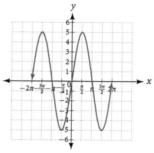

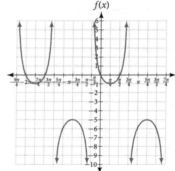

Chapter 8 Practice Test

1. Amplitude: 0.5; period: 2π; midline: $y = 0$

3. Amplitude: 5; period: 2π; midline: $y = 0$

27. The views are different because the period of the wave is $\dfrac{1}{25}$. Over a bigger domain, there will be more cycles of the graph.

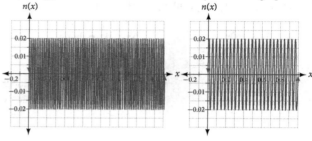

29. $\dfrac{3}{5}$

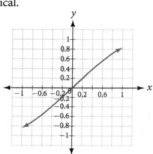

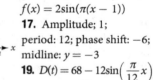

5. Amplitude: 1; period: 2π; midline: $y = 1$

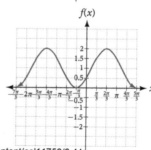

31. $\left(\dfrac{\pi}{6}, \dfrac{\pi}{3}\right), \left(\dfrac{\pi}{2}, \dfrac{2\pi}{3}\right), \left(\dfrac{5\pi}{6}, \pi\right), \left(\dfrac{7\pi}{6}, \dfrac{4\pi}{3}\right), \left(\dfrac{3\pi}{2}, \dfrac{5\pi}{3}\right), \left(\dfrac{11\pi}{6}, 2\pi\right)$

33. $f(x) = 2\cos\left(12\left(x + \frac{\pi}{4}\right)\right) + 3$ **35.** This graph is periodic with a period of 2π.

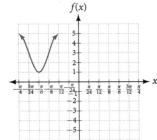

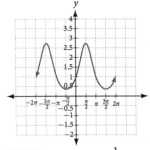

37. $\frac{\pi}{3}$ **39.** $\frac{\pi}{2}$ **41.** $\sqrt{1 - (1 - 2x)^2}$ **43.** $\frac{1}{\sqrt{1 + x^4}}$

45. $\csc t = \frac{x + 1}{x}$ **47.** False   **49.** 0.07 radians

CHAPTER 9

Section 9.1

1. All three functions, F, G, and H, are even. This is because
$F(-x) = \sin(-x)\sin(-x) = (-\sin x)(-\sin x) = \sin^2 x = F(x)$,
$G(-x) = \cos(-x)\cos(-x) = \cos x \cos x = \cos^2 x = G(x)$ and
$H(-x) = \tan(-x)\tan(-x) = (-\tan x)(-\tan x) = \tan^2 x = H(x)$.

3. When $\cos t = 0$, then $\sec t = \frac{1}{0}$, which is undefined.

5. $\sin x$ **7.** $\sec x$ **9.** $\csc t$ **11.** -1 **13.** $\sec^2 x$

15. $\sin^2 x + 1$ **17.** $\frac{1}{\sin x}$ **19.** $\frac{1}{\cot x}$ **21.** $\tan x$

23. $-4\sec x \tan x$ **25.** $\pm\sqrt{\frac{1}{\cot^2 x} + 1}$ **27.** $\pm\frac{\sqrt{1 - \sin^2 x}}{\sin x}$

29. Answers will vary. Sample proof:
$\cos x - \cos^3 x = \cos x(1 - \cos^2 x) = \cos x \sin^2 x$

31. Answers will vary. Sample proof:
$\frac{1 + \sin^2 x}{\cos^2 x} = \frac{1}{\cos^2 x} + \frac{\sin^2 x}{\cos^2 x} = \sec^2 x + \tan^2 x$
$= \tan^2 x + 1 + \tan^2 x = 1 + 2\tan^2 x$

33. Answers will vary. Sample proof:
$\cos^2 x - \tan^2 x = 1 - \sin^2 x - (\sec^2 x - 1)$
$\qquad = 1 - \sin^2 x - \sec^2 x + 1 = 2 - \sin^2 x - \sec^2 x$

35. False   **37.** False

39. Proved with negative and Pythagorean identities

41. True $3\sin^2\theta + 4\cos^2\theta = 3\sin^2\theta + 3\cos^2\theta + \cos^2\theta$
$\qquad\qquad\qquad\qquad\quad = 3(\sin^2\theta + \cos^2\theta) + \cos^2\theta$
$\qquad\qquad\qquad\qquad\quad = 3 + \cos^2\theta$

Section 9.2

1. The cofunction identities apply to complementary angles. Viewing the two acute angles of a right triangle, if one of those angles measures x, the second angle measures $\frac{\pi}{2} - x$. Then $\sin x = \cos\left(\frac{\pi}{2} - x\right)$. The same holds for the other cofunction identities. The key is that the angles are complementary.

3. $\sin(-x) = -\sin x$, so $\sin x$ is odd.
$\cos(-x) = \cos(0 - x) = \cos x$, so $\cos x$ is even.

5. $\frac{\sqrt{2} + \sqrt{6}}{4}$ **7.** $\frac{\sqrt{6} - \sqrt{2}}{4}$ **9.** $-2 - \sqrt{3}$

11. $-\frac{\sqrt{2}}{2}\sin x - \frac{\sqrt{2}}{2}\cos x$ **13.** $-\frac{1}{2}\cos x - \frac{\sqrt{3}}{2}\sin x$

15. $\csc\theta$ **17.** $\cot x$ **19.** $\tan\left(\frac{x}{10}\right)$

21. $\sin(a - b)$
$= \left(\frac{4}{5}\right)\left(\frac{1}{3}\right) - \left(\frac{3}{5}\right)\left(\frac{2\sqrt{2}}{3}\right)$
$= \frac{4 - 6\sqrt{2}}{15}$

$\cos(a + b)$
$= \left(\frac{3}{5}\right)\left(\frac{1}{3}\right) - \left(\frac{4}{5}\right)\left(\frac{2\sqrt{2}}{3}\right)$
$= \frac{3 - 8\sqrt{2}}{15}$

23. $\frac{\sqrt{2} - \sqrt{6}}{4}$ **25.** $\sin x$

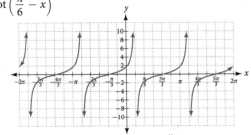

27. $\cot\left(\frac{\pi}{6} - x\right)$

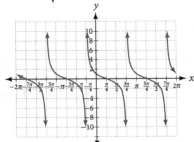

29. $\cot\left(\frac{\pi}{4} + x\right)$

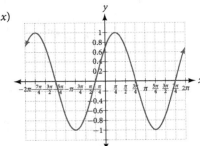

31. $\frac{\sqrt{2}}{2}(\sin x + \cos x)$

33. They are the same.   **35.** They are the different, try $g(x) = \sin(9x) - \cos(3x)\sin(6x)$ **37.** They are the same.

39. They are the different, try $g(\theta) = \frac{2\tan\theta}{1 - \tan^2\theta}$

41. They are different, try $g(x) = \frac{\tan x - \tan(2x)}{1 + \tan x \tan(2x)}$

43. $-\frac{\sqrt{3} - 1}{2\sqrt{2}}$ or -0.2588 **45.** $\frac{1 + \sqrt{3}}{2\sqrt{2}}$, or 0.9659

47. $\tan\left(x + \frac{\pi}{4}\right) = \frac{\tan x + \tan\left(\frac{\pi}{4}\right)}{1 - \tan x \tan\left(\frac{\pi}{4}\right)}$
$\qquad\qquad\quad = \frac{\tan x + 1}{1 - \tan x(1)} = \frac{\tan x + 1}{1 - \tan x}$

49. $\dfrac{\cos(a+b)}{\cos a \cos b} = \dfrac{\cos a \cos b}{\cos a \cos b} - \dfrac{\sin a \sin b}{\cos a \cos b} = 1 - \tan a \tan b$

51. $\dfrac{\cos(x+h) - \cos x}{h} = \dfrac{\cos x \cos h - \sin x \sin h - \cos x}{h} =$

$\dfrac{\cos x(\cos h - 1) - \sin x \sin h}{h} = \cos x \dfrac{\cos h - 1}{h} - \sin x \dfrac{\sin h}{h}$

53. True   **55.** True. Note that $\sin(\alpha + \beta) = \sin(\pi - \gamma)$ and expand the right hand side.

Section 9.3

1. Use the Pythagorean identities and isolate the squared term.

3. $\dfrac{1 - \cos x}{\sin x}, \dfrac{\sin x}{1 + \cos x}$, multiplying the top and bottom by $\sqrt{1 - \cos x}$ and $\sqrt{1 + \cos x}$, respectively.

5. a. $\dfrac{3\sqrt{7}}{32}$ **b.** $\dfrac{31}{32}$ **c.** $\dfrac{3\sqrt{7}}{31}$ **7. a.** $\dfrac{\sqrt{3}}{2}$ **b.** $-\dfrac{1}{2}$ **c.** $-\sqrt{3}$

9. $\cos\theta = -\dfrac{2\sqrt{5}}{5}$, $\sin\theta = \dfrac{\sqrt{5}}{5}$, $\tan\theta = -\dfrac{1}{2}$, $\csc\theta = \sqrt{5}$,

$\sec\theta = -\dfrac{\sqrt{5}}{2}$, $\cot\theta = -2$ **11.** $2\sin\left(\dfrac{\pi}{2}\right)$ **13.** $\dfrac{\sqrt{2-\sqrt{2}}}{2}$

15. $\dfrac{\sqrt{2-\sqrt{3}}}{2}$ **17.** $2 + \sqrt{3}$ **19.** $-1 - \sqrt{2}$

21. a. $\dfrac{3\sqrt{13}}{13}$ **b.** $-\dfrac{2\sqrt{13}}{13}$ **c.** $-\dfrac{3}{2}$

23. a. $\dfrac{\sqrt{10}}{4}$ **b.** $\dfrac{\sqrt{6}}{4}$ **c.** $\dfrac{\sqrt{15}}{3}$ **25.** $\dfrac{120}{169}, -\dfrac{119}{169}, -\dfrac{120}{119}$

27. $\dfrac{2\sqrt{13}}{13}, \dfrac{3\sqrt{13}}{13}, \dfrac{2}{3}$ **29.** $\cos(74°)$ **31.** $\cos(18x)$ **33.** $3\sin(10x)$

35. $-2\sin(-x)\cos(-x) = -2(-\sin(x)\cos(x)) = \sin(2x)$

37. $\dfrac{\sin(2\theta)}{1 + \cos(2\theta)} \tan^2(\theta) = \dfrac{2\sin(\theta)\cos(\theta)}{1 + \cos^2(\theta) - \sin^2(\theta)} \tan^2(\theta) =$

$\dfrac{2\sin(\theta)\cos(\theta)}{2\cos^2(\theta)} \tan^2(\theta) = \dfrac{\sin(\theta)}{\cos(\theta)} \tan^2(\theta) = \cot(\theta)\tan^2(\theta) = \tan(\theta)$

39. $\dfrac{1 + \cos(12x)}{2}$ **41.** $\dfrac{3 + \cos(12x) - 4\cos(6x)}{8}$

43. $\dfrac{2 + \cos(2x) - 2\cos(4x) - \cos(6x)}{32}$

45. $\dfrac{3 + \cos(4x) - 4\cos(2x)}{3 + \cos(4x) + 4\cos(2x)}$ **47.** $\dfrac{1 - \cos(4x)}{8}$

49. $\dfrac{3 + \cos(4x) - 4\cos(2x)}{4(\cos(2x) + 1)}$ **51.** $\dfrac{(1 + \cos(4x))\sin x}{2}$

53. $4\sin x \cos x (\cos^2 x - \sin^2 x)$

55. $\dfrac{2\tan x}{1 + \tan^2 x} = \dfrac{\dfrac{2\sin x}{\cos x}}{1 + \dfrac{\sin^2 x}{\cos^2 x}} = \dfrac{\dfrac{2\sin x}{\cos x}}{\dfrac{\cos^2 x + \sin^2 x}{\cos^2 x}}$

$= \dfrac{2\sin x}{\cos x} \cdot \dfrac{\cos^2 x}{1} = 2\sin x \cos x = \sin(2x)$

57. $\dfrac{2\sin x \cos x}{2\cos^2 x - 1} = \dfrac{\sin(2x)}{\cos(2x)} = \tan(2x)$

59. $\sin(x + 2x) = \sin x \cos(2x) + \sin(2x)\cos x$
$= \sin x(\cos^2 x - \sin^2 x) + 2\sin x \cos x \cos x$
$= \sin x \cos^2 x - \sin^3 x + 2\sin x \cos^2 x$
$= 3\sin x \cos^2 x - \sin^3 x$

61. $\dfrac{1 + \cos(2t)}{\sin(2t) - \cos t} = \dfrac{1 + 2\cos^2 t - 1}{2\sin t \cos t - \cos t}$

$= \dfrac{2\cos^2 t}{\cos t(2\sin t - 1)}$

$= \dfrac{2\cos t}{2\sin t - 1}$

63. $(\cos^2(4x) - \sin^2(4x) - \sin(8x))(\cos^2(4x) - \sin^2(4x) + \sin(8x))$
$= (\cos(8x) - \sin(8x))(\cos(8x) + \sin(8x))$
$= \cos^2(8x) - \sin^2(8x)$
$= \cos(16x)$

Section 9.4

1. Substitute α into cosine and β into sine and evaluate.

3. Answers will vary. There are some equations that involve a sum of two trig expressions where when converted to a product are easier to solve. For example: $\dfrac{\sin(3x) + \sin x}{\cos x} = 1$. When converting the numerator to a product the equation becomes: $\dfrac{2\sin(2x)\cos x}{\cos x} = 1$.   **5.** $8(\cos(5x) - \cos(27x))$

7. $\sin(2x) + \sin(8x)$ **9.** $\dfrac{1}{2}(\cos(6x) - \cos(4x))$

11. $2\cos(5t)\cos t$ **13.** $2\cos(7x)$ **15.** $2\cos(6x)\cos(3x)$

17. $\dfrac{1}{4}(1 + \sqrt{3})$ **19.** $\dfrac{1}{4}(\sqrt{3} - 2)$ **21.** $\dfrac{1}{4}(\sqrt{3} - 1)$

23. $\cos(80°) - \cos(120°)$ **25.** $\dfrac{1}{2}(\sin(221°) + \sin(205°))$

27. $\sqrt{2}\cos(31°)$ **29.** $2\cos(66.5°)\sin(34.5°)$

31. $2\sin(-1.5°)\cos(0.5°)$

33. $2\sin(7x) - 2\sin x = 2\sin(4x + 3x) - 2\sin(4x - 3x)$
$= 2(\sin(4x)\cos(3x) + \sin(3x)\cos(4x)) - 2(\sin(4x)\cos(3x) - \sin(3x)\cos(4x))$
$= 2\sin(4x)\cos(3x) + 2\sin(3x)\cos(4x) - 2\sin(4x)\cos(3x) + 2\sin(3x)\cos(4x)$
$= 4\sin(3x)\cos(4x)$

35. $\sin x + \sin(3x) = 2\sin\left(\dfrac{4x}{2}\right)\cos\left(\dfrac{-2x}{2}\right) = 2\sin(2x)\cos x$
$= 2(2\sin x \cos x)\cos x = 4\sin x \cos^2 x$

37. $2\tan x \cos(3x) = \dfrac{2\sin x \cos(3x)}{\cos x}$

$= \dfrac{2(0.5(\sin(4x) - \sin(2x)))}{\cos x}$

$= \dfrac{1}{\cos x}(\sin(4x) - \sin(2x))$

$= \sec x (\sin(4x) - \sin(2x))$

39. $2\cos(35°)\cos(23°)$, 1.5081 **41.** $-2\sin(33°)\sin(11°)$, -0.2078

43. $\dfrac{1}{2}(\cos(99°) - \cos(71°))$, -0.2410 **45.** It is an identity.

47. It is not an identity, but $2\cos^3 x$ is.

49. $\tan(3t)$ **51.** $2\cos(2x)$ **53.** $-\sin(14x)$

55. Start with $\cos x + \cos y$. Make a substitution and let $x = \alpha + \beta$ and let $y = \alpha - \beta$, so $\cos x + \cos y$ becomes
$\cos(\alpha + \beta) + \cos(\alpha - \beta) =$
$= \cos\alpha\cos\beta - \sin\alpha\sin\beta + \cos\alpha\cos\beta + \sin\alpha\sin\beta$
$= 2\cos\alpha\cos\beta$
Since $x = \alpha + \beta$ and $y = \alpha - \beta$, we can solve for α and β in terms of x and y and substitute in for $2\cos\alpha\cos\beta$ and get
$2\cos\left(\dfrac{x+y}{2}\right)\cos\left(\dfrac{x-y}{2}\right)$.

57. $\dfrac{\cos(3x) + \cos x}{\cos(3x) - \cos x} = \dfrac{2\cos(2x)\cos x}{-2\sin(2x)\sin x} = -\cot(2x)\cot x$

59. $\dfrac{\cos(2y) - \cos(4y)}{\sin(2y) + \sin(4y)} = \dfrac{-2\sin(3y)\sin(-y)}{2\sin(3y)\cos y}$

$\qquad = \dfrac{2\sin(3y)\sin(y)}{2\sin(3y)\cos y} = \tan y$

61. $\cos x - \cos(3x) = -2\sin(2x)\sin(-x) = 2(2\sin x\cos x)\sin x$
$\qquad = 4\sin^2 x\cos x$

63. $\tan\left(\dfrac{\pi}{4} - t\right) = \dfrac{\tan\left(\dfrac{\pi}{4}\right) - \tan t}{1 + \tan\left(\dfrac{\pi}{4}\right)\tan(t)} = \dfrac{1 - \tan t}{1 + \tan t}$

Section 9.5

1. There will not always be solutions to trigonometric function equations. For a basic example, $\cos(x) = -5$. **3.** If the sine or cosine function has a coefficient of one, isolate the term on one side of the equals sign. If the number it is set equal to has an absolute value less than or equal to one, the equation has solutions, otherwise it does not. If the sine or cosine does not have a coefficient equal to one, still isolate the term but then divide both sides of the equation by the leading coefficient. Then, if the number it is set equal to has an absolute value greater than one, the equation has no solution.

5. $\dfrac{\pi}{3}, \dfrac{2\pi}{3}$ **7.** $\dfrac{3\pi}{4}, \dfrac{5\pi}{4}$ **9.** $\dfrac{\pi}{4}, \dfrac{5\pi}{4}$ **11.** $\dfrac{\pi}{4}, \dfrac{3\pi}{4}, \dfrac{5\pi}{4}, \dfrac{7\pi}{4}$

13. $\dfrac{\pi}{4}, \dfrac{7\pi}{4}$ **15.** $\dfrac{7\pi}{6}, \dfrac{11\pi}{6}$ **17.** $\dfrac{\pi}{18}, \dfrac{5\pi}{18}, \dfrac{13\pi}{18}, \dfrac{17\pi}{18}, \dfrac{25\pi}{18}, \dfrac{29\pi}{18}$

19. $\dfrac{3\pi}{12}, \dfrac{5\pi}{12}, \dfrac{11\pi}{12}, \dfrac{13\pi}{12}, \dfrac{19\pi}{12}, \dfrac{21\pi}{12}$ **21.** $\dfrac{1}{6}, \dfrac{5}{6}, \dfrac{13}{6}, \dfrac{17}{6}, \dfrac{25}{6}, \dfrac{29}{6}, \dfrac{37}{6}$

23. $0, \dfrac{\pi}{3}, \pi, \dfrac{5\pi}{3}$ **25.** $\dfrac{\pi}{3}, \pi, \dfrac{5\pi}{3}$ **27.** $\dfrac{\pi}{3}, \dfrac{3\pi}{2}, \dfrac{5\pi}{3}$ **29.** $0, \pi$

31. $\pi - \sin^{-1}\left(-\dfrac{1}{4}\right), \dfrac{7\pi}{6}, \dfrac{11\pi}{6}, 2\pi + \sin^{-1}\left(-\dfrac{1}{4}\right)$

33. $\dfrac{1}{3}\left(\sin^{-1}\left(\dfrac{9}{10}\right)\right), \dfrac{\pi}{3} - \dfrac{1}{3}\left(\sin^{-1}\left(\dfrac{9}{10}\right)\right), \dfrac{2\pi}{3} + \dfrac{1}{3}\left(\sin^{-1}\left(\dfrac{9}{10}\right)\right),$
$\pi - \dfrac{1}{3}\left(\sin^{-1}\left(\dfrac{9}{10}\right)\right), \dfrac{4\pi}{3} + \dfrac{1}{3}\left(\sin^{-1}\left(\dfrac{9}{10}\right)\right), \dfrac{5\pi}{3} - \dfrac{1}{3}\left(\sin^{-1}\left(\dfrac{9}{10}\right)\right),$

35. 0 **37.** $\theta = \sin^{-1}\left(\dfrac{2}{3}\right), \pi - \sin^{-1}\left(\dfrac{2}{3}\right), \pi + \sin^{-1}\left(\dfrac{2}{3}\right),$
$2\pi - \sin^{-1}\left(\dfrac{2}{3}\right)$ **39.** $\dfrac{3\pi}{2}, \dfrac{\pi}{6}, \dfrac{5\pi}{6}$ **41.** $0, \dfrac{\pi}{3}, \pi, \dfrac{4\pi}{3}$

43. There are no solutions.

45. $\cos^{-1}\left(\dfrac{1}{3}(1 - \sqrt{7})\right), 2\pi - \cos^{-1}\left(\dfrac{1}{3}(1 - \sqrt{7})\right)$

47. $\tan^{-1}\left(\dfrac{1}{2}(\sqrt{29} - 5)\right), \pi + \tan^{-1}\left(\dfrac{1}{2}(-\sqrt{29} - 5)\right),$
$\pi + \tan^{-1}\left(\dfrac{1}{2}(\sqrt{29} - 5)\right), 2\pi + \tan^{-1}\left(\dfrac{1}{2}(-\sqrt{29} - 5)\right)$

49. There are no solutions. **51.** There are no solutions.

53. $0, \dfrac{2\pi}{3}, \dfrac{4\pi}{3}$ **55.** $\dfrac{\pi}{4}, \dfrac{3\pi}{4}, \dfrac{5\pi}{4}, \dfrac{7\pi}{4}$

57. $\sin^{-1}\left(\dfrac{3}{5}\right), \dfrac{\pi}{2}, \pi - \sin^{-1}\left(\dfrac{3}{5}\right), \dfrac{3\pi}{2}$

59. $\cos^{-1}\left(-\dfrac{1}{4}\right), 2\pi - \cos^{-1}\left(-\dfrac{1}{4}\right)$

61. $\dfrac{\pi}{3}, \cos^{-1}\left(-\dfrac{3}{4}\right), 2\pi - \cos^{-1}\left(-\dfrac{3}{4}\right), \dfrac{5\pi}{3}$

63. $\cos^{-1}\left(\dfrac{3}{4}\right), \cos^{-1}\left(-\dfrac{2}{3}\right), 2\pi - \cos^{-1}\left(-\dfrac{2}{3}\right), 2\pi - \cos^{-1}\left(\dfrac{3}{4}\right)$

65. $0, \dfrac{\pi}{2}, \pi, \dfrac{3\pi}{2}$ **67.** $\dfrac{\pi}{3}, \cos^{-1}\left(-\dfrac{1}{4}\right), 2\pi - \cos^{-1}\left(-\dfrac{1}{4}\right), \dfrac{5\pi}{3}$

69. There are no solutions. **71.** $\pi + \tan^{-1}(-2),$
$\pi + \tan^{-1}\left(-\dfrac{3}{2}\right), 2\pi + \tan^{-1}(-2), 2\pi + \tan^{-1}\left(-\dfrac{3}{2}\right)$

73. $2\pi k + 0.2734, 2\pi k + 2.8682$ **75.** $\pi k - 0.3277$

77. $0.6694, 1.8287, 3.8110, 4.9703$ **79.** $1.0472, 3.1416, 5.2360$

81. $0.5326, 1.7648, 3.6742, 4.9064$ **83.** $\sin^{-1}\left(\dfrac{1}{4}\right), \pi - \sin^{-1}\left(\dfrac{1}{4}\right), \dfrac{3\pi}{2}$

85. $\dfrac{\pi}{2}, \dfrac{3\pi}{2}$ **87.** There are no solutions. **89.** $0, \dfrac{\pi}{2}, \pi, \dfrac{3\pi}{2}$

91. There are no solutions. **93.** $7.2°$ **95.** $5.7°$ **97.** $82.4°$

99. $31.0°$ **101.** $88.7°$ **103.** $59.0°$ **105.** $36.9°$

Chapter 9 Review Exercises

1. $\sin^{-1}\left(\dfrac{\sqrt{3}}{3}\right), \pi - \sin^{-1}\left(\dfrac{\sqrt{3}}{3}\right), \pi + \sin^{-1}\left(\dfrac{\sqrt{3}}{3}\right), 2\pi - \sin^{-1}\left(\dfrac{\sqrt{3}}{3}\right)$

3. $\dfrac{7\pi}{6}, \dfrac{11\pi}{6}$ **5.** $\sin^{-1}\left(\dfrac{1}{4}\right), \pi - \sin^{-1}\left(\dfrac{1}{4}\right)$ **7.** 1 **9.** Yes

11. $-2 - \sqrt{3}$ **13.** $\dfrac{\sqrt{2}}{2}$

15. $\cos(4x) - \cos(3x)\cos x = \cos(2x + 2x) - \cos(x + 2x)\cos x$
$= \cos(2x)\cos(2x) - \sin(2x)\sin(2x) - \cos x\cos(2x)\cos x +$
$\quad \sin x\sin(2x)\cos x$
$= (\cos^2 x - \sin^2 x)^2 - 4\cos^2 x\sin^2 x - \cos^2 x(\cos^2 x - \sin^2 x)$
$\quad + \sin x(2)\sin x\cos x\cos x$
$= (\cos^2 x - \sin^2 x)^2 - 4\cos^2 x\sin^2 x - \cos^2 x(\cos^2 x - \sin^2 x)$
$\quad + 2\sin^2 x\cos^2 x$
$= \cos^4 x - 2\cos^2 x\sin^2 x + \sin^4 x - 4\cos^2 x\sin^2 x - \cos^4$
$\quad x + \cos^2 x\sin^2 x + 2\sin^2 x\cos^2 x$
$= \sin^4 x - 4\cos^2 x\sin^2 x + \cos^2 x\sin^2 x$
$= \sin^2 x(\sin^2 x + \cos^2 x) - 4\cos^2 x\sin^2 x$
$= \sin^2 x - 4\cos^2 x\sin^2 x$

17. $\tan\left(\dfrac{5}{8}x\right)$ **19.** $\dfrac{\sqrt{3}}{3}$ **21.** $-\dfrac{24}{25}, -\dfrac{7}{25}, \dfrac{24}{7}$

23. $\sqrt{2(2 + \sqrt{2})}$ **25.** $\dfrac{\sqrt{2}}{10}, \dfrac{7\sqrt{2}}{10}, \dfrac{1}{7}, \dfrac{3}{5}, \dfrac{4}{5}, \dfrac{3}{4}$

27. $\cot x\cos(2x) = \cot x(1 - 2\sin^2 x)$
$\qquad = \cot x - \dfrac{\cos x}{\sin x}(2)\sin^2 x$
$\qquad = -2\sin x\cos x + \cot x$
$\qquad = -\sin(2x) + \cot x$

29. $\dfrac{10\sin x - 5\sin(3x) + \sin(5x)}{8(\cos(2x) + 1)}$ **31.** $\dfrac{\sqrt{3}}{2}$ **33.** $-\dfrac{\sqrt{2}}{2}$

35. $\dfrac{1}{2}(\sin(6x) + \sin(12x))$ **37.** $2\sin\left(\dfrac{13}{2}x\right)\cos\left(\dfrac{9}{2}x\right)$

39. $\dfrac{3\pi}{4}, \dfrac{7\pi}{4}$ **41.** $0, \dfrac{\pi}{6}, \dfrac{5\pi}{6}, \pi$ **43.** $\dfrac{3\pi}{2}$ **45.** No solution

47. $0.2527, 2.8889, 4.7124$ **49.** $1.3694, 1.9106, 4.3726, 4.9137$

Chapter 9 Practice Test

1. 1 **3.** $\sec\theta$ **5.** $\dfrac{\sqrt{2} - \sqrt{6}}{4}$ **7.** $-\sqrt{2} - \sqrt{3}$

9. $-\dfrac{1}{2}\cos(\theta) - \dfrac{\sqrt{3}}{2}\sin(\theta)$ **11.** $\dfrac{1 - \cos(64°)}{2}$ **13.** $0, \pi$

15. $\dfrac{\pi}{2}, \dfrac{3\pi}{2}$ **17.** $2\cos(3x)\cos(5x)$ **19.** $4\sin(2\theta)\cos(6\theta)$

21. $x = \cos^{-1}\left(\dfrac{1}{5}\right)$ **23.** $\dfrac{\pi}{3}, \dfrac{4\pi}{3}$ **25.** $\dfrac{3}{5}, -\dfrac{4}{5}, -\dfrac{3}{4}$

27. $\tan^3 x - \tan x \sec^2 x = \tan x (\tan^2 x - \sec^2 x)$
$= \tan x (\tan^2 x - (1 + \tan^2 x))$
$= \tan x (\tan^2 x - 1 - \tan^2 x)$
$= -\tan x = \tan(-x) = \tan(-x)$

29. $\dfrac{\sin(2x)}{\sin x} - \dfrac{\cos(2x)}{\cos x} = \dfrac{2\sin x \cos x}{\sin x} - \dfrac{2\cos^2 x - 1}{\cos x}$
$= 2\cos x - 2\cos x + \dfrac{1}{\cos x}$
$= \dfrac{1}{\cos x} = \sec x = \sec x$

31. Amplitude: $\dfrac{1}{4}$, period $\dfrac{1}{60}$, frequency: 60 Hz

33. Amplitude: 8, fast period: $\dfrac{1}{500}$, fast frequency: 500 Hz, slow period: $\dfrac{1}{10}$, slow frequency: 10 Hz   **35.** $D(t) = 20 (0.9086)^t$ cos $(4\pi t)$, 31 second

CHAPTER 10

Section 10.1

1. The altitude extends from any vertex to the opposite side or to the line containing the opposite side at a 90° angle.   **3.** When the known values are the side opposite the missing angle and another side and its opposite angle.   **5.** A triangle with two given sides and a non-included angle.   **7.** $\beta = 72°$, $a \approx 12.0$, $b \approx 19.9$ **9.** $\gamma = 20°$, $b \approx 4.5$, $c \approx 1.6$ **11.** $b \approx 3.78$
13. $c \approx 13.70$ **15.** One triangle, $\alpha \approx 50.3°$, $\beta \approx 16.7°$, $a \approx 26.7$
17. Two triangles, $\gamma \approx 54.3°$, $\beta \approx 90.7°$, $b \approx 20.9$ or $\gamma' \approx 125.7°$, $\beta' \approx 19.3°$, $b' \approx 6.9$ **19.** Two triangles, $\beta \approx 75.7°$, $\gamma \approx 61.3°$, $b \approx 9.9$ or $\beta' \approx 18.3°$, $\gamma' \approx 118.7°$, $b' \approx 3.2$ **21.** Two triangles, $\alpha \approx 143.2°$, $\beta \approx 26.8°$, $a \approx 17.3$ or $\alpha' \approx 16.8°$, $\beta' \approx 153.2°$, $a' \approx 8.3$
23. No triangle possible   **25.** $A \approx 47.8°$ or $A' \approx 132.2°$
27. 8.6   **29.** 370.9   **31.** 12.3   **33.** 12.2   **35.** 16.0
37. 29.7°   **39.** $x = 76.9°$ or $x = 103.1°$ **41.** 110.6°
43. $A \approx 39.4$, $C \approx 47.6$, $BC \approx 20.7$ **45.** 57.1   **47.** 42.0
49. 430.2   **51.** 10.1   **53.** $AD \approx 13.8$ **55.** $AB \approx 2.8$
57. $L \approx 49.7$, $N \approx 56.1$, $LN \approx 5.8$ **59.** 51.4 feet
61. The distance from the satellite to station A is approximately 1,716 miles. The satellite is approximately 1,706 miles above the ground.   **63.** 2.6 ft   **65.** 5.6 km   **67.** 371 ft   **69.** 5,936 ft
71. 24.1 ft   **73.** 19,056 ft²   **75.** 445,624 square miles   **77.** 8.65 ft²

Section 10.2

1. Two sides and the angle opposite the missing side.   **3.** s is the semi-perimeter, which is half the perimeter of the triangle.
5. The Law of Cosines must be used for any oblique (non-right) triangle.   **7.** 11.3   **9.** 34.7   **11.** 26.7   **13.** 257.4
15. Not possible   **17.** 95.5°   **19.** 26.9°   **21.** $B \approx 45.9°$, $C \approx 99.1°$, $a \approx 6.4$ **23.** $A \approx 20.6°$, $B \approx 38.4°$, $c \approx 51.1$
25. $A \approx 37.8°$, $B \approx 43.8°$, $C \approx 98.4°$ **27.** 177.56 in²   **29.** 0.04 m²
31. 0.91 yd²   **33.** 3.0   **35.** 29.1   **37.** 0.5   **39.** 70.7°
41. 77.4°   **43.** 25.0   **45.** 9.3   **47.** 43.52   **49.** 1.41
51. 0.14   **53.** 18.3   **55.** 48.98   **57.**
59. 7.62   **61.** 85.1   **63.** 24.0 km
65. 99.9 ft   **67.** 37.3 miles   **69.** 2,371 miles

71.

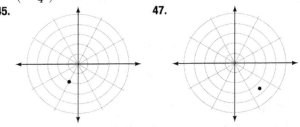

73. 599.8 miles   **75.** 65.4 cm²   **77.** 468 ft²

Section 10.3

1. For polar coordinates, the point in the plane depends on the angle from the positive x-axis and distance from the origin, while in Cartesian coordinates, the point represents the horizontal and vertical distances from the origin. For each point in the coordinate plane, there is one representation, but for each point in the polar plane, there are infinite representations.
3. Determine θ for the point, then move r units from the pole to plot the point. If r is negative, move r units from the pole in the opposite direction but along the same angle. The point is a distance of r away from the origin at an angle of θ from the polar axis.   **5.** The point $\left(-3, \dfrac{\pi}{2}\right)$ has a positive angle but a negative radius and is plotted by moving to an angle of $\dfrac{\pi}{2}$ and then moving 3 units in the negative direction. This places the point 3 units down the negative y-axis. The point $\left(3, -\dfrac{\pi}{2}\right)$ has a negative angle and a positive radius and is plotted by first moving to an angle of $-\dfrac{\pi}{2}$ and then moving 3 units down, which is the positive direction for a negative angle. The point is also 3 units down the negative y-axis.

7. $(-5, 0)$ **9.** $\left(-\dfrac{3\sqrt{3}}{2}, -\dfrac{3}{2}\right)$ **11.** $(2\sqrt{5}, 0.464)$
13. $(\sqrt{34}, 5.253)$ **15.** $\left(8\sqrt{2}, \dfrac{\pi}{4}\right)$ **17.** $r = 4\csc \theta$
19. $r = \sqrt[3]{\dfrac{\sin \theta}{2\cos^4 \theta}}$ **21.** $r = 3\cos \theta$ **23.** $r = \dfrac{3\sin \theta}{\cos (2\theta)}$
25. $r = \dfrac{9\sin \theta}{\cos^2 \theta}$ **27.** $r = \sqrt{\dfrac{1}{9\cos \theta \sin \theta}}$
29. $x^2 + y^2 = 4x$ or $\dfrac{(x - 2)^2}{4} + \dfrac{y^2}{4} = 1$; circle
31. $3y + x = 6$; line   **33.** $y = 3$; line   **35.** $xy = 4$; hyperbola
37. $x^2 + y^2 = 4$; circle   **39.** $x - 5y = 3$; line
41. $\left(3, \dfrac{3\pi}{4}\right)$ **43.** $(5, \pi)$

45. **47.**

49. **51.**

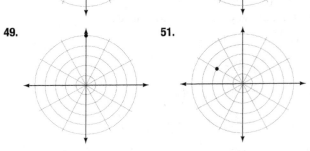

53.

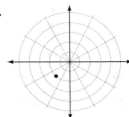

55. $r = \dfrac{6}{5\cos\theta - \sin\theta}$

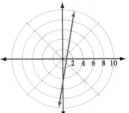

57. $r = 2\sin\theta$

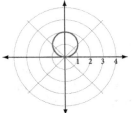

59. $r = \dfrac{2}{\cos\theta}$

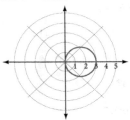

61. $r = 3\cos\theta$

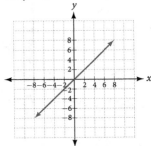

63. $x^2 + y^2 = 16$

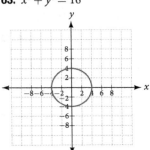

65. $y = x$

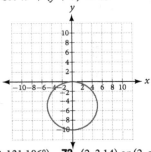

67. $x^2 + (y + 5)^2 = 25$

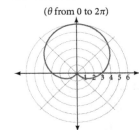

69. $(1.618, -1.176)$ **71.** $(10.630, 131.186°)$ **73.** $(2, 3.14)$ or $(2, \pi)$

75. A vertical line with a units left of the y-axis.

77. A horizontal line with a units below the x-axis.

79.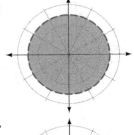

81.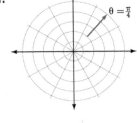

83.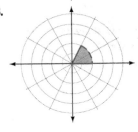

Section 10.4

1. Symmetry with respect to the polar axis is similar to symmetry about the x-axis, symmetry with respect to the pole is similar to symmetry about the origin, and symmetric with respect to the line $\theta = \dfrac{\pi}{2}$ is similar to symmetry about the y-axis.

3. Test for symmetry; find zeros, intercepts, and maxima; make a table of values. Decide the general type of graph, cardioid, limaçon, lemniscate, etc., then plot points at $\theta = 0, \dfrac{\pi}{2}, \pi$ and $\dfrac{3\pi}{2}$, and sketch the graph.   **5.** The shape of the polar graph is determined by whether or not it includes a sine, a cosine, and constants in the equation.   **7.** Symmetric with respect to the polar axis   **9.** Symmetric with respect to the polar axis, symmetric with respect to the line $\theta = \dfrac{\pi}{2}$, symmetric with respect to the pole   **11.** No symmetry   **13.** No symmetry

15. Symmetric with respect to the pole

17. Circle
(θ from 0 to 2π)

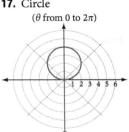

19. Cardioid
(θ from 0 to 2π)

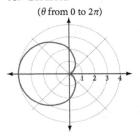

21. Cardioid
(θ from 0 to 2π)

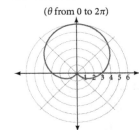

23. One-loop/dimpled limaçon
(θ from 0 to 2π)

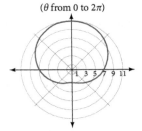

25. One-loop/dimpled limaçon
(θ from 0 to 2π)

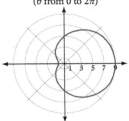

27. Inner loop/two-loop limaçon

29. Inner loop/two-loop limaçon
(θ from 0 to 2π)

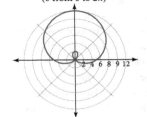

31. Inner loop/two-loop limaçon
(θ from 0 to 2π)

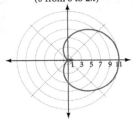

33. Lemniscate
(θ from $-\pi$ to π)

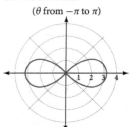

35. Lemniscate
(θ from $-\pi$ to π)

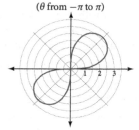

37. Rose curve

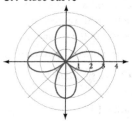

39. Rose curve
(θ from 0 to 2π)

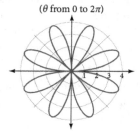

41. Archimedes' spiral
(θ from 0 to 3π)

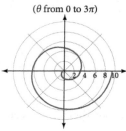

43. Archimedes' spiral
(θ from 0 to 3π)

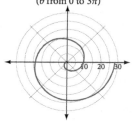

45. (θ from 0 to 8)

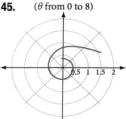

47. (θ from $-\pi$ to π)

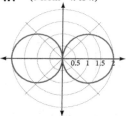

49. (θ from 0 to 2π)

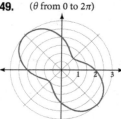

51. (θ from 0 to 3π)

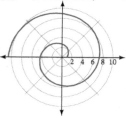

53. (θ from 0 to 2π)

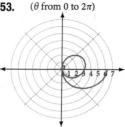

55. They are both spirals, but not quite the same.
57. Both graphs are curves with 2 loops. The equation with a coefficient of θ has two loops on the left, the equation with a coefficient of 2 has two loops side by side. Graph these from 0 to 4π to get a better picture.

59. When the width of the domain is increased, more petals of the flower are visible. **61.** The graphs are three-petal, rose curves. The larger the coefficient, the greater the curve's distance from the pole. **63.** The graphs are spirals. The smaller the coefficient, the tighter the spiral. **65.** $\left(4, \frac{\pi}{3}\right), \left(4, \frac{5\pi}{3}\right)$

67. $\left(\frac{3}{2}, \frac{\pi}{3}\right), \left(\frac{3}{2}, \frac{5\pi}{3}\right)$ **69.** $\left(0, \frac{\pi}{2}\right), (0, \pi), \left(0, \frac{3\pi}{2}\right), (0, 2\pi)$

71. $\left(\frac{\sqrt[4]{8}}{2}, \frac{\pi}{4}\right), \left(\frac{\sqrt[4]{8}}{2}, \frac{5\pi}{4}\right)$ and at $\theta = \frac{3\pi}{4}, \frac{7\pi}{4}$ since r is squared

Section 10.5

1. a is the real part, b is the imaginary part, and $i = \sqrt{-1}$
3. Polar form converts the real and imaginary part of the complex number in polar form using $x = r \cos \theta$ and $y = r \sin \theta$.
5. $z^n = r^n(\cos(n\theta) + i \sin(n\theta))$ It is used to simplify polar form when a number has been raised to a power. **7.** $5\sqrt{2}$
9. $\sqrt{38}$ **11.** $\sqrt{14.45}$ **13.** $4\sqrt{5}\text{cis}(333.4°)$
15. $2\text{cis}\left(\frac{\pi}{6}\right)$ **17.** $\frac{7\sqrt{3}}{2} + \frac{7}{2}i$ **19.** $-2\sqrt{3} - 2i$
21. $-1.5 - \frac{3\sqrt{3}}{2}i$ **23.** $4\sqrt{3}\text{cis}(198°)$ **25.** $\frac{3}{4}\text{cis}(180°)$
27. $5\sqrt{3}\text{cis}\left(\frac{17\pi}{24}\right)$ **29.** $7\text{cis}(70°)$ **31.** $5\text{cis}(80°)$
33. $5\text{cis}\left(\frac{\pi}{3}\right)$ **35.** $125\text{cis}(135°)$ **37.** $9\text{cis}(240°)$
39. $\text{cis}\left(\frac{3\pi}{4}\right)$ **41.** $3\text{cis}(80°), 3\text{cis}(200°), 3\text{cis}(320°)$
43. $2\sqrt[3]{4}\text{cis}\left(\frac{2\pi}{9}\right), 2\sqrt[3]{4}\text{cis}\left(\frac{8\pi}{9}\right), 2\sqrt[3]{4}\text{cis}\left(\frac{14\pi}{9}\right)$
45. $2\sqrt{2}\text{cis}\left(\frac{7\pi}{8}\right), 2\sqrt{2}\text{cis}\left(\frac{15\pi}{8}\right)$

47.

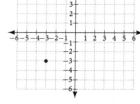

49.

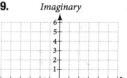

51.

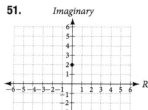

53.

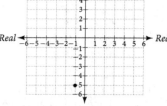
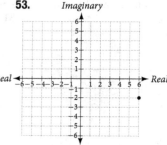

55. Plot of $1 - 4i$ in the complex plane (1 along the real axis, -4 along the imaginary axis). **57.** $3.61e^{-0.59i}$
59. $-2 + 3.46i$ **61.** $-4.33 - 2.50i$

Section 10.6

1. A pair of functions that is dependent on an external factor. The two functions are written in terms of the same parameter. For example, $x = f(t)$ and $y = f(t)$.   **3.** Choose one equation to solve for t, substitute into the other equation and simplify.

5. Some equations cannot be written as functions, like a circle. However, when written as two parametric equations, separately the equations are functions.   **7.** $y = -2 + 2x$

9. $y = 3\sqrt{\dfrac{x-1}{2}}$ **11.** $x = 2e^{\frac{1-y}{5}}$ or $y = 1 - 5\ln\left(\dfrac{x}{2}\right)$

13. $x = 4\log\left(\dfrac{y-3}{2}\right)$ **15.** $x = \left(\dfrac{y}{2}\right)^3 - \dfrac{y}{2}$ **17.** $y = x^3$

19. $\left(\dfrac{x}{4}\right)^2 + \left(\dfrac{y}{5}\right)^2 = 1$ **21.** $y^2 = 1 - \dfrac{1}{2}x$ **23.** $y = x^2 + 2x + 1$

25. $y = \left(\dfrac{x+1}{2}\right)^3 - 2$ **27.** $y = -3x + 14$ **29.** $y = x + 3$

31. $\begin{cases} x(t) = t \\ y(t) = 2\sin t + 1 \end{cases}$ **33.** $\begin{cases} x(t) = \sqrt{t} + 2t \\ y(t) = t \end{cases}$

35. $\begin{cases} x(t) = 4\cos t \\ y(t) = 6\sin t \end{cases}$; Ellipse   **37.** $\begin{cases} x(t) = \sqrt{10}\cos t \\ y(t) = \sqrt{10}\sin t \end{cases}$; Circle

39. $\begin{cases} x(t) = -1 + 4t \\ y(t) = -2t \end{cases}$ **41.** $\begin{cases} x(t) = 4 + 2t \\ y(t) = 1 - 3t \end{cases}$

43. Yes, at $t = 2$ **45.**

t	1	2	3
x	-3	0	5
y	1	7	17

47. Answers may vary:

$\begin{cases} x(t) = t - 1 \\ y(t) = t^2 \end{cases}$

and $\begin{cases} x(t) = t + 1 \\ y(t) = (t + 2)^2 \end{cases}$

49. Answers may vary:

$\begin{cases} x(t) = t \\ y(t) = t^2 - 4t + 4 \end{cases}$ and $\begin{cases} x(t) = t + 2 \\ y(t) = t^2 \end{cases}$

Section 10.7

1. Plotting points with the orientation arrow and a graphing calculator   **3.** The arrows show the orientation, the direction of motion according to increasing values of t.   **5.** The parametric equations show the different vertical and horizontal motions over time.

7.

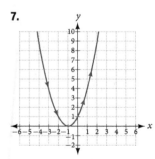

9.

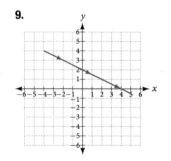

11.

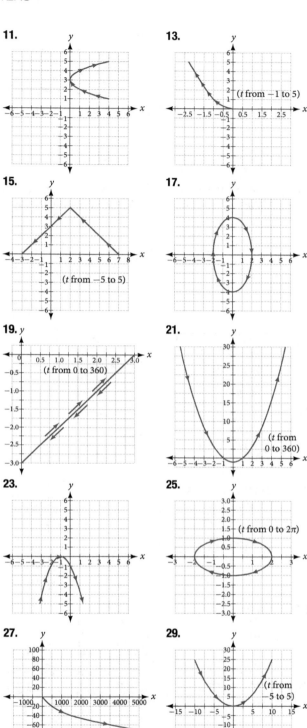

13. (t from -1 to 5)

15. (t from -5 to 5)

17.

19. (t from 0 to 360)

21. (t from 0 to 360)

23.

25. (t from 0 to 2π)

27. (t from -1 to 5)

29. (t from -5 to 5)

31. (t from 0 to 1000)

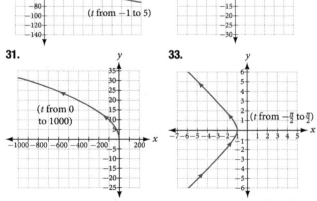

33. (t from $-\frac{\pi}{2}$ to $\frac{\pi}{2}$)

35.
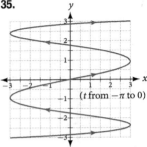
(t from −π to 0)

37.
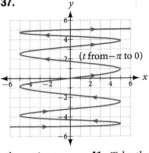
(t from −π to 0)

59.
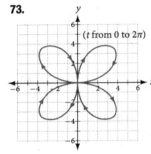
(t from −4π to 6π)

61. The y-intercept changes.

63. $y(x) = -16\left(\dfrac{x}{15}\right)^2 + 20\left(\dfrac{x}{15}\right)$

65. $\begin{cases} x(t) = 64\cos(52°) \\ y(t) = -16t^2 + 64t\sin(52°) \end{cases}$

67. Approximately 3.2 seconds

69. 1.6 seconds

39. There will be 100 back-and-forth motions. **41.** Take the opposite of the x(t) equation. **43.** The parabola opens up.

45. $\begin{cases} x(t) = 5\cos t \\ y(t) = 5\sin t \end{cases}$

47.
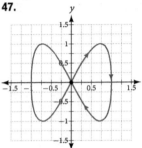

49.
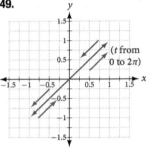
(t from 0 to 2π)

71.
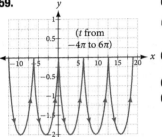
(t from 0 to 2π)

73.
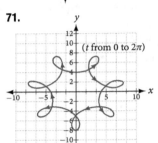
(t from 0 to 2π)

51.
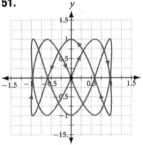

53. $a = 4, b = 3, c = 6, d = 1$

55. $a = 4, b = 2, c = 3, d = 3$

(t from 0 to 2π)

Section 10.8

1. Lowercase, bold letter, usually u, v, w   **3.** They are unit vectors. They are used to represent the horizontal and vertical components of a vector. They each have a magnitude of 1.

5. The first number always represents the coefficient of the i, and the second represents the j.   **7.** $\langle 7, -5 \rangle$ **9.** Not equal

11. Equal   **13.** Equal   **15.** $-7i - 3j$ **17.** $-6i - 2j$

19. $u + v = \langle -5, 5 \rangle, u - v = \langle -1, 3 \rangle, 2u - 3v = \langle 0, 5 \rangle$

21. $-10i - 4j$ **23.** $-\dfrac{2\sqrt{29}}{29}i + \dfrac{5\sqrt{29}}{29}j$

25. $-\dfrac{2\sqrt{229}}{229}i + \dfrac{15\sqrt{229}}{229}j$ **27.** $-\dfrac{7\sqrt{2}}{10}i + \dfrac{\sqrt{2}}{10}j$

29. $|v| = 7.810, \theta = 39.806°$ **31.** $|v| = 7.211, \theta = 236.310°$

33. -6 **35.** -12

37.
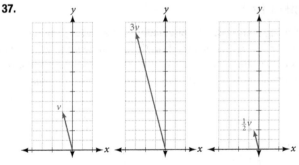

57.
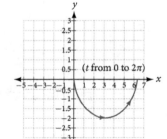
(t from 0 to 2π)

(t from 0 to 2π)

39.

41.
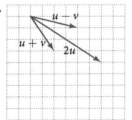

57. (cont.)
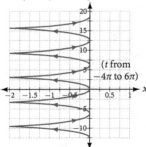
(t from −4π to 6π)

(t from −4π to 6π)

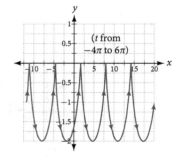
(t from −4π to 6π)

43.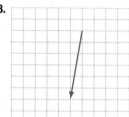
45.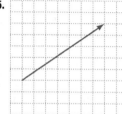

47. ⟨4, 1⟩
49. $v = -7i + 3j$
51. $3\sqrt{2}i + 3\sqrt{2}j$
53. $i - \sqrt{3}j$
55. a. 58.7; **b.** 12.5
57. $x = 7.13$ pounds,
$y = 3.63$ pounds
59. $x = 2.87$ pounds,
$y = 4.10$ pounds

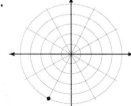

61. 4.635 miles, 17.764° N of E
63. 17 miles, 10.071 miles
65. Distance: 2.868, Direction:
86.474° North of West, or 3.526° West of North
67. 4.924°, 659 km/hr   **69.** 4.424°   **71.** (0.081, 8.602)
73. 21.801°, relative to the car's forward direction
75. Parallel: 16.28, perpendicular: 47.28 pounds
77. 19.35 pounds, 51.65° from the horizontal
79. 5.1583 pounds, 75.8° from the horizontal

Chapter 10 Review Exercises

1. Not possible   **3.** $C = 120°$, $a = 23.1$, $c = 34.1$
5. Distance of the plane from point A: 2.2 km, elevation of the
plane: 1.6 km   **7.** $B = 71.0°$, $C = 55.0°$, $a = 12.8$ **9.** 40.6 km
11.

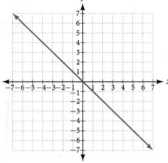

13. (0, 2)
15. (9.8489, 203.96°)
17. $r = 8$
19. $x^2 + y^2 = 7x$

21. $y = -x$ **23.** Symmetric with respect to
the line $\theta = \dfrac{\pi}{2}$

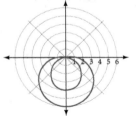

25. (θ from 0 to 2π)   **27.** (θ from 0 to 2π)

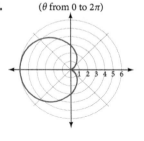

29. 5   **31.** $\text{cis}\left(-\dfrac{\pi}{3}\right)$ **33.** $2.3 + 1.9i$ **35.** $60\text{cis}\left(\dfrac{\pi}{2}\right)$
37. $3\text{cis}\left(\dfrac{4\pi}{3}\right)$ **39.** $25\text{cis}\left(\dfrac{3\pi}{2}\right)$ **41.** $5\text{cis}\left(\dfrac{3\pi}{4}\right)$, $5\text{cis}\left(\dfrac{7\pi}{4}\right)$
43.

45. $x^2 + \dfrac{1}{2}y = 1$
47. $\begin{cases} x(t) = -2 + 6t \\ y(t) = 3 + 4t \end{cases}$

49. $y = -2x^5$

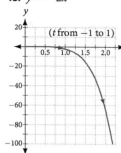

51. a. $\begin{cases} x(t) = (80\cos(40°))t \\ y(t) = -16t^2 + (80\sin(40°))t + 4 \end{cases}$
b. The ball is 14 feet high and 184 feet from where it was launched.
c. 3.3 seconds
53. Not equal   **55.** $4i$
57. $-\dfrac{3\sqrt{10}}{10}i$, $-\dfrac{\sqrt{10}}{10}j$
59. Magnitude: $3\sqrt{2}$, Direction: 225°
61. 16

63.

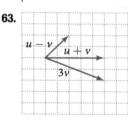

Chapter 10 Practice Test

1. $\alpha = 67.1°$, $\gamma = 44.9°$, $a = 20.9$ **3.** 1,712 miles   **5.** $(1, \sqrt{3})$
7. $y = -3$ **9.** (θ from 0 to 2π)

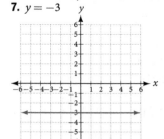   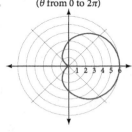

11. $\sqrt{106}$ **13.** $-\dfrac{5}{2} + \dfrac{5\sqrt{3}}{2}i$ **15.** $4\text{cis}(21°)$
17. $2\sqrt{2}\,\text{cis}(18°)$, $2\sqrt{2}\,\text{cis}(198°)$ **19.** $y = 2(x-1)^2$
21.

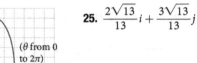

23. $-4i - 15j$
25. $\dfrac{2\sqrt{13}}{13}i + \dfrac{3\sqrt{13}}{13}j$

Chapter 11

Section 11.1

1. No, you can either have zero, one, or infinitely many. Examine graphs. **3.** This means there is no realistic break-even point. By the time the company produces one unit they are already making profit. **5.** You can solve by substitution (isolating x or y), graphically, or by addition. **7.** Yes **9.** Yes **11.** $(-1, 2)$

13. $(-3, 1)$ **15.** $\left(-\frac{3}{5}, 0\right)$ **17.** No solutions exist

19. $\left(\frac{72}{5}, \frac{132}{5}\right)$ **21.** $(6, -6)$ **23.** $\left(-\frac{1}{2}, \frac{1}{10}\right)$

25. No solutions exist. **27.** $\left(-\frac{1}{5}, \frac{2}{3}\right)$ **29.** $\left(x, \frac{x+3}{2}\right)$

31. $(-4, 4)$ **33.** $\left(\frac{1}{2}, \frac{1}{8}\right)$ **35.** $\left(\frac{1}{6}, 0\right)$

37. $(x, 2(7x - 6))$ **39.** $\left(-\frac{5}{6}, \frac{4}{3}\right)$ **41.** Consistent with one solution **43.** Consistent with one solution

45. Dependent with infinitely many solutions
47. $(-3.08, 4.91)$ **49.** $(-1.52, 2.29)$ **51.** $\left(\frac{A+B}{2}, \frac{A-B}{2}\right)$

53. $\left(-\frac{1}{A-B}, \frac{A}{A-B}\right)$ **55.** $\left(\frac{EC-BF}{AE-BD}, \frac{DC-AF}{BD-AE}\right)$

57. They never turn a profit. **59.** $(1,250, 100,000)$
61. The numbers are 7.5 and 20.5. **63.** 24,000
65. 790 sophomores, 805 freshman **67.** 56 men, 74 women
69. 10 gallons of 10% solution, 15 gallons of 60% solution
71. Swan Peak: $750,000, Riverside: $350,000 **73.** $12,500 in the first account, $10,500 in the second account **75.** High-tops: 45, Low-tops: 15 **77.** Infinitely many solutions. We need more information.

Section 11.2

1. No, there can be only one, zero, or infinitely many solutions.
3. Not necessarily. There could be zero, one, or infinitely many solutions. For example, $(0, 0, 0)$ is not a solution to the system below, but that does not mean that it has no solution.
$2x + 3y - 6z = 1 \quad -4x - 6y + 12z = -2 \quad x + 2y + 5z = 10$
5. Every system of equations can be solved graphically, by substitution, and by addition. However, systems of three equations become very complex to solve graphically so other methods are usually preferable. **7.** No **9.** Yes

11. $(-1, 4, 2)$ **13.** $\left(-\frac{85}{107}, \frac{312}{107}, \frac{191}{107}\right)$ **15.** $\left(1, \frac{1}{2}, 0\right)$

17. $(4, -6, 1)$ **19.** $\left(x, \frac{65-16x}{27}, \frac{28+x}{27}\right)$ **21.** $\left(-\frac{45}{13}, \frac{17}{13}, -2\right)$

23. No solutions exist **25.** $(0, 0, 0)$ **27.** $\left(\frac{4}{7}, -\frac{1}{7}, -\frac{3}{7}\right)$

29. $(7, 20, 16)$ **31.** $(-6, 2, 1)$ **33.** $(5, 12, 15)$

35. $(-5, -5, -5)$ **37.** $(10, 10, 10)$ **39.** $\left(\frac{1}{2}, \frac{1}{5}, \frac{4}{5}\right)$

41. $\left(\frac{1}{2}, \frac{2}{5}, \frac{4}{5}\right)$ **43.** $(2, 0, 0)$ **45.** $(1, 1, 1)$

47. $\left(\frac{128}{557}, \frac{23}{557}, \frac{28}{557}\right)$ **49.** $(6, -1, 0)$ **51.** 24, 36, 48

53. 70 grandparents, 140 parents, 190 children **55.** Your share was $19.95, Sarah's share was $40, and your other roommate's share was $22.05.

57. There are infinitely many solutions; we need more information. **59.** 500 students, 225 children, and 450 adults **61.** The BMW was $49,636, the Jeep was $42,636, and the Toyota was $47,727. **63.** $400,000 in the account that pays 3% interest, $500,000 in the account that pays 4% interest, and $100,000 in the account that pays 2% interest. **65.** The United States consumed 26.3%, Japan 7.1%, and China 6.4% of the world's oil. **67.** Saudi Arabia imported 16.8%, Canada imported 15.1%, and Mexico 15.0% **69.** Birds were 19.3%, fish were 18.6%, and mammals were 17.1% of endangered species

Section 11.3

1. A nonlinear system could be representative of two circles that overlap and intersect in two locations, hence two solutions. A nonlinear system could be representative of a parabola and a circle, where the vertex of the parabola meets the circle and the branches also intersect the circle, hence three solutions. **3.** No. There does not need to be a feasible region. Consider a system that is bounded by two parallel lines. One inequality represents the region above the upper line; the other represents the region below the lower line. In this case, no points in the plane are located in both regions; hence there is no feasible region. **5.** Choose any number between each solution and plug into $C(x)$ and $R(x)$. If $C(x) < R(x)$, then there is profit.

7. $(0, -3), (3, 0)$ **9.** $\left(-\frac{3\sqrt{2}}{2}, \frac{3\sqrt{2}}{2}\right), \left(\frac{3\sqrt{2}}{2}, -\frac{3\sqrt{2}}{2}\right)$

11. $(-3, 0), (3, 0)$ **13.** $\left(\frac{1}{4}, -\frac{\sqrt{62}}{8}\right), \left(\frac{1}{4}, \frac{\sqrt{62}}{8}\right)$

15. $\left(-\frac{\sqrt{398}}{4}, \frac{199}{4}\right), \left(\frac{\sqrt{398}}{4}, \frac{199}{4}\right)$ **17.** $(0, 2), (1, 3)$

19. $\left(-\sqrt{\frac{1}{2}(\sqrt{5}-1)}, \frac{1}{2}(1-\sqrt{5})\right), \left(\sqrt{\frac{1}{2}(\sqrt{5}-1)}, \frac{1}{2}(1-\sqrt{5})\right)$

21. $(5, 0)$ **23.** $(0, 0)$ **25.** $(3, 0)$ **27.** No solutions exist

29. No solutions exist

31. $\left(-\frac{\sqrt{2}}{2}, -\frac{\sqrt{2}}{2}\right), \left(-\frac{\sqrt{2}}{2}, \frac{\sqrt{2}}{2}\right), \left(\frac{\sqrt{2}}{2}, -\frac{\sqrt{2}}{2}\right), \left(\frac{\sqrt{2}}{2}, \frac{\sqrt{2}}{2}\right)$

33. $(2, 0)$ **35.** $(-\sqrt{7}, -3), (-\sqrt{7}, 3), (\sqrt{7}, -3), (\sqrt{7}, 3)$

37. $\left(-\sqrt{\frac{1}{2}(\sqrt{73}-5)}, \frac{1}{2}(7-\sqrt{73})\right)\left(\sqrt{\frac{1}{2}(\sqrt{73}-5)}, \frac{1}{2}(7-\sqrt{73})\right)$

39. **41.**

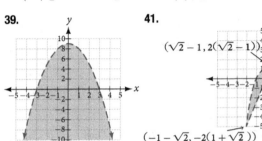

$(\sqrt{2}-1, 2(\sqrt{2}-1))$

$(-1-\sqrt{2}, -2(1+\sqrt{2}))$

43.

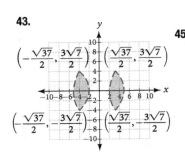

$\left(-\dfrac{\sqrt{37}}{2}, \dfrac{3\sqrt{7}}{2}\right)$ $\left(\dfrac{\sqrt{37}}{2}, \dfrac{3\sqrt{7}}{2}\right)$

$\left(-\dfrac{\sqrt{37}}{2}, -\dfrac{3\sqrt{7}}{2}\right)$ $\left(\dfrac{\sqrt{37}}{2}, -\dfrac{3\sqrt{7}}{2}\right)$

45.

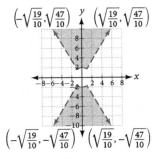

$\left(-\sqrt{\dfrac{19}{10}}, \sqrt{\dfrac{47}{10}}\right)$ $\left(\sqrt{\dfrac{19}{10}}, \sqrt{\dfrac{47}{10}}\right)$

$\left(-\sqrt{\dfrac{19}{10}}, -\sqrt{\dfrac{47}{10}}\right)$ $\left(\sqrt{\dfrac{19}{10}}, -\sqrt{\dfrac{47}{10}}\right)$

47.

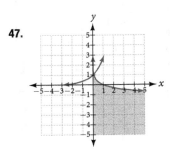

49. $\left(-2\sqrt{\dfrac{70}{383}}, -2\sqrt{\dfrac{35}{29}}\right),$
$\left(-2\sqrt{\dfrac{70}{383}}, 2\sqrt{\dfrac{35}{29}}\right),$
$\left(2\sqrt{\dfrac{70}{383}}, -2\sqrt{\dfrac{35}{29}}\right),$
$\left(2\sqrt{\dfrac{70}{383}}, 2\sqrt{\dfrac{35}{29}}\right)$

51. No solution exists

53. $x = 0, y > 0$ and $0 < x < 1, \sqrt{x} < y < \dfrac{1}{x}$

55. 12,288

57. 2–20 computers

Section 11.4

1. No, a quotient of polynomials can only be decomposed if the denominator can be factored. For example, $\dfrac{1}{x^2 + 1}$ cannot be decomposed because the denominator cannot be factored.

3. Graph both sides and ensure they are equal.

5. If we choose $x = -1$, then the B-term disappears, letting us immediately know that $A = 3$. We could alternatively plug in $x = -\dfrac{5}{3}$ giving us a B-value of -2.

7. $\dfrac{8}{x+3} - \dfrac{5}{x-8}$

9. $\dfrac{1}{x+5} + \dfrac{9}{x+2}$

11. $\dfrac{3}{5x-2} + \dfrac{4}{4x-1}$

13. $\dfrac{5}{2(x+3)} + \dfrac{5}{2(x-3)}$

15 $\dfrac{3}{x+2} + \dfrac{3}{x-2}$

17. $\dfrac{9}{5(x+2)} + \dfrac{11}{5(x-3)}$

19. $\dfrac{8}{x-3} - \dfrac{5}{x-2}$

21. $\dfrac{1}{x-2} + \dfrac{2}{(x-2)^2}$

23. $-\dfrac{6}{4x+5} + \dfrac{3}{(4x+5)^2}$

25. $-\dfrac{1}{x-7} - \dfrac{2}{(x-7)^2}$

27. $\dfrac{4}{x} - \dfrac{3}{2(x+1)} + \dfrac{7}{2(x+1)^2}$

29. $\dfrac{4}{x} + \dfrac{2}{x^2} - \dfrac{3}{3x+2} + \dfrac{7}{2(3x+2)^2}$

31. $\dfrac{x+1}{x^2+x+3} + \dfrac{3}{x+2}$

33. $\dfrac{4-3x}{x^2+3x+8} + \dfrac{1}{x-1}$

35. $\dfrac{2x-1}{x^2+6x+1} + \dfrac{2}{x+3}$

37. $\dfrac{1}{x^2+x+1} + \dfrac{4}{x-1}$

39. $\dfrac{2}{x^2-3x+9} + \dfrac{3}{x+3}$

41. $-\dfrac{1}{4x^2+6x+9} + \dfrac{1}{2x-3}$

43. $\dfrac{1}{x} + \dfrac{1}{x+6} - \dfrac{4x}{x^2-6x+36}$

45. $\dfrac{x+6}{x^2+1} + \dfrac{4x+3}{(x^2+1)^2}$

47. $\dfrac{x+1}{x+2} + \dfrac{2x+3}{(x+2)^2}$

49. $\dfrac{1}{x^2+3x+25} - \dfrac{3x}{(x^2+3x+25)^2}$

51. $\dfrac{1}{8x} - \dfrac{x}{8(x^2+4)} + \dfrac{10-x}{2(x^2+4)^2}$

53. $-\dfrac{16}{x} - \dfrac{9}{x^2} + \dfrac{16}{x-1} - \dfrac{7}{(x-1)^2}$

55. $\dfrac{1}{x+1} - \dfrac{2}{(x+1)^2} + \dfrac{5}{(x+1)^3}$

57. $\dfrac{5}{x-2} - \dfrac{3}{10(x+2)} + \dfrac{7}{x+8} - \dfrac{7}{10(x-8)}$

59. $-\dfrac{5}{4x} - \dfrac{5}{2(x+2)} + \dfrac{11}{2(x+4)} + \dfrac{5}{4(x-4)}$

Section 11.5

1. No, they must have the same dimensions. An example would include two matrices of different dimensions. One cannot add the following two matrices because the first is a 2×2 matrix and the second is a 2×3 matrix. $\begin{bmatrix} 1 & 2 \\ 3 & 4 \end{bmatrix} + \begin{bmatrix} 6 & 5 & 4 \\ 3 & 2 & 1 \end{bmatrix}$ has no sum.

3. Yes, if the dimensions of A are $m \times n$ and the dimensions of B are $n \times m$, both products will be defined **5.** Not necessarily. To find AB, we multiply the first row of A by the first column of B to get the first entry of AB. To find BA, we multiply the first row of B by the first column of A to get the first entry of BA. Thus, if those are unequal, then the matrix multiplication does not commute.

7. $\begin{bmatrix} 11 & 19 \\ 15 & 94 \\ 17 & 67 \end{bmatrix}$

9. $\begin{bmatrix} -4 & 2 \\ 8 & 1 \end{bmatrix}$

11. Undefined; dimensions do not match

13. $\begin{bmatrix} 9 & 27 \\ 63 & 36 \\ 0 & 192 \end{bmatrix}$

15. $\begin{bmatrix} -64 & -12 & -28 & -72 \\ -360 & -20 & -12 & -116 \end{bmatrix}$

17. $\begin{bmatrix} 1{,}800 & 1{,}200 & 1{,}300 \\ 800 & 1{,}400 & 600 \\ 700 & 400 & 2{,}100 \end{bmatrix}$

19. $\begin{bmatrix} 20 & 102 \\ 28 & 28 \end{bmatrix}$

21. $\begin{bmatrix} 60 & 41 & 2 \\ -16 & 120 & -216 \end{bmatrix}$

23. $\begin{bmatrix} -68 & 24 & 136 \\ -54 & -12 & 64 \\ -57 & 30 & 128 \end{bmatrix}$

25. Undefined; dimensions do not match.

27. $\begin{bmatrix} -8 & 41 & -3 \\ 40 & -15 & -14 \\ 4 & 27 & 42 \end{bmatrix}$

29. $\begin{bmatrix} -840 & 650 & -530 \\ 330 & 360 & 250 \\ -10 & 900 & 110 \end{bmatrix}$

31. $\begin{bmatrix} -350 & 1{,}050 \\ 350 & 350 \end{bmatrix}$

33. Undefined; inner dimensions do not match.

35. $\begin{bmatrix} 1{,}400 & 700 \\ -1{,}400 & 700 \end{bmatrix}$

37. $\begin{bmatrix} 332{,}500 & 927{,}500 \\ -227{,}500 & 87{,}500 \end{bmatrix}$

39. $\begin{bmatrix} 490{,}000 & 0 \\ 0 & 490{,}000 \end{bmatrix}$

41. $\begin{bmatrix} -2 & 3 & 4 \\ -7 & 9 & -7 \end{bmatrix}$

43. $\begin{bmatrix} -4 & 29 & 21 \\ -27 & -3 & 1 \end{bmatrix}$

45. $\begin{bmatrix} -3 & -2 & -2 \\ -28 & 59 & 46 \\ -4 & 16 & 7 \end{bmatrix}$

47. $\begin{bmatrix} 1 & -18 & -9 \\ -198 & 505 & 369 \\ -72 & 126 & 91 \end{bmatrix}$

49. $\begin{bmatrix} 0 & 1.6 \\ 9 & -1 \end{bmatrix}$

51. $\begin{bmatrix} 2 & 24 & -4.5 \\ 12 & 32 & -9 \\ -8 & 64 & 61 \end{bmatrix}$

53. $\begin{bmatrix} 0.5 & 3 & 0.5 \\ 2 & 1 & 2 \\ 10 & 7 & 10 \end{bmatrix}$

55. $\begin{bmatrix} 1 & 0 & 0 \\ 0 & 1 & 0 \\ 0 & 0 & 1 \end{bmatrix}$

57. $\begin{bmatrix} 1 & 0 & 0 \\ 0 & 1 & 0 \\ 0 & 0 & 1 \end{bmatrix}$

59. $B^n = \begin{cases} \begin{bmatrix} 1 & 0 & 0 \\ 0 & 1 & 0 \\ 0 & 0 & 1 \end{bmatrix}, n \text{ even,} \\ \begin{bmatrix} 1 & 0 & 0 \\ 0 & 0 & 1 \\ 0 & 1 & 0 \end{bmatrix}, n \text{ odd.} \end{cases}$

Section 11.6

1. Yes. For each row, the coefficients of the variables are written across the corresponding row, and a vertical bar is placed; then the constants are placed to the right of the vertical bar.

3. No, there are numerous correct methods of using row operations on a matrix. Two possible ways are the following: (1) Interchange rows 1 and 2. Then $R_2 = R_2 - 9R_1$. (2) $R_2 = R_1 - 9R_2$. Then divide row 1 by 9.

5. No. A matrix with 0 entries for an entire row would have either zero or infinitely many solutions.

7. $\begin{bmatrix} 0 & 16 & | & 4 \\ 9 & -1 & | & 2 \end{bmatrix}$ **9.** $\begin{bmatrix} 1 & 5 & 8 & | & 19 \\ 12 & 3 & 0 & | & 4 \\ 3 & 4 & 9 & | & -7 \end{bmatrix}$

11. $-2x + 5y = 5$
$6x - 18y = 26$

13. $3x + 2y = 13$
$-x - 9y + 4z = 53$
$8x + 5y + 7z = 80$

15. $4x + 5y - 2z = 12$
$y + 58z = 2$
$8x + 7y - 3z = -5$

17. No solutions

19. $(-1, -2)$

21. $(6, 7)$

23. $(3, 2)$ **25.** $\left(\frac{1}{5}, \frac{1}{2}\right)$ **27.** $\left(x, \frac{4}{15}(5x + 1)\right)$ **29.** $(3, 4)$

31. $\left(\frac{196}{39}, -\frac{5}{13}\right)$ **33.** $(31, -42, 87)$ **35.** $\left(\frac{21}{40}, \frac{1}{20}, \frac{9}{8}\right)$

37. $\left(\frac{18}{13}, \frac{15}{13}, -\frac{15}{13}\right)$ **39.** $\left(x, y, \frac{1}{2} - x - \frac{3}{2}y\right)$

41. $\left(x, -\frac{x}{2}, -1\right)$ **43.** $(125, -25, 0)$ **45.** $(8, 1, -2)$

47. $(1, 2, 3)$ **49.** $\left(-4z + \frac{17}{7}, 3z - \frac{10}{7}, z\right)$

51. No solutions exist.   **53.** 860 red velvet, 1,340 chocolate

55. 4% for account 1, 6% for account 2   **57.** $126

59. Banana was 3%, pumpkin was 7%, and rocky road was 2%

61. 100 almonds, 200 cashews, 600 pistachios

Section 11.7

1. If A^{-1} is the inverse of A, then $AA^{-1} = I$, the identity matrix. Since A is also the inverse of A^{-1}, $A^{-1}A = I$. You can also check by proving this for a 2×2 matrix.   **3.** No, because ad and bc are both 0, so $ad - bc = 0$, which requires us to divide by 0 in the formula.   **5.** Yes. Consider the matrix $\begin{bmatrix} 0 & 1 \\ 1 & 0 \end{bmatrix}$. The inverse is found with the following calculation:

$$A^{-1} = \frac{1}{0(0) - 1(1)}\begin{bmatrix} 0 & -1 \\ -1 & 0 \end{bmatrix} = \begin{bmatrix} 0 & 1 \\ 1 & 0 \end{bmatrix}.$$

7. $AB = BA = \begin{bmatrix} 1 & 0 \\ 0 & 1 \end{bmatrix} = I$ **9.** $AB = BA = \begin{bmatrix} 1 & 0 \\ 0 & 1 \end{bmatrix} = I$

11. $AB = BA = \begin{bmatrix} 1 & 0 & 0 \\ 0 & 1 & 0 \\ 0 & 0 & 1 \end{bmatrix} = I$ **13.** $\frac{1}{29}\begin{bmatrix} 9 & 2 \\ -1 & 3 \end{bmatrix}$

15. $\frac{1}{69}\begin{bmatrix} -2 & 7 \\ 9 & 3 \end{bmatrix}$ **17.** There is no inverse   **19.** $\frac{4}{7}\begin{bmatrix} 0.5 & 1.5 \\ 1 & -0.5 \end{bmatrix}$

21. $\frac{1}{17}\begin{bmatrix} -5 & 5 & -3 \\ 20 & -3 & 12 \\ 1 & -1 & 4 \end{bmatrix}$ **23.** $\frac{1}{209}\begin{bmatrix} 47 & -57 & 69 \\ 10 & 19 & -12 \\ -24 & 38 & -13 \end{bmatrix}$

25. $\begin{bmatrix} 18 & 60 & -168 \\ -56 & -140 & 448 \\ 40 & 80 & -280 \end{bmatrix}$ **27.** $(-5, 6)$ **29.** $(2, 0)$

31. $\left(\frac{1}{3}, -\frac{5}{2}\right)$ **33.** $\left(-\frac{2}{3}, -\frac{11}{6}\right)$ **35.** $\left(7, \frac{1}{2}, \frac{1}{5}\right)$

37. $(5, 0, -1)$ **39.** $\left(-\frac{35}{34}, -\frac{97}{34}, -\frac{77}{17}\right)$

41. $\left(\frac{13}{138}, -\frac{568}{345}, -\frac{229}{690}\right)$ **43.** $\left(-\frac{37}{30}, \frac{8}{15}\right)$

45. $\left(\frac{10}{123}, -1, \frac{2}{5}\right)$ **47.** $\frac{1}{2}\begin{bmatrix} 2 & 1 & -1 & -1 \\ 0 & 1 & 1 & -1 \\ 0 & -1 & 1 & 1 \\ 0 & 1 & -1 & 1 \end{bmatrix}$

49. $\frac{1}{39}\begin{bmatrix} 3 & 2 & 1 & -7 \\ 18 & -53 & 32 & 10 \\ 24 & -36 & 21 & 9 \\ -9 & 46 & -16 & -5 \end{bmatrix}$

51. $\begin{bmatrix} 1 & 0 & 0 & 0 & 0 & 0 \\ 0 & 1 & 0 & 0 & 0 & 0 \\ 0 & 0 & 1 & 0 & 0 & 0 \\ 0 & 0 & 0 & 1 & 0 & 0 \\ 0 & 0 & 0 & 0 & 1 & 0 \\ -1 & -1 & -1 & -1 & -1 & 1 \end{bmatrix}$ **53.** Infinite solutions

55. 50% oranges, 25% bananas, 20% apples

57. 10 straw hats, 50 beanies, 40 cowboy hats

59. Tom ate 6, Joe ate 3, and Albert ate 3

61. 124 oranges, 10 lemons, 8 pomegranates

Section 11.8

1. A determinant is the sum and products of the entries in the matrix, so you can always evaluate that product—even if it does end up being 0.   **3.** The inverse does not exist.   **5.** -2

7. 7   **9.** -4 **11.** 0   **13.** $-7,990.7$ **15.** 3   **17.** -1

19. 224   **21.** 15   **23.** -17.03 **25.** $(1, 1)$ **27.** $\left(\frac{1}{2}, \frac{1}{3}\right)$

29. $(2, 5)$ **31.** $\left(-1, -\frac{1}{3}\right)$ **33.** $(15, 12)$ **35.** $(1, 3, 2)$

37. $(-1, 0, 3)$ **39.** $\left(\frac{1}{2}, 1, 2\right)$ **41.** $(2, 1, 4)$

43. Infinite solutions   **45.** 24   **47.** 1   **49.** Yes; 18, 38

51. Yes; 33, 36, 37   **53.** $7,000 in first account, $3,000 in second account   **55.** 120 children, 1,080 adult   **57.** 4 gal yellow, 6 gal blue   **59.** 13 green tomatoes, 17 red tomatoes

61. Strawberries 18%, oranges 9%, kiwi 10%   **63.** 100 for the first movie, 230 for the second movie, 312 for the third movie

65. 20–29: 2,100, 30–39: 2,600, 40–49: 825   **67.** 300 almonds, 400 cranberries, 300 cashews

Chapter 11 Review Exercises

1. No   **3.** $(-2, 3)$ **5.** $(4, -1)$ **7.** No solutions exist

9. $(300, 60)$ **11.** $(10, -10, 10)$ **13.** No solutions exist

15. $(-1, -2, 3)$ **17.** $\left(x, \frac{8x}{5}, \frac{14x}{5}\right)$ **19.** 11, 17, 33

21. $(2, -3), (3, 2)$ **23.** No solution   **25.** No solution

27.

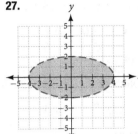

29.

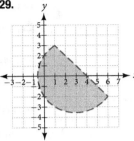

31. $-\dfrac{10}{x+2} + \dfrac{8}{x+1}$ **33.** $\dfrac{7}{x+5} - \dfrac{15}{(x+5)^2}$

35. $\dfrac{3}{x-5} + \dfrac{-4x+1}{x^2+5x+25}$ **37.** $\dfrac{x-4}{x^2-2} + \dfrac{5x+3}{(x^2-2)^2}$

39. $\begin{bmatrix} -16 & 8 \\ -4 & -12 \end{bmatrix}$ **41.** Undefined; dimensions do not match

43. Undefined; inner dimensions do not match

45. $\begin{bmatrix} 113 & 28 & 10 \\ 44 & 81 & -41 \\ 84 & 98 & -42 \end{bmatrix}$ **47.** $\begin{bmatrix} -127 & -74 & 176 \\ -2 & 11 & 40 \\ 28 & 77 & 38 \end{bmatrix}$

49. Undefined; inner dimensions do not match

51. $x - 3z = 7$

$y + 2z = -5$ with infinite solutions

53. $\begin{bmatrix} -2 & 2 & 1 & | & 7 \\ 2 & -8 & 5 & | & 0 \\ 19 & -10 & 22 & | & 3 \end{bmatrix}$ **55.** $\begin{bmatrix} 1 & 0 & 3 & | & 12 \\ -1 & 4 & 0 & | & 0 \\ 0 & 1 & 2 & | & -7 \end{bmatrix}$

57. No solutions exist   **59.** No solutions exist

61. $\dfrac{1}{8}\begin{bmatrix} 2 & 7 \\ 6 & 1 \end{bmatrix}$ **63.** No inverse exists   **65.** $(-20, 40)$

67. $(-1, 0.2, 0.3)$ **69.** 17% oranges, 34% bananas, 39% apples

71. 0   **73.** 6   **75.** $\left(6, \dfrac{1}{2}\right)$ **77.** $(x, 5x+3)$ **79.** $\left(0, 0, -\dfrac{1}{2}\right)$

Chapter 11 Practice Test

1. Yes   **3.** No solutions exist   **5.** $\left(\dfrac{1}{2}, \dfrac{1}{4}, \dfrac{1}{5}\right)$

7. $\left(x, \dfrac{16x}{5}, -\dfrac{13x}{5}\right)$

9. $\left(-2\sqrt{2}, -\sqrt{17}\right), \left(-2\sqrt{2}, \sqrt{17}\right), \left(2\sqrt{2}, -\sqrt{17}\right), \left(2\sqrt{2}, \sqrt{17}\right)$

11.

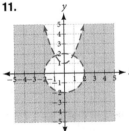

13. $\dfrac{5}{3x+1} - \dfrac{2x+3}{(3x+1)^2}$

15. $\begin{bmatrix} 17 & 51 \\ -8 & 11 \end{bmatrix}$

17. $\begin{bmatrix} 12 & -20 \\ -15 & 30 \end{bmatrix}$

19. $-\dfrac{1}{8}$

21. $\begin{bmatrix} 14 & -2 & 13 & | & 140 \\ -2 & 3 & -6 & | & -1 \\ 1 & -5 & 12 & | & 11 \end{bmatrix}$ **23.** No solutions exist.

25. $(100, 90)$ **27.** $\left(\dfrac{1}{100}, 0\right)$ **29.** 32 or more cell phones per day

CHAPTER 12

Section 12.1

1. An ellipse is the set of all points in the plane the sum of whose distances from two fixed points, called the foci, is a constant.

3. This special case would be a circle.   **5.** It is symmetric about the x-axis, y-axis, and the origin.

7. Yes; $\dfrac{x^2}{3^2} + \dfrac{y^2}{2^2} = 1$ **9.** Yes; $\dfrac{x^2}{\left(\frac{1}{2}\right)^2} + \dfrac{y^2}{\left(\frac{1}{3}\right)^2} = 1$

11. $\dfrac{x^2}{2^2} + \dfrac{y^2}{7^2} = 1$; endpoints of major axis: $(0, 7)$ and $(0, -7)$; endpoints of minor axis: $(2, 0)$ and $(-2, 0)$; foci: $\left(0, 3\sqrt{5}\right), \left(0, -3\sqrt{5}\right)$

13. $\dfrac{x^2}{(1)^2} + \dfrac{y^2}{\left(\frac{1}{3}\right)^2} = 1$; endpoints of major axis: $(1, 0)$ and $(-1, 0)$; endpoints of minor axis: $\left(0, \dfrac{1}{3}\right), \left(0, -\dfrac{1}{3}\right)$; foci: $\left(\dfrac{2\sqrt{2}}{3}, 0\right), \left(-\dfrac{2\sqrt{2}}{3}, 0\right)$ **15.** $\dfrac{(x-2)^2}{7^2} + \dfrac{(y-4)^2}{5^2} = 1$; endpoints of major axis: $(9, 4), (-5, 4)$; endpoints of minor axis: $(2, 9), (2, -1)$; foci: $\left(2 + 2\sqrt{6}, 4\right), \left(2 - 2\sqrt{6}, 4\right)$ **17.** $\dfrac{(x+5)^2}{2^2} + \dfrac{(y-7)^2}{3^2} = 1$; endpoints of major axis: $(-5, 10), (-5, 4)$; endpoints of minor axis: $(-3, 7), (-7, 7)$; foci: $\left(-5, 7+\sqrt{5}\right), \left(-5, 7-\sqrt{5}\right)$

19. $\dfrac{(x-1)^2}{3^2} + \dfrac{(y-4)^2}{2^2} = 1$; endpoints of major axis: $(4, 4), (-2, 4)$; endpoints of minor axis: $(1, 6), (1, 2)$; foci: $\left(1 + \sqrt{5}, 4\right), \left(1 - \sqrt{5}, 4\right)$ **21.** $\dfrac{(x-3)^2}{(3\sqrt{2})^2} + \dfrac{(y-5)^2}{(\sqrt{2})^2} = 1$; endpoints of major axis: $\left(3 + 3\sqrt{2}, 5\right), \left(3 - 3\sqrt{2}, 5\right)$; endpoints of minor axis: $\left(3, 5 + \sqrt{2}\right), \left(3, 5 - \sqrt{2}\right)$; foci: $(7, 5), (-1, 5)$

23. $\dfrac{(x+5)^2}{5^2} + \dfrac{(y-2)^2}{2^2} = 1$; endpoints of major axis: $(0, 2), (-10, 2)$; endpoints of minor axis: $(-5, 4), (-5, 0)$; foci: $\left(-5 + \sqrt{21}, 2\right), \left(-5 - \sqrt{21}, 2\right)$ **25.** $\dfrac{(x+3)^2}{5^2} + \dfrac{(y+4)^2}{2^2} = 1$; endpoints of major axis $(2, -4), (-8, -4)$; endpoints of minor axis $(-3, -2), (-3, -6)$; foci: $\left(-3 + \sqrt{21}, -4\right), \left(-3 - \sqrt{21}, -4\right)$.

27. Foci: $\left(-3, -1 + \sqrt{11}\right), \left(-3, -1 - \sqrt{11}\right)$ **29.** Focus: $(0, 0)$

31. Foci: $(-10, 30), (-10, -30)$

33. Center: $(0, 0)$; vertices: $(4, 0), (-4, 0), (0, 3), (0, -3)$; foci: $\left(\sqrt{7}, 0\right), \left(-\sqrt{7}, 0\right)$

35. Center $(0, 0)$; vertices: $\left(\dfrac{1}{9}, 0\right), \left(-\dfrac{1}{9}, 0\right), \left(0, \dfrac{1}{7}\right), \left(0, -\dfrac{1}{7}\right)$; foci $\left(0, \dfrac{4\sqrt{2}}{63}\right), \left(0, -\dfrac{4\sqrt{2}}{63}\right)$

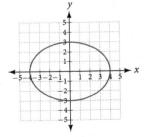

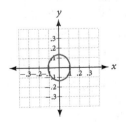

37. Center $(-3, 3)$; vertices $(0, 3)$, $(-6, 3)$, $(-3, 0)$, $(-3, 6)$; focus: $(-3, 3)$. Note that this ellipse is a circle. The circle has only one focus, which coincides with the center.

39. Center: $(1, 1)$; vertices: $(5, 1)$, $(-3, 1)$, $(1, 3)$, $(1, -1)$; foci: $\left(1, 1 + 4\sqrt{3}\right), \left(1, 1 - 4\sqrt{3}\right)$

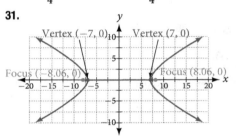

41. Center: $(-4, 5)$; vertices: $(-2, 5)$, $(-6, 5)$, $(-4, 6)$, $(-4, 4)$; foci: $\left(-4 + \sqrt{3}, 5\right), \left(-4 - \sqrt{3}, 5\right)$

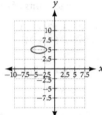

43. Center: $(-2, 1)$; vertices: $(0, 1)$, $(-4, 1)$, $(-2, 5)$, $(-2, -3)$; foci: $(-2, 1 + 2\sqrt{3}), (-2, 1 - 2\sqrt{3})$

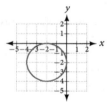

45. Center: $(-2, -2)$; vertices: $(0, -2)$, $(-4, -2)$, $(-2, 0)$, $(-2, -4)$; focus: $(-2, -2)$

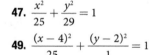

47. $\dfrac{x^2}{25} + \dfrac{y^2}{29} = 1$

49. $\dfrac{(x - 4)^2}{25} + \dfrac{(y - 2)^2}{1} = 1$

51. $\dfrac{(x + 3)^2}{16} + \dfrac{(y - 4)^2}{4} = 1$

53. $\dfrac{x^2}{81} + \dfrac{y^2}{9} = 1$

55. $\dfrac{(x + 2)^2}{4} + \dfrac{(y - 2)^2}{9} = 1$

57. Area $= 12\pi$ square units

59. Area $= 2\sqrt{5}\pi$ square units

61. Area $= 9\pi$ square units

63. $\dfrac{x^2}{4h^2} + \dfrac{y^2}{\frac{1}{4}h^2} = 1$

65. $\dfrac{x^2}{400} + \dfrac{y^2}{144} = 1$, distance: 17.32 feet

67. Approximately 51.96 feet

Section 12.2

1. A hyperbola is the set of points in a plane the difference of whose distances from two fixed points (foci) is a positive constant.
3. The foci must lie on the transverse axis and be in the interior of the hyperbola.   **5.** The center must be the midpoint of the line segment joining the foci.   **7.** Yes $\dfrac{x^2}{6^2} - \dfrac{y^2}{3^2} = 1$

9. Yes $\dfrac{x^2}{4^2} - \dfrac{y^2}{5^2} = 1$ **11.** $\dfrac{x^2}{5^2} - \dfrac{y^2}{6^2} = 1$; vertices: $(5, 0)$, $(-5, 0)$; foci: $\left(\sqrt{61}, 0\right), \left(-\sqrt{61}, 0\right)$; asymptotes: $y = \dfrac{6}{5}x, y = -\dfrac{6}{5}x$

13. $\dfrac{y^2}{2^2} - \dfrac{x^2}{9^2} = 1$; vertices: $(0, 2)$, $(0, -2)$; foci: $\left(0, \sqrt{85}\right)$, $\left(0, -\sqrt{85}\right)$; asymptotes: $y = \dfrac{2}{9}x, y = -\dfrac{2}{9}x$

15. $\dfrac{(x - 1)^2}{3^2} - \dfrac{(y - 2)^2}{4^2} = 1$; vertices: $(4, 2)$, $(-2, 2)$; foci: $(6, 2)$, $(-4, 2)$; asymptotes: $y = \dfrac{4}{3}(x - 1) + 2, y = -\dfrac{4}{3}(x - 1) + 2$

17. $\dfrac{(x - 2)^2}{7^2} - \dfrac{(y + 7)^2}{7^2} = 1$; vertices: $(9, -7)$, $(-5, -7)$; foci: $\left(2 + 7\sqrt{2}, -7\right), \left(2 - 7\sqrt{2}, -7\right)$; asymptotes: $y = x - 9, y = -x - 5$

19. $\dfrac{(x + 3)^2}{3^2} - \dfrac{(y - 3)^2}{3^2} = 1$; vertices: $(0, 3)$, $(-6, 3)$; foci: $\left(-3 + 3\sqrt{2}, 3\right), \left(-3 - 3\sqrt{2}, 3\right)$; asymptotes: $y = x + 6, y = -x$

21. $\dfrac{(y - 4)^2}{2^2} - \dfrac{(x - 3)^2}{4^2} = 1$; vertices: $(3, 6)$, $(3, 2)$; foci: $\left(3, 4 + 2\sqrt{5}\right)$, $\left(3, 4 - 2\sqrt{5}\right)$; asymptotes: $y = \dfrac{1}{2}(x - 3) + 4, y = -\dfrac{1}{2}(x - 3) + 4$

23. $\dfrac{(y + 5)^2}{7^2} - \dfrac{(x + 1)^2}{70^2} = 1$; vertices: $(-1, 2)$, $(-1, -12)$; foci: $\left(-1, -5 + 7\sqrt{101}\right), \left(-1, -5 - 7\sqrt{101}\right)$; asymptotes: $y = \dfrac{1}{10}(x + 1) - 5, y = -\dfrac{1}{10}(x + 1) - 5$

25. $\dfrac{(x + 3)^2}{5^2} - \dfrac{(y - 4)^2}{2^2} = 1$; vertices: $(2, 4)$, $(-8, 4)$; foci: $\left(-3 + \sqrt{29}, 4\right), \left(-3 - \sqrt{29}, 4\right)$; asymptotes: $y = \dfrac{2}{5}(x + 3) + 4,$ $y = -\dfrac{2}{5}(x + 3) + 4$ **27.** $y = \dfrac{2}{5}(x - 3) - 4, y = -\dfrac{2}{5}(x - 3) - 4$

29. $y = \dfrac{3}{4}(x - 1) + 1, y = -\dfrac{3}{4}(x - 1) + 1$

31.

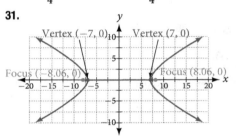

33.

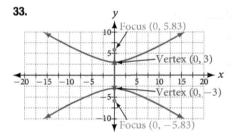

35.

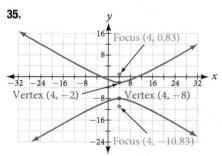

37.

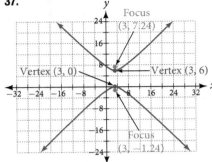

39.

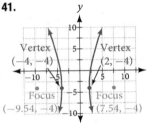

41.

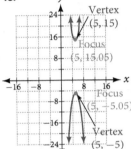

43.

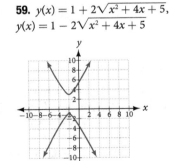

45. $\dfrac{x^2}{9} - \dfrac{y^2}{16} = 1$

47. $\dfrac{(x-6)^2}{25} - \dfrac{(y-1)^2}{11} = 1$

49. $\dfrac{(x-4)^2}{25} - \dfrac{(y-2)^2}{1} = 1$

51. $\dfrac{y^2}{16} - \dfrac{x^2}{25} = 1$

53. $\dfrac{y^2}{9} - \dfrac{(x+1)^2}{9} = 1$

55. $\dfrac{(x+3)^2}{25} - \dfrac{(y+3)^2}{25} = 1$

57. $y(x) = 3\sqrt{x^2 + 1}$, $y(x) = -3\sqrt{x^2 + 1}$

59. $y(x) = 1 + 2\sqrt{x^2 + 4x + 5}$, $y(x) = 1 - 2\sqrt{x^2 + 4x + 5}$

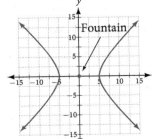

61. $\dfrac{x^2}{25} - \dfrac{y^2}{25} = 1$

63. $\dfrac{x^2}{100} - \dfrac{y^2}{25} = 1$

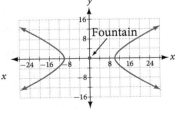

65. $\dfrac{x^2}{400} - \dfrac{y^2}{225} = 1$

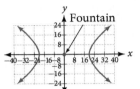

67. $\dfrac{(x-1)^2}{0.25} - \dfrac{y^2}{0.75} = 1$

69. $\dfrac{(x-3)^2}{4} - \dfrac{y^2}{5} = 1$

Section 12.3

1. A parabola is the set of points in the plane that lie equidistant from a fixed point, the focus, and a fixed line, the directrix.

3. The graph will open down.

5. The distance between the focus and directrix will increase.

7. Yes $y = 4(1)x^2$ **9.** Yes $(y-3)^2 = 4(2)(x-2)$

11. $y^2 = \dfrac{1}{8}x$, V: $(0, 0)$; F: $\left(\dfrac{1}{32}, 0\right)$; d: $x = -\dfrac{1}{32}$

13. $x^2 = -\dfrac{1}{4}y$, V: $(0, 0)$; F: $\left(0, -\dfrac{1}{16}\right)$; d: $y = \dfrac{1}{16}$

15. $y^2 = \dfrac{1}{36}x$, V: $(0, 0)$; F: $\left(\dfrac{1}{144}, 0\right)$; d: $x = -\dfrac{1}{144}$

17. $(x-1)^2 = 4(y-1)$, V: $(1, 1)$; F: $(1, 2)$; d: $y = 0$

19. $(y-4)^2 = 2(x+3)$, V: $(-3, 4)$; F: $\left(-\dfrac{5}{2}, 4\right)$; d: $x = -\dfrac{7}{2}$

21. $(x+4)^2 = 24(y+1)$, V: $(-4, -1)$; F: $(-4, 5)$; d: $y = -7$

23. $(y-3)^2 = -12(x+1)$, V: $(-1, 3)$; F: $(-4, 3)$; d: $x = 2$

25. $(x-5)^2 = \dfrac{4}{5}(y+3)$, V: $(5, -3)$; F: $\left(5, -\dfrac{14}{5}\right)$; d: $y = -\dfrac{16}{5}$

27. $(x-2)^2 = -2(y-5)$, V: $(2, 5)$; F: $\left(2, \dfrac{9}{2}\right)$; d: $y = \dfrac{11}{2}$

29. $(y-1)^2 = \dfrac{4}{3}(x-5)$, V: $(5, 1)$; F: $\left(\dfrac{16}{3}, 1\right)$; d: $x = \dfrac{14}{3}$

31.

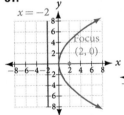

33.

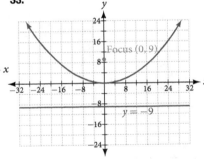

35.

37.

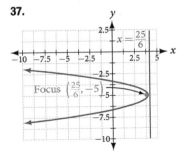

39.
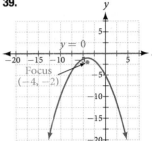

41.
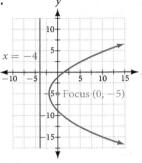

39.
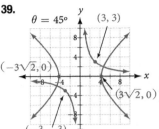

41.
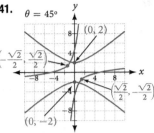

43.
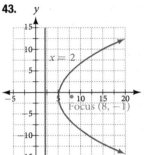

45. $x^2 = -16y$

47. $(y-2)^2 = 4\sqrt{2}(x-2)$

49. $(y+\sqrt{3})^2 = -4\sqrt{2}(x-\sqrt{2})$

51. $x^2 = y$

53. $(y-2)^2 = \dfrac{1}{4}(x+2)$

55. $(y-\sqrt{3})^2 = 4\sqrt{5}(x+\sqrt{2})$

57. $y^2 = -8x$

59. $(y+1)^2 = 12(x+3)$

61. $(0, 1)$

63. At the point 2.25 feet above the vertex   **65.** 0.5625 feet

67. $x^2 = -125(y-20)$, height is 7.2 feet   **69.** 0.2304 feet

Section 12.4

1. The xy term causes a rotation of the graph to occur.

3. The conic section is a hyperbola.   **5.** It gives the angle of rotation of the axes in order to eliminate the xy term.

7. $AB = 0$, parabola   **9.** $AB = -4 < 0$, hyperbola

11. $AB = 6 > 0$, ellipse   **13.** $B^2 - 4AC = 0$, parabola

15. $B^2 - 4AC = 0$, parabola   **17.** $B^2 - 4AC = -96 < 0$, ellipse

19. $7x'^2 + 9y'^2 - 4 = 0$ **21.** $3x'^2 + 2x'y' - 5y'^2 + 1 = 0$

23. $\theta = 60°$, $11x'^2 - y'^2 + \sqrt{3}x' + y' - 4 = 0$

25. $\theta = 150°$, $21x'^2 + 9y'^2 + 4x' - 4\sqrt{3}y' - 6 = 0$

27. $\theta \approx 36.9°$, $125x'^2 + 6x' - 42y' + 10 = 0$

29. $\theta = 45°$, $3x'^2 - y'^2 - \sqrt{2}x' + \sqrt{2}y' + 1 = 0$

31. $\dfrac{\sqrt{2}}{2}(x'+y') = \dfrac{1}{2}(x'-y')^2$ **33.** $\dfrac{(x'-y')^2}{8} + \dfrac{(x'+y')^2}{2} = 1$

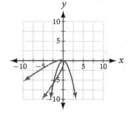

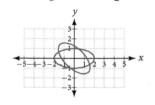

35. $\dfrac{(x'+y')^2}{2} - \dfrac{(x'-y')^2}{2} = 1$ **37.** $\dfrac{\sqrt{3}}{2}x' - \dfrac{1}{2}y' =$

$\left(\dfrac{1}{2}x' + \dfrac{\sqrt{3}}{2}y' - 1\right)^2$

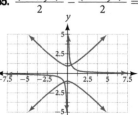

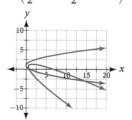

39.
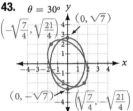

41.
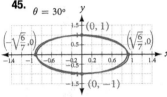

43. $\theta = 30°$
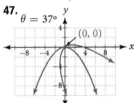

45. $\theta = 30°$
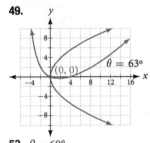

47. $\theta = 37°$
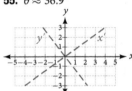

49.
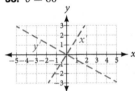

51. $\theta = 45°$
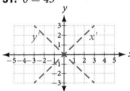

53. $\theta = 60°$

55. $\theta \approx 36.9°$

57. $-4\sqrt{6} < k < 4\sqrt{6}$

59. $k = 2$

Section 12.5

1. If eccentricity is less than 1, it is an ellipse. If eccentricity is equal to 1, it is a parabola. If eccentricity is greater than 1, it is a hyperbola.   **3.** The directrix will be parallel to the polar axis.

5. One of the foci will be located at the origin.   **7.** Parabola with $e = 1$ and directrix $\dfrac{3}{4}$ units below the pole.   **9.** Hyperbola with $e = 2$ and directrix $\dfrac{5}{2}$ units above the pole.   **11.** Parabola with $e = 1$ and directrix $\dfrac{3}{10}$ units to the right of the pole.

13. Ellipse with $e = \dfrac{2}{7}$ and directrix 2 units to the right of the pole.

15. Hyperbola with $e = \dfrac{5}{3}$ and directrix $\dfrac{11}{5}$ units above the pole.

17. Hyperbola with $e = \dfrac{8}{7}$ and directrix $\dfrac{7}{8}$ units to the right of the pole.   **19.** $25x^2 + 16y^2 - 12y - 4 = 0$

21. $21x^2 - 4y^2 - 30x + 9 = 0$ **23.** $64y^2 = 48x + 9$

25. $25x^2 - 96y^2 - 110y - 25 = 0$ **27.** $3x^2 + 4y^2 - 2x - 1 = 0$

29. $5x^2 + 9y^2 - 24x - 36 = 0$

31.

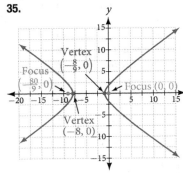

33.

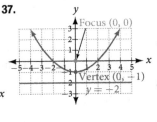

35.

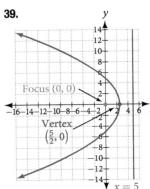

37.

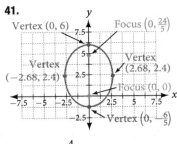

39.

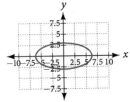

41.

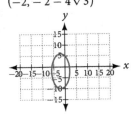

43. $r = \dfrac{4}{5 + \cos\theta}$

45. $r = \dfrac{4}{1 + 2\sin\theta}$ **47.** $r = \dfrac{1}{1 + \cos\theta}$ **49.** $r = \dfrac{7}{8 - 28\cos\theta}$

51. $r = \dfrac{12}{2 + 3\sin\theta}$ **53.** $r = \dfrac{15}{4 - 3\cos\theta}$ **55.** $r = \dfrac{3}{3 - 3\cos\theta}$

57. $r = \pm\dfrac{2}{\sqrt{1 + \sin\theta\cos\theta}}$ **59.** $r = \pm\dfrac{2}{4\cos\theta + 3\sin\theta}$

Chapter 12 Review Exercises

1. $\dfrac{x^2}{5^2} + \dfrac{y^2}{8^2} = 1$; center: $(0, 0)$; vertices: $(5, 0)$, $(-5, 0)$, $(0, 8)$, $(0, -8)$; foci: $(0, \sqrt{39})$, $(0, -\sqrt{39})$ **3.** $\dfrac{(x + 3)^2}{1^2} + \dfrac{(y - 2)^2}{3^2} = 1$

$(-3, 2)$; $(-2, 2)$, $(-4, 2)$, $(-3, 5)$, $(-3, -1)$; $(-3, 2 + 2\sqrt{2})$, $(-3, 2 - 2\sqrt{2})$

5. Center: $(0, 0)$; vertices: $(6, 0)$, $(-6, 0)$, $(0, 3)$, $(0, -3)$; foci: $(3\sqrt{3}, 0)$, $(-3\sqrt{3}, 0)$

7. Center: $(-2, -2)$; vertices: $(2, -2)$, $(-6, -2)$, $(-2, 6)$, $(-2, -10)$; foci: $(-2, -2 + 4\sqrt{3})$, $(-2, -2 - 4\sqrt{3})$

9. $\dfrac{x^2}{25} + \dfrac{y^2}{16} = 1$ **11.** Approximately 35.71 feet

13. $\dfrac{(y + 1)^2}{4^2} - \dfrac{(x - 4)^2}{6^2} = 1$; center: $(4, -1)$; vertices: $(4, 3)$, $(4, -5)$; foci: $(4, -1 + 2\sqrt{13})$, $(4, -1 - 2\sqrt{13})$

15. $\dfrac{(x - 2)^2}{2^2} - \dfrac{(y + 3)^2}{(2\sqrt{3})^2} = 1$; center: $(2, -3)$; vertices: $(4, -3)$, $(0, -3)$; foci: $(6, -3)$, $(-2, -3)$

17.

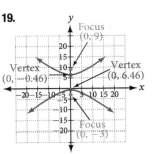

19.

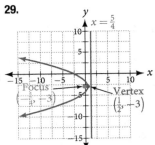

21. $\dfrac{(x - 5)^2}{1} - \dfrac{(y - 7)^2}{3} = 1$ **23.** $(x + 2)^2 = \dfrac{1}{2}(y - 1)$; vertex: $(-2, 1)$; focus: $\left(-2, \dfrac{9}{8}\right)$; directrix: $y = \dfrac{7}{8}$

25. $(x + 5)^2 = (y + 2)$; vertex: $(-5, -2)$; focus: $\left(-5, -\dfrac{7}{4}\right)$; directrix: $y = -\dfrac{9}{4}$

27.

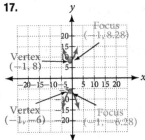

29.

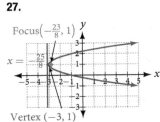

31. $(x - 2)^2 = \left(\dfrac{1}{2}\right)(y - 1)$

33. $B^2 - 4AC = 0$, parabola   **35.** $B^2 - 4AC = -31 < 0$, ellipse

37. $\theta = 45°$, $x'^2 + 3y'^2 - 12 = 0$

39. $\theta = 45°$

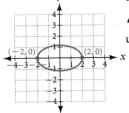

41. Hyperbola with $e = 5$ and directrix 2 units to the left of the pole.

43. Ellipse with $e = \dfrac{3}{4}$ and directrix $\dfrac{1}{3}$ unit above the pole.

45.

47.

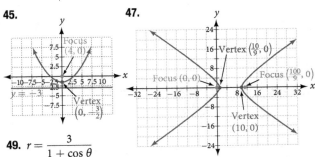

49. $r = \dfrac{3}{1 + \cos\theta}$

Chapter 12 Practice Test

1. $\dfrac{x^2}{3^2} + \dfrac{y^2}{2^2} = 1$; center: $(0, 0)$; vertices: $(3, 0)$, $(-3, 0)$, $(0, 2)$, $(0, -2)$; foci: $\left(\sqrt{5}, 0\right), \left(-\sqrt{5}, 0\right)$

3. Center: $(3, 2)$; vertices: $(11, 2)$, $(-5, 2)$, $(3, 8)$, $(3, -4)$; foci: $\left(3 + 2\sqrt{7}, 2\right), \left(3 - 2\sqrt{7}, 2\right)$

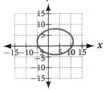

5. $\dfrac{(x-1)^2}{36} + \dfrac{(y-2)^2}{27} = 1$

7. $\dfrac{x^2}{7^2} - \dfrac{y^2}{9^2} = 1$; center: $(0, 0)$; vertices $(7, 0)$, $(-7, 0)$; foci: $\left(\sqrt{130}, 0\right), \left(-\sqrt{130}, 0\right)$; asymptotes: $y = \pm\dfrac{9}{7}x$

9. Center: $(3, -3)$; vertices: $(8, -3)$, $(-2, -3)$; foci: $\left(3 + \sqrt{26}, -3\right)$, $\left(3 - \sqrt{26}, -3\right)$; asymptotes: $y = \pm\dfrac{1}{5}(x-3) - 3$

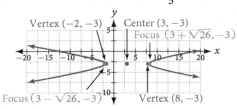

11. $\dfrac{(y-3)^2}{1} - \dfrac{(x-1)^2}{8} = 1$

13. $(x-2)^2 = \dfrac{1}{3}(y+1)$; vertex: $(2, -1)$; focus: $\left(2, -\dfrac{11}{12}\right)$; directrix: $y = -\dfrac{13}{12}$

15.

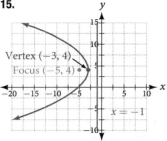

17. Approximately 8.48 feet

19. Parabola; $\theta \approx 63.4°$

21. $x'^2 - 4x' + 3y' = 0$

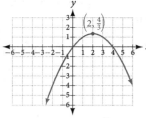

23. Hyperbola with $e = \dfrac{3}{2}$, and directrix $\dfrac{5}{6}$ units to the right of the pole.

25.

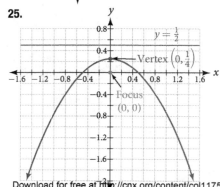

CHAPTER 13

Section 13.1

1. A sequence is an ordered list of numbers that can be either finite or infinite in number. When a finite sequence is defined by a formula, its domain is a subset of the non-negative integers. When an infinite sequence is defined by a formula, its domain is all positive or all non-negative integers.   **3.** Yes, both sets go on indefinitely, so they are both infinite sequences.

5. A factorial is the product of a positive integer and all the positive integers below it. An exclamation point is used to indicate the operation. Answers may vary. An example of the benefit of using factorial notation is when indicating the product It is much easier to write than it is to write out $13 \cdot 12 \cdot 11 \cdot 10 \cdot 9 \cdot 8 \cdot 7 \cdot 6 \cdot 5 \cdot 4 \cdot 3 \cdot 2 \cdot 1$.

7. First four terms: $-8, -\dfrac{16}{3}, -4, -\dfrac{16}{5}$ **9.** First four terms: $2, \dfrac{1}{2}, \dfrac{8}{27}, \dfrac{1}{4}$ **11.** First four terms: $1.25, -5, 20, -80$

13. First four terms: $\dfrac{1}{3}, \dfrac{4}{5}, \dfrac{9}{7}, \dfrac{16}{9}$ **15.** First four terms: $-\dfrac{4}{5}, 4, -20, 100$ **17.** $\dfrac{1}{3}, \dfrac{4}{5}, \dfrac{9}{7}, \dfrac{16}{9}, \dfrac{25}{11}, 31, 44, 59$

19. $-0.6, -3, -15, -20, -375, -80, -9375, -320$

21. $a_n = n^2 + 3$ **23.** $a_n = \dfrac{2^n}{2n}$ or $\dfrac{2^{n-1}}{n}$ **25.** $a_n = \left(-\dfrac{1}{2}\right)^{n-1}$

27. First five terms: $3, -9, 27, -81, 243$ **29.** First five terms: $-1, 1, -9, \dfrac{27}{11}, \dfrac{891}{5}$ **31.** $\dfrac{1}{24}, 1, \dfrac{1}{4}, \dfrac{3}{2}, \dfrac{9}{4}, \dfrac{81}{4}, \dfrac{2187}{8}, \dfrac{531,441}{16}$

33. $2, 10, 12, \dfrac{14}{5}, \dfrac{4}{5}, 2, 10, 12$ **35.** $a_1 = -8, a_n = a_{n-1} + n$

37. $a_1 = 35, a_n = a_{n-1} + 3$ **39.** 720   **41.** 665,280

43. First four terms: $1, \dfrac{1}{2}, \dfrac{2}{3}, \dfrac{3}{2}$

45. First four terms: $-1, 2, \dfrac{6}{5}, \dfrac{24}{11}$

47.

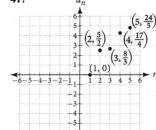

49.

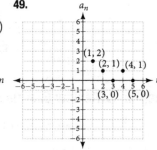

51.

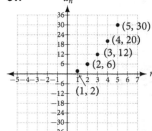

53. $a_n = 2^{n-2}$

55. $a_1 = 6, a_n = 2a_{n-1} - 5$

57. First five terms: $\dfrac{29}{37}, \dfrac{152}{111}, \dfrac{716}{333}, \dfrac{3188}{999}, \dfrac{13724}{2997}$

59. First five terms: $2, 3, 5, 17, 65537$

61. $a_{10} = 7,257,600$

63. First six terms: $0.042, 0.146, 0.875, 2.385, 4.708$

65. First four terms: $5.975, 32.765, 185.743, 1057.25, 6023.521$

67. If $a_n = -421$ is a term in the sequence, then solving the equation $-421 = -6 - 8n$ for n will yield a non-negative integer. However, if $-421 = -6 - 8n$, then $n = 51.875$ so $a_n = -421$ is not a term in the sequence.

69. $a_1 = 1, a_2 = 0, a_n = a_{n-1} - a_{n-2}$

71. $\dfrac{(n+2)!}{(n-1)!} = \dfrac{(n+2) \cdot (n+1) \cdot (n) \cdot (n-1) \cdots \; \cdot 3 \cdot 2 \cdot 1}{(n-1) \cdots \; \cdot 3 \cdot 2 \cdot 1}$

$$= n(n+1)(n+2) = n^3 + 3n^2 + 2n$$

Section 13.2

1. A sequence where each successive term of the sequence increases (or decreases) by a constant value.   **3.** We find whether the difference between all consecutive terms is the same. This is the same as saying that the sequence has a common difference.   **5.** Both arithmetic sequences and linear functions have a constant rate of change. They are different because their domains are not the same; linear functions are defined for all real numbers, and arithmetic sequences are defined for natural numbers or a subset of the natural numbers.   **7.** The common difference is $\frac{1}{2}$ **9.** The sequence is not arithmetic because $16 - 4 \neq 64 - 16$.   **11.** $0, \frac{2}{3}, \frac{4}{3}, 2, \frac{8}{3}$ **13.** $0, -5, -10, -15, -20$

15. $a_4 = 19$ **17.** $a_6 = 41$ **19.** $a_1 = 2$ **21.** $a_1 = 5$ **23.** $a_1 = 6$ **25.** $a_{21} = -13.5$ **27.** $-19, -20.4, -21.8, -23.2, -24.6$ **29.** $a_1 = 17; a_n = a_{n-1} + 9; n \geq 2$ **31.** $a_1 = 12; a_n = a_{n-1} + 5; n \geq 2$ **33.** $a_1 = 8.9; a_n = a_{n-1} + 1.4; n \geq 2$ **35.** $a_1 = \frac{1}{5}; a_n = a_{n-1} + \frac{1}{4}; n \geq 2$ **37.** $a_1 = \frac{1}{6}; a_n = a_{n-1} - \frac{13}{12}; n \geq 2$ **39.** $a_1 = 4; a_n = a_{n-1} + 7; a_{14} = 95$

41. First five terms: $20, 16, 12, 8, 4$ **43.** $a_n = 1 + 2n$ **45.** $a_n = -105 + 100n$ **47.** $a_n = 1.8n$ **49.** $a_n = 13.1 + 2.7n$ **51.** $a_n = \frac{1}{3}n - \frac{1}{3}$ **53.** There are 10 terms in the sequence.

55. There are 6 terms in the sequence.
57. The graph does not represent an arithmetic sequence.

59.
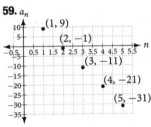

61. $1, 4, 7, 10, 13, 16, 19$

63.
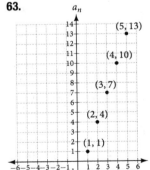

65.
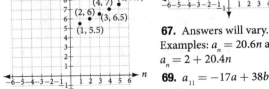

67. Answers will vary. Examples: $a_n = 20.6n$ and $a_n = 2 + 20.4n$ **69.** $a_{11} = -17a + 38b$

71. The sequence begins to have negative values at the 13ᵗʰ term, $a_{13} = -\frac{1}{3}$ **73.** Answers will vary. Check to see that the sequence is arithmetic. Example: Recursive formula: $a_1 = 3$, $a_n = a_{n-1} - 3$. First 4 terms: $3, 0, -3, -6; a_{31} = -87$

Section 13.3

1. A sequence in which the ratio between any two consecutive terms is constant.   **3.** Divide each term in a sequence by the preceding term. If the resulting quotients are equal, then the sequence is geometric.   **5.** Both geometric sequences and exponential functions have a constant ratio. However, their domains are not the same. Exponential functions are defined for all real numbers, and geometric sequences are defined only for positive integers. Another difference is that the base of a geometric sequence (the common ratio) can be negative, but the base of an exponential function must be positive.

7. The common ratio is -2 **9.** The sequence is geometric. The common ratio is 2.   **11.** The sequence is geometric. The common ratio is $-\frac{1}{2}$.   **13.** The sequence is geometric. The common ratio is 5.   **15.** $5, 1, \frac{1}{5}, \frac{1}{25}, \frac{1}{125}$ **17.** $800, 400, 200, 100, 50$

19. $a_4 = -\frac{16}{27}$ **21.** $a_7 = -\frac{2}{729}$ **23.** $7, 1.4, 0.28, 0.056, 0.0112$ **25.** $a = -32, a_n = \frac{1}{2}a_{n-1}$ **27.** $a_1 = 10, a_n = -0.3\,a_{n-1}$ **29.** $a_1 = \frac{3}{5}, a_n = \frac{1}{6}a_{n-1}$ **31.** $a_1 = \frac{1}{512}, a_n = -4a_{n-1}$ **33.** $12, -6, 3, -\frac{3}{2}, \frac{3}{4}$ **35.** $a_n = 3^{n-1}$ **37.** $a_n = 0.8 \cdot (-5)^{n-1}$ **39.** $a_n = -\left(\frac{4}{5}\right)^{n-1}$ **41.** $a_n = 3 \cdot \left(-\frac{1}{3}\right)^{n-1}$ **43.** $a_{12} = \frac{1}{177,147}$

45. There are 12 terms in the sequence.
47. The graph does not represent a geometric sequence.

49.
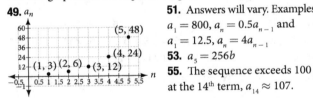

51. Answers will vary. Examples: $a_1 = 800, a_n = 0.5a_{n-1}$ and $a_1 = 12.5, a_n = 4a_{n-1}$ **53.** $a_5 = 256b$ **55.** The sequence exceeds 100 at the 14ᵗʰ term, $a_{14} \approx 107$.

57. $a_4 = -\frac{32}{3}$ is the first non-integer value
59. Answers will vary. Example: explicit formula with a decimal common ratio: $a_n = 400 \cdot 0.5^{n-1}$; first 4 terms: $400, 200, 100, 50$; $a_8 = 3.125$

Section 13.4

1. An nth partial sum is the sum of the first n terms of a sequence.   **3.** A geometric series is the sum of the terms in a geometric sequence.   **5.** An annuity is a series of regular equal payments that earn a constant compounded interest.

7. $\displaystyle\sum_{n=0}^{4} 5n$ **9.** $\displaystyle\sum_{k=1}^{5} 4$ **11.** $\displaystyle\sum_{k=1}^{20} 8k + 2$ **13.** $S_5 = \frac{25}{2}$

15. $S_{13} = 57.2$ **17.** $\displaystyle\sum_{k=1}^{7} 8 \cdot 0.5^{k-1}$

19. $S_5 = \dfrac{9\left(1 - \left(\frac{1}{3}\right)^5\right)}{1 - \frac{1}{3}} = \dfrac{121}{9} \approx 13.44$

21. $S_{11} = \dfrac{64(1 - 0.2^{11})}{1 - 0.2} = \dfrac{781,249,984}{9,765,625} \approx 80$

23. The series is defined. $S = \dfrac{2}{1 - 0.8}$

25. The series is defined. $S = \dfrac{-1}{1 - \left(-\frac{1}{2}\right)}$

27.

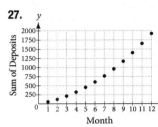

29. Sample answer: The graph of S_n seems to be approaching 1. This makes sense because $\displaystyle\sum_{k=1}^{\infty}\left(\frac{1}{2}\right)^k$ is a defined infinite geometric series with $S = \dfrac{\frac{1}{2}}{1-\left(\frac{1}{2}\right)} = 1$.

31. 49   **33.** 254   **35.** $S_7 = \dfrac{147}{2}$ **37.** $S_{11} = \dfrac{55}{2}$

39. $S_7 = 5208.4$ **41.** $S_{10} = -\dfrac{1023}{256}$ **43.** $S = -\dfrac{4}{3}$

45. $S = 9.2$ **47.** \$3,705.42   **49.** \$695,823.97

51. $a_k = 30 - k$ **53.** 9 terms   **55.** $r = \dfrac{4}{5}$

57. \$400 per month   **59.** 420 feet   **61.** 12 feet

Section 13.5

1. There are $m + n$ ways for either event A or event B to occur.
3. The addition principle is applied when determining the total possible of outcomes of either event occurring. The multiplication principle is applied when determining the total possible outcomes of both events occurring. The word "or" usually implies an addition problem. The word "and" usually implies a multiplication problem.   **5.** A combination;

$C(n, r) = \dfrac{n!}{(n-r)!r!}$ **7.** $4 + 2 = 6$ **9.** $5 + 4 + 7 = 16$

11. $2 \times 6 = 12$ **13.** $10^3 = 1{,}000$ **15.** $P(5, 2) = 20$
17. $P(3, 3) = 6$ **19.** $P(11, 5) = 55{,}440$ **21.** $C(12, 4) = 495$
23. $C(7, 6) = 7$ **25.** $2^{10} = 1{,}024$ **27.** $2^{12} = 4{,}096$
29. $2^9 = 512$ **31.** $\dfrac{8!}{3!} = 6{,}720$ **33.** $\dfrac{12!}{3!2!3!4!}$ **35.** 9

37. Yes, for the trivial cases $r = 0$ and $r = 1$. If $r = 0$, then $C(n, r) = P(n, r) = 1$. If $r = 1$, then $r = 1$, $C(n, r) = P(n, r) = n$.
39. $\dfrac{6!}{2!} \times 4! = 8{,}640$ **41.** $6 - 3 + 8 - 3 = 8$ **43.** $4 \times 2 \times 5 = 40$
45. $4 \times 12 \times 3 = 144$ **47.** $P(15, 9) = 1{,}816{,}214{,}400$
49. $C(10, 3) \times C(6, 5) \times C(5, 2) = 7{,}200$ **51.** $2^{11} = 2{,}048$
53. $\dfrac{20!}{6!6!8!} = 116{,}396{,}280$

Section 13.6

1. A binomial coefficient is an alternative way of denoting the combination $C(n, r)$. It is defined as $\binom{n}{r} = C(n, r) = \dfrac{n!}{r!(n-r)!}$.

3. The Binomial Theorem is defined as $(x + y)^n = \displaystyle\sum_{k=0}^{n}\binom{n}{k}x^{n-k}y^k$ and can be used to expand any binomial.

5. 15   **7.** 35   **9.** 10   **11.** 12,376
13. $64a^3 - 48a^2b + 12ab^2 - b^3$ **15.** $27a^3 + 54a^2b + 36ab^2 + 8b^3$
17. $1024x^5 + 2560x^4y + 2560x^3y^2 + 1280x^2y^3 + 320xy^4 + 32y^5$
19. $1024x^5 - 3840x^4y + 5760x^3y^2 - 4320x^2y^3 + 1620xy^4 - 243y^5$
21. $\dfrac{1}{x^4} + \dfrac{8}{x^3y} + \dfrac{24}{x^2y^2} + \dfrac{32}{xy^3} + \dfrac{16}{y^4}$ **23.** $a^{17} + 17a^{16}b + 136a^{15}b^2$
25. $a^{15} - 30a^{14}b + 420a^{13}b^2$

27. $3{,}486{,}784{,}401a^{20} + 23{,}245{,}229{,}340a^{19}b + 73{,}609{,}892{,}910a^{18}b^2$
29. $x^{24} - 8x^{21}\sqrt{y} + 28x^{18}y$ **31.** $-720x^2y^3$
33. $220{,}812{,}466{,}875{,}000y^7$ **35.** $35x^3y^4$
37. $1{,}082{,}565a^3b^{16}$ **39.** $\dfrac{1152y^2}{x^7}$
41. $f_2(x) = x^4 + 12x^3$ **43.** $f_4(x) = x^4 + 12x^3 + 54x^2 + 108x$

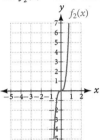
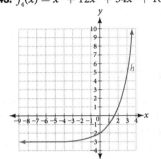

45. $590{,}625x^5y^2$

47. $k - 1$

49. The expression $(x^3 + 2y^2 - z)^5$ cannot be expanded using the Binomial Theorem because it cannot be rewritten as a binomial.

Section 13.7

1. Probability; the probability of an event is restricted to values between 0 and 1, inclusive of 0 and 1.
3. An experiment is an activity with an observable result.
5. The probability of the *union of two events* occurring is a number that describes the likelihood that at least one of the events from a probability model occurs. In both a union of sets A and B and a union of events A and B, the union includes either A or B or both. The difference is that a union of sets results in another set, while the union of events is a probability, so it is always a numerical value between 0 and 1.   **7.** $\dfrac{1}{2}$
9. $\dfrac{5}{8}$ **11.** $\dfrac{5}{8}$ **13.** $\dfrac{3}{8}$ **15.** $\dfrac{1}{4}$ **17.** $\dfrac{3}{4}$ **19.** $\dfrac{3}{8}$
21. $\dfrac{1}{8}$ **23.** $\dfrac{15}{16}$ **25.** $\dfrac{5}{8}$ **27.** $\dfrac{1}{13}$ **29.** $\dfrac{1}{26}$ **31.** $\dfrac{12}{13}$
33.

	1	2	3	4	5	6
1	(1, 1) 2	(1, 2) 3	(1, 3) 4	(1, 4) 5	(1, 5) 6	(1, 6) 7
2	(2, 1) 3	(2, 2) 4	(2, 3) 5	(2, 4) 6	(2, 5) 7	(2, 6) 8
3	(3, 1) 4	(3, 2) 5	(3, 3) 6	(3, 4) 7	(3, 5) 8	(3, 6) 9
4	(4, 1) 5	(4, 2) 6	(4, 3) 7	(4, 4) 8	(4, 5) 9	(4, 6) 10
5	(5, 1) 6	(5, 2) 7	(5, 3) 8	(5, 4) 9	(5, 5) 10	(5, 6) 11
6	(6, 1) 7	(6, 2) 8	(6, 3) 9	(6, 4) 10	(6, 5) 11	(6, 6) 12

35. $\dfrac{5}{12}$ **37.** 0.   **39.** $\dfrac{4}{9}$ **41.** $\dfrac{1}{4}$ **43.** $\dfrac{3}{4}$

45. $\dfrac{21}{26}$ **47.** $\dfrac{C(12, 5)}{C(48, 5)} = \dfrac{1}{2162}$ **49.** $\dfrac{C(12, 3)C(36, 2)}{C(48, 5)} = \dfrac{175}{2162}$

51. $\dfrac{C(20, 3)C(60, 17)}{C(80, 20)} \approx 12.49\%$ **53.** $\dfrac{C(20, 5)C(60, 15)}{C(80, 20)} \approx 23.33\%$

55. $20.50 + 23.33 - 12.49 = 31.34\%$

57. $\dfrac{C(40000000, 1)C(277000000, 4)}{C(317000000, 5)} = 36.78\%$

59. $\dfrac{C(40000000, 4)C(277000000, 1)}{C(317000000, 5)} = 0.11\%$

Chapter 13 Review Exercises

1. $2, 4, 7, 11$ **3.** $13, 103, 1003, 10003$

5. The sequence is arithmetic. The common difference is $d = \dfrac{5}{3}$.

7. $18, 10, 2, -6, -14$ **9.** $a_1 = -20, a_n = a_{n-1} + 10$

11. $a_n = \dfrac{1}{3}n + \dfrac{13}{24}$ **13.** $r = 2$ **15.** $4, 16, 64, 256, 1024$

17. $3, 12, 48, 192, 768$ **19.** $a_n = -\dfrac{1}{5} \cdot \left(\dfrac{1}{3}\right)^{n-1}$

21. $\displaystyle\sum_{m=0}^{5}\left(\dfrac{1}{2}m + 5\right)$ **23.** $S_{11} = 110$ **25.** $S_9 \approx 23.95$

27. $S = \dfrac{135}{4}$ **29.** \$5,617.61   **31.** 6 **33.** $10^4 = 10,000$

35. $P(18, 4) = 73,440$ **37.** $C(15, 6) = 5,005$

39. $2^{50} = 1.13 \times 10^{15}$ **41.** $\dfrac{8!}{3!2!} = 3,360$ **43.** $490,314$

45. $131,072a^{17} + 1,114,112a^{16}b + 4,456,448a^{15}b^2$

47.

	1	2	3	4	5	6
1	1, 1	1, 2	1, 3	1, 4	1, 5	1, 6
2	2, 1	2, 2	2, 3	2, 4	2, 5	2, 6
3	3, 1	3, 2	3, 3	3, 4	3, 5	3, 6
4	4, 1	4, 2	4, 3	4, 4	4, 5	4, 6
5	5, 1	5, 2	5, 3	5, 4	5, 5	5, 6
6	6, 1	6, 2	6, 3	6, 4	6, 5	6, 6

49. $\dfrac{1}{6}$ **51.** $\dfrac{5}{9}$ **53.** $\dfrac{4}{9}$ **55.** $1 - \dfrac{C(350, 8)}{C(500, 8)}) \approx 94.4\%$

57. $\dfrac{C(150, 3)C(350, 5)}{C(500, 8)} \approx 25.6\%$

Chapter 13 Practice Test

1. $-14, -6, -2, 0$ **3.** The sequence is arithmetic. The common difference is $d = 0.9$.   **5.** $a_1 = -2, a_n = a_{n-1} - \dfrac{3}{2}$; $a_{22} = -\dfrac{67}{2}$ **7.** The sequence is geometric. The common ratio is $r = \dfrac{1}{2}$.   **9.** $a_1 = 1, a_n = -\dfrac{1}{2} \cdot a_{n-1}$ **11.** $\displaystyle\sum_{k=-3}^{15}\left(3k^2 - \dfrac{5}{6}k\right)$

13. $S_7 = -2,604.2$ **15.** Total in account: \$140,355.75; Interest earned: \$14,355.75   **17.** $5 \times 3 \times 2 \times 3 \times 2 = 180$

19. $C(15, 3) = 455$ **21.** $\dfrac{10!}{2!3!2!} = 151,200$ **23.** $\dfrac{429x^{14}}{16}$

25. $\dfrac{4}{7}$ **27.** $\dfrac{5}{7}$ **29.** $\dfrac{C(14, 3)C(26, 4)}{C(40, 7)} \approx 29.2\%$

Index

A

AAS (angle-angle-side) triangle 644
absolute maximum 205, 267
absolute minimum 205, 267
absolute value 189, 247
absolute value equation 137, 151, 250
absolute value function 187, 247, 250
absolute value inequality 146, 147
addition method 880, 885, 972
Addition Principle 1100, 1126
addition property 143
adjacent side 633
algebraic expression 11, 66
altitude 762, 865
ambiguous case 764, 865
amplitude 645, 646, 688
angle 576, 605, 633
angle of depression 599, 633
angle of elevation 599, 633, 762
angle of rotation 1031, 1049
angular speed 633, 634
annual interest 1095
annual percentage rate (APR) 472, 565
annuity 1095, 1126
apoapsis 1040
arc 579
arc length 580, 586, 605, 633
arccosine 688, 378
Archimedes' spiral 811, 865
arcsine 688, 678
arctangent 688, 678
area 104, 151
area of a circle 360
area of a sector 587, 633
argument 818, 865
arithmetic sequence 1069, 1070, 1072, 1073, 1088, 1089, 1126
arithmetic series 1089, 1126
arrow notation 414, 453
associative property of addition 8, 66
associative property of multiplication 8, 66
asymptotes 998
augmented matrix 934, 938, 939, 951, 972
average rate of change 196, 267
axes of symmetry 998
axis of symmetry 344, 347, 453, 1020, 1021

B

base 6, 66
binomial 42, 66, 395, 1126
binomial coefficient 1110
binomial expansion 1111, 1113, 1126
Binomial Theorem 1111, 1112, 1126
break-even point 887, 972

C

cardioid 804, 865
carrying capacity 544, 565
Cartesian coordinate system 74, 151
Cartesian equation 794
Celsius 254
center of a hyperbola 998, 1049
center of an ellipse 983, 1049
central rectangle 998
change-of-base formula 523, 524, 565
circle 905, 907
circular motion 653
circumference 579
co-vertex 983, 998
co-vertices 985
coefficient 41, 42, 66, 360, 404, 453
coefficient matrix 934, 936, 953, 972
cofunction 714
cofunction identities 597, 714
column 923, 972
column matrix 924
combination 1105, 1110, 1126
combining functions 210
common base 527
common difference 1069, 1088, 1126
common logarithm 494, 565
common ratio 1079, 1091, 1126
commutative 211
commutative property of addition 8, 66
commutative property of multiplication 8, 66
complement of an event 1121, 1126
completing the square 124, 125, 151
complex conjugate 116, 151
Complex Conjugate Theorem 408
complex number 112, 113, 151, 815

complex plane 112, 151, 815
composite function 209, 210, 211, 267
compound inequality 145, 151
compound interest 472, 565
compression 292, 484, 506
conditional equation 87, 151
conic 982, 997, 1046
conic section 832, 1049
conjugate axis 998, 1049
consistent system 876, 972
constant 11, 41, 42, 66
constant of variation 447, 453
constant rate of change 309
continuous 375
continuous function 370, 453
convex limaçon 805, 865
coordinate plane 1015
correlation coefficient 327, 334
cosecant 620, 633, 664
cosecant function 665, 698
cosine 697, 732, 733
cosine function 605, 633, 643, 644, 646, 653, 664
cost function 209, 886, 972
cotangent 620, 633, 670
cotangent function 670, 698
coterminal angles 584, 586, 633
Cramer's Rule 961, 964, 968, 972
cube root 361
cubic function 187, 438
curvilinear path 826

D

De Moivre 815, 820
De Moivre's Theorem 821, 822, 865
decompose a composite function 217
decomposition 913
decreasing function 201, 267, 282
decreasing linear function 283, 334
degenerate conic sections 1027
degree 42, 66, 365, 453, 577, 633
dependent system 877, 885, 897, 972
dependent variable 160, 267
Descartes 815
Descartes' Rule of Signs 409, 453
determinant 961, 963, 964, 972
difference of squares 46, 66

dimpled limaçon 805, 865
direct variation 447, 453
directrix 1015, 1018, 1020, 1041, 1045, 1046, 1049
discriminant 127, 151
displacement 588
distance formula 80, 151, 999, 1015
distributive property 8, 66
diverge 1092, 1126
dividend 394
Division Algorithm 394, 395, 402, 453
divisor 394
domain 160, 168, 180, 181, 267
domain and range 180, 258
domain of a composite function 216
dot product 857, 865
double-angle formulas 721, 753, 719
doubling time 537, 541, 565
Dürer 806

E

eccentricity 1041, 1049
electrostatic force 199
elimination 906
ellipse 839, 906, 983, 984, 985, 987, 990, 1014, 1041, 1045, 1049
ellipsis 1056
end behavior 362, 423, 453
endpoint 198, 576
entry 923, 972
equation 13, 66, 166
equation in quadratic form 138
equation in two variables 76, 151
equations in quadratic form 151
Euler 815
even function 233, 267, 624, 697
even-odd identities 699, 753, 719
event 1117, 1126
experiment 1117, 1126
explicit formula 1057, 1073, 1082, 1126
exponent 6, 66
exponential 480
exponential decay 464, 470, 479, 537, 539, 542, 552
exponential equation 526
exponential function 464

exponential growth 464, 467, 537, 541, 543, 552, 565
exponential notation 6, 66
extraneous solution 134, 151, 530, 565
extrapolation 324, 325, 334

F

factor by grouping 51, 66
Factor Theorem 403, 453
factorial 1064
factoring 119
Fahrenheit 254
feasible region 909, 972
finite arithmetic sequence 1074
finite sequence 1057, 1126
foci 983, 985, 998, 1049
focus 983, 1015, 1018, 1020, 1040, 1045, 1046
focus (of an ellipse) 1049
focus (of a parabola) 1049
FOIL 44, 114
formula 13, 66, 166
function 161, 189, 267
function notation 162
Fundamental Counting Principle 1102, 1126
Fundamental Theorem of Algebra 407, 408, 453

G

Gauss 815, 892, 934
Gaussian elimination 892, 937, 972
general form 345
general form of a quadratic function 345, 453, 454
Generalized Pythagorean Theorem 776, 865
geometric sequence 1079, 1081, 1091, 1126
geometric series 1091, 1126
global maximum 387, 388, 453
global minimum 387, 388, 453
graph in two variables 76, 151
gravity 842
greatest common factor 49, 66, 119

H

half-angle formulas 725, 726, 753
half-life 533, 537, 539, 565
Heaviside method 915
Heron of Alexandria 781
Heron's formula 781
horizontal asymptote 416, 417, 422, 453
horizontal compression 237, 267, 747
horizontal line 95, 297, 298, 334
horizontal line test 173, 267

horizontal reflection 229, 230, 267
horizontal shift 225, 267, 482, 503, 643
horizontal stretch 237, 267
hyperbola 997, 1000, 1001, 1002, 1005, 1006, 1009, 1015, 1042, 1044, 1049
hypotenuse 633, 634

I

identities 615, 625, 626, 633
identity equation 87, 151
identity function 187
identity matrix 947, 951, 972
identity property of addition 9, 66
identity property of multiplication 9, 66
imaginary number 111, 112, 151, 453, 454
inconsistent equation 87, 151
inconsistent system 877, 884, 896, 972
increasing function 201, 267, 282
increasing linear function 283, 334
independent system 876, 877, 972
independent variable 160, 267
index 36, 66
index of summation 1087, 1088, 1126
inequality 908
infinite geometric series 1092
infinite sequence 1057, 1126
infinite series 1092, 1126
initial point 847, 850, 865
initial side 577, 633
inner-loop limaçon 806, 865
input 160, 267
integers 2, 5, 66
intercepts 79, 151
Intermediate Value Theorem 385, 453
interpolation 324, 334
intersection 1119
interval 142, 151
interval notation 142, 151, 180, 184, 201, 267
inverse cosine function 678, 688
inverse function 255, 267, 435, 438
inverse matrix 951, 953
inverse of a radical function 441
inverse of a rational function 443
inverse property of addition 9, 66
inverse property of multiplication 9, 66
inverse sine function 678, 688

inverse tangent function 678, 688
inverse trigonometric functions 677, 678, 680, 684
inverse variation 448, 453
inversely proportional 448, 453
invertible function 437, 453
invertible matrix 947, 961
irrational numbers 3, 5, 66

J

joint variation 450, 453

K

Kronecker 815

L

latus rectum 1015, 1020, 1049
Law of Cosines 777, 865
Law of Sines 763, 777, 865
leading coefficient 42, 66, 365, 453
leading term 42, 66, 365, 453
least common denominator 60, 66, 89
least squares regression 325, 334
lemniscate 807, 865
limaçon 805, 806
linear equation 87, 151
Linear Factorization Theorem 408, 453
linear function 280, 294, 309, 334
linear growth 464
linear inequality 151
linear model 310, 322
linear relationship 322
linear speed 589, 633, 634
local extrema 200, 267
local maximum 200, 267, 388
local minimum 200, 267, 388
logarithm 492, 565
logarithmic equation 531
logarithmic model 555
logistic growth model 544, 565
long division 393
lower limit of summation 1087, 1088

M

magnitude 189, 224, 816, 847, 849, 865
main diagonal 936, 972
major and minor axes 985
major axis 983, 987, 1049
matrix 923, 924, 928, 934, 972
matrix multiplication 928, 948, 953
matrix operations 924
maximum value 344
measure of an angle 577, 633

midline 645, 646, 688
midpoint formula 82, 151
minimum value 344
minor axis 983, 987, 1049
model breakdown 324, 334
modulus 189, 818, 865
monomial 42, 67
Multiplication Principle 1101, 1102, 1126
multiplication property 143
multiplicative inverse 949
multiplicative inverse of a matrix 947, 972
multiplicity 379, 453
mutually exclusive events 1120, 1126

N

n factorial 1064, 1126
natural logarithm 496, 529, 565
natural numbers 2, 5, 67, 160
negative angle 577, 603, 614, 633
Newton's Law of Cooling 542, 565
nominal rate 472
non-right triangles 762
nondegenerate conic section 1027, 1029, 1049
nonlinear inequality 908, 972
nth partial sum 1087, 1126
nth root of a complex number 822
nth term of a sequence 1057, 1126

O

oblique triangle 762, 865
odd function 233, 267, 624, 697
one-loop limaçon 805, 865
one-to-one 480, 492, 517, 523
one-to-one function 170, 257, 267, 677
opposite side 633, 634
order of magnitude 538, 565
order of operations 6, 67
ordered pair 75, 151, 160, 181
ordered triple 892
origin 75, 151, 248
outcomes 1117, 1126
output 160, 267

P

parabola 344, 350, 838, 909, 1014, 1019, 1021, 1040, 1043, 1049
parallel 96
parallel lines 96, 298, 299, 334
parallelograms 851
parameter 826, 865
parametric equation 827, 837, 839

parametric form 840
parent function 503
partial fraction 913, 972
partial fraction decomposition 913, 972
Pascal 806
Pascal's Triangle 1112
perfect square trinomial 45, 67
periapsis 1040
perimeter 104, 151
period 628, 633, 643, 659, 661, 739
periodic function 628, 643, 688
permutation 1102, 1126
perpendicular 96
perpendicular lines 97, 299, 334
pH 516
phase shift 647, 688
piecewise function 189, 190, 267, 1060
point-slope form 285, 334
point-slope formula 98, 1003
polar axis 788, 865
polar coordinates 788, 790, 791, 792, 799, 865
polar equation 794, 800, 801, 865, 1041, 1049
polar form 816
polar form of a complex number 817, 865
polar form of a conic 1046
polar grid 788
pole 788, 865
polynomial 41, 42, 67, 404
polynomial equation 133, 151
polynomial function 364, 375, 382, 386, 454
position vector 847, 849
positive angle 577, 584, 633
power function 360, 454
power rule for logarithms 519, 523, 565
principal nth root 36, 67
principal square root 31, 67
probability 1117, 1126
probability model 1117, 1126
product of two matrices 928
product rule for logarithms 517, 519, 565
product-to-sum formula 734, 753, 719
profit function 887, 972
properties of determinants 967
Proxima Centauri 538
Pythagoras 815
Pythagorean identities 699, 753, 719
Pythagorean Identity 607, 627, 633, 707
Pythagorean Theorem 80, 127, 152, 721, 748, 776, 841

Q

quadrant 74, 152
quadrantal angle 578, 633, 634
quadratic 138, 917, 919
quadratic equation 119, 120, 123, 125, 152, 743
quadratic formula 125, 126, 152, 743
quadratic function 187, 347, 349
quotient 394
quotient identities 699, 753, 719
quotient rule for logarithms 518, 565

R

radian 580, 581, 633
radian measure 581, 586, 633
radical 31, 67
radical equation 134, 135, 152
radical expression 31, 67
radical functions 437
radicand 31, 67, 134
radiocarbon dating 540
range 160, 267, 678
rate of change 196, 267, 280
rational equation 89, 90, 152
rational exponents 37
rational expression 58, 67, 89, 913, 919
rational function 418, 425, 428, 454
rational number 89
rational numbers 2, 5, 67
Rational Zero Theorem 404, 454
ray 576, 633
real number line 4, 67
real numbers 4, 67
reciprocal 96, 255, 361
reciprocal function 188, 414
reciprocal identities 664, 670, 699, 753, 719
reciprocal squared function 188
rectangular coordinates 788, 790, 791, 792
rectangular equation 794, 831
rectangular form 817, 840
recursive formula 1062, 1072, 1081, 1127
reduction formulas 753, 719
reference angle 584, 613, 614, 615, 623, 633
reflection 485, 508
regression analysis 552, 555, 558
regression line 326
relation 160, 267
remainder 394
Remainder Theorem 402, 454
removable discontinuity 421, 454

restricting the domain 262
resultant 851, 866
revenue function 886, 972
Richter Scale 491
right triangle 593, 677
roots 345, 454
rose curve 809, 866
row 923, 972
row matrix 924
row operations 936, 940, 950, 951, 952, 972
row-echelon form 936, 938, 972
row-equivalent 936, 972

S

sample space 1117, 1127
SAS (side-angle-side) triangle 776
scalar 852, 866, 926
scalar multiple 926, 972
scalar multiplication 852, 866, 926
scatter plot 322
scientific notation 25, 26, 27, 67
secant 620, 633, 664
secant function 664
sector of a circle 587
sequence 1056, 1069, 1127
series 1087, 1127
set-builder notation 142, 183, 184, 268
sigma 1087
sine 697, 733, 734
sine function 605, 624, 633, 642, 647, 652, 654
sinusoidal function 644, 688
slope 92, 93, 152, 281, 282, 284, 334
slope-intercept form 281, 334
smooth curve 370, 454
solution set 87, 152, 893, 972
solving systems of linear equations 878, 880
special angles 611, 706
square matrix 924, 961
square root function 188
square root property 123, 152
SSA (side-side-angle) triangle 762
SSS (side-side-side) triangle 776
standard form 95
standard form of a quadratic function 346, 454, 455
standard position 577, 633, 847, 866
stretch 484
stretching/compressing factor 660, 661
substitution method 879, 972

sum and difference formulas for cosine 708
sum and difference formulas for sine 709
sum and difference formulas for tangent 711
sum-to-product formula 753, 719
summation notation 1087, 1088, 1127
surface area 435
symmetry test 800
synthetic division 397, 406, 454
system of equations 935, 936, 938, 939, 953
system of linear equations 315, 876, 878, 879, 973
system of nonlinear equations 903, 973
system of nonlinear inequalities 909, 973
system of three equations in three variables 964

T

tangent 620, 633, 659
tangent function 660, 661, 662, 672, 698
term 1056, 1070, 1127
term of a polynomial 41, 42, 67
term of a polynomial function 364, 454
terminal point 847, 850, 866
terminal side 577, 633
transformation 222, 292
translation 1019
transverse axis 998, 1049
trigonometric equations 831, 832
trigonometric functions 593, 625
trigonometric identities 777
trinomial 42, 67
turning point 368, 383, 454

U

union of two events 1119, 1127
unit circle 581, 594, 605, 608, 612, 624, 633, 740
unit vector 854, 866
upper limit of summation 1087, 1088, 1127
upper triangular form 892

V

variable 11, 67
varies directly 447, 454
varies inversely 448, 454
vector 847, 866
vector addition 851, 866
vertex 344, 454, 633, 634, 983, 1015, 1021

vertex form of a quadratic
    function 346, 454
vertical asymptote 416, 419,
    423, 454, 678
vertical compression 234, 268
vertical line 95, 297, 298, 334
vertical line test 171, 268
vertical reflection 229, 230, 268
vertical shift 222, 223, 268, 293,
    481, 504, 542, 647
vertical stretch 234, 268, 292,
    506
vertices 983, 985
volume 104, 152
volume of a sphere 360

W

whole numbers 2, 5, 67

X

x-axis 74, 152
x-coordinate 75, 152
x-intercept 79, 152, 296

Y

y-axis 74, 152
y-coordinate 75, 152
y-intercept 79, 152, 281, 282,
    291, 296

Z

zero-product property 120, 152
zeros 345, 376, 379, 404, 454,
    802